D1105110

# HISTORICAL DICTIONARIES OF LITERATURE AND THE ARTS

## Jon Woronoff, Series Editor

# Historical Dictionary of
# American Cinema

M. Keith Booker

The Scarecrow Press, Inc.
Lanham • Toronto • Plymouth, UK
2011

Published by Scarecrow Press, Inc.
A wholly owned subsidiary of The Rowman & Littlefield Publishing Group, Inc.
4501 Forbes Boulevard, Suite 200, Lanham, Maryland 20706
http://www.scarecrowpress.com

Estover Road, Plymouth PL6 7PY, United Kingdom

British Library Cataloguing in Publication Information Available

**Library of Congress Cataloging-in-Publication Data**
Booker, M. Keith.
  Historical dictionary of American cinema / M. Keith Booker.
    p. cm. — (Historical dictionaries of literature and the arts)
  Includes bibliographical references.
  ISBN 978-0-8108-7192-2 (cloth : alk. paper) -- ISBN 978-0-8108-7459-6 (ebook)
  1. Motion pictures—United States—Dictionaries. I. Title.
  PN1993.5.U6B653 2011
  791.430973'03—dc22

                                                                    2010048178

For Benjamin Booker, Skylor Booker, and Adam Booker

# Contents

# Editor's Foreword

American cinema was not the first on the scene, but it quickly became the foremost in terms of the number of films, variety of genres, technological innovation, certainly marketing clout, and sometimes (although not always) quality. Since its earliest steps in the age of silent film to the present days of computer-generated imagery, it has undergone ups and downs both commercially and artistically, and it has also come under political pressure on occasion. There were times when it was overshadowed by other cinemas, particularly in Europe with regard to quality, and more recently Hollywood has slipped in terms of sheer quantity compared to Bollywood. Still, while not always the trendsetter, and even when it misses out on new technologies or fashions, it quickly catches up and often pulls ahead. Thus American cinema—the concept as well as the reality—has long been and remains at the top of the list, constantly generating films that are shown almost everywhere and whose directors, producers, and especially actors are known around the world.

So this *Historical Dictionary of American Cinema*, although appearing later than works on other national cinemas, is certainly a crucial volume that has to fill a very big gap. This it does more than adequately. First, the historical span of nearly a century and a half is traced in the chronology. Then, the introduction provides a broader overview, following its evolution from one era to the next, right down to the very latest events. The dictionary section, large and densely packed with information, looks into many of the essential details with hundreds of entries on the main actors, directors, producers, scriptwriters, composers, and others who contribute to the making of a film, as well as a few dozen on the main types of films. Some of the best-known films get their own entries, as do the major and some independent studios, certain technical aspects, and the most prestigious awards. For cinema buffs, the bibliography is hardly the least, since it includes references to further reading on all these topics and more.

This latest addition to the subseries on cinema was written by M. Keith Booker, who is the James E. and Ellen Wadley Roper Professor of English and also the director of the Program in Comparative Literature and Cultural

Studies at the University of Arkansas. In a long and fruitful career, he has written and lectured not only on literature but also popular culture more generally, with a definite emphasis on cinema as well as television and related fields. The genre he has dealt with most is science fiction, and he is the author of the recently published *Historical Dictionary of Science Fiction Cinema* as well as a number of other books on that topic. All in all, he has written several dozen books in this circle of topics, which have made him a recognized authority. It is thus fortunate that he has written this volume in which he can refer to so many areas that will doubtlessly interest not only students and academics but movie buffs as well.

Jon Woronoff
Series Editor

# Preface

There is a scene in Billy Wilder's *Sunset Blvd.* (1950), one of the classic films about the Hollywood film industry, in which jaded screenwriter Joe Gillis (William Holden) walks with innocent, aspiring screenwriter Betty Schaefer (Nancy Olson) through the Paramount studio lot, strolling down a street lined with fake buildings. Looking around her, Schaefer acknowledges the artificiality of what she sees but admires it nevertheless: "Look at this street," she tells Gillis. "All cardboard, all hollow, all phony, all done with mirrors. You know, I like it better than any street in the world."

Schaefer's comment is a perfect summary of America's love affair with the movies, even if the film in which she appears is, as a whole, a bit cynical in its vision of the film industry as a cutthroat enterprise that uses people for its own ends, then casts them aside when they are no longer useful. A similar duality, in fact, can be found in the entire cultural history of American cinema, which has been seen by many as perhaps the most glorious expression of the American dream, yet has also been viewed with suspicion and disdain as a potentially unsavory form of entertainment.

In addition, American movies have been criticized as the ultimate example of commodified culture, designed and produced primarily with a concern for profit potential. After all, major films now often have budgets upward of $200 million and can generate more than a billion dollars in gross box-office receipts, not to mention merchandising and video sales. In point of fact, however, the movie business has been a business from the very beginning, even when the stakes were much lower. Pioneers such as famed inventor Thomas Edison led the way in thinking of filmmaking primarily as a way of using technology to generate income rather than a way of using talent and creativity to generate art. Meanwhile, critics of movies have long seen this concern with profit as detrimental to the production of films with genuine artistic merit or responsible social messages.

American cinema has, of course, survived such criticisms to become the world's most important cinema and one of the most powerful forces in world culture, popular (yet still often controversial) around the globe. American filmmakers have mastered a visual and narrative language that seems to have almost universal appeal. At the same time, this widespread popularity has drawn additional criticism from those who see the global distribution of American films as a form of cultural imperialism that contributes to an overall commodification, homogenization, and Americanization of world culture.

I share many of the concerns of critics who see the business aspect of the American film industry as a potentially negative cultural force. Yet I still, even though (or perhaps because) I have been watching movies for more than 50 years, share some of Betty Schaefer's wide-eyed wonder and amazement at the magic that American filmmakers sometimes manage to put on the screen despite it all. I am also frequently impressed at the social critique and commentary that sometimes manage to creep into American films, even though the film industry is so thoroughly implicated in the system that is being criticized, partly because movies are so rich and complex that it is never quite possible entirely to engineer or anticipate the reactions that audiences might have to them.

While no single volume can be comprehensive in its coverage of the more than a century that now constitutes the history of American cinema, it is hoped that this historical dictionary can capture some of the complexity and diversity of both the American film industry and American films themselves.

# Acronyms and Abbreviations

| | |
|---|---|
| 3D | Three dimensional |
| ABC | American Broadcasting Company |
| AFI | American Film Institute |
| AIP | American International Pictures |
| AMPAS | Academy of Motion Picture Arts and Sciences |
| ASCAP | American Society of Composer, Authors and Publishers |
| CBS | Columbia Broadcasting System (initially) |
| CGI | Computer-generated imagery |
| DGA | Director's Guild of America |
| FBI | Federal Bureau of Investigation |
| HBO | Home Box Office |
| HUAC | House Un-American Activities Committee |
| ILM | Industrial Light & Magic |
| IMP | Independent Moving Pictures Company |
| MGM | Metro-Goldwyn-Mayer |
| MPAA | Motion Picture Association of America |
| MPPDA | Motion Picture Producers and Distributors of America |
| MPPC | Motion Picture Patents Company |
| MTV | Music Television |
| NAACP | National Association for the Advancement of Colored People |
| NBC | National Broadcasting Company |
| PBS | Public Broadcasting System |
| RCA | Radio Corporation of America (originally) |
| SAG | Screen Actors Guild |
| sf | Science fiction |
| SIMPP | Society of Independent Motion Picture Producers |
| WGA | Writers Guild of America |
| WGAE | Writers Guild of America East |
| WGAW | Writers Guild of America West |

# Reader's Note

In the following text, the years associated with films are the year of first release of the film in the United States. Unless otherwise indicated, any individual associated with a film in the possessive (as in Orson Welles's *Citizen Kane*) is the director of that film. Any item in boldface within a given entry is also covered in an entry of its own. "*See also*" designations also provide cross references to related entries in the text.

The term "Hollywood" is frequently used in this volume (as it is throughout American culture) as a synonym for the mainstream American film industry. Geographically, Hollywood is a district located in the northwest quadrant of Los Angeles, California. Though the American film industry had its origins in the New York and New Jersey area, filmmakers quickly moved to California, where it was cheaper and easier to make films, partly because the area was less developed than New York and partly because of better weather conditions. The Biograph company began shooting films in the Los Angeles area as early as 1906, though filmmaking in Hollywood proper did not start until 1910, when D. W. Griffith shot the film *In Old California* there for Biograph. From that point forward, the Hollywood-based film industry grew rapidly. By 1920, the identification of the name "Hollywood" with American film in general was common worldwide. Though the American film industry has significantly dispersed in recent years, substantial film-related activity is still centered in Hollywood proper, and the Hollywood name remains synonymous with American filmmaking, even for films that are not actually made in Hollywood.

This volume frequently mentions the popular lists of various sorts of distinction in American film that are published by the American Film Institute (AFI). Those lists can be found in their entirety on the AFI website at http://connect.afi.com/site/PageServer?pagename=100YearsList.

# Chronology

**1878**  Eadweard Muybridge uses multiple cameras to produce a series of still photographs that can be combined to show a horse in motion.

**1888**  Thomas Edison announces his plans to develop a device for recording and displaying motion pictures.

**1889**  Edison's planned device is formally named the "kinetoscope."

**1891**  First public demonstrations of prototype kinetoscopes, single-viewer machines that allow the viewing of brief films inside the unit.

**1893**  Muybridge exhibits films of animals in motion to a paying audience at the World's Columbian Exposition (World's Fair) in Chicago. At the same exposition, Edison exhibits the first completed kinetoscope film, made at Edison's "Black Maria," the first American movie studio, in West Orange, New Jersey.

**1894**  Edison makes *Fred Ott's Sneeze*, which becomes the first copyrighted motion picture. The first public kinetoscope parlor opens in New York City, featuring 10 machines, each showing a different short film. Similar parlors are soon opened in Chicago and San Francisco.

**1895**  A new device, the Eidoloscope, is used for the first commercial screening of a projected motion picture in the United States. The American Mutoscope Company is founded, becoming the first American company devoted exclusively to the production and exhibition of films.

**1896**  The Edison Company's projection system, the Vitascope, is used for its first commercial exhibition, making it clear that projection is the future of film exhibition. However, American Mutoscope's Biograph projector offers superior image quality.

**1899**  American Mutoscope becomes the American Mutoscope and Biograph Company.

**1903**  The Edison Company produces Edwin S. Porter's *The Great Train Robbery*, often credited as the first American narrative film of significant length (11 minutes).

**1904** Marcus Loew founds the theater chain that will grow into Loew's Theatres, which will last until 2006, when it merges with AMC Theaters under the name of the latter.

**1906** Biograph opens its own movie studio in New York City.

**1908** Edison spearheads the formation of the Motion Picture Patents Company (MPPC), an amalgamation of the nine leading U.S. motion picture companies. Eastman Kodak (the country's only manufacturer of film stock) agrees to sell film stock only to the members of the MPPC. D. W. Griffith becomes the film director for Biograph, one of the members of the MPPC.

**1909** The Selig Polyscope Company (a member of the MPPC) opens the first Los Angeles–area film studio and releases the first film, *In the Sultan's Power*, made entirely on the West Coast.

**1910** Actors in American films begin to be identified in onscreen credits as part of an attempt on the part of Carl Laemmle and his Independent Moving Pictures Company (IMP) to use recognized stars to market films (and thus better to compete with the MPPC). Griffith's film *In Old California* for Biograph, is the first film made in Hollywood, a district of Los Angeles. Hollywood rapidly becomes the center of the film industry.

**1911** The independent New Jersey–based Centaur Company builds the first Hollywood film studio. By 1920, the once-sleepy hamlet would be the center of the American film industry.

**1912** The U.S. government initiates an antitrust action against the MPPC, but by this time the company had already lost its stranglehold on the rapidly growing U.S. film industry. Famous Players Film Company (the forerunner of Paramount Pictures) is founded, ultimately making Paramount the oldest of the five major studios of the Golden Age of Hollywood. In the same year, Laemmle merges IMP with other studios to form Universal, arguably the first major studio.

**1914** In the debut of an actor who would arguably become the most important actor of the silent-film era, Charles Chaplin appears in the first of his films for Mack Sennett's Keystone Film Company. In addition to numerous short films, Chaplin appears in the first feature-length comedy in this year, Keystone's *Tillie's Punctured Romance*.

**1915** Griffith's feature-length *The Birth of a Nation*, made for the new Triangle Film Corporation, thrusts the United States to the forefront of the international film industry. The MPPC is ordered dissolved after it is found guilty of antitrust violations; the Supreme Court will verify the ruling in 1918.

**1916** *Intolerance*, Griffith's follow-up to *Birth of a Nation*, is even more ambitious, but is a commercial failure.

**1917** The United States enters World War I. Theda Bara stars in the first film version of *Cleopatra*. Buster Keaton makes his first appearance in film. Mack Sennett leaves Keystone Studios to form his own independent production company; Keystone's business subsequently declines.

**1918** World War I ends. The four Warner Brothers open their first West Coast studio.

**1919** Chaplin, Griffith, Douglas Fairbanks, and Mary Pickford form United Artists in an attempt to give artists greater creative control over their work.

**1920** *The Mark of Zorro*, starring Fairbanks, is the first film released by United Artists.

**1921** With a 68-minute runtime, *The Kid* can be considered Chaplin's first feature-length film, signaling the growing dominance of that form in the film industry. Griffith's *Dream Street* experiments with the limited use of integrated sound in its prologue.

**1922** Robert Flaherty's *Nanook of the North* is the first feature-length documentary.

**1923** Cecil B. DeMille's first version of *The Ten Commandments* is the most expensive film made to that time

**1924** The major studio MGM is formed from an amalgamation of Metro Pictures, Goldwyn Pictures, and Louis B. Mayer Pictures. The company will eventually become the biggest of the major studios of the Golden Age of Hollywood.

**1925** *The Lost World* includes the most advanced special effects of the silent film era. *The Big Parade*, set during World War I, is a classic antiwar drama. MGM's *Ben-Hur: A Tale of the Christ* grosses $9 million.

**1926** Warner Bros. releases *Don Juan* with an integrated musical sound track (but no dialogue).

**1927** *The Jazz Singer* makes use of synchronized sound and video (including limited dialogue), initiating a trend that would soon mean the end of the silent film era. The film helps make struggling Warner Bros. a major studio and heralds the coming of the sound film era. However, 1927 is a banner year for silent film and includes the release of such classics as Buster Keaton's *The General* and German director F. W. Murnau's *Sunrise*, a film that indicates a growing migration of top European directors to Hollywood. Louis B. Mayer is the prime force behind the founding of the Academy of Motion Picture Arts and Sciences.

**1928**  The new sound film technology is instrumental in the founding of RKO Pictures, largely to aid in the marketing of sound film equipment developed by its parent, Radio Corporation of America (RCA). Paramount becomes the first studio to announce that it will henceforth produce only sound films.

**1929**  The Academy Awards are first given, with the first Oscar for Best Picture going to William Wellman's silent film *Wings* (1927). It will be the only silent film ever to win the award. The awards themselves will go on to become the most prestigious honors in the film industry. **October 29:** The stock market crash heralds the beginning of the Great Depression in the United States; it will not truly end until World War II.

**1930**  Originally conceived as a silent film, *All Quiet on the Western Front* is released as a sound film; it is an impressive technical achievement that suggests the great potential of the new form. In answer to controversies over the potentially objectionable content of Hollywood films, the Production Code is established by the film industry as a form of self-censorship, though it will not be fully enforced until 1934.

**1931**  With sound film now almost entirely dominant, Chaplin's *City Lights* is one of the last silent features. New trends in film emerge with Universal's monster movie *Frankenstein* and Warner Bros.' gangster films *Public Enemy* and *Little Caesar*.

**1933**  *King Kong* is a major step forward in special effects technology. *Gold Diggers of 1933*, choreographed by Busby Berkeley, and *42nd Street* are major milestones in the evolution of the movie musical.

**1934**  Frank Capra's *It Happened One Night* sweeps the major Academy Awards (Best Picture, Director, Screenplay, Actor, and Actress) and launches the classic period of the screwball comedy. *Bright Eyes* makes six-year-old Shirley Temple a star. Full enforcement of the Production Code goes into effect, curtailing the representation of sex and violence on the screen.

**1935**  The Fox Film Corporation and Twentieth Century Pictures merge to form Twentieth Century Fox. *Becky Sharp* is the first feature film shot entirely in three-strip Technicolor.

**1936**  With *Modern Times*, even Chaplin finally joins the sound era, though the film still includes very limited dialogue. The Western feature *The Trail* *of the Lonesome Pine* features the first outdoor sequences shot in three-strip Technicolor.

**1937** Walt Disney's *Snow White and the Seven Dwarfs* becomes the first feature-length animated film—and the top-grossing film of the year. Its success proves the viability of animated features, while also providing a boost to the three-strip Technicolor process. MGM's Louis B. Mayer is reportedly the highest-paid individual in America.

**1939** The Civil War epic *Gone with the Wind* will go on to gross over $190 million, at that time easily the most in history. When adjusted for inflation, it is still the top box-office draw of all time in 2010. *The Wizard of Oz* is less of a hit when first released but will go on to become one of the iconic works of American popular culture. John Ford's *Stagecoach* is a landmark in the evolution of the Western genre. Its star, John Wayne, will go on to become an icon of the genre. Films such as *Ninotchka, Mr. Smith Goes to Washington,* and *Wuthering Heights* are also released, making this arguably the greatest year in American film history.

**1940** Ford's *The Grapes of Wrath* is a surprisingly faithful adaptation of John Steinbeck's novel, the author's most radical political statement about conditions during the Depression. *Rebecca* is Alfred Hitchcock's first American film. Charles Chaplin's anti-Nazi satire *The Great Dictator* is the director's first genuine talkie and one of Hollywood's first openly antifascist films.

**1941** Twenty-five-year-old Orson Welles directs and stars in *Citizen Kane,* still often regarded as the greatest film ever made. The film has very limited success, largely due to the efforts of newspaper mogul William Randolph Hearst (widely acknowledged to be the model for Kane) to suppress it. Bette Davis becomes the first female president of the Academy of Motion Picture Arts and Sciences, but soon resigns after clashes with other members of the organization's ruling board. The United States enters World War II at the end of the year. Many will leave Hollywood for military service, while the film industry is mobilized to make films that support the war effort.

**1942** *Casablanca* is the epitome of the classic Hollywood style. Jacques Tourneur's *Cat People,* produced by Val Lewton for RKO Pictures, initiates an important cycle of Lewton-produced horror films. *The Magnificent Ambersons,* Welles's follow-up to *Citizen Kane,* is released by RKO but with a revised (happy) ending reshot by the studio without Welles's participation or approval.

**1945**   World War II ends, though war films are still among Hollywood's leading products, including *The Story of G. I. Joe* and *They Were Expendable*. Billy Wilder's *The Lost Weekend* is another highlight of the year.

**1946**   Director Frank Capra returns from wartime military service to make *It's a Wonderful Life*. Not a hit at the time, it will later become his most beloved film. *The Best Years of Our Lives* is an important commentary on the domestic social consequences of the war's end. French critics Nino Frank and Jean-Pierre Chartier coin the term "film noir" in reference to wartime American films such as *The Maltese Falcon* (1941), *Double Indemnity* (1944), *Laura* (1944), *Murder, My Sweet* (1944), and *The Lost Weekend* (1945).

**1947**   The House Un-American Activities Committee (HUAC) begins questioning members of the film industry in a declared effort to root out communist influence in Hollywood. The investigation will soon lead to the blacklisting of those in the industry suspected of "subversive" activities, especially in the highly publicized case of a group known as the "Hollywood Ten." Chaplin's *Monsieur Verdoux* bombs at the box office, partly because of public suspicions concerning Chaplin's possible pro-communist sympathies. Welles goes into self-imposed exile in Europe to escape the repressive political climate in the United States.

**1948**   In the Paramount Antitrust Case, the U.S. Supreme Court finds that the ownership and control of extensive theater chains by Hollywood's major films studios is a violation of federal antitrust laws. The studios are subsequently forced to divest themselves of their theater holdings, leading to a major shake-up in the industry. *Rope* is Hitchcock's first color feature.

**1950**   The Hollywood Ten begin serving prison sentences, and the blacklist is in full swing. *Destination Moon* and *Rocketship X-M* initiate a surge in the production of American science fiction films. Billy Wilder's *Sunset Blvd.* is one of Hollywood's great works of self-commentary. *All about Eve* is an even darker commentary on the ethos of show business. Going against the tradition of having stars work strictly under studio contracts for fixed salaries, James Stewart signs a freelance deal to star in the Western *Winchester '73*, working for a percentage of the film's profits.

**1951**   *The Day the Earth Stood Still* achieves a new level of thematic seriousness in science fiction film—and goes against the grain of American society by criticizing the Cold War arms race. *A Streetcar Named Desire* makes Marlon Brando a star. The Best Picture Oscar is from this point awarded to a film's producers rather than the studio, indicating the decline of the old studio system.

**1952** *Singin' in the Rain* will become perhaps the most highly regarded musical of all time. The classic Western *High Noon* is interpreted by many as a commentary on Hollywood's lack of courage in standing up to the blacklist. The introduction of high-quality color film by Eastman Kodak signals the beginning of the end for black-and-white film as the dominant mode in Hollywood. 3D films (especially horror and science fiction) begin to appear as an attempt to counter the growing appeal of television; Paramount's big-screen Cinerama process debuts as part of the same effort. Neither of these attempts will be successful.

**1953** Twentieth Century Fox releases *The Robe* in the newly developed CinemaScope format. The film is a major success that encourages the use of such wide-screen formats as a mode of competing with television for audiences. Otto Preminger's *The Moon Is Blue* becomes the first studio-produced film to be released without approval of the Motion Picture Production Code since its full implementation in 1934. The film is nevertheless a big hit. George Stevens's *Shane* is a classic Western.

**1954** Elia Kazan's *On the Waterfront* wins the Academy Award for Best Picture, though many see it as an attempt to justify the director's cooperative testimony before HUAC. Alfred Hitchcock's *Rear Window* is one of the key films of the decade. Michael Curtiz's *White Christmas* is the first film released in Paramount's new VistaVision wide-screen format. Dorothy Dandridge's performance in *Carmen Jones* wins her an Oscar nomination for Best Actress in a Leading Role, the first Oscar nomination for an African American.

**1955** *Rebel without a Cause* signals the growing prominence of teenagers in film and in American culture as a whole; its star, James Dean, is killed in an auto accident at the age of 26, securing his legendary status as an icon of disaffected youth. The noir film *Killer's Kiss* marks the debut of director Stanley Kubrick.

**1956** *Invasion of the Body Snatchers* captures the paranoid tenor of the mid-1950s. John Ford's *The Searchers* is one of the greatest Westerns in film history. *Forbidden Planet* is another science fiction classic. Cecil B. DeMille's *The Ten Commandments* (a remake of his own 1923 film) is perhaps the greatest of the biblical epics released in the decade. *Giant* is a more contemporary epic, posthumously starring Dean. *Rock around the Clock* endorses the new rock music, while playing to the growing teen audience for film. *The Wizard of Oz* becomes the first feature-length film broadcast on television; its annual showings on television soon become an American institution.

**1957** RKO Pictures, one of the major studios of the Golden Age of Hollywood, ceases active production, becoming the biggest casualty of the crisis that pervaded the film industry in the 1950s.

**1958** Hitchcock's *Vertigo* begins a key three-year sequence in which the director would release three consecutive classics. Orson Welles's *Touch of Evil* will be considered by many to be the last film in the original film noir cycle.

**1959** Wilder's *Some Like It Hot* will come to be regarded as one of the funniest films of all time. Hitchcock's *North by Northwest* is his second consecutive masterpiece.

**1960** The blacklist is effectively broken when Hollywood Ten member Dalton Trumbo receives onscreen credit for writing both Otto Preminger's *Exodus* and Stanley Kubrick's *Spartacus*. Hitchcock's *Psycho* begins the new decade with what will become one of the director's most admired films, though it is shocking to many at the time. *The Apartment* wins triple Oscars for Wilder, as its writer, director, and producer.

**1961** *The Misfits* is Marilyn Monroe's last completed film. *El Cid* is one of the last of the historical epics that became popular in the 1950s. TWA begins showing regular in-flight movies on cross-continental flights; NBC's *Saturday Night at the Movies* premieres, indicating a growing trend toward broadcasting Hollywood films on television, part of a consolidation of the film and television industries.

**1962** Monroe dies of an apparent drug overdose. The American–British co-production of *Lawrence of Arabia* is perhaps the high point in the cycle of wide-screen epics that began in the 1950s as an answer to the growing popularity of television. *Dr. No* initiates the James Bond film franchise. Marlon Brando becomes the first actor to be paid more than a million dollars to star in a film, for *Mutiny on the Bounty*. Kubrick's controversial *Lolita* is the first of his films to be made in Great Britain, a practice he would continue through the remainder of his career.

**1963** *Cleopatra* is the highest-grossing film of the year but loses money due to its high production costs. Elizabeth Taylor becomes the first female star to be paid a million dollars for her role in the film. Sidney Poitier stars in *Lilies of the Field*, which will make him the first African American to win the Academy Award for Best Actor.

**1964** Kubrick's *Dr. Strangelove* is an absurdist satire of the Cold War arms race that becomes a key marker of the beginning of a decline in nuclear anxiety in the United States. Don Siegel's *The Killers* is the last film of actor Ronald Reagan.

**1965** *The Sound of Music* wins the Best Picture Oscar and surpasses *Gone with the Wind* as the top-grossing film of all time.

**1966** Sweeping revisions to the Production Code allow *Who's Afraid of Virginia Woolf?* to use levels of profanity unprecedented in American feature film.

**1967** Showing the influence of the French New Wave, *Bonnie and Clyde* breaks new ground in Hollywood film. *The Graduate* and *In the Heat of the Night* indicate a growing willingness on the part of Hollywood studios to make films that criticize certain aspects of American society. Clint Eastwood stars in *A Fistful of Dollars*, the first spaghetti Western.

**1968** *Planet of the Apes* and Kubrick's *2001: A Space Odyssey* make this year a landmark in the evolution of science fiction film. *Rosemary's Baby* and *Night of the Living Dead* do much the same for the horror film. The Motion Picture Association of America institutes a new system for rating films on the basis of age-group suitability, effectively replacing the Production Code.

**1969** The success of the countercultural film *Easy Rider* suggests new directions for Hollywood film and helps to usher in the New Hollywood era. Sam Peckinpah's *The Wild Bunch* portrays unprecedented levels of violence. *Butch Cassidy and the Sundance Kid* updates the Western for new, hipper audiences. *Midnight Cowboy* becomes the first X-rated film to win the Oscar for Best Picture, though the rating is later revised to R. The Woodstock music festival is held, providing a key monument of the 1960s counterculture.

**1970** Robert Altman's *MASH*, set in the Korean War, is an important antiwar comedy generally interpreted as a commentary on the U.S. involvement in Vietnam. *Woodstock*, about the previous year's music festival, becomes one of the most successful documentaries of all time.

**1971** Melvin Van Peebles's *Sweet Sweetback's Baadasssss Song* (1971) initiates the blaxploitation film cycle.

**1972** *The Godfather* is perhaps the greatest work of the "New Hollywood," making director Francis Ford Coppola a major figure in that movement. Burglars connected to the Committee to Re-Elect the President (Republican Richard Nixon) break into Democratic Party Headquarters in the Watergate office complex in Washington, D.C., triggering a major political scandal.

**1973** Altman's *The Long Goodbye* helps to begin the resurrection of film noir in the new mode known as "neo-noir." The science fiction thriller *Westworld* is the first film to employ computer-generated imagery (CGI).

**1974** Nixon is forced to resign from office due to fallout from the Watergate scandal. That scandal will soon help to inspire a wave of paranoid thrillers in film, of which Coppola's *The Conversation* (released four months before the resignation) is one of the first. Coppola's *The Godfather: Part II* becomes the first sequel to win the Oscar for Best Picture. Roman Polanski's *Chinatown* is perhaps the greatest of the neo-noir films.

**1975** *Jaws* is a breakthrough film for director Steven Spielberg; one of the first films to open nationwide rather than slowly building toward national distribution, it contributes to a growing emphasis on blockbusters among Hollywood studios. *One Flew over the Cuckoo's Nest* sweeps the top five Academy Awards, the first film to do so since *It Happened One Night*. The U.S. military withdrawal leads to the fall of Saigon and the end of the war in Vietnam, which will subsequently become the subject matter of some of the key films of the coming years.

**1976** *Taxi Driver* makes stars of actor Robert De Niro and director Martin Scorsese. It will become one of the best-known and most influential works of the New Hollywood, including playing a role in the fantasy world of John Hinckley that will inspire him to attempt the assassination of President Ronald Reagan in 1981. *All the President's Men* is inspired directly by the Watergate scandal. Sylvester Stallone's *Rocky* goes against the typical cynicism of 1970s film and becomes a major hit, winning the Academy Award for Best Picture.

**1977** Spielberg's *Close Encounters of the Third Kind* and (especially) George Lucas's *Star Wars* initiate a major renaissance in science fiction film. The latter, in particular, points toward the growing importance of special effects in the film industry in the coming years. *Annie Hall* is director Woody Allen's biggest hit.

**1978** John Carpenter's independently produced low-budget horror film *Halloween* is a surprise hit that initiates the teen slasher subgenre. *Superman* is the first major film featuring a comic-book superhero.

**1979** Coppola's *Apocalypse Now* is the first major post–Vietnam War film about that conflict; initially greeted with mixed responses, it will go on to become an acclaimed masterpiece. Ridley Scott's *Alien* initiates a major science fiction franchise.

**1980** Former Hollywood B-movie actor Ronald Reagan is elected president of the United States. Scorsese's *Raging Bull*, a biopic about boxer Jake La-Motta, will become the most highly regarded sports film and the most highly regarded biopic of all time. Michael Cimino's *Heaven's Gate* is an expensive box-office failure that for many signals the end of the New Hollywood era.

**1981** Spielberg's *Raiders of the Lost Ark* (executive produced by Lucas) is a huge hit that initiates the Indiana Jones film franchise.

**1982** Spielberg's *E.T.: The Extra-Terrestrial* continues the ongoing resurgence in the popularity of science fiction films, extending its appeal to younger audiences. *Star Trek II: The Wrath of Khan* takes the use of computer-generated imagery to a new level.

**1984** *The Terminator* continues a string of important science fiction films released since 1977 and makes stars of both director James Cameron and actor Arnold Schwarzenegger.

**1986** Oliver Stone's *Platoon* becomes one of the most respected films about the Vietnam War, winning the Oscar for Best Picture and making its director a major figure in Hollywood. The campy, but effectively satirical, *Robocop* is a hit, but announces the beginning of the end of the science fiction renaissance of the decade.

**1987** Stone's *Wall Street* becomes the definitive cinematic exploration of capitalist greed during the Reagan years.

**1988** *Who Framed Roger Rabbit* achieves a new level of sophistication in combining live action and animated images. Pixar's *Tin Toy* becomes the first computer-animated film to win an Academy Award (for Best Animated Short). The National Film Preservation Act establishes the National Film Registry to ensure the preservation of culturally significant films.

**1989** *The Little Mermaid* is the first major animated hit for Disney in decades, signaling the beginnings of a renaissance for Disney and for animated film as a whole. Tim Burton's *Batman* resurrects the superhero film genre, but in a darker mode.

**1990** *Dances with Wolves* is the year's Best Picture Oscar winner, revising the Western genre from the point of view of Native Americans.

**1991** Stone's *JFK* suggests possible CIA involvement in the assassination of President John F. Kennedy and becomes one of the most controversial films of the 1990s. Cameron's *Terminator 2: Judgment Day* is the first film to exceed $100 million in production costs. *Beauty and the Beast* is another huge hit for Disney and becomes the first animated film to be nominated for an Academy Award for Best Picture. John Singleton becomes the first African American nominated for the Best Director Oscar, for *Boyz 'n the Hood*. *The Silence of the Lambs* becomes the third film to sweep the top five Academy Awards.

**1992** Clint Eastwood's *Unforgiven* becomes the second Western in three years to win the Best Picture Oscar, proving that Westerns can still succeed in Hollywood.

**1993**   Spielberg's *Schindler's List* will become the director's most respected film and win him his first Academy Award for Best Director. *Philadelphia* is the first major Hollywood film to deal extensively with the AIDS issue.

**1994**   *The Lion King*, with a domestic gross of over $300 million, is Disney's biggest commercial success to date; that success helps Disney to become the first studio to exceed one billion dollars in gross domestic box-office receipts for the year. *Forrest Gump* wins the Best Picture Oscar and breaks new ground in the manipulation of images to insert its actors into existing historical footage.

**1995**   Pixar's *Toy Story* is the first feature-length film generated entirely by computer animation, which will quickly become the dominant form of film animation.

**1997**   Cameron's *Titanic* will become the biggest box-office film of all time—and will remain so until supplanted by Cameron's *Avatar* in 2010. *Good Will Hunting* makes a major splash and introduces Matt Damon and Ben Affleck to film audiences.

**1998**   Spielberg's *Saving Private Ryan* brings new levels of realism to the war film. *Antz* is the first animated film from DreamWorks.

**1999**   The much anticipated *Star Wars: Episode 1—The Phantom Menace* is a huge hit that initiates the second *Star Wars* trilogy, a prequel to the first. Another science fiction film, *The Matrix*, sets new standards for computer-enhanced action sequences.

**2000**   Steven Soderbergh's *Erin Brockovich* is a highlight of the year, winning a Best Actress Oscar for star Julia Roberts. *X-Men* is the first major film adapted from a leading Marvel comics franchise. Its success initiates a highly successful sequence of Marvel adaptations.

**2001**   *Lord of the Rings: The Fellowship of the Ring* initiates a landmark film trilogy based on the novels of J. R. R. Tolkien. DreamWorks's *Shrek* wins the first Academy Award for Best Animated Feature, mounting a challenge to Disney's dominance in that genre. Denzel Washington stars in *Training Day*, Halle Berry in *Monster's Ball*; the roles will make them the first African Americans to win Oscars for Best Actor and Best Actress in the same year.

**2002**   *Chicago* proves that the musical is still a viable film genre—and goes on to become the first musical to win the Oscar for Best Picture since *Oliver!* (1969). *Star Wars: Episode II—Attack of the Clones* is the first big-budget Hollywood feature shot entirely in digital video.

**2003**   U.S. military forces invade and occupy Iraq. *Finding Nemo* becomes Pixar's biggest hit to date and wins the Oscar for Best Animated Feature. Pixar is clearly the new industry leader in children's animation, ending decades of dominance by Disney (though Disney distributes the film). *Terminator* star Arnold Schwarzenegger becomes governor of California.

**2005**   *Chicken Little* is the first Disney-branded film produced entirely by computer animation and the first film released using the new Disney Digital 3D process, signaling a coming wave of 3D films using new digital processes.

**2006**   Disney acquires Pixar, reestablishing its position as the industry leader in animated films for children.

**2007**   The Writers Guild of America initiates a three-month strike that has severe repercussions throughout the entertainment industry. The strike is mainly concerned with such issues as writers' residuals for sales of film and television programs on DVD and in new media.

**2008**   Christopher Nolan's *The Dark Knight* is a huge hit, becoming the top-grossing superhero film of all time.

**2009**   Disney and DreamWorks announce plans to release all subsequent children's animated films in digital 3D formats. DreamWorks's *Monsters vs. Aliens* is the first film released under this new program. *Up* is the first Pixar film to be released in the Disney Digital 3D format. It is also the third consecutive Pixar film to win the Oscar for Best Animated Feature. Cameron's 3D science fiction film *Avatar* breaks new technological ground—and will become the highest-grossing film of all time. However, the Iraq occupation drama *The Hurt Locker* wins the Academy Award as the year's Best Picture.

**2010**   Tim Burton's *Alice in Wonderland* mixes live actors with computer animation and is released in Disney Digital 3D. It becomes Disney's second-highest-grossing film both domestically and worldwide, exceeded only by *Pirates of the Caribbean: Dead Man's Chest* (2006). Nolan's science fiction thriller *Inception* is one of the year's highlights.

# Introduction

One of the most powerful forces in world culture, American cinema now has a long and complex history that stretches through more than a century. This history not only includes a legacy of hundreds of important films but also the evolution of the film industry itself, which is in many ways a microcosm of the history of American society as a whole. The time-honored and widely held notion of Hollywood as a "dream factory" encapsulates many of the complexities of this history. Like much great art, American films often have a dreamlike quality, transporting audiences to other worlds (sometimes pleasant, sometimes nightmarish). But these films are expensive commodities, designed and manufactured through the cooperative efforts of numerous individuals, generally under the management and with the financing of large corporate entities whose principal goal is the generation of profits.

American films, then, are almost always produced through a complex series of negotiations between aesthetic aspirations and commercial interests, which often involve conflicts between the talented artists involved in making the films and the studios (and, more recently, the corporate owners of those studios) producing the films. Meanwhile, the relationship between American film and American society is complex as well; from the beginning, many observers have suspected films of having an unsavory effect on their audiences, while others have seen film as a glorious expression of American values. In any case, American films have often reflected important phenomena in the world at large, sometimes exercising an influence on those events.

By the 1920s, the studio system emerged to give corporate structure to the film industry, often treating actors, directors, and other artists simply as marketable commodities to be exploited for maximum profit. In response, artists have long struggled in a variety of ways to gain greater creative control over their work, including the founding of creator-controlled studios such as United Artists and the evolution of a variety of forms of "independent" film. Still, most artists in the film industry remained under the control of the corporate-dominated studio system into the 1950s, bound to specific studios

1

by long-term and highly restrictive contracts. In that decade, however, the original studio system collapsed beneath the weight of federal antitrust laws, the rise of television, and controversies over potential communist infiltration of the film industry. That collapse led to decades of reshuffling in the film industry, though by the early years of the 21st century the situation had somewhat stabilized, with all of the major studios owned by large multimedia conglomerates.

The (sometimes antagonistic) intermingling of art and commerce in the film industry is accompanied by a similarly complex relationship between art and technology. Indeed, the earliest film audiences seemed more interested in the technological novelty of moving pictures than in the actual content of the pictures, though rapid increases in technology for the recording and projection of pictures also meant that the individual films could be made more interesting. Of course, the increasingly high-tech nature of filmmaking also made film production more expensive, even as the increasing popularity of film made the business more lucrative. Thus, from the beginning, the relationship between art and technology in film was closely connected to the relationship between art and commerce. Technology has often had a major impact on the business of filmmaking, as when the new sound film technologies pioneered by Warner Bros. in the late 1920s made the small, struggling studio a major Hollywood power. Indeed, the coming of sound film at the end of the 1920s provided probably the single greatest watershed in American film history, though subsequent developments in color film technologies, wide-screen processes, and (eventually) computer-generated effects (including three-dimensional ones) were crucial to the history of American film as well.

The complexities of the American film business are easily matched by the complexity and variety of the films themselves. American films can be funny or sad, comforting or thought-provoking. They often provide cheery, feel-good entertainment, and they can transport audiences to idealized versions of their own world or to different worlds entirely. Yet they also often provide trenchant commentary on very real social and political issues. While the best-known films today tend to be megabudget spectacles driven by expensive computer-generated special effects, many of the best films are smaller efforts, earnest and thoughtful. While certain genres (such as fantasy and science fiction) have tended to dominate at the box office in recent decades, American films can be of any genre and can tackle virtually any subject matter. There is, in the films themselves, ample reason for both the praise and the criticism that have been aimed at the American film industry over the decades

## THE EMERGENCE OF AMERICAN CINEMA

Forms of projected images (some of them even with limited movement) go back to the magic lantern shows of the 18th century. But what we think of as the cinema begins in the late 19th century with the development of new techniques for recording and displaying moving images via film. The American film industry, now the most powerful and influential in the world, was also one of the earliest, with the company headed by Thomas Edison leading the way with the introduction of kinetoscope "peep shows" in 1891. In the 1890s, French filmmakers were at the forefront of the development of motion picture technology and technique, with the Lumière brothers (Auguste and Louis) pioneering the use of realistic photography and magician Georges Méliès developing a number of "trick" techniques that were the forerunners of modern special effects. In 1893, the Edison Company introduced the Vitascope projection camera (invented by Thomas Armat and C. Francis Jenkins, but widely attributed to Edison, largely for marketing purposes), used to exhibit large-screen motion pictures by early 1896; it was quickly followed by former Edison employee W. K. L. Dickson's Biograph projector in the fall of 1896.

For Edison and other early film companies, the technology that allowed for the display of moving images was regarded as their central product, while films themselves merely provided material for the demonstration of that technology. As a result, the same companies that were involved in the early development of filmmaking technologies were also involved in the production of films, though these early films were typically brief, displaying little in the way of plot or inventiveness (with the exception of the "trick" films of Méliès, which were quickly imitated by Edison and others). In 1903, however, the Edison Company released Edwin S. Porter's *The Great Train Robbery*, which introduced greater narrative richness and pointed the way for the more complex films that followed. Meanwhile, by this time the technology for recording and exhibition of films was becoming mature enough that more attention was being paid to the films themselves.

## AMERICAN CINEMA IN THE SILENT FILM ERA

After the success of *The Great Train Robbery*, narrative soon became the dominant mode, and genres such as the Western quickly evolved and developed a following. Most films remained short, however, and companies such as Biograph, with director D. W. Griffith leading the way, cranked out dozens of films (many now lost) per year. Other stars, such as Charles Chaplin, emerged during this early period as well. Then, in 1915, Griffith released *The Birth of a Nation* through his own company. This three-hour epic proved the potential of feature-length films, which became the dominant mode by the 1920s.

During that decade, Soviet and German filmmakers were widely regarded as the world leaders in cinematic artistry, but the Hollywood studios were already at the economic forefront of the film industry, and they began to use their economic strength to import European directors in a quest for greater legitimacy, especially among the middle and upper classes, who often looked upon filmgoing as an unsavory activity engaged in primarily by working-class (and often immigrant) viewers. Numerous American silent films of the 1920s are still regarded as classics, including dramas such as King Vidor's *The Big Parade* (1925) and *The Crowd* (1928) and F. W. Murnau's *Sunrise* (1927). The decade was also a key one for silent film comedy, with Chaplin, Buster Keaton, and Harold Lloyd emerging as major stars.

## THE COMING OF SOUND AND HOLLYWOOD'S GOLDEN AGE

Though Chaplin's most highly respected film, *City Lights*, was released in 1931, the silent film era was by this time essentially at an end due to the rapid rise of "talkies" after the breakout success of *The Jazz Singer*, with Al Jolson in 1927. This film allowed the upstart Warner Bros. to make a successful bid to become a major studio by being on the forefront of new technology for the production of integrated sound and picture. This technology quickly caught on and swept the industry, taking the film industry into the sound era with Hollywood now at the forefront of world cinema, a position the American film industry has yet to relinquish. In fact, Hollywood's dominance was extended and solidified during the 1930s, as the studio system for film production was fully established and the "Hollywood style" became fully developed. This style involved what came to be known as "invisible editing," which sought to make technical factors such as camera placement and movement and cuts between scenes as unnoticeable as possible, encouraging audiences to focus on characters and narrative and to ignore the status of a film as a crafted artifact.

American film in the 1930s, of course, was dominated by the looming reality of the Depression, as can be seen in such classic statements as Charles Chaplin's *Modern Times* (1936), which also addresses the potential threat to film art of the coming of sound, including the famous shot of the Tramp caught in the gears of factory machinery, looking like film going through a projector. Studios such as Warner Bros. led the way in developing gritty, realistic dramas such as gangster films and "social problem" dramas that addressed the hardships of life in the Depression, while documentary film, which addressed the Depression even more directly, also enjoyed an unprecedented prominence. On the other hand, such films of the early 1930s brought protests from some circles with regard to their content, leading to the implementation, by 1934, of the Motion Picture Production Code, which seriously limited the kinds of materials (especially related to crime and sex) that could be featured in American films for the next three decades.

Other fare of the 1930s was lighter, as studios such as MGM had great success during the decade with lavish escapist spectacles, especially musicals, designed to take audiences away from the reality of the Depression, if only for a short while. The Depression also contributed to the rise of particular forms of comedy that provided another sort of escape from conditions during the Depression. For example, the anarchic films of the Marx Brothers, perhaps best represented by the 1933 *Duck Soup*, can only be understood in relation to their Depression setting. Meanwhile, 1930s film comedy is probably best remembered for the rise of the so-called screwball comedy, in which a sequence of mishaps and misunderstandings complicates a budding romance (often between members of different classes), only to be resolved in the end.

The mid-1930s were marked by advances in color film technology, especially via the three-strip Technicolor process. In 1937, Disney's *Snow White and the Seven Dwarfs* proved the viability of animated feature films as well as demonstrating the potential of color films. The 1930s then ended with a particularly successful year in 1939, with the release of such films as the romantic historical epic *Gone with the Wind* and the musical fantasy *The Wizard of Oz*, both of which would go on to become among the most admired films in American history. The Hollywood style remained dominant through the 1940s, as the major studios became more and more entrenched as the industry's trendsetters. Meanwhile, film itself became ever more firmly situated as a crucial element of American popular culture, while movie stars, actively promoted by the studios as a branding and marketing tool, became some of the best-known individuals in the world. Most of the leading films of the 1940s epitomized the Hollywood style, as in the case of *Casablanca* (1942), sometimes regarded as the quintessential example of the style. On the other hand, the most highly regarded films of the decade (and, in many circles, of all time) was Orson Welles's *Citizen Kane* (1941), a film that achieves its effects largely by violation of the conventions of the Hollywood style (with an overtly constructed nonlinear plot, intrusive camera angles, mixtures of genres, and so on).

The first half of the 1940s, of course, was dominated by World War II, which affected Hollywood in a number of ways, including the fact that numerous prominent figures within the film industry served actively in the military during the war, effectively putting their film careers on hold. Films themselves, meanwhile, often addressed the reality of the war, as pro-war, anti-Nazi, and even pro-Soviet films came to the fore, initiated even before the U.S. entry into the war by the 1940 release of Chaplin's anti-Hitler satire *The Great Dictator.*

The war years also saw the rise of the phenomenon that would come to be known as "film noir," though the genre would not be identified as such until after the war when French critics, without access to American films during most of the war, were surprised to find the new, dark, stylish, and gritty films about crime and corruption that had appeared in the United States during the war. Films such as John Huston's *The Maltese Falcon* (1941) and Billy Wilder's *Double Indemnity* (1944) employed low-key lighting and moody black-and-white photography reminiscent of the German expressionist films of the 1920s to produce atmospheric effects that reinforced their dark subject matter and helped to inspire an extensive cycle of such films over the first postwar decade.

## THE 1950S AND THE END OF THE GOLDEN AGE

As the film industry sought to move forward after the end of the war—and directly responded to postwar social realities in such films as *The Best Years of Our Lives* (1946)—the industry was sent reeling when hearings before the House Un-American Activities Committee (HUAC) in October 1947 suggested (though with little real evidence) extensive communist influence in the film industry. The industry was then thrown into further turmoil when a 1948 U.S. Supreme Court ruling against the industry in the Paramount Antitrust Case forced the major Hollywood studios to divest themselves of their self-owned chains of movie theaters over the next several years. In the meantime, the industry responded to charges of communist influence by establishing an extensive blacklist of individuals with suspected political leanings, making it impossible for hundreds of screenwriters, directors, producers, and actors to work in Hollywood film until the blacklist finally fell apart in the early 1960s.

The American film industry experienced additional pressures when television began its meteoric rise as a force within American culture in the early 1950s. The industry responded by attempting to produce lavish, full-color, wide-screen spectacles (such as biblical epics), employing technologies that could create viewing experiences unavailable on television. It also gradually began to introduce subject matter that might be deemed unacceptable on television, though the combination of the Production Code and the repressive political climate of the 1950s placed severe limitations on how far film could go in this sense. Meanwhile, films by "prestige" directors, such as Alfred Hitchcock and Billy Wilder, gained a new importance, marketed as material of a quality far beyond what could be found on television—though by 1955 Hitchcock was hosting his own weekly anthology series on television, indicating the gradual merger of the two industries, as Hollywood film studios, strapped for cash, began to produce more and more programming for the rival medium.

The decline of the Golden Age studio system also opened up opportunities in the 1950s for smaller, independent studios, which often sought niche audiences through the production of genre films, especially science fiction and the Western. By the late 1950s, an unprecedented emphasis, especially among lower-budget films, was being placed on teenage audiences, with the notion that such viewers would attend films as a social or dating experience that could not be attained from watching television. Many of these films were poorly and quickly made, especially given the sense that teens were coming to movies for the social experience, with relatively little regard for the actual content of the films. Still, some of the landmark films of the decade, such as Nicholas Ray's *Rebel without a Cause* (1955), were teen-oriented films, while others among the decade's finest films were genre films, such as the science fiction classic *The Day the Earth Stood Still* (1951) or Westerns such as *High Noon* (1952) and *The Searchers* (1956).

## THE 1960S AND THE 1970S:
## THE COMING OF THE NEW HOLLYWOOD

The 1960s continued the decline of the old studio system as the film industry went through a number of corporate reshufflings, meanwhile still seeking to redefine its product as something that could compete with television. Most of the decade was marked by diversity and variety, including a new air of open-mindedness that was signaled by the breaking of the blacklist, beginning with *Spartacus* (1960), based on a novel by the leftist novelist Howard Fast and scripted by blacklisted screenwriter Dalton Trumbo. Meanwhile, Arthur Penn's *Bonnie and Clyde* (1967) showed a new willingness on the part of Hollywood directors to borrow techniques from French and other international films. By the latter years of the 1960s, the political activism of the decade was reflected in an increasing emphasis on films containing social and political commentary, such as Mike Nichols's *The Graduate* or Norman Jewison's *In the Heat of the Night* (both released in 1967). The film industry then took some important turns at the end of the decade as films such as the science fiction classic *2001: A Space Odyssey* (1968) and the Western *Butch*

*Cassidy and the Sundance Kid* (1969) challenged the usual conventions of genre films, while the surprise success of *Easy Rider* (1969) indicated the economic viability of films made from the point of view of the 1960s counterculture.

Such films took the industry into the 1970s in a mood that was highly receptive to innovation, just as most of the leading directors of Hollywood's Golden Age were ending their careers and a whole new generation of filmmakers, educated in film schools, moved to the forefront of the industry in the phenomenon that came to be known as the New Hollywood. These intensely self-conscious directors produced a number of notable films, making the decade, in the minds of many, the richest in Hollywood history.

New Hollywood filmmakers of the 1970s continued to challenge the conventions of established genres, as in Robert Altman's update of the war film in *MASH* (1970). One important genre revision came with films such as Altman's *The Long Goodbye* (1973) and Roman Polanski's *Chinatown* (1974), which revived the film noir with new energies and triggered a new cycle of "neo-noir" films, including such important films of the 1980s as *Body Heat* (1981) and *Blade Runner* (1982). The New Hollywood also produced important works of social commentary, such as Altman's exploration of the violent tendencies in American society (via an excursion into the country music industry) in *Nashville* (1975). The most important of such films, however, were those that commented on the recent American experience in Vietnam, including Hal Ashby's *Coming Home* (1978), Michael Cimino's *The Deer Hunter* (1978), and Coppola's *Apocalypse Now* (1979). Meanwhile, Martin Scorsese's *Taxi Driver* (1976) linked the legacy of Vietnam to the contemporary violence in American society.

The horror genre was particularly rich in the 1970s, as were several others; it was at this time that Francis Ford Coppola breathed new life into the gangster film genre with what might be its two greatest works, *The Godfather* (1972) and *The Godfather: Part II* (1974). These films were also huge commercial successes that indicated the growing importance of blockbusters to the business plans of the major studios, a trend that was continued with the huge success of Steven Spielberg's *Jaws* (1975) and George Lucas's *Star Wars* (1977). The latter, along with Spielberg's *Close Encounters of the Third Kind*, released in the same year, triggered a major renaissance in science fiction film that lasted into the mid-1980s. On the other hand, many felt that the new emphasis on special effects in such films was ultimately detrimental to the production of genuinely thoughtful works of science fiction cinema, just as the emphasis on production of blockbusters that marked the end of the 1970s was ultimately detrimental to the production of fine works of cinematic art in general.

## THE 1980S AND 1990S

The key films of the 1980s included such early blockbusters as Spielberg's *Raiders of the Lost Ark* (1981), which triggered a succession of successful sequels, and *E.T.: The Extra-Terrestrial* (1982), which contributed to the ongoing science fiction renaissance, a phenomenon that would soon include such films as the first two *Star Trek* sequels and James Cameron's *The Terminator* (1984) and *Aliens* (1986). One of the classic films of the 1980s was *Tootsie* (1982), a role-reversal film that responded to changing attitudes toward gender in American society. Meanwhile, the Vietnam War films of the 1970s were followed by such works as Oliver Stone's *Platoon* (1986) and Kubrick's *Full Metal Jacket* (1987), while the gangster film cycle triggered by *The Godfather* continued with Brian De Palma's *Scarface* (1983).

Scorsese also started out the decade on a high note, with *Raging Bull* (1980), perhaps now his most admired film. Still, the early 1980s began with the apparent exhaustion of the New Hollywood in the commercial failure of films such as Cimino's *Heaven's Gate* (1980), and the decade as a whole was marked by financial instability among many of the major studios and a general decline in the number of truly remarkable films relative to the 1970s. On the other hand, films such as Stone's *Wall Street* (1987) provided important commentary on the social and economic climate of the Reagan years, while new independent filmmakers such as John Sayles—with *Matewan* (1987) and *Eight Men Out* (1988)—showed that important, politically engaged films could be made outside the mainstream Hollywood system.

The 1980s ended on a positive note, as 1989 saw the release of such films as Cameron's *The Abyss* (1989), another important science fiction film, while Spike Lee's *Do the Right Thing* (1989) signaled the emergence of a major new African American filmmaker. That same year, Tim Burton's *Batman* revived the superhero movie and put its director on the road to stardom. Disney's return to success in animated films for children began with *The Little Mermaid* (1989), triggering a Disney renaissance that was one of the crucial phenomena in American film of the 1990s. Such positive signs at the end of the 1980s foreshadowed a rich and varied decade in the 1990s, which saw continued growth in the success of children's film (buoyed by the emergence of computer-animated films), an explosive expansion of the independent film industry, and the continued strength of individual blockbusters, such as Spielberg's *Jurassic Park* (1993) and Cameron's *Titanic* (1997), which went on, at the time, to become the top-grossing film of all time.

Both *Jurassic Park* and *Titanic* made heavy use of computer-generated special effects, the rapid development of which was one of the crucial driving factors of American film in the 1990s, leading by the end of the decade to such effects-driven science fiction films as *The Matrix* (1999). One of the most important developments in computer-generated imagery, however, was the evolution of techniques to generate entire animated films by computer, beginning with *Toy Story* (1995), a film the success of which put the upstart Pixar on the road to becoming the leading player in the children's film industry, driving Disney (long skeptical of the possibilities of computer animation) and others in that direction as well.

More conventional filmmaking continued apace as well, and major directors from earlier decades continued to produce important works. Coppola's *The Godfather: Part III* (1990) was something of a disappointment, but Scorsese's *Goodfellas* (1990) was another important gangster film classic. Altman's Hollywood satire *The Player* (1992) was a key film of the early 1990s, while, in addition to *Jurassic Park*, Spielberg scored major successes with *Schindler's List* (1993) and *Saving Private Ryan* (1998). In 1991, Stone's *JFK* became one of the most talked-about films of the decade, as did his *Natural Born Killers* (1994), a critique of violence in American culture that many saw as a glorification of violence in its own right. The latter was based on a story by Quentin Tarantino, who had made an impressive directorial debut with *Reservoir Dogs* (1992), following with *Pulp Fiction* (1994), the film that made him a top Hollywood director and helped to fuel the surge in independent film that marked the decade. Other key directors gained prominence in the 1990s as well, include the brother team of Joel and Ethan Coen, who released such films as *Barton Fink* (1991), *The Hudsucker Proxy* (1993), *Fargo* (1996), and *The Big Lebowski* (1998) in the decade.

Other highly successful films of the 1990s included such varied fare as the tense thriller *The Silence of the Lambs* (1991), the Western *Unforgiven* (1992), the prison drama *The Shawshank Redemption* (1994), and the unusual romantic drama *Forrest Gump* (1994). Meanwhile, the horror genre gained a new level of self-consciousness with such works as Wes Craven's three *Scream* films (1996, 1997, 2000), while *The Blair Witch Project* (1999) pointed toward a coming wave of grittier, low-budget horror films.

## AMERICAN FILM IN THE 21ST CENTURY

By the early years of the 21st century, decades of corporate instability in the film industry were coming to an end as large and powerful media conglomerates gained solid control of the major studios. By the end of the first decade of the century, Disney had become the largest of these, while Paramount was a subsidiary of Viacom, Twentieth Century Fox of Newscorp, and Warner Bros. of Time Warner. This development brought a certain economic stability to the industry, while positioning film to take its place among the proliferation of "new media" that marked the new century.

Probably the most important film phenomenon of the early years of the 21st century was the year-by-year release of the *Lord of the Rings* trilogy in 2001, 2002, and 2003, elaborate adaptations of J. R. R. Tolkien's classic fantasy novels made possible by the availability of highly sophisticated computer-generated imagery. The year 2001 also saw the release of the first film adaptation of the Harry Potter novels, beginning a major film franchise that would include the release of eight films in the next 10 years. Meanwhile, Disney's *Pirates of the Caribbean* franchise (with films released in 2003, 2006, and 2007) continued the domination of big-budget effects-driven fantasy films at the box office, usurping the place once held by science fiction, though science fiction would reclaim the box-office crown with Cameron's *Avatar*, released at the end of 2009, an environmentalist science fiction epic that went on easily to surpass *Titanic* as the top-grossing film of all time.

The growing importance of franchises in the new century was part of a tendency, begun in the 1990s, toward more and more sequels to and remakes of earlier successful films, a trend that some saw as indicative of a lack of creative energy or, alternatively, of a greater emphasis on profitability than creativity. Meanwhile, other trends were also viewed by many with alarm, as in the proliferation of grisly, low-budget slasher films such as the *Saw* sequence, which stretched to seven films from 2004 to 2010. Still, directors such as Tarantino, Burton, and the Coens continued to produce impressive work, while art-director David Lynch moved more into the mainstream with *Mulholland Dr.* (2001), widely considered to be his finest film. Meanwhile, older directors continued to produce interesting films as well, such as Scorsese's *Gangs of New York* (2002), *The Aviator* (2004), and *The Departed* (2006).

Serious films were also produced in response to events such as the 9/11 bombings and the subsequent U.S. "war on terror" and invasion of Iraq. Among the more important of these were *Jarhead* (2005), *In the Valley of Elah* (2007), *Lions for Lambs* (2007), *Redacted* (2007), *Body of Lies* (2008), *The Hurt Locker* (2008, a Best Picture Oscar winner), and *The Messenger* (2009). Most of these films, however, did not do well at the box office, perhaps because they reflected serious matters with which many filmgoers would prefer not to deal. Other serious, politically engaged films of the century's first decade sometimes did a bit better, including several featuring actor George Clooney, such as *Good Night, and Good Luck* (2005), *Syriana* (2005), and *Michael Clayton* (2007), the first of which he also directed.

Though the Disney renaissance of the 1990s had cooled, children's animated films continued to score big at the box office, with Pixar (acquired by Disney in 2006) leading the way with such films as *Finding Nemo* (2003),

*The Incredibles* (2004), and *WALL-E* (2008), while DreamWorks scored big with its *Shrek* sequence (four films from 2001 to 2010), and Fox/Blue Sky Studios had major hits with the *Ice Age* films (released in 2002, 2006, and 2009). By the end of the decade, all major animated children's films were being released via newly developed digital 3D processes, representing a major change in film-viewing technologies. One of these new 3D films was Burton's 2010 remake of Disney's classic *Alice in Wonderland*, which employed a combination of live actors and computer animation to become the top-grossing children's film of all time, only to be surpassed a few months later by the 3-D feature *Toy Story 3*.

The new 3D revolution, employing digital technologies far superior to the original 3D processes of the 1950s, moved well beyond children's film with such works as *Avatar*. New digital technologies were beginning to have large impacts on other aspects of 21st-century American film as well, as films of all kinds were increasingly being shot in digital video instead of on film. Film distributors were also increasingly mulling the potential of beaming films digitally from satellites to theaters, rather than distributing conventional reels of film. All in all, given the decline of the American economy in the first decade of the new century, the U.S. film industry was doing well indeed—and looking forward to a bright future in which a climate of technological change would offer both challenges and opportunities.

# A

***2001: A SPACE ODYSSEY.*** Still widely regarded as the film that first demonstrated the potential of **science fiction** film to be genuine art, *2001: A Space Odyssey* (dir. Stanley Kubrick, 1968) has exercised a powerful influence on the look and feel of countless subsequent films in its genre. Though greeted with mixed reviews from critics on its initial release, the film has enjoyed a growing prestige over time and certainly helped to open the way for increased production of sf films in the 1970s, after a relatively slow decade in the 1960s. The striking classical **music** soundtrack of *2001* (including an overture and an intermission) openly declares its aspiration to the status of high art, but it is ultimately the visuals of the film that make it important. The film's representation of the futuristic technology of space travel remains effective and impressive even today, though the film was made without the aid of the kinds of computer-generated imageries that are indispensible to science fiction film in the 21st century. Images from the film (perhaps most importantly its renegade computer, HAL, and its central musical theme, Richard Strauss's *Also Sprach Zarathustra*) have become an integral part of contemporary American popular culture.

 *2001* is a complex film that leaves many aspects open to interpretation. Based on a short story by sf master Arthur C. Clarke (who co-wrote the script with director Kubrick), the film hints that a superhuman alien presence has been monitoring the evolution of the human race from its very beginning, perhaps subtly intervening when the time is right for the race to make a major new step in its development. The bulk of the film is set during one of those turning points, as an expedition into deep space apparently leads to an encounter with the aliens and a return to Earth of a mysterious infant, seen by most as a Star Child who is supposed to help bring about the next stage in the evolution of the human species. The film thus deals with the kind of weighty matters that are appropriate to its considerable artistic merit, helping to open the way for a variety of serious issues to be dealt with in the sf films that followed it.

**ABBOTT, BUD (1895–1974) AND COSTELLO, LOU (1906–1959).** Bud Abbott and Lou Costello first met while working in vaudeville theaters in the 1930s and officially became a team in 1935. They went on to gain greater exposure on radio, and then appeared in their first film in 1940 with their supporting roles in *One Night in the Tropics*. Their performance in that film featured a shortened version of what would become one of their signature routines, the baseball sketch "Who's on First?" They were an immediate hit with audiences and went on, with Abbott playing the straight man and Costello the funny man, somewhat in the mold of **Stan Laurel and Oliver Hardy**, to become one of the great **comedy** teams in Hollywood history. Their first starring role came in 1941 with *Buck Privates*, a film that helped them to become one of Hollywood's top starring acts during World War II. By the time of *Dance with Me, Henry* (1956), the duo had made three dozen films together. In addition, they continued to appear on radio throughout the 1940s and starred in their own television series from 1952 to 1958.

Abbott and Costello specialized in films that were spoofs of popular Hollywood genres, including **science fiction**, **horror**, **Westerns**, and **war films**. Much of the comedy in their films came from the use of skits and routines that they had earlier performed on stage. Many of their films were also punctuated by lavish **musical** production numbers, indicating the importance with which their films were regarded by **Universal Pictures**, the studio for which most of their films were made. Some of the more popular films of Abbott and Costello included *Hold That Ghost* (1941), *Who Done It?* (1942), *Pardon My Sarong* (1942), *The Naughty Nineties* (1945), *The Time of Their Lives* (1946), and *Buck Privates Come Home* (1947). They also starred in a number of films that essentially spoofed the classic Universal **monster movies** of the 1930s, including *Abbott and Costello Meet Frankenstein* (1948), *Abbott and Costello Meet the Killer, Boris Karloff* (1949), and *Abbott and Costello Meet the Invisible Man* (1951).

Abbott and Costello broke up in 1957 after both had experienced financial difficulties due to demands from the Internal Revenue Service for payment of back taxes. This event, which forced both partners to sell off numerous assets, came after years in which relations between the two had been strained and in which their popularity was on the wane. Abbott performed very little after the split, but Costello worked more extensively, performing stand-up comedy and starring in one solo film, *The 30 Foot Bride of Candy Rock* (1959).

**ACADEMY AWARD.** The Academy Awards, given annually by the **Academy of Motion Picture Arts and Sciences** (AMPAS) for outstanding performance in a variety of categories, are the world's most prestigious awards for achievement in the film industry. Winners of the award are given a gold-plated statuette known as an "**Oscar**" (the origin of the term is disputed), and the awards themselves are also popularly known as the "Oscars." They have been given every year since 1929, though the categories covered by the awards have varied slightly over time. Originally consisting of a relatively small private luncheon, the awards ceremonies have been telecast since 1953 and now constitute a major annual television event, attended in person by hundreds of Hollywood's elite and seen worldwide by tens of millions of viewers.

Typically, the most prestigious Academy Awards have been those for Best Picture, Best Director, Best Actor in a Leading Role, Best Actress in a Leading Role, and Best Writing, all of which have been given since 1927. However, since 1940, the writing award has involved separate awards for Best Adapted Screenplay (for a screenplay adapted from material formerly appearing in another medium) and Best Original Screenplay (for a screenplay written directly for the screen). Other important awards include those for Best Supporting Actor and Actress, Best Cinematography, Best Art Direction, Best Costume Design, Best Makeup, Best Musical Score, Best Song, Best Visual Effects, Best Film Editing, Best Sound Mixing, and Best Sound Editing. In addition to the main Best Film category, there are now also separate categories for Best Foreign Language Film, Best Animated Feature, Best Documentary Feature, Best Live Action Short Film, Best Animated Short Film, and Best Documentary Short Subject.

The Academy also occasionally grants honorary awards, typically to individuals it feels have deserved a regular award but have failed to win one. In addition, the Academy grants a number of awards outside the main categories of the Academy Awards. The most prestigious of these is the **Irving G. Thalberg** Memorial Award, given periodically for outstanding lifetime achievement. Other auxiliary awards include the Scientific and Engineering Award and the Technical Achievement Award.

**ACADEMY OF MOTION PICTURE ARTS AND SCIENCES (AMPAS).** The Academy of Motion Picture Arts and Sciences is a professional organization whose membership consists of more than 6,000 individuals who work in the film industry. Founded in 1927 as the brainchild of **Louis B. Mayer,** the Academy is dedicated to advancing the art of film and is involved in a number of film-related educational and promotional activities. For example, it operates the Samuel Goldwyn Theater in Beverly Hills, a state-of-the-art facility designed to display films with the optimum available technology. The Academy is best known, however, for bestowing the annual **Academy Awards** for outstanding contributions to the field of motion pictures.

**ACTION FILM.** Though a great deal of action is common in American film as a whole, there is an identifiable genre of American film that depends primarily on spectacular action sequences to achieve its effects. Such films have their roots in the "swashbuckling" adventures of the 1930s, in which actors such as **Douglas Fairbanks** and **Errol Flynn** became major stars. Crime dramas also often featured considerable amounts of action, and many of the **spy films** that arose during the Cold War (especially the James Bond sequence) employed spectacular action scenes to great effect as well. But it was not until the end of the 1970s that action film became a true genre of its own, as technological advances, especially in **computer-generated imagery**, made it possible to produce action sequences never before imaginable on screen.

Science fiction films such as *Star Wars* (1977), *Alien* (1979), and *The Terminator* (1984) led the way in the rise of more spectacular action scenes in American film. The sword-and-sorcery **fantasy** cycle that began with *Conan the Barbarian* (1982) made a major contribution to the rise of the action genre as well, and it is no coincidence that both *Conan* and *The Terminator* starred **Arnold Schwarzenegger**, who would go on to become the leading action star as action grew into an identifiable genre in its own right. In addition to starring in several other high-action sf films, Schwarzenegger also starred in the ultraviolent *Commando* (1985), *Raw Deal* (1986), and *Red Heat* (1988), though by the time of *The Last Action Hero* (1993) and *True Lies* (1994) his films were beginning to parody themselves, suggesting the beginning of the end of his particular cycle of action films.

The other major star who helped to establish the action genre in the 1980s was **Sylvester Stallone**, whose attempts at sf film were largely unfortunate, but who found a niche for himself in the ultraviolent *Rambo* sequence, beginning with *First Blood* (1982) and following with the even more successful *Rambo: First Blood Part II* (1985). Stallone became even better known for *Rocky* and its sequels (which spanned a 30-year period from 1976 to 2006), but those were not action films per se. Lesser figures, such as the Belgian martial artist Jean-Claude Van Damme, attempted to become Schwarzenegger-type action stars as well, but with limited success.

Police action dramas also became popular in the 1980s, led by the efforts of actors such as **Bruce Willis**, whose starring role in *Die Hard* (1988) led to similar roles in both a series of sequels and a series of similar films, which typically feature a courageous lone protagonist battling highly organized groups of villains, including terrorists. **Mel Gibson** had similar success with the *Lethal Weapon* (1987) series of films, though these contained considerable comic elements that pointed the way toward more **comedy** in recent action films, such as those featuring Chinese martial arts star Jackie Chan.

Another key development, again spurred by science fiction via the performances of Sigourney Weaver in the *Alien* films and Linda Hamilton in *Terminator 2: Judgment Day* (1991), has been the rise of female action stars, especially beginning in the 1990s. Taking their cue partly from Hong Kong martial arts films, which often feature female protagonists, films such as *Point of No Return* (1993), a remake of the 1990 French film *Nikita*, began to feature strong women who employed martial arts and various weapons in action roles. By the end of the decade, characters such as Trinity (Carrie-Anne Moss) in *The Matrix* (1999) were making formidable women a standard feature of action films. Subsequently, the new century has featured a number of key action performances by women, including Angelina Jolie as the title character in *Laura Croft: Tomb Raider* (2001), Uma Thurman as "the Bride" in the two *Kill Bill* films (2003 and 2004), and Milla Jovovich as the lead character in the three *Resident Evil* films (2002–2007).

Recent **spy films** have also proved fertile ground for action sequences, including the growth of more and more spectacular action in the James Bond sequence, as well as such new film sequences as the *Mission Impossible* films, beginning in 1996. Increasing action has also marked other genres (such as the **Western**) as well, to the point that the action film as a distinct genre is becoming harder to distinguish from any of the other genres that it touches upon.

**ALDRICH, ROBERT (1918–1983).** The American director, writer, and producer Robert Aldrich began his work in film as an assistant director, then quickly moved into the director's chair with the **sports movie** *Big Leaguer* (1953) and the **Western** *Apache* (1954). The latter was part of a contemporary trend toward more sympathetic portrayal of Native Americans in film, indicating a tendency toward progressive political ideas that marked many of Aldrich's films. Among the best known of Aldrich's early films is *Kiss Me Deadly* (1955), a **film noir** classic that he both directed and produced. Based on a novel by Mickey Spillane, this film is an offbeat effort that in many ways challenges Spillane's reactionary politics. Aldrich also directed and produced *The Big Knife* (1955), a film noir that satirizes the Hollywood film industry. *Attack* (1956) was a politically engaged **war film** exploring the role of social class in the U.S. military.

In a commercial sense, Aldrich was particularly successful in the 1960s, directing a series of high-profile films that included the **biblical epic** *Sodom and Gomorrah* (1962), *Whatever Happened to Baby Jane?* (1962), *Hush, Hush, Sweet Charlotte* (1964), and *The Dirty Dozen* (1967). The latter was so profitable that Aldrich was able to establish his own film production company, though it met with little success; one of its productions, *Ulzana's Raid*

(1972), was a notable progressive Western that focused on the genocidal extermination of Native Americans after the Civil War, at the same time indirectly commenting on the U.S. involvement in Vietnam.

By the time of his next hit, *The Longest Yard* (1974), Aldrich was again working for a **major studio** (**Paramount Pictures**), though retaining his progressive politics in a sports movie that satirizes numerous aspects of life in corporate-dominated, Nixon-era America. Aldrich returned to his critique of the U.S. involvement in Vietnam with *Twilight's Last Gleaming* (1977), a thriller that suggests corruption in the highest echelons of the U.S. government.

Aldrich is noted for his attention to detail and for his innovative use of techniques such as the split screens of *The Longest Yard* and *Twilight's Last Gleaming*. He was nominated for numerous international awards, including a nomination for the Golden Palm at the Cannes Film Festival for *Whatever Happened to Baby Jane?* However, he was never nominated for an **Academy Award**, despite being considered by critics to be a genuine film auteur.

**ALLEN, WOODY (1935– ).** Born Allen Stewart Konigsberg, Woody Allen would go on to become one of the most distinctive and prolific directors in American film, generally also writing and frequently starring in his own films. Most of Allen's films center on the Jewish milieu of New York City (where he himself was born and grew up); they typically revolve around his most representative protagonist (usually played by himself), who is neurotic, whining, and sexually insecure, but intelligent and talented. Allen has worked in a variety of genres, typically working quickly and with a fairly low budget, but able to attract talented and well-known actors to his projects because of the critical esteem in which his work is held.

Having attended (but not graduated from) New York University and City College of New York, Allen got his start as a television script writer and stand-up comedian. He moved into film with *What's New Pussycat* (1965), for which he wrote the screenplay and in which he played a supporting role as an actor. He had his directorial debut in *What's Up, Tiger Lilly?* (1966), an inventive effort in which an actual Japanese spy movie is redubbed into English with a completely different (and comic) script, co-written by Allen. In the next few years he established himself as a director, writer, and actor with a series of farcical **comedies**, marked by clever one-liners, broad **slapstick** humor, and parodic engagement with the conventions of Hollywood film. These initial films included *Take the Money and Run* (1969), *Bananas* (1971), *Everything You Always Wanted to Know about Sex * But Were Afraid to Ask* (1972), and *Sleeper* (1973), all of which featured actress Louise Lasser, Allen's first wife and the first of several actress-muses who would play important roles in his career. During this period, Allen also wrote and starred in **Herbert Ross**'s *Play It Again, Sam* (1972) and starred in **Martin Ritt**'s *The Front* (1976).

The bittersweet **romantic comedy** *Annie Hall* (1977), widely regarded as Allen's finest achievement, marked the pinnacle of his many early collaborations with actress **Diane Keaton**, while winning Allen **Academy Awards** for Best Director and Best Original Screenplay. This film also signaled a turn toward more serious subjects, even when still treated in the comic mode. Keaton's period of close collaboration with Allen then ended with the much-admired *Manhattan* (1979), a black-and-white homage to the city that provides the locale for so many of Allen's films. These films continued to grow more serious while also becoming more identifiably postmodernist and self-consciously artistic over the next years, often paying homage to European directors he admired, such as Sweden's Ingmar Bergman and Italy's Federico Fellini. Thus, *Stardust Memories* (1980) is essentially a postmodern pastiche of Fellini's *8 1/2* (1963), while *Zelig* (1983) and *The Purple Rose of Cairo* (1985) are postmodern meditations on the instability of personal identity and of the boundary between fiction and reality in the contemporary world. Films such as *Interiors* (1978) and *Another Woman* (1988) are somber efforts made in the mode of Bergman, while *Shadows and Fog* (1992) pays homage to German expressionism.

Most of Allen's films from *A Midsummer Night's Sex Comedy* (1982) to *Husbands and Wives* (1992) featured actress Mia Farrow, with whom he had a longtime personal relationship. Highlights during this period included *Hannah and Her Sisters* (1986), for which Allen won a second Best Original Screenplay **Oscar**, and *Radio Days* (1987), which nostalgically looks back to Allen's own childhood while also recalling Fellini's *Amarcord* (1973).

Allen continued to be an active and critically admired director through the 1990s, though shifting back to a more comic mode with films such as *Bullets over Broadway* (1994), *Mighty Aphrodite* (1995), *Everyone Says I Love You* (1996), *Deconstructing Harry* (1997), and *Celebrity* (1998). The more serious *Sweet and Lowdown* (1999), which reflected Allen's lifelong serious interest in jazz **music**, was also a critical success.

Beginning with *The Curse of the Jade Scorpion* (2001), Allen experienced a series of critical and commercial failures, which came on the heels of considerable controversy in his personal life as well, especially involving his romantic relationship with young Soon-Yi Previn, the adopted daughter of his longtime lover, actress Mia Farrow. However, he rebounded strongly in 2005 with *Match Point*, one of his most successful films and the film that marked his first collaboration with new muse Scarlett Johansson. Johansson also starred in Allen's *Scoop* (2006) and *Vicky Cristina Barcelona* (2008). In addition to his three Oscar wins, Allen has had a total of 14 Oscar nominations for Best Screenplay, six for Best Director, and one for Best Actor (for *Annie Hall*). *See also* POSTMODERNISM; NYKVIST, SVEN.

**ALTMAN, ROBERT (1925–2006).** One of the most distinguished American film directors of his generation, Robert Altman began his career as the director of numerous industrial films and **documentaries**, then moved into feature film as the writer and director of *The Delinquents* (1957), a low-budget teen **exploitation film** that nevertheless showed flashes of Altman's future promise as a director. Subsequently, Altman worked extensively as a writer and director for a number of different television series through the 1960s, a decade in which his only feature film was the unsuccessful *The Cold Day in the Park* (1969).

Altman's career took a dramatic turn with the release of *MASH* (1970), a Korean War film that clearly served as a commentary on the U.S. involvement in Vietnam as well. This major critical and commercial success catapulted Altman into the Hollywood mainstream, and he followed it with a string of some of the most acclaimed films of the 1970s, including the revisionary **Western** *McCabe & Mrs. Miller* (1971), the **neo-noir** film *The Long Goodbye* (1973), *Thieves Like Us* (1974), and *Nashville* (1975). The latter, which focuses on the country **music** industry but satirically explores numerous aspects of contemporary American society, is still widely regarded as his greatest achievement. All of these films contain considerable social and political commentary, and all show Altman's trademark technique of constructing complex plots from numerous interrelated storylines, highlighted by scenes of highly realistic dialogue in which characters' speeches often overlap.

Altman's career began to take a downturn with the release of *Buffalo Bill and the Indians, or Sitting Bull's History Lesson* (1976), another biting **satire** of the media-saturated society of the 1970s America but one that met with little commercial success, despite **Paul Newman**'s virtuoso performance as Buffalo Bill Cody. Working with his own film production company, Lion's Gate Films, Altman made increasingly eccentric films in the late 1970s, falling out of favor with audiences. His attempt to return to the mainstream with *Popeye* (1980), a somewhat bizarre live-action **musical** adaptation of the classic comic and cartoon, was a critical and commercial disaster.

Through the 1980s, Altman made a series of small, rather obscure films that got little attention, though his 1988 political mockumentary for HBO, *Tanner '88*, was widely lauded for its satirical commentary on the American political process. Altman then returned to the limelight with the much-acclaimed Hollywood satire *The Player* (1992), which skewers the pretentions and greed of the Hollywood film industry. Among other things, this film features numerous cameo appearances by major Hollywood actors, suggesting their endorsement of Altman's assessment of the film industry. Once again a name to reckon with, Altman remained active as a director throughout the rest of his life, making a number of films that bore his distinctive stamp and that consistently refused to succumb to Hollywood cliché. Among his later films, *Short Cuts* (1993), *Ready to Wear (Prêt à Porter)* (1994), and *Gosford Park* (2001) were particularly successful, the latter scoring seven **Academy Award** nominations and winning Altman a Director of the Year award from the **American Film Institute**. That film also won Altman his fifth Academy Award nomination as Best Director, though he never won that award. He was, however, awarded an honorary **Oscar** for lifetime achievement in 2006.

**AMBLIN ENTERTAINMENT.** Amblin Entertainment is a film and television production company that was founded in 1981 by director–producer **Steven Spielberg**, along with producers Kathleen Kennedy and Frank Marshall. Their first production was the **romantic comedy** *Continental Divide*, but the young company became an important force with the 1982 release of Spielberg's *E.T.: The Extra-Terrestrial*, which went on to become one of the biggest hits in film history. Nevertheless, Amblin has remained a relatively small company, usually producing its films in conjunction with a larger studio and also contracting with others (especially **Universal Pictures**) to distribute their films.

Amblin has helped to produce a number of major films directed by Spielberg, including *The Color Purple* (1985), *Jurassic Park* (1993), *Schindler's List* (1993), *The Lost World: Jurassic Park* (1997), *A.I.: Artificial Intelligence* (2001), *Minority Report* (2002), and *War of the Worlds* (2005). Most of Spielberg's Amblin-produced films have been **science fiction**, and the company has scored big successes with sf films from other directors as well, such as Barry Sonnenfeld's sf **comedies** *Men in Black* (1997) and *Men in Black II* (2002). Amblin has also been involved in the production of a number of other high-profile films, many of them aimed at younger audiences. These include *Gremlins* (1984), *The Goonies* (1985), *Young Sherlock Holmes* (1985), and the *Back to the Future* trilogy (1985, 1989, 1990). Amblin has also been involved in a number of important **animated films**, including *An American Tail* (1986) and *The Land before Time* (1988), as well as *Who Framed Roger Rabbit* (1988), which involves an innovative combination of animation and live action.

After producing or co-producing 30 films in the 1990s, Amblin somewhat scaled back its production schedule in the first decade of the 21st century. However, it continues to produce important films, such as **Clint Eastwood**'s paired **war films** *Flags of Our Fathers* (2006) and *Letters from Iwo Jima* (2007).

**AMERICAN FILM INSTITUTE (AFI).** Somewhat modeled on the British Film Institute (which had been founded by royal charter in 1933), the American Film Institute was established by the National Endowment for the Arts in 1967 as an independent, nonprofit organization dedicated to preserving the history of American film and to helping educate new generations of filmmakers and filmgoers. In 1969, AFI established the Center for Advanced Film Studies in Beverly Hills, California; that center eventually grew into the AFI Conservatory, a fully accredited graduate school dedicated to education in the art of film.

The AFI also maintains an online database devoted to American film history and conducts a special Directing Workshop for Women, as well as film festivals and a variety of other research and cultural exchange programs. In recent years, AFI has drawn especially extensive attention for its "top 100" lists (compiled by polling a wide variety of experts), beginning with its list of the 100 Best American Films, first published in 1998 and updated in 2007. Other lists (generally first announced during annual television specials devoted to them), include a list of the 25 greatest male and 25 greatest female stars of all time (1999), a list of the 100 funniest films (2000), the 100 top "thrillers" (2001), the top 100 cinematic love stories (2002), the top 50 movie heroes and top 50 villains (2003), the top 100 movie songs (2004), the top 100 movie quotes (2005), the top 100 film scores (2005), the top 100 **musicals** (2006), the top 100 most inspiring movies (2006), and a list of the 10 top films in each of 10 different genres.

**AMERICAN INTERNATIONAL PICTURES (AIP).** Though a relatively small operation, American International Pictures made a huge contribution to the **science fiction** film boom of the 1950s, especially in the turn toward more teen-oriented fare in the latter half of the decade. The company was founded in 1956, when James H. Nicholson and Samuel Z. Arkoff decided to convert their American Releasing Corporation into a film production company that would focus on low-budget films for mostly teen audiences. Using focus groups to determine what kinds of films would appeal to these audiences, it developed a very market-oriented approach that put more emphasis on working within formulas that had proven to be marketable than on creativity or artistic merit. Nevertheless, their typically tawdry productions sometimes had flashes of brilliance, especially in the hands of their leading producer, **Roger Corman**, who also often directed, making highly marketable films very quickly and very cheaply, especially in the genres of **horror** and science fiction.

AIP made a variety of teen exploitation films in the late 1950s, often cashing in on contemporary fear about juvenile delinquency, but from a teen perspective that winked at the paranoia displayed by the older generation toward their own children. Teen culture films such as hot rod films and beach party films were also a staple of the company's output. In the realm of science fiction, Corman was definitely the company's leading light, though films such as *It Conquered the World* (1956) often contained horror elements as well, and Corman would ultimately become better known for horror films—such as the cycle of eight Edgar Allan Poe adaptations that he did for AIP from 1960 to 1964. Director Bert I. Gordon also worked with AIP on a number of sf films of the late 1950s.

In the mid-1960s, AIP also moved into television production, though without great success. After Corman left to found his own production company in 1970, AIP did less work with science fiction and instead explored new territory such as **blaxploitation** films, including *Blacula* (1972), which combined this new endeavor with their traditional focus on horror. In science fiction, AIP moved in the latter part of the 1970s into bigger-budget, more mainstream science fiction with such films as *The Island of Dr. Moreau* (1977) and *Meteor* (1979). AIP was the American distributor for a version of *Mad Max* (1979) that was dubbed into American English. Arkoff retired in 1979 and AIP was sold to Filmways, Inc., which was later bought by **Orion Pictures**. Most of the AIP library is now owned by **Metro-Goldwyn-Mayer** (MGM), which bought the financially troubled Orion in 1997.

**AMERICAN ZOETROPE.** Founded in 1969 by young directors **Francis Ford Coppola** and **George Lucas**, American Zoetrope was envisioned as an effort to give directors greater creative control over their films. While not a major financial success, the company has produced a number of important films, including Lucas's first two films, *THX 1138* (1971) and *American Graffiti* (1973). Perhaps their most significant film has been the Coppola-directed *Apocalypse Now* (1978); they have produced a number of less-important Coppola films, including *The Outsiders* (1983), *Rumble Fish* (1983), *The Cotton Club* (1984), *Peggy Sue Got Married* (1986), *The Godfather: Part III* (1990), and *Bram Stoker's Dracula* (1992). American Zoetrope has also been involved in the production of films by a number of prominent international directors, such as Akira Kurosawa, Jean-Luc Godard, and Wim Wenders. Many of their most interesting recent productions have been directed by Coppola's daughter, Sofia Coppola, including *The Virgin Suicides* (1999), *Lost in Translation* (2003), and *Marie Antoinette* (2006). The company is now owned by Sofia Coppola and her brother Roman Coppola.

**ANARCHIC COMEDY.** Anarchic comedy (sometimes referred to as "wacky comedy") is a form of **comedy** in which events occur in a rapid, non-sequitur fashion, often upsetting the status quo. The form is related to the centuries-old tradition of the carnival in that it involves a suspension of the normal rules of logic and behavior. It also has more recent roots in such forms as vaudeville and burlesque. However, the form is particularly well suited to modern film, in which established techniques of cutting from one scene to another make it particularly easy to construct nonsensical sequences of events. The chaos of the anarchic comedy film is often created by a protagonist who, either by choice or by simple ignorance, refuses to follow accepted patterns of behavior; the objects of the humor are often stodgy authority figures who insist on maintaining order and reason—to the point of unreason. As a result, established rules of conduct are often shown to be arbitrary or, worse, tools for control on the part of those in power. This type of comedy thus has considerable potential for political commentary.

While **silent film** artists such as the Keystone Kops or **Buster Keaton** often engaged in anarchic comedy (frequently in conjunction with **slapstick**, which might be considered a special type of anarchic comedy), the form reached its zenith in the early days of sound film, especially in the films of the **Marx Brothers**, including such classics as *Animal Crackers* (1930) and *Duck Soup* (1933). Anarchic comedy remained an important element of many comedies in the following decade but declined over time as a principal mode of humor in American films.

Anarchic comedy made something of a comeback in the 1970s, with the films of such directors as **Woody Allen** and Mel Brooks leading the way. The films of the mostly British comedy troupe Monty Python, beginning with *Monty Python and the Holy Grail* (1975), were also important to this revival in anarchic comedy. Films such as *National Lampoon's Animal House* (1978) and *Caddyshack* (1980) also made important contributions to this resurgence, as did *Kentucky Fried Movie* (1977)—essentially a sequence of almost unrelated skits—and *Airplane!* (1980)—a spoof of the **disaster** film genre that is really just a sequence of (mostly awful) one-liners and sight gags, strung only loosely together by the basic narrative. Though intentionally low brow, *Airplane!* was a great success; it was named the 10th funniest film of all time in a 2000 poll conducted by the **American Film Institute**.

*Airplane!* gave rise to one direct sequel, *Airplane II: The Sequel* (1982). Its success also helped to spur a whole series of films much in the same mode, including the three *Naked Gun* films (1988, 1991, 1994), all of which starred Leslie Nielsen, who had also been one of the stars of *Airplane!*. This subgenre of films that are really little more than a loosely connected series of gags has, in recent years, been dominated by films that are farcical parodies of particular film genres, looking back to the genre parodies of Brooks, such as the **Western** spoof *Blazing Saddles* (1974), the monster movie parody

*Young Frankenstein* (1974), and the **science fiction** spoof *Spaceballs* (1987). The immensely popular **horror** movie spoof *Scary Movie* (2000, with sequels in 2001, 2003, and 2006) led the way in this regard. Other recent examples include *Epic Movie* (2007), *Meet the Spartans* (2008), and *Superhero Movie* (2008).

**Tim Burton**, with films such as *Pee-Wee's Big Adventure* (1986) and *Mars Attacks!* (1996), and **Joel and Ethan Coen**, with films such as *Raising Arizona* (1987) and *The Big Lebowski* (1998), are among important filmmakers who have made contributions to the evolution of contemporary anarchic comedy. Other directors, such as the Farrelly Brothers (Bobby and Peter), have also been crucial to this evolution, culminating in their 2012 update film *The Three Stooges*. Finally, the recent resurgence in anarchic comedy has seen the rise of such new stars of the form as **Jim Carrey** (in virtually all of his films) and Mike Myers, the latter especially in the two *Wayne's World* films (1992, 1993) and the three *Austin Powers* films (1997, 1999, 2002), though Myers's turn as the title character in *The Cat in the Hat* (2003) was not a success, despite being one of the purest examples of anarchic comedy in recent years.

**ANDERSON, PAUL THOMAS (1970– ).** After early work as a production assistant, Paul Thomas Anderson began his career as a feature-film director with the crime drama *Sydney*, later retitled as *Hard Eight* (1996). Anderson gained major critical attention with the release of *Boogie Nights* (1997), a complex drama about the pornographic films industry with a structure reminiscent of the films of **Robert Altman**. It won Anderson an **Academy Award** nomination for Best Screenplay Written Directly for the Screen. His next film, *Magnolia* (1999), was similarly complex and drew even more critical praise, winning Anderson his second **Oscar** nomination for Best Screenplay. The **comedy–romance** *Punch Drunk Love* (2002) was a commercial failure, though it drew a number of positive reviews. Anderson then scored another critical hit (and significant box-office success) with the oil-industry drama *There Will Be Blood* (2007), based on Upton Sinclair's 1927 novel *Oil*. Dedicated to the recently deceased Altman, this film won Anderson his greatest critical acclaim to date, garnering eight Academy Award nominations, including one for Anderson for Best Achievement in Directing. Anderson, who has written the screenplays for all of his feature films to date, also won an Oscar nomination for Best Screenplay Based on Material Previously Produced or Published for *There Will Be Blood*.

**ANIMATED FILM.** Though short animated films had been made for some time, feature-length animated films began with **Disney**'s *Snow White and* *the Seven Dwarfs* (1937). Since that time, animated film and **children's film** have remained inseparable in the public consciousness in the United States. As a result, animated films made for more mature audiences have typically had a great deal of difficulty in reaching anything beyond small, niche audiences. Indeed, animated films for adult audiences in the United States were virtually nonexistent until animator-director **Ralph Bakshi** began to produce such films as *Fritz the Cat* (1972), based on the innovative countercultural "comix" of artist–writer R. Crumb. Bakshi went on to create a number of other interesting animated films, including the postapocalyptic fantasy *Wizards* (1977) and *The Lord of the Rings* (1978), a partial adaptation of the novels of J. R. R. Tolkien. By the time of *American Pop* (1981), an ambitious multigenerational family epic that also aspires to being a history of American popular **music**, Bakshi (who had never enjoyed major commercial success) began to fade as a factor in American film.

Bakshi later directed *Cool World* (1992), a relatively prominent film that switches between live action and animation. By this time, *Who Framed Roger Rabbit* (1988), which combines live action and animation in innovative ways, had also gained considerable attention, but neither that film nor Bakshi's efforts triggered a major interest in animation for adults, partly because the beginning of the "Disney Renaissance" with *The Little Mermaid* (1989) reclaimed animation for children's film. Some of the most notable subsequent animated films for adults have been in the realm of **science fiction**, including such films as *Titan A.E.* (2000) and *Battle for Terra* (2007), but such films have never really caught on with American audiences, even though animated sf films for adults have been extremely popular elsewhere, especially in Japan. It should be noted, however, that the increasing use of **computer-generated imagery** in science fiction film and elsewhere has gradually eroded the boundary between animation and live action, so that most major science fiction, **fantasy**, and **action films** contain a great deal of animation, even when they use live actors. *See also* BIRD, BRAD; DISNEY, WALT; LASSETER, JOHN; PIXAR.

**ARBUCKLE, ROSCOE "FATTY" (1887–1933).** Comedian Roscoe "Fatty" Arbuckle was one of the pioneers of the **silent film** era. He began his career in short films for the Selig Polyscope Company in 1909 and also appeared in films for **Biograph** before moving to the **Keystone Film Company** in 1913. There, he quickly became a star, appearing in dozens of films between 1913 and 1916, when health problems began to threaten his career. During this period, he also became a mentor to future silent film stars **Charles Chaplin** and **Buster Keaton**.

After recovering from his health problems, Arbuckle briefly started his own film company, Comique, but soon transferred control of the company to Keaton after Arbuckle himself accepted a lucrative offer to make feature-length films for **Paramount**. Arbuckle was a success at Paramount, but his career was virtually destroyed after he was accused of raping and accidentally killing actress Virginia Rappe during a party hosted by Arbuckle. Attempts to prosecute Arbuckle were highly publicized, and his career never recovered, even after he was officially vindicated. From 1924 to 1932, he directed nearly 50 short **comedies** under the pseudonym "William Goodrich." A promising comeback as an actor (under his own name) in the early 1930s was cut short by his death at age 46.

**ARNOLD, JACK (1916–1992).** Born Jack Arnold Waks in New Haven, Connecticut, Jack Arnold was one of the leading directors of the **science fiction** film explosion of the 1950s. Like many sf films of the period, Arnold's films were generally low-budget affairs, but several of his films stand out for their interesting cinematography, well-crafted scripts, and thoughtful exploration of contemporary social issues. Arnold's first directorial effort was the 1950 **documentary** *With These Hands*, which was nominated for an **Academy Award** for Best Documentary Feature. Its exploration of working conditions in the New York garment industry showed the social consciousness that would continue to mark Arnold's later sf films, which began with *It Came from Outer Space* (1953), one of the most thoughtful (and least xenophobic) of the alien invasion films of the 1950s. Arnold is perhaps best remembered for *The Creature from the Black Lagoon* (1954) and its sequel *Revenge of the Creature* (1955), a pair of unusually cerebral examples of the **monster movie**. (A second sequel, 1956's *The Creature Walks among Us*, was directed by John Sherwood.) Also particularly important in Arnold's directorial oeuvre is *The Incredible Shrinking Man* (1957), which effectively deals not only with Cold War nuclear fears but also with anxieties about contemporary threats to traditional masculine roles. *Tarantula* (1955) was a better than average science-themed monster movie, though Arnold's later attempts to move into youth-market science fiction produced largely forgettable films such as *The Space Children* (1958) and *Monster on the Campus* (1958).

In 1959, Arnold went to England to direct the Peter Sellers vehicle *The Mouse That Roared*. In the 1960s and 1970s, he worked mostly in television, directing numerous episodes of such well-known series as *Gilligan's Island* and *The Brady Bunch*. In 1985, Arnold won the President's Award (for lifetime achievement) from the Academy of Science Fiction, Fantasy, and Horror Films.

**ARONOFSKY, DARREN (1969– ).** Darren Aronofsky established himself as director of promise with the innovative *Pi* (1998), a low-budget, black-and-white effort that won the Directing Award at the 1998 Sundance **Film Festival**. This quirky film features Max Cohen, a young mathematics genius who seeks to understand the world (and predict the stock market) by seeking out numerical patterns, leading to plot complications and pushing Max toward such dangerous discoveries that he ultimately lobotomizes himself to keep the information he has learned from being revealed. *Requiem for a Dream* (2000) was a much more expensive effort with a first-rate cast. One of the most powerful and inventive films of the turn of the century, its bitterly satirical treatment of contemporary society was too strong for many viewers. *The Fountain* (2006) was Aronofsky's most ambitious film to date, intertwining three different plot strands from widely separated historical periods in the past, present, and future. The film is stunning, but its complex plot seemed muddled and incomprehensible to many viewers.

Aronofsky turned to a much more mainstream effort with *The Wrestler* (2008), which tells the tragic story of an aging professional wrestler, presenting the wrestling world as a microcosm of the contemporary world of American capitalism. The film drew considerable critical acclaim and drew numerous awards and award nominations, though most of those were for the performances of actors Mickey Rourke and Marisa Tomei. Aronofsky is reportedly now at work on a number of projects, including a remake of the classic 1987 **science fiction** film *Robocop*.

**ARTHUR, JEAN (1900–1991).** The comic actress Jean Arthur started her career in **silent film**, but established herself as a major force in screen **comedy** in the sound era, when her trademark squeaky voice made almost any line she spoke seem inherently funny. Yet she often played roles with a serious edge, typically playing an ordinary working girl whose spunk and independent spirit often got her into trouble, but generally got her out as well. She consistently worked with directors who were among the best in Hollywood history. For example, her film debut came in the 1923 silent *Cameo Kirby* (1923), directed by **John Ford**. Her breakthrough role came in Ford's *The Whole Town's Talking* (1935), but she became a true star thanks to her performances in a sequence of films directed by **Frank Capra**, including *Mr. Deeds Goes to Town* (1936), *You Can't Take It with You* (1938), and *Mr. Smith Goes to Washington* (1939). Arthur was especially associated with the genre of **screwball comedy**, in which she was arguably the most important actress. Other important roles in the 1930s included **Cecil B. DeMille**'s **Western** *The Plainsman* (1936), the screwball comedy *Easy Living* (1937), and the adventure *Only Angels Have Wings* (1939), directed by **Howard Hawks**. Her most notable films of the 1940s included *The Devil and Miss Jones* (1941) and **George Stevens**'s *The Talk of the Town* (1942), comedies that also engaged in serious social and political commentary. She scored her only Best Actress **Academy Award** nomination for her performance in Stevens's *The More the Merrier* (1943). Arthur performed only sporadically after her contract with **Columbia Pictures** expired in 1944. Her most notable late roles included a turn as a congresswoman in **Billy Wilder**'s *A Foreign Affair* (1948) and a dramatic performance as the rancher's wife in the classic Western *Shane* (1953), again directed by Stevens.

**ASHBY, HAL (1929–1988).** Though Hal Ashby's career as a film director was relatively short and though he was never quite thought of as one of Hollywood's elite directors, he nevertheless directed some of the most memorable works of American film during the 1970s. Ashby first gained recognition as a film editor in the late 1960s, winning an **Academy Award** for Best Film Editing for *In the Heat of the Night* (1968). He gained attention as a director with the offbeat **romantic comedy** *Harold and Maude* (1971) and scored another success with the comedy–drama *The Last Detail* (1973), starring **Jack Nicholson**. Ashby's biggest commercial success came with the **Warren Beatty** vehicle *Shampoo* (1975), a social **satire** over which Beatty reportedly exercised considerable creative control. Ashby followed with *Bound for Glory* (1976), a politically charged **biopic** focusing on the life of folk singer Woody Guthrie, then gained his greatest critical acclaim for the Vietnam War drama *Coming Home* (1978), for which he won his only Best Director **Oscar** nomination. Ashby's next film, the satirical dark **comedy** *Being There* (1979), has developed a growing critical reputation over the years as an effective commentary on the growing penetration of the media into every aspect of American life. It was, however, Ashby's last success. His few films of the 1980s were commercial and critical failures, while his growing reputation for unreliability made it harder and harder for him to find work.

**ASTAIRE, FRED (1899–1987).** Though he lacked movie-star good looks and was not a particularly gifted actor, Fred Astaire parlayed his dancing abilities and considerable onscreen charisma to become one of Hollywood's top leading men during a career that spanned more than 30 films, including some of the best-known **musicals** in film history. Named the fifth greatest male star of all time in a 1999 **American Film Institute** poll, Astaire used his dancing skills and innovative choreography to produce some of the greatest and most influential dance scenes in the history of American film. He was paired with partner **Ginger Rogers** in 10 films, the two becoming probably the best-known dance duo in film history.

Dancing on stage from an early age, Astaire had appeared prominently in Broadway and London stage shows by the time he was lured to Hollywood by **RKO Pictures** to participate in the rising wave of movie musicals that had been ushered in by the coming of sound. He appeared in his first film, *Flying Down to Rio*, in 1933. His breakthrough film came with *The Gay Divorcee* (1934), his first starring role and his second film with Rogers. He and Rogers scored an even bigger hit with *Top Hat* (1935), one of their greatest successes, and they followed with such hits as *Follow the Fleet* (1936) and *Swing Time* (1936), revolutionizing the role of dance in film. By the end of the 1930s, rising production costs meant that the elaborate Astaire–Rogers musicals were no longer profitable, and the team broke up, though they reunited in 1949 in *The Barkleys of Broadway*.

Astaire would never again achieve the heights he had reached in the 1930s, but he continued to be a top Hollywood star through the 1940s. *Broadway Melody of 1940* (1940) contains one of Astaire's most famous dance sequences (performed with Eleanor Powell), while *Holiday Inn* (1942), in which he costarred with **Bing Crosby**, is one of Astaire's best-known films. Astaire also costarred with Crosby in *Blue Skies* (1946), in which Astaire performed one of his signature dance numbers, to the song *Puttin' on the Ritz*. In *Ziegfeld Follies* (1945), Astaire performed a dance routine with **Gene Kelly**, the only movie dancer whose reputation rivaled his own.

Though he announced his retirement from film in 1946, Astaire later returned, scoring several more major successes. Films from the 1950s such as *The Band Wagon* (1953, with Cyd Charisse), *Daddy Long Legs* (1955, with Leslie Caron), *Funny Face* (1957, with **Audrey Hepburn**), and *Silk Stockings* (1957, again with Charisse) made a major contribution to Astaire's legacy as a film star. After 1957, he continued to work as an actor, but did little dancing on screen, though *Finian's Rainbow* (1968) was a return to the musical form. Among the best-known films in which Astaire appeared only as an actor are the postapocalyptic film *On the Beach* (1959) and the **disaster** film *The Towering Inferno* (1974), for which he received an **Academy Award** nomination for Best Supporting Actor. This was his only **Oscar** nomination, though he received an honorary Oscar for lifetime achievement in 1950. Astaire's legacy was boosted by the inclusion of clips from his earlier films in popular 1970s compilations such as *That's Entertainment* (1974).

**AUTRY, GENE (1907–1998).** The Texas-born Gene Autry began his career as a singing cowboy when he signed his first recording contract with Columbia Records in 1929. Subsequent success with recordings and radio performances drew the attention of Hollywood, and he made his first appearance in a film with *In Old Santa Fe* (1934). In 1935, he starred in the 12-part serial *The Phantom Empire* and also made his debut in a starring role in feature film with *Tumbling Tumbleweeds*. The latter featured Smiley Burnette as Autry's sidekick, a role Burnette would continue to play (as the character "Frog Millhouse") in most of the more than 40 B-**Westerns** that Autry made for **Republic Pictures** over the next several years. Autry, meanwhile, played himself in these films, or at least established a screen persona by the name of "Gene Autry" who toted both a guitar and a gun, singing and fighting villains as a courageous and virtuous hero.

Autry quickly became the leading Western film star, a role he did not relinquish until he left Hollywood to serve as a pilot in World War II. In the meantime, Autry remained a star in radio into the mid-1950s; he became a television pioneer as well, starring in his own show beginning in 1950. By the time he retired from show business in 1964, Autry was a legend in several media, having made nearly 100 films and over 600 recordings, in addition to his numerous appearances on radio and television. Autry wrote many of his own songs, though he did not write his best-known recording, "Rudolph, the Red-Nosed Reindeer," still a Christmas staple. He did, however, write "Here Comes Santa Claus," another song of which his recording is a Christmas favorite.

After his retirement, Autry's extensive investments of the money made in his earlier career made him one of the richest men in Hollywood. In his later years he was most visible as the owner of the Los Angeles Angels baseball team from their inception in 1961 until he sold controlling interest in the team to the Walt **Disney** Company in 1996.

*AVATAR. Avatar* (dir. **James Cameron**, 2009) is a 3D **science fiction** epic that went on to become the biggest commercial hit of all time, easily surpassing the $2 billion mark in global box-office receipts. *Avatar* is an ambitious film that deals with a number of topical issues, though both its plot and its treatment of these issues are ultimately predictable. The film is also fairly weak on characterization, lacking the memorable iconic characters who have populated many of the greatest sf films. It is, however, an impressive visual spectacle that employs groundbreaking technologies to present audiences with an unprecedented filmgoing experience.

The plot of *Avatar* focuses on the efforts of colonizing forces from Earth to exploit the mineral resources of the distant planet Pandora, a project that is complicated by the fact that Pandora is already inhabited by an intelligent species, the tall, blue-skinned Na'vi. Further, the Na'vi live in total harmony with their environment, which they treat with reverence, but which is threatened with large-scale destruction by the human mining efforts. The humans do attempt some communication with the Na'vi by having humans inhabit artificial Na'vi bodies (the "avatars" of the title) in order to try to negotiate with the natives on their own terms, but there is little common ground between the two sides. The insensitivity of the humans (and their tendency to resort to brute military force to achieve their objectives) inevitably leads to conflict.

The story is in many ways a familiar one, and the Na'vi rather obviously represent Native Americans, while to an extent serving as a sort of allegorical stand-in for non-Western peoples as a whole. In this case, however, the history of colonialism on Earth is reversed, and the Na'vi are able to win a decisive military victory over the humans invaders, with the help of a group of renegade humans and of the resources of the planet itself. *Avatar* thus provides a fairly conventional critique of colonialism, supplemented by a strong emphasis on environmentalist themes. Indeed, the environment of Pandora, represented using breakthrough techniques of 3D photography and digital animation, may be the most important "character" in the film.

*Avatar* is first and foremost a technological masterpiece, a striking demonstration of the way in which the most impressive technologies in a science fiction film can sometimes be the technologies that went into the making of the film itself, which in this case include a seamless integration of live action and computer animation, but most importantly involve three-dimensional imagery that is superior to that seen in any previous film, thanks to special cameras and processing that Cameron and his crew developed in the years-long process of planning and making the film. The enthusiastic response of audiences to the film suggests that these new technologies have a promising future in sf films of the coming years.

# B

**BACALL, LAUREN (1924– ).** Having debuted as an actress on Broadway in 1942, Lauren Bacall broke into film with a memorable role opposite **Humphrey Bogart** in *To Have and Have Not* (1944). She and Bogart quickly became a couple and married the following year, in which Bacall also had a lead role in *Confidential Agent*. She followed with a series of classic **film noir** roles opposite Bogart, including *The Big Sleep* (1946), *Dark Passage* (1947), and *Key Largo* (1948).

Bacall's roles in the 1950s showed considerable range, from her turn as a femme fatale in *Young Man with a Horn* (1950), to comic roles in *How to Marry a Millionaire* (1953) and *Designing Woman* (1957), to a dramatic turn in the tearjerker *Written on the Wind* (1956). In the 1960s and 1970s, Bacall did her most notable work on the stage on Broadway and in Chicago, though she did appear in several high-profile films, including *Sex and the Single Girl* (1964), *Harper* (1966), *Murder on the Orient Express* (1974), and *The Shootist* (1976, the last film of **John Wayne**).

Bacall continued to appear sporadically in film well into the 21st century, winning her only **Academy Award** nomination (for Best Supporting Actress) for her role in *The Mirror Has Two Faces* (1996). In 1999, a poll conducted by the **American Film Institute** named her the 20th greatest female film legend in Hollywood history.

**BAKSHI, RALPH (1938– ).** Born in Palestine, the animator and director Ralph Bakshi immigrated to the United States during World War II and grew up in New York City. In his early career he worked extensively on animated programming for television, especially for the Terrytoons unit of CBS. His major career breakthrough came in 1972 with the release of the **animated film** *Fritz the Cat* (1972), based on the innovative countercultural "comix" of artist–writer R. Crumb. Until the release of this decidedly adult-oriented film, animated films had typically been regarded as being primarily for children. Bakshi then continued to make virtually the only adult-oriented animated feature films in the United States, following with *Heavy Traffic* (1973), about an underground cartoonist, and *Coonskin*

(1975), a **satire** about race relations in the United States. Bakshi's next major breakthrough, though, came with the ambitious postapocalyptic **fantasy** *Wizards* (1977). Bakshi's *The Lord of the Rings* (1978), a partial adaptation of the novels of J. R. R. Tolkien, was equally ambitious and is now something of a **cult** favorite, but poor contemporary responses to the film ultimately made it impossible for Bakshi to make the planned follow-up that would have completed the adaptation.

*American Pop* (1981), an ambitious multigenerational family epic that also aspires to be a history of American popular **music**, was a moderate success, but the 1950s period piece *Hey Good Lookin'* (1982) was less so. Then, *Fire and Ice* (1983) was an animated sword-and-sorcery fantasy so unsuccessful that it drove Bakshi into temporary retirement. He returned to television animation by the end of the 1980s but did not direct another film until *Cool World* (1992), a relatively big-budget effort that switches between live action and animation. After numerous production battles between Bakshi and **Paramount Pictures**, this film was a bust with both audiences and critics. It would be Bakshi's last feature-length theatrical film.

**BARA, THEDA (1885–1955).** One of the biggest stars of the **silent film** era, the Cincinnati-born Theda Bara (née Theodosia Burr Goodman) was one of the earliest sex symbols in American film. Often scantily dressed on the screen, Bara typically played sexually aggressive women with dark agendas, making her the forerunner of the femme fatale of **film noir**, while earning her the nickname "The Vamp." The studios for which she worked played up this image, conducting extensive publicity campaigns to create an image of Bara as being more like the characters she played than she really was.

Unfortunately, only six of the more than 40 films that Bara made between 1914 and 1926 remain extant, and only four of those are feature length. These include *The Stain* (1914), *A Fool There Was* (1915), *East Lynne* (1916), and *The Unchastened Woman* (1925). Only a few brief fragments remain from what is probably her best-known film, *Cleopatra* (1917), which was remade in 1963 with **Elizabeth Taylor** in the lead role. In 1994, Bara's image appeared on a U.S. postal stamp to honor her contribution to the development of American film.

**BAXTER, ANNE (1923–1985).** The granddaughter of famed architect Frank Lloyd Wright, Anne Baxter began appearing in films at the age of 17, then had her breakthrough role in **Orson Welles**'s *The Magnificent Ambersons* (1942). She was one of Hollywood's leading actresses over the next two decades, during which she appeared in more than 30 films. She won an **Academy Award** nomination for Best Actress in a Supporting Role for *The*

*Razor's Edge* (1946), then won the **Oscar** for Best Actress in a Leading Role for *All about Eve* (1950). Other prominent roles included that of the Egyptian princess Nefretiri in *The Ten Commandments* (1956). After her performance in **Edward Dmytryk**'s *Walk on the Wild Side* (1962), Baxter appeared mostly on television, where she made numerous guest appearances; she then topped off her career with an extended role as heiress Victoria Cabot in the series *Hotel* (1983–1986).

**BEATTY, WARREN (1937– ).** A high-school football star who turned down numerous offers of athletic scholarships in order to study drama at Northwestern University, Warren Beatty began his acting career in a number of off-Broadway productions, then won a Tony Award in 1960 for his only performance on Broadway. He made several television appearances in the late 1950s before breaking into film with a lead role in **Elia Kazan**'s *Splendor in the Grass* (1961). Beatty won a **Golden Globe** nomination for Best Actor for this film; he then had several more leading roles in unimportant films before his breakthrough performance as legendary bank robber Clyde Barrow in *Bonnie and Clyde* (1967). This film, one of the iconic works of 1960s cinema, won Beatty an **Academy Award** nomination as Best Actor and firmly established him as a Hollywood star.

Beatty also produced *Bonnie and Clyde* out of a desire to have more control over the projects in which he was involved. He subsequently played leading roles in a string of important films, including **Robert Altman**'s *McCabe & Mrs. Miller* (1971), *The Parallax View* (1974), and *Shampoo* (1975), serving as both producer and co-writer in the latter. Beatty made his (**Oscar-**nominated) directorial debut with the highly successful *Heaven Can Wait* (1978), in which he also starred, but it was with *Reds* (1981), an epic **biopic** about radical journalist Jack Reed (played by Beatty) that Beatty established himself as a major director, winning his second consecutive Best Director Oscar nomination. He also won Oscar nominations for Best Actor in a Leading Role and Best Screenplay Written Directly for the Screen for that film, which was also nominated in the Best Picture category, giving Beatty those four major nominations for a second straight film, having garnered them for *Heaven Can Wait* as well.

*Reds* was an exhausting project, and Beatty did not return to film until 1987, when he starred with **Dustin Hoffman** in the disastrous *Ishtar*. Beatty followed as the director and star of *Dick Tracy* (1990), generally panned by critics, though a box-office success. Beatty returned to both critical and commercial success as an actor and producer with *Bugsy* (1991), a biopic in which he played gangster Bugsy Siegel, which won a Best Picture Oscar nomination, as well as another Best Actor nomination for Beatty. Beatty starred opposite wife Annette Bening in *Love Affair* (1994), then once again gained substantial acclaim for the political **satire** *Bulworth* (1998), which he directed, wrote, and starred in. That film won Beatty still another Oscar nomination for Screenwriting, his fourth, though he never won in that category. Among numerous other honors, *Bulworth* won the Golden Globe for Best Motion Picture—**Comedy/Musical**. In 2000, Beatty won the **Irving G. Thalberg** Memorial Award for lifetime achievement in filmmaking. *See also* MACLAINE, SHIRLEY.

**BENNETT, JOAN (1910–1990).** Actress Joan Bennett's long and illustrious career began in **silent films** when she was a mere six years old and extended into roles in television films when she was in her seventies. In between, Bennett appeared in more than 70 films, including such early highlights as the **musical** *Puttin' on the Ritz* (1931) and two 1932 films with **Spencer Tracy**, *She Wanted a Millionaire* and *Me and My Gal.*

At the behest of producer **Walter Wanger**, the naturally blonde Bennett dyed her hair dark in 1938 and subsequently moved into roles as a femme fatale, most notably in **film noirs** directed by **Fritz Lang**, including *Man Hunt* (1941), *The Woman in the Window* (1934), and *Scarlet Street* (1945). Later, Bennett again shifted gears, appearing as the mother of the bride (again opposite Tracy) in two classic comedies directed by **Vincente Minnelli**, *Father of the Bride* (1950) and *Father's Little Dividend* (1951). Bennett worked only sparingly in the rest of the 1950s, as studios avoided hiring her after an incident in late 1951 in which Wanger, then Bennett's husband, shot and wounded her longtime agent, whom he suspected of having an affair with Bennett.

Bennett made a comeback on television in the 1960s, making numerous appearances that were highlighted by her role as Elizabeth Collins Stoddard in the gothic soap opera *Dark Shadows* (1966–1971). She appeared in several made-for-television movies between 1972 and 1982, though her most notable performance in the 1970s came in the Italian **horror** classic *Suspiria* (1977), directed by Dario Argento.

**BERGMAN, INGRID (1915–1982).** The international film star Ingrid Bergman was born in Stockholm, Sweden, and spent much of her career in Europe. However, it was in American films that she achieved her greatest successes; a 1999 poll of the **American Film Institute** ranked her the fourth greatest female star in Hollywood history.

Having established herself as a film actress in Sweden, Bergman was brought to Hollywood in 1939 by producer **David O. Selznick**. Her first film, *Intermezzo: A Love Story* (1939) was a remake of her recent Swedish hit and quickly established her as a star in American film. A series of moderate successes followed, but it was in *Casablanca* (1942) that she played her most memorable role, opposite **Humphrey Bogart**. Starring roles in a string of high-profile hits followed, including *For Whom the Bell Tolls* (1943), *Gaslight* (1944), *Joan of Arc* (1948), and three films with director **Alfred Hitchcock**: *Spellbound* (1945), *Notorious* (1946), and *Under Capricorn* (1949).

Now at the very pinnacle of Hollywood stardom, Bergman experienced a sudden downfall when scandal erupted over her affair with Italian director Roberto Rosselini, with whom she was making the Italian–American coproduction *Stromboli* (1950). Bergman and Rosselini, both married to others at the time, both quickly divorced their previous spouses and married each other, but, given the conservative mores of 1950 America, great damage was done to Bergman's reputation, especially when it was revealed that she had been impregnated by Rosselini before their marriage. She was essentially driven into European exile, working in a series of Italian films directed by Rosselini through most of the 1950s.

Bergman made a triumphant return to Hollywood film in *Anastasia* (1956), for which she won her second **Academy Award** for Best Actress in a Leading Role, an award she had also won for *Gaslight*. She followed with another success in *Indiscreet* (1958). From that point forward, however, Bergman worked rather sparingly in film, though she still made a number of important appearances, including those in *The Inn of the Sixth Happiness* (1968), *Cactus Flower* (1969), *Murder on the Orient Express* (1974), and Ingmar Bergman's *Autumn Sonata* (1978). *Murder* won her an Academy Award for Best Supporting Actress, while her performance in *Autumn Sonata* led to her fourth **Oscar** nomination for Best Actress in a Leading Role, in addition to her two wins. She also performed on stage and television in her later years, winning both an Emmy and a Tony Award.

**BERKELEY, BUSBY (1895–1976).** After an extensive career as a choreographer on Broadway, Busby Berkeley moved to Hollywood, where his distinctive designs of elaborate production numbers involving the arrangement of large choruses of dancers into intricate geometric patterns were an immediate hit. His earliest films, a series of **musicals** starring Eddie Cantor and produced by **Samuel Goldwyn**, also established his signature technique of shooting his carefully arranged dancers from an overhead camera.

As a choreographer, Berkeley became a major figure in Hollywood with the success of *42nd Street* and *Gold Diggers of 1933*, both released in 1933. In that same year, he graduated to the director's chair with *She Had to Say Yes*. Berkeley also directed three sequels to *Gold Diggers*, remaining Hollywood's top designer of dance production numbers through the 1930s, typically directing the films for which he did choreography. By the end of the decade, however, elaborate numbers such as those designed by Berkeley were becoming more and more expensive and less popular with audiences.

Berkeley continued to work as a choreographer into the 1960s but also tried his hand at straight directing as musicals became less popular. The **John Garfield** vehicle *They Made Me a Criminal* (1939) was a particularly successful drama directed by Berkeley, though his most successful films continued to be musicals such as *Babes on Broadway* (1941), *The Gang's All Here* (1943), and *Take Me Out to the Ball Game* (1949). He also designed important production numbers for films such as *Girl Crazy* (1943), on which he began as director, but was fired after a series of disagreements with star **Judy Garland**. Berkeley never won an **Academy Award**, but he did score three nominations for Best Dance Direction.

**BERNSTEIN, ELMER (1922–2004).** Elmer Bernstein was one of Hollywood's leading composers of film scores, writing the scores for a wide variety of films, from the **biblical epic** *The Ten Commandments* (1956); to dramas such as *The Man with the Golden Arm* (1955), *To Kill a Mockingbird* (1962), and *Hud* (1963); to the **war film** *The Great Escape* (1963); to the **Westerns** such as *The Magnificent Seven* (1960) and *True Grit* (1969); to the **horror** film *An American Werewolf in London* (1981); to light **comedies** such as *Meatballs* (1979), *Airplane!* (1980), and *Ghostbusters* (1984). Bernstein was just coming into his own as a composer at the beginning of the 1950s, when the anticommunist purges in Hollywood at that time caused his career to get off to a slow start due to his leftist political leanings. Once he got a chance to work on such films as *The Man with the Golden Arm*, he caught on quickly and worked widely, however, ultimately scoring more than 200 films and television programs.

Bernstein won a total of 14 **Academy Award** nominations for Best Score or Best Song, beginning with a Best Score nomination for *The Man with the Golden Arm* and ending with a similar nomination for *Far from Heaven* (2002), nearly half a century later. His only **Oscar** win, however, was for the score for *Thoroughly Modern Millie* (1967). He was not related to composer/conductor Leonard Bernstein.

**BERRY, HALLE (1966– ).** Initially known primarily for her stunning looks, the former beauty queen Halle Berry eventually gained critical respect for her acting abilities, becoming the first African American woman to win the **Academy Award** for Best Actress for her performance in *Monster's Ball* (2001). Actually, Berry first attracted attention as an actor for her performance in a supporting role in **Spike Lee's** *Jungle Fever* (1991).

That same year, she also had supporting roles in *Strictly Business* and *The Last Boy Scout*, and it was clear that she was a new talent to be reckoned with.

After winning a major role in the prime-time television soap *Knot's Landing*, Berry graduated to bigger film roles with her performance in *Boomerang* (1992). She followed with important roles in such films as *The Flintstones* (1994), *Losing Isaiah* (1995), and *Executive Decision* (1996). However, it was not until her role in *Bulworth* (1998), opposite **Warren Beatty**, that she began to become a true Hollywood star. She then gained major attention as the star of the much-acclaimed television movie *Introducing Dorothy Dandridge* (1999), which she also co-produced. That film won her an Emmy Award, a **Golden Globe** Award, a **Screen Actors' Guild** Award, and an NAACP Image Award.

Now a widely recognized Hollywood name (and face), Berry was cast in a leading role in the blockbuster hit *X-Men* (2000); she followed with a major role in the **action** thriller *Swordfish* (2001) and with her award-winning role in *Monster's Ball* that same year. She followed in 2002 by achieving one of the pinnacles of female film stardom: playing a "Bond girl" in *Die Another Day* (2002). *X2* (2003), the sequel to *X-Men*, was another major commercial success, but both *Gothika* (2003) and (especially) *Catwoman* (2004) were critical and commercial failures. Berry again starred in the third X-Men film, *X-Men: The Last Stand* (2006), but she never regained the star-power momentum that she had had coming off of her Academy Award. Her starring roles in *Perfect Stranger* (2007), *Things We Lost in the Fire* (2007), and *Frankie and Alice* (2009, which she also co-produced) drew relatively little attention.

**BIBLICAL EPIC.** Films based on the Old and New Testaments of the Judeo–Christian Bible were prominent even in the earliest days of American **silent film**. However, a distinctively new version of the Bible-based film began to appear in the 1950s as advances in filmmaking technology made it more feasible to produce elaborate stagings of biblical stories just as the encroaching threat of television caused Hollywood filmmakers to seek new film forms that would far outstrip anything that could be seen on the small, black-and-white screens of the new medium. The result was a series of epic biblical films that were self-consciously grand, not only in their subject matter but also in their wide-screen, full-color presentation of spectacular events featuring casts of thousands.

Early examples of this new wave of biblical films tended to merge the biblical epic and historical epic and to be based on specific historical novels, rather than the Bible directly. These included *Quo Vadis* (1951), which focuses on the conflict between emergent Christianity and the decadent Roman

Empire of the first century A.D., and *The Robe* (1953), which tells the story of the aftermath of the crucifixion of Christ from the point of view of the Roman military tribune who commanded the unit that carried out the execution.

With **Cecil B. DeMille**'s *The Ten Commandments* (1956), the biblical epic reached a new level of grandeur, while turning more directly to the Old Testament for inspiration in its retelling of the story of Moses (played by **Charlton Heston**). On the other hand, biblical epics based on historical novels continued to appear as well, most notably including **William Wyler**'s *Ben-Hur* (1959), in which Heston played the title character, a heroic Jewish prince who runs afoul of the Roman Empire during the time of Christ—and who at several points briefly crosses paths with Christ himself.

It was not, however, until **Nicholas Ray**'s *King of Kings* (1961) that the biblical epic attempted to focus on the Christ story itself, though this film was essentially a remake of DeMille's 1927 silent film *The King of Kings*. Here, Jeffrey Hunter became the first modern American actor extensively to portray Christ on the screen. In 1965, George Stevens undertook to retell the Christ story with an even larger budget and elaborate presentation, but *The Greatest Story Ever Told* (1965, with Swedish actor Max von Sydow as a solemn Christ) was not a commercial success. **Robert Aldrich**'s return to the Old Testament with *Sodom and Gomorrah* (1962) had not been a success either, and the changing times of the 1960s meant that the biblical epic was essentially a thing of the past.

Subsequent returns to biblical themes in American film have achieved mixed critical and commercial results. For example, **Martin Scorsese**'s focus on the human side of Christ in *The Last Temptation of Christ* (1988) caused widespread protests, including complaints of blasphemy by the Catholic Church. **Mel Gibson**'s *The Passion of the Christ* (2004), on the other hand, was a huge commercial success and met with Catholic approval, but its negative portrayal of the role of the Jews in the execution of Christ struck many as anti-Semitic, while its fascination with the suffering of Christ struck some critics and viewers as lurid, decadent, and exploitative. Meanwhile, *Prince of Egypt* (1998), an **animated film** retelling the Moses story for children, was critically and commercially unsuccessful. *See also* HISTORICAL EPIC.

**BIGELOW, KATHRYN (1951– ).** Kathryn Bigelow is one of the most prominent female directors in Hollywood history, a status that is made all the more remarkable by the fact that she has specialized in particularly masculine-dominated genres such as **science fiction**, **horror**, and **action films**. She began her career as a director of feature film by co-directing the biker movie *Loveless* (1982). She next directed (and co-wrote) the vampire film *Near Dark* (1987), which has subsequently gained something of a **cult**

following. Bigelow moved into the Hollywood mainstream as the director of the action films *Blue Steel* (1990) and *Point Break* (1991), though neither was a big commercial hit.

Bigelow next directed the cyberpunk science fiction film *Strange Days* (1995), which was written and produced by **James Cameron**, to whom she had been married from 1989 to 1991. This film drew considerable attention for its stylish presentation but was again not a commercial success. *The Weight of Water* (2000) was a "relationship" film that departed from Bigelow's typical emphasis on action, an emphasis to which she returned in the nuclear-submarine thriller *K-19: The Widowmaker* (2002), a **Harrison Ford** vehicle that was unsuccessful both critically and commercially. Her gripping 2009 film *The Hurt Locker* (2009), about postinvasion Iraq, was again not a commercial hit, though it drew considerable critical praise. Winner of a Best Picture **Academy Award**, it made Bigelow the first woman to be named Best Director by the Directors Guild of America as well as the first woman to win a Best Director **Oscar**.

**BIOGRAPH COMPANY.** Founded in 1895 as the American Mutoscope Company, Biograph was the first independent company in the United States whose sole business was the production and exhibition of films. The company changed its name to the American Mutoscope and Biograph Company in 1899 to emphasize the importance of its Biograph film projector, introduced in 1896. It changed its name simply to the Biograph Company in 1909. The company was one of the leading pioneers of the **silent film** era, ultimately producing more than 3,000 short films and a dozen feature films by the time it ceased production in 1928.

From 1895 to 1903, the company concentrated on brief "actualities," then turned (with the rest of the film industry) to an emphasis on narrative films in 1903; it moved into a new indoor studio in Manhattan in 1906, the first studio in the world to use all artificial light. In 1908, the company joined with eight other leading U.S. motion picture companies to form the Motion Picture Patents Company (MPPC) in an attempt to establish their control of the American film industry. The company then received a major creative boost that same year when pioneering filmmaker **D. W. Griffith** became its principal director, producing a sequence of innovative short films. However, Griffith left the company in 1913 because of its resistance to making the feature-length films that he wanted to pursue.

Griffith's subsequent work helped to establish the feature-length film as the dominant form in the American film industry, while Biograph's slow entry into that market ultimately spelled the downfall of the company, which declined in importance through the 1920s. Its studios and film laboratory facilities were acquired by Herbert Yates and made a part of his Consolidated Film Industries in 1928, effectively putting an end to the Biograph Company.

**BIOPIC.** Short for "biographical picture," the term "biopic" refers to films that narrate the life stories or significant portions of the life stories of real-world individuals. Of course, when these individuals are of substantial historical importance, the genre of the biopic overlaps with genres such as the **historical epic**. The biopic can overlap with other genres as well, as when *The Great Ziegfeld* (1936) relates the life story of American stage impresario Florenz Ziegfeld, including elaborate stagings that make the film very much a **musical**. Nevertheless, the biopic is usually recognizable for its specific focus on the biography of a single individual, though such films have often been criticized for bending (or outright changing) the facts for dramatic (or even comic) effect, in accordance with the expectations of a variety of other Hollywood genres.

Biographical narratives are typically complex, so it is not surprising that the genre did not become prominent until the sound era, when more complex narration than had been feasible in **silent film** became possible. The form rose quickly, however, and the biopic enjoyed a particular prominence in the 1930s, when such films were often regarded as prestige projects that might help to overcome Hollywood's reputation for producing low-brow, escapist fare. For example, both *The Great Ziegfeld* and **William Dieterle**'s *The Life of Emile Zola* (1937) won Best Picture **Oscars**. Dieterle was something of a biopic specialist during the period, also directing *Madame du Barry* (1934), *The Story of Louis Pasteur* (1935), and *Juarez* (1939).

Dieterle's biopics tended to be highly romanticized. Meanwhile, John Ford's *Young Mr. Lincoln* (1939) is an almost entirely fictionalized account of an incident early in the career of Abraham Lincoln that is clearly designed as much as anything to be a feel-good patriotic salute to American virtue. Sam Wood's sentimental *Pride of the Yankees* (1942, about Lou Gehrig), meanwhile, went against the tendency of biopics to focus on political leaders, artists, and scientists, opening the way for a number of biopics about sports figures, especially baseball players and boxers, with **Martin Scorsese**'s *Raging Bull* (1980) serving as the leading example and with *The Jackie Robinson Story* (1950) being notable for featuring the baseball star as himself. Boxer Muhammad Ali would also later play himself in *The Greatest* (1977), though the major biopic about Ali would come much later with **Will Smith** in the title role in **Michael Mann**'s *Ali* (2001).

Biopics declined in popularity after World War II, though notable examples did continue to appear, including **Victor Fleming**'s *Joan of Arc* (1948), **Elia Kazan**'s *Viva Zapata!* (1954, with **Marlon Brando** as the

Mexican revolutionary leader), **Billy Wilder**'s *The Spirit of St. Louis* (1957, with **James Stewart** as Charles Lindbergh), and **George Stevens**'s *The Diary of Ann Frank* (1959). The **biblical epic** *The Ten Commandments* (1957), meanwhile, is essentially a biopic about Moses, with **Charlton Heston** in that role. Heston also played Michelangelo in *The Agony and the Ecstasy* (1965), one of the key biopics of the 1960s, among which might also be numbered the biblical epics *King of Kings* (1961) and *The Greatest Story Ever Told* (1965), which are biopics about Christ. The greatest biopic of the 1960s, however, was surely David Lean's *Lawrence of Arabia* (1962), a joint British–American production.

Like *Lawrence of Arabia*, *Patton* (1970), a biopic about American General George S. Patton, with **George C. Scott** in the title role, won the **Academy Award** for Best Picture, suggesting that biopics still carried a certain prestige. In keeping with the times, *Patton* was a complex film that contained certain antiwar elements and was not entirely positive in its portrayal of the famed World War II leader. Meanwhile, other biopics of the period tended to focus on countercultural figures as opposed to the establishment icons of the past. Biopics in this vein included Bob Fosse's *Lenny* (1974, with **Dustin Hoffman** as controversial comic Lenny Bruce), **Hal Ashby**'s *Bound for Glory* (1976, about left-leaning folk singer and activist Woody Guthrie), and, most notably, **Warren Beatty**'s *Reds* (1981, about radical journalist John Reed).

**Milos Forman**'s *Amadeus* (1984), which won the Best Picture Oscar, was a lively account that depicted composer Wolfgang Amadeus Mozart as a somewhat countercultural figure in his own time. **Spike Lee**'s *Malcolm X* (1992) also focused on an antiestablishment figure. Other major biopics of the 1990s included *Hoffa* (1992, about the long-time labor leader), **Oliver Stone**'s *Nixon* (1995, about the problematic U.S. president), and Forman's *Man on the Moon* (1999, about short-lived comedian Andy Kaufman). Such films particularly strove for greater biographical realism in their depiction of the lives of their protagonists than had been typical of the classic biopics of the 1930s. In particular, they tended to focus on the complexities of their multifaceted subjects, rather than simply heroizing them.

Perhaps fueled by the success of this new turn toward complexity and realism, the biopic has experienced something of a resurgence in recent years. In addition to *Ali*, key biopics of the 21st century have included *Pollock* (2000, focusing on artist Jackson Pollock), *A Beautiful Mind* (2001, about troubled, but brilliant, mathematician John Nash), Julie Taymor's *Frida* (2002, about the Mexican artist and activist Frida Kahlo), *American Splendor* (2003, concerning comics writer Harvey Pekar), Scorsese's *The Aviator* (2004, about aviation pioneer and entrepreneur Howard Hughes), *Ray* (2004, on blues singer and musician Ray Charles), *Good Night, and Good Luck* (2005, on pioneering television journalist Edward R. Murrow), *Capote* (2005, about writer Truman Capote), *Marie Antoinette* (2006), and *Milk* (2008, about gay politician and activist Harvey Milk).

**BIRD, BRAD (1957– ).** Brad Bird became interested in **animation** at an early age and later attended the California Institute of the Arts on a scholarship from the **Disney Company**. There, he met fellow student **John Lasseter**, the future chief of **Pixar**. After graduation, Bird worked briefly as an animator for Disney on *The Fox and the Hound* (1981), then worked mostly in television for several years, though he did coscript the live-action **science fiction** film *\*batteries not included* in 1987.

Bird's breakthrough in feature film came in 1999 when he directed and helped to write the animated science fiction film *The Iron Giant*. Though not a commercial success, this film garnered considerable critical praise and has become something of a **cult** film over the years. In addition, *The Iron Giant* drew the attention of Lasseter and Pixar and opened the way for Bird to write and direct the animated **superhero film** *The Incredibles* (2004) for Pixar, based on an idea Bird had pitched to the company, making it the first Pixar film to originate outside ideas conceived by their own staff.

*The Incredibles* was a commercial and critical success, winning the **Academy Award** for Best Animated Feature and winning Bird an additional **Oscar** nomination for Best Original Screenplay. It also won for Best Achievement in Sound Editing and was nominated for Best Achievement in Sound Mixing. Bird subsequently assumed the helm of the Pixar feature *Ratatouille* (2007), taking over from original director Jan Pinkava at the request of the company. That film was another success, scoring big at the box office and winning another Academy Award for Best Animated Feature. It also garnered four other Oscar nominations, including one for Best Screenplay Written Directly for the Screen, which Bird shared with Pinkava and Jim Capobianco.

Bird has since been at work on *1906*, a live-action film dealing with events surrounding the 1906 San Francisco earthquake. Slated to be co-produced by Pixar, *1906* would be the company's first foray into live-action film, though production has been delayed by budgetary concerns.

***THE BIRTH OF A NATION.*** *The Birth of a Nation*, D. W. Griffith's epic story (1915) of the end of the Civil War and its aftermath, was the highest grossing film of the **silent film** era. With a run-time of more than three hours, it is also often credited as the first feature-length film, and its success certainly contributed to a growing emphasis on the production of longer films. The film also introduced a number of technical and aesthetic innovations that eventually became common practice. It was, however, controversial even in its day for its subject matter, which includes the depiction of the Restoration South as a postapocalyptic landscape in which rampaging and rapacious blacks torment innocent whites, who have only the heroic Ku Klux Klan to protect them.

*The Birth of a Nation* was based on a 1905 novel and play entitled *The Clansman*, by Thomas Dixon, and indeed the film originally premiered under Dixon's title. Showings of the film often triggered protests, which in some cases led to rioting. Several major cities refused to allow the film to be shown at all. Nevertheless, the film received substantial critical acclaim as well, and President Woodrow Wilson famously proclaimed that it was like "writing history with lightning." The ambitious film contains a number of complex and elaborate scenes that go beyond anything previously put on film. Further, as the final title suggests, Griffith clearly saw the film as a sort of national allegory, narrating the emerging of the United States as a new modern nation out of the chaos of the Civil War.

Praise for the technical innovations of the film has long been tempered by concerns over its racist message. Nevertheless, the film was named the 44th greatest film of all time in the 1997 poll conducted by the **American Film Institute** (AFI). Interestingly enough, however, the film did not appear on the updated top 100 films list published by the AFI in 2007. Instead, Griffith's even more ambitious follow-up, *Intolerance* (1916), which included an anti-racist message, joined the list at number 49.

**BITZER, BILLY (1872–1944).** Gottfried Wilhelm "Billy" Bitzer was one of the pioneering cinematographers in film history, shooting nearly 1,000 films during the **silent film** era. Bitzer is known especially for his work with director **D. W. Griffith**, including the groundbreaking features *The Birth of a Nation* (1915) and *Intolerance* (1916). However, his contributions to cinematography probably lie less in individual films than in the fact that he initiated so many practices that would become standard tools of the Hollywood cinematographer. The first cinematographer to shoot films entirely in artificial light, his innovations also included techniques of soft focus photography, the use of fade outs and irises to mark scene transitions, and the development of a number of mood-setting devices. The greatest master of silent film cinematography, Bitzer was unable to make a successful transition to sound, and his career ended soon after the coming of sound. In 2003, he was named one of the 10 most influential cinematographers of all time in a poll conducted by the International Cinematographers Guild.

**BLACK COMEDY.** Sometimes also referred to as "dark" **comedy**, black comedy is a comic form that derives humor from the depiction of events that, in a different context, would generally be seen as tragic, horrifying, or just plain disgusting. These events are often of a grim or gruesome nature and include such topics as rape, death, murder, mutilation, illness, insanity, and warfare. Because of their flagrant violation of accepted standards of propriety, black comedies typically have an antiestablishment and antiauthoritarian orientation. They can sometimes also make particularly powerful satirical points because the shock created by their seemingly inappropriate subject matter can make audiences view important subjects in a new light—or at least think about subjects that would ordinarily be taboo.

Black humor was rare in American film before the 1950s, though examples did occur, such as Frank Capra's *Arsenic and Old Lace* (1944), featuring kindly but murderous old ladies. However, black humor became prominent in American literature in the 1950s and 1960s (in the work of writers such as Kurt Vonnegut, Joseph Heller, and Thomas Pynchon), and American film followed suit. **Alfred Hitchcock**'s *The Trouble with Harry* (1955), a comedy dealing with the difficulties of disposing of a dead body, was an important landmark in the rise of black comedy in American film. By the beginning of the 1960s **Roger Corman**'s *Little Shop of Horrors* (1960) pushed the hybrid genre of comic horror films—previously dominated by light fare such as many of the films of **Bud Abbott and Lou Costello**—in a darker direction. This genre has since produced such landmarks as Mel Brooks's *Young Frankenstein* (1974) and *Dracula: Dead and Loving It* (1995). Zombies seem to be particularly effective as a focus for **horror** comedy, as in *My Boyfriend's Back* (1993) and *Zombieland* (2009), though the British film *Shaun of the Dead* (2004) and the Canadian film *Fido* (2006) may be the best examples of this particular subgenre.

Cinematic black comedy reached what was probably its zenith with **Stanley Kubrick**'s *Dr. Strangelove or: How I Learned to Stop Worrying and Love the Bomb* (1964), a hilarious farce about the nuclear destruction of modern civilization. In 1970, *Catch-22* and *MASH* followed suit as black comedies about warfare, while **Hal Ashby**'s *Harold and Maude* (1971) soon afterward brought black humor to **romantic comedy**. British film has been particularly good at black comedy, often influencing American film. For example, the mostly British comedy troupe Monty Python exercised an important influence on the growth of black comedy in film in the 1970s, including their own British-produced films, beginning with *Monty Python and the Holy Grail* (1975). American Python member **Terry Gilliam** went on to direct a series of films that include a considerable amount of black humor, especially in his comic dystopian film *Brazil* (1985). Other highlights in black comedy in the 1980s include the cannibalism farce *Eating Raoul* (1982), which particularly well illustrates the potential of black comedy for producing **cult** films.

That year (1982) also saw the release of *Porky's* (with sequels in 1983 and 1985), a teen comedy that helped to initiate a related form of humor often referred to as "gross-out" comedy, relying heavily on crude sexual or toilet humor. Teen gross-out comedy has also been central to such films as *American Pie* (1999) and its sequels, though a more conventional form of black humor has been used in teen films such as *Heathers* (1988). A certain amount of gross-out humor is also central to *Weekend at Bernie's* (1989), in which the theme of a comical dead body looks back to *The Trouble with Harry*.

Virtually all of the films of **Joel and Ethan Coen** employ black comedy, and their films have constituted some of the most important examples of the genre in recent years, including *Raising Arizona* (1987), *Fargo* (1996), *The Big Lebowski* (1997), *The Ladykillers* (2004), and *Burn after Reading* (2008). Many of the films of **Tim Burton** feature black comedy as well, as in *Beetlejuice* (1988) and *Corpse Bride* (2005). Other recent black comedies include *Don't Tell Mom the Babysitter's Dead* (1991), *Death Becomes Her* (1992), *Serial Mom* (1994), *8 Heads in a Duffle Bag* (1997), *Very Bad Things* (1998), *Happiness* (1998), *Bamboozled* (2000), and *Life during Wartime* (2009).

**BLACKLIST.** *See* HOLLYWOOD TEN; HOUSE UN-AMERICAN ACTIVITIES COMMITTEE.

**BLAXPLOITATION.** The term "blaxploitation" is applied to a family of films, mostly appearing in the 1970s, that were focused on black urban life and targeted to black urban audiences. Formed from the combination of "black" and "exploitation," the term indicates the way in which these (mostly low-budget) films were designed to exploit the economic potential of this market, which was not being addressed in mainstream Hollywood film. At the same time, many of these films came to be regarded as expressions of genuine African American cultural energies, providing inspiration for later generations of black filmmakers. They were also particularly influential in their groundbreaking use of jazz and soul **music** in the soundtracks.

One of the founding films of the blaxploitation cycle was the defiantly anti-establishment **independent film** *Sweet Sweetback's Baadasssss Song* (1971), written, produced, scored, directed by, and starring Melvin Van Peebles, who also largely financed the making of the film. That same year, the detective drama *Shaft* (1971) got studio backing from **Metro-Goldwyn-Mayer** (MGM) and brought the blaxploitation phenomenon to larger audiences. The year 1972 saw the release of the blaxploitation classic *Super Fly* and *Blacula*, a film about a black vampire that extended the phenomenon into the genre of **horror**. *Black Caesar* (1973) then took blaxploitation film into the **gangster**

**film** genre, while *Coffy* (1973) established Pam Grier as the biggest female blaxploitation star.

By the mid-1970s, the cycle was on the wane, and few films that might be classified as blaxploitation films have been made since the end of the 1970s. Nevertheless, later African American filmmakers such as **Spike Lee** and **John Singleton** (who remade *Shaft* in 2000) have been heavily influenced by the cycle, and even parodies of blaxploitation films—such as *I'm Gonna Git You Sucka* (1988) and *Pootie Tang* (2001)—show a certain fondness for them. Meanwhile, later films that are not parodies, such as **Quentin Tarantino**'s *Jackie Brown* (1997), pay open homage to the blaxploitation cycle.

**B-MOVIE.** The term "B-movie" is widely used in the film industry to indicate a low-budget film with modest (or no) artistic aspirations. The term originated in the 1930s, when films were typically distributed and exhibited as double features, one feature of which would be a more ambitious, higher-budget effort, the other of which would be the lower-budget B-movie. B-movies can be of virtually any type or genre, but they have been most closely associated with specific popular genres, such as the **Western** (especially in the 1930s and 1940s), **science fiction** (especially in the 1950s), and **horror** (especially in the 1960s and beyond).

While the original B-movies were often produced by **major studios** for distribution alongside their more prestigious products, several smaller studios (such as the so-called **Poverty Row** studios) came to specialize in the production of such films. By the 1950s, B-movies came more and more to be associated with specific market niches, especially the youth market, as "teen exploitation" films produced by new studios such as **American International** came to be the center of the B-movie industry, with producer/director **Roger Corman** emerging as perhaps the greatest auteur of the B-movie.

B-movies sometimes flew under the radar of Hollywood's moral arbiters and ultimately played a major role in the liberalization of film **censorship** and the ultimately downfall of the **Production Code**, helping to keep the film industry in step with the changing values of American society in the 1960s and 1970s. Indeed, directors such as Russ Meyer became widely known for the salacious content of their B-movies. Meanwhile, specializing in venues such as drive-ins or marginal urban "grindhouse" theaters, B-movies came more and more during this period to be marked by their focus on sex and spectacular violence, while also moving into socially important areas such as the **blaxploitation** film, making the 1970s as a whole a particularly rich period for the B-movie.

The market for theatrical B-movies declined during the 1980s as soaring production costs (and increasing focus on big-budget blockbusters) increasingly made former B-genres such as science fiction into high-end products. The emerging cable industry, however, provided a fertile venue for less expensive films, and the kinds of B-movies that had formerly began exhibited in theaters came increasingly to be made strictly for television and home video—though such films have sometimes been called "C-movies" to indicate that they are lower in quality than the typical older B-movies. Meanwhile, studios such as Troma Pictures, founded to take advantage of the B-movie boom of the 1970s, continued to thrive by pushing their content to ridiculous, campy, self-parodic extremes. Such films draw upon the legacy of ultracheap, ultrabad films such as those made by director Ed Wood in the 1950s that have more recently come to be enjoyed for their camp value, leading to their designation as a separate category, the "Z-movie."

The rise of **independent film** in the 1990s created a focus on artistically ambitious low-budget fare that further pushed B-movies out of the theatrical market, though some successful directors, most notably **Robert Rodriguez** and **Quentin Tarantino**, openly paid homage to earlier B-movies in their own films. Meanwhile, technical advances in computer-generated imagery and digital video have made it possible to produce relatively slick-looking films at a relatively low cost, leading to phenomena such as "mockbusters," low-budget films that are unapologetic rip-offs of recent big-budget films, especially science fiction films.

**BOGART, HUMPHREY (1899–1957).** A 1999 poll conducted by the **American Film Institute** named Humphrey Bogart the greatest male screen legend of all time, and it would be hard to disagree. Neither tall, handsome, nor particularly gifted as an actor, Bogart had an onscreen charisma virtually unmatched in film history. He established a tough-guy persona (sometimes with a heart of gold, sometimes not) that served him well through dozens of film roles, including some of the most memorable roles of all time. His trademark lisp (possibly caused by a scar to his lip, possibly cultivated intentionally) gave him one of the most iconic voices in Hollywood history.

Bogart started as a Broadway actor in the 1920s, then moved to film with a number of relatively unimportant roles until he first gained major attention with his role as gangster Duke Mantee in *The Petrified Forest* (1936). *Dead End* (1937) was another important role, but Bogart only truly became a star in 1941 with his roles in *High Sierra* and *The Maltese Falcon*, one of the founding works of **film noir**, of which Bogart would become the leading star. It was, however, with *Casablanca* (1942) that Bogart perfected his screen persona and reached the very pinnacle of Hollywood stardom.

The next several years saw Bogart star in such notable films as *To Have and Have Not* (1944), *The Big Sleep* (1946), *Dark Passage* (1947), and *Key*

*Largo* (1948), all with **Lauren Bacall**, whom Bogart married in 1945. Among Bogart's most memorable roles were his star turns in *The Treasure of the Sierra Madre* (1948), *Knock on Any Door* (1949), *In a Lonely Place* (1950), and *The African Queen* (1951), for which he won his only Best Actor **Academy Award**, though he was also nominated for *Casablanca* and for *The Caine Mutiny* (1954). One of his few comic roles was in **Billy Wilder**'s *Sabrina* (1954).

Though critical of the harassment of Hollywood by the **House Un-American Activities Committee** (HUAC), Bogart managed to avoid the **blacklist** and to work actively through the first half of the 1950s, appearing in three memorable films in 1955 alone: **Michael Curtiz**'s *We're No Angels*, **Edward Dmytryk**'s *The Left Hand of God*, and **William Wyler**'s *The Desperate Hours*. Bogart's last role was as sportswriter Eddie Willis in the boxing film *The Harder They Fall* (1956), after which cancer led to his early death in 1957.

**BOGDANOVICH, PETER (1939– ).** Peter Bogdanovich had already established a reputation as a film critic and scholar when he was tapped by **Roger Corman** to direct *Targets* (1968), an inventive thriller that deals with the **horror film** industry, though it is not, strictly speaking, a horror film itself. That same year Bogdanovich also directed the Corman-produced *Voyage to the Planet of Prehistoric Women*, an English-language adaptation based on pre-existing footage from the 1962 Russian **science fiction** film *Planeta Bur*.

Bogdanovich's breakthrough came with *The Last Picture Show* (1971), a highly acclaimed effort that gained eight **Academy Award** nominations, including one for Best Picture and one for Bogdanovich as Best Director and another for him as the co-writer of the screenplay. This film also established Bogdanovich as a leading member of Hollywood's New Wave of young directors, a group that also included such figures as **Francis Ford Coppola**, **George Lucas**, **Brian De Palma**, **Martin Scorsese**, and **Steven Spielberg**. Bogdanovich followed as the director of the **romantic comedy** *What's Up, Doc?* (1972), which showed the clear influence of the **screwball comedies** of earlier decades, indicating the strong influence of film history on Bogdanovich's own filmmaking.

Bogdanovich next directed the comedy *Paper Moon* (1973), which not only looked back to earlier films but was set in the 1930s. This film was produced by the Director's Company, a group formed by Bogdanovich, Coppola, and William Friedkin to produce films in conjunction with **Paramount Pictures**, but over which the directors would have essentially complete artistic control. The Director's Company also produced Bogdanovich's *Daisy Miller* (1974), a rather unsuccessful adaptation of the novel by Henry James.

Several subsequent Bogdanovich films met with mediocre success, though the drama *Mask* (1985) was a standout. However, *Texasville* (1990), the much-anticipated sequel to *The Last Picture Show*, was generally regarded as a disappointment.

The 1992 comedy *Noises Off* has gained something of a following as a **cult** film, and *The Cat's Meow* (2001) relates some interesting aspects of Hollywood history (and legend). However, Bogdanovich has done little directing since the failure of *Texasville*, preferring instead to return to his original focus as a scholar and critic of film. He has also continued his occasional acting appearances, with roles in both film and television.

***BONNIE AND CLYDE.*** *Bonnie and Clyde* (dir. **Arthur Penn**, 1967) was one of the most important and influential films of the 1960s. Its innovative aesthetic, strongly influenced by the French New Wave, itself exerted a powerful influence on **New Hollywood** films that followed it. Meanwhile, the film made stars of its lead actors, **Warren Beatty** (who also produced the film) and **Faye Dunaway**; it also received a total of 10 **Academy Award** nominations, including for the key categories of Best Picture, Best Director, Best Screenplay, Best Actor, and Best Actress. However, it won **Oscars** only for Best Cinematography and Best Actress in a Supporting Role (Estelle Parsons).

*Bonnie and Clyde* is a rather romanticized account of the lives (and deaths) of Depression-era outlaws Clyde Barrow (Beatty) and Bonnie Parker (Dunaway), who move across the American Southwest with their small gang, robbing banks and attempting to evade the law. In the process, they become famous, feared for their violence, but also admired as Robin Hood–like figures of the Common Man battling against the rich and powerful. The subject matter of the film thus recalls such earlier works as **Fritz Lang**'s *You Only Live Once* (1937), **Nicholas Ray**'s *They Live by Night* (1948), and Joseph H. Lewis's *Gun Crazy* (1950). But *Bonnie and Clyde* is very much a film of the 1960s, and its antiestablishment tone derives less from the economic hardships of the Depression than from prevailing cultural attitudes at the time the film was made. Indeed, while numerous aspects of the film carefully place it in its proper historical context (as when the characters attend a screening of *Gold Diggers of 1933*), the film is shot in richly splendid colors that seem more suggestive of the 1960s counterculture than of 1930s poverty.

The antiauthoritarian tone of *Bonnie and Clyde* is enhanced by its flaunting of a number of the conventions of the Hollywood commercial film, especially in its complex mixture of different moods and genres. In this sense, it is reminiscent of the work of French New Wave directors such as Jean-Luc Godard and François Truffaut, each of whom contributed to the development of the project and was at one time or another considered as a possible director for the film. On the other hand, the film at times seems overly taken with its own stylistic play, which may enhance its overt celebration of nonconformism but which tends to diminish its potential anticapitalist message.

**BRACKETT, CHARLES (1892–1969).** Charles Brackett was one of Hollywood's most honored screenwriters, winning **Academy Awards** for Best Screenplay for *The Lost Weekend* (1945), *Sunset Blvd.* (1950), and *Titanic* (1953), as well as writing nominations for the screenplays of *Ninotchka* (1939), *Hold Back the Dawn* (1941), *A Foreign Affair* (1948), and *The King and I* (1956). All of these through *Sunset Blvd.* were coscripted with **Billy Wilder**, with whom Brackett had a fruitful partnership that saw them collaborate on 13 films between 1938 and 1950. Their earliest collaborations were directed by others, including *Bluebeard's Eighth Wife* (1938) and *Ninotchka*, by Ernst Lubitsch, and *Ball of Fire* (1941), by **Howard Hawks**. Beginning with *The Major and the Minor* (1942), the films written by Brackett and Wilder were generally directed by Wilder, including *Five Graves to Cairo* (1943) and *The Emperor Waltz* (1948).

Brackett also received an **Oscar** nomination for Best Original Story for *To Each His Own* (1946), directed by Mitchell Leisen, who directed several films written by Brackett. Brackett served as the president of the **Screen Writers Guild** in 1938–1939. He was president of the **Academy of Motion Picture Arts and Sciences** from 1949 to 1955. In 1958, he was given an honorary award for outstanding service to the Academy.

**BRANDO, MARLON (1924–2004).** Marlon Brando burst into stardom in the early 1950s with his dynamic starring performances in **Elia Kazan**'s *A Streetcar Named Desire* (1951) and *On the Waterfront* (1954) ), with important starring roles in Kazan's *Viva Zapata!* (1952), *The Wild One*, and *Julius Caesar* (1953) sandwiched in between. Brando followed with a string of notable, but sometimes eccentric performances in such films as *Guys and Dolls* (1955), *The Young Lions* (1958), and *One-Eyed Jacks* (1961, the only film directed by Brando). For his role in *Mutiny on the Bounty* (1962), Brando was paid the record sum of $1.25 million. He subsequently starred in *The Ugly American* (1963), *Reflections in a Golden Eye* (1967), and *Burn!* (1969), a commercial failure that seemed to confirm the decline of Brando's star power.

Ultimately, however, Brando's most memorable role was probably as Vito Corleone, the title character of **Francis Ford Coppola**'s *The Godfather* (1972). Brando won his second **Academy Award** for Best Actor for that film (the first was for *On the Waterfront*), but famously refused to accept the award because he felt that Hollywood was complicit in the persecution of Native Americans in the United States. Brando followed with starring roles in Bernardo Bertolucci's critically acclaimed, but controversial *Last Tango in Paris* (released in the United States in 1973), then starred with **Jack Nicholson** in the **Western** *The Missouri Breaks* (1976).

Brando had relatively small but important roles in *Superman: The Movie* (1978) and in Coppola's *Apocalypse Now* (1979), both of which attempted to capitalize on Brando's stature as a Hollywood legend. He was highly paid for both films, but his soaring weight began, with these films, to limit the kinds of roles he could play. He also filmed scenes for *Superman II* (1980), but refused to allow them to be used after a dispute with the producers over his payment. Brando received a Best Actor **Oscar** nomination for *A Dry White Season* (1989), but his performances in such later films as *The Freshman* (1990), *Don Juan DeMarco* (1994), and *The Score* (2001) were unremarkable. *The Island of Dr. Moreau* (1996) was a particular critical and commercial disappointment.

Brando was nominated for a total of eight Best Actor Oscars, including the two that he won. A 1999 poll conducted by the **American Film Institute** named him the fourth greatest male screen legend in Hollywood history.

**BRAT PACK.** Teen film reached a new height of prominence in Hollywood in the 1980s, and the numerous teen films of the decade were dominated by an ensemble of young actors who collectively came to be known as the "Brat Pack," in reference to the earlier group of performers known as the "**Rat Pack.**" Various members of the Brat Pack made repeated appearances with each other in a sequence of films in the 1980s, thus the popular recognition of them as a group. **John Hughes**'s *The Breakfast Club* (1985) and Joel Schumacher's *St. Elmo's Fire* (1985) were perhaps the two most important teen films of the decade; they were also the central Brat Pack films, and Brat Packers Emilio Estevez, Judd Nelson, and Ally Sheedy appeared in both films. Other central members of the Brat Pack included Andrew McCarthy, Rob Lowe, and Molly Ringwald, while Anthony Michael Hall and Demi Moore are generally considered members as well. All of these actors appeared in either *The Breakfast Club* or *St. Elmo's Fire*. Other young actors sometimes associated with the Brat Pack include Jon Cryer, John Cusack, **Robert Downey Jr.**, Jami Gertz, **Sean Penn**, and James Spader.

**BREEN, JOSEPH (1888–1965).** Joseph Ignatius Breen became an important figure in the American cinema when he was hired, in 1934, to enforce the **Production Code** that had been adopted by the motion picture industry in 1930, but which had hitherto been only loosely enforced. As head of the

Production Code Administration (popularly known as the "Breen Office") from 1934 until 1954, Breen was the film industry's chief censor, charged with reviewing individual films to ensure that they adhered to the production code. In 1941, Breen served briefly as the head of **RKO Pictures**. When he retired in 1954, he was given an honorary **Academy Award** for his contribution to the film industry. *See also* CENSORSHIP.

**BRIDGES, JEFF (1949– ).** The son of actor Lloyd Bridges and the younger brother of actor Beau Bridges, Jeff Bridges would go on to establish a solid career as a film actor, starring in a wide variety of films. An extremely natural actor, he typically makes flawed and problematic characters into extremely likeable figures on the screen. After numerous television appearances as a child actor, Bridges made his first major film appearance in *The Last Picture Show* (1971), for which he received an **Academy Award** nomination for Best Supporting Actor. He followed with important roles in a number of interesting films over the next decade and a half, including such highlights as *Thunderbolt and Lightfoot* (1975), for which he received a second Best Supporting Actor nomination; he also had an important supporting role in *Heaven's Gate* (1980) and starring roles in *Stay Hungry* (1976), *King Kong* (1976), *TRON* (1982), and *Against All Odds* (1984) during this period.

Bridges received a Best Actor **Oscar** nomination for his performance in *Starman* (1984). Numerous starring roles followed, mostly in dramas such as *Tucker: The Man and His Dream* (1988), *The Fisher King* (1991), *The Vanishing* (1993), and *Fearless* (1993). However, Bridges's most memorable role in the 1990s was probably that of "The Dude" in the **cult** classic **comedy** *The Big Lebowski* (1998).

Bridges received another Best Supporting Actor Oscar nomination for *The Contender* (2000). Other important films featuring Bridges in the 2000s include *Seabiscuit* (2003), *Tideland* (2005), *Iron Man* (2008), and *The Men Who Stare at Goats* (2009). He won his first Oscar, for Best Actor, for his performance as an aging country **music** singer in *Crazy Heart* (2009).

**BROWN, CLARENCE (1890–1987).** Clarence Brown began his career as an assistant to the pioneering French-born director Maurice Tourneur, with whom he shared directing credit on such early **silent films** as *The Great Redeemer* (1920) and *The Last of the Mohicans* (1920). Brown received his first solo directorial credit for *The Light in the Dark* (1922) and directed several other silent films before transitioning to sound in 1930 as the director of *Anna Christie* (1930), which featured **Greta Garbo** in her first speaking role. Brown received an **Academy Award** nomination for Best Director for that year for his work on that film and on *Romance*, the first of five such nominations he would receive in the course of his career.

Known as a director who worked well with actors, Brown directed numerous films for **Metro-Goldwyn-Mayer** (MGM) over the next two decades, working frequently with such female stars as Garbo and **Joan Crawford**. Particular highlights included such films as *Anna Karenina* (1935, featuring Garbo), *The Human Comedy* (1943, starring **Mickey Rooney**), *National Velvet* (1944, starring Rooney and a young **Elizabeth Taylor**), and *The Yearling* (1946, featuring **Gregory Peck**). Brown retired from directing after *The Plymouth Adventure* (1952), having become a wealthy man due to judicious investments of his income as a director and producer.

**BRUCKHEIMER, JERRY (1945– ).** Producer Jerry Bruckheimer began his career directing television commercials, then moved into film with a series of minor films until such efforts as *Flashdance* (1983), *Beverly Hills Cop* (1984), and *Top Gun* (1986) made him a leading Hollywood producer. He is known for slickly produced, highly commercial films and has produced some of the biggest-grossing films of all time, specializing in high-**action** crime and adventure films. His most successful films are the *Pirates of the Caribbean* trilogy (2003, 2006, 2007), all made by **Disney**, with which Bruckheimer has had a particularly rich association. Other key films produced by Bruckheimer include *Days of Thunder* (1990), *Bad Boys* (1995), *Dangerous Minds* (1995), *The Rock* (1996), *Con Air* (1997), *Armageddon* (1998), *Enemy of the State* (1998), *Pearl Harbor* (2001), *Black Hawk Down* (2001), and the *National Treasure* films (2004, 2007).

In the late 1990s, Bruckheimer moved into television and has executive produced some of the most successful television programs aired since that time, especially *CSI: Crime Scene Investigation* (2000– ) and its spinoffs, *CSI: Miami* (2002– ) and *CSI: NY* (2004– ). Despite his commercial success in film, Bruckheimer has never been nominated for an **Academy Award**. He has, however, had numerous Emmy nominations and wins for *CSI: Crime Scene Investigation* and for the reality series *The Amazing Race*, which he has executive produced since 2001.

**BRYNNER, YUL (1920–1985).** Though perhaps known most prominently as the greatest entirely bald movie star of all time, the Russian-born Yul Brynner was in fact a versatile actor who played some of the most memorable roles in Hollywood history. His first (and still best-known) major film role was probably as the king of Siam in *The King and I* (1956), for which he won his only **Academy Award** for Best Actor in a Leading Role, bringing to the screen a role he had already played many times in the Broadway play on which the film was based. That same year, Brynner had important roles in *The Ten Commandments* and *Anastasia*, marking one of the most impressive debut years in Hollywood history.

Over the next several years, Brynner established a niche for himself as Hollywood's leading actor for roles that required a vaguely foreign or exotic appearance. However, he went against type as an aging gunslinger in the **Western** *The Magnificent Seven* (1960), demonstrating his versatility. He would appear in several more Westerns, including the sequel *Return of the Seven* (1966) and *Villa Rides* (1968), in which he returned to "exotic" character types as the Mexican bandit and revolutionary leader Pancho Villa.

Other important films in which Brynner played major roles ranged from the satirical comedy *The Madwoman of Chaillot* (1969) to the thriller *The Light at the Edge of the World* (1971), in which he played a sadistic pirate. He even made an (uncredited) appearance as a transvestite cabaret singer in the **satire** *The Magic Christian* (1969). Two of Brynner's most prominent late roles were in the groundbreaking **science fiction** films *Westworld* (1973) and *Futureworld* (1976).

**BURTON, RICHARD (1925–1984).** After a celebrated early career on the British stage, Richard Burton turned to film, becoming one of the top stars in Hollywood. Though perhaps as well known for his tempestuous personal relationship with superstar actress **Elizabeth Taylor** as for his acting, Burton appeared in a number of the most notable films of his era, reaching the pinnacle of his success in the 1960, when he became Hollywood's highest-paid actor.

Burton received an **Academy Award** nomination for Best Actor in a Supporting Role for his performance in *My Cousin Rachel* (1952), then received considerable attention for his lead role in the **biblical epic** *The Robe* the following year. That performance earned him the first of his six **Oscar** nominations (without a win) for Best Actor in a Leading Role. His film career developed slowly in the 1950s, though his performance in *Look Back in Anger* (1959) won much critical praise.

Burton's performances in the 1960s won him a string of Oscar nominations, including those for *Becket* (1964), *The Spy Who Came in from the Cold* (1965), *Who's Afraid of Virginia Woolf?* (1966, opposite Taylor), and *Anne of the Thousand Days* (1969). His performance in *Night of the Iguana* (1964) was another critical success. However, he was perhaps best known in the 1960s for his hard drinking and for his tempestuous relationship with Taylor, with whom he also starred in the **historical epic** *Cleopatra* (1963, a notorious failure), as well as *The Sandpiper* (1965), *The Taming of the Shrew* (1967), *The Comedians* (1967), and *Dr. Faustus* (1967).

Burton won another Oscar nomination for his lead role in *Equus* (1977), but by this time his career was in decline, largely due to health problems exacerbated by alcohol. His performance as O'Brien in *Nineteen Eighty-Four* was, however, a late highlight.

**BURTON, TIM (1958– ).** The former **Disney** animator Tim Burton made his debut as a director of feature films with *Pee-Wee's Big Adventure* (1985), an interesting postmodern pastiche of children's films that is clearly aimed more at adults. He followed with *Beetle Juice* (1988), a comic supernatural thriller that similarly straddles the boundary between children's and adult's films. These films set the stage for many of Burton's subsequent films, which often seem aimed at children but which, on closer inspection, seem more appropriate for adults. Burton then made his commercial breakthrough with the highly successful *Batman* (1989), a brooding version of the Batman story set in a Gotham City that seemed taken straight out of **film noir**.

Burton followed with *Edward Scissorhands* (1990), a fairy-tale film that was the first of what would be many films with actor **Johnny Depp**. *Batman Returns* (1992), a sequel to the 1989 *Batman*, was also a critical and commercial success, though Burton then turned to more eccentric and less commercial projects. In 1994, he directed *Ed Wood* (1994), a **biopic** about the notoriously bad 1950s director of the title, and in 1996 he paid more general homage to the **science fiction** films of the 1950s with the alien invasion spoof *Mars Attacks!* (1996), which also served as a parodic rejoinder to *Independence Day* (1996), which had appeared only months earlier.

In 1993, Burton was the writer and producer (but not director) of the extremely inventive stop-motion **animation** film *The Nightmare before Christmas*, a film that was to be distributed by Disney, but which Disney elected to distribute under its Touchstone Pictures label for fear that the film would be seen as inappropriate for children. Over time, this brilliant film became a favorite with children and adults alike; it was ultimately released on DVD under the Disney brand name, helping to draw Burton back into the Disney fold.

*Sleepy Hollow* (1999, again starring Depp), *Planet of the Apes* (2001, a remake of the 1968 classic), and *Big Fish* (2003) were reasonably mainstream films that still contained offbeat touches. None of these films were major hits, but they were successful enough to put Burton at the helm of *Charlie and the Chocolate Factory* (2005), an extremely eccentric (and expensive) remake of the 1971 children's classic *Willy Wonka and the Chocolate Factory*. This film stirred some controversy, especially for Depp's decidedly strange portrayal of Willy Wonka, but it was visually brilliant and profitable at the box office.

Also in 2005, Burton directed *Corpse Bride*, a stop-motion film that was something of a follow-up to *The Nightmare before Christmas*. Then, in 2007, he directed Depp in *Sweeney Todd: The Demon Barber of Fleet Street*, a darkly gruesome comedy about a cynical serial killer. With this film, it was for once clear that the intended audience of a Burton film did not include children. In 2009, Burton was a producer for 9, a stop-motion animated posta-pocalyptic film that was also not really for children, but in 2010 he returned to directing with the big-budget, high-profile *Alice in Wonderland*, a stylish remake (again produced by Disney) of the 1951 classic Disney adaptation of the work of Lewis Carroll, with Depp as the Mad Hatter. That film was a huge international success, grossing more than $1 billion in worldwide box office receipts. *See also* BLACK COMEDY; POSTMODERNISM.

**BUTCH CASSIDY AND THE SUNDANCE KID.** *Butch Cassidy and the Sundance Kid* (dir. **George Roy Hill**, 1969) was probably the central work in the spate of revisionary **Westerns** that appeared at the end of the 1960s and beginning of the 1970s, substantially renewing the genre under the influence of the 1960s counterculture. Like many of these Westerns, *Butch Cassidy* is set at the end of the 19th century and thus at a time when capitalist modern-ization is leading to the closing of the frontier and to the waning of the Wild West world of which outlaws such as Butch and Sundance, presented in the film as charming and lovable rogues, were a central part.

As the film opens, Butch (**Paul Newman**) and Sundance (**Robert Redford**) are already worrying that the modern world is passing them by; in particular, they quickly find that the forces of law and order that oppose them are becom-ing increasingly efficient and professional. Ultimately, the two outlaws decide to travel to Bolivia, which they hope will still have some of the wildness they once enjoyed in North America. Butch and Sundance resume their careers as robbers in Bolivia, but eventually find that even there the authoritarian forces arrayed against individualist outlaws are now insurmountable. The film ends as Butch and Sundance are surrounded by police, then rush from their hiding place with guns blazing, hoping to shoot their way to freedom, only to find that the police who surround them have been reinforced by hundreds of troops from the Bolivian army, thus making the situation hopeless.

In this sense, the story of Butch and Sundance is largely a tragic one, though, in keeping with the film's generally light tone, Hill chooses to es-chew the violent final scenes of near-contemporary films that influenced it, such as ***Bonnie and Clyde*** (1967). Instead, *Butch Cassidy* ends with a freeze frame of the two outlaws charging forth, their final demise indicated only in the gunfire of the film's continuing soundtrack. The film, despite its vague tone of 1960s rebelliousness, ultimately depicts opposition to capitalist mod-ernization as hopeless and quixotic.

*Butch Cassidy and the Sundance Kid* received seven **Academy Award** nominations, including for Best Picture and Best Director; it won **Oscars** for Best Screenplay, Best Original Score, Best Original Song, and Best Cinema-tography.

# C

**CAGNEY, JAMES (1899–1986).** One of the great stars of American film history, James Cagney began his career as a dancer and comedian in vaudeville. He then moved into stage acting, drawing the attention of **Warner Bros.**, who quickly signed him to a film contract. He began his film career in *Sinners' Holiday* (1930), the film adaptation of the play *Penny Arcade*, in which Cagney had starred on Broadway. He was then propelled to major stardom as tough-guy gangster Tom Powers in *The Public Enemy* (1931), one of his signature roles and the one that served as the prototype for many tough-guy roles that followed for Cagney. One of the key films in the early 1930s **gangster film** cycle, *The Public Enemy* features one of the most famous scenes in film history, in which Cagney's Powers smashes a grapefruit into the face of his moll, played by actress Mae Clarke.

Cagney was one of Hollywood's most versatile stars of the 1930s, performing in lead roles in such **comedies** as *Blonde Crazy* (1931) and *Lady Killer* (1933) in addition to crime dramas such as *Angels with Dirty Faces* (1938), which won him his first **Academy Award** nomination for Best Actor. He eventually won that award for *Yankee Doodle Dandy* (1942), in which he returned to his show-business roots by displaying his musical talents.

Cagney used his tough-guy image to good effects in such postwar **film noir** dramas as *White Heat* (1949) and *Kiss Tomorrow Goodbye* (1950). He continued to perform in **musicals** as well, including lead roles in *The West Point Story* (1950) and *Love Me or Leave Me* (1955). The latter won him his third and last Academy Award nomination for Best Actor. However, now in his mid-50s, Cagney began to appear less regularly, though he did have several notable roles in the late 1950s, including the lead role in *Man of a Thousand Faces* (1957), a **biopic** about actor Lon Chaney. Cagney returned to crime drama at the end of the decade in *Never Steal Anything Small* (1959). He then essentially finished his film career with a flurry of films, demonstrating his ongoing versatility as an actor, starring in an oddly whimsical drama about the 1921 Irish Revolution, *Shake Hands with the Devil* (1959); in a biopic about U.S. Navy Admiral William Halsey, *The Gallant Hours* (1960); and in **Billy Wilder**'s Cold War comedy *One, Two, Three* (1961). Cagney did, however, return for an important role as the tough police commissioner in *Ragtime* (1981).

Cagney was listed as the eighth greatest male film star of all time in a list compiled by the **American Film Institute** in 1999.

**CAMERON, JAMES (1954– ).** After beginning his feature-film career working in the low-budget shop of **Roger Corman**, the Canadian-born director James Cameron went on to direct high-budget blockbusters, including *Titanic* (1997), then the biggest box-office hit of all time and a film that won 11 **Academy Awards**, including Best Picture and Best Director. However, it is for his contributions to **science fiction** film that Cameron is likely to be most remembered in the long run. After supervising the **special effects** for Corman's *Battle beyond the Stars* (1980), Cameron made his directorial debut the next year with *Piranha II: The Spawning*, also produced by Corman. However, Cameron's first major directorial effort came with the landmark sf film *The Terminator* (1984), which would be followed by the equally important sequel *Terminator II: Judgment Day* (1991). In between, Cameron helmed two other major science fiction films, *Aliens* (1986, the second entry in the *Alien* franchise) and *The Abyss* (1989). In 1994, he directed the tongue-in-cheek **action film** *True Lies*.

Cameron has written or co-written all of his major films, which are marked by excellent special effects, engaging storytelling, and the development of compelling characters. He has also occasionally written films for other directors, including *Rambo: First Blood Part II* (1985) and *Strange Days* (1995). Much of Cameron's time after *Titanic* was devoted to making **documentaries** and to developing new 3D camera technologies, the latter of which would ultimately come to be used in another megabudget sf film, *Avatar* (2009), composed mostly of **computer-generated images**. *Avatar* received nine **Oscar** nominations, including Best Picture and Best Director, though it won in only three technical categories. Another 3D sf film directed by Cameron, *Battle Angel*, is currently scheduled for release in 2011.

**CAPRA, FRANK (1897–1991).** The Sicilian-born Frank Capra moved to the United States in his early childhood. He began his professional career as a prop man in **silent film**, then became a silent-film director before going on, in the sound era, to direct some of the best-known and most-loved films in American film history. Marked by what some have seen to be a rather corny form of populist faith in the basic goodness of human beings (the term "Capra-corn" has sometimes been used to describe his films), Capra's films typically feature ordinary protagonists who triumph over diversity through their own hard work, ingenuity, common sense, and fundamental virtuousness.

Capra first became a major Hollywood figure as the director of *Lady for a Day* (1933), which won him an **Academy Award** nomination for Best Director, as well as being nominated for Best Picture. Capra then followed in 1934 with *It Happened One Night*, a key **screwball comedy** that swept the top five Academy Awards, winning Capra his first Best Director **Oscar**, as well as Oscars for Best Picture, Best Screenplay, Best Actor (**Clark Gable**), and Best Actress (**Claudette Colbert**).

Subsequently, Capra moved away from screwball comedy, directing such memorable films as *Mr. Deeds Goes to Town* (1936, winning Capra a Best Director Oscar), *Lost Horizon* (1937), *You Can't Take It with You* (1938, yielding Capra's third and final best Director Oscar), *Mr. Smith Goes to Washington* (1939, winning Capra his fifth Oscar nomination for Best Director), and *Meet John Doe* (1941). Commissioned as a major in the U.S. Army Signal Corps during World War II, Capra was employed primarily in the war years in making propaganda films for the U.S. government, including the important seven-episode *Why We Fight* series. He did, however, return to screwball comedy in 1944 with *Arsenic and Old Lace* (1944), a film with decidedly dark undertones.

A similar underlying darkness can be found in *It's a Wonderful Life* (1946), which marked Capra's postwar return to full-time commercial directing. The film won Capra his sixth and final Best Director Oscar but was a box-office failure at the time of its first release. However, it has gone on to become a Christmas staple on television, where most viewers have appreciated its sweetly sentimental surface narrative while ignoring an underlying pessimism that sets the film apart from Capra's earlier work. *State of the Union* (1948) was a notable political comedy, but from this point forward Capra was no longer a major force in Hollywood. He directed only four more feature films, ending with *Pocketful of Miracles* (1961).

**CARPENTER, JOHN (1948– ).** Though perhaps best known as a master of the **horror** genre, thanks to the success of such efforts as *Halloween* (1978), John Carpenter has actually worked as much in **science fiction** as in horror, and many of his films combine the two genres. The first major film directed by Carpenter was the sf comedy *Dark Star* (1974), a genre to which he has occasionally returned, as in *Memoirs of an Invisible Man* (1992). However, after his first film, Carpenter did not return to science fiction until the 1981 postapocalyptic film *Escape from New York*. In the meantime, he had established himself as a horror director with *Halloween* (1978) and *The Fog* (1980).

Carpenter followed in 1982 with *The Thing*, a slickly produced remake of *The Thing from Another World* (1951) that combines science fiction with horror. In 1983, he returned to straight horror with *Christine*. *Starman* (1984) is a much-praised alien invasion narrative with a more benevolent alien, while *They Live* (1988) is a low-budget sf **satire** that is highly effective in its critique of modern consumer capitalism. *Big Trouble in Little China* (1986) was a box-office flop that combines elements of numerous genres, including science fiction. It has since become something of a **cult** favorite on home video. *Escape from L.A.* (1996) is a sequel to *Escape from New York*, relocated to the West Coast, while the high-**action** thriller *Ghosts of Mars* (2001) again combines the horror and science fiction genres. Other horror films directed by Carpenter include the 1998 film *Vampires*, a minor classic of its genre.

Carpenter has written both the scripts and the **music** for most of the films he has directed. Many of Carpenter's films have stood the test of time; sometimes regarded as a maker of low-budget exploitation films, Carpenter now has a growing critical reputation as a genre-film auteur.

**CARREY, JIM (1962– ).** The Canadian-born actor and comedian Jim Carrey had appeared in supporting roles in a number of films when he rose to national prominence as a regular performer on the television skit-comedy series *In Living Color* from 1990 to 1994. That exposure gained him the lead role in a series of **comedies** released in 1994, including *Ace Ventura: Pet Detective*, *The Mask*, and *Dumb & Dumber*. Now a recognized star, he employed his rubber-faced, over-the-top acting style as the Riddler in *Batman Forever* (1995). Carrey went on to become one of Hollywood's highest-paid stars, maintaining his stature with lead roles in such comedies as *Ace Ventura: When Nature Calls* (1995), *The Cable Guy* (1996), *Liar Liar* (1997), *Me, Myself & Irene* (2000), *How the Grinch Stole Christmas* (2000), and *Bruce Almighty* (2003).

In the meantime, however, Carrey also moved into more serious roles in *The Truman Show* (1998) and *Man on the Moon* (1999), both of which won him Best Actor **Golden Globe** awards. He was also nominated for that award three times for his comic performances and again for a serious role in *Eternal Sunshine of the Spotless Mind* (2004), perhaps his most critically admired film. Carrey's films of recent years have seen only moderate success relative to his earlier hits, though his comic performances as Count Olaf in *Lemony Snicket's A Series of Unfortunate Events* (2004) and as the lead character in *Yes Man* (2008) have helped him remain a leading comic actor. More serious roles in *The Majestic* (2001) and *The Number 23* (2007) have not been especially well received. In 2008, he voiced the lead character in the commercially successful **animated film** *Dr. Seuss' Horton Hears a Who!*, and in 2009 he starred (via performance capture animation) in the not-so-successful **Disney** film adaptation of the classic Charles Dickens story *A Christmas Carol*, playing Scrooge at various ages as well as the ghosts of Christmas past and future.

*CASABLANCA.* One of the paradigmatic films of the classic period of Hollywood film, *Casablanca* (dir. **Michael Curtiz**, 1942) is one of the best known and most beloved films in American cinema history. As an antifascist drama set at about the time of the beginning of the American involvement in World War II, *Casablanca* is very much a film of its time. In this sense it can be seen as the story of the conversion (or reversion) of cynical American Rick Blaine (**Humphrey Bogart**) to antifascist activism due to his recognition that the fight against fascism transcends personal concerns. On the other hand, part of the secret of the film's enduring popularity is the fact that it is also a very romantic story centering on Blaine's ill-fated love for Norwegian refugee Ilsa Lund (**Ingrid Bergman**), whom he gives up so that she can provide support for her husband Victor Laszlo (Paul Henreid), an important antifascist leader.

*Casablanca* is a quintessential classic Hollywood film that employs entirely conventional camera work and editing and uses highly recognizable big-name stars to tell a fairly predictable and even clichéd story, cobbled together from elements of various film genres. For example, in addition to its obvious generic associations, the film derives considerable energy from conventions of the **Western**, as when Casablanca itself is depicted as a sort of lawless Wild West frontier town. That the film is so effective is a testament to the charisma of its stars and to the power of classic Hollywood conventions, to which this film adheres quite closely.

*Casablanca* was nominated for eight **Academy Awards**, winning in the key categories of Best Picture, Best Director, and Best Screenplay. In a 2007 poll conducted by the **American Film Institute**, it was named the third greatest film of all time.

**CASSAVETES, JOHN (1929–1989).** Though best remembered as the director of a number of groundbreaking **independent films**, John Cassavetes also wrote most of the films he directed and had an extensive career as an actor in television and mainstream Hollywood films, as well as his own films. He began his acting career with numerous television appearances in the 1950s, culminating in his starring role in the series *Johnny Staccato* (1959–1960). His appearances in films other than those he directed included major roles in **Don Siegel**'s 1964 remake of the **film noir** classic *The Killers*, *The Dirty Dozen* (1967, winning him an **Academy Award** nomination for Best Supporting Actor), and (perhaps most memorably) *Rosemary's Baby* (1968).

Using handheld cameras that lent an air of cinema verité realism to the gritty dramas he directed, Cassavetes established himself as a director with the film *Shadows* (1959), in which he played only a small (uncredited) role as an actor. Other important films that helped to establish his trademark style include *Faces* (1968, for which Cassavetes's screenplay won an **Oscar** nomination), *Husbands* (1970), *A Woman under the Influence* (1974, winning Cassavetes an Oscar nomination for Best Director), *Opening Night* (1978), and *Gloria* (1980), all of which featured his wife, actress Gena Rowlands (who won two Oscar nominations for Best Actress in his films), in central roles. *The Killing of a Chinese Bookie* (1976) was a key Cassavetes-directed film that featured neither him nor Rowlands as actors, but did feature Ben Gazzara, who appeared in several Cassavetes films.

As a director, Cassavetes was a major inspiration for the rising independent film movement, financing his films partly from his own income as an actor. His **documentary**-style realism was influential on studio films as well, as were his own method acting style and tendency to give actors considerable improvisational freedom in interpreting the scripts that he wrote for them.

**CENSORSHIP.** Though most observers agree that film is a form of speech protected under the First Amendment to the United States Constitution, American film has, in fact, been subjected to a number of forms of censorship over the years. Of course, filmmakers have always exercised some sort of judgment concerning the content of their films, which amounts to a form of self-censorship, though the most prominent form of self-censorship in the American film industry took the form of the **Production Code**, adopted in 1930 (but not fully enforced until 1934) in response to widely expressed concerns that films might be exerting a detrimental moral influence on Americans, especially younger ones. This code, which severely limited the content of films (especially in relation to the depiction of sex and, to a lesser extent, violence), remained in force until 1968, though it had been eroding for some time by that point.

The Production Code was backed through much of its time in force by a variety of state and local antipornography laws that placed similar restrictions on the content of films and other forms of popular entertainment. However, these laws also eroded through the 1960s, many being declared in violation of the First Amendment. In 1968, the Production Code was replaced by a ratings system instituted by the **Motion Picture Association of America (MPAA)**, indicating the suitability of individual films for audiences of various ages. In particular, films deemed to have extremes of graphic sex or violence were given an X rating, generally considered to be box-office poison, relegating such films to the pornography market. This designation was later replaced by an NC-17 designation (indicating that no one under 17 should be permitted to view the film), which carries less of a stigma and allows for the possibility that serious, nonpornographic films might still be suitable only for adult audiences.

The most overt political censorship of American films occurred in the years after World War II, when the **House Un-American Activities Committee** (HUAC) launched investigations, beginning in 1947, into supposed communist influence in the American film industry. These investigations led to the establishment of an extensive **blacklist** of individuals, such as the **Hollywood Ten**, whose suspected leftist political sympathies made them unemployable in Hollywood. Hollywood films, meanwhile, became increasingly reluctant to tackle any issues that might draw the attention of anticommunist zealots in Washington.

The blacklist was broken at the beginning of the 1960s, and subsequent censorship in Hollywood has resided primarily in the self-censorship of the ratings system. For example, filmmakers (and the studios who back them) generally seek to avoid the NC-17 rating, which imposes severe limits on the commercial potential of film. Filmmakers often seek to avoid even the R rating, with the result that that ratings system, while not banning any specific representations in film, has the effect of imposing substantial limits on film contents, and the ratings system strongly encourages self-censorship. In another form of self-censorship, filmmakers also often seek to avoid controversies of various kinds, as numerous special-interest groups have historically been involved in launching public protests against films of which they disapprove.

Numerous groups have historically been involved in such protests, one of the most important of which has been the National Legion of Decency, founded (as the Catholic Legion of Decency) by the Catholic Church in 1933 to protest what they saw as objectionable content in films. The Catholic Church had earlier been an important driving force behind the adoption of the Production Code, and this new group was instrumental in forcing stricter enforcement of the code beginning in 1934, the year the organization changed its name to the National Legion of Decency to indicate that it also had substantial Protestant support. By the 1960s, however, that support had eroded and the organization was again renamed, as the National Catholic Office for Motion Pictures, in 1966. Its influence fading, the organization was eventually incorporated into the U.S. Conference of Catholic Bishops, which still maintains its own ratings system for films, though these ratings are little heeded by the general public.

**CHANDLER, RAYMOND (1888–1959).** Novelist Raymond Chandler is notable in American film history first and foremost because of the influence his hard-boiled detective novels (featuring detective Philip Marlowe) exerted on Hollywood in general, especially in the evolution of **film noir**. Several of Chandler's novels have been directly adapted to the screen, including *The Big*

*Sleep* (1939), which became a classic film of the same title in 1946 (and was adapted again in 1978), and *Farewell, My Lovely* (1940), which was memorably adapted as *Murder, My Sweet* in 1944. The latter was also the basis for the films *The Falcon Takes Over* (1942) and *Farewell, My Lovely* (1975). Chandler's *The High Window* (1942) and *Lady in the Lake* (1943) were adapted to film under the same titles in 1942 and 1947, respectively, while his novel *The Long Goodbye* (1954) became an important **neo-noir** film of the same title under the direction of **Robert Altman** in 1973.

Chandler also worked extensively as a screenwriter, most notably as the co-writer (with **Billy Wilder**) of the film noir classic *Double Indemnity* (1944), for which he received an **Academy Award** nomination. He received a similar nomination for his original screenplay for *The Blue Dahlia* (1946). Among Chandler's other screenwriting credits, the most notable was as the co-writer of the script for **Alfred Hitchcock**'s *Strangers on a Train* (1951).

**CHAPLIN, CHARLES (1889–1977).** The British-born Charles Chaplin is widely regarded as one of the few true geniuses of American cinema. The son of **music** hall performers, Chaplin himself began as a child performer in British music halls, first coming to the United States with a touring troupe in 1910–1912. During a second tour of the United States, Chaplin was seen by **Mack Sennett** and signed to a contract to appear in films for Sennett's Keystone Film Company. After a slow start, Chaplin debuted his "Little Tramp" character in the 1914 silent film *Kid Auto Races at Venice*. This character would go on to become his signature role and one of the most beloved characters in film history; he was the key figure in a large number of classic **silent films**, including such **comedies** written and directed by Chaplin as *The Kid* (1921), *City Lights* (1931), and *Modern Times* (1936), the latter of which marked Chaplin's belated farewell to the silent era and the beginning of his move into sound.

The vast majority of Chaplin's films were made for Keystone and other studios before he founded **United Artists**—along with **D. W. Griffith**, **Douglas Fairbanks**, and **Mary Pickford**—in 1919 in order to give artists an opportunity for greater creative control over their work. After that point, Chaplin made fewer films, putting more time and effort into both the creation and the marketing of each, though even his earlier, hastier productions featured many well-remembered classics, such as *The Floorwalker* (1916) and *The Rink* (1916).

Having finally (and reluctantly) joined the move to sound film, Chaplin wrote, produced, directed, and starred in another comedy classic, *The Great Dictator* (1940), which lampooned Adolf Hitler and the German Nazis and sought to generate sympathy for the Popular Front effort to mobilize international opposition to fascism. Though a recognized classic, this film would contribute to Chaplin's reputation as a leftist sympathizer, and would eventually draw the attention of the **House Un-American Activities Committee** and drive Chaplin into European exile; he lived in Switzerland from 1952 until his death.

Chaplin made the dark comedy *Monsieur Verdoux* in 1947, alienating many of his fans with his portrayal of the title character, a sociopath who is willing to kill to make money. The overt critique of capitalism embedded in this film added to Chaplin's troubles, as did controversies over his personal life. The 1952 film *Limelight*, his last film made in America, was hardly released at all in the United States until 1972, winning Chaplin his only competitive **Academy Award** at that time for co-writing the film's **musical** score. However, Chaplin was given honorary **Oscars** in both 1929 and 1972, the latter of which he accepted on a triumphant return to the United States after 20 years of exile. He also won Oscar nominations for Best Actor and Best Director for *The Great Dictator* and for the screenplay of *Monsieur Verdoux*.

Chaplin's last two films as a director, *A King in New York* (1957) and *A Countess from Hong Kong* (1967), were made in Great Britain and were not widely seen in the United States. However, while he also starred in the first of these, he appeared only in a brief cameo role in the latter, which featured **Marlon Brando** and Sophia Loren in the lead roles and was Chaplin's only film to be made in color.

**CHAYEFSKY, PADDY (1923–1981).** Paddy Chayefsky was a successful playwright, novelist, and television scriptwriter in addition to his critically acclaimed career as a screenwriter. Actually, Chayefsky wrote relatively few screenplays, but nearly half his screenplays won **Academy Award** nominations for Best Screenplays. Of his total of four nominations, he won three **Oscars**, for *Marty* (1955), *The Hospital* (1971), and *Network* (1976). He was also nominated for the screenplay *The Goddess* (1958). Other screenplays written by Chayefsky include those for *The Bachelor Party* (1957), *The Americanization of Emily* (1964), *Paint Your Wagon* (1969), and *Altered States* (1980), the latter based on his own novel.

Chayefsky is credited as being a pioneer in bringing greater realism to television drama in the 1950s, somewhat along the lines of the contemporary British movement known as "kitchen sink realism." He brought much of the same grittiness to his film dramas.

**CHILDREN'S FILM.** The Walt **Disney** Company established itself in the first half of the 1930s with a series of critically acclaimed, award-winning short animated films for children. The company then moved into feature film with the 1937 classic *Snow White and the Seven Dwarfs*, which has some claim to being the first children's feature film. Meanwhile, that this film was also the first feature-length **animated film** is no coincidence but indicates the close relationship that has existed ever since between children's film and animated film.

Of course, films that might appeal to children are essentially as old as film itself; the entire medium had such an unsavory reputation in its early years that, in the eyes of many, filmgoing was by definition an unacceptable activity for children. It was not until the 1930s that feature-length films that might be characterized as children's films began to emerge as an identifiable cultural phenomenon. Even then, many of these films, which often featured child stars such as **Shirley Temple**, **Mickey Rooney**, and **Judy Garland**, were not oriented so much toward children as toward families, hoping to appeal to parents while at the same time assuring parents that it was okay to bring along the kids. The same might be said for *The Wizard of Oz* (1939), a live-action **musical** that might still be the most highly regarded film that seems aimed largely at children.

Meanwhile, the Disney Company maintained its dominance in the realm of children's animated film for decades, producing such classics of the form as *Pinocchio* (1941), *Dumbo* (1941), *Bambi* (1942), *Cinderella* (1950), *Alice in Wonderland* (1951), *Peter Pan* (1953), and *Sleeping Beauty* (1959). In the meantime, however, Disney had switched mostly to live-action films, largely due to their lower production costs. Most of their live-action films were more forgettable than the animated classics, but some—including *Treasure Island* (1950), *20,000 Leagues under the Sea* (1954), *Old Yeller* (1957), *Swiss Family Robinson* (1960), and *The Absent-Minded Professor* (1961)—remain an important part of American children's culture. Of the live-action films made during the lifetime of company founder **Walt Disney**, *Mary Poppins* (a 1964 film that includes some brief animated sequences) was by far the most commercially successful.

After Disney's death in 1966, his company seemed to lack direction and began to lose its dominance in the world of children's film. Thus, while they continued to produce some interesting films, the door was opened for competitors. As early as 1968, *Chitty Chitty Bang Bang*, a British-produced film (distributed in the United States by **United Artists**) was a key hit that openly drew upon the success of *Mary Poppins*; for example, *Chitty Chitty Bang Bang* starred Dick Van Dyke and featured songs by the Sherman brothers, just as *Mary Poppins* had done. Other challenges to Disney's control of the children's film industry arose here and there, largely through adaptations of well-known children's books. The year 1971, for example, saw the release of *Willy Wonka and the Chocolate Factory* (distributed by **Paramount Pic-**

**tures**), a somewhat sanitized film version of the 1964 novel *Charlie and the Chocolate Factory* by Roald Dahl (who had, incidentally, coscripted *Chitty Chitty Bang Bang*). Meanwhile, one of the most important non-Disney films of the early post-Walt years was the animated film *Charlotte's Web* (1973), also distributed by Paramount and based on a novel by E. B. White, who had staunchly refused to let Disney adapt his book.

Perhaps the biggest turn away from Disney in children's film came with the release of *E.T.: The Extra-Terrestrial* (1982), a huge hit that launched director **Steven Spielberg** (and his production company, **Amblin Entertainment**) as a major player in children's film. Amblin (with Spielberg as executive producer) subsequently made such hits as *Gremlins* (1984), *Goonies* (1985), *The Land before Time* (1988, directed by former Disney animator Don Bluth), and *Who Framed Roger Rabbit* (1988), which featured a groundbreaking mixture of live action and animation. The latter incidentally, was co-produced by Disney and distributed by Disney's Touchstone Pictures unit (on the premise that the faux noir subject matter of this innovative mixture of live action and animation was a bit too mature to carry the Disney logo).

Other notable children's films of the 1980s included Bluth's animated *The Secret of N.I.M.H.* (1982) and the live-action *Pee-Wee's Big Adventure* (1985), directed by future superstar director (and another former Disney animator) **Tim Burton**. It was, however, the Disney company itself that topped off the decade with *The Little Mermaid* (1989), an animated fairy tale that self-consciously looked back to the early Disney classics and ushered in what has come to be known as the "Disney Renaissance," which included a string of animated hits that included *Beauty and the Beast* (1991), *Aladdin* (1992), and *The Lion King* (1994). Later works such as *Pocahontas* (1995), *The Hunchback of Notre Dame* (1996), *Hercules* (1997), *Mulan* (1998), and *Tarzan* (1999) are also generally considered to be part of the Renaissance, though the energy of Disney's comeback was clearly beginning to fade a bit by the end of the decade.

In the meantime, Disney's unprecedented commercial success with animated children's films in the 1990s also encouraged other studios to get into the game. Ultimately, though, the most important of these new players was **Pixar**, an upstart company devoted to computer animation whose features were initially distributed by Disney and which was acquired by Disney as a wholly owned subsidiary in 2006. Pixar's first film, *Toy Story* (1995), was also the first film to be produced entirely by **computer-generated imagery** (CGI), starting a trend that would make this form of animation a dominant force in American children's film. Under the creative leadership of former Disney animator **John Lasseter**, Pixar followed with a string of successes that has made all of their films major blockbuster hits as well as critical successes regarded by audiences as instant classics.

Pixar's films have included two sequels to *Toy Story* (in 1999 and 2010), *A Bug's Life* (1998), *Monsters, Inc.* (2001), *Finding Nemo* (2003), *The Incredibles* (2004), *Cars* (2006), *Ratatouille* (2007), *WALL-E* (2008), and *Up* (2009). The success of these films has encouraged other studios to produce major computer-animated features as well. Disney itself has switched almost completely to computer animation, though the films released under the Disney brand name in the 21st century—which have shown a particular proclivity toward **science fiction**, as in *Lilo & Stitch* (2002), *Chicken Little* (2005), and *Meet the Robinsons* (2007)—have clearly taken a back seat to Pixar. Since the introduction of the **Academy Award** for Best Animated Feature in 2001, for example, no Disney-branded film has won that honor, though Pixar has won four times.

The most prominent competitor to Disney–Pixar has been the animation unit of **Dreamworks**, a studio founded by Spielberg, record mogul David Geffen, and former Disney executive Jeffrey Katzenberg. Their animated films have met with somewhat mixed success, though the sequence of films that began with *Shrek* in 2001 has been a colossal success. As of this writing, in fact, *Shrek 2* (2004) remains the top-grossing animated film of all time. *Shrek the Third* (2007) and *Shrek Forever After* (2010) have been smash hits as well, while the hip, irreverent style of the *Shrek* films (filled with pop-cultural references, they are conceived essentially as parodic rejoinders to the classic Disney fairy-tale films) has been hugely influential on other recent animated films. Other notable Dreamworks efforts include *Antz* (1998), *Madagascar* (2005), *Madagascar: Escape 2 Africa* (2008), and *Kung Fu Panda* (2008).

Other than the *Shrek* sequence, the most lucrative franchise in children's film in recent years has been the *Ice Age* sequence, produced and distributed by **Twentieth Century Fox**, with computer animation by Blue Sky Studios, acquired by Fox in 1997. While not as critically acclaimed as the *Shrek* films, this sequence—including *Ice Age* (2002), *Ice Age: The Meltdown* (2006), and *Ice Age: Dawn of the Dinosaurs* (2009)—has rivaled even the *Shrek* films in commercial success, with the third *Ice Age* film now standing second only to *Shrek 2* in worldwide box-office receipts among animated films. Meanwhile, the shift to computer animation has opened the field to a number of smaller studios, while Pixar and the major animation studios have continued to push the technological envelope, including the recent introduction of much-improved versions of three-dimensional (3D) computer animation.

Live-action films have continued to be produced for children as well, but none have rivaled the top animated films in prominence as cultural artifacts since the beginning of the Disney Renaissance in 1989. Interestingly, one of the most successful live-action films for children in recent years has been Disney's own *Enchanted* (2007), which shows a clear *Shrek* influence in poking gentle fun at the Disney animated classics, though it ultimately embraces (while slightly updating) the messages of those earlier films. Meanwhile, *Enchanted* features some animated sequences, while other recent successful live-action family films, such as *Stuart Little* (1999) and *Alvin and the Chipmunks* (2007) have featured computer-animated characters interacting with live actors.

*CHINATOWN*. *Chinatown* (dir. **Roman Polanski**, 1974) was one of the key films in resurrecting many of the motifs of **film noir** and is often considered the definitive work of **neo-noir**, the film that brought film noir into the **New Hollywood** and helped to inspire a resurgence of noir motifs in Hollywood film. In fact, despite being shot in color, *Chinatown* is in many ways a classic film noir, combining a complex detective story plot with a general air of corruption and a darkly claustrophobic look and atmosphere. In many ways, the protagonist, J. J. Gittes (**Jack Nicholson**), is a typical film noir detective, willing to bend the rules but ultimately sincere in his quest for the truth. Similarly, the central female character, Evelyn Mulwray (**Faye Dunaway**), seems the quintessential film noir femme fatale, seductive but dangerous, largely because of her mysterious past. In some ways, however, *Chinatown* is even darker than the typical film noir. Gittes succeeds in solving the film's mystery, but he is no match for the mighty forces that are arrayed against him, powerless to prevent the realization of the complex, evil plot that his investigation uncovers. Ultimately, Gittes becomes a figure of the lone individual, entirely overmatched by the powerful forces arrayed against him, embodied in the central villain, Noah Cross (played by film noir pioneer **John Huston**).

The film is set in 1937 and employs exquisite period detail to make that setting clear. In addition, it is based on actual Los Angeles water scandals dating back to the first decade of this century. Nevertheless, *Chinatown* is very much a film of the 1970s, both in its underlying ecological concerns and in its cynicism about the possibility of opposing the ruthless and greedy quest for profit that constitutes the context of the film. In its blurring of boundaries between different historical periods and in its self-conscious pastiche of film noir, *Chinatown* can be considered a representative work of **postmodernism**. One of the most highly praised films of the 1970s, *Chinatown* garnered 11 **Academy Award** nominations but won only for **Robert Towne**'s screenplay. It was named the 21st greatest film of all time in a 2007 poll conducted by the **American Film Institute**.

***CITIZEN KANE.*** *Citizen Kane* (dir. **Orson Welles**, 1941) is quite widely considered to be the greatest film ever made, coming in first in the all-time greatest film lists compiled by the **American Film Institute** in both 1997 and 2007. The film was remarkable at the time for its innovative use of deep-focus photography and for the way its unusual camera placements and editing called attention to themselves, as opposed to the "Hollywood style" of "invisible editing," in which audiences are encouraged to become immersed in the story rather than thinking about decisions made in the filming and editing process. Audience immersion in the story of *Citizen Kane* is further complicated by the highly nonlinear, modernist construction of the plot and by the presentation of the title character, a complex and flawed figure with whom it is difficult to identify fully.

The technical and stylistic innovations in *Citizen Kane*—the first film by its 25-year-old director—ultimately made it one of the most influential films in Hollywood history. However, the content of the film is important as well. The plot essentially involves the life story of newspaper tycoon Charles Foster Kane, with Welles delivering a dazzling performance in the lead role. This story, however, is related indirectly, almost as a detective story, as a magazine reporter attempts to unravel the mysteries of the life of the recently deceased Kane.

Welles famously based Kane primarily on newspaper magnate William Randolph Hearst, who was enraged by the film and attempted to suppress it using the power of his media empire. However, though the film is unsentimental in its presentation of Kane's life, it does humanize him to an extent, thus producing a certain amount of sympathy for a man who himself has little sympathy for anyone else. But Kane's story is not merely a personal one. It comments in important ways on the rise of the modern American media and on the dehumanizing and alienating consequences of capitalism, whatever its material benefits. Indeed, Kane is an allegorical figure of modern American society, a fact apprehended in Welles's use during filming of working titles such as "American" and "John Citizen, U.S.A."

*Citizen Kane*, despite Hearst's attempts to suppress it, received nine **Academy Award** nominations, including Best Picture and Best Director and Best Actor nominations for Welles. However, it won only for the screenplay by Welles and Herman Mankiewicz.

***CITY LIGHTS.*** *City Lights* (dir. **Charles Chaplin**, 1931) is one of the greatest films of the silent era and is perhaps the most admired film of Chaplin, its esteemed director and star. *City Lights* was also Chaplin's last fully **silent film**, made at a time when sound film had already become the industry standard. As such, it can be taken as Chaplin's nostalgic farewell to silent film, which he felt was superior to sound film as an artistic medium.

*City Lights* is well tuned to the Depression era, as two of the central figures are Chaplin's always-poor Tramp and a penniless blind girl (played by Virginia Cherrill). The plot involves the Tramp's efforts to help the girl, with whom he falls in love. These efforts, meanwhile, centrally involve the Tramp's relationship with a hard-drinking millionaire, who befriends the Tramp when drunk but abuses him when sober. There is thus a great deal of potential social commentary about the treatment of the poor by the rich in this film, but it is best remembered for its touching love story and for Chaplin's trademark **slapstick comedy**, which combine to give the film the rather complex, bittersweet tone that is typical of much of Chaplin's comedy.

*City Lights* was named the 11th greatest film of all time in a 2007 poll conducted by the **American Film Institute** (AFI). Further, it was named the greatest **romantic comedy** of all time in a 2008 poll conducted by the AFI.

**CLIFT, MONTGOMERY (1920–1966).** Montgomery Clift burst on the Hollywood scene with a memorable performance as a sensitive younger cowboy who is somewhat brutalized by **John Wayne**'s character in *Red River* (1948). Subsequently, he played a series of intense roles, generally involving similarly sensitive and often tormented characters, including a role in *The Search*, also in 1948, for which he received an **Academy Award** nomination for Best Actor. He received similar nominations for *A Place in the Sun* (1951) and *From Here to Eternity* (1953), and received a nomination for Best Supporting Actor for *Judgment at Nuremburg* (1961).

Clift also had prominent roles in such films as *Lonelyhearts* (1958) and *The Young Lions* (1958), in which he starred opposite **Marlon Brando**, and *The Misfits* (1961), in which he costarred with **Clark Gable** and **Marilyn Monroe**. A major Hollywood heartthrob whose own personal life was troubled by problems with alcohol and drugs, as well as his own complex sexuality, Clift appeared in relatively few films but nevertheless left an indelible impression on audiences.

**CLOONEY, GEORGE (1961– ).** George Clooney had made numerous minor appearances when he finally began to draw more attention for his semiregular role in the *Roseanne* television series (1988–1991). He then gained major exposure as Dr. Doug Ross on the hit television medical drama *ER* (1994–1999). By the time he left that series to pursue a full-time career in film, he had already starred in the offbeat horror film *From Dusk till Dawn* (1996) and had a high-profile (but widely panned) role as Batman in *Batman & Robin* (1997). It was, however, his performance in **Steven Soderbergh**'s stylish **neo-noir** film *Out of Sight* (1998) that really got his film career off to a successful start, especially when it was immediately followed by an outstanding performance in the quirky **war film** *Three Kings* (1999).

Clooney's potential as a comic actor was especially demonstrated in **Joel and Ethan Coen**'s *O Brother, Where Art Thou?* (2000), where he partly channels **Clark Gable** in an over-the-top performance as a loveable prison escapee and con man. His performance in *The Perfect Storm* (2000) was less interesting but still showed that he could manage a lead role in a big-budget blockbuster, as did Soderbergh's heist film *Ocean's Eleven* (2001). *Confessions of a Dangerous Mind* (2002, which Clooney directed), Soderbergh's **science fiction** remake *Solaris* (2002), and the Coens' *Intolerable Cruelty* (2003) were all interesting projects that helped to display Clooney's versatility as an actor, even if they were less than fully successful.

Having starred in the sequel *Ocean's Twelve* in 2004, Clooney made a major step forward into Hollywood superstardom in 2005 when he played an important supporting role and also directed and co-wrote the critically acclaimed *Good Night, and Good Luck*, winning **Academy Award** nominations for Best Director and for the screenplay. That same year, Clooney also had an important supporting role in the complex political drama *Syriana* (2005), which won him the **Oscar** for Best Supporting Actor. He had another important supporting role in Soderbergh's *The Good German* (2006) and gained additional critical recognition for his starring role in *Michael Clayton* (2007), which won him an Oscar nomination for Best Actor in a Leading Role.

In 2008, Clooney directed the comedic **sports film** *Leatherheads*, in which he also starred and produced, having served as an executive producer on several previous projects. That same year he returned for his third film with the Coen Brothers in the comedic **spy film** *Burn after Reading*. He was particularly busy in 2009, when he provided the lead voice in the **animated film** *Fantastic Mr. Fox*, produced and starred in *The Men Who Stared at Goats*, and starred in the much-acclaimed *Up in the Air*.

**COEN, JOEL (1954– ) AND ETHAN (1957– ).** Working so closely throughout their careers that they are typically thought of as a composite entity, brothers Joel and Ethan Coen have made some of the most distinctive works of the American cinema since their entry into the field with the 1984 **neo-noir** film *Blood Simple*. For that film, Joel was credited as the director and Ethan as the producer, with both brothers credited as the authors of the screenplay. That arrangement continued until *The Ladykillers* (2004), from which point both brothers have been given credits as directors, producers, and writers on their films. It has been widely recognized, however, that the brothers have played these roles for all of their films.

The Coens followed in 1987 with *Raising Arizona*, a sort of combination of the **screwball comedy** with a heist narrative, with hilarious results that led the film to be named the 31st funniest film of all time in a 2000 poll conducted by the **American Film Institute**. They have gone on to make a career of producing innovative variations on established film genres, sometimes combining two or more genres in a single film. *Miller's Crossing* (1990), for example, is their take on the **gangster film**, while *Barton Fink* (1991), which won the Palm D'or at the Cannes Film Festival, is an offbeat drama about the Hollywood film industry, with elements of **comedy** and **horror** thrown in as well.

*The Hudsucker Proxy* (1994) saw a return to screwball comedy, though this relatively big-budget film received mixed reviews, partly because many critics felt that it relied too heavily on its pastiche of earlier films, such as **Howard Hawks's** *His Girl Friday* (1940). However, the Coens achieved their greatest critical success to date with their next film, *Fargo* (1996), a return to neo-noir spiced with comic elements. This film won an **Academy Award** for Best Screenplay for the brothers, as well as a Best Actress **Oscar** for Joel's wife, Frances McDormand, who had also starred in *Blood Simple* and who has had smaller roles in several of the Coen brothers' films.

*The Big Lebowski* (1998) is a broad crime farce that has gained a substantial **cult** following over the years, while *O Brother, Where Art Thou?* (2000), a crime comedy set in the 1930s, again gained considerable critical attention, especially for its innovative bluegrass-based soundtrack. Critics were less enthusiastic about *The Man Who Wasn't There* (2001), though this black-and-white **film noir** pastiche (with elements of **science fiction** tossed in for good measure) is highly interesting in its meticulous recreation of the texture of late-1940s noir films.

The Coens' next two films were comedies, but *Intolerable Cruelty* (2003) and *The Ladykillers* (2004) were among their least successful efforts. They rebounded in good style, however, with *No Country for Old Men* (2007), a stylish, but relatively conventional (by the Coens' standards) thriller that scored a total of eight Academy Award nominations and won four Oscars, including Best Picture and Best Directing and Best Screenplay Oscars for the brothers. Their follow-up, *Burn after Reading* (2008) is a rather farcical take on the genre of the **spy film**, while *A Serious Man* (2009) is a low-budget **black comedy** about a Jewish academic family, a milieu in which the Coens themselves grew up.

**COHN, HARRY (1891–1958).** Harry Cohn (along with his brother Jack Cohn) was one of the founding partners of **Columbia Pictures** when it was constituted in 1924 from an earlier partnership between the Cohns and Joe Brandt. Harry Cohn was the president of the new company and oversaw its production of films in Hollywood. Initially, Columbia had a reputation for low-budget, low-brow fare, but the company's fortunes improved in the 1930s with director **Frank Capra** as their most important creative figure. Capra films such as *It Happened One Night* (1934) and *Mr. Smith Goes to Washington* (1939) improved the company's public image, but Cohn continued to place emphasis on low-budget affairs such as serials, which were quite profitable for the company.

An autocratic executive with reported ties to organized crime, Cohn ran Columbia with an iron hand, always with an eye toward the bottom line. He was an efficient manager, though his management style, which often included the intentional humiliation of subordinates, alienated many. Cohn's sudden death from a heart attack in 1958 left Columbia in a state of disarray from which it took two decades to recover.

**COLBERT, CLAUDETTE (1903–1996).** Born in France, Claudette Colbert grew up in New York City and began her career as an actress on Broadway in the 1920s. She soon transitioned to film and gained major attention after her performance in the **screwball comedy** *It Happened One Night* (1934), which won her an **Academy Award** for Best Actress. Colbert also had another high-profile role in 1934 as the title character in **Cecil B. DeMille**'s *Cleopatra*, and she followed in 1935 with a lead role in the drama *Private Worlds* (1935), which won her another **Oscar** nomination and solidified her status as one of Hollywood's top stars.

In the second half of the 1930s, Colbert starred in a series of successful, if unremarkable, films. In 1940, she declined to renew her lucrative contract with **Paramount**, instead becoming a freelance performer, paving the way for other actors eventually to do the same. She was successful in the effort, continuing to star in major films such as *Boom Town* (1940), **Preston Sturges**'s *The Palm Beach Story* (1942), and *Since You Went Away* (1944), for which she won her third and final Oscar nomination for Best Actress.

After the successful **comedy** *Bride for Sale* (1949), Colbert's stardom began to decline. From the mid-1950s, she worked primarily on television or the stage. She was nominated for an Emmy Award for her supporting performance in the 1987 television miniseries *The Two Mrs. Grenvilles*.

**COLUMBIA PICTURES.** Columbia Pictures is now part of the Columbia TriStar Motion Picture Group, which is itself a subsidiary of **Sony Pictures Entertainment**. However, Columbia is one of the oldest "brand" names in American film. Originally founded as Cohn-Brandt-Cohn Film Sales, the company adopted the Columbia Pictures name in 1924. While never one of the "majors" of the era, the company grew in importance in the late 1920s and through the 1930s, when it became one of the leading producers of **screwball comedies** such as *It Happened One Night* (1934). In addition to that film, most of director **Frank Capra**'s other films of the 1930s were made for Columbia, giving the company newfound prestige.

In the late 1930s, the company found another niche in serials, which they continued making until 1956. Meanwhile, with **Rita Hayworth** as its leading star, the company did well in general through the 1940s and into the 1950s, producing such important films as *Gilda* (1946) and *From Here to Eternity* (1953). In addition, when the 1948 **Paramount Antitrust Case** forced the majors to divest themselves of the theater chains they owned, Columbia (which had never owned such a chain) gained competitive power.

In 1958, studio chief **Harry Cohn**, who had been with the company since its inception, died suddenly, and Columbia Pictures subsequently entered a crisis of leadership and direction. The company seemed unsure of its response to the sweeping changes in American society in the 1960s, and by the early 1970s the company was nearly bankrupt. A reorganization and new management team somewhat restored the company's financial health, leading to a purchase of the company by the Coca-Cola Company in 1982. All of the operations of Columbia Pictures (which increasingly included a significant amount of production of programming for television) were then sold to Sony in 1989.

Initially a near disaster for Sony, the takeover eventually proved profitable as Columbia rebounded to become one of the top-grossing studios by the end of the 1990s. The company became even more profitable in the early 2000s with the release of the *Spider-Man* franchise of **superhero films**. By 2006, Columbia established a new record annual domestic box-office gross for a single studio.

**COMEDY.** In its broadest sense, dating back to its use in ancient Greece, the term "comedy" simply refers to a work with a happy ending. In contemporary usage, however, the term is generally applied to humorous works that are intended to provoke laughter and amusement. As such, it is a major category of American film and includes numerous subcategories as well. For one thing, virtually all genres of American film contain comedies, including such examples as comic **Westerns, science fiction** comedies, comic **horror** films, even comic **war films** and comic **film noirs**. Many of these films are parodies of their own genre or of specific well-known works within the genre.

In addition, some kinds of films are virtually always comic in nature, such as **children's films**, especially children's **animated films**. But there are also a wide variety of American film comedies that do not necessarily belong to genres other than comedy itself. These latter "pure" comedies can themselves be separated into numerous subgenres, including **satire, anarchic comedy, slapstick, black comedy**, and **romantic comedy**, each of which can itself be divided into a number of subgenres.

**COMPUTER-GENERATED IMAGERY (CGI).** Computer-generated imagery involves the use of computer graphics to produce special visual effects for film, television, and video games. Such images have become increasingly important in **science fiction** film over the past several decades because they can be used to produce effects that are far more convincing and elaborate than those that could be created by physical techniques (such as the use of sets and models) on the same budget. As a result, science fiction films have long been on the forefront of the development of CGI, though the technique is now widely used in other films (especially **action films**) as well.

Computer-generated images were first used in the dystopian film *Westworld* in 1973; they were then used more extensively in that film's sequel, *Futureworld* (1976). However, the real breakthrough in the use of CGI came in 1977 with the release of ***Star Wars***, which employed far more elaborate CGI than had ever been used before. From that point forward, CGI was used more and more in sf film, often generated by special companies devoted to the generation of such images, such as **George Lucas's Industrial Light and Magic**, which created the effects for his *Star Wars* sequence but branched out to create effects for numerous other films as well.

**Steven Spielberg's** *Jurassic Park* (1993) was the next major milestone in the development of CGI for sf film, employing the technique to create highly believable dinosaurs—and to generate huge profits at the box office. Two years later, **Pixar** (formerly a subsidiary of **Lucasfilm**, but now an independent studio) released *Toy Story*, the first animated film to be generated entirely by computer graphics—though the voices of the characters were supplied by live actors. Since that time, computer animation has become entirely dominant in the world of animated film. Meanwhile, increasingly elaborate computer-generated **special effects** have been used to enhance live-action films as well, including more and more use of green screen technologies, in which live actors are filmed in front of a blank screen, with the background images filled in later by computer. This tendency culminated in 2004 with the release of several films that were shot essentially entirely in front of green screens and even included some computer-generated characters, including Enki Bilal's *Immortel (ad Vitam)*, the Japanese film *Casshern*, the low-budget U.S. film *Able Edwards*, and the relatively big-budget *Sky Captain and the World of Tomorrow*.

Increases in the power of computer hardware and the sophistication of computer software continue to enable steady improvement in the quality and complexity of computer-generated images. The generation of attractive and believable human characters by computer has thus far proved elusive, however, and audiences have tended to find computer-generated characters such as those in the film *Final Fantasy: The Spirits Within* (2001) subtly disturbing. Thus, a film such as Pixar's *WALL-E* (2008), which employs some of the most impressive computer-generated machinery and backgrounds ever put on film, employs human characters that are mere caricatures, far removed from realistic depiction, the only realistic human character being portrayed by a live actor.

**CONNERY, SEAN (1930– ).** Although he had made several film and television appearances—including a major role in the **Disney** film *Darby O'Gill and the Little People* (1959)—the Scottish actor Sean Connery was still a virtual unknown when he was cast in the lead role in *Dr. No* (1962), the first James Bond film. He would go on to star in six more Bond films over the next two decades, and it is for those films that he will probably forever be best known. However, he has appeared in numerous other films in a long and versatile acting career that has seen him become one of Hollywood's best-known figures. In these films he has shown talents that go well beyond the rugged onscreen sex appeal that made his Bond films so successful.

Connery won an **Academy Award** for Best Supporting Actor for his performance in *The Untouchables* (1987). Connery has, in fact, played a number of important supporting roles, perhaps most notably as the father of Indiana Jones in *Indiana Jones and the Last Crusade* (1989). Other key supporting roles have included those in *Murder on the Orient Express* (1974), *A Bridge Too Far* (1977), and *The Avengers* (1998).

Other career highlights include starring roles in such films as **Alfred Hitchcock**'s *Marnie* (1964), *The Molly Maguires* (1970), *The Wind and the Lion* (1975), *Robin and Marian* (1976), the media **satire** *Wrong Is Right* (1982), the European-produced *The Name of the Rose* (1986), *The Presidio* (1988), *The Russia House* (1990), *The Hunt for Red October* (1990), *First Knight* (1995), *The Rock* (1996), *Entrapment* (1999), and *Finding Forrester* (2000). He has also starred in several **science fiction** films, including *Zardoz* (1974), *Meteor* (1979), and *Outland* (1981), while playing key supporting roles in such **fantasy** films as *Time Bandits* (1981) and *Highlander* (1986).

Connery was knighted in 2000 in recognition of his career achievements.

**COOPER, GARY (1901–1961).** Famed for his laconic, restrained acting style, Gary Cooper was one of Hollywood's top leading men during his career, starring in a number of important films, especially **Westerns**. Cooper began his work in Hollywood in 1925 as an extra. By 1926 he had landed a contract with **Paramount** and had begun playing major roles in **silent films**, graduating to sound as the title character in *The Virginian* (1929). Lead roles in films such as *A Farewell to Arms* (1932) and *Mr. Deeds Goes to Town* (1936) cemented his status as one of Hollywood's top stars. The latter won him the first of his five **Academy Award** nominations for Best Actor.

Cooper followed with lead roles in a number of now-classic dramas, including *The Plainsman* (1936), *Meet John Doe* (1941), *Sergeant York* (1941, for which he won his first Best Actor **Oscar**), *Pride of the Yankees* (1942), and *For Whom the Bell Tolls* (1943), the latter two of which also won him Oscar nominations for Best Actor. He went against type in his role as a befuddled English professor in **Howard Hawks's screwball comedy** *Ball of Fire* in 1941, proving that he could be successful in that genre as well.

An avowed anticommunist, Cooper testified as a friendly witness before the **House Un-American Activities Committee** (HUAC) in 1947. His career was somewhat on the wane by the time he played the lead role of Marshal Will Kane in *High Noon* (1952), a performance that would ultimately come to be regarded as his greatest and that won him his second Best Actor Oscar. That film, ironically, would come to be seen by many as a subtle critique of the HUAC-led Hollywood witch hunts in which Cooper himself had willingly participated.

Cooper continued to appear regularly in films through the 1950s, with his role as a Quaker farmer in **William Wyler's** *Friendly Persuasion* (1956) providing a highlight. He received an honorary Academy Award for lifetime achievement in 1961, shortly before his death from cancer.

**COPPOLA, FRANCIS FORD (1939– ).** A leading member of the New Wave of directors who rose to prominence in Hollywood in the 1970s, Francis Ford Coppola began his career making low-budget films for **Roger Corman** in the 1960s, such as the 1963 horror film *Dementia 13*. Coppola moved into the direction of more mainstream films with late 1960s efforts such as the **musical** *Finian's Rainbow* (1968), but first rose to true Hollywood prominence as the co-writer of *Patton* (1970), which won him an **Academy Award** for Best Screenplay. He then became a truly major figure as the director (and co-writer) of *The Godfather* (1972), one of the seminal films of American cinematic history, ranked the second greatest film of all time in a 2007 list published by the **American Film Institute** (AFI).

Coppola followed with *The Conversation* (1974), an interesting thriller, and *The Godfather: Part II* (1974), which some critics felt was even better than the first *Godfather* film. He then finished out the decade of the 1970s with *Apocalypse Now* (1979), a film that initially got mixed reviews but that has established a growing critical reputation, coming in at No. 30 on the 2007 AFI list of greatest films, two notches ahead of *The Godfather: Part II*.

During the 1970s, Coppola also served as a producer of his own films, as well as of **George Lucas**'s *American Graffiti* (1973), with which he became involved via **American Zoetrope**, the production company he had founded with Lucas in 1969. American Zoetrope also produced *Apocalypse Now*, as well as a number of late, but less prominent Coppola films, such as *The Outsiders* (1983), *Rumble Fish* (1983), *The Cotton Club* (1984), *Peggy Sue Got Married* (1986), *The Godfather: Part III* (1990), and *Bram Stoker's Dracula* (1992). Since 1992, Coppola has worked less often as a director, working more frequently as a producer and executive producer of films directed by others, including *The Virgin Suicides* (1999), *Lost in Translation* (2003), and *Marie Antoinette* (2006), all directed by his daughter, Sofia Coppola.

Coppola has only won one **Oscar** for Best Director (for *The Godfather: Part II*). However, he received Best Director nominations for *The Godfather*, *Apocalypse Now*, and *The Godfather: Part III*. He won a Best Picture Oscar as the producer of *The Godfather: Part II*; of the films he has produced, *American Graffiti*, *The Conversation*, *Apocalypse Now*, and *The Godfather: Part III* also scored Best Picture Oscar nominations. In addition to *Patton*, Coppola has won Best Screenplay Oscars for co-writing (with Mario Puzo) *The Godfather* and *The Godfather: Part II*. He received Best Screenplay nominations for *The Conversation* and *Apocalypse Now*.

**CORMAN, ROGER (1926– ).** Educated as an industrial engineer at Stanford University, Roger Corman has put that training to use to produce entertaining films quickly, cheaply, and efficiently, almost in assembly-line fashion. Corman got his big start in the film business directing a series of **science fiction** films (many in the **monster movie** subgenre) for **American International Pictures** (AIP), beginning in 1955. These films included such efforts as *It Conquered the World* (1956), *Attack of the Crab Monsters* (1957), *Teenage Cave Man* (1958), and *The Wasp Woman* (1959). They were largely aimed at youthful audiences, and Corman quickly showed an ability to put together formulaic films that would appeal to teenage moviegoers. He also quickly showed that he was more talented as a producer than as a director, and most of his work beyond the 1960s has been as the producer or executive producer of what is now a total of almost 400 films.

Of all of these, Corman is perhaps best known for the series of **horror** film adaptations of the work of Edgar Allan Poe that he directed and produced for AIP in the early 1960s, largely based on scripts written by Richard Matheson. After that, most of Corman's films were made by his own production companies, of which there have been several, beginning with New World

Pictures in 1970. Despite their perceived status as B-movies and exploitation films, Corman's films often deal with important topical issues. Though he has increasingly specialized in horror films in the latter part of his career, science fiction has remained a crucial part of his output as well. Several of Corman's later productions have been remakes of his own early films, playing up the campy aspects of those films.

The low-budget nature of most of Corman's films has often made it possible (or even necessary) for him to hire young, unknown talent to work on them. His judgment of the potential of young talent has been impressive. Thus, in addition to his numerous films, Corman has been an important force in the American film industry because of the number of prominent actors, writers, and (especially) directors who have gotten started in the industry working on his films. Directors **Peter Bogdanovich**, **James Cameron**, **Francis Ford Coppola**, Jonathan Demme, **Ron Howard**, **John Sayles**, and **Martin Scorsese** all worked for Corman at the beginnings of their careers, as did actors David Carradine, Bruce Dern, Peter Fonda, **Dennis Hopper**, **Robert De Niro**, and **Jack Nicholson**.

**COSTELLO, LOU.** *See* ABBOTT, BUD AND COSTELLO, LOU.

**CRABBE, BUSTER (1908–1983).** A gifted athlete who was a member of the U.S. Olympic swimming teams in 1928 and 1932, Buster Crabbe went on to make more than 100 film appearances, most notably in serials of the 1930s and 1940s. Crabbe is best known as the star of the three Flash Gordon **science fiction** serials—*Flash Gordon: Space Soldiers* (1936), *Flash Gordon's Trip to Mars* (1938), and *Flash Gordon Conquers the Universe* (1940)—as well as the 1939 serial *Buck Rogers*. He began his career in serials as the title character in the 1933 serial *Tarzan the Fearless*. He also played a number of other "jungle man" roles, including the leads in the features *King of the Jungle* (1933) and *Jungle Man* (1941) and the 1952 serial *King of the Congo*. Most of Crabbe's appearances in the 1940s were in a series of B-**Westerns** in which he played either Billy the Kid or Billy Carson. Most of his appearances after 1952 were guess spots on television, though he did star in his own ongoing series, *Captain Gallant of the Foreign Legion*, from 1955 to 1957.

**CRAVEN, WES (1939– ).** One of the leading writers and directors of American **horror** films, Wes Craven is best known as the creator of the *Nightmare on Elm Street* horror franchise. A former college English teacher, Craven began his career in film with two important horror films in the 1970s, *The Last House on the Left* (1972) and *The Hills Have Eyes* (1977), both of which he also wrote. Several less successful films followed, but Craven had his big breakthrough in 1984 as the writer and director of *The Nightmare on Elm Street*, a reality-bending horror film that introduced the iconic character of Freddy Krueger and founded an extensive franchise; although 1994's *New Nightmare* is the only other film in the sequence directed by Craven, he did co-write the screenplay for *A Nightmare on Elm Street 3: Dream Warriors* (1987). *The People under the Stairs* (1991) is another important horror film written and directed by Craven, and one that contains considerable social commentary. His most important works of recent years have been the three *Scream* films (1996, 1997, 2000), which he directed but did not write. The *Scream* films are works of **postmodernism** that include a strong element of clever self-conscious commentary on the horror genre, as well as being legitimate horror films in their own right.

**CRAWFORD, JOAN (1908–1977).** Named the 10th greatest female star of all time in a 1999 poll conducted by the **American Film Institute**, Joan Crawford began her career in **silent film**, struggling toward stardom in the late years of that era. She transitioned smoothly into the sound era, and by the time of her role in *Grand Hotel* (1932), she had become a top star of sound film as well. In 1934, she starred in three major commercial hits, *Sadie McKee*, *Chained*, and *Forsaking All Others*. Her popularity declined in the late 1930s, however, and by 1943 her lucrative contract with **Metro-Goldwyn-Mayer** (MGM) had been terminated.

Switching to **Warner Bros.**, Crawford rebounded in good fashion, however, as the star of the 1945 **film noir** classic *Mildred Pierce*, for which her portrayal of the title character won her her only **Academy Award** for Best Actress. Some of her most distinguished roles followed, including **Oscar**-nominated lead roles in the noir films *Possessed* (1947) and *Sudden Fear* (1952). Her role in the off-beat noir **Western** *Johnny Guitar* (1954) was also notable, but her career subsequently declined, and by the 1960s she was largely relegated to B-grade **horror** films such as *I Saw What You Did* (1965) and *Berserk* (1967), though she did experience one last career highlight in the **Robert Aldrich** thriller *What Ever Happened to Baby Jane* (1962), in which she starred opposite her longtime rival **Bette Davis**.

In 1978, Crawford became the subject of posthumous controversy when her adopted daughter, Christine, published a memoir in which she charged Crawford with mental and physical abuse. Many of Crawford's longtime friends and associates denounced the book, but *Mommie Dearest* became a bestseller and later became a 1981 film, starring **Faye Dunaway** as Crawford.

**CRONENWETH, JORDAN (1935–1996).** Cinematographer Jordan Cronenweth began his film career with **Robert Altman**'s *Brewster McCloud*

(1970) and subsequently worked on a wide variety of important films. He was the cinematographer on *Altered States* (1980), *Gardens of Stone* (1987), *Get Back* (1991), and *Final Analysis* (1992). His only **Academy Award** nomination for Best Cinematography came for **Francis Ford Coppola**'s *Peggy Sue Got Married* (1986), but he is best known as the cinematographer for *Blade Runner* (1982), one of the most visually inventive and influential films of all time. In 2003, Cronenweth was named one of the 10 most influential cinematographers of all time in a poll conducted by the International Cinematographers Guild.

**CROSBY, BING (1903–1977).** Crooner Bing Crosby was a hugely successful recording artist from the late 1920s until his style of **music** was largely supplanted by rock 'n' roll in the late 1950s. He also parlayed his popularity as a singer into a major career in film, starring in a number of commercially successful films, mostly **musicals** in which he also sang. He is probably best remembered for the series of "*Road*" buddy pictures in which he starred with comedian **Bob Hope**, including five films between 1940 and 1947, beginning with *Road to Singapore* (1940) and extending through *Road to Rio* (1947); this series was then continued with *Road to Bali* (1952) and *The Road to Hong Kong* (1962). These light musical **comedies** were hugely popular with audiences; however, Crosby had already appeared in numerous films in the 1930s before teaming with Hope and actually had his greatest success as an actor in films in which he starred without Hope during the term of their onscreen partnership.

In 1944, Crosby starred as a priest in the musical comedy *Going My Way*, winning an **Academy Award** for Best Actor for the role. The next year, he reprised the role in a sequel, *The Bells of St. Mary's*, winning another Best Actor **Oscar** nomination. Later, he won his third and final Best Actor Oscar nomination for *The Country Girl* (1954), in which he starred opposite **Grace Kelly**. Crosby's greatest commercial success in film also came in 1954, with his starring role in **Michael Curtiz**'s *White Christmas*, whose title song (first performed on film by Crosby as part of his starring role in the 1942 film *Holiday Inn*) was Crosby's biggest musical hit and is still a perennial holiday favorite.

Though his popularity as a film star had waned by the 1960s, Crosby continued to make numerous appearances on musical variety shows on television. He also continued to exert a major influence on the entertainment business, both through the legacy of his own music and films and through the results of his work as a show-business entrepreneur and advocate of new recording technologies.

**CROWE, RUSSELL (1964– ).** The New Zealand–born Russell Crowe began his career starring in Australian films such as *The Crossing* (1990),

*Proof* (1991), and *Romper Stomper* (1992), all of which won him Best Actor nominations from the Australian Film Institute, and the latter two of which were wins. By 1995, he had moved into American film, making prominent appearances in four different films that year. He drew major attention for his performance in *L.A. Confidential* (1997), then catapulted to the top ranks of stardom with lead roles in *The Insider* (1999), *Gladiator* (2000), and *A Beautiful Mind* (2001), all of which gained him **Academy Award** nominations for Best Actor, an award that he won for *Gladiator*.

Crowe's subsequent roles have gained considerable attention as well, including starring roles in *Master and Commander: The Far Side of the World* (2003), *3:10 to Yuma* (2007), and *American Gangster* (2007), as well as a supporting role in *Body of Lies* (2008). In 2010, he starred as the title character in *Robin Hood*, his fourth film with director **Ridley Scott**. He has also sometimes performed as a rock musician.

**CRUISE, TOM (1962– ).** Tom Cruise began his film acting career with two supporting roles in 1981, then burst into stardom in 1983 with a key role in *The Outsiders* and lead roles in *Losin' It*, *All the Right Moves*, and (especially) *Risky Business*. A series of major roles followed, and his performances in films such as *Top Gun* (1986), *The Color of Money* (1986, opposite **Paul Newman**), *Rain Man* (1988, opposite **Dustin Hoffman**), and *Born on the Fourth of July* (1989) solidified Cruise's position as one of the top young stars in Hollywood, the latter winning him his first **Academy Award** nomination for Best Actor.

Cruise also scored a Best Actor **Oscar** nomination for *Jerry Maguire* (1996), as well as a Best Supporting Actor nomination for *Magnolia* (1999). Roles such as that one established his ability to play interesting character parts, as did his over-the-top comic performance in *Tropic Thunder* (2008). However, Cruise has remained primarily a leading man in big-budget films, such as **Steven Spielberg**'s **science fiction** thrillers *Minority Report* (2001) and *War of the Worlds* (2005), and the three *Mission Impossible* films (1996, 2000, 2006).

Other notable lead roles played by Cruise include those in *Interview with the Vampire* (1994), *Eyes Wide Shut* (1999), *The Last Samurai* (2003), *Collateral* (2004), and *Valkyrie* (2008). Cruise has also served as a producer on more than a dozen films.

**CUKOR, GEORGE (1899–1983).** George Cukor came to Hollywood in 1928 after early experience as a stage manager and stage director. After a brief apprenticeship, he made his solo directorial debut in 1931 with *Tarnished Lady*, for **Paramount**. However, a dispute over directorial credit for *One Hour with You* (1932) led Cukor to leave Paramount for **RKO**, where he directed a string of highly successful films, including *What Price Hollywood?* (1932), *A Bill of Divorcement* (1932), *Dinner at Eight* (1933), and *Little Women* (1933), before moving on (with studio executive **David O. Selznick**) to **Metro-Goldwyn-Mayer** (MGM) to direct such films as *David Copperfield* (1935), *Romeo and Juliet* (1936), and *Camille* (1937).

Cukor was originally slated by Selznick to direct *Gone with the Wind* (1939), but was replaced early in the production by Victor Fleming. Though disappointed, Cukor rebounded with several strong films for MGM in the next few years, including *The Women* (1939), *The Philadelphia Story* (1941), and *Gaslight* (1944), cementing his reputation as an actor's director and as one who worked particularly well with strong women actors, such as **Greta Garbo** and **Katharine Hepburn**.

Subsequently, Cukor had a particularly rich partnership with screenwriters Garson Kanin and Ruth Gordon, with whom he made a string of successful films, including *Adam's Rib* (1949), *Born Yesterday* (1950), *The Marrying Kind* (1952), and *It Should Happen to You* (1954). Also in 1954, Cukor directed *A Star Is Born* for Warner Bros., but production was plagued by the instability of leading lady **Judy Garland**, and Cukor had considerable battles with the studio over the length of the film, which was ultimately reduced without his participation.

Cukor worked less frequently in subsequent years, though he directed two successful films—*Les Girls* and *Wild Is the Wind*—in 1957. In 1962, Cukor was directing *Something's Got to Give* for **Twentieth Century Fox**, but that production was plagued with difficulties, including problems with star **Marilyn Monroe**. The film was eventually scrapped, and Monroe would be found dead only a few weeks later. From that point, Cukor's career was in decline, though the **musical** *My Fair Lady* (1964) was a notable late success.

Cukor won his only **Academy Award** for Best Director for *My Fair Lady*, though he had four other nominations—for *Little Women*, *The Philadelphia Story*, *A Double Life* (1947), and *Born Yesterday*. In addition, he has the distinction of having directed more films featuring Best Acting **Oscar** winners than any other director.

**CULT.** A cult film is one that has acquired an unusually devoted following among a specific subgroup of fans. The name derives from the fact that such films sometimes become so important to their fans that the fan group begins to function almost in the manner of a religious cult. Cult films usually lie outside the Hollywood mainstream, going against the normal conventions of film in style, content, or both. On the other hand, relatively conventional (and even initially popular) films can sometimes attain cult status well after their initial release.

The widespread availability of home video spurred the growth of the cult film phenomenon in the 1980s, when such films as *Reefer Madness* (1936) and *Plan 9 from Outer Space* (1959) gained cult followings precisely because they were so notoriously bad and patently silly. **Science fiction** films (often low-budget efforts from the 1950s) led the way in this phenomenon, ultimately giving rise to the television series *Mystery Science Theater 3000* (1988–1999), which lovingly lampooned bad sf films from the past. Meanwhile, even hugely successful mainstream sf films (such as those in the **Star Wars** franchise) have often attained cult status due to the intensity of the fandom that follows them.

Because of the excess that is central to the genre, **horror** films such as **George Romero**'s *Night of the Living Dead* (1968) have often also had extended lives as cult films, while the **musical**/science fiction/horror film *The Rocky Horror Picture Show* (1975) may be the biggest cult film of all time, combining virtually all of the elements (stylistic excess, outrageous premise, over-the-top performances, and unusual sexual content) that go into the making of a cult film. The cult status of this film was particularly spurred by its popularity as a midnight feature in movie theaters, as the midnight movie phenomenon joined the home video market as a major venue for cult films in general during the 1980s.

By the 1980s, some directors and studios, especially in the case of science fiction and horror films, seemed to be producing films with the explicit goal of achieving cult status. The production company Troma Entertainment, for example, has specialized in low-budget horror and sf films with campy elements typical of cult films, such as *The Toxic Avenger* (1984). The offbeat sf film *Repo Man* (1984) belongs in the category of the intentional cult film, as does the sequence of *Evil Dead* horror films, beginning in 1981. The same can be said for *Brazil* (1985) and most of the other films of **Terry Gilliam**, especially *Fear and Loathing in Las Vegas* (1998). Indeed, the films of certain directors have attained almost automatic cult status, whether it involved the avant-garde aesthetics of the films of David Lynch, the intentionally offensive bad taste of the films of **John Waters**, or the unconventional narrative structures of the films of **Jim Jarmusch**.

Young audiences have been particularly drawn to cult films, and many such films are understandably youth oriented. Several of the teen-oriented films of writer–director **John Hughes** in the 1980s have become cult favorites, as have such films as *Fast Times at Ridgemont High* (1982) and *Dazed & Confused* (1993). Meanwhile, films that combine a focus on teen life with other cultish genres—such as the sf teen film *Donnie Darko* (2001)—have often attained cult status as well. Dark comedies aimed at teen audiences—from *Heathers* (1989) to *Jennifer's Body* (2009)—seem designed to become cult films, while offbeat, often dark, comedies in general have frequently found cult followings, as in the case of **Hal Ashby**'s *Harold and Maude* (1971), Todd Solondz's *Happiness* (1998), or **Joel and Ethan Coen**'s *Raising Arizona* (1987) and *The Big Lebowski* (1998).

Films that appeal to particular subcultures also frequently attain cult status, as when *Ghost World* (2001) functions both as a teen-life narrative and as a narrative that appeals to the comic-book subculture. The cult film phenomenon has been particularly important in the gay and lesbian community, whether it involve the "adoption" of mainstream hits such as *The Wizard of Oz* (1939) and *Singin' in the Rain* (1951) or the enthusiastic viewing of films with explicitly gay, lesbian, or cross-dressing characters or subtexts, such as *The Rocky Horror Picture Show*, films of Waters that feature the drag queen Divine, or the Australian drag film *The Adventures of Priscilla, Queen of the Desert* (1994).

**CURTIS, TONY (1925–2010).** The versatile actor Tony Curtis (born Bernard Schwartz) made frequent, if unremarkable, appearances in film from 1949 until he made a major impact with breakthrough dramatic performances in *Sweet Smell of Success* (1957) and *The Defiant Ones* (1958), the latter of which won him his only **Academy Award** nomination for Best Actor. He then followed with a notable comic performance in *Some Like It Hot* (1959), named in a 2000 poll by the **American Film Institute** as the funniest movie ever made.

Curtis would never again star in such important films, though he played a key supporting role in *Spartacus* (1960) and continued to make frequent film appearances (usually in lead roles) for the next decade. By the first half of the 1970s, most of his appearances were guest spots on television, though he rebounded with a number of film roles in the second half of the 1970s, as in **Elia Kazan**'s *The Last Tycoon* (1976). He continued to appear regularly on both film and television well into the 21st century, though his later film roles were typically in questionable low-budget films such as *The Mummy Lives* (1993), in which he played the lead role.

**CURTIZ, MICHAEL (1886–1962).** One of Hollywood's most reliable and durable directors, Michael Curtiz began his career directing **silent films** in his native Austro–Hungary, then came to Hollywood in the 1920s and later transitioned smoothly into the sound era, typically directing several films per year through the 1930s. Of these, among the best known are those in the series of swashbuckling adventure films that he directed featuring **Errol Flynn**, beginning with *Captain Blood* (1935), which won Curtiz his first **Academy Award** nomination for Best Director. Curtiz also directed Flynn in *The Charge of the Light Brigade* (1936), *The Adventures of Robin Hood* (1938), and *The Sea Hawk* (1940). Curtiz scored another Best Director **Oscar** nomination in the decade for *Angels with Dirty Faces* (1938).

Curtiz received Best Director Oscar nominations for films released in 1942: *Yankee Doodle Dandy* and **Casablanca**. He won the Oscar for the second of these, which is one of the most beloved films in American history, ranking third on the list of all-time great films published by the **American Film Institute** in 2007 after coming in second in their original 1997 list.

Curtiz would never again enjoy such critical success, but he remained busy as the competent director of numerous films in a variety of genres through the 1950s, including the **film noir** classic *Mildred Pierce* (1945), the hit **musical** *White Christmas* (1954), the **Humphrey Bogart** vehicle *We're No Angels* (1955), and the Elvis Presley vehicle *King Creole* (1958). Curtiz ended his directing career with *The Comancheros* (1961), a **Western** starring **John Wayne**.

# D

**DAMON, MATT (1970– ).** Since bursting onto the scene as the star and co-writer of *Good Will Hunting* in 1997, Matt Damon has proven himself one of the most versatile and popular actors in Hollywood. Damon had had supporting roles in such films as *Mystic Pizza* (1988), *School Ties* (1992), and *Geronimo: An American Legend* (1993) and even starred in *The Rainmaker* (1997), put into full release two months before *Good Will Hunting*. But it was the latter film that made him a star, winning him an **Academy Award** nomination for Best Actor in a Leading Role and an **Oscar** for Best Screenplay. Damon followed by solidifying his star status as the title character in **Steven Spielberg**'s *Saving Private Ryan* (1998).

Starring roles in *Rounders* (1998) and *The Talented Mr. Ripley* (1999) were less successful, though the latter did attract considerable attention. After several subsequent supporting roles, Damon suddenly reinvented himself as a successful action hero in the sequence of Jason Bourne **spy films**, based on the novels of Robert Ludlum. These highly successful films have thus far included *The Bourne Identity* (2002), *The Bourne Supremacy* (2004), and *The Bourne Ultimatum* (2007). In the meantime, he had a major supporting role in *Syriana* (2005) and lead roles in such important films as *The Departed* (2006) and *The Good Shepherd* (2006). Damon also had important roles in all three of **Steven Soderbergh**'s "Ocean's" films, including *Ocean's Eleven* (2001), *Ocean's Twelve* (2004), and *Ocean's Thirteen* (2007).

Though a top box-office draw, Damon has shown a continuing willingness to play supporting roles, winning an **Oscar** nomination for Best Actor in a Supporting Role for his performance in *Invictus* (2009). He has also shown a willingness to star in smaller, independent productions, as in the case of Soderbergh's *The Informant!* (2009).

Damon is also known for his philanthropic and humanitarian projects, including aid to Africa and other areas of the former Third World, as well as support for novice filmmakers.

**DANDRIDGE, DOROTHY (1922–1965).** Beginning her career as a touring child performer on the stage, Dorothy Dandridge made her first film appearance in a 1935 *Our Gang* short. Subsequently, she had a small role in the Marx Brothers' *A Day at the Races* (1937), but remained confined to minor, stereotypical black roles until her breakthrough performance in **Otto Preminger**'s *Carmen Jones* (1954). For that film, she became the first African American performer to win an **Academy Award** nomination for Best Actress.

Unfortunately, good roles for African American actresses remained rare, and the nomination opened few doors, though Dandridge did make notable appearances in subsequent films such as *Island in the Sun* (1957) and *Porgy and Bess* (1959). A talented singer, she also had a significant career as a recording artist, but the latter part of her life was marked by personal tragedies, and she herself died of an accidental drug overdose at the age of 42.

Largely forgotten, Dandridge came to the attention of a new generation of film fans when **Halle Berry** played her in the award-winning 1999 HBO movie *Introducing Dorothy Dandridge*. Three years later, Berry would ironically become the first African American to win the **Oscar** for Best Actress.

**DAVIS, BETTE (1908–1989).** A versatile actress who could play both heroes and villains, Bette Davis was a strong, independent woman who was noted for her clashes with the studios for which she worked, especially during her long tenure as a contract performer for **Warner Bros.** She was also, according to a 1999 poll conducted by the **American Film Institute**, the second greatest female film star of all time.

Davis began appearing in films in 1931. After a slow start, she first gained major critical attention in 1934, a year in which she appeared in no less than six films. The most important of these appearances was her performance as Mildred Rogers in *Of Human Bondage*, an unsympathetic character the portrayal of which established Davis's willingness and ability to play characters that other Hollywood leading ladies were hesitant to tackle.

Davis was nominated for an **Academy Award** for Best Actress for her performance in *Of Human Bondage*, then followed by winning that award for her role in *Dangerous* (1935). She followed with another notable role in *The Petrified Forest* (1936), but was by this time increasingly unhappy with the roles she was being offered. A controversial legal battle followed, but Davis was unable to get out of her contract with Warner Bros., which she described as a form of slavery.

Nevertheless, Davis, often playing opposite **Humphrey Bogart**, as in *Marked Woman* (1937) and *Dark Victory* (1939), continued her rise to top stardom. Her performance in *Jezebel* (1938) earned her her second Best Actress **Oscar**. Davis also won Best Actress nominations for *Dark Victory*; *The Letter* (1940); *The Little Foxes* (1941); *Now, Voyager* (1942); *Mr. Skeffington*

(1944); *All about Eve* (1950); *The Star* (1952); and *Whatever Happened to Baby Jane?* (1962). She thus had a total of 11 such nominations, though she scored only two wins. In 1941, Davis became the first female president of the **Academy of Motion Picture Arts and Sciences**, but soon resigned after clashes with other members of the organization's ruling board.

After critics panned Davis's performance in *Beyond the Forest* (1949), Davis was finally released from her contract with Warners. She soon followed with her performance as aging actress Margo Channing in *All about Eve*, perhaps her greatest role. She continued to be a leading star well into her fifties. Other important films starring Davis include *The Private Lives of Elizabeth and Essex* (1939), *Watch on the Rhine* (1943), *The Virgin Queen* (1955), *Storm Center* (1956), and *Hush, Hush, Sweet Charlotte* (1964). She continued to perform in both film and television until shortly before her death.

**DAY, DORIS (1922– ).** Having already had some success as a singer, Doris Day began her film career with *Romance on the High Seas*, in which she had originally been cast in a supporting role but was thrust into the lead after star Betty Hutton was forced to withdraw. A series of roles in minor **musicals** followed, though Day gained mainstream attention for her starring role in *Calamity Jane* (1953), in which her performance of "Secret Love" won an **Academy Award** for Best Original Song.

Now a star, Day had a notable role in **Alfred Hitchcock**'s *The Man Who Knew Too Much* (1956), in which her performance of "Que Sera, Sera" won another Best Original Song **Oscar**. She has several other dramatic roles in the 1950s as well, but she became known primarily for her roles in **romantic comedies**, in which her squeaky-clean image helped her to gain the title of "America's Sweetheart." Films in this vein included *The Pajama Game* (1957), *Teacher's Pet* (1958), and *Pillow Talk* (1959), the latter of which won her her only Best Actress Oscar nomination and firmly reestablished her considerable box-office appeal, which had been on the wane.

Doris also paired with close friend **Rock Hudson** in *Lover Come Back* (1961) and *Send Me No Flowers* (1964) and had success in such films as *Please Don't Eat the Daisies* (1960) and *That Touch of Mink* (1962). However, her image was decidedly out of step with the changing times of the 1960s, and her popularity quickly declined as the decade proceeded. Her film career ended with her performance in *With Six You Get Eggroll* (1968), though she subsequently made a number of television appearances, including a five-year run as the star of *The Doris Day Show* from 1968 to 1973. In her latter years, she has been known primarily as a vigorous advocate of animal rights, though recent years have also seen a revival of critical and popular interest in her films.

**DEAKINS, ROGER (1949– ).** The British-born cinematographer began his career as a cameraman for **documentaries** around the world, especially in Africa. He also worked as a director and cinematographer of **music** videos and as a cinematographer on feature films such as *Sid and Nancy* (1986), *Stormy Monday* (1988), *The Kitchen Toto* (1987), and *White Mischief* (1987), the latter two of which were set in Africa. He began his career in Hollywood with the 1990 feature *Mountains of the Moon* (1990), also set in Africa. Since that time he has had a distinguished career in American film, gaining eight **Academy Award** nominations for Best Cinematography, though he has never won that award.

In 1991, Deakins was the chief cinematographer on the **Joel and Ethan Coen** film *Barton Fink*, beginning a rich association that has seen him do the cinematography for almost all of the Coen brothers' films since that time, four of which—*Fargo* (1996); *O Brother, Where Art Thou?* (2000); *The Man Who Wasn't There* (2001); and *No Country for Old Men* (2007)—have won **Oscar** nominations for Deakins's cinematography. Deakins has also scored Oscar nominations for *The Shawshank Redemption* (1994), *Kundun* (1997), *The Assassination of Jesse James by the Coward Robert Ford* (2007), and *The Reader* (2008). Other prominent films photographed by Deakins include *The Hurricane* (1999), *A Beautiful Mind* (2001), *House of Sand and Fog* (2003), *The Village* (2004), *Jarhead* (2005), *Doubt* (2008), and *Revolutionary Road* (2008).

**DEAN, JAMES (1931–1955).** In his brief but spectacular career, James Dean's intense performances made him a top Hollywood star, while his early death at the age of 24 actually served to enhance his status as a Hollywood legend. After a series of minor performances (mostly on television), Dean burst into the popular consciousness of American film audiences with his performance as Caleb Trask in **Elia Kazan**'s *East of Eden* (1955). He then cemented his image as a figure of youthful protest against the conformist inclinations of the 1950s with his signature role as troubled and rebellious (but ultimately virtuous) teenager Jim Stark in **Nicholas Ray**'s *Rebel without a Cause* (1955).

Now a major star, Dean costarred with **Rock Hudson** and **Elizabeth Taylor** in the 1956 oil-industry epic *Giant* (1956). Shortly after filming was completed, however, Dean was killed in an auto accident while driving his Porsche racing vehicle on a California highway. He received posthumous Best Actor **Academy Award** nominations for both *East of Eden* and *Giant*, further adding to his reputation as a tragic figure and to his status as a cultural icon.

**DE HAVILLAND, OLIVIA (1916– ).** Olivia de Havilland first gained attention in Hollywood as Hermia in the film adaptation of *A Midsummer Night's*

*Dream* (1935), a role she had played earlier on the stage. She followed the same year with a starring role opposite **Errol Flynn** in *Captain Blood*, then again starred opposite Flynn in *The Charge of the Light Brigade* (1936) and (perhaps most memorably) *Robin Hood* (1938). Altogether she appeared in eight films with Flynn (ending with the Custer's-Last-Stand **Western** *They Died with Their Boots On* in 1941), establishing something of a niche for herself as a damsel in distress waiting for the heroic Flynn to come to the rescue.

De Havilland received her first **Academy Award** nomination for her supporting role in *Gone with the Wind*. This was followed with a Best Actress **Oscar** nomination for her lead role in *Hold Back the Dawn* (1941)—though she lost out that year to her younger sister, **Joan Fontaine**. Still, she was unhappy with the quality of the roles she was offered. Meanwhile, supported by the **Screen Actors Guild**, she mounted a successful legal challenge to her contract with **Warner Bros.** in 1943, paving the way for other actors to have greater autonomy and marking an important milestone in the decline of the power of the studios over actors. A switch to **Paramount** helped de Havilland receive better roles, and the late 1940s were marked by a series of Oscar nominations that would make her one of Hollywood's most respected actresses of the period. She was also nominated for *The Snake Pit* (1948) and won for *To Each His Own* (1946) and *The Heiress* (1948).

De Havilland worked less frequently after 1950, though she did continue to appear in both television and film up until her retirement in 1988. As late as 1986, her performance in the television miniseries *Anastasia: The Mystery of Anna* won her an Emmy nomination for Best Supporting Actress.

**DEMILLE, CECIL B. (1881–1959).** Cecil B. DeMille became a legendary director during the **silent film** era, making dozens of films, including such high-profile **biblical epics** as *The Ten Commandments* (1923) and *King of Kings* (1927). DeMille worked far less frequently in the sound era; nevertheless, some of his sound films have become recognized classics of the American cinema.

In the 1930s, DeMille attempted ambitious **historical epics** such as *Cleopatra* (1934) and *The Crusades* (1935), with limited success. Smaller films, such as *This Day and Age* (1933, an obscure **cult** favorite), *The Plainsman* (1936), and *North West Mounted Police* (1940) were actually more successful during this period. The latter film featured DeMille's first use of three-strip Technicolor, and his use of vivid Technicolor in his subsequent films would become a trademark.

DeMille memorably appeared as himself in **Billy Wilder**'s *Sunset Blvd.* (1950), indicating DeMille's own star status. Interestingly, though, the films for which he is today best remembered were still ahead of him. The circus film *The Greatest Show on Earth* (1952) won him his only **Academy Award** for Best Director, while also winning the **Oscar** for Best Picture. The 1956 remake of his own earlier silent film *The Ten Commandments* (1956) also won a Best Picture Oscar and is today regarded as DeMille's masterpiece, making particularly good use of his knack for designing and executing large, complex scenes involving spectacular action and large numbers of extras.

**DE NIRO, ROBERT (1943– ).** After beginning his career with appearances in several minor films—including director **Brian De Palma**'s *Greetings* (1968), *The Wedding Party* (1969, but filmed in 1963) and *Hi, Mom!* (1970)—Robert De Niro was catapulted into stardom in 1973 with his effective performances in *Bang the Drum Slowly* and *Mean Streets* (both 1973), the latter of which was the beginning of a rich collaboration with director **Martin Scorsese**. De Niro, famed for his method acting style and fierce immersion in his roles, would go on to become one of the most respected American film actors of his generation.

De Niro won an **Academy Award** for Best Supporting Actor for his portrayal of the young Vito Corleone in **Francis Ford Coppola**'s *The Godfather: Part II* (1974). Through his career he would become especially well known for his roles in **gangster films**, including *Once upon a Time in America* (1984) and Scorsese's *Goodfellas* (1990) and his turn as Al Capone in De Palma's *The Untouchables* (1987). However, in *A Bronx Tale* (1993), which he also directed, De Niro plays a virtuous father who attempts to keep his son away from involvements with mobsters, while in *Analyze This* (1999) and *Analyze That* (2002) he plays a comic gangster who is in some ways a lampoon of De Niro's earlier gangster roles. The same might be said for Don Lino, a gangster shark voiced by De Niro in the 2004 **animated film** *Shark Tale.*

De Niro has also done effective comic turns in *Meet the Parents* (2000) and *Meet the Fockers* (2004), indicating his versatility as an actor. However, his two signature roles are his intensely dramatic performances in the Scorsese films *Taxi Driver* (1976), for which De Niro was nominated for a Best Actor **Oscar**, and *Raging Bull* (1980), for which he won that award for his portrayal of boxer Jake La Motta, famously gaining 60 pounds to play an aging La Motta in part of that film. De Niro also scored Best Actor Oscar nominations for *The Deer Hunter* (1978), *Awakenings* (1990), and *Cape Fear* (1991).

De Niro has continued to appear frequently in film in recent years, including an interesting supporting role in **Quentin Tarantino**'s *Jackie Brown* (1997), a role opposite **Dustin Hoffman** in *Wag the Dog* (1997), and two roles opposite **Al Pacino**: in *Heat* (1995) and *Righteous Kill* (2008). Along the way, De Niro has played everything from a would-be comedian in *The King of Comedy* (1983), to a working-class man struggling to learn to read in *Stanley & Iris* (1990), to the monster in *Frankenstein* (1994), to Fearless Leader in *The Adventures of Rocky & Bullwinkle* (2000), to a father attempting to reunite with his grown children in *Everybody's Fine* (2009). In addition to *A Bronx Tale*, he also directed the successful 2006 **spy film** *The Good Shepherd*.

**DE PALMA, BRIAN (1940– ).** An intensely self-conscious director, Brian De Palma is widely regarded as a key member of the "Film School" generation of new directors who rose to prominence in the 1970s, a group that also include such luminaries as **Peter Bogdanovich, Francis Ford Coppola, George Lucas, Martin Scorsese,** and **Steven Spielberg,** all of whom are in one way or another intensely aware of their relationship with the works of earlier filmmakers. De Palma began his career with several small films (all starring a young **Robert De Niro**) that experiment with technique and that can in one way or another be taken as commentaries on filmmaking itself: *Greetings* (1968), *The Wedding Party* (1969, but filmed in 1963) and *Hi, Mom!* (1970). He then continued his commentaries on **show business** with *Get to Know Your Rabbit* (1972) and *Phantom of the Paradise* (1974), essentially a rock remake of *Phantom of the Opera* that also includes elements derived from *Faust*, Oscar Wilde's *The Picture of Dorian Gray*, **John Frankenheimer**'s *The Manchurian Candidate* (1962), and **Alfred Hitchcock**'s *Psycho* (1960).

De Palma established his reputation with a series of thrillers that crucially rely on their pastiche of the work of Hitchcock. These include *Sisters* (1973), *Obsession* (1976), *Dressed to Kill* (1980), *Body Double* (1984), and *Raising Cain* (1992), all of which function fairly well as thrillers in their own right, but none of which can be properly understood without understanding their dialogue with classic Hitchcock films—especially **Vertigo** (1958), *Rear Window* (1954), and *Psycho*—making them key works of cinematic **postmodernism.**

*Body Double*, however, serves virtually as a parody of De Palma's other engagements with Hitchcock, further indicating the extent of his self-consciousness as a director. Other De Palma films relying crucially on their dialogue with earlier works include *Blow Out* (1981), which is essentially a reworking of Michelangelo Antonioni's *Blow Up* (1966) through **Francis Ford Coppola**'s *The Conversation* (1974). *Scarface* (1983), meanwhile, is an ultraviolent reworking of the 1932 classic **gangster film.**

De Palma has also adapted classic television series to film in *The Untouchables* (1987) and *Mission: Impossible* (1996). He has also made a number of genre films that engage in interesting dialogues with predecessors in their genre. These include the gangster film *Carlito's Way* (1993) and the gangster film spoof *Wise Guys* (1987), as well as the **horror** film *Carrie* (1976), the Vietnam **war film** *Casualties of War* (1989), the **science fiction** film *Mission to Mars* (2000), and the **neo-noir** films *Snake Eyes* (1998), *Femme Fatale* (2002) and *The Black Dahlia* (2006). *Redacted* (2007), meanwhile, is a critique of media coverage of the American invasion of Iraq in 2003.

**DEPP, JOHNNY (1963– ).** After beginning his career with a supporting role in the **horror** film *A Nightmare on Elm Street* (1984), Johnny Depp rose to prominence as a teen idol in the television series *12 Jump Street* (1987–1991). He then had his breakthrough as a film actor with lead roles in two decidedly different films in 1990: John Waters's *Cry-Baby* and **Tim Burton's** *Edward Scissorhands*. Since that time, Depp has established himself as one of the world's leading film actors, starring in some of the biggest blockbusters of all time, but also starring in a number of decidedly quirky and offbeat films.

Depp's biggest box-office hits have been the three *Pirates of the Caribbean* films (2003, 2006, 2007), in which he memorably plays pirate Captain Jack Sparrow. These films have reportedly made Depp the world's highest-paid film actor, though he has also shown a willingness to appear in small films for little pay. Meanwhile, he won an **Academy Award** nomination for Best Actor for the first *Pirates of the Caribbean* film, a nomination he also won for less commercial projects in *Finding Neverland* (2004) and in Burton's decidedly nonmainstream **musical** *Sweeney Todd: The Demon Barber of Fleet Street* (2007), a singing role that won Depp a **Golden Globe** Award for Best Actor in a Musical or Comedy.

Depp has, in fact, had a particularly rich association with Burton, in whose films he has had many of his most important roles. Other Burton films in which he has starred include *Ed Wood* (1994), *Sleepy Hollow* (1999), *Charlie and the Chocolate Factory* (2005), and *Alice in Wonderland* (2010). Depp also provided the voice of the lead character in Burton's **animated film** *Corpse Bride* (2005).

Depp's career has been marked by a willingness to play a wide variety of roles, demonstrating a versatility that has allowed him to star in films as different as **Jim Jarmusch's** offbeat **Western** *Dead Man* (1995); **Terry Gilliam's** *Fear and Loathing in Las Vegas* (1998), a fictionalized **biopic** about gonzo journalist Hunter S. Thompson; a variety of horror films, such as **Roman Polanski's** *The Ninth Gate* (1999), *The Astronaut's Wife* (1999), *From Hell* (2001), and *The Secret Window* (2004); and **gangster films** of various types, including *Donnie Brasco* (1997), *Blow* (2001), *Once Upon a Time in Mexico* (2003), and *Public Enemies* (2009). In 2009, Depp appeared in Gilliam's *The Imaginarium of Doctor Parnassus* (2009), helping (along with Jude Law and Colin Farrell) to fill in the role originally played by Heath Ledger, who died during filming.

**DICAPRIO, LEONARDO (1974– ).** Beginning his career as a teen actor, Leonardo DiCaprio first got wide exposure as a recurring cast member of the television sitcom *Growing Pains* (1991–1992). In 1993, he had important and critically acclaimed roles in *This Boy's Life* (1993) and *What's Eating Gilbert Grape* (1993), the latter of which won him an **Academy Award** nomination for Best Supporting Actor. Lead roles in *The Basketball Diaries* (1995) and *Romeo + Juliet* (1996) followed, establishing DiCaprio as a rising actor in Hollywood. He then became a major box-office (and tabloid) star with his performance as Jack Dawson in *Titanic* (1997), though the films that immediately followed, including *The Man in the Iron Mask* (1998) and *The Beach* (2000), were somewhat disappointing.

In 2002, DiCaprio starred in two critical hits, **Steven Spielberg**'s *Catch Me If You Can* (2002) and **Martin Scorsese**'s *Gangs of New York* (2002), the latter of which established a fruitful working relationship between DiCaprio and Scorsese that saw DiCaprio go on to star in Scorsese's *The Aviator* (2004), a **biopic** about Howard Hughes; *The Departed* (2006), a **gangster film**; and *Shutter Island* (2010), a mystery with **horror** elements. Shunned by the Academy for his work in *Titanic* (which scored **Oscar** nominations in almost every category other than Best Actor), DiCaprio did win Best Actor nominations for *The Aviator* and for his role in the thriller *Blood Diamond* (2006). He has also starred in **Ridley Scott**'s *Body of Lies* (2008) and **Sam Mendes**'s *Revolutionary Road* (2009).

DiCaprio served as an executive producer on *The Aviator* and has since worked as a producer on a number of projects, including the environmentalist documentary *The 11th Hour* (2007), which he also narrated.

**DIETERLE, WILLIAM (1893–1972).** William Dieterle was an established director in his native Germany before he came to Hollywood to direct *The Last Flight* (1931), a powerful and unusual psychologically oriented **war film**. From that point, he became one of **Warner Bros.**' top directors, assigned to such prestige projects as the Shakespeare adaptation *A Midsummer Night's Dream* (1935) and the **biopics** *Madame du Barry* (1934), *The Story of Louis Pasteur* (1935), and *The Life of Emile Zola* (1937), the latter of which won an **Academy Award** for Best Picture, while winning Dieterle his only **Oscar** nomination for Best Director.

In 1938, Dieterle left Warner Bros. to make the Spanish Civil War film *Blockade*, though he was back at Warners to make *Juarez* (1939), a biopic about the 19th-century Mexican revolutionary leader Benito Juarez that was in a somewhat similar political vein. That same year he directed the literary adaptation *The Hunchback of Notre Dame* for **RKO Pictures**.

Dieterle worked less frequently in the 1940s, but continued to score successes with films such as *All That Money Can Buy* (1941, aka *The Devil and Daniel Webster*), *Love Letters* (1945), and *Portrait of Jennie* (1948). By the end of the 1940s, the politics of *Blockade* and *Juarez* put Dieterle under suspicion amid the anticommunist purges sweeping Hollywood. He was never **blacklisted**, but worked even less frequently in the 1950s, eventually returning to Germany by the end of the decade to complete his career where it had begun.

**DIETRICH, MARLENE (1901–1992).** Marlene Dietrich had made several **silent film** appearances when she made her breakthrough in the early German talkie *The Blue Angel* (1930), a film that was made both in this English-language version and in German as *Der blaue Engel*. This **musical** included Dietrich's performance of "Falling in Love Again," which would become her signature song. It was directed by **Josef von Sternberg**, who would encourage Dietrich to move to Hollywood, where she landed a contract with **Paramount Pictures**. She began her American career in Von Sternberg's *Morocco* (1931), a film that won her her only **Academy Award** nomination for Best Actress.

Dietrich followed with starring roles in *Dishonored* (1931), *Shanghai Express* (1932), *Blonde Venus* (1933), *The Scarlet Empress* (1934), and *The Devil is a Woman* (1935), all directed by Von Sternberg for Paramount. This sequence marked the peak of her stardom in Hollywood, though she would continue to make notable appearances for decades to come. Highlights after the Von Sternberg period include a role opposite **James Stewart** in the comic **Western** *Destry Rides Again* (1939), lead roles in **Alfred Hitchcock**'s *Stage Fright* (1950) and **Fritz Lang**'s *Rancho Notorious* (1952), and a small but memorable role as a Mexican gypsy in Orson Welles's *Touch of Evil* (1958).

During World War II, Dietrich, now an American citizen, made anti-Nazi recordings and performed live for Allied troops in Europe. She made her last American film appearance in a supporting role in *Judgment at Nuremberg* (1961), though she continued to tour internationally performing live, until a fall from a stage in Australia in 1975 resulted in a broken leg and ended her career as an active show-business performer, though she had a minor role in the 1978 German film *Just a Gigolo*. The award-winning 1984 **documentary** *Marlene* effectively narrates the story of her life.

**DISASTER.** Films relating natural disasters such as floods, fires, earthquakes, or volcano eruptions have formed a major genre of American film since the early 1970s, when films such as *The Towering Inferno* (1974, produced by Irwin Allen, the "Master of Disaster") and *Earthquake* (1974) were major box-office hits. Sometimes, these disasters involve the failure of man-made systems, such as the sinking of an ocean liner or the crash of an airliner. Thus, *Airport* (1970) is sometimes considered to be the beginning of the 1970s cycle of disaster films, while *The Poseidon Adventure* (1972, also produced by Allen) is one of the best known of these films. In this sense, **James Cameron**'s *Titanic* (1997), the largest-grossing film of all time, can be considered a disaster film. Such films employ a classic disaster film structure in which a large cast of characters is introduced at the beginning of the film, followed by the announcement of a looming disaster, followed by a narration of the various ways in which the characters we have come to know deal with the disaster. In most cases, these films cannot really be considered to be **science fiction**, even though the high stakes involved in disaster films are similar to those that are often found in science fiction film.

Many disaster films, however, clearly move into the realm of science fiction. For example, the 1970s cycle of disaster films was topped off in 1979 with the much maligned *Meteor* (1979), about a giant asteroid that threatens to collide with the Earth, and thus a film that is rightly considered science fiction. The postapocalyptic film cycle of the 1950s, as well as the **monster movie** boom of that decade, are both heavily informed by sf conceits, such as the destruction of society by advanced technologies or the production of monsters by unrestrained scientific inquiry. Meanwhile, a classic case of the sf disaster film can be found as early as 1951 with *When Worlds Collide*, in which the Earth is destroyed in a collision with another planet—though a few humans manage to survive by rocketing to still another planet that conveniently happens to be passing by as well. Val Guest's *The Day the Earth Caught Fire* (1961) is also a good example of the early sf disaster film, this time involving a perturbation in the Earth's orbit (caused by nuclear testing) that sends the planet hurtling toward the sun.

Such cosmic catastrophes are typical of the sf disaster film, which came to particular prominence in the 1990s, as advances in **computer-generated imagery** made it possible to produce convincing **special effects** for the depiction of such disasters. One of the first films of this disaster film renaissance was Roland Emmerich's *Independence Day* (1996), an alien invasion drama that employs the classic structure of the disaster film. A cycle of more conventional cosmic disaster films followed, including *Deep Impact* and *Armageddon*, both released in 1998, in which the Earth is threatened by impending collision with a comet and an asteroid, respectively, while scientists and astronauts scramble to avert the collisions. In *The Core* (2003), sf disaster turns inward as scientists tunnel into the Earth to try to restart the rotation of the Earth's core. Meanwhile, Danny Boyle's *Sunshine* (2007) is more typical of sf disaster films, as scientists travel into space to prevent disaster, this time to try to restart the dying sun. Meanwhile, *Knowing* (2009), looks back to *When Worlds Collide* as a solar event wipes out life on Earth, but a small group of humans manage to escape (this time with the help of advanced aliens) to another planet.

Emmerich has become perhaps the central figure in this latest cycle of sf disaster films, though Michael Bay, the director of *Armageddon*, has employed many elements of the disaster film structure in his two *Transformers* films (2007, 2009). Emmerich followed *Independence Day* by resurrecting the classic Japanese movie monster Godzilla and setting it upon New York City, but his 1998 film *Godzilla* was not a big success. Emmerich had better success in 2004 with *The Day after Tomorrow*, a work with a theme of environmentalism, as global warming causes catastrophic weather events across the United States. Finally, Emmerich's *2012* (2009) deals with the ultimate global catastrophe; based on ancient Mayan predictions of the end of the world in 2012, Emmerich's film deals with the realization of those predictions—and with human attempts to preserve the race nonetheless.

**DISNEY.** The Walt Disney Company, generally referred to simply as "Disney," is now the largest media-oriented corporate entity in the world. Originally founded in 1923 by brothers Roy and **Walt Disney** as Disney Brothers Cartoon Studio, the company was re-incorporated as Walt Disney Productions in 1929, subsequently becoming a leading maker of cartoon shorts in the 1930s. The company then achieved a major milestone in film history in 1937 by releasing **Snow White and the Seven Dwarfs** as the first feature-length **animated film.**

While remaining a relatively small studio, Disney maintained its niche as the leading maker of feature-length animated films for the next 30 years, under the leadership of cofounder Walt Disney until his death in 1966. However, from the beginning of the 1950s onward, the company concentrated more and more on live-action films, which were much simpler and cheaper to produce. The company also began to branch out into other media, becoming one of the first movie studios to think of television as a new marketing opportunity rather than simply as a competitor. In 1955, the company opened the Disneyland theme park in Anaheim, California, an enterprise that proved extremely lucrative in its own right, while also providing a major boost to the company's already astute efforts at branding and comarketing among different media.

After Walt Disney's death, the Disney Company underwent a crisis of direction and leadership that kept it in disarray until the late 1980s, though the opening of the Walt Disney World Resort near Orlando, Florida, in 1971 was a major success. However, under the management of studio chief **Michael Eisner**, the company's film business underwent a major resurgence when it returned to an emphasis on animated films for children, beginning with *The Little Mermaid* (1989) and *Beauty and the Beast* (1991). The "Disney Renaissance" then remained in full swing through the 1990s, including the release in 1994 of *The Lion King*, at that time easily the highest-grossing film in the history of the company.

By this time, Disney was also beginning to build a cable television empire, beginning with the establishment of the Disney Channel in 1983. Disney's television holdings are now managed by their subsidiary, the Disney-ABC Television Group (founded 2004); these holdings now include several Disney-branded cable channels, as well as the ABC broadcast network (acquired in 1996), the ABC Family cable network, and the family of ESPN sports-oriented cable networks.

By the end of the 1990s, Disney's television empire had become far more lucrative than its film business, though Disney was also diversifying its offerings in film, beginning with the establishment in 1984 of the Touchstone Pictures label for the release of films oriented toward more mature audiences than the family audiences typically targeted by the Disney label. In addition, the profits of the Disney Renaissance (and associated gains in capital via the increasing value of the company's stock) were being plowed into a series of acquisitions, beginning with the purchase of **Miramax** in 1993 and extending through the acquisition of **Pixar** in 2006 and Marvel Entertainment in 2009. Disney has also increasingly served as a distributor for films made by other studios, as in their 2009 agreement to distribute (over a period of five years) 30 live-action films from **DreamWorks** through their Touchstone label.

The rancorous ouster of Eisner in 2004 generated considerable publicity but did not slow the growth of Disney toward its current position as the world's largest media company. This expansion has been aided by the huge success of the *Pirates of the Caribbean* film franchise (2003, 2006, 2007), which was inspired by a ride at Disneyland. Their media empire now extends into radio, publishing, and **music**, as well as television, film, and theme parks around the world.

In recent years, Disney has led the way in the resurgence of 3D filmmaking, beginning with the release of *Chicken Little* in their new Disney Digital 3D format in 2005. In 2009, the Pixar film *Up* was released in the process and the company announced plans to release all subsequent animated films in 3D. **Tim Burton**'s 3D remake of *Alice in Wonderland* was a huge hit in 2010.

**DISNEY, WALT (1901–1966).** Walt Disney was the principal founding force behind the Walt Disney Company (commonly referred to simply as

**Disney**), now the world's largest media conglomerate. In addition, though he never received screen credit as a director, Disney is regarded as one of the great creative forces behind the evolution of American popular culture, effectively producing (with or without screen credit) over 600 films while also making pioneering innovations in television and the theme park industry. Disney is associated particularly closely with the evolution of **animated film**, in which he became interested as a teenager in Kansas City. Along with his collaborator Ub Iwerks, Disney began making short animated films in Kansas City, including *Alice's Wonderland* (1923), which mixed live action and animation and became the founding work in a series of 50 *Alice* shorts between 1923 and 1927, fueling Disney's move to Hollywood and founding, along with his brother Roy, of his own studio there.

In 1927, Disney and Iwerks created the animated character Oswald the Lucky Rabbit, which seemed to have great commercial potential until they lost the rights to the character in a dispute with **Universal Pictures**. Disney and Iwerks then conceived Mickey Mouse as a replacement, and that character would become the foundation of the Disney empire. Beginning in 1928, when he appeared in the shorts *Steamboat Willie*, *Plane Crazy*, and *The Gallopin' Gaucho*, Mickey would go on to become one of the greatest icons of American popular culture. Meanwhile, the Disney Company became the dominant force in the production of short animated films, typically screened in theaters just before the main feature.

Disney himself received an honorary **Academy Award** in 1932 for the creation of Mickey Mouse. From 1932 through 1940, films made by the Disney Company scored a total of 15 Academy Award nominations for Best Short Subject, Cartoons. Disney won that award in 1932, then again in every year from 1934 through 1940. By this time, however, the company had made film history with the release of the first feature-length animated film, *Snow White and the Seven Dwarfs* (1937). This film, scoffed at before its release as "Walt's folly," became the founding work of the **children's film** industry and was named as late as 2008 as the greatest animated film of all time by the **American Film Institute**. Six of the other top 10 animated films on this list were made by Disney as well, and two others were made by **Pixar**, now a Disney subsidiary.

Disney guided his company carefully through the next three decades, as it remained the dominant force in children's film and in animated film throughout the rest of his life, even as he himself gradually steered the company more and more into less expensive live-action productions. Indeed, the company remained relatively small during Walt's life, especially as a film studio, though its cultural influence was always far greater than its economic clout. The company continued to be an **Oscar** darling, even as its critical reputation began to wane during the 1950s, winning numerous short-subject awards and nominations during that decade. The company received its first Best Picture nomination for the mostly live-action film *Mary Poppins* (1964) the year before Disney died, though it did not win the award. Disney himself remained very much the public face of the company from its beginnings until his death, and for many he was also the face of wholesomeness and virtue, a steward of American values. Since his death, however, concerns over his right-wing political views and exploitation of his own workers have marred his reputation to some extent, even as the company he founded has, in the past two decades, grown immensely in economic power.

**DMYTRYK, EDWARD (1908–1999).** The Canadian-born Edward Dmytryk established himself as a Hollywood director with numerous films in the 1940s, including the **film noir** classics *Murder, My Sweet* (1944) and *Crossfire* (1947), the latter of which centrally deals with the theme of American anti-Semitism and is typical of the political orientation of many of Dmytryk's early films. In particular, his films made during and just after World War II, including *Hitler's Children* (1943), *Tender Comrade* (1943), and *Cornered* (1945), tended to feature anti-Nazi themes that some interpreted as pro-communist. This orientation brought Dmytryk to the attention of the **House Un-American Activities Committee** (HUAC) in 1947, when his refusal to testify ultimately landed him in prison as a member of the **Hollywood Ten**. Soon afterward, Dmytryk subsequently relented and testified, including naming the names of 26 others in Hollywood with radical political connections.

As a result of this testimony, Dmytryk was able to escape the blacklist and to resume his directorial career. He subsequently made several interesting films, including the **Westerns** *Broken Lance* (1954) and *Warlock* (1959), *The Caine Mutiny* (1954), *The Young Lions* (1958), and *Walk on the Wild Side* (1962), but these films never quite achieved the intensity of some of his earlier efforts. Many in the industry resented his earlier HUAC testimony, making him something of an outsider in Hollywood. In the 1970s, he left filmmaking to become an academic, teaching film studies at the University of Texas in Austin. Dmytryk was nominated for the **Academy Award** for Best Director for *Crossfire*.

**DOCUMENTARY.** Many of the earliest films were brief, reality-based "actualities" that simply recorded sights and events for later viewing by filmgoers who might not otherwise be able to experience them. The term "documentary" was first applied to the more complex reality-based films that gradually evolved from these beginnings in a 1926 review of Robert Flaherty's film *Moana* (1926, filmed in Samoa). However, Flaherty (widely regarded as the father of the documentary film) had already made the first widely distributed feature-length documentary film in 1922 with *Nanook of the North*, about the Inuit people and culture.

Flaherty's films, though based on footage of real-world cultures, tended to romanticize and exoticize those cultures, while staging many shots to further the narratives being created in the films. By the 1930s, meanwhile, it was well established that documentaries could be very effective for the promotion of specific political agendas, sometimes carefully manipulating the truth in order to do so. For example, in Nazi Germany, Leni Riefenstahl's *Triumph of the Will* (1935) elevated the political propaganda documentary to an art form. Meanwhile in the United States, a number of documentaries were made with government sponsorship, including **Pare Lorentz**'s *The Plow That Broke the Plains* (1936) and *The River* (1938), which promoted the programs of Franklin D. Roosevelt's New Deal, though from political perspectives that seemed to the left of Roosevelt's own. Meanwhile, Ralph Steiner and Willard Van Dyke's *The City* (1939), sponsored by the Institute of City Planners and funded by a grant from the Carnegie Foundation, avoided explicit political statement but still managed to make a powerful comment about the negative impact of capitalist modernization and industrial development on American cities.

Numerous propagandistic documentaries were made on both sides during World War II. In the United States, **Frank Capra**'s *Why We Fight* films (1942–1944) were a particular highlight in this regard. In the immediate postwar years, however, the documentary form experienced something of a downturn; the most successful documentaries of the 1950s were the series of heavily romanticized nature documentaries produced by **Disney** in its "True Life Adventures" series, which won three Best Documentary **Oscars** during the decade. On the other hand, fiction films of the 1950s, seeking a greater air of realism, began to show the influence of the documentary style.

From the 1960s forward, the most successful documentaries tended to be intensely political in tone. Barbara Kopple's prolabor documentaries *Harlan County, U.S.A.* (1976) and *American Dream* (1990) were two of the highlights in documentary film of the latter part of the 20th century, both winning **Academy Awards** for Best Documentary Feature. The 1970s were also marked by such antiestablishment documentaries as Michael Wadleigh's *Woodstock* (1970), about the legendary 1969 countercultural **music** festival, and Peter Davis's *Hearts and Minds* (1974), an anti–Vietnam War documentary.

The year 1989 saw the release of **Michael Moore**'s *Roger & Me* (1989), about the damage done to the city of Flint, Michigan, by the policies of the General Motors Corporation, perhaps the first documentary to attain the status of a **cult** film. Moore became the leader of a new generation of politically committed documentary filmmakers with such efforts as *The Big One* (1997), another documentary about corporate greed; the Oscar-winning *Bowling for Columbine* (2003), a study of American gun culture that attempted to shed light on the Columbine High School shootings of 1999; *Fahrenheit 9/11* (2004), a film about the George W. Bush administration's "war on terror" that became the top-grossing documentary of all time; *Sicko* (2007), an Oscar-nominated documentary about America's scandalous health-care system; and *Capitalism: A Love Story* (2009), about the corporate machinations that led to the near collapse of the U.S. financial system in 2007–2009.

The popularity of Moore's films has helped to usher in a sort of Golden Age of documentary film, a phenomenon that has also been spurred by the much acclaimed documentary work of Errol Morris, beginning with the classic *Gates of Heaven* (1978), which used a study of the pet cemetery industry to explore issues of ethics, mortality, and the afterlife. *The Thin Blue Line* (1988), about Randall Dale Adams, a man who had been sentenced to die for a murder he did not commit, became one of the most acclaimed documentaries of all time, meanwhile helping to exonerate Adams and get him freed from prison. The failure of *The Thin Blue Line* to be nominated for an Oscar caused something of a scandal, but Morris would later win the Academy Award for Best Documentary Feature for *The Fog of War: Eleven Lessons from the Life of Robert S. McNamara* (2003).

Morris's interview-based films have joined Moore's quest to make his films entertaining as major influences on the recent surge in documentary film production. That phenomenon was also fed by the policies of the Bush administration, which presented ample opportunity for critical inquiry, beginning with *Unprecedented: The 2000 Presidential Election* (2002), a documentary that explored the questionable circumstances under which Bush was elected in the first place. This film was executive produced by Robert Greenwald, who would go on to produce and direct an important series of documentaries, including *Uncovered: The Whole Truth about the Iraq War* (2003) and *Iraq for Sale: The War Profiteers* (2006), about the U.S. invasion and occupation of Iraq, and the corporate exposés *Outfoxed: Rupert Murdoch's War on Journalism* (2004) and *Wal-Mart: The High Cost of Low Price* (2005).

Other key recent documentaries include Morgan Spurlock's *Super Size Me* (2004), an exposé of the fast-food industry focusing on the McDonald's chain of restaurants, and Robert Kenner's *Food, Inc.* (2008), on corporate management of the food industry as a whole. Meanwhile, the French nature documentary *March of the Penguins* (2005) was a big hit in the United States, where it won the Best Documentary Oscar, while Davis Guggenheim's *An Inconvenient Truth* (2006), featuring the activist efforts of former U.S. vice president Al Gore to draw attention to the global-warming crisis, gained major media attention and also won an Oscar for Best Documentary Feature.

**DONEN, STANLEY (1924– ).** Stanley Donen began his movie career as a dancer and choreographer, then went on to direct some of Hollywood's best-loved **musicals**, including *Singin' in the Rain* (1952), which he co-directed with **Gene Kelly**. Donen also co-directed *On the Town* (1949) and *It's Always Fair Weather* (1955) with Kelly. Other well-known musicals directed by Donen include *Royal Wedding* (1951), *Seven Brides for Seven Brothers* (1954), *Funny Face* (1957), *The Pajama Game* (1957), and *Damn Yankees!* (1958). He also directed nonmusicals, usually in a comic vein, including *Indiscreet* (1958), *Charade* (1963), and *Bedazzled* (1967).

Though he was never nominated for a regular **Oscar**, Donen received an honorary lifetime achievement award from the **Academy of Motion Picture Arts and Sciences** in 1998.

**DONNER, RICHARD (1930– ).** Richard Donner had an extensive career as a television director, but had worked only sparingly in film when he burst into the Hollywood limelight as the director of the **horror** film *The Omen* in 1976. The success of that film led him to be tapped as the director of *Superman: The Movie* (1978), probably his most important film. Donner then began work on the sequel, *Superman II*, but was ultimately fired after now-legendary battles with the film's producers. He subsequently directed a number of moderately successful films, such as *The Toy* (1982), *Ladyhawke* (1985), *The Goonies* (1985), and *Scrooged* (1988). However, his next major success came as the director of the four *Lethal Weapon* films (1987, 1989, 1992, 1998), a series of lively thrillers that include strong comic elements.

*DOUBLE INDEMNITY.* *Double Indemnity* (dir. **Billy Wilder**, 1944) is often considered to be the quintessential **film noir**. It contains all the key visual elements of the genre, including low-key lighting, black-and-white photography, and strategic uses of patterns of light and shadow. Its snappy, rapid-fire dialogue is precisely the kind for which noir films often strive. And its basic story contains elements and characters that are iconic of the genre, including a sultry femme fatale (Phyllis Dietrichson, played by Barbara Stanwyck) who lures a reasonably good but weak man (Walter Neff, played by **Fred Mac-Murray**) into murderous misbehavior and ultimate doom.

*Double Indemnity* was co-written by director Billy Wilder and Raymond Chandler, and based on a book by James M. Cain; it thus has impeccable noir credentials. However, it also adds elements that are not necessarily typical of film noir, such as the relationship between the insurance salesman Neff and Barton Keyes (Edward G. Robinson), the head claims investigator at Pacific All Risk, the insurance company for which Neff works. Keyes, in particular, is a complex figure, honest and reliable, but also so devoted to his duties in the service of his corporate employer that he can seem heartless and inhuman. He thus joins Dietrichson and Neff as characters who have, in their various ways, been emotionally crippled by modern life.

Though *Double Indemnity* was nominated for seven **Academy Awards** (including Best Picture, Best Director, Best Actress, and Best Screenplay), it won none. It has, however, gained stature over the years as a classic of American cinema and especially of film noir. It was named the 29th greatest film of all time in a 2007 poll conducted by the **American Film Institute**.

**DOUGLAS, KIRK (1916– ).** Born Issur Danielovich, the cleft-chinned actor Kirk Douglas made an immediate impression in his first film role, as District Attorney Walter O'Neil in the **film noir** classic *The Strange Love of Martha Ivers* (1946). He followed with a key role in another noir thriller, *Out of the Past* (1947), and also appeared in the noir film *I Walk Alone* (1948), the first of seven onscreen collaborations with fellow actor **Burt Lancaster**. In the beginning of his career, Douglas tended to play villains, and it was not until the boxing film *Champion* (1949) that Douglas truly emerged as a leading man, and even then he tended to play flawed and often unpleasant characters.

Douglas refined his tough-guy screen image in a variety of films in the 1950s, though his performances of the decade in such films as the noirish media critique *Ace in the Hole* (1951), the **science fiction** adventure *20,000 Leagues under the Sea* (1954), the **war film** *Paths of Glory* (1957), and the **Western** *Gunfight at the O.K. Corral* (1957) indicated his versatility as an actor. Then, in 1960, he emerged as a heroic figure in what was probably his greatest role, that of the title character in **Stanley Kubrick**'s *Spartacus* (1960). Douglas continued to be a recognized star and to appear regularly in mainstream films, including such highlights as *Seven Days in May* (1964), *In Harm's Way* (1965), *The Light at the Edge of the World* (1971), and the Australian film *The Man from Snowy River* (1981). In 1986, he teamed with Lancaster one last time for *Tough Guys*, a comic **gangster film** that drew considerable comic energy from its play with the once-tough screen images of both aging actors. Slowed by a 1996 stroke that left his speech impaired, Douglas has nevertheless since returned to acting. He is also the author of a number of books, both fiction and nonfiction.

Douglas directed two films—*Scalawag* (1973) and *Posse* (1975)—and produced several others. In addition to *Champion*, he was nominated for **Academy Awards** for Best Actor for *The Bad and the Beautiful* (1952) and *Lust for Life* (1956), but he never won. However, in 1996, he was given an honorary award for lifetime achievement by the **Academy of Motion Picture Arts and Sciences**. In 1999, he was ranked 17th on a list of the all-time greatest male movie stars compiled by the **American Film Institute**.

**DOUGLAS, MICHAEL (1944– ).** The son of legendary actor **Kirk Douglas**, Michael Douglas had his first important success in film as the producer of such films as *One Flew over the Cuckoo's Nest* (1975) and *The China Syndrome* (1979). In the meantime, he became known as an actor for his starring role in the television series *The Streets of San Francisco* (1972–1976). He also played an important role in *The China Syndrome* and starred in such films as *Coma* (1978) and *Romancing the Stone* (1984). It was, however, as the greedy investor Gordon Gecko in **Oliver Stone**'s *Wall Street* (1987) that Douglas had his breakthrough into true stardom as an actor.

Douglas won the **Academy Award** for Best Actor in a Leading Role for *Wall Street*. Since that time he has starred in numerous films, while also still occasionally working as a producer. Highlights of his recent acting career include *Basic Instinct* (1992), one of the iconic films of the 1990s, as well as such key films as *Falling Down* (1993), *Traffic* (2000), and *Solitary Man* (2009).

Douglas reprised the role of Gekko in the 2010 sequel *Wall Street: Money Never Sleeps*.

**DOWNEY, ROBERT, JR. (1965– ).** The son of a film director, Robert Downey Jr. began appearing in his father's films at the age of five. A series of mostly small roles followed, including appearances in such teen films as *Tuff Turf* (1985), *Weird Science* (1985), and *The Pick-Up Artist* (1987), as Downey became a sort of peripheral member of the 1980s **Brat Pack**. Downey then began to establish himself as one of Hollywood's most promising young actors with his major supporting role in *Less Than Zero* (1987). Unfortunately, that film's focus on drug use among the young and wealthy mirrored Downey's own troubled experience with drug use, which would shadow his career for years to come.

Downey built his credentials as an actor with important supporting roles in such films as *True Believer* (1989) and *Air America* (1990), then had a breakthrough as the title character in *Chaplin* (1992), a **biopic** about **Charles Chaplin**. That performance won Downey an **Academy Award** nomination for Best Actor. Unfortunately, substance abuse problems (including a series of highly publicized arrests) prevented Downey from moving immediately into major stardom, though he continued to work regularly in supporting roles, often in important films, including **Oliver Stone**'s *Natural Born Killers* (1995), Mike Figgis's *One Night Stand* (1997), *U.S. Marshals* (1998), and *Wonder Boys* (2000). He also had a lead role in *Restoration* (1995).

After release from a prison drug rehab facility in 2000, Downey gained considerable attention for his Emmy-nominated supporting role on the television series *Ally McBeal*. More drug use and another arrest followed, however, and Downey began to lose work because his unreliability made it difficult to get insurance bonds for films in which he appeared. His career was resurrected, however, with his outstanding performance in the lead role in *The Singing Detective* (2003), for which his longtime friend **Mel Gibson** personally put up his insurance bond. Downey followed with lead roles in such films as *Gothika* (2003) and *Kiss Kiss Bang Bang* (2005), while continuing to perform in supporting roles as well.

Downey's career then took a dramatic turn with his performance as the title character in the big-budget **superhero film** *Iron Man* (2008), a box-office and critical success that made Downey a genuine movie star. Starring roles in the big-budget **action films** *Sherlock Holmes* (2009) and *Iron Man 2* (2010) have solidified that position, though Downey also appeared in a quirky supporting role (performing entirely in blackface) in the comedy *Tropic Thunder* (2008), a performance that won him an **Oscar** nomination for Best Supporting Actor.

**DREAMWORKS.** DreamWorks Pictures represents one of the most ambitious efforts to found a new Hollywood studio since the **silent film** era. Founded as a joint effort of director–producer **Steven Spielberg** and entertainment industry executives Jeffrey Katzenberg and David Geffen, the new studio showed considerable early promise and has scored some notable successes, though it has also experienced troubles that show just how difficult the movie business can be.

The former **Paramount** executive Katzenberg became the head of **Disney**'s motion picture division in 1984 and oversaw a strong resurgence in Disney's film business over the next decade. When he failed to receive a promotion to president of the overall Disney Company when that position was vacated in 1994, Katzenberg left Disney with considerable rancor (and with $280 million won in a lawsuit against Disney for his treatment there). Subsequently, he banded together with **music** industry mogul David Geffen and superstar director and producer Steven Spielberg (aided by a $500 million investment from Microsoft cofounder Paul Allen) to form DreamWorks SKG, a new state-of-the-art movie studio that would also be active in the production of music, television programming, and video games..

In the beginning, DreamWorks seemed to have an extremely bright future as they sought to inject some new energy into the Hollywood film industry. And the company has met with considerable success, such as the winning of consecutive **Academy Awards** for Best Picture, for *American Beauty* (1999), *Gladiator* (2000), and *A Beautiful Mind* (2001). However, some of the company's most ambitious plans (such as the building of a vast studio campus that would include elaborate on-site housing for many of the principals) never came into the being. By the end of 2005, the company's financial troubles had forced it to agree to sell off its live-action operations to Viacom-Paramount, though DreamWorks Animation was spun-off into a separate, independent entity. The deal between DreamWorks and Paramount has subsequently expired; the live-action operations of DreamWorks are now again independent, with the backing of an Indian investment firm and with a long-term deal for most of their films to be distributed by Disney, their old rival.

DreamWorks Animation, however, has remained a separate and autonomous entity all along, and it has been in the realm of **animated film** that DreamWorks has probably made its most substantial contributions, making DreamWorks the first studio to pose a genuine threat to Disney's dominance in the realm of animation and of **children's film** as a whole. DreamWorks entered the fray with a direct challenge to Disney–Pixar, releasing the computer-animated *Antz* in October 1998, the month before the release of *A Bug's Life*. The company then immediately followed in December with the release of the traditionally animated *The Prince of Egypt*, thus quickly staking a claim to be a major player in animated film.

Among other things, DreamWorks has shown a consistent ability to "scoop" Disney by releasing their animated films shortly before similar films by Disney. The most obvious case is the release of the highly successful *Madagascar* (2005) by DreamWorks a year before *The Wild*, but the tendency goes all the way back to the release of DreamWorks's first animated film, *Antz* just weeks before the similarly themed Disney–Pixar release *A Bug's Life* in 1998. Similarly, DreamWorks released their "South American" film *The Road to El Dorado* in 2000, nine months before Disney's *The Emperor's New Groove*, while Disney's *Home on the Range* appeared two years after DreamWorks's much more serious (and successful) Western, *Spirit: Stallion of the Cimarron*.

DreamWorks has also been on the forefront of developments in animation technology. Beginning with *Monsters vs. Aliens* (2009), for example, they have begun to distribute all of their animated films for children in stereoscopic 3D, and plan to do so for the foreseeable future. Their greatest success in the realm of animation, however, has been with the *Shrek* franchise, which now includes four films: *Shrek* (2001), *Shrek 2* (2004), *Shrek the Third* (2007), and *Shrek Forever After* (2010). These irreverent films, which draw heavily upon references to contemporary pop culture in conducting what is essentially an ongoing parody of the classic Disney fairy-tale films, have been a huge critical and commercial success. The first *Shrek* film won the first ever Academy Award for Best Animated Feature Film, while the franchise as a whole has grossed over $3 billion in worldwide box-office receipts.

**DUNAWAY, FAYE (1941– ).** Faye Dunaway burst upon the Hollywood scene with her **Oscar**-nominated performance as Bonnie Parker in *Bonnie* *and Clyde* (1967). She also had key roles in films such as *The Thomas Crown Affair* (1968) and *Little Big Man* (1970) before solidifying her status as one of Hollywood's leading actresses with her Oscar-nominated performance in *Chinatown* (1973). She won a third **Academy Award** nomination for Best Actress for her performance in *Network* (1976), for which she scored her only Oscar win.

Specializing in playing women who were sexy but often cold, troubled but often powerful, Dunaway was especially prominent in the 1970s, when she also appeared in such films as *The Towering Inferno* (1974), *Three Days of the Condor* (1975), and *Eyes of Laura Mars* (1978). In 1980, however, her performance as **Joan Crawford** in *Mommie Dearest* won her a **Razzie Award** for Worst Actress. Most of her appearances in the remainder of the 1980s were in supporting roles or in questionable films, though her starring role in *Barfly* (1987) did win her a **Golden Globe Award** for Best Actress. The majority of her appearances since 1990 have been on television.

**DUVALL, ROBERT (1931– ).** After numerous appearances on television and the stage in the 1950s, Robert Duvall managed to land supporting roles in a number of major films in the 1960s, including ***To Kill a Mockingbird*** (1962), *Bullitt* (1968), and *True Grit* (1969). However, he was still regarded primarily as a television actor until his roles in *MASH* (1970) and *THX* (1971) drew major attention, followed by a performance as Tom Hagen in **Francis Ford Coppola**'s ***The Godfather*** (1972) that won him an **Academy Award** nomination for Best Supporting Actor. He reprised the same role in Coppola's *The Godfather: Part II* (1974) and also had important supporting roles in such major 1970s films as *Network* (1976) and Coppola's *Apocalypse Now* (1979), which won him his second Best Supporting Actor **Oscar** nomination.

The year 1979 also saw Duvall star in *The Great Santini*, in a performance that won him his first Oscar nomination for Best Actor in a Leading Role. He then won that award for his performance in *Tender Mercies* (1983) and would later be nominated for it again for his lead role in *The Apostle* (1997), a film he also wrote and directed. Duvall scored his third Best Supporting Actor nomination for *A Civil Action* (1998).

A versatile actor who has proven able both to carry films in starring roles and to provide important support as a character actor, Duvall has remained extremely busy in Hollywood film through the first decade of the 21st century (and through the eighth decade of his life), though he has moved primarily into supporting roles in his seventies.

# E

**EASTWOOD, CLINT (1930– ).** Clint Eastwood has enjoyed dual careers as a leading Hollywood actor and, increasingly, as one of Hollywood's most respected directors. However, Eastwood's movie career took off slowly, with his most notable role through the early 1960s being that of Rowdy Yates in the television **Western** *Rawhide* (1959–1965). However, Eastwood's career took a dramatic turn when he gained major attention for his appearances in a sequence of Italian-made "spaghetti" Westerns, including *A Fistful of Dollars* (1964), *For a Few Dollars More* (1965), and *The Good, the Bad, and the Ugly* (1966). These performances established a tough, laconic onscreen image as something of an antihero that Eastwood was able to continue in a series of performances in American film in the 1970s, especially in Westerns such as *Hang 'Em High* (1968), *Two Mules for Sister Sara* (1970), *High Plains Drifter* (1973), and *The Outlaw Josey Wales* (1976).

The 1970s also saw Eastwood establish what is perhaps his best remembered role, that of rule-breaking police inspector "Dirty" Harry Callahan, in *Dirty Harry* (1971), *Magnum Force* (1973), and *The Enforcer* (1976), a role he would reprise in *Sudden Impact* (1983) and *The Dead Pool* (1988). Eastwood also showed increasing versatility as an actor in films such as *Play Misty for Me* (1971), *The Eiger Sanction* (1975), and the **comedy** *Every Which Way but Loose* (1978). He also moved into directing many of his own films in the early 1970s, even beginning to direct films in which he did not star with *Breezy* (1973).

In the 1980s, Eastwood began producing many of his films. He also starred in everything from the action thriller *Firefox* (1982), to the two additional "Dirty Harry" films, to the Western *Pale Rider* (1985), to the action comedy *Pink Cadillac* (1989). He also continued to direct, including films in which he did not star, such as the **biopic** *Bird* (1988). Long a major movie star, Eastwood then finally achieved major critical acclaim for the Western *Unforgiven* (1992), which won the **Academy Award** for Best Picture, while winning Eastwood the **Oscar** for Best Director and a nomination for Best Actor.

Subsequently, Eastwood won the **Irving G. Thalberg** Award for lifetime achievement from the Academy in 1995, but his achievement was far from over. Indeed, though he had directed 19 films as of 1995, his greatest days as a director were still ahead of him. Eastwood would go on to win another Best Director Oscar for *Million Dollar Baby* (2004), a film that also won Best Picture and for which Eastwood also received his second Best Actor nomination. Best Director and Best Picture nominations also went to Eastwood's *Mystic River* (2003) and *Letters from Iwo Jima* (2006). Eastwood gained additional critical praise as the director and star of *Gran Torino* (2008) and as the director of *Invictus* (2009).

**EBERT, ROGER (1942– ).** Through his film review column in the *Chicago Sun-Times* and a series of successful film review programs on television, Roger Ebert has become one of the best-known critics in the history of American film. In recent years, Ebert's reviews have also had a prominent online presence, while he has also published a series of successful books about film, including a sequence of annual "movie yearbooks" that are primarily compilations of his reviews from the year before.

Ebert began his career as the film critic for the *Sun-Times* in 1967 and subsequently achieved major success in that role. In 1975, Ebert began cohosting (with Gene Siskel of the *Chicago Tribune*) a film review show on local television in Chicago. That program, entitled *Sneak Previews*, was picked up for national broadcast on the Public Broadcasting System (PBS) in 1978. They shifted to national syndication in 1982, retitling the show *At the Movies with Gene Siskel and Roger Ebert*. With that show growing in popularity, the duo entered an agreement with **Disney**'s Buena Vista Television unit to produce their show as *Siskel and Ebert and the Movies*. Known for their "thumbs up/thumbs down" review summaries, Siskel and Ebert became an increasingly prominent part of American popular culture until Siskel's death in 1999.

The show continued as *Roger Ebert & the Movies*, hosted by Ebert and a series of guest cohosts until September 2000, when Ebert's fellow *Chicago Sun-Times* columnist Richard Roeper became the permanent cohost and the show was renamed *At the Movies with Ebert & Roeper*. Complications from thyroid cancer, diagnosed in 2002, limited Ebert's participation in the program, which he eventually left altogether in 2006 when complications from the surgery to treat Ebert's cancer rendered him unable to speak. He has, however, continued to write reviews both for the *Sun-Times* and online.

Though sometimes accused of showing elitist tastes, Ebert has in fact often been a champion of more low-brow film forms, feeling that all films should be judged within the context of other films of the same type. For example, early in his career, Ebert became a supporter of the **sexploitation films** of director Russ Meyer, eventually entering into a working partnership with Meyer. Ebert subsequently wrote the scripts for three Meyer-directed films:

*Beyond the Valley of the Dolls* (1970), *Up!* (1976), and *Beneath the Valley of the Ultra-Vixens* (1979).

Indeed, Ebert has long had the reputation of being more of a film industry insider than is typical for film critics. Since 1999, he has sponsored his own film festival in Champaign, Illinois, and in 2005 he became the first film critic to be awarded a star on the Hollywood Walk of Fame. Among his more influential efforts has been a series of reviews of "Great Movies," which he began in 1994 and which has now extended to more than 300 films.

**EDISON, THOMAS (1847–1931).** Thomas Alva Edison was probably the most famous inventor in American history, though he was at least as important as a businessman and entrepreneur, particularly adept at converting his (and others') inventions into marketable (and profitable) products. Though perhaps best known for his innovations in telegraphy and as the inventor of the phonograph, the light bulb, and practical systems for the distribution of electricity, Edison also contributed to the development of a number of key pieces of motion picture technology. Devices such as the Kinetograph (one of the first motion picture cameras) and the Kinetoscope (a device for the viewing of motion pictures by a single viewer) were developed in Edison's labs, though much of the credit for these inventions surely belongs to William Kennedy Dickson, the company's official photographer, who was assigned by Edison to develop these devices based on his preliminary conceptualizations.

Edison and his company also pioneered in the production of motion pictures to provide content for their display devices. In 1893, they opened the Black Maria in West Orange, New Jersey. This was the world's first motion picture studio, though it was closed and replaced in 1901 by a new, glass-enclosed, rooftop studio in New York City. In 1908, Edison spearheaded the formation of the Motion Picture Patents Company among the leading film producers, hoping to corner the market on film production. The company, also known as the Edison Trust, was unsuccessful in preventing the growth of the industry beyond their control; it was formally dissolved in 1915 by federal court order as being in violation of antitrust laws. Edison was subsequently not a major player in the film industry.

**EDUCATIONAL PICTURES.** Educational Pictures (or Educational Film Exchanges, Inc.) was a film production and distribution company founded in 1915 by Earle Hammons. Taking its name from Hammons's original intention to focus on the making and distribution of educational films to schools, the company soon shifted to the more lucrative theatrical market, with a special emphasis on **comedies**.

Educational's **silent film** comedies of the 1920s were particularly successful, and the company entered the sound era as the distributor for the films of comedy pioneer **Mack Sennett**. After Sennett left (his own studio was in financial difficulty), the company continued to have success with a series of comedies starring **Buster Keaton**. Nevertheless, financial problems eventually forced the company into bankruptcy. Their final film was released in 1939 and their surviving film library was auctioned off in 1940—though many of their silent films had been destroyed in a 1937 fire.

**EDWARDS, BLAKE (1922– ).** Blake Edwards had a long and varied career in film, beginning as an unsuccessful actor in the 1940s, then moving into a career as a writer, producer, and director that culminated in his receipt, in 2004, of an honorary award for his achievement in those areas from the **Academy of Motion Picture Arts and Sciences.** His first major film as a director was the military comedy *Operation Petticoat* (1959). He then became a frontline Hollywood director with his work in the more serious *Breakfast at Tiffany's* (1961) and *Days of Wine and Roses* (1962). It was, however, the farcical comedy *The Pink Panther* (1963), which he both directed and co-wrote, that would become his signature film.

That film was the beginning of an important franchise that would see Edwards go on to write and direct six sequels: *The Return of the Pink Panther* (1975), *The Pink Panther Strikes Again* (1976), *Revenge of the Pink Panther* (1978), *Trail of the Pink Panther* (1982), *Curse of the Pink Panther* (1983), and *Son of the Pink Panther* (1993). He also produced all but the last of these films, which formed the core of his film career, though he directed a number of other important **comedies**, typically writing and directing them as well. Edwards's other films include *The Great Race* (1965), *10* (1979), *S.O.B.* (1981), *Victor Victoria* (1982), *Micki & Maude* (1984), *Blind Date* (1987), *Skin Deep* (1989), and *Switch* (1991).

**EISNER, MICHAEL (1942– ).** Media executive for both NBC and CBS before moving to the ABC television network, where he advanced to the position of senior vice president in charge of programming and development, Michael Eisner entered the film business in 1976 when he was hired as the president and chief operating officer (CEO) of **Paramount Pictures.** In 1984, Eisner made his most important career move, becoming the CEO of **Disney**, then somewhat in disarray. Eisner quickly got Disney onto a firmer footing and oversaw the company's return to its roots in fairy-tale-based **animated films** for children. The subsequent success of *The Little Mermaid* (1989) and *Beauty and the Beast* (1991) marked the beginning of the so-called Disney Renaissance, which ran through the 1990s, reaping unprecedented profits for Disney's film business.

Perhaps even more important, however, was Eisner's management of Disney's expansion in areas outside of film, especially television. It was this expansion that would ultimately build the once-struggling Disney into the world's largest media corporation. On the other hand, this expansion (combined with Eisner's sometimes acerbic personal style) led many in the corporation to become unhappy with his leadership, feeling that his unstinting focus on the bottom line was a betrayal of the legacy of company founder **Walt Disney**. A group led by Walt's nephew, Roy E. Disney, managed to oust Eisner as the chairman of the board of Disney in 2004, and he resigned his post as CEO a year later.

**ELFMAN, DANNY (1953– ).** The leader of the successful rock band Oingo Boingo from 1976 to 1995, Danny Elfman has also become one of America's leading composers of **music** for film and television. Elfman's single best known piece of music is probably the theme to *The Simpsons* television program; he was nominated for an Emmy for that theme in 1990 and won an Emmy in 2005 for composing the theme to the series *Desperate Housewives*. It is, however, for his versatile and highly entertaining film scores—especially in the films of director **Tim Burton**—that Elfman is best known.

Elfman first tried his hand at scoring for film with *Forbidden Zone* (1982), directed by his brother, Richard Elfman. He then moved more into the Hollywood mainstream by writing the score for Burton's first feature film, *Pee-Wee's Big Adventure* (1985). Since that time, he has scored all but two of Burton's films, from the soaring and dramatic score of *Batman* (1989); to the score of *Mars Attacks!* (1996), with its numerous allusions to the scores of 1950s **science fiction** films; to the romantic score for *Big Fish* (2003), the only Burton film for which Elfman has received an **Academy Award** nomination for Best Original Score. However, Elfman has also received Best Original Score nominations for the non-Burton films *Men in Black* (1997), *Good Will Hunting* (1997), and *Milk* (2008). Other particularly prominent films for which Elfman has written scores include *To Die For* (1995), *A Simple Plan* (1998), *Chicago* (2002), the first two *Spider-Man* films (2002, 2004), *Hulk* (2003), and *Terminator Salvation* (2009).

Elfman has sometimes also performed his own music in films, perhaps most notably in the Burton-produced *Nightmare before Christmas* (1993, directed by Henry Selick), in which Elfman provides the singing voice for Jack Skellington, as well as writing one of his most entertaining scores. Elfman also provides the voice for one of the characters in Burton's *Corpse Bride* (2005), a sort of follow-up to *The Nightmare before Christmas*. Finally, Elfman provides all the vocals for the **musical** performances by the Oompa-Loompas in Burton's *Charlie and the Chocolate Factory* (2005), which he also scored.

***E.T.: THE EXTRA-TERRESTRIAL.*** Conceived largely as a **science fiction** film for children, *E.T.* (dir. **Steven Spielberg**, 1982) was a huge critical and commercial success and is now regarded as a classic of both sf film and **children's film**. Like *Close Encounters of the Third Kind* (1977), its predecessor in Spielberg's oeuvre, *E.T.* is an alien invasion narrative that features benevolent aliens who have come to Earth on a peaceful mission. Indeed, one could almost describe *E.T.* as a children's version of *Close Encounters*, emphasizing the same general themes but for a younger audience. In the case of *E.T.*, the aliens, presented as vulnerable and harmless, seem simply to be gathering scientific data. Interrupted by a sinister-seeming group of humans, the aliens flee back to their ship, taking off in such haste that they leave one of their number behind. This alien, the film's title character, then spends the rest of the film struggling both to survive on Earth and to find a way to get back home, despite the efforts of certain humans to capture it, presumably for study.

Indeed, this film quite consistently reverses the terms of the classic alien invasion narrative, making the alien sympathetic, while making most humans (especially those in positions of authority) seem villainous. Children, on the other hand, are treated more sympathetically, and eventually a group of them helps E.T. to summon a ship to take him back to his home planet.

This relatively simple narrative is punctuated by a number of memorable scenes that help to make *E.T.* probably the most beloved of all of Spielberg's films. In addition to its tremendous box-office success, it won **Oscars** for Best Original Musical Score, Best Sound, Best Sound Effects Editing, and Best Visual Effects (especially for Carlo Rambaldi's design of the mechanical figure used to represent E.T., who is very much the star of the film). Indeed, the lovability of the central alien is one of the secrets of the success of the film, which centrally depends on sympathy for E.T. in delivering its message of tolerance toward the Other. Meanwhile, the film delivers a considerable amount of commentary on American society, though this aspect of the film is considerably muted relative to the sometimes sharp critique in *Close Encounters*. Moreover, *E.T.* includes, among other things, a number of allusions to other films (such as ***Star Wars***), making it a tribute to the power of the movies and to the central role played by movies in shaping the popular American imagination.

**EVANS, ROBERT (1930– ).** Though he has been directly credited as the producer of relatively few films, Robert Evans has been involved in a number of especially high-profile projects as either a producer or studio executive. In the process, he has become one of the most famous figures in Hollywood, though perhaps as much for his high-rolling lifestyle (including seven marriages) as for his professional body of work. Evans's only **Academy Award** nomination came as the producer of *Chinatown* (1974), which was nominated for Best Picture. However, by this time, he had, as the head of **Paramount Pictures** (a position he held from 1966 to 1974), already been involved in the production of several highly successful films, including *Rosemary's Baby* (1968), *The Odd Couple* (1968), *Love Story* (1970), *The Godfather* (1972), and *Serpico* (1973).

During this period, Evans came to be seen as an important force behind the **New Hollywood** innovations that were sweeping the film industry. On the other hand, several of the films he produced after stepping down as the head of Paramount were notable flops, including *Urban Cowboy* (1980), *Popeye* (1980), and *The Cotton Club* (1984), which Evans had originally planned to direct but which had to be finished by **Francis Ford Coppola** due to production difficulties. Evans made something of a comeback in the 1990s and has continued to produce into the 21st century, though none of his latter films — including *The Two Jakes* (1990), *Sliver* (1993), *Jade* (1995), *The Phantom* (1996), *The Saint* (1997), *The Out-of-Towners* (1999), and *How to Lose a Guy in 10 Days* (2003) — have been particularly successful, either critically or commercially.

In the late 1950s, Evans appeared in several films as an actor, including a role as legendary studio executive **Irving Thalberg** in *Man of a Thousand Faces* (1957). Evans's notoriety has been enhanced by a number of legal problems, including an arrest for attempting to buy cocaine during the production of *Popeye*. This notoriety has also led to numerous references to him in popular culture; for example, the unscrupulous Hollywood producer played by **Dustin Hoffman** in the **satire** *Wag the Dog* (1998) was clearly based on Evans. In 2003, Evans provided the voice for a character based on himself in the short-lived animated television series *Kid Notorious*.

**EXPLOITATION FILMS.** *See* BLAXPLOITATION; SEXPLOITATION.

# F

**FAIRBANKS, DOUGLAS (1883–1939).** The dashing and athletic star of swashbuckling **silent film** classics such as *The Mark of Zorro* (1920), *Robin Hood* (1922), and *The Thief of Baghdad* (1924), Douglas Fairbanks was one of the world's first major movie stars. Fairbanks was also very interested in maintaining artistic control of his own work, founding his own production company as early as 1916. In 1919, he founded (along with **D. W. Griffith**, **Charles Chaplin**, and Fairbanks's wife-to-be **Mary Pickford**) United Artists, a new studio dedicated to providing creative autonomy for actors and directors.

In 1920, Fairbanks married Pickford and the two became Hollywood's first celebrity couple. In 1926, Fairbanks starred in another swashbuckler, *The Black Pirate*, which had the distinction of being the first Technicolor film. He starred with Pickford in his first talkie, *The Taming of the Shrew* (1929). However, Fairbanks did not transition well into the sound era, starring in only three films in the 1930s, ending with the British production *The Private Life of Don Juan* (1934).

In 1927, Fairbanks was elected the first president of the **Academy of Motion Picture Arts and Sciences**, a post he held until 1929.

**FAMILY FILM.** *See* CHILDREN'S FILM.

**FANTASY.** The literary genre of fantasy generally involves tales that are set in imaginary worlds that differ substantially from our own and that contain phenomena (such as magic) and creatures (such as dragons) that do not occur in our real world. Moreover, the differences between our world and the world of a work of fantasy are typically stipulated, with no scientific or rational explanation offered or required. Aside from major exceptions such as *The Wizard of Oz* (1939), fantasy has not been a traditionally strong genre within American film. Even *The Wizard of Oz* has been widely perceived as a film for children, and most fantasies in the history of American film have been **children's films**, including the various fairy-tale-based films produced by **Disney**. Fantasy–adventure films such as *The 7th Voyage of Sinbad* (1958) and *Jason and the Argonauts* (1962), both featuring **special effects** by Ray Harryhausen, provided occasional exceptions, though these tended to be at least as popular with children as with adults. There had long been other films that contained strong fantasy elements, such as the swashbuckling adventure films of the 1930s or **Frank Capra**'s *It's a Wonderful Life* (1946), but fantasy for adult audiences was rare in American film until **Ralph Bakshi**'s *Wizards* (1977), an **animated film** (not for children) that combined fantasy with postapocalyptic **science fiction**.

Bakshi's ambitious follow-up was *The Lord of the Rings* (1978), an animated partial adaptation of the similarly titled trilogy of novels by J. R. R. Tolkien, perhaps the most important fantasy works of all time. This film is now something of a **cult** classic, but lukewarm responses at the time made it impossible for Bakshi to make the follow-up film that would have completed the adaptation. Bakshi's animated sword-and-sorcery fantasy *Fire and Ice* (1983) was largely panned by critics and ignored by audiences, and his career as a maker of animated fantasy films that could appeal to adult audiences was at an end.

Still, by this time, fantasy was becoming more and more common in American film. *Superman* (1978) and *Superman II* (1980) were successful **superhero films** that were a form of fantasy, but additional sequels soon foundered. The early 1980s did, however, see the release of successful fantasy films such as *The Beastmaster* (1982) and *Conan the Barbarian* (1982), suggesting that there was indeed a market for fantasy films for adults. The biggest landmark of this era, however, was **Steven Spielberg**'s *Raiders of the Lost Ark* (1981), an adventure fantasy that spawned one of the most successful film franchises in history. Later in the decade, films such as *The Princess Bride* (1987) and *Willow* (1988) demonstrated the potential of "straight" fantasy film, as opposed to adventure and sword-and-sorcery.

The 1980s also saw the debut of **Tim Burton**, many of whose films—such as *Beetle Juice* (1988), *Edward Scissorhands* (1990), *Sleepy Hollow* (1999), *Big Fish* (2003), and *Charlie and the Chocolate Factory* (2005)—contain strong fantasy elements. In addition, Burton's *Batman* (1989) and *Batman Returns* (1992) helped to initiate a resurgence in superhero movies that would eventually become a full-blown box-office phenomenon, led by the *X-Men* (2000, 2003, 2006) and *Spider-Man* (2002, 2004, 2007) trilogies, while the form would reach even greater box-office success when the Batman franchise (which had foundered under the weight of two sequels to Burton's films, campily directed by Joel Schumacher) was resurrected by British director Christopher Nolan with *Batman Begins* (2005) and *The Dark Knight* (2008).

A variety of other forms of fantasy film appeared in the 1990s, but fantasy really hit its stride in the new century, when, in addition to numerous superhero films, several new fantasy sequences joined the most successful franchises of all time. Peter Jackson's *Lord of the Rings* **trilogy** (2001, 2002, 2003), a New Zealand–U.S. co-production, was the first full cinematic adaptation of Tolkien's trilogy. It was also a hugely successful demonstration of the ability of state-of-the-art **computer-generated imagery** to bring fantasy to life on the screen. These films were based on a revered work of literary fantasy and thus had something of a built-in audience, but the *Pirates of the Caribbean* trilogy (2003, 2006, 2007), based on a more pedestrian source (a Disneyland theme ride), gained even more commercial success. Finally, the Harry Potter films (a total of eight between 2001 and 2011), based on the hugely popular novels of J. K. Rowling, became one of the most durable (and highest-grossing) film franchises of all time.

The success of these franchises has spurred the production of a number of recent fantasy films, many based on successful sequences of fantasy books, most notably the *Chronicles of Narnia* series of C. S. Lewis. However, the only other fantasy films to have approached the commercial success of the central franchises are the *Twilight* films, based on the novels of Stephanie Meyer. Vampire narratives that are clearly more fantasy than **horror**, these films seem aimed largely at teenage girls but have attracted older audiences as well. Many of the other recent fantasy films seem aimed largely at children but contain elements that are clearly designed to appeal to adults as well.

**FIELD, SALLY (1946– ).** Sally Field rose to national prominence as a television actress with starring roles in *Gidget* (1965–1966) and *The Flying Nun* (1967–1979). She made a number of additional television appearances in the first half of the 1970s, culminating in a starring role in the television movie *Sybil* (1976), which won her an Emmy Award and drew the attention of Hollywood. She then moved into her first lead role in a feature film with *Smokey and the Bandit* (1976), the beginning of several major roles that eventually led to her performance as the title character in **Martin Ritt**'s *Norma Rae* (1979), which won her an **Academy Award** for Best Actress in a Leading Role.

Now a top star, Field had lead roles in a number of important films of the 1980s, including *Absence of Malice* (1981), *Murphy's Romance* (1985), and *Steel Magnolias* (1989). The highlight of her work in that decade was her performance in *Places in the Heart* (1984), for which she won her second Best Actress **Oscar**.

Entering the 1990s in her mid-40s, Field increasingly found lead roles in film hard to come by, though she had interesting supporting roles in such films as *Soapdish* (1991), *Mrs. Doubtfire* (1993), and *Forrest Gump* (1994). Since the mid-1990s, she has frequently returned to television, where she has had her most important roles of recent years. Between 2000 and 2009, she scored a total of six Emmy Awards for Best Actress in various categories, winning twice. Over the years, Field has won 10 **Golden Globe** nominations in various acting categories, winning twice (for *Norma Rae* and *Places in the Heart*).

**FIELDS, W. C. (1880–1946).** Former vaudevillian W. C. Fields (born William Claude Dukenfield) was one of Hollywood's top comic performers in the 1930s and early 1940s. Fields made a number of **silent films**, but his trademark sarcastic asides worked best in sound film, and it was in the sound era that he rose to true stardom. Fields continued to star in short films—such as *The Dentist* (1932), *The Pharmacist* (1933), and *The Barber Shop* (1933), even after Hollywood had shifted almost all of its emphasis to features. However, it was in features such as *International House* (1933) that he rose to major stardom.

For a brief period, from 1933 to 1936, Fields starred in such films as *You're Telling Me!* (1934), *It's a Gift* (1934), *Man on the Flying Trapeze* (1935), and *Poppy* (1936), often playing cynical charlatans or con men. However, his most memorable performances during this period were probably in supporting roles, as when he played Humpty-Dumpty in *Alice in Wonderland* (1933) or Mr. Micawber in *David Copperfield* (1935). Health problems, exacerbated by alcohol, forced Fields to take a hiatus from film from 1936 to 1938, though he eventually returned with a vengeance.

After the relatively forgettable *The Big Broadcast of 1938* (1938), Fields starred in a string of what are possibly his four best-remembered films: *You Can't Cheat an Honest Man* (1939), *My Little Chickadee* (1940), *The Bank Dick* (1940), and *Never Give a Sucker an Even Break* (1941). However, battles with Universal Pictures over the final film led him to be released by the studio that, combined with health and weight problems, effectively ended his career in film.

The title (but supporting) role in **The Wizard of Oz** (1939) was written with Fields in mind, but he declined to appear in the film, concentrating on his own starring projects instead.

**FILM FESTIVALS.** Film festivals are organized events, usually taking place over several days in a single location, that are designed to spotlight specific types of films or just film in general. In recent years, festivals have gained increasing importance in the film industry, providing venues in which independent filmmakers can showcase their films, often with the goal of attracting distributors. As such, film festivals have been an important part of the boom in independent filmmaking since the beginning of the 1990s.

Film festivals originated in Europe, beginning with the Venice Film Festival in 1932. Important annual festivals in cities such as Berlin and Edinburgh were established over the coming years, with the Edinburgh festival, held annually since 1947, currently being the longest continually operated festival in the world. Probably the most prestigious festival, however, is the Cannes Film Festival, which was founded in 1946, but which missed several years in its early history due to budgetary problems. This festival highlights films that are soon to be released, sometimes by **major studios**, and is much watched in Hollywood, though it is international in nature.

The most important North American film festival is the Toronto Film Festival, though numerous festivals are held in the United States as well. The best known of these is probably the Sundance Film Festival, which was founded in 1978 in Salt Lake City and now takes place annually in several different Utah locales. This festival, particularly noted for its focus on **independent films**, has long been associated with its inaugural chairperson, actor **Robert Redford**, and takes its name from his character in *Butch Cassidy and the Sundance Kid* (1969). It has, in recent years, grown into a major media spectacle attended by numerous Hollywood celebrities, though the actual films featured at the festival still come mainly from little-known filmmakers seeking attention for their latest projects.

The success of the Sundance Festival has led to the growth of other important festivals focusing on independent film, including the Telluride Film Festival, Austin's South by Southwest festival, and New York's Tribeca Film Festival.

**FILM NOIR.** The term "film noir" was coined by the French critics Nino Frank and Jean-Pierre Chartier in 1946, when they declared wartime films such as **John Huston**'s *The Maltese Falcon* (1941), **Billy Wilder**'s *Double Indemnity* (1944) and *The Lost Weekend* (1945), **Otto Preminger**'s *Laura* (1944), and **Edward Dmytryk**'s *Murder, My Sweet* (1944) to be the vanguard of a new breakthrough in film realism. To this list, one might add such early examples as **Raoul Walsh**'s *High Sierra* (1941), **Michael Curtiz**'s *The Sea Wolf* (1941), Josef von Sternberg's *The Shanghai Gesture* (1941), Stuart Heisler's *The Glass Key* (1942), Frank Tuttle's *This Gun for Hire* (1942), Richard Wallace's *The Fallen Sparrow* (1943), **Fritz Lang**'s *Hangmen Also Die* (1943), and Herman Shumlin's *Watch on the Rhine* (1943), films which together demonstrate that film noir was well established as a genre by the end of World War II, even if it had yet to be given a name.

In both their cynical tone and focus on such subjects as murder and corruption, such films clearly owed a great deal to the hard-boiled fiction of such American writers of the 1930s as **Raymond Chandler**, Dashiell Hammett, and James M. Cain, writers who had gained relatively little high-brow literary respect by the 1950s but whose ascendant reputations since that time parallel the growing critical respect that has been gained by film noir, some of the best examples of which have been directly adapted from their novels. However, film noirs had already, in the 1950s, come to be recognized by many as respected products of cinematic art, even as others saw them as lowly and crude, combining to make film noir seem something like an illegitimate offspring of pulp fiction and high modernism. For example, the visual texture of film noir, with its low-key lighting and ominous shadows, clearly owes a great deal to earlier German expressionist films, such as Robert Wiene's *The Cabinet of Dr. Caligari* (1919) and Lang's *Metropolis* (1926), while Lang's *M* (1931) is a clear forerunner of film noir both visually and thematically.

The critical reception of film noir has been schizophrenic ever since the French approvingly applied the term to American film in 1946. On the one hand, respected directors such as Wilder and **Orson Welles** were intimately associated with the genre. On the other hand, many of the film noirs that have enjoyed the most positive and lasting critical reputations are offbeat, low-budget cult classics such as **Edgar Ulmer**'s *Detour* (1945) and the noir films of **Samuel Fuller**. Meanwhile, some of the greatest works of film noir, such as Wilder's *Sunset Blvd.* (1950) and (especially) Welles's *Touch of Evil* (1958), openly parody the conventions of the genre, while others, such as **Robert Aldrich**'s *Kiss Me Deadly* (1955), adapted from a novel by the outrageous Mickey Spillane, are strongly skeptical of, if not downright antagonistic toward, the pulp fictions on which they are based.

The ambivalence shown film noir by critics mirrors the duality and ambivalence of the films themselves, which are shot through with a skepticism and cynicism far too thorough to allow an unequivocal commitment to any particular ideal. Film noirs tend to break down easy distinctions, especially between good and evil, creating an effect of confusion that disorients viewers. In addition, film noir as a form is extremely self-conscious and conducts an ongoing subversive critique of the more saccharine products of Hollywood in the 1930s and 1940s. But this self-conscious skepticism toward film as a medium extended, from the very beginning, to film noir itself. Even an early work such as *The Maltese Falcon*, one of the very first full-fledged film noirs, is highly cynical, yet also highly stylized, even campy, intensely aware of its own status as a performance.

That film noir was already moving into self-parody by the time of *Sunset Blvd.* indicates the self-consciousness and staginess that pervade even the straightest of film noirs. For example, *Murder, My Sweet*, the other great private-eye film noir of the war years, is even campier than *The Maltese Falcon*. In *Murder, My Sweet*, baby-faced crooner Dick Powell does a surprisingly good imitation of Chandler's tough-but-weary Marlowe, and the very fact that it is obviously an imitation only adds to the fun in a film that may be the stagiest of the "straight" film noirs, outdone in theatricality only by noir parodies such as *Touch of Evil*.

Given its self-consciousness, it is perhaps not surprising that some of the most successful examples of film noir have literally been about the Hollywood film industry. *Sunset Blvd.* (whose two central figures are an aging actress and an aspiring screenwriter) is a key example of this phenomenon, as is *In a Lonely Place* (1950), starring **Humphrey Bogart** as troubled and embittered screenwriter Dixon Steele. Another key example is Aldrich's *The Big Knife* (1955), about the self-destruction of a prominent Hollywood actor.

Film noir is also a surprisingly versatile form, lending itself to everything from pure entertainment to incisive commentary on capitalism and American society, and on the roles played by race, class, gender, and other factors in that society. A given film, of course, can do both. Thus, a boxing film such as Robert Rossen's *Body and Soul* (1949) could be highly entertaining but also serve as a trenchant commentary on the dehumanizing competition and greed driving modern capitalism. Meanwhile, a film such as **Samuel Fuller**'s *Pickup on South Street* (1953) was an overtly anticommunist **spy film**, while many film noirs of the war years were explicitly antifascist. The legacy of antifascism also continued to influence the film noir well after the end of the war. Thus, works such as Dmytryk's *Cornered* (1945), **Alfred Hitchcock**'s *Notorious* (1946), and Welles's *The Stranger* (1946) all dealt with a postfascist world, but one in which fascists still posed a threat to the safety and security of right-thinking individuals in the victorious West. Film noir can be quite funny at times, as in the moments of over-the-top dialogue that punctuate otherwise serious films such as *Double Indemnity*. But film noir can also be genuinely terrifying, as in certain moments in *The Sound of Fury* (1950, aka *Try and Get Me*) and *The Night of the Hunter* (1955).

Film noir, despite its distinctive visual style, also produced a variety of looks and an array of iconic visual images, such as the trademark shadow pattern thrown on a wall by a light shining through a venetian blind, to the often-seen reflection of street lights on wet city streets at night. Similarly, film noir produced a variety of representative characters, from deranged and heartless killers such as Richard Widmark's psychopathic gangster in *Kiss of Death* (1947), to the completely innocent man wrongly accused, as in **Henry Fonda**'s portrayal of the title character in Alfred Hitchcock's *The Wrong Man* (1956). One of the most representative film noir protagonists is the basically good man who makes one mistake and can never quite escape the consequences of that single misstep, as in **Burt Lancaster**'s portrayal of Swede Andersen in **Robert Siodmak**'s *The Killers* (1946) or in **Robert Mitchum**'s Jeff Bailey in **Jacques Tourneur**'s *Out of the Past* (1947).

Perhaps the most iconic film noir character is the femme fatale, the dangerous and alluring woman who tempts men to their doom—and who is typically the central source of the sexual charge for which film noirs are famous. The femme fatale was sometimes a figure of almost pure evil, as in Barbara Stanwyck's portrayal of Phyllis Dietrichson in *Double Indemnity*, while others were more morally complex, as in **Rita Hayworth**'s portrayal of the title character in *Gilda* (1946). Others were simply so mysterious and enigmatic that it was virtually impossible to judge their morality or motivations in any conclusive way, as with Hayworth's portrayal of the title character Elsa in Welles's *The Lady from Shanghai* (1947) or with Ava Gardner's Kitty Collins in *The Killers* (1946). In any case, the femme fatale was a figure of feminine strength and power seldom before seen in American film.

By the time of *Touch of Evil* and such later noir films by Fuller as *Shock Corridor* (1963) and *The Naked Kiss* (1964), film noir seemed to have descended into self-parody and thus perhaps to have run its historical course. It quickly returned in updated form, however, with the release of such films as **Robert Altman**'s *The Long Goodbye* (1973) and *Thieves like Us* (1974) and **Roman Polanski**'s *Chinatown* (1974), films that announced the arrival of a **"neo-noir"** style that self-consciously drew upon, but often played with, the codes and conventions of film noir. Lawrence Kasdan's *Body Heat* (1981) was another notable example of the emergent neo-noir form, which quickly spread to a number of genres, as in the noir-inflected style of the **science fiction** classic *Blade Runner* (1982). Since the success of that film, numerous sf films have drawn upon the noir visual style, as well as incorporating thematic elements typical of film noir, initiating a new subgenre known as "future noir" or "tech noir." Meanwhile, the dimly lit noir visual style has had a pervasive influence on recent American film and television.

Neo-noir films have generally been made in color, rather than the typical black-and-white of the film noir, though occasional examples of the neo-noir film, such as **Joel and Ethan Coen**'s *The Man Who Wasn't There* (2001), are in black and white, in this case as part of a meticulous recreation of the film noir visual style in a film that is set in 1947, the peak of the noir cycle in Hollywood. Other recent examples of neo-noir look back on the original noir films more thematically than visually, as in the case of David Lynch's *Mulholland Dr.* (2001), which looks back on earlier noir critiques of the Hollywood film industry, or David Cronenberg's *A History of Violence* (2005), which revisits the theme of a good man haunted by a dark past. *See also* SODERBERGH, STEVEN.

**FINCHER, DAVID (1964– ).** Like many directors of his generation, David Fincher began his career directing television commercials and **music** videos, including videos for such major artists as Madonna and the Rolling Stones. Fincher's debut as a director of feature films was a high-visibility project, *Alien³*, the third film in the *Alien* sequence of **science fiction** films. He next moved to the shocking thriller *Seven* (1995), showing some of the same flair for darkly atmospheric visual compositions that had marked *Alien³*.

Now clearly identified as a rising director to be reckoned with, Fincher next directed the relatively conventional (and disappointing) thriller *The Game* (1997), though this film still contained mind-bending twists that set it apart from most films of its genre. The impressive but controversial *Fight Club* (1999) did even more to challenge the audience's perceptions of reality (and of the film they were seeing). It also added substantially to Fincher's growing critical reputation. *Panic Room* (2002) and *Zodiac* (2007) were again relatively bland and conventional thrillers, but the decidedly unusual *The Curious Case of Benjamin Button* (2008) gained widespread attention and garnered Fincher his first **Academy Award** nomination for Best Director. He then followed with *The Social Network* (2010), something of a **biopic** about the founders of the online social networking site Facebook.

**FLEMING, RHONDA (1924– ).** Rhonda Fleming's first screen credit was for a supporting role in **Alfred Hitchcock**'s *Spellbound* (1945); she quickly followed with a supporting role in **Robert Siodmak**'s *The Spiral Staircase* in the same year, getting her career off to an impressive start. Afterward, while she never won an **Academy Award** nomination or soared to the highest levels of Hollywood stardom, Fleming established herself as a dependable and versatile actress with key roles in a number of important films. She also gained a reputation as a dazzling beauty whose flaming red hair helped to gain her the nickname "Queen of Technicolor."

Fleming was the femme fatale in the classic **film noir** *Out of the Past* (1947) and played the female leads opposite **Bob Hope** in *The Great Lover* (1949) and opposite **Bing Crosby** in *A Connecticut Yankee in King Arthur's Court* (1949). But it was in the 1950s when she truly hit her stride as a film actress, appearing in more than two dozen films in both supporting and leading roles. Among the most notable of these was her starring turn as Cleopatra in *Serpent of the Nile* (1953), along with female lead roles in **Fritz Lang**'s film noir *While the City Sleeps* (1956) and in the classic Western *Gunfight at the O.K. Corral* (1957).

By the 1960s, Fleming was relegated mostly to guest appearances on television, though she did have a major supporting role in film as late as 1980 in the comedy *The Nude Bomb*, a spin-off of the *Get Smart* television series.

**FLEMING, VICTOR (1889–1949).** If he had worked only in 1939, Victor Fleming would have been a historically important Hollywood director, for in that year he directed both *Gone with the Wind* (for which he won his only **Academy Award** for Best Director) and *The Wizard of Oz* (the latter with an assist from producer **Mervyn LeRoy**), two of the biggest films of all time. Nothing else in Fleming's career would approach the importance of those two films. Before 1939, however, he had directed more than three dozen films, beginning with **silent films** in 1919 and extending through important films of the 1930s such as *Treasure Island* (1934), *Reckless* (1935), and *Captains Courageous* (1937). He directed only a handful of films after 1939, including *Dr. Jekyll and Mr. Hyde* (1941), *Tortilla Flat* (1942), and *Joan of Arc* (1948). The latter film received a total of seven **Oscar** nominations, though Fleming was not nominated as the director; Fleming died soon after it was completed.

**FLYNN, ERROL (1909–1959).** Though **Douglas Fairbanks** had established the swashbuckling adventure as an important film genre in the **silent film** era, it was Errol Flynn who brought the genre to the pinnacle of its popularity with his roles in a number of such films in the 1930s. Flynn was born in Tasmania, Australia, and began his acting career in Great Britain, but it was his roles in such Hollywood films as *Captain Blood* (1935), *The Charge of the Light Brigade* (1936), and *The Adventures of Robin Hood* (1938) that made him an icon of onscreen adventure, known especially for his elaborate and fast-paced onscreen swordfights. He became a top box-office draw, even if he never received extensive critical acclaim for his acting.

Flynn remained a popular leading man through the 1940s, expanding into other genres, especially the **war film** and the **Western**. His films of the decade were increasingly secondary, however, and the 1950s saw his career descend even further as years of hard living took their toll on his health. He did, however, receive critical praise for his supporting role in *The Sun Also Rises* (1957) and for his lead role in *Too Much Too Soon* (1958).

**FONDA, HENRY (1905–1982).** Henry Fonda was one of Hollywood's most dependable and durable stars in a film acting career that spanned over 100 films and nearly 50 years. He had a starring role in his very first film, *The Farmer Takes a Wife* (1935), and seemed destined for major stardom by the time of **Fritz Lang**'s **film noir** *You Only Live Once* (1937), by which time he had begun to establish his trademark persona of a simple, ordinary, plainspoken individual, often caught up in troubles not of his own making. In 1939, he had one of his most memorable roles, as a young Abraham Lincoln (still plainspoken, but now quite eloquent) in **John Ford**'s *Young Mr. Lincoln* (1939). He then followed with what probably remains his best known role, that of Tom Joad in Ford's *The Grapes of Wrath* (1940), for which he won his first **Academy Award** nomination for Best Actor.

Though his acting career was interrupted when he enlisted for military service during World War II, Fonda still starred in a number of important films in 1940s, especially in **Westerns** such as **William Wellman**'s *The Ox-Bow Incident* (1943) and Ford's *My Darling Clementine* (1946) and *Fort Apache* (1948). He also starred in the **screwball comedy** *The Lady Eve* (1941) and in the drama *Daisy Kenyon* (1947). The first half of the 1950s was a slow period for Fonda on film, as he returned largely to stage acting. However, he returned to film in the latter half of the decade with some of his greatest roles, from his starring turn in the comedic **war film** *Mister Roberts* (1955), to his compelling performance as an innocent man wrongly accused in **Alfred Hitchcock**'s film noir *The Wrong Man* (1956), to his powerful performance in the legal drama *12 Angry Men* (1957), a film for which he also served as the producer, winning an **Oscar** nomination for Best Picture.

In his mid-50s as the 1960s began, Fonda began to move more into supporting roles, but he still continued to play important parts in films such as *Advise & Consent* (1962); *The Longest Day* (1962); *Spencer's Mountain* (1963); *The Best Man* (1964); *Fail-Safe* (1964); *In Harm's Way* (1965); *Madigan* (1968); and *Yours, Mine, and Ours* (1968). By the 1970s, however, Fonda's career was in decline, and he was relegated to roles in such films as the **horror** film *The Swarm* (1978) and the **science fiction disaster** film *The Meteor* (1979). He even performed in such films as the Italian horror film *Tentacoli* (1977), though *Midway* (1976), in which he had an important supporting role, was a fairly major war film.

Fonda did, however, make one last splash with his starring role opposite **Katharine Hepburn** in *On Golden Pond* (1981), for which the 76-year-old Fonda became the oldest recipient of the Academy Award for Best Actor in a Leading Role. It was his only competitive Oscar win, though he did receive a special honorary award in 1981. Hepburn won for Best Actress for the same film. Moreover, Henry's daughter, **Jane Fonda**, received an Oscar nomination for Best Supporting Actress for the same film, in which she played the daughter of Henry's character. Henry Fonda was also the father of actor Peter Fonda.

**FONDA, JANE (1937– ).** The daughter of distinguished film actor **Henry Fonda**, Jane Fonda established solid credentials of her own in the 1960s with her lead roles in such films as *Cat Ballou* (1965) and *Barefoot in the Park*

(1967). Her notorious role in the campy **science fiction** sex romp *Barbarella* (1968, directed by her then husband Roger Vadim) was something of a detour, though that film has become a **cult** classic. Fonda then achieved major critical success with her role in *They Shoot Horses, Don't They?* (1969), which gained her her first **Academy Award** nomination for Best Actress. Fonda then won that award with her next film, *Klute* (1971).

By this time, however, Fonda was becoming more famous for her political activism (especially for her opposition to the Vietnam War) than for her acting, and her trip to Hanoi in 1972, while making her an icon to many in the antiwar movement, also made her a widely despised figure whom many accused of treason. She did not have another major film role until the heist comedy *Fun with Dick and Jane* (1977). She quickly followed that, however, with a critically acclaimed (and **Oscar**-nominated) role in *Julia* (1977), followed by an Oscar-winning performance in the 1978 anti–Vietnam War film *Coming Home* (1978). Fonda continued her string of Oscar-nominated performances with *The China Syndrome* (1979) and *On Golden Pond* (1981), in which she played the daughter of the character played by Henry Fonda, who won a Best Actor Oscar for the role.

Fonda received an additional Best Actress Oscar nomination for *The Morning After* (1986). Other key films in which she has appeared include *Nine to Five* (1980), *Agnes of God* (1985), and *Stanley & Iris* (1990). Fonda then announced her retirement from film, though she continued to appear in the string of highly successful exercise videos that she made from 1982 to 1995. She returned to film acting in *Monster-in-Law* (2005) and starred in *Georgia Rule* (2007). In 1984, Fonda won an Outstanding Lead Actress Emmy for her performance in *The Dollmaker* (1984).

**FONTAINE, JOAN (1917– ).** Joan Fontaine made a number of relatively minor film appearances in the 1930s before finally bursting into stardom with her **Academy Award**–nominated lead role in *Rebecca* (1940), the first American film by British director **Alfred Hitchcock**. She then followed by winning the Best Actress **Oscar** for Hitchcock's *Suspicion* (1941), thus becoming the only actor who would win an Oscar under Hitchcock's direction.

Fontaine was also nominated for Best Actress for her performance in *The Constant Nymph* (1943). She had leading roles in such other major films of the 1940s as *Jane Eyre* (1944), *Ivy* (1947), and *The Emperor Waltz* (1948). Highlights of the 1950s included *Ivanhoe* (1952) and *Island in the Sun* (1957), but by this time Fontaine's performances were shifting more and more to stage and television. From the 1960s onward, she appeared primarily in guest spots on television, winning a Daytime Emmy nomination for a recurring role on the soap opera *Ryan's Hope* in 1980.

**FORD, GLENN (1916–2006).** The Canadian-born Glenn Ford moved to California at age eight and ultimately became one of Hollywood's most versatile actors in a career that spanned over a half a century, from 1937 to 1991. A likeable figure on the screen, he usually played sympathetic characters, often ordinary men thrust into extraordinary circumstances. Ford was still struggling to find a foothold in Hollywood when military service during World War II slowed his career. It was not, in fact, until after the war, in the classic **film noir** *Gilda* (1946), that he made his first real move toward stardom.

Ford was particularly prominent as a film actor in the 1950s and 1960s, playing important roles in film noirs such as *The Big Heat* (1953) and *The Blackboard Jungle* (1955), as well as in **comedies** such as *The Teahouse of the August Moon* (1956) and *The Courtship of Eddie's Father* (1963). He was particularly successful in **Westerns**, appearing in such films as *The Redhead and the Cowboy* (1951), *The Violent Men* (1955), *3:10 to Yuma* (1957), *Cimarron* (1960), and *Heaven with a Gun* (1969).

In the 1970s, Ford began to appear more and more on television, though his role as Jonathan Kent, the adopted father of Clark Kent, in *Superman* (1978) was prominent and well received. He continued to perform in film and on television until 1991, at which time his career was ended by ill health that made it impossible for him to work during the last years of his life.

**FORD, HARRISON (1942– ).** When he was cast as Han Solo in *Star Wars* (1977), Harrison Ford was a virtual unknown who had labored in Hollywood obscurity for more than a decade. The role, reenacted by Ford in the next two *Star Wars* film as well, propelled Ford to stardom, though between the second and third *Star Wars* films he also starred as Indiana Jones in *Raiders of the Lost Ark* (1981), probably his best-known role. He had also starred as android hunter Rick Deckard in *Blade Runner* (1982), perhaps his most important role in a **science fiction** film. After *Star Wars Episode VI: Return of the Jedi* (1983), Ford moved away from science fiction, concentrating on big-budget **action** thrillers (including several more Indiana Jones films) to become one of Hollywood's most bankable leading men.

In the drama *Witness* (1985), Ford scored his only **Academy Award** nomination for Best Actor; he also appeared in **Roman Polanski**'s stylish thriller *Frantic* (1988) and has appeared in a number of **comedies**, including *Working Girl* (1988) and *Sabrina* (1995). But his most effective roles have been in action thrillers, including *Patriot Games* (1992), *Clear and Present Danger* (1994), *Air Force One* (1997), *What Lies Beneath* (2000), and *Firewall* (2006).

**FORD, JOHN (1884–1973).** John Ford directed more than 60 **silent films** (most of which are now lost), performing with particular distinction as a director of **Westerns**. He then moved seamlessly into the sound era, becoming one of the most honored and prolific directors of the early years of the talkies. He gained significant critical attention as the director of the literary adaptation *Arrowsmith*, which scored four **Academy Award** nominations, including Best Picture, though Ford did not receive a Best Director nomination. However, he won the **Oscar** for Best Director for *The Informer* (1935), the first of his record four Best Director Oscars.

A master craftsman renowned for his efficiency on the set, Ford directed his last silent Western in 1926; he returned to that genre in 1939 with *Stagecoach*, a film that resuscitated the Western genre from low-budget oblivion and that made Ford protégé **John Wayne** a star. Ford also directed such notable films as *Drums along the Mohawk* and *Young Mr. Lincoln* in 1939. He was again nominated by the Academy as Best Director for *Stagecoach*, but did not win; he did, however, win that award for his next two films, *The Grapes of Wrath* (1940) and *How Green Was My Valley* (1941).

During World War II, Ford served in the U.S. Navy and made **documentaries** for the Department of the Navy. He returned to features in the **war film** *They Were Expendable* (1945), then returned to the Western with *My Darling Clementine* (1946), starring **Henry Fonda**, another Ford favorite. Indeed, Ford was known for repeatedly using the same actors (and crew) in his films, establishing an unusual continuity from one film to the next. In the following years, Ford had some failures, but scored solid successes with such films as *Wagon Master* (1950) and *The Quiet Man* (1952), which won Ford his fourth Best Director Oscar. Also important during these years was his so-called "Calvary Trilogy" of Westerns, comprising *Fort Apache* (1948), *She Wore a Yellow Ribbon* (1949), and *Rio Grande* (1950), all starring Wayne.

*Mogambo* (1953) was a major commercial success, but production of *Mister Roberts* (1955) was marred by Ford's battles with alcohol and with his star, Fonda; the film had to be completed by **Mervyn LeRoy**. Ford rebounded quickly, scoring what was perhaps his greatest artistic success with *The Searchers* (1956), a complex film that starred Wayne and that is now regarded as possibly the greatest Western ever made, though it was underappreciated at the time, failing at the box office and winning no Oscar nominations. It was, however, named the 12th greatest film of all time in the 2007 list compiled by the **American Film Institute** (AFI), 15 places ahead of *High Noon* (1952), the second highest-ranking Western. Not surprisingly, *The Searchers* was named the greatest Western of all time in the genre lists compiled by the AFI in 2008.

Among other things, *The Searchers* marked a clear turn away from Ford's earlier participation in Hollywood's stereotypical depiction of Native Americans as murderous savages. This trend culminated in the decidedly pro-Indian

*Cheyenne Autumn* (1964), his last Western. In between, *The Man Who Shot Liberty Valance* (1962) was another complex Western that is highly regarded by critics, though it did not deal with Native Americans.

Ford wrote a number of his films and produced even more of them. His films from *The Fugitive* (1947) to *The Sun Shines Bright* (1953) were produced through Ford's own independent production company, Argosy Pictures, which he founded with longtime associate Merian C. Cooper. In 1973, the American Film Institute gave Ford its first award for lifetime achievement.

**FOREMAN, CARL (1914–1984).** Though his early career was interrupted by service in the U.S. military during World War II, Carl Foreman had written a number of screenplays when he emerged as a leading Hollywood writer in 1949 with the scripts for *Home of the Brave* (a **war film** exploring racism in the U.S. military during the recent world war) and *Champion* (a **noir** boxing film rife with social commentary). The latter film won Foreman an **Academy Award** nomination for Best Screenplay. He received similar nominations for *The Men* (1950) and *High Noon* (1952), a classic **Western** that was seen by many as an allegory about the McCarthyite purges then sweeping Hollywood. Ironically, by the time this film had been released, Foreman himself had been called as a witness before the **House Un-American Activities Committee** (HUAC) because of the political content of his films and his earlier membership in the American Communist Party. He then joined the Hollywood **blacklist** after his refusal to name the names of others in Hollywood with radical political inclinations caused him to be labeled an unfriendly witness. However, he did received screen credit for writing *High Noon* despite the desire of some (including producer Stanley Kramer) that his name should be removed for political reasons.

Unable to work in Hollywood for the next six years, Foreman moved to England, where he scripted several films that were ultimately produced in Hollywood, though he was unable to receive screen credit because of the blacklist. His most important contribution during this period was as the co-writer (along with Michael Wilson, who was also blacklisted) of the joint British–American production *The Bridge on the River Kwai* (1957). This classic war film won the **Oscar** for Best Screenplay, though the blacklist prevented Foreman and Wilson from being named in the award, which instead went to Pierre Boulle, who wrote the novel on which the screenplay was based but who did not know English. The award was amended to include the names of Foreman and Wilson in 1984, by which time both had died.

Foreman received his first post-blacklist screen credit as the writer of *The Key* (1958), then received his first credit in a major Hollywood production for *The Guns of Navarone* (1961), which he both wrote and produced and for which he received Oscar nominations for Best Screenplay and as producer of the Best Picture. Foreman continued to live and work in Great Britain, however, where he was ultimately named a Commander of the Order of the British Empire for his contributions to film. He worked sparingly, even after his return from the blacklist, though he did write and produce such films as *The Victors* (1963), *Mackenna's Gold* (1969), and *Young Winston* (1972), for which he received his sixth Oscar nomination as a writer.

**FORMAN, MILOS (1932– ).** Milos Forman directed a number of films in his native Czechoslovakia in the 1960s, then moved to the United States after incurring political problems in his homeland related to the events there of 1968. He became a film professor at Columbia University, while also pursuing a career in American film that eventually saw him achieve success with the celebrated *One Flew over the Cuckoo's Nest* (1975), which won Forman an **Academy Award** as Best Director. It also won four other **Oscars**, including Best Picture, as well as an additional four nominations. He followed with high-profile films in *Hair* (1979) and *Ragtime* (1981), though neither was a huge success.

*Amadeus* (1984), however, won Forman another Best Director Oscar as well as the Best Picture Oscar, surpassing even *Cuckoo's Nest* with its 11 Oscar nominations and seven wins. *Valmont* (1989) and *The People vs. Larry Flynt* (1996) were less successful, though the latter did win Forman another Oscar nomination for Best Director. *Man on the Moon* (1999), a **biopic** about comic Andy Kaufman, won no Oscar nominations but did received considerable critical praise.

**FOSTER, JODIE (1962– ).** Jodie Foster had already made numerous appearances, mostly on television, when she leapt into the public eye for her role as a young prostitute in Martin Scorsese's *Taxi Driver* (1976). Her status as a rising young star was further enhanced with appearances in three more films that same year: *Bugsy Malone*, *Freaky Friday*, and *The Little Girl Who Lives Down the Lane*.

Foster's performance in *Taxi Driver* not only won her an **Academy Award** nomination for Best Supporting Actress at the tender age of 14, but also famously drew the attention of John Hinckley Jr., who claimed he was trying to impress Foster with his assassination attempt on U.S. President Ronald Reagan in 1981. Meanwhile, she cut back on her acting schedule in the early 1980s to attend Yale University, from which she graduated in 1985. She had several key roles in the late 1980s, most notably in the 1988 drama *The Accused*, for which she won the **Oscar** for Best Actress in a Leading Role. Her status as a full-blown adult star was then solidified with her role as FBI agent Clarice Starling in the thriller *Silence of the Lambs* (1991), which won her another Best Actress Oscar.

Foster also received a Best Actress Oscar nomination for her role in *Nell* (1994); she has also starred in such films as *Contact* (1997), *Anna and the King* (1999), *Panic Room* (2002), *Flightplan* (2005), *Inside Man* (2006), and *Nim's Island* (2008). In 1991, she made her directorial debut with *Little Man Tate*, in which she also acted. Other directorial credits include *Home for the Holidays* (1995) and *The Beaver* (2010).

**FOX, WILLIAM (1879–1952).** Born in Hungary as Vilmos Fried, William Fox was brought to the United States in his infancy; his name was changed at that time. One of the pioneers of the film industry, he entered the film business in 1904, when he purchased his first nickelodeon. By 1915, he had founded his own studio, the Fox Film Corporation. By 1929, this company had become one of the largest studios in Hollywood, also operating its own chain of theaters. In that year, however, Fox was badly injured in an automobile accident; soon afterward, the stock market crash largely wiped out Fox's personal wealth, leading to years of legal struggles over bankruptcy. His misfortunes continued into 1930, when he lost control of Fox Film in a hostile takeover. He lost the remainder of his interests in Fox Film (which had by this time merged with Twentieth Century Pictures to form **Twentieth Century Fox**) when his bankruptcy case was settled in 1936. In addition, he was convicted of perjury and attempted bribery of the judge during those proceedings, eventually serving six months in prison, after which he retired from the film business.

**FRANKENHEIMER, JOHN (1930–2002).** John Frankenheimer began his career by directing more than 100 episodes of various television series in the 1950s. He moved into feature film with *The Young Stranger* in 1957 and *The Young Savages* (1961), but made his big breakthrough in 1962, when he directed *All Fall Down* and *Birdman of Alcatraz*, both starring **Burt Lancaster**, with whom Frankenheimer would work regularly over the next several years. The year 1962 also saw the release of Frankenheimer's most admired film, *The Manchurian Candidate*, still considered one of the classics of Cold War culture. *Seven Days in May* (1964) was also an effective Cold War thriller, and Frankenheimer continued the peak period of his career with the World War II film *The Train* (1964), the **science fiction** film *Seconds* (1966, now a **cult** classic), and the auto-racing drama *Grand Prix* (1966).

Frankenheimer would never again achieve the success he enjoyed in the period 1962–1966. Films such as *The Extraordinary Seamen* (1967), *The*

*Horsemen* (1971), and *Black Sunday* (1977) were disappointing, both critically and commercially. By the time of the latter, Frankenheimer was battling a serious alcohol problem that curtailed his subsequent output, which included such films as *Prophecy* (1979), *52 Pick-Up* (1986), *Dead Bang* (1989), *The Fourth War* (1991), and *The Island of Dr. Moreau* (1996), which received some of the worst reviews of his career. *Ronin* (1998) fared a bit better with critics and audiences, but the most critically respected work of Frankenheimer's late career was done on television, particularly in a series of made-for-TV films that he did for the HBO cable network: *Against the Wall* (1994), *The Burning Season* (1994), and *Path to War* (2002). He also directed the successful TV movies *Andersonville* (1996) and *George Wallace* (1997) for the TNT network.

**FRANKENSTEIN.** *Frankenstein* (dir. **James Whale**, 1931) is one of the founding films of the modern **monster movie** genre and one of the most important films in the history of American cinema. It provided some of the best-known images of American popular culture in the 20th century and served as the prototype not only for the dozens of Frankenstein movies that would be made in subsequent years but of the mad scientist **horror** film in general. Based loosely on Mary Shelley's 1818 novel (but more directly on a 1930 stage adaptation of Shelley's novel by Peggy Webling), this story of the pitfalls of unbridled scientific inquiry expressed some of American society's anxieties over the rapid scientific and technological advances that had occurred in the first three decades of the 20th century. Constructed from the spare parts of dead bodies and brought to life with a jolt of electricity by scientist Henry Frankenstein (Colin Clive) and his hunchback assistant, Fritz (Dwight Frye), the monster turns out accidentally to have been given the brain of a hardened criminal, with predictably disastrous results. Still, though dangerous, the film's shambling monster (Boris Karloff) is mostly just confused and misunderstood.

As the film ends, the monster, having committed a series of killings, is pursued by an angry mob and apparently driven to a fiery death, though in Whale's 1935 sequel, *The Bride of Frankenstein* (considered by many the greatest of the *Frankenstein* movies), it would be revealed that the monster actually escaped death by taking refuge from the flames in a water-filled cellar. Meanwhile, the shots of the sinister, deranged townspeople who constitute the mob at the end of *Frankenstein* are among the most interesting in the film. These shots clearly contribute to the audience's potential sympathy for the monster, despite his malevolent appearance and grisly origins. A lone, one-of-a-kind individual whose only crimes have been either accidental or in self-defense, the monster becomes an odd sort of Byronic hero.

**FREEMAN, MORGAN (1937– ).** Though he had made occasional support-ing appearances in film, Morgan Freeman was primarily known prior to his fifties for his appearances in the children's educational television series *The Electric Company* (1971–1977), where he played a variety of characters, and for his regular role as Dr. Roy Bingham on the soap opera *Another World* (1982–1984). His film career began to pick up in the late 1980s, especially after his performances in *Street Smart* (1987) and *Driving Miss Daisy* (1989) won him **Academy Award** nominations for Best Supporting Actor and Best Actor in a Leading Role, respectively.

Freeman has since made numerous appearances, typically as a wise, fa-therly type, becoming one of the most distinguished African American actors of his generation. Among the many films in which he has appeared are *Unfor-given* (1992), *Seven* (1995), *Amistad* (1997) *Under Suspicion* (2000), *Batman Begins* (2005), *The Bucket List* (2007), and *The Dark Knight* (2008). Free-man has often played characters, such as police and military officials, who are figures of authority; he even played God in the comedies *Bruce Almighty* (2003) and *Evan Almighty* (2007). He won a second Best Actor nomination for *The Shawshank Redemption* (1994), then won a Best Supporting Actor **Oscar** for **Clint Eastwood**'s *Million Dollar Baby* (2004) and received Best Actor in a Leading Role Oscar nomination for his role as Nelson Mandela in Eastwood's *Invictus*.

**FULLER, SAMUEL (1912–1997).** Known as something of a B-movie au-teur, Samuel Fuller put his personal stamp on a number of low-budget genre films, making important contributions in the areas of the **war film**, **film noir**, and the **Western**. He began as a screenwriter with *Hats Off* (1936) and had several more screenwriting credits before transitioning into directing with the Western *I Shot Jesse James* (1949), which he also wrote. He then made his first major impression with his next film, the Korean War drama *The Steel Helmet* (1951). By 1953, he had made the film noir *Pickup on South Street*, thus quickly establishing himself in all three of the genres for which he would become known.

Other Westerns directed by Fuller include *The Baron of Arizona* (1950), *Run of the Arrow* (1957), and *Forty Guns* (1957). His war films include *Fixed Bayonets!* (1951), *Merrill's Marauders* (1962), and *The Big Red One* (1980), considered something of a classic of the genre. His greatest achievement, however, was probably in the genre of film noir, where he made such films as *House of Bamboo* (1955) and *Underworld U.S.A.* (1961) before making what are perhaps his two most famous films, *Shock Corridor* (1963) and *The Naked Kiss* (1964), over-the-top film noirs that are often considered as having ended the film noir cycle proper, while setting the stage for **neo-noir**.

Fuller's only major directorial credit between *The Naked Kiss* and *The Big Red One* was the thriller *Shark!* (1969); his last feature film was *Street of No Return* (1989) made in Portugal with French backing. Indeed, he moved to France (where he had a lofty reputation among critics as a major influence on the New Wave) in 1982 after a dispute with **Paramount Pictures** over the racial connotations of his film *White Dog* (1982), which would not be released in the United States until its DVD premiere in 2008. Fuller found this controversy insulting considering the antiracist messages of many of his films.

# G

**GABLE, CLARK (1901–1960).** Clark Gable had an undistinguished career with several minor roles in **silent film** in the 1920s, but began to get more prominent roles in the sound era in films such as *Red Dust* (1932), the first of several pairings with actress **Jean Harlow** that helped to make him the top leading man at **Metro-Goldwyn-Mayer** (MGM). He then achieved truly major stardom in the **screwball comedy** *It Happened One Night* (1934), for which MGM lent him out to **Columbia Pictures** and for which he received his only **Academy Award** for Best Actor. He followed with another Best Actor nomination back at MGM the following year for *Mutiny on the Bounty* (1935).

A string of successful but unremarkable films followed, until 1939, when he played his greatest role, that of Rhett Butler in *Gone with the Wind*, which gained him his third (and last) Best Actor **Oscar** nomination. That same year, Gable married actress **Carole Lombard**, beginning a period of great happiness that ended in early 1942 with her death in an air crash. That event and his own subsequent military service curtailed his acting career in the 1940s. Then his first postwar film, *Adventure* (1945), was a critical and commercial failure, signaling that his days as Hollywood's top male star were over.

The Madison Avenue **satire** *The Hucksters* (1947) was a critical success for Gable. However, by 1953 he left MGM in dissatisfaction with the roles he was being offered in their films, though his lead role helped to make **John Ford**'s *Mogambo* a box-office hit for MGM that year. Going out on his own did little to revitalize Gable's career. *Teacher's Pet* (1958) and *Run Silent Run Deep* (1958) were moderate successes, but the highlight of his late career might have been his last film, *The Misfits* (1961), which was not released until after his death. Gable received considerable critical praise for his performance in that film, which was also the last completed by his costar, **Marilyn Monroe**, before her own death. Thus, Gable's career as a leading man spanned the great era of Hollywood's blonde bombshells, from the rise of Harlow to the fall of Monroe.

In 1999, Gable was named the seventh greatest male film star of all time in a poll conducted by the **American Film Institute**.

**GANGSTER FILM.** Films about gangsters and organized crime became a sudden rage in the early 1930s when such films as *Public Enemy* (1931), *Little Caesar* (1931), and *Scarface* (1932) resonated with the experience of Depression-era audiences by depicting individuals forced to go outside the legal boundaries of the capitalist system in order to seek economic opportunity. In addition, these films, by depicting crime as an organized business, potentially suggested that there was a fundamentally criminal aspect to the operations of capitalism itself. Thus, though popular, these films immediately raised concerns in some circles, where it was felt that they were glamorizing their often violent criminal protagonists and making them heroes. Such concerns, along with the coming of the **Production Code**, led to a quick curtailment of the genre. Gangster films produced later in the 1930s, such as *Marked Woman* (1937) and *Angels with Dirty Faces* (1938), were less violent and focused more on the inevitable defeat of the gangsters; other films of the era, such as the boxing film *The Golden Boy* (1939), featured gangsters in secondary roles only.

Few gangster films were produced in the 1940s and 1950s, when the world of criminality was represented primarily through **film noir**. However, some noir films, such as **Raoul Walsh**'s *White Heat* (1949), could also be considered gangster films. Meanwhile, 1960s films such as *Bonnie and Clyde* (1967) did depict criminal gangs but were still more concerned with the depiction of their protagonists as individualist outlaws rather than as organized gangsters. The genre did not see a real resurgence until the appearance of **Francis Ford Coppola**'s *The Godfather* (1972), a landmark film that raised the gangster genre to the level of high art, while depicting its organized criminals as real human beings with considerable psychological depth and complexity. When Coppola followed with the equally successful *The Godfather: Part II* in 1974, it was clear that the genre had great potential both for the depiction of human drama and for social and political commentary, as the line between "legitimate" business and criminal enterprise was increasingly shown to be a fine one.

Other notable examples of gangster films followed, including Brian De Palma's ultraviolent *Scarface* (1983), a remake of the 1932 film that was only loosely related to the original, focusing on a Cuban-American drug lord. Sergio Leone's *Once upon a Time in America* (1984), a joint U.S.–Italian production, moved the emphasis back to Italian–American gangsters. De Palma himself followed with a comic version of the gangster film in *Wise Guys* (1986), which suggested that the conventions of the genre were familiar enough to make it a target of parody. This development, however, was not a sign of the demise of the genre but of the rise of a new subgenre of comic gangster films, which has since seen the release of such films as **Woody Allen**'s *Bullets over*

*Broadway* (1994), as well as *Analyze This* (1999) and *Analyze That* (2002), the latter two featuring gangster film icon **Robert De Niro**.

De Palma himself followed with *The Untouchables* (1987), focusing on the efforts of government agents to curb the power of gangster Al Capone during Prohibition, thus deviating from the tendency of gangster films to feature the gangsters (rather than their adversaries) as protagonists. In 1990, Coppola's *The Godfather: Part III* was generally considered inferior to the first two *Godfather* films, but Martin Scorsese's *Goodfellas* (1990), based on the story of a real-life gangster, was an outstanding addition to the genre. That same year, **Joel and Ethan Coen** put their own particular spin on the gangster genre with *Miller's Crossing*.

In 1991, *Bugsy* combined the gangster film with the **biopic** by relating the story of notorious gangster Bugsy Siegel. De Palma returned to the genre in 1993 with *Carlito's Way*, the same year in which De Niro directed *A Bronx Tale*, in which he plays a father struggling to keep his son out of the mob. **Quentin Tarantino's** *Pulp Fiction* (1994), focuses (among other things) on the activities of two mob hit men. Scorsese's *Casino* (1995) stars De Niro in a film that focuses on the gambling operations of the mob in Las Vegas. *Donnie Brasco* (1997), meanwhile, focuses on the efforts of an FBI infiltrator to gather evidence on the mob—and on the mixed sympathies experienced by the infiltrator as he becomes more and more immersed in the mob.

In the 21st century, the most prominent gangster drama has probably been the HBO television series *The Sopranos* (1999–2007). However, gangster films have remained an important Hollywood genre, appearing with great regularity. Recent films such as **Steven Soderbergh's** *Traffic* (2000) and Ted Demme's *Blow* (2001) have focused effectively on the organized drug trade, while the graphic-novel adaptation *Road to Perdition* (2002) is a sympathetic look at a war raged against the mob by a former mob hit man. Scorsese's *The Departed* (2006) is a particularly complex look at Irish–American gangsterism in Boston, while *Public Enemies* (2009) returns to the Depression era by focusing on official efforts to hunt down gangster John Dillinger.

**GARBO, GRETA (1905–1990).** Having begun her acting career in her native Sweden, Greta Garbo (born Greta Gustafsson), appeared in only a few American **silent films**, beginning with *Torrent* in 1926. Nevertheless, her subsequent roles in films such as *The Temptress* (1926), *Flesh and the Devil* (1926), *Love* (1927), and *The Mysterious Lady* (1928) made her one of silent film's greatest stars. Her transition to sound in *Anna Christie* (1930), marketed with the slogan "Garbo Talks," was a major media event, and she subsequently became a top star in the talkies as well, despite the fact that English was not her native language.

Both *Anna Christie* and *Romance*, also released in 1930s, won Garbo **Academy Award** nominations for Best Actress. Major roles in *Mata Hari* (1931) and *Grand Hotel* (1932) solidified her status and helped her to gain a new contract with **Metro-Goldwyn-Mayer** (MGM) that gave her greater creative control over her projects. Key films of the mid-1930s included *Anna Karenina* (1935) and *Camille* (1936), the latter of which is considered by many to be her finest performance. Her only other **Oscar** nomination for Best Actress, however, came for her performance in the **Ernst Lubitsch comedy** *Ninotchka* (1939), which attempted to make her seem more accessible after years playing mysterious, distant, and formidable women. The follow-up comedy *Two-Faced Woman* (1941) was panned by critics, however, and Garbo afterward retired from acting.

Despite appearing in relatively few films, Garbo's mystique was such that she was named the fifth greatest female screen legend of all time in a 1999 poll conducted by the **American Film Institute**.

**GARDNER, AVA (1922–1990).** After several relatively minor supporting roles, Ava Gardner drew major attention for her performance as sultry femme fatale Kitty Collins in the **film noir** *The Killers* (1946). She made subsequent major performances in *The Hucksters* (1947), *Show Boat* (1951), *The Barefoot Contessa* (1954), *Bhowani Junction* (1956), and *The Sun Also Rises* (1957), establishing herself as one of Hollywood's most glamorous leading ladies, a reputation enhanced by her own high-profile love life, especially her relationship with Frank Sinatra, to whom she was married from 1951 to 1957, but which began when he was married to someone else.

Gardner scored an **Academy Award** nomination for Best Actress for her role in *Mogambo* (1953) and worked frequently in the 1950s, though she began to appear less often in the 1960s. Her performance in *The Night of the Iguana* (1964), however, won critical praise. Gardner made high-profile appearances in *Earthquake* (1974) and *The Cassandra Crossing* (1976) in the 1970s, but health problems eventually curtailed her career. Most of her appearances of the 1980s were on television, and two strokes in 1986 ended her career.

Gardner was named the 25th greatest female screen legend of all time in a 1999 poll conducted by the **American Film Institute**.

**GARFIELD, JOHN (1913–1952).** Having been a member of New York's leftist Group Theater in the 1930s, John Garfield came to Hollywood and scored an immediate success, winning an **Academy Award** nomination for Best Supporting Actor in his first film, *Four Daughters* (1938). He then had his first starring role in 1939 in *They Made Me a Criminal*. This film established Garfield as a promising and charismatic actor, able to evince sympathy with his portrayals of ordinary men embattled by extraordinary circumstances. His dynamic performances in such films as *Juarez* (1939), *The Sea Wolf* (1941), and *Tortilla Flat* (1942) solidified his reputation as an electric onscreen presence, though all were in supporting roles.

Garfield had lead roles, however, in *The Postman Always Rings Twice* (1946), *Body and Soul* (1947), and *Force of Evil* (1948), a series of **film noirs** that made him one of the leading stars of that genre. *Body and Soul* also won him his only **Oscar** nomination for Best Actor in a Leading Role. Other key appearances by Garfield during the late 1940s were in *Humoresque* (1946) and *Gentlemen's Agreement* (1947). By the 1950s, however, his uncooperative testimony before the **House Un-American Activities Committee**, before which he had been called because of his liberal political activism, led him to be placed on the **blacklist**. Garfield's last film was another classic film noir, *He Ran All the Way* (1951). He died at the age of 39, due to a long-term heart condition reportedly exacerbated by the stress of the blacklisting.

**GARLAND, JUDY (1922–1969).** Young Judy Garland became a teen star in the 1930s, performing in a series of **musicals** that allowed her to showcase her considerable singing talents. She was especially successful in her teamings with young **Mickey Rooney**, which began with *Thoroughbreds Don't Cry* (1937) and eventually extended through a total of nine films, including such early efforts as *Love Finds Andy Hardy* (1938) and *Babes in Arms* (1939). It was also in 1939, of course, that Garland had her greatest role (and one of the greatest roles of all time) as Dorothy Gale in *The Wizard of Oz.*

In 1940, Garland received a special "juvenile" **Academy Award** for her performances of the previous year. During the next decade, she gradually transitioned to more adult roles in films such as *Meet Me in St. Louis* (1944), *Ziegfeld Follies* (1945), *Easter Parade* (1948), and *Summer Stock* (1950). She still performed primarily in musicals but honed her skills as a dramatic actress as well, eventually winning an **Oscar** nomination for Best Actress for the musical *A Star Is Born* (1954). She received a similar nomination for her dramatic performance in her next film, the nonmusical *Judgment at Nuremberg* (1961).

By this time, however, Garland's career was increasingly plagued by problems with drug addiction and with psychological instability, problems that had first become clear in 1947, when she had a nervous breakdown during the filming of *The Pirate* (1947). She provided the voice of the lead character in the animated film *Gay Purr-ee* (1962) and starred in *A Child Is Waiting* and *I Could Go on Singing*, both in 1963. In 1963 and 1964, she starred in a self-titled (and critically acclaimed) television variety show, though it was canceled after a single season due to low ratings.

Garland would never return to film and died of what was apparently an accidental drug overdose shortly after her 47th birthday in 1969. She was named the eighth greatest female screen legend of all time in a 1999 poll conducted by the **American Film Institute**.

**GARSON, GREER (1904–1996).** Though she had appeared on stage and even in early experimental television broadcasts in her native Great Britain, Greer Garson got a late start as a Hollywood film actress, making her first appearance in *Goodbye, Mr. Chips* (1939). That performance won her the first of what would ultimately be seven **Academy Award** nominations for Best Actress. She was one of the top stars for **Metro-Goldwyn-Mayer** (MGM) in the 1940s, wining consecutive **Oscar** nominations in the years 1942 to 1946 for her performances in *Blossoms in the Dust* (1941), *Mrs. Miniver* (1942, her only Oscar win), *Madame Curie* (1943), *Mrs. Parkington* (1944), and *The Valley of Decision* (1945).

Following this Oscar run, Garson's career began to decline, especially after the much-hyped *Adventure* (1945), in which she starred with a **Clark Gable** returning from war, was a disappointment. Her appearances were especially few and far between after her MGM contract expired in 1954. She did, however, have a few important later roles, such as her performance as Eleanor Roosevelt in *Sunrise at Campobello* (1960). Her last appearance in film was in *The Happiest Millionaire* (1967), though she continued to make occasional television appearances as late as 1982.

**GIBSON, MEL (1956– ).** Though born in Peekskill, New York, the actor and director Mel Gibson grew up in Australia, where he also started his acting career, getting his big break when he was cast in the lead role of the postapocalyptic film *Mad Max* (1979). Gibson's voice was actually dubbed in the United States release of that film, but he gained considerable attention with *Mad Max 2*, released in the United States as *The Road Warrior* (1981). By the time Gibson returned to the role for *Mad Max beyond Thunderdome* (1985), he had starred in several more mainstream films in both Australia and the United States and was rapidly becoming an important film star worldwide.

In 1987, Gibson costarred with Danny Glover in *Lethal Weapon*, an **action**-thriller with strong comic elements that helped to make Gibson a top box-office draw. That franchise has now extended through four successful films, the last in 1998. In addition, Gibson has starred in a wide variety of other films, from an adaptation of Shakespeare's *Hamlet* (1990), to the comic **Western** *Maverick* (1994), to the **romantic comedy** *What Women*

*Want* (2000), to the Vietnam **war film** *We Were Soldiers* (2002), to M. Night Shyamalan's alien invasion film *Signs* (2002).

Gibson made his debut as a film director with *The Man without a Face* (1993), in which he also starred. He followed by winning the **Academy Award** for Best Director for *Braveheart*, which also won the **Oscar** for Best Picture in 1995 and which he also produced and starred in. His next directorial effort was the box-office hit *The Passion of the Christ* (2004), which he did not act in. Controversy over the potentially anti-Semitic implications of that film and subsequent troubles in Gibson's private life have tarnished his image in recent years, though *Apocalypto* (2006), which he directed, was a moderate success.

**GILLIAM, TERRY (1940– ).** Terry Gilliam, widely known as the only American member of the British Monty Python comedy troupe, has also established a reputation as a visionary director of **fantasy** films with a unique visual style. Actually, he mixed the two careers in his first feature-length directorial effort, *Monty Python and the Holy Grail* (1975), a British film in which he also performed. His *Jabberwocky* (1977), based on the writings of Lewis Carroll, was also a British production in which he appeared. It was not really, however, until *Time Bandits* (1981) that he began to establish the quirky and outlandish visual style for which he would become known.

Gilliam returned to the Python group as the co-director of *The Meaning of Life* (1983), in which he played several parts. He then scored his first truly major critical success as a director with the offbeat dystopian film *Brazil* (1985), which has since become a **cult** favorite and for which Gilliam received an **Academy Award** nomination as the co-writer of the screenplay. *The Adventures of Baron Munchausen* (1988) was less successful, though it did extend Gilliam's reputation for spectacular visual style and inventive fantasy content. His next film, *The Fisher King* (1991), was probably his most mainstream, though it still contains fantasy elements; it was also his first American production. The **science fiction** film *Twelve Monkeys* (1995), which mixed time travel and postapocalyptic elements, was another American production and Gilliam's biggest box-office success.

Gilliam continued his string of American productions with *Fear and Loathing in Las Vegas* (1998), a decidedly strange narrative based on the writings of gonzo journalist Hunter S. Thompson. It was not a commercial success in theaters but has become a cult favorite on home video. *The Brothers Grimm* (2005) was an ambitious and expensive attempt based on the fairy-tale collections of the brothers of the title, but it was panned by critics and spurned by filmgoers. *Tideland*, released in the same year was a more low-key fantasy, a British–Canadian production that got little mainstream attention.

Gilliam has become notorious for his battles with the studios backing his films and for production problems during the making of his films. The latest of these was the death of actor Heath Ledger during the filming of *The Imaginarium of Doctor Parnassus* (2009). Ultimately, though, the film was completed, with **Johnny Depp**, Jude Law, and Colin Farrell pitching in to complete Ledger's role. Having renounced his U.S. citizenship in 2006, Gilliam is only allowed to spend a maximum of 30 days per year in the United States; beginning with *The Brothers Grimm*, he has returned to making his films in Great Britain and other European locations.

**GISH, LILLIAN (1893–1993).** Lillian Gish was one of the great stars of **silent film**, appearing particularly prominently in the films of director **D. W. Griffith**, including the groundbreaking *The Birth of a Nation* (1915), the much-respected *Intolerance* (1916), and the iconic *Way Down East* (1920). However, Gish did not transition well to the talkies and made only a few more film appearances before her performance in the **Western** *Duel in the Sun* (1946) won her an **Academy Award** nomination for Best Supporting Actress.

Gish made a number of television appearances in the early 1950s and 1960s. She occasionally appeared in films as well in these decades, most importantly in the **film noir** *Night of the Hunter* (1955). She made her last film appearance in *The Whales of August* (1987), thus giving her film career a span of 75 years. In 1999, Gish was named the 17th greatest female screen legend of all time in a poll conducted by the **American Film Institute**, the only actress on their list of 25 known primarily for her performances in silent film. She was given an honorary Academy Award in 1971 for her contributions to film.

**GODDARD, PAULETTE (1910–1990).** Born Pauline Marion Levy, Paulette Goddard had been a child fashion model and a Ziegfeld Girl when she began to appear in films in 1929, but she was relegated to a series of bit parts until her breakthrough starring role in **Charles Chaplin**'s *Modern Times* (1936). Apparently married to Chaplin from 1936 to 1942 (though some mystery surrounds the actual status of their relationship), she also appeared opposite him in *The Great Dictator* (1940), their only other film together. However, though she reportedly narrowly lost out in her bid to land the role of Scarlett O'Hara in *Gone with the Wind* (1939), she did appear in dozens of other films in various genres; she was particularly at home in **comedies**.

Goddard's star turn opposite **Bob Hope** in *The Cat and the Canary* (1939) was a particularly important landmark in her career. Other important roles of the 1930s included her appearances in such films as *The Young in Heart*

(1938) and *The Women* (1939), but it was in the 1940s that she reached her greatest stardom, appearing in some of **Paramount**'s most important productions of the decade and winning an **Academy Award** nomination for Best Supporting Actress for her role in *So Proudly We Hail!* (1943). Films in which Goddard starred in the decade included *Nothing but the Truth* (1941, again opposite Hope), *Reap the Wild Wind* (1942), *Standing Room Only* (1944), and *On Our Merry Way* (1948, opposite her then-husband Burgess Meredith).

Goddard's career cooled in the 1950s, though she did star in such films as *Babes in Bagdad* (1952) and *Sins of Jezebel* (1953). After *Charge of the Lancers* (1954) and the British film *The Stranger Came Home* (1954), her appearances in the latter half of the 1950s were on television. By this time, she was living primarily in Europe. In 1958 she married German novelist Erich Maria Remarque and lived with him in Europe until his death in 1970. During this time, she was essentially retired from acting, though she did appear in the television film *The Phantom* (1961) and the Italian film *Gli indifferenti* (1964). In 1972, she had a supporting role in the American television film *The Snoop Sisters*.

**THE GODFATHER.** Widely recognized as one of the greatest of all American films, *The Godfather* (dir. **Francis Ford Coppola**, 1972) was named the third greatest film of all time in a poll conducted by the **American Film Institute** (AFI) in 1998, then moved up to second on their 2007 update of the poll. Of a total of 11 **Academy Awards** that the film received, it won for Best Picture and Best Adapted Screenplay, while star **Marlon Brando** won the **Oscar** for Best Actor. The film combines an engaging narrative, impressive acting performances, and visual and thematic richness to produce a work that is both compelling and thought-provoking. Its story of the operations of the Corleone family adds to an already rich tradition of American **gangster films**, while making especially clear that this organized crime family of Italian immigrants is a quintessentially American phenomenon, pursuing the American dream in ways that are paradigmatic of modern capitalist society.

In addition to its own great commercial and critical success, *The Godfather* spawned an immediate sequel in *The Godfather: Part II* (1974), widely regarded as one of the finest sequels in film history. Together, these first two *Godfather* films narrate a story of capitalist modernization, as Don Vito Corleone (Brando) is replaced as leader of the Corleone crime family by his son Michael (Al Pacino), an Ivy League graduate and recent war hero, who oversees the conversion of the family's operations into a modern, efficient business. In this and other ways, *The Godfather* seeks in numerous ways to suggest parallels between the operations of organized crime and of capitalist business in general. Its gangsters continually refer to themselves as business-men, once pointing out that their goal is pure profit, because "after all, we're not communists." Moreover, the representation of the Corleone family as quite literally a *family* before its appropriation by capitalist modernization suggests a utopian vision of an older and more humane form of social orga-nization that is no longer available in contemporary America.

A third *Godfather* film, made reluctantly by Coppola in 1990, is widely considered to be less successful than the first two. However, *The Godfather: Part II* is a much respected film in its own right, coming in at 32nd on the AFI greatest films lists in both 1998 and 2007.

**GOLDEN AGE.** The term "Golden Age" or "Golden Age of Hollywood," is used to refer to the period from the beginning of the sound era to the 1950s, when the **major studios** maintained a firm control of the film industry and the film industry remained the dominant force in the American entertainment business. The Golden Age was marked not only by the emergence of distinc-tive "house" tendencies among the major studios (effectively establishing film "brands") but also by the emergence of a "star" system in which the studios promoted the careers of individual stars (whom they had under con-tractual control) for marketing purposes. The Golden Age was also marked by the evolution of an overall "classical style," also referred to as the "Hol-lywood style," that emphasized "invisible" editing designed to encourage audiences to suspend their disbelief and to become immersed in the narratives of the films they were watching, rather than focusing on technical aspects such as editing or camera placement and movement. Meanwhile, the content of Golden Age films was kept under strict control by a **Production Code** that emphasized wholesomeness and encouraged films to avoid troubling or controversial material.

The coming of television and shake-ups within the film industry due to the **Paramount Antitrust Case** of 1948 effectively brought an end to the Golden Age but also helped to bring about a more diversified American film industry with greater variety in both style and content of films. Thus, while 23 films on the **American Film Institute**'s 2007 list of the top 100 films of all time were released in the peak Golden Age decade of the 1930s and 1940s, 33 of the films on the list were released in the 1950s and 1960s, when the film industry was in corporate disarray.

**GOLDEN GLOBE.** The Golden Globe Awards are a series of awards given annually by the Hollywood Foreign Press Association in a variety of catego-ries related to both film and television. Because the Golden Globe winners are announced each year a few weeks before the **Academy Awards,** they are often regarded as a predictor of the winners of those more prestigious awards, though the Golden Globes also have something of a reputation for eccentricity.

First given in 1944, the Golden Globe now includes such film categories as Best Director, Best Supporting Actor, Best Supporting Actress, and Best Screenplay, much like the Academy Awards. However, in the categories of Best Picture, Best Actor, and Best Actress, the Golden Globes include dual awards, one for drama and one for **musical** or **comedy**. The most prestigious of the Golden Globe awards is the **Cecil B. DeMille** Award for Lifetime Achievement in Motion Pictures, given annually since 1952 (except 1976).

Although the award recognizes all categories of achievement, it has tended to give a certain preference to actors. DeMille himself was the first winner of the award, to be followed by such luminaries as **Walt Disney** (1953), **Fred Astaire** (1961), **John Wayne** (1966), **Charlton Heston** (1967), **Kirk Douglas** (1968), **Alfred Hitchcock** (1972), **Henry Fonda** (1980), **Laurence Olivier** (1983), **Paul Newman** (1984), **Audrey Hepburn** (1990), **Jack Nicholson** (1999), **Al Pacino** (2001), **Steven Spielberg** (2009), and **Martin Scorsese** (2010).

**GOLDMAN, WILLIAM (1931– ).** William Goldman's second screenplay, for *Harper* (1966), won a Best Screenplay award from the Mystery Writers of America. In addition, he was already a successful Broadway playwright and novelist who had had two of his own novels adapted (by others) to film when he burst into true prominence as a screenwriter with own third screenplay, for *Butch Cassidy and the Sundance Kid* (1969), which won him the **Academy Award** for Best Original Screenplay. Goldman's next screenplay, for *The Hot Rock* (1972), drew little attention, but the one after was for *The Stepford Wives* (1975), which became one of the most discussed films of the 1970s, even if it did not receive extensive critical acclaim.

Now firmly established as a top Hollywood screenwriter, Goldman subsequently scripted a number of important films, including *All the President's Men* (1976), for which he won a second Best Screenplay **Oscar**. Other notable films for which Goldman wrote the screenplay include *Marathon Man* (1976), *A Bridge Too Far* (1977), *Heat* (1986), *The Princess Bride* (1987), *Misery* (1990), *Chaplin* (1992), *Absolute Power* (1997), and *Dreamcatcher* (2003).

**GOLDWYN, SAMUEL (1879–1974).** Producer and executive Samuel Goldwyn was a principal driving force behind the founding of several Hollywood studios, and indeed of the Hollywood film industry itself. Born Schmuel Gelbfisz in Warsaw, Poland, he arrived in the United States in 1898. After initially working as a salesman and sales executive in the garment industry, he moved into the film industry by 1913 when he and partner Jesse L. Lasky hired a young **Cecil B. DeMille** to direct films for the company that would eventually evolve into **Paramount Pictures**.

Having left this original partnership, Gelbfisz (Goldfish) formed a second company with Broadway producers Edgar and Archibald Selwyn in 1916. The company, combining the names of its founders, was called Goldwyn Pictures Corporation; Gelbfisz, meanwhile, legally changed his name to Samuel Goldwyn to match the name of the company. He was, however, soon forced out of the company by his partners, going on to found his own self-named company, Samuel Goldwyn, Inc. This new company then opened its own Samuel Goldwyn Studio in Hollywood by renting the facilities of the existing studio founded by **silent film** legends **Mary Pickford** and **Douglas Fairbanks**. They then expanded by acquiring the facilities of the failing **Triangle Film Corporation**.

The Goldwyn company produced some of the most successful films in Hollywood during the 1920s and 1930s, all of which were released through **United Artists**, the company of which Pickford and Fairbanks had been founding partners. Of the dozens of films produced by Goldwyn during this period, films such as *Arrowsmith* (1931), *Dodsworth* (1936), *Dead End* (1937), and *Wuthering Heights* (1939) received **Academy Award** nominations for Best Picture, though none of them won the award.

Beginning with *The Little Foxes* (1941), another **Oscar** nominee for Best Picture, Goldwyn's films were distributed by **RKO Radio Studios**. One of Goldwyn's films distributed through RKO, *The Best Years of Our Lives* (1946), finally won the Oscar for Best Picture at the 1947 award ceremonies, during which Goldwyn himself received the **Irving G. Thalberg** Memorial Award for his lifetime contributions to the film industry.

Goldwyn scaled back his work as a producer in the 1950s, during which his most notable productions were a pair of unusual **musicals**, *Guys and Dolls* (1955) and *Porgy and Bess* (1959). He retired from active work as a producer after the failure of the latter film. However, his name remains prominent in Hollywood thanks to the ongoing operations of the Samuel Goldwyn Company, founded by Goldwyn's son Samuel Jr. in 1979. This company produced numerous **independent films** of its own, as well as acquiring the rights to all of the elder Goldwyn's previous productions before itself being acquired by **Metro-Goldwyn-Mayer** (MGM) in 1997. The younger Goldwyn then founded Samuel Goldwyn films, which began producing its own independent films in 2001.

**GRAHAME, GLORIA (1923–1987).** After beginning her career in *Blonde Fever* (1944) and *Without Love* (1945), Gloria Grahame had what would ultimately be one of her most important roles in **Frank Capra**'s *It's a Wonderful Life* (1946), though that film was not a great success on its initial release. Her first major critical recognition came in the **film noir** *Crossfire* (1947), for which she received an **Academy Award** nomination for Best Supporting Actress. She followed with a series of successful roles in noir films such as *In a Lonely Place* (1950), *Sudden Fear* (1952), and *The Big Heat* (1953), though her greatest critical recognition came for *The Bad and the Beautiful* (1952), in which she won the Best Supporting Actress **Oscar**.

Grahame had a lead role in the classic **musical** *Oklahoma!* (1955) and got some good reviews for her lead performance in the **war film** *The Man Who Never Was* (1956), then returned to film noir in *Odds against Tomorrow* (1959). Most of her roles from 1960 onward, however, were on television. When she did have starring roles in film it was in minor films, such as the B-grade **horror** movies *Blood and Lace* (1971) and *Mansion of the Damned* (1976).

**GRANT, CARY (1904–1986).** Born in Great Britain, Archibald Leach went to Hollywood in 1931, where he adopted the professional name of Cary Grant and subsequently became one of Hollywood's most durable and versatile leading men. Handsome and debonair, but agile and athletic, Grant played a variety of memorable roles, getting off to a fast start as a leading man opposite **Marlene Dietrich** in *Blonde Venus* (1932) and opposite Mae West in *She Done Him Wrong* (1933) and *I'm No Angel* (1933). In those films, however, he was somewhat overshadowed by his better-known leading ladies, and his career did not really take off until he starred in his first **comedies**, *Topper* and *The Awful Truth*, in 1937. Subsequently, he would become one of the top comic actors in Hollywood, especially in **screwball comedies** such as *Bringing Up Baby* (1938), *His Girl Friday* (1940), *The Philadelphia Story* (1940), *Arsenic and Old Lace* (1944), and *Monkey Business* (1952).

Other key comedies in which Grant starred include the adventure film *Gunga Din* (1939); the **romantic comedies** *Indiscreet* (1958), *That Touch of Mink* (1962), and *Father Goose* (1964); and the military comedy *Operation Petticoat* (1959). On the other hand, many of his most memorable roles were in thrillers directed by **Alfred Hitchcock**, including *Suspicion* (1941), *Notorious* (1946), *To Catch a Thief* (1955), and *North by Northwest* (1959).

Grant's only two **Academy Award** nominations for Best Actor came for *Penny Serenade* (1941) and *None but the Lonely Heart* (1944), two films that would not ultimately become among his best known. He never won that award, partly because he was the first major Hollywood star to go independent, controlling his own career rather than working under contract to studios. He did, however, receive an honorary award in 1970 for his long acting career. In a

1999 poll conducted by the **American Film Institute**, Grant was named the second greatest male film star of all time.

**THE GRAPES OF WRATH.** *The Grapes of Wrath* (dir. **John Ford**, 1940) is one of the rare examples in American cultural history of a truly classic film that is an adaptation of one of the classics of American literature, in this case John Steinbeck's 1939 novel of the same title. Meanwhile, this timely late-Depression work is also unusual among major works of American cinema in its relatively unstinting look at the realities of the lives of America's poor. Granted, the film excises or tempers many of the book's more radical political messages, but the ongoing popularity of the film has also helped the book to find new readers over the decades.

Like the novel, the film follows the members of the impoverished Joad family as they lose their farm in dust-bowl Oklahoma, then travel cross-country, seeking opportunity in the promised land of California. The film's central figure is young Tom Joad (**Henry Fonda**), who returns at the beginning of the film from a prison sentence unjustly received when he killed a man in self-defense, setting the stage for a thorough indictment of the current social and economic system that runs throughout the film. Indeed, after the family suffers exploitation and abuse in California, Tom ends the film again on the run from the law. The film's most famous image of working-class perseverance and resistance (and one of the most famous scenes in American film history) occurs as Tom bids good-bye to his mother (played by Jane Darwell) before taking flight. Tom vows to devote himself to the fight for justice, telling his mother in a famous scene that, while she may never again see him in the flesh, he will be symbolically present wherever there is injustice or resistance to it. "I'll be there," he tells her. "Wherever there's a fight so hungry people can eat, . . . whenever there's a cop beating a guy, I'll be there."

The first volume of Ford's "poor folks" trilogy (which continued with *How Green Was My Valley* and *Tobacco Road*, both released in 1941), *The Grapes of Wrath* is by far the best and most important film of the three, both for its deft use of imagery and narrative and for its genuine sympathy with those who have suffered from the abuses of capitalism in one of its darkest hours. The film was nominated for **Academy Awards** in all of the major categories, including Best Picture, Best Actor (Fonda), and Best Screenplay (**Nunnally Johnson**). However, it won only for Best Director and Best Supporting Actress (Darwell).

**GREEN, JOHNNY (1908–1989).** Though he also had an extensive career as a songwriter, composer, and conductor outside of film, Johnny Green had one of the most distinguished composing careers in the history of Hollywood.

The recipient of a total of 12 **Academy Award** nominations for Best Original Score, he won that award four times: for *Easter Parade* (1948), *An American in Paris* (1951), *West Side Story* (1961), and *Oliver!* (1968). However, his single best-known piece of "film" **music** may be for the jazzy "Body and Soul," which he co-wrote in 1930 but which was used as the theme to the 1947 **film noir** of the same title and which has since been used in numerous other films as well.

Green served as the music director at **Metro-Goldwyn-Mayer** (MGM) from 1949 to 1959, contributing to the music for numerous films during that period, though the orchestrations for the music he wrote for films were usually done by someone else. He conducted the orchestras that recorded the music for numerous films as well.

**GRIFFITH, D. W. (1875–1948).** One of the most legendary directors in Hollywood history, D. W. Griffith is credited with virtually having invented the feature-length film narrative in such early works as *The Birth of a Nation* (1915) and *Intolerance* (1916). He was, however, also an incredibly prolific (and innovative) director of shorter **silent films**, of which he had directed more than 500 by the time he made *Birth of a Nation*. That film is still much admired for its advances in cinematic technique and was a commercial hit, but was controversial even at the time for its racist implications and its glorification of the Ku Klux Klan. *Intolerance* can be seen as something of an answer to criticism of the politics of *Birth of a Nation*, though it was a long and complex work that did not do well commercially and that many found simply confusing. However, while *Birth of a Nation* did not appear in the 2007 list of the 100 greatest films of all time compiled by the **American Film Institute**, *Intolerance* was ranked 47th.

Griffith's films through *Brute Force* (1914) were made for **Biograph**, one of the pioneering companies of the film industry. However, his desire to make feature-length films (and the company's lack of commitment to such films) led him to leave Biograph to form the Mutual Film Corporation, meanwhile founding, with Harry Aitken, Reliance-Majestic Studios as the production company for Mutual's films. The financial failure of *Intolerance*, however, contributed to the dissolution of the production agreement with Aitken. Griffith moved on, eventually founding **United Artists** in 1919, along with actors **Charles Chaplin**, **Douglas Fairbanks**, and **Mary Pickford**—in the hope of giving artists greater creative control over their work.

*Broken Blossoms* (1919) and *Way Down East* (1920) were successes with United Artists, but the box-office failure of *Isn't Life Wonderful* (1924) led Griffith to leave the company. He directed several more silent films and two unsuccessful sound films, *Abraham Lincoln* (1930) and *The Struggle* (1931).

At that point, his career as a director was over; he thus never really made a direct impact on the talkies, but his influence on other directors in the sound era was immense.

**GRINDHOUSE.** Grindhouse cinemas were urban theaters, popular mostly in the 1970s, known for specializing in ultraviolent exploitation films of various kinds, including slasher and other **horror** films, **blaxploitation** films, and **sexploitation** films. Grindhouse theaters were named for their similarity to earlier burlesque theaters, where strippers often performed "bump and grind" routines. They were typically older single-screen theaters that fell out of the mainstream as multiplexes became more popular. Though many grindhouse films often displayed as double or even triple features and were of low quality, relying on bizarre or sensational content to attract audiences, many of the films exhibited in such theaters have since become **cult** classics. The wide availability of movies on home video or cable beginning in the 1980s essentially eliminated the market for grindhouse theaters, which have since virtually disappeared, sometimes becoming objects of nostalgia, as in the 2007 "Grindhouse" double feature directed by **Quentin Tarantino** and **Robert Rodriguez.**

**HACKMAN, GENE (1930– ).** Gene Hackman had appeared only in minor film roles and in guest spots on television when his role as Buck Barrow in *Bonnie and Clyde* (1967) thrust him into the Hollywood spotlight, winning him an **Academy Award** nomination for Best Supporting Actor. He garnered the same nomination for *I Never Sang for My Father* (1970), then transitioned mostly into starring roles, though he has continued to appear in supporting roles throughout his career. He became especially popular as a lead actor after his performance in *The French Connection* (1971) won him the **Oscar** for Best Actor.

Other important films featuring Hackman in the 1970s included *The Conversation* (1974), *Night Moves* (1975), *A Bridge Too Far* (1977), and *Superman* (1978), in which he played arch-villain Lex Luthor. He reprised that role in *Superman II* (1980) and had a supporting role in *Under Fire* (1983), then starred in such films as *Uncommon Valor* (1983) and *Hoosiers* (1986) before winning another Best Actor Oscar nomination for his role in *Mississippi Burning* (1988).

Hackman remained a popular actor moving into the 1990s (and into his sixties), especially after his performance in the **Western** *Unforgiven* (1992) won him a Best Supporting Actor Oscar, propelling him into roles in other Westerns, such as *Wyatt Earp* (1994) and *The Quick and the Dead* (1995). Other memorable films of the 1990s featuring Hackman included *The Firm* (1993), *Get Shorty* (1995), *Absolute Power* (1997), and *Enemy of the State* (1998). *Under Suspicion* (2000), *Heist* (2001), and *The Royal Tenenbaums* (2001) got Hackman off to a fast start in the 21st century, but, after the unsuccessful comedy *Welcome to Mooseport* (2004), he announced his retirement from acting.

**HAGGIS, PAUL (1953– ).** The Canadian-born Paul Haggis spent more than 20 years as a writer and producer for television before he turned to feature film with one of the most auspicious beginnings of any screenwriter in history. Though Haggis had written the screenplay for *Red Hot* (1993), an obscure Canadian film, his first Hollywood screenplay was for **Clint**

**Eastwood**'s *Million Dollar Baby* (2004), for which Haggis won the 2005 **Academy Award** for Best Adapted Screenplay. That film, meanwhile, won the **Oscar** for Best Picture. Then, his second screenplay, for *Crash* (2004), won the Oscar for Best Original Screenplay, making Haggis the first screenwriter to win writing Oscars in back-to-back years for films that also won Best Picture Oscars. Furthermore, Haggis took home the Best Picture Oscar as the producer of *Crash* and received a Best Director Oscar nomination for that film as well, in his Hollywood directorial debut (though he had also directed *Red Hot*).

Haggis has remained a top name in Hollywood ever since his debut there. He wrote the screenplay for the **romantic comedy** *The Last Kiss* (2006). That same year, he also co-wrote the screenplays for the James Bond film *Casino Royale* and for Eastwood's World War II films *Flags of our Fathers*, while writing the original story for Eastwood's *Letters from Iwo Jima*, the latter of which earned Haggis another Oscar nomination for original writing. In 2007, he wrote, directed, and produced *In the Valley of Elah*. He then co-wrote the screenplay for a second Bond film, *Quantum of Solace* (2008).

**HALL, CONRAD L. (1926–2003).** Conrad L. Hall was one of the most distinguished cinematographers in Hollywood history in a career that spanned more than four decades and a total of 10 **Academy Award** nominations (including three wins) for Best Cinematography. Hall came to prominence in the mid-1960s, winning Academy Award nominations as the cinematographer for such films as *Morituri* (1965), *The Professionals* (1966), and *In Cold Blood* (1967). He then won his first **Oscar** for *Butch Cassidy and the Sundance Kid* (1969).

Hall shot a number of mainstream commercial films in the 1970s, but won only one Oscar nomination in that decade, for *The Day of the Locust* (1975). After a 10-year hiatus from 1977 to 1987, he returned to work as a cinematographer and did some of his best work in his sixties and seventies. He received Best Cinematography Oscar nominations for *Tequila Sunrise* (1988), *Searching for Bobby Fischer* (1993), and *A Civil Action* (1998). He then capped off his career by winning Best Cinematography Oscars for *American Beauty* (1999) and *Road to Perdition* (2002). In 2003, he was named one of the 10 most influential cinematographers of all time in a poll conducted by the International Cinematographers Guild.

**HANKS, TOM (1956– ).** After gaining considerable exposure as the wacky sidekick in the television sitcom *Bosom Buddies* (1980–1982) and in guest spots on other television series, Tom Hanks gained immediate attention as a comic actor in film for his lead role in the **romantic comedy** *Splash* (1984).

He followed with lead roles in a string of light **comedies**, including *Bachelor Party* (1984) and *The Money Pit* (1986), meanwhile proving that he could play dramatic roles with his performance in *Nothing in Common* (1986).

Hanks scored a major success in the fantasy *Big* (1988), which won him his first **Academy Award** nomination for Best Actor in a Leading Role. He then starred in a string of indifferent films before his performances in *A League of Their Own* (1992) and *Sleepless in Seattle* (1993) again made him a top leading man in Hollywood comedies. It was, however, with his **Oscar**-winning dramatic role as a lawyer afflicted with AIDS in *Philadelphia* (1993) that Hanks truly came into his own as an actor, especially after he followed with his second consecutive Best Actor Oscar for *Forrest Gump* (1994).

Hanks provided the voice of the cowboy doll Woody in *Toy Story* (1995) and *Toy Story 2* (1999), meanwhile starring in the critically acclaimed *Apollo 13* (1995) and winning still another Best Actor Oscar nomination for his performance in **Steven Spielberg**'s **war film** *Saving Private Ryan* (1998), beginning an association that later saw Hanks and Spielberg work together as executive producers of the television miniseries *Band of Brothers* (2001), also about World War II. Hanks also directed one episode of *Band of Brothers*, having earlier helped with the direction of the miniseries *From the Earth to the Moon* (1998), on which he served as executive producer, and directing the feature film *That Thing You Do* (1996).

Hanks's career as a director has never taken off, but he has had a successful career as the producer or executive of such films as *My Big Fat Greek Wedding* (2002), *The Polar Express* (2004), *The Ant Bully* (2006), *Charlie Wilson's War* (2007), *Mamma Mia!* (2008), and *Where the Wild Things Are* (2009). In the meantime, he has continued his successful acting career. *You've Got Mail* (1998) was a successful follow-up to *Sleepless in* Seattle, while Hanks won his fifth Best Actor Oscar nomination for *Cast Away* (2000).

Key films in which Hanks has starred in recent years include *Road to Perdition* (2002), Spielberg's *Catch Me if You Can* (2002) and *The Terminal* (2004), *The Da Vinci Code* (2006), and *Angels & Demons* (2009), as well as a return to provide the voice of Woody in *Toy Story 3* (2010). Hanks is immensely likeable on the big screen, and many of his films have been major box-office hits; indeed, with a lifetime cumulative gross of over $3.5 billion, he is the leading career box-office draw of all time.

**HARLOW, JEAN (1911–1937).** After a slow start in film, Jean Harlow became an international sensation for her role in *Hell's Angels* (1930). She made another important appearance in *The Public Enemy* (1931), and was becoming prominent enough that the film *Platinum Blonde* (1931) was retitled to emphasize that it featured Harlow and her trademark platinum blonde hair.

After her contract was bought by **Metro-Goldwyn-Mayer** (MGM) in 1932, Harlow began to get better roles and was propelled into a brief but spectacular stint as a superstar, beginning with such initial films as *Red-Headed Woman* (1932, for which she wore a wig) and the critically praised *Red Dust* (1932), in which she began to show skills as a comic actress.

*Red Dust* was Harlow's first film with **Clark Gable**, and the two proved to be a particularly successful team, also appearing together in *Hold Your Man* (1933), *China Seas* (1935), and *Wife vs. Secretary* (1936). In 1937, shortly after 26th birthday, Harlow collapsed on the set of *Saratoga* (1937), which she was also filming with Gable. She died soon afterward, under somewhat mysterious circumstances.

Harlow partly played herself when she starred as a sexy film actress in *Bombshell* (1933); she is widely regarded as Hollywood's first great "blonde bombshell" and is partly responsible for establishing the trend toward blonde actresses as Hollywood sex symbols.

**HAWKS, HOWARD (1896–1977).** Though he began his career in the late days of **silent film**, it was in the sound era that Howard Hawks established himself as one of the directors who helped to define the new medium of sound film. A master of technique renowned for working quickly and efficiently, he made important contributions in a variety of genres, beginning with the **gangster film** *Scarface* (1932) and ending with the **John Wayne Westerns** *Rio Bravo* (1959), *El Dorado* (1966), and *Rio Lobo* (1970), all three of which are essentially variations on the same film. In between, Hawks made especially important contributions to the development of the **screwball comedy**, directing such films as *Bringing Up Baby* (1938), *His Girl Friday* (1940), *Ball of Fire* (1941), and *Monkey Business* (1952).

Other important films directed by Hawks include *Twentieth Century* (1934), *Only Angels Have Wings* (1939), *To Have and Have Not* (1944), *The Big Sleep* (1946), *Red River* (1948), and *Gentlemen Prefer Blondes* (1953). He also helped out with the direction of the **science fiction** classic *The Thing from Another World* (1951), though he did not receive screen credit. Hawks's only **Academy Award** nomination for Best Director came for the **biopic/war film** *Sergeant York* (1941). However, he was given an honorary award by the **Academy of Motion Pictures Arts and Sciences** in 1975 in recognition of his distinguished creative contributions to world cinema.

**HAYWARD, SUSAN (1917–1975).** A young New York fashion model by the name of Edythe Marrenner traveled to Hollywood in 1937, hoping to land the much-coveted role of Scarlett O'Hara in the upcoming *Gone with the Wind* (1939). She failed to do so, but did win a contract with **Warner Bros.**, changing her professional name to Susan Hayward and subsequently playing a series of bit parts until 1939, when she moved to **Paramount** and was given an important supporting role in *Beau Geste* (1939). During World War II, she continued to play substantial supporting parts, and even moved into starring roles in films such as *The Hairy Ape* (1944). Then, she received an **Academy Award** nomination for her leading role in *Smash-Up: The Story of a Woman* (1947), and stardom was achieved at last.

Hayward also won Best Actress **Oscar** nominations for *My Foolish Heart* (1949), *With a Song in My Heart* (1952), and *I'll Cry Tomorrow* (1955), but did not win the award until her fifth (and final) nomination, for *I Want to Live!* (1958). She remained busy through the 1950s, but her roles began to decline in quality and frequency in the 1960s. She appeared in both *Valley of the Dolls* and *The Honey Pot* in 1967, but then did not appear onscreen again until 1972, when she appeared in a minor role in *The Revengers* (1972) and starred in two television movies, *Heat of Anger* and *Say Goodbye, Maggie Cole*. The latter was intended as the pilot for a series, but by this time Hayward had been diagnosed with the brain cancer that would take her life three years later, and she made no further appearances as an actress.

**HAYWORTH, RITA (1918–1987).** Rita Hayworth was one of Hollywood greatest sex symbols of the 1940s, when her acting career was at its peak. Actually, Hayworth (born Carmen Cansino) appeared in nearly three dozen films in the 1930s, mostly B-movies in which she had secondary roles, though her important secondary performance in **Howard Hawks**'s *Only Angels Have Wings* (1939) helped her to begin to move into better roles. A talented dancer, Hayworth was well equipped to star in **musicals** such as *Music in My Heart* (1940) and *Cover Girl* (1944, with **Gene Kelly**), even though her singing voice was dubbed.

It was, in fact, Hayworth's dancing with **Fred Astaire** in *You'll Never Get Rich* (1941) that propelled her to stardom. She again danced with Astaire in *You Were Never Lovelier* (1942) and was also effective in comedies such as **Raoul Walsh**'s *The Strawberry Blonde* (1941), but it was in the **film noir** *Gilda* (1946), in which she also performed musically, that she achieved her greatest success as a steamy onscreen presence. She also had a prominent femme fatale role in *The Lady from Shanghai* (1947), opposite director **Orson Welles**, to whom Hayworth was married from 1943 to 1948.

In 1949, Hayworth married Prince Aly Khan of Pakistan and retired from film until after their 1951 divorce. She successfully returned to film with *Affair in Trinidad* (1952), her first film in four years, then followed with additional hits in *Salome* (1953) and *Miss Sadie Thompson* (1953), after which she had another four-year hiatus from film due to her tumultuous personal life. She made another return to film in 1957, with *Fire Down Below* (1957) and the musical *Pal Joey* (1957), with **Frank Sinatra**. However, she, never quite recovered the momentum of her earlier career, though her performance in *Circus World* (1964) gained considerable critical praise. She appeared in only a few more films, ending with *The Wrath of God* (1972).

In a 1999 poll conducted by the **American Film Institute**, Hayworth was named the 19th greatest female screen legend of all time.

**HECHT, BEN (1894–1964).** Also a successful playwright and novelist, Ben Hecht was one of the most prolific and respected screenwriters in Hollywood history, producing an output that earned him the nickname "The Shakespeare of Hollywood." Hecht began writing for films at the very beginning of the sound era, debuting by writing the story and screenplay for **Josef von Sternberg**'s **gangster film** *Underworld* (1927), for which Hecht won the first **Academy Award** for Best Story. Hecht also scored his first major success in the gangster genre as the screenwriter for **Howard Hawks**'s *Scarface* (1932). In the mid-1930s, Hecht won back-to-back Best Writing **Oscar** nominations for *Viva Villa!* (1934) and *The Scoundrel* (1935), winning for the latter.

Hecht would receive additional Best Screenplay Oscar nominations for *Wuthering Heights* (1939), *Angels over Broadway* (1940, which he also directed and produced), and **Alfred Hitchcock**'s *Notorious* (1946). Other key films for which he received writing credits include Hitchcock's *Spellbound* (1945), the **film noir** classics *Kiss of Death* (1947) and *Where the Sidewalk Ends* (1950), the **screwball comedy** *Monkey Business* (1952), and the literary adaptation *A Farewell to Arms* (1957). His stage play *The Front Page* (co-written by Charles MacArthur, who also worked with Hecht on several screenplays) was adapted to the screen multiple times, first under its own title in 1931, but most memorably as Hawks's screwball comedy *His Girl Friday* (1940).

Hecht was the consummate professional screenwriter, working with famous rapidity in virtually every genre, though he had his greatest successes with crime and gangster films and screwball comedies. He made uncredited contributions to numerous screenplays, sometimes as a script doctor and sometimes because his political activism as a Zionist caused his films to be banned in Great Britain for a time in the 1930s and 1940s; studios thus began to release his films without his name so that they could be screened in Great Britain. Hecht worked without screen credit on such screenplays as *Twentieth Century* (1934), *A Star Is Born* (1937), *Angels with Dirty Faces* (1938), *Gone with the Wind* (1939, reportedly rewriting the entire screenplay as a script doctor), *Stagecoach* (1939), *Dual in the Sun* (1946), *Rope* (1948), *The Thing from Another World* (1951), and *Strangers on a Train* (1951).

Several of Hecht's scripts have been used as the basis for remakes. Thus, he was still receiving screen credit as late as 1995 for the remake of *Kiss of Death*.

**HECKERLING, AMY (1954– ).** Also a writer and producer, Amy Heckerling is best known as one of the leading women film directors of her generation. Her directorial debut in feature film came in 1982 with the immensely successful teen film *Fast Times at Ridgemont High*, still considered one of the classics of its genre. She followed with the comedies *Johnny Dangerously* (1984) and *European Vacation* (1985), which were not highly successful. The talking-baby romantic comedies *Look Who's Talking* (1989) and *Look Who's Talking Too* (1990) got little critical respect but were highly successful at the box office.

Heckerling scored another major success in the teen film genre with *Clueless* (1995), a clever reworking of Jane Austen's *Emma* within the context of a modern Beverly Hills high school. This hit spun off into a television series created by Heckerling. She also wrote and directed the feature films *Loser* (2000) and *I Could Never Be Your Woman* (2007).

**HELLMAN, LILLIAN (1905–1984).** Though best known for her distinguished career as a playwright, Lillian Hellman was also extensively involved in the American film industry. Hellman herself wrote a number of screenplays, while a number of her stage plays were adapted to the screen, sometimes by herself. However, her Hollywood career was curtailed when she was **blacklisted** after her uncooperative testimony before the **House Un-American Activities Committee** (HUAC) in 1950. Hellman's experiences with HUAC and the blacklist are outlined in her memoir *Scoundrel Time* (1976).

Hellman began her Hollywood career by writing the screenplay for *The Dark Angel* (1935). She also wrote the screenplay for **William Wyler**'s crime drama *Dead End* (1937), a film that helped to make **Humphrey Bogart** a star. Hellman adapted her own play to the screen in Wyler's *Little Foxes* (1941), receiving an **Academy Award** nomination for Best Screenplay. She received a Best Original Screenplay **Oscar** nomination for *North Star* (1943) and worked with longtime lover Dashiell Hammett to adapt her play *Watch on the Rhine* to film in that same year. Hellman's best-known screenplay, however, is probably for Wyler's *The Children's Hour* (1961), which Hellman again adapted from her own stage play. Hellman herself (played by **Jane Fonda**) figures as a lead character in the 1977 film *Julia*, based on Hellman's 1973 autobiographical novel *Pentimento*.

**HEPBURN, AUDREY (1929–1993).** The Belgian-born Audrey Hepburn spent much of her childhood in the Netherlands, though she also spent time attending school in Great Britain. She moved to London in 1948 to pursue a career as a ballerina but soon switched to acting. She made her film debut in 1951, when she appeared in four British films and two French films, mostly in small parts. Having subsequently starred in the Broadway play *Gigi*, Hepburn moved into a more important supporting role in the British film *The Secret People* (1952), which allowed her to use her ballet skills on screen. This performance drew the attention of Hollywood and helped gain her the starring role (opposite **Gregory Peck**) in the classic **romantic comedy** *Roman Holiday* (1953). This performance won her the **Academy Award** for Best Actress, and a star was born.

Hepburn followed with another **Oscar**-nominated lead performance in *Sabrina* (1954), then moved into a lead dramatic role in the prestige project *War and Peace* (1956), an adaptation of Leo Tolstoy's classic novel. She then again used her dancing skills onscreen, opposite **Fred Astaire** in *Funny Face* (1957). More major films followed, including a lead dramatic role in *A Nun's Story* (1959) that won Hepburn her third Best Actress nomination. Another Oscar followed for the romantic comedy *Breakfast at Tiffany's* (1961), one of the films for which she is best remembered.

A string of additional successful films in the 1960s solidified Hepburn's reputation as one of the world's top stars; she was the epitome of grace and dignity on the screen, yet able to play impish roles as well. Her important films of the 1960s included *The Children's Hour* (1961), *Paris—When It Sizzles* (1964), *How to Steal a Million* (1966), and *Wait until Dark* (1967), the latter of which won her a fifth Oscar nomination for Best Actress. In the coming years, she scaled back her acting and devoted most of her time to humanitarian projects, though her performance as Marian opposite **Sean Connery**'s Robin Hood in *Robin and Marian* (1976) was another memorable role.

The **Academy of Motion Picture Arts and Sciences** named Hepburn the winner of their Jean Hersholt Humanitarian Award shortly before her death in 1993. In 1999, a poll conducted by the **American Film Institute** named her the third greatest female screen legend of all time.

**HEPBURN, KATHARINE (1907–2003).** In a Hollywood career that spanned more than six decades, Katharine Hepburn starred in many memorable films and won a total of 12 **Academy Award** nominations for Best Actress. This impressive body of work, along with her unique onscreen presence, helped her to be named the top female screen star of all time in a 1999 poll conducted by the **American Film Institute**.

Hepburn began her career with a major supporting role in **George Cukor**'s *A Bill of Divorcement* (1931) and would work with Cukor many times in the coming years, including his *Little Women* (1933), in which she had one of her first starring roles. That same year, she also starred in the drama *Morning Glory* (1933), which won her the first of her four Best Actress **Oscars**. Unfortunately, Hepburn's unconventional looks, strong opinions, and onscreen persona made it difficult for her studio, **RKO Pictures**, to decide just what to do with her, and most of her films of the next few years were not successful, though she won a second Oscar nomination for her performance in *Alice Adams* (1935). Her move into **comedy** in such films as *Bringing Up Baby* (1938), *The Philadelphia Story* (1940), and *Woman of the Year* (1942) was a critical success, though, and the latter two won her Oscar nominations for Best Actress.

*Woman of the Year* was also Hepburn's first appearance with **Spencer Tracy**, with whom she subsequently formed an ongoing partnership, both on screen and off; the two became a legendary onscreen couple, even though the Catholic Tracy refused to divorce his estranged wife and thus never married Hepburn, forcing them to keep their off-screen relationship a secret from the public. Despite potential controversy, they remained together until his death in 1967. In the meantime, they starred together in a number of films, typically playing couples who were involved in intricate psychological fencing matches as they struggled to find terms on which a relationship could succeed. Key films starring Hepburn and Tracy included *Keeper of the Flame* (1942), *Adam's Rib* (1949), *Pat and Mike* (1952), *Desk Set* (1957) and *Guess Who's Coming to Dinner* (1967), for which Hepburn won her second Best Actress Oscar.

Hepburn followed with her third Oscar win for *The Lion in Winter* (1968), keeping her at the top ranks of Hollywood stardom even as she entered her 60s. In the meantime, she had won additional Oscar nominations for *The African Queen* (1951), *Summertime* (1955), *The Rainmaker* (1956), *Suddenly, Last Summer* (1959), and *Long Day's Journey into Night* (1962). Hepburn's starring role in *The Madwoman of Chaillot* (1969) was another memorable performance, though she did subsequently scale back her acting schedule, appearing sparingly in the 1970s, mostly on television, including a role in Cukor's television movie *Love among the Ruins* (1975) that won her a Best Lead Actress Emmy. She returned to center stage on film, however, with *On Golden Pond* (1981) in which she won her fourth Best Actress Oscar starring opposite fellow legend **Henry Fonda**. That was Hepburn's last major appearance, though she starred in the television movie *One Christmas* and had a supporting role in the theatrical film *Love Affair* as late as 1994.

**HERRMANN, BERNARD (1911–1974).** Bernard Herrmann began his Hollywood career by composing the **music** for *Citizen Kane* (1941), for which he received an **Academy Award** nomination for Best Music. Ironically, he did not win for that film, instead winning the same award for his work on *All That Money Can Buy* that same year. After this fast start, Herrmann went on to become one of the best-known composers of music in film history, topping off his career as he had begun it, with double Best Music **Oscar** nominations in 1977 for *Taxi Driver* and *Obsession*, both released posthumously in 1976. He is especially well known for his collaboration with director **Alfred Hitchcock**, having composed the scores for all of Hitchcock's films from *The Trouble with Harry* (1955) through *Marnie* (1964), including such classics as *Vertigo* (1958), *North by Northwest* (1959), and *Psycho* (1960).

Herrmann was known for his use of instruments not usually used in film music, including the innovative electronic music for *The Day the Earth Stood Still* (1951), which helped to establish the musical style of **science fiction** film soundtracks for decades to come. He was also nominated for a Best Music Oscar for *Anna and the King of Siam* (1946).

**HESTON, CHARLTON (1923–2008).** The American actor Charlton Heston rose to major stardom when he played Moses in the 1956 **biblical epic** *The Ten Commandments*, a performance that he followed by playing the title character in *Ben-Hur* (1959), which won him an **Academy Award** for Best Actor in his only nomination for that award. He remained best known for these two roles for the rest of his life, though he played many roles in many genres in a long and prolific career.

In 1961, Heston starred in the **historical epic** *El Cid*. He also starred in the **Western** *Major Dundee* (1965) and had a supporting role as John the Baptist in *The Greatest Story Ever Told* (1965), looking back to his earlier performances in biblical epics. Particularly important was his lead role in the **science fiction** classic *Planet of the Apes* (1968), a role that helped to make him a top sf action star in the years that followed, with lead roles in such films as *The Omega Man* (1971) and *Soylent Green* (1973).

At this point, Heston had reached the pinnacle of his stardom, and the quality of his roles was in decline. In 1973, he had a supporting role as Cardinal Richelieu in *The Three Musketeers*, and he had a lead role in the 1974 **disaster** film *Earthquake*. He also starred in the thriller *Two-Minute Warning* (1976), but was increasingly relegated to supporting roles, including an appearance in **James Cameron**'s *True Lies* (1994) in the following years. Heston directed the films *Antony and Cleopatra* (1972) and *Mother Lode* (1982), in both of which he also starred.

Active since the 1950s in a number of progressive political causes, Heston was awarded the Jean Hersholt Humanitarian Award by the **Academy of Motion Picture Arts and Sciences** in 1978. Subsequently, however, he swung to the right politically and gained considerable attention as the pro-gun president of and spokesman for the National Rifle Association from 1998 to 2003. Ironically, one of Heston's last roles was a small (uncredited) part as an aging ape who warns against the dangers of guns in **Tim Burton's** 2001 remake of *Planet of the Apes*.

*HIGH NOON*. One of the classic **Westerns** of all time, *High Noon* (Dir. **Fred Zinnemann**, 1952) includes numerous elements that are typical of the genre, including gunplay between a virtuous lawman and a gang of ruthless outlaws, but it also explores a number of serious ethical and political issues, giving it a depth sometimes lacking in the genre. The action takes place in the town of Hadleyville, a formerly wild and dangerous town that Marshal Will Kane (**Gary Cooper**) has tamed, making it a good place to live and raise a family. One of his major accomplishments in this regard was the arrest and conviction, for murder, of local bad-man Frank Miller (Ian McDonald), sent away to state prison five years earlier. But, as the film begins, Miller has just inexplicably been pardoned and is now headed back to Hadleyville to seek revenge on Kane. The townspeople urge Kane and his new Quaker wife Amy (**Grace Kelly**) to flee, but Kane decides to stay to face Miller and his gang and to protect the town, despite the fact that the townspeople provide him with little support. He then defeats the outlaws in a running gun battle, after which he and Amy leave town without a word to the townspeople, Kane tossing his badge with disgust into the dusty street.

Viewed as a straightforward Western, *High Noon*, with its individualist hero and its disdain for the masses who inhabit the town, hardly seems like a leftist film, especially with the virulent anticommunist Cooper in the lead role. However, it is generally recognized that the film also functions as an allegory about the anticommunist purges sweeping Hollywood, with Kane functioning as the rare individual who stands up against persecution, while all around him are taking the easy road and giving in. Miller and his gang thus play the role of anticommunist investigators, casting the **House Un-American Activities Committee** (HUAC) as a gang of ruthless thugs. This reading is reinforced by the fact that the film was written by **Carl Foreman**, who would soon join the **blacklist** and who was almost denied onscreen credit for the film because of controversy surrounding his politics.

*High Noon* won four **Academy Awards** and received a total of seven nominations, including Best Picture, Best Director, and Best Screenplay, though it did not win in those three categories. A 2007 poll conducted by the **American Film Institute** named *High Noon* the 27th greatest film of all time; a 2008 AFI poll named it the second greatest Western of all time.

**HILL, GEORGE ROY (1921–2002).** George Roy Hill had worked primarily as a television director when he broke into feature film with *Period of Adjustment* (1962), based on a play by Tennessee Williams. He then followed with another adaptation, *Toys in the Attic* (1963), based on a play by **Lillian Hellman**. Hill moved into **comedy** with *The World of Henry Orient* (1964), into the **historical epic** with *Hawaii* (1966), and into the **musical** with *Thoroughly Modern Millie* (1967), demonstrating considerable versatility as a director, though his box-office success was uneven. It was, however, with the immensely successful revisionary **Western** *Butch Cassidy and the Sundance Kid* (1969), that Hill became a truly major Hollywood director, winning an **Academy Award** nomination for Best Director for the film, which was itself nominated for Best Picture.

Hill followed the success of *Butch Cassidy* with the offbeat **science fiction** film *Slaughterhouse-Five* (1972), then reunited with *Butch Cassidy* stars **Paul Newman** and **Robert Redford** in the comic con-man film *The Sting* (1973), another major success that won Hill the Best Director **Oscar** and that won a total of seven Oscars, including Best Picture. Hill again worked with Redford in *The Great Waldo Pepper* (1975), a film that was something of a disappointment, then returned to work with Newman in *Slap Shot* (1977), an ice hockey film that has become a **cult** classic.

*A Little Romance* (1979) won an Oscar for its score and another nomination for its screenplay, but otherwise got relatively little attention. Hill scored another hit with *The World According to Garp* (1982), but *The Little Drummer Girl* was not a hit, while Hill's last film, *Funny Farm* (1988), was an unsuccessful comedy.

**HILLER, ARTHUR (1923– ).** The Canadian-born director Arthur Hiller had worked widely in television in the 1950s but had only directed a few minor films when he first gained major attention as the director of *The Americanization of Emily* (1964). After that, Hiller worked regularly as a director of mainstream Hollywood productions for more than three decades.

Hiller's output was particularly rich from the mid-1960s to the mid-1970s. Among the highlights of this period of Hiller's career are the **war film** *Tobruk* (1967), the **comedies** *Popi* (1969) and *The Out of Towners* (1970), the tearjerker *Love Story* (1970), the **romantic comedy** *Plaza Suite* (1971), the drama *The Hospital* (1971), and the classic comedy *Silver Streak* (1976). His later films have been primarily comedies, though he did director *Babe* (1992), a **biopic** about baseball slugger Babe Ruth.

Hiller received an **Academy Award** nomination for Best Director for *Love Story*. In 2002, the Academy gave him its Jean Hersholt Humanitarian award for his charitable and philanthropic work.

**HISTORICAL EPIC.** Large-scale films based on historical events have been a part of American film since the **silent film** era, with **D. W. Griffith**'s *Birth of a Nation* (1915) and *Intolerance* (1916) perhaps being the most notable early examples. However, due to the expense and difficulty of making such films (*Intolerance* itself was a financial disaster), true historical epics were rare until the 1950s, with exceptions such as *Gone with the Wind* (1939) being heavily romanticized. In the 1950s and 1960s, however, epics became more popular as the film industry actively sought to produce films that could only be appreciated on the big screens of theaters, thus providing an experience that audiences could not achieve at home watching television. Crucially important to this phenomenon was the **biblical epic**, in which stories based on the Bible or other religious traditions were presented on film, but many epics of the period were simply based on historical events and were not religious in nature.

Historical epics and biblical epics are, of course, closely interrelated: many biblical epics presumably portray real historical events, while many popular historical epics, especially in the 1950s are set in biblical times, the antiquity of which was felt to have a certain exotic attraction. In some notable cases, such as *Ben-Hur* (1959), the two genres overlapped. Other historical epics were more clearly secular, however, as in the case of *Spartacus* (1960), *El Cid* (1961), *Lawrence of Arabia* (1962), and *Cleopatra* (1963). Because of the intentionally grand nature of their conception, several of these historical epics are among the most highly regarded films of all time; however, the expense of making such films also made them highly risky endeavors, and films such as *Cleopatra* were critical and commercial failures that soon drove the genre back out of favor.

There were occasional attempts to revive the genre or bring it more up to date in the coming years—as in **Stanley Kubrick**'s *Barry Lyndon* (1975), set in the 18th century, or Richard Attenborough's British film *Gandhi* (1982), set in the 20th. **War films** such as *Patton* (1970) also occasionally took on epic proportions, as did multigenerational crime sagas such as the *Godfather* sequence, beginning in 1972. In general, however, the historical epic fell out of favor by the mid-1960s and remained rare for the next three decades. **Mel Gibson**'s *Braveheart* (1995), a highly romanticized epic set in medieval Scotland, was a commercial and critical success that many have credited with reviving the genre, though **James Cameron**'s even more romanticized *Titanic* (1997), at the time the biggest commercial hit ever, was even more important in its indication of the box-office potential of nostalgia-driven historical epics.

Despite the promise indicated by such films, it was the growth of **computer-generated imagery** soon afterward—as perhaps best embodied in the *Lord* *of the Rings* **Trilogy** (2001–2003), an epic fantasy sequence—that gave the biggest boost to epics of all kinds, by making it far easier and less expensive to make such films. Historical epics (often again highly romanticized and often using fictional epics such as *Lord of the Rings* as a generic model) have subsequently become much more common in Hollywood.

Important recent historical epics have included **Ridley Scott**'s *Gladiator* (2000) and *Kingdom of Heaven* (2005), Wolfgang Petersen's *Troy* (2004), and **Oliver Stone**'s *Alexander* (2004). Such films have been hit-or-miss affairs, however, and some of the most successful, such as the graphic-novel adaptation *300* (2006), have relied more on **fantasy** and adventure elements than historical accuracy. That such epics were collectively spoofed in *Meet the Spartans* (2008) suggests both their recent popularity and the possibility that the latest cycle of epics is nearing an end.

**HITCHCOCK, ALFRED (1899–1980).** The renowned British director Alfred Hitchcock is one of the most distinctive (and most respected) directors in film history. He began his career in his native Great Britain in the **silent film** era, directing such films as *The Lodger: A Story of the London Fog* (1927), a major critical and commercial success that established his affinity for thrillers. He began work on *Blackmail* (1929) as a silent film, but the studio decided to make it a sound film, which he then completed as one of the first British films of the sound era. He went on to complete a series of important British films in the 1930s, including *Juno and the Paycock* (1930), *The Man Who Knew Too Much* (1934), *The 39 Steps* (1935), *Secret Agent* (1936), *The Lady Vanishes* (1938), and *Jamaica Inn* (1939). Hitchcock was then recruited by **David O. Selznick** to come to America to make films for the latter's Selznick International Pictures.

Hitchcock's first American film (set in England, starring British actor **Laurence Olivier**, and based on a book by British novelist Daphne du Maurier) was *Rebecca* (1940), a great success that would be the only film directed by Hitchcock to win the **Academy Award** for Best Picture. Hitchcock garnered the first of his five Best Director **Oscar** nominations for that film, though he would never win that award. Under contract to Selznick, Hitchcock's subsequent output in the 1940s was unusually diverse, partly because he worked for a number of different studios to whom Selznick loaned him out. Hitchcock's films of the next decade included the thrillers *Suspicion* (1941), *Spellbound* (1945), and *Notorious*; the **romantic comedy** *Mr. and Mrs. Smith* (1941), the **film noir** *Shadow of a Doubt* (1943), the war-related drama *Lifeboat* (1944), the courtroom drama *The Paradine Case* (1947), and the murder-related dramas *Rope* (1948) and *Stage Fright* (1950).

By this time Hitchcock had developed the distinctive style that made his films easily recognizable as his own, combining technical innovations with intricate, witty plots and psychologically complex characterization. He worked repeatedly with some of Hollywood's top stars (despite his reputedly low opinion of actors), including **Cary Grant, James Stewart,** and **Grace Kelly** (one of a series of "Hitchcock blondes" who would become a trademark of his films), while also continuing his habit (established in the 1930s) of making brief cameo appearances in his own films. During the next decade, Hitchcock continued to produce one memorable film after another, including a series of psychological thrillers that are now established classics of world cinema. These films include *Rear Window* (1954), ***Vertigo*** (1958), *North by Northwest* (1959), and *Psycho* (1960). However, many of Hitchcock's other films of this period are important in their own right, including *Strangers on a Train* (1951), *Dial M for Murder* (1954), *It Takes a Thief* (1955), *The Trouble with Harry* (1955), and *The Wrong Man* (1956).

The *Birds* (1963), a **horror** film in which ordinary birds inexplicably attack a California town en masse, was another success, though Hitchcock's output was beginning to decrease by this time. He would make five more films, from *Marnie* (1964) to *Family Plot* (1976), all interesting and watchable, but none quite up to the level of his previous work. In 1968, the **Academy of Motion Picture Arts and Sciences** gave Hitchcock its **Irving G. Thalberg** Memorial Award for his lifetime achievement in film.

**HOFFMAN, DUSTIN (1937– ).** Dustin Hoffman had made several appearances on television and had won acclaim as a stage actor when he burst onto the scene as a film actor with his starring role in *The Graduate* (1967). That performance won him the first of what have now been seven nominations for the **Academy Award** for Best Actor. He would be nominated again two years later for *Midnight Cowboy* (1969), making him one of Hollywood's most highly regarded actors going into the 1970s. He also won that nomination for *Lenny* (1974) and finally won the **Oscar** for Best Actor for *Kramer vs. Kramer* (1979). Other notable films in which he was featured in the 1970s included *Little Big Man* (1970), *Straw Dogs* (1971), *Papillon* (1973), *All the President's Men* (1976), and *Marathon Man* (1976).

A gifted dramatic actor, Hoffman changed directions in 1982, winning another Oscar nomination for his performance as a cross-dressing actor in the **comedy** *Tootsie* (1982), solidifying his position as one of Hollywood's top leading men, despite his small stature and lack of conventional movie star looks. However, though he did win an Emmy for his performance as Willy Loman in a 1985 television adaptation of *Death of a Salesman*, Hoffman did not return to film until the disastrous *Ishtar* in 1987. He rebounded strongly, however, winning another Oscar for Best Actor for his compelling performance as an obsessive autistic savant in *Rain Man* (1988).

Hoffman was hilarious as the gangster Mumbles in the largely unsuccessful *Dick Tracy* (1990); he next starred in *Billy Bathgate* (1991) and *Hook* (1991), both of which were unsuccessful. The **science fiction** thriller *Outbreak* (1995) was a box-office hit, though the later sf film *Sphere* (1998) was not as successful. In between, Hoffman starred in two 1997 works of political **satire**, both focusing on the negative consequences of contemporary media culture: *Mad City* and *Wag the Dog*, the latter of which won him his seventh Oscar nomination for Best Actor.

Moving into the 21st century (and into his own mid-sixties) Hoffman continued to work frequently. His supporting role in *Finding Neverland* (2004) was a highlight of these years, as was his supporting comic turn in the farce *Meet the Fockers* (2004). Hoffman has also done a substantial amount of voiceover work in **animated films**, including prominent roles in *Kung Fu Panda* (2008) and *The Tale of Despereaux* (2008).

**HOLDEN, WILLIAM (1918–1981).** William Holden began his career in Hollywood with an impressive starring performance as Joe Bonaparte, a sensitive violinist driven by economic necessity to become a boxer, in *The Golden Boy* (1939). His career developed slowly during the 1940s, partly due to his military service during World War II. He became a true star, however, as screenwriter Joe Gillis in **Billy Wilder**'s *Sunset Blvd.* (1950), in which he began to establish the cynical and detached (but still sympathetic) persona that would mark many of his subsequent roles.

Holden received an **Academy Award** nomination for Best Actor for *Sunset Blvd.*, then followed by winning that award for his performance in Wilder's *Stalag 17* (1953). He proceeded to become one of Hollywood's top leading men of the 1950s, when he starred in such important films as *Executive Suite* (1954), *Sabrina* (1954), *The Bridges at Toko-Ri* (1954), *Picnic* (1955), and *The Bridge on the River Kwai* (1957). His career cooled somewhat in the 1960s, though he continued to appear as a reliable leading man, and even topped off the decade with another important lead performance in *The Wild Bunch* (1969).

In the 1970s, Holden had a leading role in *The Towering Inferno* (1974), then came up with one of his most memorable performances as world-weary television executive Max Schumacher in Sidney Lumet's *Network* (1976), one of the key films of the decade. Holden received his third Best Actor **Oscar** nomination for that performance, which would prove to be the capstone of his career. He did, however, subsequently star in *Damien: Omen II* (1978), *The Earthling* (1980), and Blake Edwards's *S.O.B.* (1981), one of Holden's few comic performances.

Holden was named in the 25th greatest male film star of all time in a 1999 poll conducted by the **American Film Institute**.

**HOLLYWOOD TEN.** The Hollywood Ten were a group of Hollywood professionals who became the central figures in the anticommunist witch-hunts and subsequent blacklist that swept the film industry in the years after World War II. This group (Alvah Bessie, Herbert Biberman, Lester Cole, **Edward Dmytryk**, **Ring Lardner Jr.**, Howard Lawson, Albert Maltz, Samuel Ornitz, Adrian Scott, and **Dalton Trumbo**) was called to testify before the **House Un-American Activities Committee** (HUAC) in October of 1947, then refused to answer the committee's questions about their political affiliations, believing such inquiries to be a violation of their constitutional rights. The Ten were subsequently cited for contempt of Congress and imprisoned.

Dmytryk soon repented and provided testimony about his political affiliations and those of other members of the film industry. He was thus released from prison, removed from the blacklist, and allowed to continue his film career. The other members of the Ten served out their one-year prison sentences, then subsequently found themselves unable to work in Hollywood due to the blacklist. Biberman subsequently directed the **independent** leftist-film *Salt of the Earth* (1954), but this effort to establish a film industry outside of official Hollywood did not go beyond that single (but important) film. Others went abroad to find work or wrote for film or television under pseudonyms or using fronts.

The blacklist would remain in place until 1960, when director **Otto Preminger** announced that Trumbo (who had actually written the screenplays for more than a dozen Hollywood films in the 1950s, without onscreen credit) had written the screenplay for his upcoming film *Exodus*, insisting that Trumbo receive onscreen credit. Trumbo also received credit in 1960 for writing the screenplay for **Stanley Kubrick**'s *Spartacus* (1960), largely at the insistence of star **Kirk Douglas**.

**HOPE, BOB (1903–2003).** Though born in London, England, Bob Hope moved to the United States at the age of five, ultimately becoming an American cultural icon. A star in various media, Hope was perhaps best known in his later years for his performances on television and for the live shows he hosted to entertain members of the U.S. military. However, Hope also had a substantial and successful career in film **comedy**—though he himself poked considerable fun at his lack of film success (and especially at his inability to win an **Academy Award**), especially during the record 18 times that he hosted the annual Academy Award ceremonies.

Hope got his start in film as the star of several comic shorts beginning in 1934, before graduating to feature film in a supporting role in the **W. C. Fields** vehicle *The Big Broadcast of 1938* (1938). His breakthrough role as the star of *The Cat and the Canary* (1939), opposite **Paulette Goddard**, then launched him on a major film career in which he remained one of the biggest stars of **Paramount Pictures** for the next two decades. He again starred opposite Goddard in *Nothing but the Truth* (1941); in between, he starred with **Bing Crosby** in *Road to Singapore* (1940), beginning one of the best-known partnerships in American film. Hope and Crosby teamed up for four more "Road" pictures from *Road to Zanzibar* in 1941 and extending through *Road to Rio* (1947); this series was then continued with *Road to Bali* (1952) and *The Road to Hong Kong* (1962).

These popular light **musical** comedies helped to make Hope one of the most recognizable comic performers in America. Highlights of his film career apart from Crosby included the **film noir** spoof *My Favorite Brunette* (1947), *Fancy Pants* (1950), *The Seven Little Foys* (1955), and *I'll Take Sweden* (1965). His last starring role in a feature film came in 1972 in *Cancel My Reservation*.

Though he was never even nominated for a competitive Academy Award, Hope did win four honorary awards from the Academy (over a period from 1941 to 1966), as well as its Jean Hersholt Humanitarian Award in 1960.

**HOPKINS, ANTHONY (1937– ).** The distinguished Welsh actor Anthony Hopkins has played important roles in dozens of American films. After a promising beginning in the British theater, Hopkins had his first major film role as Richard I in the British-produced *The Lion in Winter* (1968). Numerous other roles in British film and (especially) television followed, including a starring role in David Lynch's *The Elephant Man* (1980), but it was not until *The Silence of the Lambs* that Hopkins would become widely known to American film audiences. A string of both leading and supporting roles in major films followed, including (in addition to the films for which he received **Oscar** recognition) *Surviving Picasso* (1996), *Titus* (1999), *The World's Fastest Indian* (2005), *Fracture* (2007), and *The Wolfman*.

Renowned for seemingly effortless performances achieved by immersing himself in the roles that he plays, Hopkins is probably best known in the United States for his performance as psychotic killer Hannibal Lecter in *The Silence of the Lambs* (1991), which won him an **Academy Award** for Best Actor. He would memorably reprise that role in *Hannibal* (2001) and *Red Dragon* (2002). He also won Best Actor Oscar nominations for *The Remains of the Day* (1993) and *Nixon* (1995), and a Best Supporting Actor nomination for *Amistad* (1997).

**HOPPER, DENNIS (1936–2010).** Beginning in 1955, Dennis Hopper had numerous roles on television, as well as supporting roles in such important films as *Rebel without a Cause* (1955), *Giant* (1956), *Gunfight at the O.K.*

*Corral* (1957), and *Cool Hand Luke* (1967). It was, however, as the costar, director, and co-writer of the hugely successful countercultural film *Easy Rider* (1969) that Hopper became a major figure in American film. Hopper received an **Academy Award** nomination for Best Screenplay for *Easy Rider*. Several starring roles followed, including one in *The Last Movie* (1971), which he also directed. It was not, however, until his performance as a freaked-out photojournalist in **Francis Ford Coppola**'s *Apocalypse Now* (1979) that Hopper made his next appearance in a major American film.

Erratic behavior fueled by an almost legendary intake of drugs and alcohol continued to slow the development of Hopper's career, though his performances in films such as *Rumble Fish* (1983) and *The Osterman Weekend* (1983) were notable. It was in 1986, however, that he had what has become perhaps his best-known role, that of manic psycho-killer Frank Booth in David Lynch's *Blue Velvet*. That same year, Hopper received an **Oscar** nomination for Best Supporting Actor for his role in *Hoosiers*.

Subsequently, Hopper directed *Colors* (1988), a successful film in which he did not act, but he continued to be known primarily as an actor. However, he continued to work primarily as an actor, appearing in dozens of films (mostly in supporting roles, often as a sinister villain) after 1986, including such highlights as *Red Rock West* (1993), *True Romance* (1993), *Speed* (1994), *Waterworld* (1995), *Space Truckers* (1996), *Land of the Dead* (2005), and *Elegy* (2008).

**HOPPER, HEDDA (1885–1966).** After an early career as an actress, Hedda Hopper became a nationally known gossip columnist whose reports on the Hollywood movie scene made her one of the most powerful people in the film industry. Hopper's influential column, "Hedda Hopper's Hollywood," could go a long way toward making or breaking careers in Hollywood, and Hopper herself relished her power, becoming a prominent figure who hobnobbed with film royalty, always with an eye out for a scoop. Widely known for her large, flamboyant hats, Hopper was no stranger to controversy, engaging, among other things, in a high-profile feud with former friend and fellow gossip columnist **Louella Parsons**, her only real rival for the title of most powerful gossip columnist in Hollywood.

Hopper also courted attention with her anticommunist activism, which included providing the **House Un-American Activities Committee** (HUAC) with the names of those in the film industry she felt had leftist sympathies. Chief among these was **Charles Chaplin**, against whom Hopper conducted such a diatribe in her columns that many felt she was a central contributing factor to his decision to leave the United States for Europe in 1952. Chaplin, however, was only one among many in Hollywood who regarded Hopper as an enemy.

In her later years, Hopper played upon her fame to return to acting in a series of small roles, including a cameo as herself in *Pepe* (1960).

**HORNER, JAMES (1953– ).** James Horner is one of the most successful composers in film history, having scored more than 100 films, including the two biggest box-office hits of all time, **James Cameron**'s *Titanic* (1997) and *Avatar* (2009). Horner also wrote the well-known (and widely excerpted) score for Cameron's *Aliens* (1986) and has written **music** for a number of other **science fiction** films as well. Indeed, he began his career working for **Roger Corman**, leading to his first screen credit as a composer for the Corman-produced *Battle beyond the Stars* (1980), a low-budget space opera. Other science fiction films scored by Horner include *Star Trek II: The Wrath of Khan* (1982), *Krull* (1983), *Star Trek III: The Search for Spock* (1984), *Cocoon* (1985), *Honey, I Shrunk the Kids* (1989), *Deep Impact* (1998), and *Bicentennial Man* (1999).

Horner has composed for numerous other films as well, including *Patriot Games* (1992). *Searching for Bobby Fischer* (1993), *Courage under Fire* (1996), *The Perfect Storm* (2000), *A Beautiful Mind* (2001), *House of Sand and Fog* (2003), and *Apocalypto* (2006). In addition to 14 ASCAP Film and Television Music awards, he has received a total of eight **Academy Award** nominations for Best Score, though he won only for *Titanic*. Known for making effective use of vocal music within his scores, he has also received two **Oscar** nominations for Best Song, again winning for *Titanic* with "My Heart Will Go On." Though sometimes criticized for sampling heavily from his own previous scores and from the works of classical composers (such as Sergei Prokofiev and Dmitri Shostakovich), Horner has produced some of the most dramatically effective music in recent film history.

**HOUSE UN-AMERICAN ACTIVITIES COMMITTEE (HUAC).** The House Un-American Activities Committee (also known as the House Committee on Un-American Activities, but better known simply as HUAC) was originally formed as a special committee in 1938 to investigate supposed subversive activities of various kinds, especially possible German American involvement in the Nazi Party and the Ku Klux Klan. However, under the leadership of its inaugural chairman, Texas Congressman Martin Dies Jr., the committee soon turned its focus on possible communist activity within the United States.

HUAC became a standing committee of Congress in 1945 and soon broadened the scope of its investigations of supposed communist activity, famously turning its attention to such activity within the film industry with an initial nine days of hearings in October 1947, followed by a second round of hearings concerning the film industry in 1951. These investigations led to an extensive blacklist in which over 300 individuals who had been working in film (especially screenwriters) were made unemployable in Hollywood—at least under their real names—because aspersions had been cast on their possible leftist political sympathies.

The highest-profile members of this blacklist were the **Hollywood Ten**, who were convicted of contempt of Congress for their refusal to cooperate with the committee and consigned to one-year prison terms in 1950s. Ironically, two members of the Hollywood Ten—Lester Cole and **Ring Lardner Jr.**—were joined during their stay at Connecticut's Danbury Prison by former Congressman J. Parnell Thomas, who chaired HUAC during the initial Hollywood hearings but who had later been convicted of corruption charges. Meanwhile, the blacklist itself remained in effect until the beginning of the 1960s, by which time HUAC had lost considerable prestige and the anticommunist hysteria of the 1950s had greatly calmed.

In 1969, HUAC was renamed the House Committee on Internal Security, and in 1975 it was abolished altogether. *See also* DMYTRYK, EDWARD; FOREMAN, CARL; HELLMAN, LILLIAN; *HIGH NOON*; KAZAN, ELIA; SCHULBERG, BUDD; *SPARTACUS*; TRUMBO, DALTON.

**HOWARD, RON (1954– ).** Ronny Howard had an extensive career as a child and young-adult actor, especially as Opie Taylor in *The Andy Griffith Show* (1960–1968) and as the star of *Happy Days* (1974–1984). The latter was a follow-up to **George Lucas**'s *American Graffiti* (1973), in which Howard had the most important of his numerous film roles. It was, however, as the highly competent director of numerous mainstream Hollywood films that Ron Howard would ultimately become best known. His films have now accumulated a domestic box-office gross of more than $1.7 billion, making him the third-rated director of all time in terms of that statistic.

Howard began his directorial career with *Grand Theft Auto* (1977), in which he starred and which he co-wrote with his father, Rance Howard. He then established a solid track record in the 1980s as the director of a series of successful **comedies**, including *Night Shift* (1982), *Splash* (1984), *Cocoon* (1985), *Gung Ho* (1986), and *Parenthood* (1989). Meanwhile, the **fantasy** *Willow* (1988), the drama *Backdraft* (1991), the romance *Far and Away* (1992), and the reality-based drama *Apollo 13* (1993) established his ability to do other genres as well.

Howard won the **Academy Award** for Best Director for *A Beautiful Mind* (2001), which also won the **Oscar** for Best Picture. He was nominated for the Best Director Oscar for *Frost/Nixon* (2008), which was also nominated for Best Picture. Other successful films directed by Howard include *Ransom*

(1996), *How the Grinch Stole Christmas* (2000), *Cinderella Man* (2005), *The Da Vinci Code* (2006), and *Angels and Demons* (2009).

**HOWE, JAMES WONG (1899–1976).** Born in China, James Wong Howe was brought to the United States in 1904. He would go on to become one of the most prolific cinematographers in Hollywood history in a career that began in the **silent film** era and stretched to the middle of the 1970s. A pioneer in the use of deep-focus photography, Howe was a particular master of black-and-white photography. He won the first of his 10 **Academy Award** nominations for Best Cinematography for *Algiers* (1938); he received his 10th nomination for *Funny Lady* (1975), nearly 40 years later. In between, he won Best Cinematography **Oscars** for *The Rose Tattoo* (1955) and *Hud* (1963) and shot many of the most important films in Hollywood history, ultimately serving as the cinematographer on well over 100 films.

Among Howe's other Oscar-nominated films were *Abe Lincoln of Illinois* (1940), *The North Star* (1943), and *The Old Man and the Sea* (1958, his first nominated film to be shot in color). Other important films for which he served as cinematographer include *They Made Me a Criminal* (1939), *Yankee Doodle Dandy* (1942), *Body and Soul* (1947), *He Ran All the Way* (1951), and *Sweet Smell of Success* (1957). In 2003, he was named one of the 10 most influential cinematographers of all time in a poll conducted by the International Cinematographers Guild.

**HORROR.** One of the oldest and most popular genres of American film, horror films have been around since early **silent films** such as the 1910 adaptation of *Frankenstein* and have included such major works of cinematic art as *Rosemary's Baby* (1968) and *The Exorcist* (1973). Though often considered a low-brow form of cinematic art and frequently made on low budgets for teen audiences, the horror genre is actually quite diverse in both content and style. Horror film also includes a number of distinctive subgenres, including Gothic horror, supernatural and occult horror, and the slasher film (and the related splatter film). It also sometimes overlaps with other genres, such as **fantasy**, **science fiction**, and the **disaster** film.

In the silent film era, horror film was especially important in European film, where it was central to the development of the German expressionist style in cinema. In the United States, horror film emerged early as well, building upon the Gothic tradition in European literature with such works as the 1910 adaptation of *Frankenstein*. By the 1920s, Lon Chaney emerged as America's first horror-film star, with roles in such silent films as *The Hunchback of Notre Dame* (1923), *The Monster* (1925), and (most importantly) *The Phantom of the Opera* (1925). It was, however, with the coming of the sound era that American horror movies hit their stride, especially in a series of films produced by **Universal Pictures**, including such well-remembered classics as *Frankenstein* (1931), *Dracula* (1931), *The Mummy* (1932), and *Bride of Frankenstein* (1935).

Less well known, but also notable among the Universal films of the first half of the 1930s, was **Edgar G. Ulmer**'s *The Black Cat* (1934), a low-budget classic that featured both **Boris Karloff** and **Béla Lugosi**, who had already emerged as Hollywood's two leading horror-film stars of the early sound era. In the second half of the 1930s (partly due to stricter enforcement of the **Production Code**), horror films became less popular, though important horror films continued to be produced in the 1940s, perhaps most notably the low-budget horror films produced by Val Lewton for **RKO Pictures**, including *Cat People* (1942), *I Walked with a Zombie* (1943), and *The Body Snatcher* (1945).

In the 1950s, the horror film experienced a renaissance, though much of the impetus behind the resurgence of the genre came from Great Britain's Hammer Film Productions, which released a series of popular Gothic horror films, many featuring the same monsters as the Universal films of the early 1930s. In the United States, the 1950s also saw the rise of teen-oriented horror films designed to attract the young audiences that were becoming increasingly important to the Hollywood film industry. Many of these were low-budget efforts from new studios such as **American International Pictures** (AIP), whose leading light, **Roger Corman**, went on to become one of the key figures in the evolution of the horror-film genre. Corman was particularly successful with a series of film adaptations of the work of Edgar Allan Poe that he directed and produced for AIP in the early 1960s. However, by the end of the 1960s, he had gone out on his own and would subsequently work more as a producer than as a director.

Through most of the 1960s, horror remained mostly a low-budget film genre, though occasional A-list films could be classified as horror, such as **Alfred Hitchcock**'s *Psycho* (1960) and *The Birds* (1963). On the other hand, some of these low-budget efforts produced important films, such as **George A. Romero**'s low-budget, black-and-white **independent film** *Night of the Living Dead* (1968), which spawned an extensive franchise and demonstrated the ability of horror film to produce serious social and political commentary.

That same year, horror film attained a newfound respectability with the release of **Roman Polanski**'s occult-themed *Rosemary's Baby*, a chilling horror film with excellent production values and high artistic aspirations. That film (along with the demise of the Production Code) helped to trigger a particularly rich period in American horror film, making the 1970s one of the most interesting decades in the history of the genre. Occult horror films such as William Friedkin's *The Exorcist* (1973) and **Richard Donner**'s *The Omen* (1976) were big-budget efforts with the backing of **major studios** (in this case, **Warner Bros.** and **Twentieth Century-Fox**, respectively). However, some of the decade's most interesting horror films came from low-budget **independent** filmmakers such as Larry Cohen, with *It's Alive* (1974); Tobe Hooper, with *The Texas Chain Saw Massacre* (1974); and **Wes Craven**, with *The Last House on the Left* (1972) and *The Hills Have Eyes* (1977).

The late 1970s also saw the release of Romero's *Dawn of the Dead* (1978), a sequel that announced the further evolution of an important zombie-film franchise, and **John Carpenter**'s *Halloween* (1978), the beginning of another extensive horror sequence and one that particularly demonstrated the potential of the slasher film subgenre of the horror film now that the Production Code was a thing of the past. Add in the horror/science fiction hybrid *Alien* (1979) and the slasher film *Friday the 13th* (1980), which would inspire multiple sequels of their own, and the great age of horror franchises was underway.

The year 1980 saw the release of **Stanley Kubrick**'s *The Shining* (1980), an artistically ambitious horror film that in many ways sought to do what Kubrick's *2001: A Space Odyssey* (1968) had earlier done for science fiction film. Horror moved further into the Hollywood mainstream with Hooper's *Poltergeist* (1982), a supernatural horror film written and produced by **Steven Spielberg** with the backing of **Metro-Goldwyn-Mayer** (MGM). Craven also moved more into the mainstream as the writer and director of *The Nightmare on Elm Street* (1984), founding still another major horror franchise, this time with a reality-bending twist on the slasher premise.

The success of the horror film, along with its often extreme subject matter, naturally led to the production of self-conscious variants that parodied, or at least commented upon, the genre to which they belong. Sam Raimi's *Evil Dead* (1981) was among the first important films in this category. It was followed by two sequels, *Evil Dead II: Dead by Dawn* (1987) and *Army of Darkness* (1992), both also directed by Raimi. All three films starred Bruce Campbell, who became a sort of **cult** film legend. Campbell also starred in *Bubba Ho-Tep* (2002), one of the more off-beat of the horror-film spoofs.

The 1990s and 2000s saw a number of such self-conscious horror films, most of which, following in the footsteps of their 1950s predecessors, increasingly catered to younger audiences, typically featuring groups of teenage and college-age protagonists threatened by some sort of evil, supernatural or otherwise. Particularly notable here are the three *Scream* films (1996, 1997, 2000), all directed by Craven. These films were successful enough to become an important franchise in their own right, in the meantime reenergizing the teen horror genre as a whole and triggering a spate of imitators, the most notable of which was *I Know What You Did Last Summer* (1997). Most of these self-conscious films still functioned to some extent as legitimate horror films, but the *Scary Movie* franchise (2000, 2001, 2003, 2006), took the horror spoof into the realm of almost pure **comedy**.

The last two decades in horror film have also brought a new level of variety to the genre. For example, *The Blair Witch Project* (1999) presented as a grainy documentary shot by amateurs with a handheld video camera, achieved exceptional success; that basic approach has since been used in such horror-related films as Romero's *Diary of the Dead* (2007), the **monster movie** *Cloverfield* (2008), and *Paranormal Activity* (released at **film festivals** in 2007, then put in general release—with surprising box-office success—in 2009). New levels of bloodiness came to horror in such films as the *Saw* franchise (currently consisting of six films released from 2004 to 2009), which brings graphic scenes of torture to a level that some regard as pornographic.

Traditional variants of the horror film such as zombie movies and vampire movies have remained strong in recent years, though they have sometimes moved to new levels of violence, as in the comic-book vampire tale adaptation *30 Days of Night* (2007). The ultraviolent British zombie film *28 Days Later* (2002) has been particularly influential on American horror films in this regard. On the other hand, films such as *Interview with the Vampire* (1994) have presented more sympathetic, even romanticized views of vampires, anticipating the later appearance of the *Twilight* vampire films, which are really more **fantasy**/romance than horror.

Meanwhile, the major slasher film franchises have been joined in recent years by successful second-tier franchises, such as *Child's Play* (five films, 1988–2004) and *Leprechaun* (five films, 1993–2000), while the major franchises have been extended and updated with remakes of their initial entries. Thus, the *Halloween* franchise now includes 10 films, with updates of the first two films in 2007 and 2009; *Friday the 13th* includes 11 films, with a 2009 update of the original film; and *Nightmare on Elm Street* includes seven films through 1994, plus a remake of the first film in 2010. A crossover between the latter two franchises also appeared in 2003 with *Freddy vs. Jason*. The new century has also seen updated (higher budget) remakes of such classic 1970s horror films as *The Texas Chainsaw Massacre* (2003), *Dawn of the Dead* (2004), *The Hills Have Eyes* (2006), and *The Last House on the Left* (2009).

**HUDSON, ROCK (1925–1985).** Rock Hudson struggled for several years in his attempt to be a Hollywood actor, then finally broke through with his lead role in *Magnificent Obsession* (1954), subsequently becoming one of Hollywood's handsomest and most popular leading men. He followed with a number of mostly dramatic roles, including the lead role in *Giant* (1956), though it was ultimately in **romantic comedies**, especially opposite **Doris Day**, that he ultimately had his greatest success. Hudson's films with Day included *Pillow Talk* (1959), *Lover Come Back* (1961), and *Send Me No Flowers* (1964).

Hudson appeared in a number of other films as well, including the **science fiction** thriller *Seconds* (1966), the **war film** *Tobruk* (1967), and the **spy film** *Ice Station Zebra* (1968). However, his film career was in decline by the end of the 1960s, and his most notable role in the 1970s was on television as Police Commissioner Stewart McMillan in *McMillan and Wife* (1971–1977). Hudson continued to appear regularly on television through the first half of the 1980s. After years of poor health, including heart ailments, he died of AIDS in 1985. The later revelation of Hudson's long-term gay lifestyle gained considerable media attention.

**HUGHES, HOWARD (1905–1976).** One of the most enigmatic (and one of the most famous) Americans of the 20th century, Howard Hughes made important contributions as an aviator, inventor, industrialist, and philanthropist, in addition to his work in film, first as an independent producer, then later as the head of **RKO Pictures**. Along the way, Hughes became one of the richest men in the world, though he grew increasingly eccentric and reclusive in his later years.

Hughes began his film career in the **silent film** era, serving as the producer and "presenter" of *Two Arabian Knights* (1927) and *The Racket* (1928), a **gangster film**. He moved into directing with the big-budget aviation film *Hell's Angels* (1930), though he would work primarily as a producer and executive producer throughout his involvement with film. The Hughes-produced **gangster film** *Scarface* (1932) is a classic of its genre. It was also highly controversial at the time, when many felt that it glorified organized crime. Hughes afterward left the film business for the rest of the decade, returning in 1941 to produce and direct *The Outlaw*, starring his new find **Jane Russell**. However, controversies over Russell's costuming in the film (particularly related to her displays of cleavage) kept the film out of release until 1943 and out of wide release until 1946.

Hughes, long regarded as something of a rebel against the Hollywood establishment, became a member of that establishment when he acquired a controlling interest in struggling **RKO Pictures** in 1948. Unfortunately, Hughes's capricious management style was not suited to running a **major studio**, especially in the environment of crisis in which the film industry found itself after the **Paramount Antitrust Case** of 1948 and the initial **House Un-American Activities Committee** hearings about possible subversive activity in Hollywood, which began in October 1947.

Though RKO had some successes during Hughes's tenure, the studio came under increasing financial pressure. Himself under pressure from stockholders, Hughes bought most of them out by the end of 1954, then sold the studio to General Tire and Rubber in 1955, reportedly making a tidy profit, despite the studio's troubles. That sale essentially ended Hughes's career in film, though films begun at RKO under his tenure continued to appear until 1957.

In addition to his own work in film, Hughes has appeared as a character in a number of films, most notably including *Melvin and Howard* (1980) and *The Aviator* (2004).

**HUGHES, JOHN (1950–2009).** Though he actually worked more widely as a producer and screenwriter, John Hughes is best known as the director of a sequence of popular films of the 1980s, largely oriented toward teen audiences. Films such as *Sixteen Candles* (1984), *The Breakfast Club* (1985), *Pretty in Pink* (1986), and *Ferris Bueller's Day Off* (1986) have become iconic cinematic representations of teen life in the mid-1980s. However, his attempts to branch out into films for older audiences — such as *Planes, Trains, and Automobiles* (1987) and *Uncle Buck* (1989) — were less successful.

Hughes's last directorial effort was *Curly Sue*, in 1991. However, he continued to work as a writer and producer, most notably of *Home Alone* (1990) and its first two sequels (1992 and 1997).

**HUSTON, JOHN (1906–1987).** Though also an accomplished actor and screenwriter, John Huston is best known as the director of such classic films as *The Treasure of the Sierra Madre* (1948), for which he won **Academy Awards** for Best Director and Best Screenplay. Indeed, Huston won a total of eight **Oscar** nominations as a screenwriter, as opposed to five nominations for Best Director, and had worked in Hollywood as a successful screenwriter for more than a decade before he made his directorial debut with the **film noir** classic *The Maltese Falcon* (1941).

Huston was especially adept as a film noir director, also helming such key noir films as *Key Largo* (1948) and *The Asphalt Jungle* (1950). However, Huston worked in a number of genres and was one of Hollywood's top directors through the early to mid-1950s, when he directed such notable films as *The African Queen* (1951), *The Red Badge of Courage* (1952), *Moulin Rouge* (1952), *Beat the Devil* (1953), and *Moby Dick* (1956).

While his directorial career began to cool a bit in the late 1950s, Huston still directed a number of important films from that point forward, including *The Misfits* (1961), *The Night of the Iguana* (1964), *Reflections in a Golden Eye* (1967), and the *MacKintosh Man* (1973). Indeed, as late as 1985 he was nominated for an Oscar for Best Director for the tongue-in-cheek **gangster film** *Prizzi's Honor*. Several of his later films were adaptations of well-known literary works, including *The Man Who Would Be King* (1975), *Wise Blood* (1979), *Under the Volcano* (1984), and *The Dead* (1987).

Huston made dozens of appearances as an actor in Hollywood films (as well as in several Italian films), including a role in *The Cardinal* (1963) that won him an Oscar nomination as Best Supporting Actor. However, as an actor Huston is probably best remembered for his performance as the wealthy and cynical Noah Cross in **Roman Polanski**'s *Chinatown* (1974). In addition to his own work in film, Huston was the subject of the documentary *John Huston: The Man, the Movies, the Maverick* (1989) and the inspiration for **Clint Eastwood**'s 1990 film *White Hunter Black Heart*.

Huston had the distinction of directing both his famous father, Walter Huston, and his famous daughter, Angelica Huston, in Oscar-winning performances (*The Treasure of the Sierra Madre* and *Prizzi's Honor*, respectively).

# I

**INDEPENDENT FILM.** The term "independent film" refers to any film made outside the normal studio-dominated system of Hollywood. The concept originated in the early **silent film** days (leading to such efforts as the artist-controlled **United Artists**), but gained particular prominence during the heyday of the **studio system** in Hollywood, when the studios, especially the five **major studios** (**Metro-Goldwyn-Mayer**, **Paramount**, **Fox**, **Warner Bros.**, and **RKO**) exercised almost total dominance in the film industry, often paying more attention to economics than to art or social responsibility. The concept gained particular traction with the founding, in 1941, of the Society of Independent Motion Picture Producers (SIMPP) by **Mary Pickford** and **Charlie Chaplin** (who had been instrumental in the founding of United Artists), joined by Hollywood newcomer **Orson Welles** and such producers as **Walt Disney**, **Samuel Goldwyn**, and **David O. Selznick**.

The efforts of the SIMPP helped to spur the production of independent films such as *Little Fugitive* (1953), which won an **Academy Award** nomination for Best Writing, the first **Oscar** nomination for an independent film in any category. SIMPP's most important contribution, however, was the filing of a suit that led to the landmark 1948 U.S. Supreme Court's decision in the **Paramount Antitrust Case** that broke the monopolistic power of the studios over film distribution and exhibition. Moving forward, films such as *Salt of the Earth* (1954) were made entirely outside the studio system for political reasons, though most "independent" films were actually made by small upstart studios such as **American International Pictures**. Still, filmmakers such as **John Cassavetes** made almost entirely independent films, in this case financing them largely from the proceeds of his successful acting career in mainstream films, thus foreshadowing the work of such later independent filmmakers as **John Sayles**, who has helped to finance his own films with the income from his work as a mainstream screenwriter.

In the 1960s, independent filmmakers such as **Roger Corman** and **George Romero** had particular success in the realm of **horror** films. By the end of the 1960s, as a new generation of filmmakers started to emerge from film schools, Hollywood studios began to give greater independence to young filmmakers, which led to the production of successful "independent" films such as *Easy Rider* (1969, made with the backing of **Columbia Pictures**); however, this phenomenon also began to blur the boundary between studio films and independent films. By the end of the 1970s, however, this new paradigm was already coming apart, partly due the fact that the huge commercial successes scored by **New Hollywood** directors such as **George Lucas** and **Steven Spielberg** caused studios to concentrate more on commercial blockbusters than on innovative filmmaking. Meanwhile, **film festivals** such as the Sundance Film Festival (first held in 1978) began to provide venues for the screening of independent films, often leading to distribution deals with companies such as Miramax (founded in 1979), which specialized in the distribution of independent films.

Miramax also began to participate in the production of films as well. However, by the time of what was perhaps their greatest success, ***Pulp Fiction*** (1994), Miramax had been acquired by **Disney**, though they were still allowed to operate with relative independence. From this point forward, more and more studios began to operate their own "independent" film units, designed to produce the same kind of daring and unusual films for which truly independent filmmakers had become known over the years. Thus, most "independent" films today are made either by subsidiaries of major studios or by smaller independent studios, rather than by literally independent individuals.

Independent film remains a vital element of the American film industry, focusing in recent years on traditional independent niches such as horror, as well as on "relationship" films that are perhaps more subtle and less formulaic than those designed for box-office appeal by the bigger studios. Independent film has especially been spurred in recent years by advances in relatively inexpensive filmmaking technologies, such as digital video and computer editing, which have made it possible to make professional-looking films with little more equipment than a digital camera and a personal computer. *See also* JARMUSCH, JIM; LIONSGATE; NEW LINE CINEMA; POVERTY ROW.

**INDUSTRIAL LIGHT & MAGIC (ILM).** Founded by **George Lucas** in 1975 specifically to make the **special effects** for the upcoming *Star Wars* (1977) movie, Industrial Light & Magic has gone on to become one of Hollywood's preeminent special effects design and production studios, remaining on the cutting edge of new developments in special effects technology. Still a subsidiary of **Lucasfilm** Limited, the company has been especially important in the development of techniques for the **computer-generated imagery** (CGI) in **science fiction** films, and in films in general. In recent years, in fact, they have focused almost exclusively on CGI effects. In addition to creating the special effects for Lucas's own productions—including the *Star Wars* films and the Indiana Jones films—the company has now produced special effects for more than 200 other films and has won more than three dozen Academy Awards in the Best Visual Effects and other technical categories. In addition to their work on the *Star Wars* sequence, some of ILM's most notable achievements in effects for sf films include the genesis effect in *Star Trek: The Wrath of Khan* (1982), the aqueous pseudopod for *The Abyss* (1989), the liquid metal effects for the T-1000 terminator in *Terminator 2: Judgment Day* (1991), the computer-generated dinosaurs for *Jurassic Park* (1993), and the urban destruction effects for the **disaster** film *The Day after Tomorrow* (2004).

***IT HAPPENED ONE NIGHT.*** One of the founding works of the **screwball comedy** genre, *It Happened One Night* (dir. **Frank Capra**, 1934) was a great commercial and critical success, winning **Academy Awards** for Best Picture, Best Director, Best Screenplay, Best Actor, and Best Actress. In the film, spoiled heiress Ellen Andrews (**Claudette Colbert**) escapes from her father's yacht off the Florida coast when he holds her there to try to convince her to annul her recent marriage to a famed aviator. In Miami, Ellie catches a bus for New York, where she plans to rejoin her new husband. On the same bus is hard-drinking newspaper reporter Peter Warne (**Clark Gable**), headed north in search of opportunity, having just been fired from his job with a New York newspaper.

The developing relationship between Andrews and Warne as they travel cross-country includes numerous classic elements of the screwball comedy, including its focus on a central couple who experience strong sexual attraction but who try to deny this attraction because they appear completely mismatched due to their great differences in background, experience, and social class. Meanwhile, the film wryly comments on the newly enforced **Production Code** by assuring viewers that no sex is occurring as the two protagonists travel cross-country, sharing lodgings. Thus, at night they remain discreetly separated by curtains constructed of ropes and blankets, which they refer to as the "Walls of Jericho."

After numerous disagreements and misadventures, however, each protagonist comes to better understand the other. Warne and Andrews wind up married and set out on their honeymoon; the film ends as Warne blows a trumpet to announce to his new bride that the Walls of Jericho can now come tumbling down. This wall, sexual innuendo notwithstanding, is largely one of class, and the collapse of this barrier at the end of *It Happened One Night* is a classic example of the consistent tendency of American films, especially screwball comedies, to try to deny or efface class difference.

In 2007, the **American Film Institute** (AFI) ranked *It Happened One Night* as the 46th greatest film of all time; in 2008, an AFI poll rated the film as the third greatest **romantic comedy** of all time.

**IT'S A WONDERFUL LIFE.** *It's a Wonderful Life* (dir. **Frank Capra**, 1946) was not a big commercial success upon its initial release, though it did receive five **Academy Award** nominations, including Best Picture, Best Director, and Best Actor. The film was then reincarnated in the 1970s as Christmas programming for television. It has subsequently become standard Christmas viewing for millions of Americans and is now one of the most beloved of American films. The film has also gained critical respect during the last few decades and is now regarded as one of the finest and most effective films in the history of American cinema.

*It's a Wonderful Life* is ostensibly the simple and sentimental tale of George Bailey (James Stewart), a good-hearted citizen of the small town of Bedford Falls, who continually forgoes his own hopes and dreams in order to help others. When money troubles drive Bailey to the brink of suicide, a kindly angel intervenes to allow him to see what Bedford Falls would have been like without Bailey's efforts to make things better. In particular, without Bailey, sinister banker Henry Potter (Lionel Barrymore) would have been able to gain full dominance over the town, transforming it into the dystopian Pottersville, a sinful city of garish neon lights that advertise the bars, strip joints, and gambling houses that seem almost the only businesses in town. Meanwhile, almost everyone Bailey had known has come to a bad end, and all of the working people Bailey had helped to achieve decent housing are now forced to live in slums owned by Potter.

Bailey realizes that his life has been worthwhile and cancels his suicide plans. Further, his money troubles are almost magically solved with the help of the people of the town, allowing the Bailey family to have a Merry Christmas. The film thus appears to end as sentimental holiday fare and is usually received that way by viewers. However, much of the film is unremittingly bleak as well as strongly cynical in its depiction of capitalism. After all, the alternative vision of Bedford Falls/Pottersville presented in the film is an image of a society in which capitalism has been given its head, allowed to pursue its goals without opposition. The result is the ultimate product of capitalist modernization: a debased and spiritually bankrupt society completely devoid of tradition, morals, or meaningful human relationships.

*It's a Wonderful Life* was named the 20th greatest film of all time in a 2007 poll conducted by the **American Film Institute**.

**IVENS, JORIS (1898–1989).** The Dutch **documentary** film director Joris Ivens was a committed communist who worked in the Soviet Union in the early 1930s. However, his most important film before coming to the United States was probably *The New Earth* (1934), a documentary focusing primarily on Dutch efforts to reclaim land from the Zuiderzee. From 1936 to 1945,

Ivens worked in the United States, during which time he made a number of important nonfiction films, perhaps most notably *The Spanish Earth* (1937), a documentary (narrated by Ernest Hemingway) that was designed to stimulate support for the Republican side in the Spanish Civil War, and *The Power and the Land* (1940), a documentary (produced by the U.S. Film Service for the Department of Agriculture's Rural Electrification Administration) that sought to demonstrate the importance of rural electrification.

Ivens worked largely in Eastern Europe in the years following World War II, though from 1965 to 1977 he filmed important documentaries in North Vietnam and China. Ivens was awarded the Lenin Peace Prize for 1967.

# J

**JACKSON, SAMUEL L. (1948– ).** After an active involvement with the Civil Rights movement in the 1960s and early 1970s, Samuel L. Jackson struggled for years trying to get his acting career off the ground until his role in **Spike Lee**'s *Do the Right Thing* (1989) finally got the attention of Hollywood. From that point forward he has worked frequently, including roles in Lee's *Mo' Better Blues* (1990) and *Jungle Fever* (1991). In the meantime, he established a solid track record as a supporting actor in such films as *Goodfellas* (1990), *Strictly Business* (1991), *Patriot Games* (1992), *Menace II Society* (1993), and *Jurassic Park* (1993). It was, however, with his **Oscar**-nominated supporting role as Julius Winnfield in **Quentin Tarantino**'s *Pulp Fiction* (1994) that Jackson became a truly major name in Hollywood. From that point forward, he has been one of Hollywood's most successful (and durable) actors, appearing in what is now a total of more than 100 films.

Jackson's next several films after *Pulp Fiction* were generally panned by critics, but he gained renewed attention for his major supporting role in *A Time to Kill* (1996), which propelled him into lead roles in such films as *Eve's Bayou* (1997), Tarantino's *Jackie Brown* (1997), and *The Negotiator* (1998). His major role as a scientist in the unsuccessful *Sphere* (1998) at least showed range in the characters he could portray, and he further extended his **science fiction** credentials the next year with a major supporting role as Jedi Master Mace Windu in *Star Wars: Episode I—The Phantom Menace* (1999). He portrayed that character in the next two *Star Wars* films (in 2002 and 2005) as well, reaching the largest audiences of his career.

Other notable appearances made by Jackson in the 2000s include *Unbreakable* (2000), his title role in the remake of *Shaft* (2000), and starring roles in *S.W.A.T.* (2003), *Black Snake Moan* (2006), and *Soul Men* (2008). Also in 2008, Jackson made a small appearance as Nick Fury in *Iron Man*, presaging a major new phase of his career as an **action** star in comic-book films. He had major supporting roles as Fury in *Iron Man 2* (2010) and *Thor* (2011) and is slated to star as Fury in the upcoming *Nick Fury* film and to appear as Fury in *The Avengers* (both scheduled for release in 2012).

**JARMUSCH, JIM (1953– ).** Director Jim Jarmusch has been one of America's leading makers of **independent films** since his debut with *Permanent Vacation* (1980), though it was with his second film *Stranger Than Paradise* (1982) that he first began to draw widespread attention. Through *Down by Law* (1986) and *Mystery Train* (1989), Jarmusch's unusual films, which eschew many of the conventions of commercial Hollywood cinema, gained increasingly positive critical attention. These "small" films were not designed to seek widespread commercial success, but they did become popular with "art house" audiences.

By the time of *Night on Earth* (1991), some critics felt that Jarmusch's films had become less daring and more predictable. However, the Western *Dead Man* (1995), starring **Johnny Depp**, was one of Jarmusch's most unusual and enigmatic efforts, even if it did have a somewhat larger production budget (a still low $9 million) than his earlier films. *Ghost Dog: The Way of the Samurai* (1999) was another highly unusual experiment with genre, combining the samurai **action film** with the **gangster film** to produce a result that differs dramatically from the usual examples of either genre.

*Coffee and Cigarettes* (2003) is a sequence of vignettes that are connected mainly in that they involve the items of the title, with no narrative connection. *Broken Flowers* (2005), on the other hand, was a move back toward more mainstream filmmaking, though still with a decidedly "indie" film feel with its unusual focus on relationships as a middle-aged man reviews the loves of his past. The crime film *The Limits of Control* (2009) is another exercise in genre-bending.

**JARRE, MAURICE (1924–2009).** French composer Maurice Jarre is probably best known for his film scores for British director David Lean, including *Lawrence of Arabia* (1962), *Doctor Zhivago* (1965), and *A Passage to India* (1965), all three of which won **Academy Awards** for Best Music. These three films feature grand, orchestral musical schemes. From the 1980s forward, however, Jarre became particularly known for his electronic scores, making heavy use of synthesizers.

The prolific Jarre scored more than 150 films and television programs. In addition to his three **Oscar** wins, he was nominated for six other Best Music Oscars. Though he began his career in French film and worked on a number of international productions, most of his films were American productions or co-productions with American involvement. Oscar-nominated films scored by Jarre include *The Life and Times of Judge Roy Bean* (1972), *Witness* (1985), *Gorillas in the Mist* (1988), and *Ghost* (1990). He also received an Oscar nomination for the **music** for *The Message* (1976), a variant on the "biblical" epic that tells the story of the prophet Mohammad.

Other prominent films scored by Jarre include *The Professionals* (1966), *Plaza Suite* (1971), *The Year of Living Dangerously* (1982), *Mad Max beyond Thunderdome* (1985), *Fatal Attraction* (1987), *Dead Poets Society* (1989), and *Jacob's Ladder* (1990).

**JEWISON, NORMAN (1926– ).** The Canadian-born director and producer Norman Jewison worked widely in television in the 1950s and early 1960s before moving into feature film with *40 Pounds of Trouble* (1962). He followed as the director of other **comedies**, such as the **Rock Hudson–Doris Day** vehicle *Send Me No Flowers* (1964). He both produced and directed the Cold War comedy *The Russians Are Coming, the Russians Are Coming* (1966), which received an **Academy Award** nomination for Best Picture. Jewison himself received an **Oscar** nomination for Best Director for the drama *In the Heat of the Night* (1967), firmly establishing himself as a major figure in Hollywood.

In 1968, Jewison directed and produced *The Thomas Crown Affair*, and he received another Best Picture Oscar nomination as the producer of *Fiddler on the Roof* (1971), for which he also received a Best Director nomination. The countercultural **musical** *Jesus Christ Superstar* (1973), the **science fiction** thriller *Rollerball* (1975), and the labor drama *F.I.S.T.* (1978) demonstrated Jewison's versatility, and he continued his success as a director and producer through the 1980s, when *A Soldier's Story* (1984) and *Moonstruck* (1987) both won Best Picture Oscar nominations, while the latter gained Jewison his third Best Director nomination. *Agnes of God* (1985) and *In Country* (1989) were also notable films he directed and produced during the decade.

Jewison's output declined in the 1990s, though the satire *Other People's Money* (1991) and the **biopic** *The Hurricane* were notable films that he directed and produced. In 1999, he received the **Irving G. Thalberg** Award for lifetime achievement from the **Academy of Motion Picture Arts and Sciences**.

**JOHANSSON, SCARLETT (1984– ).** Scarlett Johansson made her first appearance in film with a small role in *North* (1994). Several other childhood roles followed, and she made a major impression with her performance in **Joel and Ethan Coen**'s *The Man Who Wasn't There* (2001). She followed with a lead role in *Ghost World* (2001), then solidified her status as an actress on the rise with starring roles in *Lost in Translation* (2003) and *Girl with a Pearl Earring* (2003).

Johansson became the latest muse of director **Woody Allen** with her performances in his *Match Point* (2005), *Scoop* (2006), and *Vicky Cristina Barcelona* (2008). By this time, she had also become known as a sex symbol, perhaps an heir to the tradition of **Marilyn Monroe**, whom she was chosen to play in the **biopic** *Sinatra* (2011). Her efforts in *The Black Dahlia* (2006) and *The Prestige* (2006) reinforced her sex symbol status, but her attempts to become a major box-office star in the **science fiction** film *The Island* (2005) and the **superhero film** *The Spirit* (2008) were not successful. Her role as Natasha Romanova (aka The Black Widow) in the superhero film *Iron Man 2* (2010) does suggest her potential as a leading actress in blockbusters, however.

**JOHNSON, NUNNALLY (1897–1977).** After beginning his career as a journalist, Nunnally Johnson moved to Hollywood and became one of the most successful screenwriters in film history. Hired to work full-time as a writer for **Twentieth Century Fox** in 1935, Johnson made his breakthrough as the writer of the screenplay for **John Ford's** *The Grapes of Wrath* (1940), for which Johnson received an **Academy Award** nomination for Best Screenplay. He followed by writing the screenplay for Ford's *Tobacco Road* (1941), then received another **Oscar** nomination for Best Screenplay for *Holy Matrimony* (1943).

Johnson remained prolific as a writer of screenplays through the 1950s, scripting such notable films as the **film noir** classic *The Woman in the Window* (1944), the **romantic comedy** *How to Marry a Millionaire* (1953), the high-profile literary adaptation *The Man in the Gray Flannel Suit* (1956), and the multiple-personality drama *The Three Faces of Eve* (1957). Johnson also directed the latter two of these films, as well as several others, and he served as a producer for more than three dozen films, most of which he also wrote.

Johnson was less productive in the 1960s, but did write one of the important films of the decade when he scripted the **war film** *The Dirty Dozen* (1967), the last film that he wrote. Johnson also wrote the screen adaptation of *The World of Henry Orient* (1964), based on a novel by his daughter, Nora Johnson.

**JOHNSON, VAN (1916–2008).** Van Johnson was a highly serviceable actor who, after a number of supporting roles beginning in 1940, became one of the most reliable stars for **Metro-Goldwyn-Mayer** (MGM) in the years after World War II. Actually, Johnson graduated to leading roles as early as 1944, with *Thirty Seconds over Tokyo*. He also continued to play supporting roles after the war in such films as *State of the Union* (1948). By this time, however, his likeable onscreen persona helped him to gain mostly leading roles, though his performances in such films as *In the Good Old Summer Time* (1949), *The Big Hangover* (1950), and *When in Rome* (1952) never quite took him to the top levels of Hollywood stardom.

Though dropped by MGM in 1954, Johnson continued to appear regularly throughout the 1950s. Performing in **war films, comedies, musicals**, and other genres, Johnson appeared in a total of more than two dozen films in the 1950s. After the 1960s, however, he appeared mostly in guest spots on television, while his occasional film roles were mostly in B-grade films.

**JONES, JENNIFER (1919–2009).** Jennifer Jones struggled to get her Hollywood career off the ground, but finally made her breakthrough when she landed the title role in *The Song of Bernadette* (1943), her performance in which won her the **Academy Award** for Best Actress. She followed with an **Oscar** nomination for Best Supporting Actress for *Since You Went Away* (1944), and then received Best Actress nominations for her performances in *Love Letters* (1945) and *Duel in the Sun* (1946), produced by movie impresario **David O. Selznick**.

After this sequence of Oscar-nominated roles, Jones's career slowed a bit. In 1949, however, she married Selznick, who subsequently took charge of her career, seeing to it that she was placed in starring roles in a series of high-profile, prestige projects. These included *Madame Bovary* (1949), *Carrie* (1952), *Beat the Devil* (1953), and *Love Is a Many-Splendored Thing* (1955), for which she received still another Oscar nomination for Best Actress.

Jones continued to specialize in literary adaptations with appearances in *The Man in the Gray Flannel Suit* (1956), *A Farewell to Arms* (1957), and *Tender Is the Night* (1962). After Selznick's death in 1965, she appeared in a couple of minor films, then topped off her career with a supporting role in *The Towering Inferno* (1974).

**JONZE, SPIKE (1969– ).** Born Adam Siegel, Spike Jonze gained his pseudonym as a nickname in high school. A highly successful director of **music** videos and television commercials, he broke into feature film with the highly unusual *Being John Malkovich* (1999), which won him an **Academy Award** nomination for Best Director. That film was written by **Charlie Kaufman**, who also wrote Jonze's next film, *Adaptation* (2002). In 2009, Jonze directed the much-anticipated adaptation of Maurice Sendak's children's classic *Where the Wild Things Are* (2009), the screenplay for which Jonze co-wrote.

Jonze has made several appearances as an actor, most notably in a key role in *Three Kings* (1999). He has also performed as a dancer, while his credits in various media include co-creating the successful MTV series *Jackass* (2000–2002).

# K

**KAMINSKI, JANUSZ (1959– ).** The Polish-born Janusz Kaminski immigrated to the United States at the age of 21, then later attended college and the Conservatory of the **American Film Institute** to prepare for a career in film. He began his career as a cinematographer in a series of minor films in the early 1990s, then served as the cinematographer for **Steven Spielberg**'s *Schindler's List* (1993), winning an **Academy Award** for Best Cinematography for that film. He has served as the cinematographer for all of Spielberg's films since that time, including *Amistad* (1997), for which he received another **Oscar** nomination for Best Cinematography, and *Saving Private Ryan* (1998), for which he again won that award. He received a fourth Oscar nomination for Best Cinematography for the French–U.S. co-production *The Diving Bell and the Butterfly* (2007).

**KARLOFF, BORIS (1887–1969).** Born William Henry Pratt in London, England, Boris Karloff assumed his well-known pseudonym as early as 1912, when he was performing on stage. He appeared in dozens of **silent films** in the 1920s and appeared in more than a dozen films in 1931 alone. It was only, however, with his role as the monster in **Universal Pictures**' *Frankenstein* (1931) that his career was really launched. Though that role required Karloff to do little more than lumber around and grunt, it established him as a **horror** icon, a status that was solidified by his follow-up performance as Imhotep in *The Mummy* (1932).

Karloff made two more appearances as Frankenstein's monster, in *Bride of Frankenstein* (1935) and *Son of Frankenstein* (1939). In the meantime, often loaned out by Universal to other studios, he had appeared in any number of other horror films, including *The Mask of Fu Manchu* (1932), *The Ghoul* (1933), *The Black Cat* (1934, with fellow horror icon **Béla Lugosi**), *The Raven* (1935), *The Walking Dead* (1936), *The Man Who Changed His Mind* (1936), and *The Man They Could Not Hang* (1939). On the other hand, by the time of *The Invisible Menace* (1938), Karloff had begun to appear in **comedies** that derived their humor from poking fun at his usually dour horror characters, an aspect of his career that would culminate in the 1949 film

*Abbott and Costello Meet the Killer, Boris Karloff*, a film that indicated the way in which Karloff had become indistinguishable in the public mind from the characters he played in horror films.

Karloff's key films of the 1940s included another Frankenstein film, *House of Frankenstein* (1944), though this time he played a mad scientist rather than the monster. He appeared again with Lugosi in *Black Friday* (1940) and *The Body Snatcher* (1945); the latter was one of three horror films from **RKO Pictures** in which Karloff appeared in the mid-1940s. In the 1950s, Karloff appeared primarily on television, generally playing on his status as a horror icon, which often became the target of humor. In the 1960s, however, he made something of a comeback in film, appearing in several low-budget horror films for **American International Pictures**. Though his last appearance in film was in the posthumously released 1971 U.S.–Mexican co-production *The Incredible Invasion* (1971), his career was to an extent capped off with his appearance in **Peter Bogdanovich's** *Targets* (1968), in which he played an aging star of horror films, clearly based on himself.

**KASDAN, LAWRENCE (1949– ).** Lawrence Kasdan began his film career as a screenwriter when he sold his script for *The Bodyguard* in the mid-1970s, though that film would not be made until 1992 (with Kasdan as producer). In the meantime, he built some impressive writing credits as the co-writer of the screenplay for *Star Wars: Episode V — The Empire Strikes Back* (1980) and as the writer of the screenplay for *Raiders of the Lost Ark* (1981). He then made an auspicious directorial debut with the definitive **neo-noir** film *Body Heat* (1981), for which he also wrote the screenplay.

Kasdan followed as the writer, director, and producer of *The Big Chill* (1983), for which he received an **Academy Award** nomination for Best Screenplay. His next film, the **Western** *Silverado* (1985), was less successful, but *The Accidental Tourist* (1988) won him another Best Screenplay **Oscar** nomination, as well as winning an Oscar nomination for Best Film. In 1990 Kasdan directed *I Love You to Death*, one of only two films he has directed but did not write, the other being *French Kiss* (1995).

Kasdan returned to writing his films with *Grand Canyon* (1991), for which he won another Best Screenplay Oscar nomination, along with wife Meg Kasdan, who co-wrote the script for that film. Subsequent films that he wrote, directed, and produced include the Western *Wyatt Earp* (1994), the comedy-drama *Mumford* (1999), and *Dreamcatcher* (2003), a hybrid of **science fiction** and **horror**.

**KAUFMAN, CHARLIE (1958– ).** Screenwriter Charlie Kaufman came to the film business rather late and has written relatively few films. But he has established a reputation as one of Hollywood's most brilliant and inventive writers, scripting a series of successful films, noted for their complexity and literariness. After writing a number of television episodes, he made his film debut with the highly unusual *Being John Malkovich* (1999), directed by **Spike Jonze**. This film immediately established Kaufman as a talent to be reckoned with. Kaufman's scripts never follow the Hollywood norm and have typically shown a rare ability to combine the sensibilities of **independent film** and literary fiction with relatively widespread box-office appeal.

Kaufman's second script, for Michel Gondry's *Human Nature* (2001), was at least as unusual as his first, though it got less mainstream attention. He followed, however, with a string of complex and unusual films that gained wide attention and did well at the box office. These include **George Clooney**'s *Confessions of a Dangerous Mind* (2002), Jonze's *Adaptation* (2003), and Gondry's *Eternal Sunshine of the Spotless Mind* (2004).

Kaufman received **Academy Award** nominations for Best Screenplay for both *Being John Malkovich* and *Adaptation*. He then won that award for *Eternal Sunshine of the Spotless Mind*. He both wrote and directed *Synecdoche, New York* (2008), perhaps the most unusual of all of his films, and one that received very little mainstream attention, though it was nominated for the prestigious Palme d'Or at the Cannes Film Festival.

**KAZAN, ELIA (1909–2003).** Very active on the cultural left in the 1930s, Elia Kazan had worked extensively in the leftist theater scene in New York when he made his debut in film as the director of *People of the Cumberland* (1937), produced by Frontier Films, an **independent film** company formed by a group of leftists aligned with the Popular Front. He subsequently directed such politically charged films as *A Tree Grows in Brooklyn* (1945) and *Gentleman's Agreement* (1947), which won him the **Academy Award** for Best Director. He thus had extensive credentials as a leftist filmmaker by the time the **House Un-American Activities Committee** (HUAC) focused its investigations of communist activity on Hollywood in 1947. When Kazan, a former communist, cooperated with the committee by naming the names of others in Hollywood with leftist sympathies, he helped to secure his own career but also helped to send others onto the **blacklist**, making him a controversial figure from that point forward.

Kazan's first major post-HUAC film was *A Streetcar Named Desire* (1951), which won him another Best Director **Oscar** nomination. That film starred **Marlon Brando**, who also starred in Kazan's next two films, *Via Zapata!* (1952) and *On the Waterfront* (1954). The latter won Kazan his second Best Director Oscar (as well as seven other Oscars, including Best Picture) and is widely regarded as Kazan's finest film, although it is still controversial in some circles for the way in which certain aspects of the film can be read as defenses of his cooperation with HUAC.

Kazan next directed *East of Eden* (1955), another important film notable for its introduction of **James Dean** to film audiences. *Baby Doll* (1956) was perhaps Kazan's strangest and most eccentric film, while *A Face in the Crowd* (1957) was a minor classic, providing an early critique of the negative impact of the mediatization of American society by television. As the blacklist fell apart in the 1960s, Kazan fell out of favor in Hollywood; he directed only four films in the 1960s, the most important of which was *Splendor in the Grass* (1961).

Kazan's last film was *The Last Tycoon*, in 1976. In 1999, he was given an honorary lifetime achievement award from the **Academy of Motion Picture Arts and Sciences**, an award on which many on the Hollywood left of the time looked upon with disdain.

**KEATON, BUSTER (1895–1961).** The former Vaudevillian Buster Keaton was one of the greatest actors and directors of the **silent film** era. Keaton was known as "The Great Stone Face" because of the characteristic deadpan expression with which he faced even the most outrageous **slapstick** encounters on film. He got his start in *The Butcher Boy* (1917), opposite Roscoe "Fatty" Arbuckle, who became an early mentor. Keaton soon graduated to his own production unit, however, directing a series of successful short **comedies** that paved the way for his entry into feature-length film, beginning with *Three Ages* in (1923).

Keaton would go on to direct and star in some of the most enduring comedies of the silent film era, often writing his own material and conceiving and performing his own (sometimes highly dangerous) stunts. His best-known films of the silent era included *Our Hospitality* (1923), *The Navigator* (1924), *Sherlock Jr.* (1924), *Seven Chances* (1925), *The Cameraman* (1928), *The General* (1927), and *Steamboat Bill Jr.* (1928). Keaton continued to perform regularly after the coming of sound, though his career as a director was essentially over at that point.

Alcoholism and problems in his personal life plagued Keaton throughout the 1930s, when he acted primarily in short films and occasionally worked as a (mostly uncredited) gag writer for others, including the **Marx Brothers**. In the 1940s and early 1950s, Keaton appeared in a number of supporting roles in feature films, though his best remembered role of the period might be his small cameo (as himself) in *Sunset Blvd.* (1950). In 1952, he appeared with **Charles Chaplin** in the latter's *Limelight*, the only film in which Keaton and Chaplin, the two greatest comedians of silent film, appeared together.

Appearances on television in the 1950s helped Keaton to remain a well-known figure. He made a number of small appearances in the mid-1960s in films such as *Beach Blanket Bingo* (1965), essentially trading on the recognizability of his wooden visage. He finished his film career, however, with an important supporting role in *A Funny Thing Happened on the Way to the Forum* (1966).

**KEATON, DIANE (1946– ).** Born Diane Hall, Diane Keaton had made one minor film appearance and several television appearances when she gained wide exposure as Kay Adams-Corleone in *The Godfather* (1972) and *The Godfather: Part II* (1974). In the meantime, however, she had also starred in *Play It Again, Sam* (1972) and *Sleeper* (1973), launching her as the muse of writer–director **Woody Allen**, which also led her to star in several more films directed by Allen, including *Annie Hall* (1977), for which she won an **Academy Award** for Best Actress.

Keaton won another **Oscar** nomination for Best Actress for her role in *Reds* (1981). Now established as one of Hollywood's most distinguished leading ladies, Keaton continued to star in a variety of films over the next years, including such serious films as *The Little Drummer Girl* (1984) and *The Good Mother* (1988), the **black comedy** *Crimes of the Heart* (1986), and still another film with Allen in *Manhattan Murder Mystery* (1993). Then, after a 15-year gap, she won her third Oscar nomination for Best Actress, for her performance in *Marvin's Room* (1996).

Keaton has continued to appear regularly in film well into her sixties, primarily in **romantic comedies** such as *Because I Said So* (2007) and *Mad Money* (2008). She won a fourth Best Actress Oscar nomination for her role in the **romantic comedy** *Something's Gotta Give* in 2003.

**KELLY, GENE (1912–1996).** Actor, director, and choreographer Gene Kelly is best known as a dancer in movie **musicals**, rivaled only by the more graceful (but less athletic) **Fred Astaire** for the title of greatest male dancer in film history. Beginning his career on the stage in New York, Kelly did not move into film until 1942, with a successful performance in *For Me and My Gal*. His contract now picked up by **Metro-Goldwyn-Mayer** (MGM), he starred in a number of films over the next few years, including *Anchors Aweigh* (1945), which won him an **Academy Award** nomination for Best Actor, the only competitive **Oscar** nomination he would ever receive. However, he did win a special honorary award in 1952 for the versatility of his contributions to film.

After brief military service at the end of World War II, Kelly struggled to regain the momentum of his acting career, finally scoring a success in the swashbuckling adventure *The Pirate* (1948), establishing a new screen persona that he also put to use in *The Three Musketeers* (1948). But Kelly really wanted to do musicals, including directing them. He finally got the chance in *On the Town* (1949), co-directed by **Stanley Donen**, hired by Kelly to be his assistant choreographer. Kelly followed with starring roles in two of the greatest musicals in Hollywood history, *An American in Paris* (1951) and ***Singin' in the Rain*** (1952), the latter of which he again co-directed with Donen.

Unfortunately, by this time, the popularity of the musical as a genre was in decline. Kelly did continue to make notable musicals—including *It's Always Fair Weather* (1956) and *Les Girls* (1957)—but the decline of the genre contributed to his split from MGM in 1957. From this point forward, most of Kelly's work was on the stage or on television, though he did have a notable dramatic role in the film *Inherit the Wind* in 1960.

In addition to his own performances, Kelly is remembered for a number of technical innovations in the representation of dance in film, such as the use of split screens and the combination of live dancing with animation.

**KELLY, GRACE (1929–1982).** Though her film career spanned a mere five years and some 11 films, Grace Kelly remains one of the best-remembered figures in Hollywood history. A 1999 poll conducted by the **American Film Institute** named her the 13th greatest female screen legend of all time.

After early experience on the stage and on television, the fresh-faced beauty Grace Kelly had a relatively small part in the film *Fourteen Hours* (1951), then moved into an important supporting role in the classic **Western** *High Noon* (1952). Soon afterward, she landed a starring role in **John Ford**'s *Mogambo* (1953), along with a long-term contract with **Metro-Goldwyn-Mayer** (MGM). Her performance in that film won her an **Academy Award** nomination for Best Actress. When she won that award the next year for *The Country Girl* (1954), it was clear that she had arrived as one of the top stars in Hollywood.

That year (1954) was a banner year for Kelly. She also had a notable appearance in *The Bridges at Toko-Ri*. More importantly, 1954 also saw her star in two films directed by **Alfred Hitchcock**: *Dial M for Murder* and *Rear Window*. It is, in fact, as perhaps the greatest of the "Hitchcock blondes" that Kelly is most remembered as an actress. She also starred in Hitchcock's *To Catch a Thief* in 1955. She starred in two films in 1956: *The Swan* and *High Society*. However, it was also in that year that she abruptly retired from film in order to marry Prince Rainier III of Monaco. Attempts to lure her back into acting proved unsuccessful, though she remained a popular and highly visible figure throughout the remainder of her life, which was cut short by a fatal automobile accident that occurred after she suffered a stroke while driving.

**KEYSTONE STUDIOS.** Founded by **Mack Sennett** in Edendale, California, in 1912, Keystone Studios was one of the companies that helped to establish the business and production models for the American film industry as a whole. Backed by Adam Kessell and Charles O. Bauman, Keystone established the world's first fully enclosed film studio, where they produced numerous short **silent films** with factory-like quickness and efficiency. In its earliest years, the company was very much dominated by Sennett, who produced and directed most of their films, while acting in many of them as well.

The studio was especially successful in the realm of **comedy**, as "Keystone Comedies" became one of the first recognizable "brand names" in American film. Specializing in **slapstick** sequences such as wildly anarchic chase scenes, the company made successful early film series such as those featuring the "Keystone Kops," and also became known for the "Sennett Bathing Beauties," a collection of young actresses who adorned many of the early films.

Keystone was also highly successful in discovering new talents, a list that would eventually include such luminaries as **Fatty Arbuckle**, **W. C. Fields**, **Harold Lloyd**, Mabel Normand, and **Gloria Swanson**. Their most important early star was **Charles Chaplin**, who joined the company in 1913 and soon (after a difficult beginning) became their biggest star as an actor; he also began to supplant Sennett as the studio's most important director. In 1915, Sennett joined with **D. W. Griffith** and Thomas Ince to form **Triangle Pictures Corporation**, with Keystone continuing to operate as an autonomous unit under Sennett's direction.

Sennett left Keystone in 1917 to form his own independent production center. From that point, the studio was in decline and never regained its earlier importance. It was dissolved in bankruptcy proceedings in 1935. The name "Keystone Studios" was used for the fictional studio featured in the 1994 Hollywood **satire** *Swimming with Sharks*. A new independent company with the name Keystone Studios was founded in 2005 but is related to the earlier Keystone only in name.

**KIDMAN, NICOLE (1967– ).** Born in Hawaii to Australian parents, Nicole Kidman moved to Australia when her parents returned there when she was four years old. She grew up in Australia and began her acting career there. However, she achieved major success only after moving back to the United States and making films there, though she first gained the attention of Hollywood for her lead role in the Australian film *Dead Calm* (1989). Subsequent lead roles opposite **Tom Cruise** in *Days of Thunder* (1990) and *Far and Away* (1992) propelled her to stardom, while her 1990 marriage to Cruise created one of Hollywood's most prominent couples.

Kidman's rise to major stardom was completed in 1995 when she played the female lead in the big-budget *Batman Forever* and won critical acclaim for her lead role in **Gus Van Sant**'s *To Die For*. Her performance opposite Cruise in **Stanley Kubrick**'s *Eyes Wide Shut* (1999) drew considerable attention as well, but it was with *Moulin Rouge* (2001) that Kidman scored her first **Academy Award** nomination for Best Actress, just after her divorce from Cruise. She also starred in high-profile films such as *The Others* (2001) and *Cold Mountain* (2003), while winning more critical praise for her roles in smaller films such as *Dogville* (2003) and *The Hours* (2002), in which her performance as Virginia Woolf won her her first **Oscar** for Best Actress.

Kidman continues to be a major name in Hollywood. Other recent films in which she has starred include *The Stepford Wives* (2004), *The Interpreter* (2005), *Bewitched* (2005), *The Invasion* (2007), and *The Golden Compass* (2007). None of these, however, were major successes.

*KING KONG.* One of the founding films of the American **monster movie** genre, *King Kong* (dir. Merian C. Cooper and Ernest B. Schoedsack, 1933) made its title figure an American cultural icon. The film established a formula for the genre that would be imitated in countless other films, including a number of direct sequels. It also established female lead Ann Darrow (Fay Wray) as the paradigm of the threatened victim, while setting a standard for **special effects** and visual trickery, thanks to the stop-motion special effects of Willis O'Brien that was unsurpassed for decades. Perhaps most important is the film's treatment of the giant ape Kong, however alien and dangerous he may be, as a sympathetic figure, thus making him a sort of tragic hero. Indeed, he is treated even more sympathetically than the monster in *Frankenstein* (1931), who, though constructed of human parts, ultimately lacks the humanity with which Kong is endowed in the 1933 film.

The film's opposition between Kong as an emblem of primitive power who is ultimately no match for the forces of modern technology makes the film a sort of parable of the power (and danger) of modernity. In addition, the film is enriched by its open acknowledgment of its background in Depression-era America, and much of the action is motivated by hardship-driven economic necessity. The film can also be read as a cautionary tale about Hollywood, Denham's unfettered ambition to produce an exciting film having created a dangerous monster much in the way that Dr. Frankenstein's unfettered scientific curiosity did. Finally, the sympathetic portrayal of Kong can be taken as an enactment of the American admiration for the outlaw hero. In the end, he becomes a sort of paradigm of the lone individual, the only creature of his kind, meaning well but misunderstood by all.

*King Kong* was remade in 1976, with Jessica Lange in the role that had been played by Wray. It was remade again in 2005 in a mega-budget version directed by Peter Jackson, then coming off the huge success of his *Lord of the Rings* trilogy. Though this latest version received a tremendous amount of fanfare, the film barely made back its $207 million production budget at the U.S. box office. However, receipts of over $300 million outside the United States still made it a commercial success.

**KOCH, HOWARD (1901–1995).** Howard Koch began writing plays while working as a practicing attorney in the 1920s. He was a co-writer of the script for **Orson Welles**'s radio adaptation of *The War of the Worlds* (1938), then moved on to Hollywood at the beginning of the 1940s. He then achieved mainstream success as the co-writer of the screenplay for *Sergeant York* (1941), for which he won an **Academy Award** nomination for Best Screenplay. He then followed by winning the Best Screenplay **Oscar** as the co-writer of *Casablanca* (1942), one of the most beloved films in Hollywood history.

Koch scripted a number of films during World War II, including *Mission to Moscow* (1943), an avowedly pro-Soviet film made in response to U.S. government requests that Hollywood make films to generate support for America's Soviet allies. Unfortunately, this film also drew the attention of the **House Un-American Activities Committee** (HUAC) and contributed to Koch's placement on the **blacklist** at the beginning of the 1950s, virtually ending his career as a screenwriter. Moving to Great Britain, Koch did manage to script the B-movie *The Intimate Stranger* in 1956, using the name "Peter Howard," which he continued to use in the 1960s, even after the blacklist was effectively broken, though he also used his own name as well. His films of the 1960s, including *The War Lover* (1962) and *The Fox* (1967), were relatively minor, however.

**KOVÁCS, LÁSZLÓ (1933–2007).** The Hungarian-born cinematographer László Kovács came to the United States in the late 1950s, becoming a naturalized U.S. citizen in 1963. He began his career as a Hollywood cinematographer working in low-budget films, largely for **Roger Corman**. He then gained major attention for another low-budget feature, the groundbreaking *Easy Rider* (1969), which he quickly followed with *Five Easy Pieces* (1970), another film that helped to set the stylistic tone for the **New Hollywood** of the 1970s. He was also an influential figure in that movement proper, shooting a total of six films for key New Hollywood director **Peter Bogdanovich**: *Targets* (1968), *What's Up, Doc?* (1972), *Paper Moon* (1973), *At Long Last Love* (1975), *Nickelodeon* (1976), and *Mask* (1985).

Other prominent films shot by Kovács include *Shampoo* (1975), *New York, New York* (1977), *F.I.S.T.* (1978), *Ghost Busters* (1984), *Say Anything* (1989), *Radio Flyer* (1992), *My Best Friend's Wedding* (1997), and *Miss Congeniality* (2000). Altogether, he served as the cinematographer for over

70 films, sometimes using the names Lester Kovacs or Leslie Kovacs. While Kovács never received an **Academy Award** nomination, he was honored with a lifetime achievement award for cinematography from the American Society of Cinematographers in 2002.

**KRAMER, STANLEY (1913–2001).** Stanley Kramer began his career in Hollywood as a producer, including work on such notable films as *Champion* (1949) and *Home of the Brave* (1949), two films that anticipated the later, politically engaged "message" movies for which Kramer would become known as a director. Kramer also produced **High Noon** (1952), though he became involved in controversies surrounding that film when he attempted (unsuccessfully) to prevent writer **Carl Foreman**, headed for the **blacklist**, from receiving onscreen credit for the screenplay. Then, beginning in the mid-1950s, Kramer turned to directing and eventually directed a series of some of the most important message-oriented films in Hollywood history, including *The Defiant Ones* (1958), *On the Beach* (1959), *Inherit the Wind* (1960), and *Judgment at Nuremberg* (1961).

Kramer moved into **anarchic comedy** in 1963 as the director and producer of *It's a Mad Mad Mad Mad World*. *Ship of Fools* (1965) contains a great deal of social commentary but is also a period drama that seeks to portray aspects of 1930s European society that led the continent into World War II. Kramer returned to the straight message movie in 1967 with *Guess Who's Coming to Dinner* (1967). The World War II **comedy**–drama *The Secret of Santa Vittoria* (1969) is also a notable film, but by this time Kramer's career was in decline, and his subsequent films—through *The Runner Stumbles* (1979)—did not reach the level of his earlier efforts.

Kramer never won an **Academy Award**, though his directorial efforts gained him three nominations—for *The Defiant Ones*, *Judgment at Nuremberg*, and *Guess Who's Coming to Dinner*. In addition, six films produced by Kramer scored **Oscar** nominations for Best Picture, including *High Noon*, *The Caine Mutiny* (1954), *The Defiant Ones*, *Judgment at Nuremberg*, *Ship of Fools* (1965), and *Guess Who's Coming to Dinner*.

**KUBRICK, STANLEY (1928–1999).** An American filmmaker who often worked in Great Britain (where he lived during most of the last 40 years of his life), Stanley Kubrick was one of the most respected film directors of his generation. A versatile director, producer, and writer who made groundbreaking works in a number of genres, Kubrick directed several minor films before hitting his stride with *Killer's Kiss* (1955) and *The Killing* (1956), two notable works of late **film noir**. He directed only 10 more films after these, but each is a classic of its kind.

*Paths of Glory* (1957) is a World War I film that is now much admired, though it got relatively little attention at the time. Kubrick's next film, the **historical epic *Spartacus*** (1960) gained great attention, however, both for its merits as a film and for its role in helping to break the **blacklist** by giving onscreen credit to blacklisted screenwriter **Dalton Trumbo**. *Lolita* (1962) also gained significant attention, mostly for its controversial subject matter, though it is in many ways a comic tour-de-force. It was also the first of Kubrick's films to be made in Great Britain, a practice he subsequently followed through the rest of his career.

Kubrick next directed *Dr. Strangelove or: How I Learned to Stop Worrying and Love the Bomb* (1964), a masterpiece of satirical cinema that lampoons the paranoid mentality of Cold War America, at the same time making serious points about the madness of the Cold War arms race. This film was the first of Kubrick's three important contributions to **science fiction** film. He also holds an important position in the history of science fiction film, having directed three films in the genre, all of which are classics of their kind. Kubrick's next film was ***2001: A Space Odyssey*** (1968), a philosophical space opera in a much more serious mode that has been widely credited as the first film to demonstrate that a sf film could be a true work of art. It also helped to revitalize sf cinema and to establish a number of new conventions for the visual representation of travel in outer space. Kubrick followed in 1971 with this third straight work of science fiction, the stylish and disturbing dystopian film *A Clockwork Orange*. Kubrick produced no more works of science fiction in his lifetime. However, one of the projects that was in the planning stage at his death was the film that became *Artificial Intelligence: AI*, directed by **Steven Spielberg** and released in 2001.

*Barry Lyndon* (1975) was one of the least successful of Kubrick's mature films, though it is still a notable (and visually lavish) historical epic. It also became the third of Kubrick's films to be nominated for an **Academy Award** for Best Picture, following *Dr. Strangelove* and *A Clockwork Orange*. *The Shining* (1980) is a classic of the **horror** genre, and *Full Metal Jacket* (1987) is one of the most respected films about the war in Vietnam. Kubrick ended his career with the controversial *Eyes Wide Shut* (1999), a sort of combination of the art film and soft-core pornography that received mixed initial reviews but that has gained something of a **cult** following over the years.

Kubrick's only **Oscar** win was for the **special effects** for *2001*, but he was nominated for Best Director for *Dr. Strangelove*, *2001*, *A Clockwork Orange*, and *Barry Lyndon*. He also received Best Screenplay nominations for those four films, as well as for *Full Metal Jacket*.

# L

**LADD, ALAN (1913–1964).** The Arkansas-born Alan Ladd struggled for years to get a footing in the film business before finally landing a major role as the complex villain of the **film noir** thriller *This Gun for Hire* (1942), showing considerable chemistry with the female lead, **Veronica Lake**. Though small in stature and though his blonde good looks were not those of the traditional tough guy, Ladd went on to play a number of roles as gangsters or conflicted villains, bringing a new type of energy to such roles. He solidified his position as an important new figure in Hollywood with his role in *The Glass Key* (1942, again with Lake), then followed with a string of leading roles, appearing in three major films in 1946 alone: *Two Years before the Mast*, *The Blue Dahlia* (also with Lake), and *O.S.S.* His title role in *The Great Gatsby* (1949) was also important.

Ladd's rise to stardom culminated in his performance in the title role in *Shane* (1953), probably his greatest single role. After *Shane*, the quality and frequency of his roles began to decline. He did, however, continue to play starring roles in the latter part of the 1950s, including *Boy on a Dolphin* (1957) and *The Badlanders* (1958). His career was in definite decline by the time he died, at age 50, of what was ruled an accidental drug overdose.

**LAEMMLE, CARL (1867–1939).** The German-born Carl Laemmle went on to become the founder of **Universal Studios** and was a leading force behind the early evolution of the American film industry as a whole. Laemmle came to the United States in 1884, working for years in Chicago as a bookkeeper and office manager. Eventually, he moved into the film business by buying a series of nickelodeons, then formed his own production company, Independent Moving Pictures (IMP) in 1909, with the goal of producing films for his own nickelodeons. This company later merged with several others to form, in 1914, the Universal Motion Picture Manufacturing Company, which evolved into Universal Studios after incorporating as Universal Pictures Company, Inc., in 1925, with Laemmle as its head.

Laemmle, notorious for his nepotism in hiring relatives, made his son Carl Jr. the head of Universal Pictures in 1928 as a 21st birthday present. The younger Laemmle proved to be a fairly effective studio chief, convincing his father to modernize the studio and its operations and overseeing the production of films such as Universal's highly successful **monster movies** of the early 1930s, as well as more prestigious productions, such as the classic **war film** *All Quiet on the Western Front* (1930). However, Carl Jr.'s move into more expensive productions in the mid-1930s ultimately spelled the end for himself and his father at Universal. By 1936, production problems with the lavish **musical** *Show Boat* led to the ouster of both Laemmles from Universal by its creditor Standard Capital Corporation, even though the picture would ultimately, and ironically, prove to be a great critical and commercial success.

**LAKE, VERONICA (1922–1973).** Born Constance Ockelman, Veronica Lake gained considerable attention in Hollywood while still a teenager for her roles in *I Wanted Wings*, *Hold Back the Dawn*, and *Sullivan's Travels*, all in 1941. The **film noir** *This Gun for Hire* (1942) was another major success in which Lake showed considerable chemistry with actor **Alan Ladd**, opposite whom she also appeared in the noir films *The Glass Key* (1942) and *The Blue Dahlia* (1946). Though a major star in the **Paramount** stable through the 1940s, Lake drew little critical praise for her acting and meanwhile gained a reputation for being temperamental and difficult to work with. Her career quickly declined after leaving Paramount near the end of the 1940s, and her subsequent roles were primarily on television. Her last film appearance came in the low-budget **science fiction/horror** film *Flesh Feast* (1970). Audiences were reminded of Lake's legacy through repeated references to her in the 1997 **neo-noir** film *L.A. Confidential*.

**LAMOUR, DOROTHY (1914–1996).** After her breakthrough performance as the title character in *The Jungle Princess* (1936), Dorothy Lamour went on to become one of **Paramount Pictures'** top contract stars over the next decade and a half, often playing exotic beauties from various distant locales. Most notably, she starred alongside **Bing Crosby** and **Bob Hope** in their hugely successful series of "Road" pictures, generally as an indigenous woman from whatever exotic locales they happened to be visiting at the time.

Perhaps because of her central association with these films, Lamour was always more of a movie star and sex symbol than a respected actress. She was never nominated for an **Academy Award**, for example, though she did prove a reliable player in a variety of roles, especially in **comedies** and **musicals**. In 1952, she starred in her last Road picture, *Road to Bali*, as well as playing a major role in *The Greatest Show on Earth*, which won the **Oscar** for Best Picture. She did not appear in another film for more than a decade, however, spending that time performing primarily on the stage and in nightclubs, making an occasional appearance on television variety shows.

Lamour returned to film with a supporting role in *Donovan's Reef* (1963) and subsequently made a number of appearances as an actress, usually on television. In 1987, her last performance, in the anthology film *Creepshow 2*, won her a Saturn Award nomination from the Academy of Science Fiction, Fantasy, and Horror Films as Best Supporting Actress.

**LANCASTER, BURT (1913–1994).** Though initially featured primarily in roles designed to utilize his muscular and athletic physique, Burt Lancaster gradually developed into one of America's most respected film actors. After a brief career as a circus acrobat, Lancaster entered the military during World War II; after the war, he began his acting career with an excellent performance in **Robert Siodmak's film noir** classic *The Killers* (1946). He then built his credentials with several solid performances in notable films over the next several years, including another important film noir with Siodmak, *Criss Cross* (1949); **Jacques Tourneur's** *The Flame and the Arrow* (1950); and **Michael Curtiz's biopic** *Jim Thorpe—All American* (1951). Lancaster then achieved full-blown Hollywood stardom with his performance in **Fred Zinneman's** *From Here to Eternity* (1953), for which he received the first of his four **Academy Award** nominations for Best Actor.

Lancaster appeared in a number of important films in a variety of genres in the remainder of the 1950s, including *Gunfight at the O.K. Corral* and *Sweet Smell of Success*, both in 1957. He then won his first (and only) Academy Award for Best Actor for his performance in *Elmer Gantry* (1960). He followed with performances in such notable films as *Judgment at Nuremberg* (1961), *Birdman of Alcatraz* (1963, for which he received another **Oscar** nomination for Best Actor), *Seven Days in May* (1964), and *The Professionals* (1966).

Especially known for his pairings with fellow actor **Kirk Douglas** (with whom he appeared in seven films), Lancaster continued to appear in interesting films beyond the mid-1960s, many of them openly espousing liberal political agendas. Such films include *Ulzana's Raid* (1972), which uses the genre of the **Western** to comment on the U.S. involvement in Vietnam; *Buffalo Bill and the Indians, or Sitting Bull's History Lesson* (1976), which uses the career of Western legend Buffalo Bill Cody to comment on U.S. media culture; and *Twilight's Last Gleaming* (1977), which warns of the dangers of militarism.

Lancaster received his fourth and final Oscar nomination for Best Actor for *Atlantic City* (1980). From that point forward, however, he appeared mostly in supporting roles. In a 1999 poll conducted by the **American Film Institute**, he was named the 19th greatest male film legend of all time.

**LANG, FRITZ (1890–1976).** Born in Vienna, the important screenwriter and director Fritz Lang was one of the pioneers of German cinema during the important period in which the influential expressionist style was being developed. This style was especially influential on the later American **film noir** movement, in which Lang became an important director. But it has also exercised an influence in **science fiction**. Indeed, one of the great works of German expressionist cinema was Lang's own *Metropolis* (1927), one of the founding works of modern sf film. While working in Germany, Lang also directed *M* (1931), still regarded as a classic crime thriller, and *The Testament of Dr. Mabuse* (1933), a film with clearly anti-Nazi implications.

In 1934, Lang fled Nazi Germany for Paris, subsequently moving on to the United States. His work in the United States was primarily as a director, mostly as one of the architects of film noir. His first two American films, *Fury* (1936) and *You Only Live Once* (1937), were both important forerunners of film noir. He later directed such notable noir films as *The Woman in the Window* (1944), *Scarlet Street* (1945), *Cloak and Dagger* (1946), *Secret beyond the Door* (1948), *Clash by Night* (1952), *The Blue Gardenia* (1953), and *The Big Heat* (1954). During World War II he directed the noirish anti-Nazi thriller *Hangmen Also Die!* (1943), which Lang co-wrote with John Wexley and exiled German playwright Bertolt Brecht.

Lang also worked in other genres, as in the case of the **Western** *Rancho Notorious* (1952). His films became increasingly dark and pessimistic through the 1950s, culminating in *While the City Sleeps* (1956) and *Beyond a Reasonable Doubt* (1956), perhaps the bleakest of his American noir films. Lang returned to Germany in 1957 and remained there through the rest of his life and career.

**LANGE, JESSICA (1949– ).** Young Jessica Lange gained considerable attention when she was cast to star in the 1976 remake of *King Kong*. Unfortunately, the negative critical response to that film (and to Lange's performance in it) almost derailed her career just as it was beginning. She did not appear in another film until *All That Jazz* (1979), a film that also received mostly negative reviews. Lange, however, was praised for her performance in the 1981 remake of the **film noir** classic *The Postman Always Rings Twice*, and she was on the road to stardom at last.

Finally, 1982 was a particularly big year for Lange. Her performance that year in *Frances* gained her an **Academy Award** nomination for Best Actress in a Leading Role, while her performance in *Tootsie* won her the **Oscar** for Best Actress in a Supporting Role. She received Oscar nominations for Best Actress for three more films in the 1980s, including *Country* (1984), *Sweet Dreams* (1985), and *Music Box* (1989), and she was one of Hollywood's top leading ladies throughout the decade. In the 1990s, she had leading roles in such films as *Cape Fear* (1991) and *Rob Roy* (1995), winning the Oscar for Best Actress for her performance in *Blue Sky* (1994). She continued to appear regularly in films through the first decade of the 21st century, though mostly in supporting roles.

**LARDNER, RING, JR. (1915–2000).** Screenwriter Ring Lardner Jr. was one of the most prominent members of the **Hollywood Ten,** who were at the very center of the Hollywood blacklist of the 1950s. Lardner has the distinction of winning **Academy Awards** for Best Screenplay both before—for *Woman of the Year* (1942)—and after—for *MASH* (1970)—going on the blacklist. Other notable films written by Lardner before the blacklist include **Fritz Lang's** *Cloak and Dagger* (1946) and **Otto Preminger's** *Forever Amber* (1947). He also contributed to the script for the **film noir** classic *Laura* (1944), though without screen credit. However, his uncooperative testimony before the **House Un-American Activities Committee** (HUAC) in October of 1947 effectively removed him from the film business for nearly two decades.

Lardner did occasionally write for film and television during the blacklist using pseudonyms, but he did not produce another script under his own name until *The Cincinnati Kid* in 1965. His next (and last major script) was for *MASH,* though he also scripted the Muhammad Ali **biopic** *The Greatest* (1977, starring Ali himself). He also contributed (without screen credit) to the script for the **sports movie** *Semi-Tough* (1977).

**LASSETER, JOHN (1957– ).** A former **Disney** animator who had been fired by that studio in the 1980s due to his insistence on pursuing the possibilities offered by **computer-generated imagery,** as opposed to conventional hand-drawn animation, John Lasseter quickly found employment with the Computer Graphics Group of Lucasfilm. This group eventually evolved into **Pixar,** with Lasseter as its leading light. When the Lasseter-directed *Toy Story* (1995) became a hit as the first feature-length film to be fully animated by computer, Lasseter's devotion to computer animation was vindicated.

Lasseter subsequently directed *A Bug's Life* (1998), *Toy Story 2* (1999), and *Cars* (2005), but meanwhile put more and more of his energy into his work as the head of Pixar, executive producing such films as *Monsters, Inc.* (2001), *Finding Nemo* (2003), and *The Incredibles* (2004). When Disney acquired Pixar in 2006, they reacquired Lasseter's services as well. In fact, as part of the acquisition deal, Lasseter was named chief creative officer of the animation studios of both Disney and Pixar. In addition, Lasseter, who had once worked as a Jungle Cruise skipper at Disneyland, was named principal creative advisor to Walt Disney Imagineering, in which capacity he helps design new theme park attractions.

Since the acquisition, Lasseter has executive produced such Disney **animated films** as *Meet the Robinsons* (2007), *Bolt* (2008), *The Princess and the Frog* (2009), and *Rapunzel* (2010), as well as the Pixar films *Ratatouille* (2007), *WALL-E* (2008), *Up* (2009), and *Toy Story 3* (2010). A great admirer of the Japanese animation director Hayao Miyazaki, Lasseter has also served as the executive producer for the English-dubbed versions of several of Miyazaki's films, overseeing their subsequent distribution in the United States by Disney.

**LAUREL, STAN (1890–1965), AND HARDY, OLIVER (1892–1957).** Laurel and Hardy were one of the best-known **comedy** teams in film history. Though they appeared together in the **silent film** *The Lucky Dog* and worked separately for the same production company (under **Hal Roach**) for the next several years, they did not officially become a team until 1927, when they appeared together in a number of Roach-produced shorts. Continuing to work for Roach, they moved into longer films with *Pardon Us* (1931) and soon became Roach's most profitable product.

Employing a mode of comedy relying on **slapstick** and on relatively normal situations getting entirely out of hand, the two also achieved additional comedy through their contrasting appearances, with Laurel appearing rather diminutive beside the tall and portly Hardy. Both played rather dimwitted characters; innocent and affable, they tended to maintain their good spirits in the face of adversity, though Hardy was often frustrated with Laurel and they often got into altercations with each other in addition to their battles with others. The pair continued to make shorts for Roach, including *The Music Box* (1932), which won the **Academy Award** for Best Short Subject. However, they shifted more and more to features with such films as *Sons of the Desert* (1933), *The Bohemian Girl* (1936), *Way Out West* (1937), and *Block-Heads* (1938).

After parting ways with Roach in 1940, Laurel and Hardy made a series of **B-movies** for **Twentieth Century Fox** and **Metro-Goldwyn-Mayer** (MGM) but found themselves relegated to the status of hired talent, whereas they had made more creative contributions under Roach. Though these films were quite successful commercially, the pair became frustrated with the movie business; they left film and concentrated on stage performances in Europe after 1945, though they did return for one French film, *Atoll K*, in 1951 (released in English as *Utopia* in the United States in 1954).

With both partners having health problems, the duo performed less often after 1950, and Laurel refused to perform alone after Hardy's death in 1957.

Laurel did, however, receive an honorary **Academy Award** in 1961. Laurel and Hardy have posthumously become an even more important part of the legacy of American culture, thanks to the screening of their films on television and at classic film revivals.

**LAWSON, JOHN HOWARD (1894–1977).** Screenwriter John Howard Lawson was perhaps the most genuinely radical member of the **Hollywood Ten**, one of the few members of the Hollywood blacklist of the 1950s to have actual Marxist sympathies and inclinations. During the 1920s, Lawson wrote and directed plays in New York, becoming involved with the radical theater scene there. He turned to writing for film in 1928 and contributed to the scripts for a number of mainstream films over the next few years, though perhaps his most important contribution to Hollywood history was his founding, along with Lester Cole and Samuel Ornitz, of the **Screen Writers Guild** in 1933.

Lawson joined the American Communist Party in 1934 and soon became the head of its Hollywood division. Lawson received an **Academy Award** nomination for Best Writing for writing the story for *Blockade* (1938), a film about the Spanish Civil War that was designed to generate sympathy for the Spanish Republicans in that conflict. That same year he also wrote the script for *Algiers* (1938), another notable film.

Lawson was particularly prominent as a writer of **war films** during World War II, scripting the **Humphrey Bogart** vehicles *Action in the North Atlantic* (1943) and *Sahara* (1943), as well as *Counter-Attack* (1945), a film made in support of the wartime alliance between the United States and the Soviet Union. After the war, Lawson scripted *Smash-Up: The Story of a Woman* (1947), but his output was soon curtailed after his uncooperative testimony before the **House Un-American Activities Committee** (HUAC) in 1947 led to his imprisonment and blacklisting.

Lawson never again worked in Hollywood, leaving for Mexico after his release from prison. There, working under pseudonyms, he wrote the screenplays for *Cry, the Beloved Country* (1952) and *The Careless Years* (1957). However, most of his post-blacklist writing consisted of Marxist commentaries on film and drama. The most important of these is *Film in the Battle of Ideas* (1953), a critique of the representation of class and gender in Hollywood film that was dismissed as extremist at the time but that now seems rather moderate (and accurate), anticipating many directions in academic film critique of later decades.

**LEE, SPIKE (1957– ).** Spike Lee got off to a fast start as a director of feature films when his low-budget debut (as a director, producer, and actor), *She's*

*Gotta Have It* (1985), drew rave reviews. He followed with a string of critical successes that established him as the preeminent African American film director of his generation. These films included *School Daze* (1988), *Do the Right Thing* (1989), *Mo' Better Blues* (1990), and *Jungle Fever* (1991), which together demonstrated Lee's ability to address race and other potentially controversial issues with stylistic flair.

In 1992, Lee moved into bigger budget filmmaking with the **biopic** *Malcolm X*, a three-hour-plus epic starring **Denzel Washington**, at the time a rising star, who had also had the lead in *Mo' Better Blues*. Lee then followed with a series of less successful films—including *Crooklyn* (1994), *Clockers* (1995), and *Girl 6* (1996)—that for many critics did not live up to the promise of his earlier work. On the other hand, he received an **Academy Award** nomination as the producer of the **documentary** feature *4 Little Girls* (1997). The basketball drama *He Got Game* (1998), again starring Washington, was then something of a return to form for Lee as a director of fictional films.

Lee has continued to direct regularly since that time, while his production company 40 Acres & A Mule Filmworks, has produced films directed by others as well. Highlights of his recent directorial career include *Summer of Sam* (1999), *Bamboozled* (2000), *25th Hour* (2002), *She Hate Me* (2004), *Inside Man* (2006). Lee has also been a successful director of television commercials, most notably in a series of Nike commercials in which he himself appeared, alongside basketball star Michael Jordan.

**LEHMAN, ERNEST (1915–2005).** Though he wrote the stories or scripts for only 16 films and never won a competitive **Academy Award** for writing, Ernest Lehman wrote some of the most important films in Hollywood history. He also received a total of five **Oscar** nominations for Best Writing, for his contributions to *Sabrina* (1954), *North by Northwest* (1959), *West Side Story* (1961), *Who's Afraid of Virginia Woolf?* (1966), and *Hello, Dolly!* (1969). Lehman also received a Best Picture nomination as the producer of *Who's Afraid of Virginia Woolf?*.

After a beginning as a copy writer for a public relations firm, Lehman broke into Hollywood film with *Executive Suite* (1954). Other important films written or co-written by Lehman include *Somebody Up There Likes Me* (1956), *The King and I* (1956), *Sweet Smell of Success* (1957), *The Sound of Music* (1965), and *Family Plot* (1976), **Alfred Hitchcock**'s last film. In 2001, Lehman was given an honorary Academy Award for his overall body of work.

**LEIGH, VIVIEN (1913–1967).** Born Vivian Mary Hartley in Darjeeling, India, the British actress Vivien Leigh first gained the attention of Hollywood for her performance in the British film *A Yank at Oxford* (1938), which also featured her childhood friend **Maureen O'Sullivan**. The next year, she was catapulted to the very peak of Hollywood stardom for her **Academy Award**–winning performance as Scarlett O'Hara in *Gone with the Wind* (1939). In 1940, she married British superstar **Laurence Olivier**, and the two worked together on several subsequent productions. However, mental health problems apparently related to bipolar disorder plagued Leigh in the coming years and prevented her from successfully following up on her stellar Hollywood debut.

Leigh moved back to the forefront of Hollywood stardom with her stirring performance as Blanche DuBois in *A Streetcar Named Desire* (1951), which won her a second Best Actress **Oscar**. Leigh herself would later say that the experience of playing the unbalanced DuBois pushed her from instability into madness. In any case, due to her increasing health problems (from both the bipolarity and tuberculosis), she appeared in only one more film in the 1950s. In the 1960s, she starred in *The Roman Spring of Mrs. Stone* (1961) and *Ship of Fools* (1965). She died in London of tuberculosis in 1967.

Though her reputation as an actress in American film rests almost entirely on the two films for which she won Oscars, Leigh was named the 16th greatest female screen legend of all time in a 1999 poll conducted by the **American Film Institute**, thus indicating the power of her two most important performances.

**LEMMON, JACK (1925–2001).** In a film career that spanned more than 40 years and saw him star in more than 60 movies, Jack Lemmon was one of Hollywood's most likeable and dependable stars. After numerous appearances on television, Lemmon made his official film debut with a major supporting role in **George Cukor**'s *It Should Happen to You* (1954). He then moved immediately into a starring role in Mark Robson's *Phffft* that same year. The next year, his performance in *Mister Roberts* won him an **Academy Award** for Best Supporting Actor. He made several more appearances in both leading and supporting roles until his starring performances in two films by **Billy Wilder**, *Some Like It Hot* (1959) and *The Apartment* (1960), won him back-to-back **Oscar** nominations for Best Actor, solidifying his position as a top leading man.

Lemmon received another Best Actor Oscar nomination for his dramatic performance in *Days of Wine and Roses* (1962) and continued to star in major films (mostly **comedies**) over the next several years. Other highlights of the 1960s included *Irma la Douce* (1963), *The Great Race* (1965), and *The Odd Couple* (1968), perhaps the best known of his several pairings with actor **Walter Matthau**. With *The Out of Towners* (1970), Lemmon began the

1970s with another successful comedy. He then won his first (and only) Best Actor Oscar for his dramatic performance in *Save the Tiger* (1973), marking a turn toward more concentration on dramatic roles that would also see him receive Best Actor Oscar nominations for *The China Syndrome* (1979), *Tribute* (1980), and *Missing* (1982).

In 1988, Lemmon received a Life Achievement Award from the **American Film Institute**, but his career was far from over. Subsequent to that award, he appeared in such films as *JFK* (1991), *Glengarry Glen Ross* (1992), *Short Cuts* (1993), *Grumpy Old Men* (1993), and *Grumpier Old Men* (1995), the latter two again with Matthau. In 1998, he and Matthau starred in the sequel *The Odd Couple II*.

**LEROY, MERVYN (1900–1987).** Mervyn LeRoy did a variety of film-related jobs until he finally graduated to directing with *No Place to Go* (1927). He would go on to have a long and illustrious career as a studio executive and as a producer and director in Hollywood, including an involvement in several historically important films. LeRoy directed several key films for **Warner Bros.** in the 1930s, including the **gangster film** *Little Caesar*, the social problem film *I Am a Fugitive from a Chain Gang* (1932), the **musical** *Gold Diggers of 1933* (1933), and the social drama *They Won't Forget* (1937). Known for his efficiency and organizational skills as a filmmaker, LeRoy was made head of production at **Metro-Goldwyn-Mayer** (MGM) in 1938; in this capacity he approved and oversaw the production of *The Wizard of Oz*, of which he is often considered to have been a co-director, though he was credited only as the producer.

LeRoy also continued to work as a director in his own right, receiving an **Academy Award** nomination for Best Director for *Random Harvest* (1942). He received a special honorary **Oscar** as the director and co-producer of the pro-tolerance **documentary** short *The House I Live In* (1945), though his contributions at MGM were more as an executive than as a director. In the 1950s, he moved back to Warner Bros. and revived his directorial career somewhat with films such as the **comedies** *Mister Roberts* (1955, co-directed with **John Ford**) and *No Time for Sergeants* (1958).

LeRoy received the **Irving G. Thalberg** Memorial Award in 1976.

**LESTER, RICHARD (1932– ).** The American-born director Richard Lester did much of his work in Great Britain, where he became closely associated with the "Swinging Sixties" scene, especially after directing the Beatles movies *A Hard Day's Night* (1964) and *Help!* (1965). Many of the techniques used in these films were later influential in the development of **music** videos, so much so that he was named by MTV as the "Father of the Music Video."

Lester's *The Knack . . . And How to Get It* (1965) was another key Swinging Sixties film. *How I Won the War* (1967), an antiwar film featuring Beatle John Lennon, was another expression of a quintessentially 1960s sensibility.

Lester later directed a number of other highly successful films, including *The Three Musketeers* (1973) and its sequel *The Four Musketeers* (1974) and *Robin and Marian* (1976). In 1980, he was credited as the director of *Superman II* (1980) after original director **Richard Donner** was fired in a dispute with the film's producers, though much of the film had already been shot. Lester also directed the unfortunate *Superman III* (1983), which virtually ended his directorial career, though he did direct *The Return of the Musketeers* (1989), a sequel to his earlier Musketeers films, as well as the concert tour **documentary** *Get Back* (1991), featuring former Beatle Paul McCartney.

**LEVINSON, BARRY (1942– ).** After an early career as a television writer and then screenwriter, Barry Levinson moved into directing, scoring an immediate success in his directorial debut with *Diner* (1982). Levinson directed a number of other interesting films in the 1980s, including *The Natural* (1984), *Young Sherlock Holmes* (1985), *Tin Men* (1987), and *Good Morning, Vietnam* (1987). His work of the decade then culminated in his direction of *Rain Man* (1988), for which he won the **Academy Award** for Best Director.

The **gangster film** *Bugsy* (1991) was also a critical success for Levinson, winning him his second **Oscar** nomination for Best Director and scoring a total of 10 Oscar nominations. The political **satire** *Wag the Dog* (1997) drew considerable critical attention for the timeliness of its subject matter, which concerned the manipulation of the media for political purposes. Other films directed by Levinson include *Avalon* (1990), *Toys* (1992), *Sphere* (1998), and *Man of the Year* (2006), another political satire.

In addition to his directorial work, Levinson has served as the producer or executive producer of a number of films, as well as the executive producer of a number of television programs, most notably the series *Homicide: Life on the Streets* (1993–1999) and *Oz* (HBO, 1997–2003). He has also continued to work as a writer throughout his career, receiving Best Screenplay Oscar nominations for *. . . And Justice for All* (1979), *Diner*, and *Avalon*.

**LEWIS, JOSEPH H. (1907–2000).** Working mostly with very low budgets, Joseph H. Lewis nevertheless consistently sought to invest his films with a variety of interesting visual compositions, earning himself a reputation as something of a **B-movie** auteur. Beginning mostly as a director of low-budget **Westerns** in the late 1930s and early 1940s, Lewis eventually worked in a number of genres. For example, his 1944 **musical** *Minstrel Man* is something of a low-budget classic, the success of which led Lewis to be hired to direct the musical sequences for the A-list **biopic** *The Jolson Story* (1946). Lewis also directed several **horror** films, including *Invisible Ghost* (1941, starring **Béla Lugosi**) and *The Mad Doctor of Market Street* (1942).

Lewis would ultimately become best known for his work in **film noir** in the 1940s and 1950s. His noir films include *The Falcon in San Francisco* (1945), *My Name Is Julia Ross* (1945), *So Dark the Night* (1946), *The Undercover Man* (1949), *A Lady without Passport* (1950), *Cry of the Hunted* (1953), and the much respected *The Big Combo* (1955). However, his most prominent film noir is *Deadly Is the Female* (1950, aka *Gun Crazy*), a recognized classic of the genre.

Lewis returned to the Western for his last film, *Terror in a Texas Town* (1958). His subsequent directorial efforts were all for television episodes, mostly Westerns and crime dramas, ending with episodes of *The Big Valley* and *A Man Called Shenandoah* in 1966.

**LIONSGATE.** Lionsgate Entertainment, incorporated in Canada in 1995 but now based in Santa Monica, California, is a highly successful producer and distributor of **independent films**, specializing, at least initially, in films deemed too controversial for mainstream Hollywood studios. However, as the company has grown they have moved into more mainstream fare and have recently even formed a new family film division, Lions Gate Family Entertainment, that began operation with the **animated film** *Alpha and Omega* (2010).

Lionsgate began producing and distributing films in 1997, when *Affliction* received **Academy Award** nominations for Best Leading Actor and Best Supporting Actor, winning in the second category. Their *Gods and Monsters* (1998) received an **Oscar** for both Best Actor and Best Actress, while winning the Oscar for Best Adapted Screenplay. *American Psycho* (2000) was their first big commercial hit; that same year Lionsgate was the American distributor for the critically acclaimed Mexican film *Amores Perros*, further solidifying the company's credentials as a distributor of complex, cerebral films that could appeal to both art-house crowds and general moviegoers. *Monster's Ball* (2001), meanwhile, scored Oscar nominations for Best Original Screenplay and Best Actress, with **Halle Berry** winning the award in the latter category.

Lionsgate was the American distributor for the independently produced *Crash* (2004), which received a total of six Oscar nominations, winning in three categories, including the key prize for Best Picture. The same year, they distributed **Michael Moore**'s controversial documentary *Fahrenheit 9/11*. Other prominent films produced and/or distributed by Lionsgate include

*The Rules of Attraction* (2002), *Hotel Rwanda* (2004), *Saw* (2004), *Happy Endings* (2005), *The Descent* (2006), *3:10 to Yuma* (2007), *Rambo* (2008), *W.* (2008), *Precious* (2009), *The Imaginarium of Dr. Parnassus* (2009), and *Kick-Ass* (2010).

Lionsgate Entertainment has no relationship with Lion's Gate Films, the independent production company formed by **Robert Altman** in the 1970s.

**LLOYD, HAROLD (1893–1971).** Harold Lloyd was one of the most important performers in **silent film**, exceeded in importance as an actor in silent **comedies** only by **Charles Chaplin** and **Buster Keaton**. Lloyd was particularly known for comic action sequences, performing most of his own stunts. Of the nearly 200 films in which he was credited as an actor, Lloyd is best remembered for *Safety Last!* (1923), in which a scene featuring him dangling from the hands of a giant clock high above a city street would become one of the most recognizable images in the history of American film.

Lloyd began his career in film with several uncredited roles for **Thomas Edison**'s film company in 1913. By 1915, he had moved to the new company formed by producer–director **Hal Roach**, with whom he made dozens of short films over the next four years, beginning with *Willie Runs the Park* (1915). Consciously imitative of the early films of Chaplin, these films were highly successful and established Lloyd as a star, while making his characters "Lonesome Luke" and "The Boy" figures exceeded only by Chaplin's Tramp as icons of silent film.

In the 1920s, Lloyd transitioned into longer films, while his character, still often billed as "The Boy" became a more mature figure distinguished by his heavy, round-rimmed glasses. The "Glasses Character" was a sort of American Everyman, determined to succeed despite all obstacles. Feature-length films such as *Safety Last!*, *The Freshman* (1925), and *The Kid Brother* (1927) were immense box-office successes, solidifying Lloyd's status as a major star.

Lloyd left Roach to form his own production company in 1924, producing many of his own most successful films. Unlike Chaplin, he welcomed the transition to sound; he thus converted his film *Welcome Danger* (1929), already in production as a silent, into a sound film. He followed with a series of moderately successful talkies in the 1930s, beginning with *Feet First* (1930) and *Movie Crazy* (1932), which resembled his earlier silents in many ways. Lloyd tried his hand at political **satire** in *The Cat's Paw* (1934) and at **screwball comedy** in *The Milky Way* (1936), but was never quite able to put his stamp on a distinctive brand of sound comedy as he had done with the silents.

Lloyd starred in *Professor Beware* (1938), officially produced by his company, but actually made using facilities and staff of **Paramount**. He then retired from acting, working in the early 1940s as a film producer and in the mid-1940s as director and host of the radio program *The Old Gold Comedy Hour*. He returned to acting to star in *The Sin of Harold Diddlebock* (1947), based on his own earlier character from *The Freshman*. However, production was marred by Lloyd's battles with director **Preston Sturges**, and the film was not a success. That film essentially ended Lloyd's career in film, though he did briefly return to producing in the early 1960s.

**LOEW, MARCUS (1870–1927).** Born in poverty, Marcus Loew eventually managed to acquire (in partnership with several others, including **Adolph Zukor**) a nickelodeon in New York City, which he eventually built into an extensive chain of movie theaters, beginning with the founding, in 1904, of the People's Vaudeville Company. In 1910, this expanding chain became Loew's Consolidated Enterprises. It was reorganized in 1919 under the name Loew's, Inc.

Always interested in generating films to be shown in his theaters without having to pay others for them, Loew soon forayed into film production. Between 1920 and 1924, Loew acquired controlling interest in Metro Pictures Corporation, Goldwyn Pictures Corporation (from which **Samuel Goldwyn** had already departed), and a third film production company owned by **Louis B. Mayer**. Loew merged the three into a single entity known as **Metro-Goldwyn-Mayer** (MGM), with Mayer managing its overall operations and Mayer's assistant **Irving G. Thalberg** as the production chief.

Metro-Goldwyn-Mayer (more widely known simply as MGM) would become one of the most powerful and important studios in Hollywood, though Loew's early death in 1927 prevented him from seeing the company's greatest successes. Meanwhile, these successes were partly due to their ongoing relationship with Loew's Theatres, which remained the parent company of MGM until 1959, when the outcome of the **Paramount Antitrust Case** forced studios and theater chains to become independent of one another.

Loew's Theatres remained in operation until 2006, when it merged with AMC Theatres to form (under the name of the latter) what is still the second-largest chain of movie theaters in the United States.

**LOMBARD, CAROLE (1908–1942).** In a brief career cut short by her death in a plane crash at the age of 33, Carole Lombard became one of the best known actresses in Hollywood, both for her onscreen performances and for her off-screen romance with **Clark Gable**. A 1999 poll conducted by the **American Film Institute** named Lombard the 23rd greatest female screen legend of all time.

Lombard began her career as a child actor with small roles in a number of **silent films**. She became a star after the coming of sound film, mostly in **comedies** such as *My Man Godfrey* (1936), for which she received her only **Academy Award** nomination, for Best Actress. Other key films featuring Lombard in the 1930s included *Twentieth Century* (1934) and *Bolero* (1934), for which she turned down the starring role of Ellie Andrews in *It Happened One Night* (1934). *Nothing Sacred* (1937) was another success, helping to keep Lombard at the top levels of Hollywood stardom.

The comedy *Fools for Scandal* (1938) was a notable flop, after which Lombard turned to more dramatic roles in such films as *Made for Each Other* (1939), *In Name Only* (1939), and *Vigil in the Night* (1940). She then ended her career with strong comic performances in *Mr. and Mrs. Smith* (1941) and *To Be or Not to Be* (1942).

*LORD OF THE RINGS* **TRILOGY.** The *Lord of the Rings* trilogy (dir. Peter Jackson, 2001–2003) was a major phenomenon of early 21st-century film, comprising a series of critically acclaimed box-office smashes that effectively adapted J. R. R. Tolkien's 1950s **fantasy** masterpiece to the big screen. The three movies, each corresponding to a volume of Tolkien's original trilogy, were all filmed together (in New Zealand) for budgetary and other practical reasons, then released one per year during three consecutive Christmas film seasons. The three films, all joint New Zealand–United States co-productions, are *The Lord of the Rings: The Fellowship of the Ring* (2001), *The Lord of the Rings: The Two Towers* (2002), and *The Lord of the Rings: The Return of the King* (2003).

The *Lord of the Rings* trilogy is set in Tolkien's richly imagined Middle Earth, a land of magic and titanic struggles between good and evil. It is essentially a quest narrative in which a group of lowly hobbits (a diminutive, good-hearted race that generally lives in pastoral simplicity) must take a magic ring on a long cross-country journey to the one place it can be destroyed, because this ring is the key to the power of all evil in their world. Aided by humans, wizards, elves, and dwarves, the hobbits eventually overcome all obstacles and destroy the ring, on the way encountering a variety of adventures and epic struggles brought to life by the effective **special effects** (especially **computer-generated imagery**) that made this difficult adaptation possible.

*The Fellowship of the Ring* was a sensation, receiving a total of 13 **Academy Award** nominations, including Best Picture and Best Director, though its only four **Oscar** wins were in relatively technical categories, such as Best Cinematography, Best Score, Best Visual Effects, and Best Makeup. *The Two Towers* received less critical acclaim, but did receive six Oscar nominations, including one for Best Picture, winning the awards for Best Sound

Editing and Best Visual Effects. However, *The Return of the King*, in what was clearly a sort of cumulative reaction to the trilogy as a whole, virtually swept the 2004 Oscars, winning the awards in all 11 categories in which it was nominated, including awards for Best Picture, Best Director, and Best Screenplay. The three films together grossed more than a billion dollars in U.S. box-office receipts and nearly $3 billion worldwide.

**LORENTZ, PARE (1905–1992).** Born Leonard MacTaggart Lorentz, Pare Lorentz began his career in film as a critic, then moved into the direction of **documentaries** in the 1930s, becoming one of the best-known names in the history of that genre. His career in documentaries began in 1936, when he was hired by the U.S. government (with the personal support of President Franklin J. Roosevelt) to make a film about the Oklahoma Dust Bowl. That film ultimately became *The Plow That Broke the Plains* (1936), which remains one of the most famous documentaries in American film history.

Lorentz's second major documentary for the U.S. government was *The River* (1938), a celebration of the achievements of the Tennessee Valley Authority that is perhaps his finest technical achievement. Both *The Plow That Broke the Plains* and *The River* are supportive of the New Deal government that commissioned them, though one could argue that they ultimately espouse political positions somewhat to the left of those of the Roosevelt administration.

Other documentaries made by Lorentz include *The Fight for Life* (1940), *Nuremberg* (1946), and *Rural Co-Op* (1947), as well as numerous films made for the U.S. Army, in which he served during World War II. However, postwar prosperity combined with a hostile political environment to bring Lorentz's career as a filmmaker to a halt after *Rural Co-Op*.

**LOSEY, JOSEPH (1909–1984).** Joseph Losey began his career as a theater director, having studied with the great German dramatist Bertolt Brecht. He went on to a highly successful career as a film director, though that career was interrupted when he was driven into exile in Great Britain after being placed on the **blacklist** as a result of investigations of his political leanings (including his association with the communist Brecht). Losey subsequently enjoyed a successful career in British film, though even some of his British films were directed under pseudonyms due to his controversial political reputation.

Among the most interesting of Losey's early American films are *The Boy with Green Hair* (1948), an antiracist and antiwar parable; *The Lawless* (1949), a low-budget thriller that addresses the persecution and exploitation of immigrant fruit pickers in California; and *The Prowler* (1951), a **film noir** that critiques materialistic greed. Among his first British films were *The*

*Sleeping Tiger* (1954) and *The Intimate Stranger* (1956), both directed under pseudonyms. He then returned to directing under his own name in the stylish film noir *Time without Pity* (1957), still one of his best-known films.

Losey continued to work in Great Britain even after the end of the black-list, including an association with British playwright Harold Pinter that led Losey to direct three films scripted by Pinter, including *The Servant* (1963), *The Accident* (1967), and *The Go-Between* (1971), all of which employed a number of highly influential experimental techniques, marking a move away from Losey's earlier gritty naturalism. Meanwhile, working with Losey led Pinter into a highly successful career as a screenwriter. Maintaining his connection with the world of theater, Losey also directed other film adaptations of stage plays, including *Boom!* (1968), an adaptation of a play by Tennessee Williams, as well as adaptations of Henrik Ibsen's *A Doll's House* (1973) and of Brecht's *Galileo* (1975), the original U.S. stage production of which had been co-directed by Losey and Brecht decades earlier.

Other key films directed by Losey include the **spy film** spoof *Modesty Blaise* (1966), *The Assassination of Trotsky* (1972), *Mr. Klein* (1976), and *Don Giovanni* (1979), an adaptation of the Mozart opera.

**LUBITSCH, ERNST (1892–1947).** Born in Berlin, Ernst Lubitsch developed a global reputation for his **silent films** made in Germany, before coming to Hollywood in 1922. There, he quickly established himself as a director of elegant and sophisticated **comedies**, smoothly transitioning into the sound era with a number of early **musicals**, including *The Love Parade* (1929), for which Lubitsch won an **Academy Award** nomination for Best Director. He then moved back into **romantic comedy** with *Trouble in Paradise* (1932), an innuendo-filled film that could never have been made under the dictates of the **Production Code** that went into full effect in 1934.

By 1935, Lubitsch had become the production manager at **Paramount**, in which position he subsequently produced his own films, as well as overseeing the production of films directed by others. As a result, his output as a director diminished, and he directed only two films in this capacity—*Angel* (1937) and *Bluebeard's Eighth Wife* (1938)—before moving to **Metro-Goldwyn-Mayer** (MGM) in 1939 to direct *Ninotchka* (1939), one of his best-known films. He then moved outside the **major studios** altogether, directing another classic comedy, *To Be or Not to Be* (1942). In 1943, he directed *Heaven Can Wait* (1943) for **Twentieth Century Fox**, which won him the third of his Best Director **Oscar** nominations. His activity as a director was subsequently slight, partly due to a worsening heart condition that eventually led to his death at age 55. Shortly before his death, Lubitsch was given a special Academy Award for his 25 years of achievement in Hollywood film.

**LUCAS, GEORGE (1944– ).** George Lucas is one of the leading figures of the American film industry, based largely on the immense success of the *Star Wars* science fiction franchise, which Lucas created and most of whose films he directed. Lucas's first feature (as writer and director) was the dystopian film *THX 1138* (1971), a film that already showed an excellent grasp of storytelling and visual design. Lucas moved outside of science fiction as the writer and director of *American Graffiti* (1973), his first commercial success, but then returned to sf with a flourish in 1977 with the first *Star Wars* film. In 1981, Lucas was the executive producer of *Raiders of the Lost Ark* and has remained a driving force behind the important Indiana Jones sequence ever since, though the films have been directed by Lucas's close friend **Steven Spielberg**.

In the meantime, the *Star Wars* sequence continued with the other films of the original trilogy, *Stars Wars: Episode V—The Empire Strikes Back* (1980) and *Star Wars: Episode VI—The Return of the Jedi* (1983), both of which were executive produced and partly written by Lucas, though they were directed by others. The *Star Wars* sequence was in hiatus from 1983 to 1999, when the release of *Star Wars: Episode I—The Phantom Menace* became one of the most anticipated events in global film of the late 20th century. This film also initiated a second "prequel" trilogy of *Star Wars* films that also went on to include *Star Wars: Episode II—Attack of the Clones* (2002) and *Star Wars: Episode III—Revenge of the Sith* (2005). All three films of the second sequel were directed by Lucas.

In addition to his role as the principal creative force behind the actual films, Lucas's work on the *Star Wars* sequence has also placed him in a key position as one of the leading innovators in the development of **special effects** technology for sf film in general, especially in the realm of **computer-generated imagery** (CGI). The success of *Star Wars* helped to make Lucas's own studio, **Lucasfilm**, originally founded in 1971, a major player in the film industry, whose respective visual effects and sound effects divisions, **Industrial Light & Magic** and Skywalker Sound, have become leaders in their field, producing effects not only for Lucasfilm's own films but for a wide variety of other films as well.

**LUCASFILM.** Lucasfilm is the film studio founded by **George Lucas** in 1971 after the making of his first theatrical film, the dystopian **science fiction** film *THX 1138* (1971), based on a student film school project. Lucas's next film, *American Graffiti* (1973), was the first film produced by Lucasfilm, which then co-produced *Star Wars* (1977) with **Twentieth Century Fox**. The *Star Wars* films (distributed by Twentieth Century Fox) and the Indiana Jones films (distributed by **Paramount**), all produced by Lucas himself, have remained the heart of the company's efforts in film production ever since. Lucasfilm has also been a leader in the development of innovative filmmaking technologies, especially in the area of **special effects**, where their subsidiary **Industrial Light & Magic** is an industry leader, especially in the realm of **computer-generated imagery** (CGI). Their Skywalker Sound subsidiary is an innovator in sound technology for film, and the company was responsible for the development of the industry-standard THX sound reproduction system. Lucasfilm's computer graphics group was sold to Steve Jobs in 1986, subsequently evolving into the film production company **Pixar**, now a subsidiary of **Disney**.

**LUGOSI, BÉLA (1882–1956).** One of the great stars of American **horror** movies of the 1930s, Béla Lugosi was born in a region of Austro–Hungary that is now in Romania. He began his film career in Hungarian **silent films**, then continued that career in German silents after being driven from his homeland in 1919 when his political and trade activism made his position untenable in the newly repressive regime that arose in Hungary after the collapse of Béla Kun's short-lived socialist republic there.

Lugosi immigrated to the United States in 1921 and subsequently played a number of stage roles and a few minor film roles before his breakthrough performance as the title character in *Dracula* (1931), a role he had earlier played on Broadway. From that point forward, Lugosi and fellow actor **Boris Karloff** were the two biggest stars of American horror films for years to come. The success of *Dracula* won Lugosi a studio contract with **Universal** and led to his appearance in numerous subsequent horror films, though also leading to a typecasting that made it difficult for him to get roles outside of horror.

Lugosi appeared in a number of films with Karloff, including five films for Universal: *The Black Cat* (1934), *The Raven* (1935), *The Invisible Ray* (1936), *Son of Frankenstein* (1939), and *Black Friday* (1940). Of the numerous other notable horror films in which Lugosi appeared, some of the most notable were *White Zombie* (1932), *Murders in the Rue Morgue* (1932), and *The Body Snatcher* (1945, again with Karloff). However, by the middle of the 1940s Lugosi's career was in serious decline; his last appearance in a major "horror" film was in the 1948 spoof *Bud Abbott and Lou Costello Meet Frankenstein*, in which he reprised the role of Dracula, but in a self-parodic mode.

Drug addiction and other health problems seriously curtailed Lugosi's ability to work by the 1950s, though he did famously appear in three films for the notorious Ed Wood: *Glen or Glenda* (1953), *Bride of the Monster* (1955), and even *Plan 9 from Outer Space* (1959). Lugosi died during the production of the latter, which was not released until three years after his death. Lugosi's work with Wood then gained him a new round of posthumous fame when the actor became a key character in **Tim Burton**'s *Ed Wood* (1995), in which Martin Landau won an **Academy Award** for Best Supporting Actor for his portrayal of Lugosi, an actor who ironically received little critical recognition for his own performances.

**LUPINO, IDA (1914–1995).** Ida Lupino appeared as an actress in more than 50 films and more than 50 television episodes. She also directed nine films and approximately 50 television episodes, becoming one of the first successful woman directors in Hollywood. Born in England to parents who were both performers, Lupino entered show business early and appeared in her first film at the age of 13. Numerous roles as a teen actress followed, though she quickly graduated to more adult, hard-boiled roles in such **film noir** classics as *They Drive by Night* (1940), *High Sierra* (1941), and *The Hard Way* (1943). Lupino also starred in such later noir films as *Road House* (1948) and *On Dangerous Ground* (1952), making the genre something of a specialty. She also helped (without screen credit) to direct the latter film, then followed by directing another film noir classic, *The Hitch-Hiker* (1953).

Thus becoming the only woman to make a significant contribution to film noir as a director, Lupino was also important for the groundbreaking way in which many of her films, such as the rape drama *Outrage* (1950), addressed issues related to genre. She was particularly known for subtle role-reversals in which male characters showed traits that were typical of women in Hollywood film, and vice versa. Most of Lupino's work after the early 1950s (as both an actress and a director) was in the emerging genre of television, where her directorial work made her particularly important as a pioneer among women directors.

# M

**MACLAINE, SHIRLEY (1934– ).** One of the most successful film actresses of her generation, Shirley MacLaine is also known for her belief in New Age spiritualism (and especially reincarnation) and as the sister of actor **Warren Beatty**. She got her film career off to a fast start with her appearance in **Alfred Hitchcock**'s *The Trouble with Harry* (1955), for which she won a **Golden Globe** award as the Most Promising Female Newcomer, the first of more than 20 Golden Globe wins or nominations she would ultimately receive. Important supporting roles in films such as *Around the World in Eighty Days* (1956) quickly followed, and MacLaine soon moved into starring roles, receiving an **Academy Award** nomination for Best Actress for *Some Came Running* (1958). Similar nominations followed for *The Apartment* (1960) and *Irma la Douce* (1963), firmly establishing MacLaine as one of Hollywood's leading actresses.

MacLaine followed with starring roles in such films as *Woman Times Seven* (1967, in which she played lead roles in all seven of the separate vignettes that made up the film) and *Two Mules for Sister Sara* (1970). She served as both producer and director of *The Other Half of the Sky: A China Memoir* (1975), which won an **Oscar** nomination for Best **Documentary** Feature, then scored a fourth Best Leading Actress Oscar nomination for *The Turning Point* (1977). She then won the Best Actress Oscar for *Terms of Endearment* (1983).

Other key films featuring MacLaine include *Being There* (1979), *Madame Sousatzka* (1988), *Steel Magnolias* (1989), *Postcards from the Edge* (1990), *Mrs. Winterbourne* (1996), and *Rumor Has It . . .* (2005). She has also made a number of television appearances and is the author of several best-selling books, mostly dealing with New Age spiritual beliefs.

**MACMURRAY, FRED (1908–1991).** Though he reached his widest audiences as the star of the television series *My Three Sons* (1960–1972), Fred MacMurray also appeared in nearly 100 films in a long and successful career as a film actor. Of these films, **Billy Wilder**'s **film noir** classic *Double Indemnity* (1944) is probably the most important, but MacMurray appeared in a wide variety of films, playing a diverse assortment of characters.

MacMurray had already appeared in 40 films by the time he was cast as insurance-salesman-turned-murderer Walter Neff in *Double Indemnity*, mostly in nice-guy roles and often in **comedies** and **musicals**. He continued to appear frequently on film after *Double Indemnity*, returning mostly to good-natured likeable characters, though some of his most successful roles were also as villains, as in *The Caine Mutiny* (1954) and Wilder's *The Apartment* (1960). Meanwhile, his appearance in **Disney**'s *The Shaggy Dog* (1959) brought him to a new generation of viewers as the star of a series of such family-oriented comedies, including *The Absent-Minded Professor* (1961), *Son of Flubber* (1963), and *The Happiest Millionaire* (1967).

Most of MacMurray's work from 1960 onward was in the highly successful *My Three Sons*. However, after the end of that series he did appear in two television movies and two theatrical films, including *Charley and the Angel* (1973) and *The Swarm* (1978).

**MADDOW, BEN (1909–1992).** Screenwriter Ben Maddow began his work in film in the **documentary film** movement of the 1930s, writing for such films as *Heart of Spain* (1937) and *Native Land* (1942), the latter under the pseudonym David Wolff. He moved into feature film with *Framed* (1947) and scored mainstream success with *Intruder in the Dust* (1949) and *The Asphalt Jungle* (1950), the latter of which won him his only **Academy Award** nomination for Best Screenplay. He fell victim to the **blacklist** in the 1950s, but continued to produce screenplays, either without screen credit or with credit going to front Philip Yordan. Notable films written by Maddow during this period include *The Wild One* (1953), *The Naked Jungle* (1954), *Johnny Guitar* (1954), *No Down Payment* (1957), and *God's Little Acre* (1958).

Maddow came off the blacklist in 1960, receiving screen credit for the screenplay for *The Unforgiven* and *The Savage Eye* in that year. However, he still found it difficult to find work in Hollywood and never recovered the momentum of his pre-blacklist career. Much of his subsequent writing was for television and for minor films, though he did co-write a relatively important film, *The Secret of Santa Vittoria*, released in 1969.

**MAJOR STUDIOS.** The term "major studios," or simply "majors," has been widely used to designate Hollywood's biggest and most powerful studios since the 1930s. At that time, with film entering a new era thanks to the coming of integrated sound, the "Big Five" studios **Metro-Goldwyn-Mayer (MGM)**, **Paramount**, **RKO**, **Twentieth Century Fox**, and **Warner Bros.** all commanded vast vertically integrated empires for the production, distribution, and exhibition of films. **Universal**, **Columbia**, and **United Artists** were also typically considered majors during the **Golden Age** of the 1930s and

1940s, though this "Little Three" had fewer resources, especially in terms of the control of large chains of theaters that marked the operations of the "Big Five."

The **Paramount Antitrust Case** of 1948 effectively outlawed the control of such chains by studios, leading (along with other factors, such as the coming of television) to far-reaching changes within the film industry. A long period of reorganization and changes in ownership greatly changed the structure of the business. RKO was effectively driven out of the film business, while MGM, once the largest of the majors, merged with United Artists in 1981, though the new entity ceased to be a major factor in the film business.

Today, Paramount, Twentieth Century Fox, and Warner Bros. are all still considered majors, though each is owned by a larger corporate entity: Viacom, News Corporation, and Time Warner, respectively. Universal and Columbia, controlled respectively by General Electric and **Sony Pictures Entertainment**, remain majors as well. The final major in today's Hollywood is **Disney**, once a small independent studio but now effectively the only self-owned major, though it is only a part of the vast holdings of the Walt Disney Company, the world's largest media conglomerate. Despite the rise in importance of **independent film** and the various shake-ups in the industry over the past few decades, the majors are still involved, either in production or distribution, in films that account for approximately 9 percent of all domestic box-office receipts.

**MALDEN, KARL (1912–2009).** Born Mladen George Sekulovich, Karl Malden had an acting career that spanned six decades and made him one of the most recognizable faces in American popular culture. After initial supporting roles in several films, including the important **film noirs** *Kiss of Death* (1947) and *Where the Sidewalk Ends* (1950), Malden gained considerable acclaim for his performance in **Elia Kazan**'s *A Streetcar Named Desire* (1951), for which he received an **Academy Award** for Best Supporting Actor. He received another Best Supporting Actor **Oscar** nomination for his role in Kazan's *On the Waterfront* (1954) and starred in Kazan's *Baby Doll* (1956).

Other notable films in which Malden appeared include *One-Eyed Jacks* (1961), *Birdman of Alcatraz* (1962), *How the West Was Won* (1962), *Cheyenne Autumn* (1964), and *Patton* (1970). He gained his largest audiences, however, as the costar of the television series *The Streets of San Francisco* (1972–1977). Most of his subsequent appearances were in television movies.

**MALICK, TERRENCE (1943– ).** Though he has directed only a few feature films, Terrence Malick has developed a lofty reputation among critics, who have admired each of his films. Malick began his career with *Badlands* (1974), a grisly but stylish and thoughtful thriller about a young couple on a killing spree, based on the real-life late-1950s murder spree of Charles Starkweather and his girlfriend, Caril Ann Fugate. Malick followed five years later with *Days of Heaven*, a period piece about migrant workers in the Texas Panhandle in 1916.

Malick did not release another feature film until 1998, with *The Thin Red Line*, a **war film** set during the battle of Guadalcanal in World War II, noted for its detailed and artfully depicted (but realistic) battle scenes. *The New World* (2005) is a historical drama set in the Jamestown settlement of colonial Virginia, noted for the authenticity of its detail in the depiction of the early 17th-century community, though it did modify some historical events for dramatic effect. Malick's fifth film, *The Tree of Life*, is scheduled for release in 2011.

Malick has written the screenplays for all of the films he has directed, as well as scripting several films directed by others. His films are noted for their visual artistry, and all but *Badlands* have received **Academy Award** nominations for Best Cinematography. Malick himself received **Oscar** nominations for both Best Screenplay and Best Director for *The Thin Red Line*, a film that received a total of seven Oscar nominations (including Best Picture), though it won no awards. In addition to winning the Oscar for Best Cinematography, *Days of Heaven* received nominations for Best Costume Design, Best Music, and Best Sound.

**MAMET, DAVID (1947– ).** David Mamet, one of the leading American playwrights of his generation, broke into screenwriting in 1981 when he was chosen to write the screenplay for the remake of the **film noir** classic *The Postman Always Rings Twice* (1981). That film was not notably successful, but the next film he scripted, *The Verdict* (1982), also adapted from a novel, was a bit more so, winning Mamet an **Academy Award** nomination for Best Adapted Screenplay.

The film *About Last Night* (1986) was based on Mamet's play *Sexual Perversity in Chicago*, though it was not scripted by Mamet. However, Mamet did write such films as *The Untouchables* (1987) and *We're No Angels* (1989), establishing his ability to write commercially successful films. Meanwhile, his screenwriting career moved in a new direction when he adapted *Glengarry Glen Ross* (1992) to the screen from his own play of the same title. With *American Buffalo*, Mamet similarly adapted one of his own plays to film, while his screenplay for *Wag the Dog* (1997) won him his second **Oscar** nomination for Best Screenplay.

Mamet's subsequent screenplays have produced only moderately successful films, ranging from the thriller *Ronin* (1998, written by Mamet as Richard

Weisz), to the quirky **comedy** *State and Main* (2000), to the thrillers *Hannibal* and *Heist* (both 2001). Meanwhile, Mamet has also directed a number of the films he has written, beginning with *House of Games* (1987) and *Things Change* (1988), and extending through *State and Main*, *Heist*, and *Redbelt* (2008). In so doing, he has established a highly independent style, typically financing his own films from the proceeds of his previous films.

Mamet is also a successful writer of novels and nonfiction commentaries.

**MANCINI, HENRY (1924–1994).** The American film and television composer wrote some of the most widely recognized **music** of his generation, winning numerous Grammy and **Academy Award** nominations both for his scores and for individual songs. He received his first **Oscar** nomination for Best Score for *The Glenn Miller Story* (1954), then went on to receive a total of 18 nominations for either Best Score or Best Song, winning twice in each category. By 1961, he had contributed (largely without screen credit) to the music for roughly 100 films, including several of the **science fiction** classics of the 1950s. He then achieved true prominence for his work in 1961, with three Oscar nominations, winning twice, for Best Score and Best Song (for the now-classic "Moon River") for **Blake Edwards**'s *Breakfast at Tiffany's*. Mancini would go on to compose some of his best-known music for Edwards's films, including the jazzy "Pink Panther Theme," perhaps his single best-known piece of music, first used as part of the Oscar-nominated score for *The Pink Panther* (1963).

Mancini's other two Oscar nominations were also for music written for films directed by Edwards, including Best Song for the title song from *Days of Wine and Roses* (1962) and Best Score for *Victor Victoria* (1982). Mancini scored films for numerous other directors as well, including three films for **Stanley Donen**. In 1971, he received three Oscar nominations in the same year for a second time, for Best Score and Best Song for *Darling Lili* and for Best Score for Vittorio De Sica's *I girasoli*.

Mancini also wrote widely for television, recorded over 90 albums of music in various styles and genres, and conducted hundreds of live performances of music by himself and others. He received a total of more than 70 Grammy nominations, most of them not for music from his film scores.

**MANKIEWICZ, HERMAN J. (1897–1953).** Though perhaps best known as the co-writer (with **Orson Welles**) of *Citizen Kane* (1941), Herman J. Mankiewicz was in fact already a veteran screenwriter by the time of that landmark film, having been involved in the writing of dozens of films dating back to the **silent film** era. He was especially prolific at writing the titles for dozens of silent films. However, the **Oscar** Mankiewicz shared with Welles for the screenplay of *Citizen Kane* was his first such award or nomination. He would be nominated again the next year for co-writing *The Pride of the Yankees* (1942), a classic baseball film based on the life and career of Lou Gehrig.

Mankiewicz would receive no further Oscar nominations in his career, though he did write such films as the respected **film noir** *Christmas Holiday* (1944) and another successful baseball film, *The Pride of St. Louis* (1952). Among other films scripted by Mankiewicz were *Dinner at Eight* (1933), *The Spanish Main* (1945), and *A Woman's Secret* (1949). A prodigious worker, he was also noted for making contributions to the scripts for numerous films without onscreen credit, including *The Wizard of Oz* (1939).

Mankiewicz was the brother of screenwriter, director, and producer Joseph L. Mankiewicz.

**MANKIEWICZ, JOSEPH L. (1909–1993).** Joseph L. Mankiewicz worked widely as a screenwriter in Hollywood through the middle of the 1930s, when he shifted his efforts to producing, ultimately serving as a producer for a number of classic films, including *The Philadelphia Story* (1940) and *Woman of the Year* (1942). In 1946, he became a director, directing three films in that year alone.

Known for his ability to elicit top performances from the actors who worked for him, Mankiewicz quickly became a success as the director of such notable films as *The Ghost and Mrs. Muir* (1947) and *A Letter to Three Wives* (1949). In 1950, he directed two historically important films: *No Way Out*, which featured African American actor **Sidney Poitier** in an important and groundbreaking role, and *All about Eve* (1950), Mankiewicz's most critically admired film. He also returned to screenwriting, scripting these two films, as well as *A Letter to Three Wives*.

Mankiewicz had his greatest success as a director during this early period, though he continued to direct important films in a number of genres into the 1960s, including *5 Fingers* (1952), *Julius Caesar* (1953), *The Barefoot Contessa* (1954), *Guys and Dolls* (1955), *The Quiet American* (1958), *Suddenly, Last Summer* (1959), and *Cleopatra* (1963). He worked less often after *Cleopatra*, but received an **Academy Award** nomination for Best Director for *Sleuth* (1972), his last film.

Mankiewicz won Academy Awards for both Best Director and Best Screenplay for *A Letter to Three Wives* and *All about Eve*. Altogether, he won five Best Screenplay nominations, as well as four Best Director nominations and a Best Picture nomination as the producer of *The Philadelphia Story*. He was the brother of screenwriter **Herman J. Mankiewicz**.

**MANN, ANTHONY (1906–1967).** Though often working with relatively low budgets, Anthony Mann directed some of the most memorable films in

American cinematic history, especially in the genres of the **Western** and **film noir**. Mann began his directorial career with *Dr. Broadway* (1942), a low-budget crime film that already showed flashes of the distinctive style that would later make Mann one of the key directors of film noir. Other **B-movies** followed, until Mann finally established himself with three key film noirs, all released in 1947: *T-Men*, *Railroaded!*, and *Desperate*. He quickly followed with *Raw Deal* (1948), and also directed most of *He Walked by Night* (1948), although directorial credit for that film was given to Alfred L. Werker. Mann completed his early film noir cycle with *Border Incident* (1949).

With film noir on the wane and the Western on the rise, Mann shifted most of his energies in the 1950s to the latter genre (though in ways that often showed a clear noir influence), directing such films as *Winchester '73* (1950), *Bend of the River* (1952), *The Naked Spur* (1953), *The Far Country* (1954), and *The Man from Laramie* (1955), all starring **James Stewart**. Mann also directed the Westerns *The Furies* (1950), *The Tin Star* (1957), *Man of the West* (1958), and *Cimarron* (1960). Other key films directed by Mann included *The Glenn Miller Story* (1954, again featuring Stewart) and *Men in War* (1957), both of which won him nominations for Outstanding Directorial Achievement from the Director's Guild of America (DGA).

Despite his frequent work with the megastar Stewart, it was not until he was tabbed to direct *Spartacus* (1960) that Mann seemed poised to move into truly high-profile, big-budget productions. However, disputes with star **Kirk Douglas** led to the firing of Mann soon into the filming of *Spartacus*, to be replaced by **Stanley Kubrick**. Nevertheless, Mann did move into the direction of big-budget **historical epics** soon afterward, with *El Cid* (1961, winning him his third DGA nomination for Directorial Achievement) and *The Fall of the Roman Empire* (1964). Mann died of a heart attack in Berlin while filming *A Dandy in Aspic*.

**MANN, MICHAEL (1943– ).** Though now perhaps most widely known as a director of feature films, Michael Mann has amassed an impressive résumé that includes work as a screenwriter, producer, and director in both film and television. He began his career by spending several years in London, beginning in the mid-1960s, studying at the London Film School and making television commercials and short films. Back in the United States, he moved into feature film as the director, writer, and executive producer of the crime thriller *Thief* (1981). Much of his work of the 1980s was as the executive producer of such television series as *Miami Vice* (1984–1990) and *Crime Story* (1986–1988). However, he made important contributions to film in this period as well, especially as the writer and director of *Manhunter* (1986), the first film to bring the novelist Thomas Harris's notorious character Hannibal Lecter to the big screen.

Mann wrote, directed, and produced three films in the 1990s: *The Last of the Mohicans* (1992), *Heat* (1995), and *The Insider* (1999). The latter won him **Academy Award** nominations for Best Director and Best Screenplay, as well as a Best Picture nomination. Mann also received considerable attention as the writer, producer, and director of the **biopic** *Ali* (2001). He also directed and produced the stylish **neo-noir** thriller *Collateral* in 2004, the same year he produced *The Aviator* (2004), which won a Best Picture **Oscar** nomination.

Mann wrote, directed, and produced the 2006 film adaptation of *Miami Vice*, one of his least successful films. He also directed, produced, and co-wrote the high-profile **gangster film** *Public Enemies* and produced the crime thriller *The Fields* (2010).

**MARCH, FREDRIC (1897–1975).** Fredric March appeared in more than 70 films in an acting career that spanned more than half a century. He began his career with several appearances in **silent film**, then successfully made the transition to sound, receiving an **Academy Award** nomination for Best Actor for his performance in *The Royal Family of Broadway* (1930), then winning the Best Actor **Oscar** for his role in *Dr. Jekyll and Mr. Hyde* (1931).

March also received Best Actor Oscar nominations for *A Star Is Born* (1937) and *Death of a Salesman* (1951), and won his second Best Actor Oscar for *The Best Years of Our Lives* (1946). Other notable films in which he appeared include *Executive Suite* (1954), *The Desperate Hours* (1955), *The Man in the Gray Flannel Suit* (1956), *Inherit the Wind* (1960), *Seven Days in May* (1964), and *The Iceman Cometh* (1973).

March was an accomplished stage actor who won two Tony awards for his appearances on Broadway; indeed, the frequency of his appearances in film declined after the 1930s, largely because he devoted so much time to the stage. In addition, he received three Emmy nominations for his work in television.

**MARVIN, LEE (1924–1987).** After an early career in which he played mostly villainous tough guys in a variety of supporting roles (specializing in **war films** and crime dramas), Lee Marvin went on to have a successful career as a leading man. Important early films in which Marvin had supporting roles include *The Big Heat* (1953) and *The Caine Mutiny* (1954). Most of his appearances from 1956 to 1962 were on television, though he made something of a comeback in film in *The Man Who Shot Liberty Valance* (1962), in which he played the supporting role of Valance.

Marvin then moved to more prominent roles in such films as **Don Siegel**'s remake of the **film noir** classic *The Killers* (1964), followed by his award-winning performance in *Cat Ballou* (1965), a comic **Western** in which he played two roles, a hero and a villain. That performance won Marvin the **Academy Award** for Best Actor; it also won him more prominent roles and more chances to be the hero in films such as *The Professionals* (1966) and *The Dirty Dozen* (1967), the latter of which was the first of several war films to star Marvin in the coming years. He was a villain again (but still the star) in the interesting crime drama *Point Blank* (1967), over which he was given an unusual amount of creative control. Marvin also showed versatility with his star turn opposite **Clint Eastwood** in the decidedly unusual **musical** Western *Paint Your Wagon* (1969).

In 1970, Marvin starred in the Western *Monte Walsh* (1970) as an aging cowboy who realizes that his time is past. Time was beginning to pass Marvin by as well, and his subsequent films—including *Prime Cut* (1972), *Emperor of the North Pole* (1973), *Avalanche Express* (1979), and *The Big Red One* (1980)—were somewhat less successful than his films of the 1960s. He appeared in only a few films after 1980, mostly in supporting roles.

**MARX BROTHERS.** The sons of poor Jewish immigrants on New York's Upper East Side, the Marx Brothers went on to become one of the most beloved **comedy** teams in American film history. Led by middle brother "Groucho" (born Julius Henry, 1890–1977), a total of five Marx Brothers performed at one time or another, including "Harpo" (born Adolph, later known as Arthur, 1888–1964); "Chico" (Leonard, 1887–1961); "Zeppo" (Herbert, 1901–1979); and "Gummo" (Milton, 1893–1977). Gummo, however, appeared only in their early stage act and left the group before they began their film career.

After considerable experience performing together (and with others) on stage, the Marx Brothers launched their film careers just as sound film was becoming dominant in Hollywood. Signing with **Paramount Pictures**, they began with two adaptations of Broadway plays, *The Cocoanuts* (1929) and *Animal Crackers* (1930). Both films were hits and are still considered classics. With *Monkey Business* (1931), they moved away from stage adaptations and began to perfect the zany style of **anarchic comedy** for which they have been so renowned ever since.

*Horse Feathers* (1932) and *Duck Soup* (1933) were even bigger hits; the latter, the last they would make with Paramount, is widely considered to be their greatest film. At this point, Zeppo left the act and went on to form a successful talent agency with Gummo. The remaining brothers then moved to **Metro-Goldwyn-Mayer** (MGM), where **Irving Thalberg** insisted that they develop stronger plots and more characterization, thus making their films less anarchic. Their two films made with Thalberg, *A Night at the Opera* (1935) and *A Day at the Races* (1937) were both successful and are still considered classics, but lack some of the unique energy of the earlier films.

The Marx Brothers were named the 20th greatest male screen legend in a 1999 poll conducted by the **American Screen Institute**.

**MATTHAU, WALTER (1920–1980).** After a number of appearances on television, Walter Matthau made his screen debut as a villain in *The Kentuckian* (1955). He would go on to have a distinguished and prolific career, usually playing likeable, if flawed, characters. His best-known role was probably that of the slovenly Oscar Madison in *The Odd Couple* (1968), opposite **Jack Lemmon**, with whom he appeared in a total of 10 films, including **Billy Wilder**'s *The Fortune Cookie* (1966), for which Matthau won an **Academy Award** for Best Supporting Actor. Matthau also worked with Lemmon and Wilder in *The Front Page* (1974) and *Buddy Buddy* (1981).

Matthau won **Oscar** nominations for Best Actor in a Leading Role for his performances in *Kotch* (1971, directed by Lemmon) and *The Sunshine Boys* (1975), the latter of which won him a **Golden Globe** for Best Actor in a Musical or Comedy. Other prominent films in which Matthau played prominent roles include *Fail-Safe* (1964); *Mirage* (1965); *Hello, Dolly!* (1969); *Cactus Flower* (1969); *Plaza Suite* (1971); *Charley Varrick* (1973); *The Bad News Bears* (1976), and *California Suite* (1978).

Though his career seemed on the wane in the 1980s, Matthau enjoyed something of a resurgence in the 1990s (and in his own seventies) in a series of "old-men" **comedies** in which he starred with Lemmon, including *Grumpy Old Men* (1993), *Grumpier Old Men* (1995), and *The Odd Couple II* (1998).

**MAYER, LOUIS B. (1884–1957).** Perhaps the most legendary of the legendary studio heads of the golden era of studio dominance in Hollywood, the Russian-born Louis B. Mayer exerted a powerful formative influence on the development of the American film industry. Beginning his career as the owner of a single movie theater in Haverhill, Massachusetts, in 1907, Mayer had by 1916 built that theater into an important New England chain. He had also become a founding principal of Metro Pictures Corporation in an effort to generate content for his theaters. In 1918, he left Metro to move to Los Angeles to found his own company, Louis B. Mayer Pictures Corporation. Eventually, however, he would rejoin Metro when Loew's Theatres acquired both companies, along with Goldwyn Pictures Corporation, to form **Metro-Goldwyn-Mayer** (MGM). The New York–based Nicholas Schenk was the titular head of the new company, but the Los Angeles–based Mayer was truly in charge of it as its overall West Coast head; Mayer's assistant **Irving G. Thalberg** was the new studio's production chief.

Mayer built the new company, generally known simply as MGM, into the most profitable of Hollywood's **major studios**, though he often clashed with Thalberg, who seemed more interested in the artistic merit of MGM's films, while Mayer remained focused on the bottom line. Thalberg, in ill health, was replaced as production chief in 1932 by a series of temporary stand-ins, until Mayer himself assumed the role (in addition to his role as the overall head of the studio) upon Thalberg's death in 1936.

Credited with inventing the star system, in which film marketing centered on the selling of recognizable "name-brand" stars, Mayer continued to rely on the appeal of well-known actors (many of whom regarded him as a sort of father figure) throughout his career as studio chief. Throughout the 1940s, Mayer was reportedly the highest-paid man in the United States, though he and MGM were beginning to lose some of their luster by the end of the decade. By 1951, Mayer's conflicts with new production chief **Dore Schary** led Schenk and the New York corporate management of MGM to remove Mayer as West Coast studio head. Mayer went into retirement.

**MCQUEEN, STEVE (1930–1980).** After beginning his career with a small (uncredited) role in the 1955 **Paul Newman** vehicle *Somebody Up There Likes Me* (1955), the former reformatory inmate Steve McQueen first attracted major attention as the star of *The Blob* (1958), an alien-invasion **monster movie** in which he played a clean-cut teenage hero (despite being in his late twenties). He then became well known to American audiences as the star of the television series *Wanted: Dead or Alive* (1958–1961). From there, he was propelled into a major career that saw him come to be regarded as the epitome of male onscreen coolness as the result of his numerous starring roles over the next decade and a half.

McQueen had his first big role in a major Hollywood film in *The Magnificent Seven* (1960). From there he moved into starring roles in such films as *Hell Is for Heroes* (1962), *The Great Escape* (1963), and *The Cincinnati Kid* (1965). He then received his only **Academy Award** nomination for Best Actor for his performance in *The Sand Pebbles* (1966). Now a top star, McQueen subsequently had lead roles in a series of successful films, including *The Thomas Crown Affair* (1968), *Bullitt* (1968), *The Reivers* (1969), *Junior Bonner* (1972), *The Getaway* (1972), and *Papillon* (1973).

At this point, McQueen was reputed to be the highest-paid actor in Hollywood. *The Towering Inferno* (1974) was another hit, but McQueen then all but disappeared from the public eye until the 1978 film *An Enemy of the People*, an adaptation of a play by Henrik Ibsen that was not highly successful. McQueen also starred in *Tom Horn* (1980) and *The Hunter* (1980), but was primarily known at the end of his life for his attempts to seek unconventional cancer treatments in Mexico.

**MENDES, SAM (1965– ).** The English stage and film director Sam Mendes has also made important contributions to American film. His debut feature film, *American Beauty* (1999), scored a total of eight **Academy Award** nominations, winning the award in five categories, including Best Picture and Best Director. His subsequent films have won less acclaim but have nevertheless been solid, high-profile efforts. *Road to Perdition* (2002), for example, is a stylish **gangster film**, based on the graphic novel by Max Allan Collins. *Jarhead* (2005) was an early effort at bringing the realities of the 2003 Gulf War to the screen but was not a critical success.

Revolutionary Road* (2008) is a family drama set in suburban Connecticut in the 1950s, and is thus something of a return to the material of *American Beauty*, though in a different time frame. The **comedy**–drama *Away We Go* (2009) probably received the least attention of any of Mendes's films, but he remains much in demand as a director.

**MEREDITH, BURGESS (1907–1997).** Burgess Meredith was an accomplished stage actor and director; he also appeared extensively in television, perhaps most notably in several episodes of *The Twilight Zone*, including a starring role in the classic 1959 episode "Time Enough at Last." However, he is probably best remembered for his performances in film in a long and varied career that stretched from an uncredited role in Tod Browning's *Freaks* (1932) through a supporting role in the **comedy** *Grumpier Old Men* (1995). In between, he had dozens of starring and supporting roles, winning consecutive **Academy Award** nominations for Best Supporting Actor in the 1970s, for his performances in *The Day of the Locust* (1975) and *Rocky* (1976).

By the age of 24, Meredith had already made a splash on Broadway as the star of Maxwell Anderson's hit play *Winterset*. He had made a number of appearances in film—most notably as George in *Of Mice and Men* (1939)—when he entered the military during World War II; he then received an early discharge in order to star as war correspondent Ernie Pyle in *The Story of G. I. Joe* (1945). He solidified his credentials in a number of other 1940s films as well, including three opposite then-wife **Paulette Goddard**: *Second Chorus* (1940), *Diary of a Chambermaid* (1946), and *On Our Merry Way* (1948). However, he fell victim to the Hollywood **blacklist** at the beginning of the 1950s and was relegated to appearances on television and the stage from 1950 to 1962, when he returned to film with a supporting role in **Otto Preminger**'s *Advise & Consent*.

Subsequently, Meredith appeared in a number of films directed by Preminger, including *The Cardinal* (1963), *In Harm's Way* (1965), *Hurry Sundown* (1967), *Skidoo* (1968), and *Such Good Friends* (1971). He continued to appear on television as well, and his best-known role of the 1960s was probably that of the diabolical Penguin in 21 episodes of the campy *Batman* television series (1966–1968). In the 1970s, he was prominent as Mickey Goldmill, the trainer of Rocky Balboa in the first three *Rocky* films (1976, 1979, 1982).

Meredith continued to work actively well into his eighties, including an uncredited role as the narrator of *Twilight Zone: The Movie* (1983) that looked back on his earlier classic performances in the television series. Indeed, he did extensive voiceover work throughout his career, putting his distinctive gravelly voice to good use in such roles.

**METRO-GOLDWYN-MAYER (MGM).** Metro-Goldwyn-Mayer (generally referred to simply as MGM) has been one of the most important film production and distribution companies in Hollywood since the late 1920s. The company was formed when movie theater impresario **Marcus Loew** gained control of Metro Pictures Corporation, Goldwyn Pictures Corporation, and **Louis B. Mayer** Pictures, then merged the three into a single entity known as Metro-Goldwyn-Mayer, with Mayer managing its overall West Coast operations and Mayer's assistant **Irving G. Thalberg** as the production chief, though the titular head of the new company was Nicholas Schenk, based at the official corporate headquarters in New York.

Thalberg proved an efficient production chief who nevertheless had a strong interest in aesthetic quality, often leading to conflicts with the more profit-oriented Mayer. Nevertheless, MGM quickly grew to become the most powerful and important studio in Hollywood, though Loew's early death in 1927 prevented him from seeing the company's greatest successes. Meanwhile, these successes were partly due to their ongoing relationship with Loew's Theatres, which remained the parent company of MGM until 1959, when the outcome of the **Paramount Antitrust Case** forced studios and theater chains to become independent of one another.

Known for its distinctive roaring Leo the Lion logo and its "Ars Gratia Artis" motto, MGM assumed its position as the biggest of the **major studios** by the early 1930s and maintained that position through World War II, partly due to its unmatched stable of big-name stars. Beginning in the **silent film** era, stars such as **Greta Garbo** and **Norma Shearer** helped to build the new studio's business, while the sound era saw the arrival of new MGM stars such as **Clark Gable** and **Jean Harlow**. MGM also led the way in technical innovations, especially in the use of color in films, culminating in such landmark all-color spectacles as *Gone with the Wind* and *The Wizard of Oz* (both 1939).

Releasing as much as one film per week, MGM remained profitable throughout the Depression years. However, the company began to lose ground amid the changing landscape of the film industry in the 1950s, with the loss of the Loew's Theatres connection in 1959 capping off a decade of decline in the company's market share in the film industry. Mayer was removed as West Coast chief of the company in 1951, and his replacement, **Dore Schary**, struggled to return the company to its former heights. Schary tried to move the company more toward realistic message-oriented pictures, but some of the company's most successful films under his management were actually elaborate **musicals** of the kind with which MGM had had such success in the 1930s. Films such as *An American in Paris* (1951) and *Singin' in the Rain* (1952) were box-office hits that became classics of the genre, but the historical tide was running against such films, which were becoming increasingly expensive to produce.

By 1957, MGM was losing money for the first time in its history; a new strategy that relied on the profits from a single big-budget film each year foreshadowed the later blockbuster era but had only limited success at the time. The following decades have been marked by generally declining output and a number of changes in ownership and management as the company has struggled via a number of business maneuvers to survive as an entertainment-industry entity. One of MGM's biggest hits of the 1970s was the **documentary** *That's Entertainment* (1974), which drew upon the nostalgia value of the company's golden years, again suggesting that the company's greatest days were behind it.

In 1986, Ted Turner gained ownership of MGM and **United Artists**, which had become a subsidiary of MGM in 1981; most of the company's assets were soon sold back to former owner Kirk Kerkorian, though Turner retained ownership of its most valuable property, the backlist of films produced by the company from its founding until that time. The Turner Entertainment wing of Time Warner retains ownership of that back catalog to this day, while several companies, including Time Warner, are in negotiations, as of this writing, to purchase the remainder of the assets of the struggling MGM.

**MGM.** *See* METRO-GOLDWYN-MAYER.

**MILESTONE, LEWIS (1895–1980).** The Russian-born Lewis Milestone came to the United States in 1912 and worked at a number of jobs in **silent film** after serving in the U.S. military in World War I. Many of his directorial efforts in silent film were uncredited, but he became an important figure late in the silent era, winning an **Academy Award** as Best Director in a Comedy Picture for *Two Arabian Knights* (1927). Milestone then burst into the sound era with the classic **war film** *All Quiet on the Western Front* (1930), which won him an **Oscar** as Best Director, while also winning the award as Best Picture. Milestone also received a Best Director Oscar nomination for *The Front Page* (1931).

Milestone continued to do solid work as a director of theatrical films over the next two decades, directing such films as *The General Died at Dawn* (1936), *Of Mice and Men* (1939), *The North Star* (1943), *The Strange Love of Martha Ivers* (1946), and *The Red Pony* (1949). Most of his work in the 1950s was for television, though he made something of a comeback in theatrical film at the beginning of the 1960s with *Ocean's Eleven* (1960) and *Mutiny on the Bounty* (1962). The latter, however, was his last theatrical film, and he retired from directing altogether in 1964.

**MILLAND, RAY (1907–1986).** Born in Wales, Ray Milland began his acting career on the London stage and also had several small roles in British films before moving to America after he was discovered and recruited by a Hollywood talent scout. Milland started his Hollywood career with a number of small roles, but gradually moved into lead roles in such films as *The Jungle Princess* (1936) and *Bulldog Drummond Escapes* (1937). He then continued in both starring and supporting roles in a number of films before landing what would ultimately be his greatest role as the star of **Billy Wilder**'s *The Lost Weekend* (1945); his performance in this film won Milland the **Academy Award** for Best Actor.

Over the next decade, Milland appeared in a variety of films, including starring roles in such films as the **film noir** *The Big Clock* (1948) and the **Alfred Hitchcock** thriller *Dial M for Murder* (1954). Subsequently, he began to concentrate more and more on directing for both film and television, including directing five films in which he also starred: *A Man Alone* (1955), *Lisbon* (1956), *The Safecracker* (1958), *Panic in Year Zero!* (1962), and *Hostile Witness* (1968).

From this point forward, Milland again concentrated on acting, making a number of appearances as a character actor, though most of these were either in television or in **B-movies**, including a number of **horror** movies. He did, however, have supporting roles in such prominent films as *Love Story* (1970) and *The Last Tycoon* (1976).

**MINNELLI, VINCENTE (1903–1986).** Director Vincente Minnelli had success in a number of film genres, including such films as the literary adaptation *Madame Bovary* (1949), the **comedies** *Father of the Bride* (1950) and

*Designing Woman* (1957), and the dramas *The Bad and the Beautiful* (1952), *The 4 Horsemen of the Apocalypse* (1962), and *The Sandpiper* (1965). However, it was as a director of **musicals** that Minnelli was best known, beginning with his first major film *Meet Me in St. Louis* (1944). His greatest achievement was probably the musical *An American in Paris* (1951), for which he received an **Academy Award** nomination for Best Director. He later won that award for *Gigi* (1958), another musical.

Other key musicals directed by Minnelli include *The Band Wagon* (1953), *Brigadoon* (1954), *Kismet* (1955), and *Bells Are Ringing* (1960). Though his critical reputation has been uneven in the United States, Minnelli enjoyed especially enthusiastic attention from French critics in the late 1950s and early 1960s, who saw him as an auteur of the musical form.

Also a successful stage director (especially of musicals), Minnelli was noted for bringing a theatrical sensibility to his film musicals. He was married to **Judy Garland** from 1945–1951; Liza Minnelli is his daughter with Garland.

**MIRAMAX.** Founded in 1979 by brothers Bob and Harvey Weinstein, Miramax originally built its business on the distribution of **independent films** produced by others, from both within the United States and abroad. The success of Miramax-distributed films such as *Sex, Lies, and Videotape* (1989), *The Crying Game* (1992), and **Quentin Tarantino**'s *Reservoir Dogs* (1992) made a major contribution to the independent-film boom of the 1990s. Indeed, Tarantino's ***Pulp Fiction*** (1994), both distributed and co-produced by Miramax, was perhaps the most important single film of this boom.

By this time, however, Miramax had become a subsidiary of **Disney**, though the Weinstein Brothers still managed the company with relative autonomy. Through the 1990s, Miramax had particular success with the release and distribution of English-language versions of Asian films, especially Chinese martial arts films, though the company also drew considerable criticism for its modifications of and cuts to those films. Meanwhile, growing tensions between the brothers and Disney management eventually led the Weinsteins to leave Miramax in 2005 to found their own enterprise, The Weinstein Company. This breakup came after a number of disagreements but was especially triggered by particularly rancorous battles over **Michael Moore**'s politically charged **documentary** *Fahrenheit 9/11* (2004): The brothers wanted to distribute the film, but Disney management refused, not wanting to attract controversy.

Since the departure of the Weinsteins, Miramax has gradually declined in importance as part of the Disney business. By 2009, Miramax had essentially ceased to operate as an identifiable entity, though Disney was reportedly exploring the sale of the unit, possibly back to the Weinsteins.

**MITCHUM, ROBERT (1917–1997).** A gifted and natural actor who angered some in Hollywood with his comments about how easy acting was, Robert Mitchum appeared in well over 100 films and television episodes in his long and varied career, including a number of **Westerns** and **war films**, but he is best remembered for his performances in a series of **film noirs** in the 1940s and 1950s. Mitchum's work in film noir included lead roles in such films as *Crossfire* (1947), *Out of the Past* (1947), *The Big Steal* (1949), *Where Danger Lives* (1950), *His Kind of Woman* (1951), *The Racket* (1951), and *Second Chance* (1953). He typically played sympathetic characters, though his greatest film noir performances were probably as the sinister villains in *Night of the Hunter* (1955) and *Cape Fear* (1962).

As the original film noir cycle waned, Mitchum put his tough-guy persona to work in other genres, though an aging Mitchum later starred as Raymond Chandler's detective Philip Marlowe in two **neo-noir** remakes, *Farewell, My Lovely* (1975) and *The Big Sleep* (1978). Among Mitchum's films of the 1960s were the offbeat **comedy** *The Grass Is Greener* (1960), the **musical** comedy *What a Way to Go!* (1964), the war films *The Longest Day* (1962) and *Anzio* (1968, a U.S.–Italian co-production), and the Westerns *El Dorado* (1966). In the 1970s, he starred in the romantic drama *Ryan's Daughter* (1970), in addition to the neo-noir remakes and crime dramas such as *The Friends of Eddie Coyle* (1973) and *The Yakuza* (1974). He also had important roles in the war epic *Midway* (1976) and the Hollywood **satire** *The Last Tycoon* (1976).

Mitchum continued to appear in films through the 1980s, though he was most prominent in the decade on television, especially as the star of two high-profile miniseries based on the novels of Herman Wouk, *The Winds of War* (1983) and *War and Remembrance* (1988–1989). In the 1990s he returned mostly to film, including appearances in three films in 1995 alone: the spoof *Backfire!*, **Jim Jarmusch**'s offbeat Western *Dead Man*, and the Norwegian-produced crime comedy *Pakten* (in which he had his last starring role).

**MIX, TOM (1880–1940).** One of the greatest stars of **silent film**, Tom Mix made approximately 300 silent **Westerns**, though most are now lost and the exact number is uncertain. In any case, he became the genre's first superstar and helping to define the Western as a film genre. Mix began his career with a supporting role in the Western short *The Cowboy Millionaire* (1909) for the Selig Polyscope Company. He quickly used his skills as a horseman and cattle wrangler to help him become a star for Selig, appearing in numerous shorts (most, but not all, of which were Westerns). He appeared in more than 40 films in 1913 alone. By the 1920s, feature-length films had become the dominant form, and Mix achieved his greatest stardom in the dozens of silent

Western features in which he starred in that decade, mostly for Fox Film Corporation.

Mix made the transition to sound film with *Destry Rides Again* (1932), for **Universal Pictures**. His new contract with Universal gave him unusual creative control over his projects, but he was now in his fifties and made a total of only nine films for Universal, all released in 1932 and 1933. He starred in one additional film, *The Miracle Rider* (1935), for the independent Mascot Pictures.

**MONROE, MARILYN (1926–1962).** Though she ranked sixth on the list of all-time greatest female screen legends compiled by the **American Film Institute** (AFI) in 1999, Marilyn Monroe was arguably the most legendary star in Hollywood history. Never nominated for an **Academy Award** and not particularly respected as an actress, she was nevertheless not without talent, which she was able to combine with her considerable sex appeal and onscreen charisma to build a major (if relatively brief) film career. Moreover, she was as well known for her exploits off the screen as on (including her personal relationships and her nude and partially nude modeling), creating a personal legend that became a central element of American pop cultural history.

Born Norma Jeane Mortensen, Monroe began her film career with a series of minor roles, gradually moving into larger supporting roles in important dramas such as *The Asphalt Jungle* (1950) and *All about Eve* (1950). In addition, her early roles in films such as *Monkey Business* (1952) showed considerable comedic talents. With the **film noir** *Niagara* (1953) she moved into starring roles. She subsequently starred in such films as the **Western** adventure *River of No Return* (1954), but achieved major stardom in a series of **comedies** that included *Gentlemen Prefer Blondes* (1953), *How to Marry a Millionaire* (1953), and *The Seven Year Itch* (1955). Her appearance on the cover of the first issue of *Playboy* magazine in 1953 (with a nude photo of her inside the magazine) was controversial but seemed only to increase her star power as a sex symbol. She followed with two films—*Bus Stop* (1956) and *The Prince and the Showgirl* (1957)—in which she began to receive more critical praise for her acting abilities. She then reached what many regard as the pinnacle of her career in the **Billy Wilder** comedy *Some Like It Hot* (1959), named in an AFI poll in 2000 as the funniest American movie ever made.

Monroe's next film, *Let's Make Love* (1960), was less successful, and its production was plagued by Monroe's difficulties on the set. By the time she made *The Misfits* (1961), her last completed film, Monroe's troubles with drugs and alcohol were taking a serious toll on her health. Her health worsened further during the making of *Something's Got to Give* (1962), and she was dismissed from the film by **Twentieth Century Fox** due to her frequent absences from the set. She did, however, make one of her best remembered performances during the making of this film, singing "Happy Birthday" to U.S. President John F. Kennedy during a celebration at Madison Square Garden. Meanwhile, reports of Monroe's personal relationship with Kennedy (and/or his brother Robert) have become the stuff of pop cultural legend, while her high-profile relationships (and marriages) with such figures as baseball star Joe DiMaggio and playwright Arthur Miller furthered her legend as well.

Monroe was found dead of a drug overdose less than three months after the Kennedy birthday party. The death was officially ruled a probable suicide, but a variety of rumors (including the possibility that she was murdered) have surrounded the death ever since, further adding to Monroe's legendary status.

**MONSTER MOVIES.** Though often overlapping with the **horror** genre, monster movies typically feature creatures whose origins have a scientific explanation (including monsters created by science itself). As a result, monster movies often have more in common with **science fiction** than with horror, though some of the most enduring types of movie monsters (such as vampires and zombies) have supernatural origins (or no explicable origins at all) and thus participate more in horror.

Monsters movies have been a part of American film almost from the beginning, including such early examples as the 1910 adaptation of *Frankenstein*, and were a prominent part of European **silent film**, including such examples as the classic vampire film *Nosferatu* (1922). In general, the technologies available in the silent-film era made monster movies difficult to produce, especially the kind of super-sized monsters that would be prevalent in later monster movies. An early exception was *The Lost World* (1925), which featured prehistoric creatures created by **special effects** pioneer Willis O'Brien, who would later refine these techniques in the classic 1933 monster movie *King Kong* (1933).

The early 1930s were a particularly rich period for monster movies, in which many of the conventions of the form would be established. **Universal Pictures**, with such efforts as *Frankenstein* (1931), *Dracula* (1931), *The Mummy* (1932), and *Bride of Frankenstein* (1935), led the way in monster movies of this period, though *King Kong* (from **RKO Pictures**) might have been the single most important monster movie of the era. Monster movies fell somewhat out of favor in the second half of the 1930s (partly due to increasingly strict enforcement of the **Production Code**), though Universal continued to make *Frankenstein* and *Dracula* sequels and introduced another important monster franchise in 1941 with *The Wolf Man*. They also began, in 1943, to make a series of **comedies** featuring **Bud Abbott and Lou Costello** in confrontation with some of their classic movie monsters.

The 1940s were topped off with *Mighty Joe Young* (1949), another giant ape film that was essentially a reworking of *King Kong* and whose special effects crew included Ray Harryhausen, who would go on to produce special effects for some of the best movie monsters of the 1950s. Meanwhile, the whole genre of the monster movie underwent a resurgence in the 1950s, spurred by the appearance of a number of science fictional monsters, including alien invaders such as the giant Venusian reptile of *20 Million Miles to Earth* (1957), with monster effects by Harryhausen, or in *The Blob* (1958). The most important sf movie monsters of the 1950s, however, were giant creatures (usually either insects or reptiles) produced (or, in some cases, merely freed from long entrapment) by the effects of radiation or weapons testing.

Among the giant reptiles unleashed by radiation and/or weapons testing during the decade was the giant "rhedosaurus" of *The Beast from 20,000 Fathoms* (1953), a dinosaur long frozen in the polar ice cap but freed by atomic weapons testing in the Arctic. This monster was, of course, a direct forerunner of the most famous of the radiation-induced giant reptiles of the 1950s, the Japanese Godzilla, first introduced in 1954, then made popular in the West with the its release, in 1956, as *Godzilla, King of the Monsters*, dubbed in English and with American actor Raymond Burr playing an added point-of-view character. Godzilla, of course, inspired an entire film subindustry in Japan and had numerous imitators elsewhere as well.

Giant insect (or spider) films were especially popular in American film in the 1950s. Perhaps the best of the giant insect films of the 1950s is *Them!* (1954), in which radiation produces a swarm of gigantic ants that threatens the American Southwest, eventually to be destroyed (with flamethrowers) in the sewers of Los Angeles. In Jack Arnold's *Tarantula* (1955), a scientist develops a radiation-charged nutrient that produces a giant killer spider. In *Beginning of the End* (1957), grasshoppers also dine on experimental irradiated food, then grow huge and invade Chicago. The giant insect of *The Deadly Mantis* (1957) was unusual in the 1950s in that it was a prehistoric remnant released (from the polar ice cap) by a natural geological disturbance. Meanwhile, other films of the 1950s seemed fascinated with the monstrous possibilities offered by combining humans with insects, as in *The Fly* (1958) and *The Wasp Woman* (1959), the latter directed by **Roger Corman**, who became one of the kings of B-grade monster movies during this period.

Monsters created by scientific experiments or technological devices gone awry became particularly popular in the 1950s. Frankenstein's monster itself enjoyed something of a renaissance in the decade, especially after the British Hammer Films' *The Curse of Frankenstein* (1957) became an international hit that spawned several sequels and numerous imitations.

Science fictional monster movies fell somewhat out of favor from the 1960s to the 1980s, though Japanese production of the Godzilla sequence and other films in the same vein (featuring not only the original Godzilla but also other monsters such as Rodan and Mothra) remained strong. The most important monster movies from this period involved the sequence of zombie films made by George Romero, beginning with *Night of the Living Dead* (1968) and extending through *Diary of the Dead* (2007). These films produced thoughtful political and social commentary of a kind that many have associated more with science fiction than horror and had something of the texture of postapocalyptic films, though they had no obvious science fictional explanation for the zombies. They also produced numerous imitators, including spoofs, such as the sequence of *Return of the Living Dead* films that began in 1985.

A 1976 remake of *King Kong* was one of the highlights of the genre in the 1970s, but was far less compelling than the original. Probably the most successful sf monster of the 1970s and 1980s was the "xenomorph" of the *Alien* films, though the killer cyborg of the *Terminator* films (which began to appear in 1984) is something of a monster as well. Increasing technological capabilities, especially in the realm of **computer-generated imagery**, opened new possibilities for monster movies by the end of the 1980s, though the monster movies from the 1990s onward have often relied so heavily on special effects that they have suffered in terms of plot and characterization. For example, Roland Emmerich's 1998 big-budget remake of *Godzilla* was not well received. Peter Jackson's megabudget remake of *King Kong* (2005) was more successful, though many still felt that it lacked the heart of the original.

The invading Decepticons of *Transformers* (2007) might also be considered monsters, though, as robots, they lack the personality that made monsters such as Kong so successful. Executive produced by **Steven Spielberg**, *Transformers* was in many ways reminiscent of Spielberg's own remake of *War of the Worlds* (2005), which employed state-of-the-art special effects to make H. G. Wells's invading Martians into implements of urban obliteration (in New York) that looked back to Godzilla but that also reminded many viewers of the 9/11 destruction of the World Trade Center. The innovative *Cloverfield* (2008) was also widely taken as referring to the 9/11 bombings, though that film was perhaps more notable for its use of images from a shaky handheld camera and for its effective deployment of a monster that was barely even seen on the screen. On the other hand, both *The Zombie Diaries* (2006) and *Diary of the Dead* (2007), which might be considered monster movies, came before *Cloverfield* in that respect, while all of these films owe an obvious debt to *The Blair Witch Project* (1999).

**MOORE, JULIANNE (1960– ).** Known before the 1990s primarily for her role in the television soap opera *As the World Turns* (for which she won a Daytime Emmy in 1988), Julianne Moore gradually began to build a solid portfolio of film credits with supporting roles in such films as *The Hand That Rocks the Cradle* (1992), *Benny & Joon* (1993), *The Fugitive* (1993), and *Short Cuts* (1993). Moore moved into starring roles in *Nine Months* (1995) and *The Lost World: Jurassic Park* (1997), but drew particularly positive critical attention for her role in *Boogie Nights* (1997), for which she received an **Academy Award** nomination for Best Supporting Actress. Major roles in such significant films as *The Big Lebowski* (1998) and *Magnolia* (1999) followed, and Moore received an **Oscar** nomination for Best Actress in a Leading Role for *The End of the Affair* (1999).

Moore subsequently starred in such commercial projects as *Evolution* (2001) and *Hannibal* (2001). In 2002, she scored two important successes, receiving an Oscar nomination for Best Supporting Actress for *The Hours* (2002) and a similar nomination for Best Leading Actress in *Far from Heaven* (2002). Since that time Moore has appeared in a variety of projects, ranging from **romantic comedies** such as *Laws of Attraction* (2004), to high-profile **science fiction** films such as *Children of Men* (2006) and *Next* (2007), to smaller **independent films** such as *A Single Man* (2009).

**MOORE, MICHAEL (1954– ).** Michael Moore, developing a reputation as a sort of spokesman for ordinary Americans, is the leading **documentary** filmmaker of his generation, combining exposés of corporate greed and corruption with colorful, even humorous components that make his documentaries highly entertaining. He burst onto the scene in 1989 with the release of *Roger & Me* (1989), about the damage done to the city of Flint, Michigan, by the policies of the General Motors Corporation; still widely viewed, *Roger & Me* was perhaps the first documentary to attain the status of a **cult** film.

In 1995, Moore forayed into fiction film with the satirical *Canadian Bacon* (1995), but his primary contributions remain as a documentarian. *The Big One* (1997), another documentary about corporate greed, was a moderate success, propelling Moore into a brief career in which he took his trademark documentary style to television in the series *TV Nation* (1997) and *The Awful Truth* (1999–2000). He returned to documentary feature film with *Bowling for Columbine* (2002), which attempted to understand American gun culture as background to the 1999 high school shootings in Columbine, Colorado.

*Bowling for Columbine* won the **Academy Award** for Best Documentary Feature. It was, however, with *Fahrenheit 9/11* (2004) that Moore achieved his greatest success. The film, aimed at exposing the nefarious dealings of the American Bush administration (especially in relation to the 2003 invasion of

Iraq), grossed more than $200 million worldwide, easily making it the biggest commercial success of any documentary in film history. That controversial film did not succeed in preventing the re-election of U.S. President George W. Bush, nor did it win an **Oscar** nomination, but it did succeed in making Moore perhaps the best-known documentary filmmaker in history.

Moore's next film, *Sicko* (2007), an exposé of the U.S. health-care system, was less commercially successful but did receive an Oscar nomination for Best Documentary Feature. *Captain Mike across America* (2007) documented Moore's own speaking tour of American college campuses, while *Capitalism: A Love Story* (2009) investigates the crisis in the U.S. financial system in 2007–2010; it is unusual in American culture in its suggestion that capitalism as a system (rather than simply a few bad capitalists) may be the root cause of the problem.

**MOTION PICTURE ASSOCIATION OF AMERICA (MPAA).** Founded in 1922 as the Motion Picture Producers and Distributors of America (MPPDA), the Motion Picture Association of America (MPAA) is a trade association charged with advancing the business interests of the Hollywood film industry. Its membership consists of the six biggest Hollywood studios: **Disney**, **Twentieth Century Fox**, **Sony**, **Paramount**, **Warner Bros.**, and **Universal**. The MPAA engages in a variety of public relations campaigns and antipiracy efforts, including the undertaking of legal actions against file-sharing websites that distribute videos of films.

While the sometimes controversial antipiracy efforts of the MPAA have gained considerable attention, the organization is best known for its administration of a ratings system indicating the age levels for which given films are deemed appropriate. Thus, films rated "G" by the MPAA are deemed appropriate for all ages; "PG" films are considered potentially appropriate for all ages, with the proviso that parents should use their own judgment regarding the viewing of films by younger children; a "PG-13" rating implies stronger cautions, and films with this rating are considered problematic for any children under 13, though parents are again urged to use their own judgment. An "R" rating implies that no one under 17 should be allowed to view the film in theaters without an accompanying parent or adult guardian, though enforcement of this rule has been problematic. Finally, if a film is rated "NC-17," no one under 17 is to be allowed to view the film in theaters.

This ratings system was originally put in place in 1968, though it has been modified several times over the years. It has thus proved quite durable, though it has often been criticized for being mechanical and arbitrary and for being far more concerned about sexuality and profanity than about violence. Participation in the system is officially voluntary, though the six **major studios** that make up the MPAA have agreed to submit all of their films for rating, while the release of a film without an MPAA rating (or with the NC-17 rating) is generally a recipe for commercial failure.

**MOTION PICTURE PRODUCTION CODE.** *See* PRODUCTION CODE.

**MURNAU, F. W. (1888–1931).** Friedrich Wilhelm Murnau was one of the most important directors of German **silent film**, a key developer of the German expressionist style in cinema. His *Nosferatu* (1922) is still an acknowledged classic and one of the founding works of the vampire film subgenre. *The Last Laugh* (1924) also made particularly important contributions to the development of the expressionist style.

Murnau came to Hollywood in 1926 as part of a conscious effort on the part of Hollywood studios to recruit talented European directors. Going to work for Fox Studio, Murnau's first American film was *Sunrise* (1927), which brought the expressionist style to Hollywood with great success. *Sunrise* is widely considered to be one of the greatest films of all time, and possibly the greatest of all silent films. It won three awards in the initial 1929 **Academy Awards**, including "Best Picture, Unique and Artistic Production."

Murnau moved into sound with his second American film, *4 Devils* (1928), which was not a great success and is now lost. His next sound film, *City Girl* (1930), was also unsuccessful. His last film, *Tabu: A Story of the South Seas* (1931), is a fictional film that was originally to be co-directed by pioneering documentarian Robert J. Flaherty, but Flaherty left early in the production due to artistic differences. The film was originally shot in a part-sound, part-silent version, though it was ultimately restored to an all-silent version. Murnau died a week before the film was released, due to injuries suffered in an automobile accident.

**MUNI, PAUL (1895–1967).** Though his tenure as a top Hollywood star was brief, Paul Muni was one of the biggest stars of the 1930s, playing some of the decade's most intense and memorable roles. During that decade, he was generally the first actor of choice to star in the most prestigious films produced by **Warner Bros.**, though he was also given the rare (at the time) option to choose his own roles.

After early success on the New York stage, Muni got his start in film in the now lost *Seven Faces* (1929), in which he played seven different roles. Muni received an **Academy Award** nomination for Best Actor in a Leading Role for his second film, *The Valiant* (1929). However, his breakthrough into stardom came in 1932 when he starred in the **gangster film** *Scarface* (1932) and the powerful social drama *I Am a Fugitive from a Chain Gang*, a gangster film of sorts, in which the protagonist is portrayed as the victim of a sadistic legal and penal system. Muni received his second **Oscar** nomination for Best Actor for that film.

Muni received his third Oscar nomination for Best Actor for the **biopic** *The Story of Louis Pasteur* (1935), though he had finished second in the previous year's balloting for Best Actor as a write-in candidate for his performance in *Black Fury* (1935), a labor drama directed by **Michael Curtiz**. Muni won another Oscar nomination for his lead role in *The Life of Emile Zola* (1937) and followed as the star of still another biopic in *Juarez* (1939).

From that point forward, Muni returned mostly to stage acting, though he still appeared occasionally in film. Highlights of the 1940s included *A Song to Remember* (1945) and *Angel on My Shoulder* (1946). Muni received his sixth and last Oscar nomination for his lead role in *The Last Angry Man* (1959), one of only two films in which he appeared after *Angel on My Shoulder*.

**MURRAY, BILL (1950– ).** Bill Murray has become one of the most successful comic actors of his generation, at the same time starring in a number of serious roles. He won considerable critical recognition, including an **Academy Award** nomination for Best Actor, for his performance in *Lost in Translation* (2003). It is, however, for his appearances in a number of now-classic **comedies** that Murray will probably be best remembered.

Murray began his career with Chicago's "Second City" improvisational comedy troupe, then gained national recognition as a regular cast member of the television skit comedy *Saturday Night Live* from 1977 to 1980. In the meantime, he had starred in the **anarchic comedy** *Meatballs* (1979) and *Caddyshack* (1980), the latter of which has become something of a **cult** classic and which helped to launch his post-television film career. He followed with a starring role in *Stripes* (1981) and with a major supporting role in the much-respected *Tootsie* (1982).

Murray next costarred in *Ghost Busters* (1984), solidifying his credentials in comedy, that same year also receiving good reviews for his first major dramatic role, in *The Razor's Edge*. Since that time, Murray has remained a major presence in American film (and popular culture as a whole), both as a lead actor and as a supporting actor. Subsequent comedies in which he starred, including *Scrooged* (1988), *Ghost Busters II* (1989), and *Groundhog Day* (1993), were successful, though *Quick Change* (1990) and *What About Bob?* (1991) were less so. Meanwhile, his supporting performances in films such as *Ed Wood* (1994), *Rushmore* (1998), and *Cradle Will Rock* (1999) helped to establish his credentials as a solid supporting actor in a variety of modes.

In more recent years, Murray has focused on roles in quirky **independent films**, including *Lost in Translation*, Wes Anderson's *The Life Aquatic with*

*Steve Zissou* (2004) and *The Darjeeling Limited* (2007), and **Jim Jarmusch**'s *Broken Flowers* (2005). Murray has also done voiceover work in films such as *Garfield* (2004) and *Fantastic Mr. Fox* (2009). He played himself in a cameo role in the zombie comedy *Zombieland* (2009) that many regarded as the highlight of the film.

**MUSIC.** Music has been an integral part of film since the very beginning. Indeed, **silent films** were not really silent, but were typically accompanied by music, played live from a score distributed with the film. With the rise of sound film, integrated musical sound tracks became even more important, while diegetic music also often became part of the content of films, including the rise of the **musical** as a major American film genre.

Even aside from musicals, virtually every American film from the sound era has included a soundtrack of background music that helps to set the tone and atmosphere for the scenes in which it appears. Early on, film music was dominated by composers who were heavily influenced by the European classical music tradition, especially the Romantic tradition. Many of the most important early composers (such as **Max Steiner**, **Miklós Rózsa**, **Dimitri Tiomkin**, and **Franz Waxman**) were, in fact, born in Europe.

As the film industry entered a period of crisis and change in the 1950s, film music began to change as well, generally taking on a more modern and more American flavor. Subsequently, film music was heavily influenced by the rise of rock 'n' roll and other forms of American popular music, though it continued to be standard practice in Hollywood to use original compositions in film rather than simply to important pieces of familiar popular music. However, especially beginning in the 1960s, songs from films were frequently remarketed as popular music, enjoying considerable commercial success on its own. Albums of soundtrack music, which had first been marketed in the 1940s, also became popular in the 1960s; many became bestsellers, as in the huge success of **John Williams**'s soundtrack for ***Star Wars*** (1977).

**Francis Ford Coppola**'s *Apocalypse Now* (1979) featured a soundtrack mostly consisting of well-known popular music from the 1960s, performed by such rock groups as the Doors and the Rolling Stones. Subsequently, preexisting popular music was used more and more in film, though well-known songs have often been re-recorded for film as well. The soundtrack for **Quentin Tarantino**'s ***Pulp Fiction*** (1994), consisting of previously re-corded songs that had first appeared over a period of several decades, was a key element in the success of that film and became a major bestseller in its own right. The film was an important example of the growing commercial importance of soundtrack music, which caused many film companies to open their own music divisions specifically for the distribution of soundtracks.

Sales of soundtracks have flagged along with the general depression in the music industry in the early years of the 21st century, but music remains an extremely important and integral part of American film.

The importance of film music has long been recognized by the inclusion of several music categories in the **Academy Awards**, which have included an award to the composer of the Best Original Film Score since 1934, though the exact designation of that award has changed from year to year. (During most of the 1940s and 1950s, for example, two Best Score awards were given, one for **comedies** or dramas, and one for musicals.) The top film composers have tended to be quite prolific, and many have received numerous **Oscar** nominations for Best Score, topped by **Alfred Newman** with 43 and Williams with 40.

**MUSICAL.** While virtually all American films rely on **music** for an important part of their overall impact, the musical, which involves musical performances by the characters within the diegetic world of the film (and is often thematically about music), is a distinctive genre of its own. The coming of sound film in the late 1920s led immediately to the birth of the musical, which offered one of the most obvious uses for the new technology. For example, *The Jazz Singer* (1927), often cited as the first true talkie, actually included relatively very little synchronized dialogue and was more notable for its musical performances. By the 1930s, the musical had become a major film genre, often involving elaborately staged spectacles clearly designed to supply escapist relief from the realities of life during the Depression. The genre declined during and after World War II, largely due to the expense of production, though important musicals have continued to appear.

Many early musicals were essentially filmed versions of the stage musicals that had long been popular on Broadway and elsewhere. It soon became apparent, however, that the nature of film made it possible to stage spectacular production numbers that would not be practical in live performance. Such numbers came to dominate the genre in the 1930s, most notably in the various musicals choreographed or directed by **Busby Berkeley**, beginning with *42nd Street* and *Gold Diggers of 1933*, both released in 1933. However, such films quickly fell out of favor due to the expense of production. Films featuring smaller-scale dance numbers became popular by the mid-1930s, when films such as *Top Hat* (1935) and *Swing Time* (1936) made dancer **Fred Astaire** a major Hollywood star. Meanwhile, the most important musical of the late 1930s was *The Wizard of Oz* (1939), which included the more conventional use of diegetic musical performances, relying more on the singing talents of **Judy Garland** and its other stars than on elaborate production numbers.

Few musicals were produced during the war years, but, with **Metro-Goldwyn-Mayer** (MGM) taking the lead, Hollywood attempted to resurrect the genre in the postwar years. Films such as *Easter Parade* (1948), *On the Town* (1949), *An American in Paris* (1951), **Singin' in the Rain** (1952) and *The Band Wagon* (1953) did indeed bring new life to the genre, but musicals were still expensive to produce and the historical tide was against the genre as Hollywood studios began more and more to reserve their highest budgets for **biblical epics** and **historical epics**. By the mid-to-late 1950s, the musical resurgence of the early 1950s was beginning to wane, and the most important musicals of the second half of the 1950s often had to rely on innovative premises, such as the musical **gangster film** *Guys and Dolls* (1955), or *Porgy and Bess* (1959), which featured an African American cast.

In the late 1950s and into the 1960s, Hollywood attempted to cash in on the rise of rock music with such films as *Rock around the Clock* (1956) and with an entire series of films starring rock megastar **Elvis Presley**. Such efforts saw only limited success, though the musical made another minor comeback in the early 1960s, as several important and successful musicals appeared, including *West Side Story* (1961), *The Music Man* (1962), *My Fair Lady* (1964), *Mary Poppins* (1964), and *The Sound of Music* (1965). The live-action *Mary Poppins*, for example, was easily the biggest hit yet produced by **Disney**, while it should be noted that all of Disney's previous **animated films** had really been musicals, though they are not usually thought of in that category.

The success of the early 1960s musicals encouraged studios to devote substantial resources to the genre in the late 1960s, but most of the musicals of that era were expensive flops. Films such as *Hello, Dolly!* (1969) and *Paint Your Wagon* (1969) failed to meet expectations at the box office, as it soon became clear that the success of the early 1960s films had come at least partly because musicals had by that time become a novelty. The novelty having worn off, musicals were once again out of favor in Hollywood, and the musical was soon relegated to occasional curiosities such as the self-parodic **cult** favorite *The Rocky Horror Picture Show* (1975). The most successful American musicals of the remainder of the 20th century were the animated films of the Disney Renaissance, beginning in 1989, with films such as *Beauty and the Beast* (1991) and *The Lion King* (1994) being key examples.

The musical has remained a marginal genre in the early 21st century, though several interesting examples have suggested that the genre still holds considerable potential. For example, Baz Luhrmann's *Moulin Rouge!* (2001), featuring the musical performances of well-known actors **Nicole Kidman** and Ewan McGregor, got considerable attention for its resurrection of the musical spectacle, though in a **postmodern** mode. Meanwhile, *Chicago* (2002), a film adaptation of a stage musical, won six **Academy Awards**, including Best Picture, achieving its effects partly by similarly relying on the musical talents of stars (Renée Zellweger, Catherine Zeta-Jones, and Richard Gere) who were better known as actors than as musical performers.

**Tim Burton**'s *Sweeney Todd: The Demon Barber of Fleet Street* (2007) was a particularly dark and offbeat example of the musical, suggesting its versatility, while the recent *Mama Mia!* (2008) was a surprise hit that suggested an ongoing commercial potential for the genre, though it received a lukewarm reception from critics.

# N

**NASHVILLE.** *Nashville* (dir. **Robert Altman**, 1975), widely considered one of the most important American films of the 1970s, is an impressive **satire** that uses a critical examination of Nashville's country **music** industry to comment on the violence, greed, apathy, and rampant commodification that Altman sees as characteristic of 1970s American society as a whole. The film is essentially a slice of Nashville life. However, by following an array of characters from different backgrounds (many of whom are not Nashvillians) through several days of activity in the city, the film clearly identifies Nashville as part of a larger world and as representative of larger phenomena.

Many of the characters in *Nashville* are successful country music performers, some of whom can be related to actual country stars, though it is probably better to see them as representing types rather than specific individuals. Altman also indicates the way in which, by the mid-1970s, the Nashville music industry was already extending its scope beyond traditional country music, at the same time becoming increasingly commodified. He thus includes Tom, Bill, and Mary, a trio of pop-folk singers, who are recording in Nashville.

*Nashville* culminates by bringing most of the characters together in Nashville's Centennial Park for a free concert that features several of the principals and is being held to promote the presidential campaign of third-party candidate Hall Phillip Walker, a populist with no coherent political philosophy other than dissatisfaction with the status quo, thus indicating the poverty of American political discourse. The concert (whose performers are clearly seeking to promote their own careers rather than Walker's candidacy) opens beneath a huge American flag, only to be interrupted when a mysterious figure who has floated through the entire film emerges from the audience and shoots two performers, apparently killing one of them.

Despite the momentary chaos that ensues, the concert quickly resumes. Albuquerque (Barbara Harris), an ambitious would-be star who has yet to get her big break in show business, seizes her opportunity, grabs the mike, and launches into a bluesy rendition of "It Don't Worry Me," a song whose very title indicates the growing political apathy of the American populace in the wake of Vietnam and Watergate. The performance is highly successful. Albuquerque is soon joined by a gospel choir on hand for the concert, while the audience claps and sings along, seemingly unaffected by the shooting, presumably because, by 1975, they have become so accustomed to such events as to be anesthetized to them. Popular culture, meanwhile, contributes to this anesthetic effect by providing an entertaining distraction from political reality.

*Nashville* was nominated for a total of five **Academy Awards**, including Best Picture and Best Director, but it won only in the category of Best Song, for "I'm Easy," which had become a national hit in its own right.

**NATIONAL FILM REGISTRY.** Established by the National Film Preservation Act of 1988, the National Film Registry is a list of "culturally, historically, or aesthetically significant films" designated for preservation in the Library of Congress by the National Film Preservation Board. The Film Preservation Act authorizes the board to designate up to 25 films each year to be added to the list. A film must be at least 10 years old to be added to the registry, which currently contains films ranging from *Blacksmith Scene* (1893) to *Fargo* (1996). The initial list, determined in 1989, included such classics as *Intolerance* (1916), *The General* (1927), *Sunrise* (1927), *Modern Times* (1936), **Snow White and the Seven Dwarfs** (1937), **Gone with the Wind** (1939), **The Wizard of Oz** (1939), **Citizen Kane** (1941), *The Maltese Falcon* (1941), **Casablanca** (1942), **Sunset Blvd.** (1950), **Singin' in the Rain** (1952), **High Noon** (1952), **The Searchers** (1956), and **Vertigo** (1958).

**NEO-NOIR.** *See* FILM NOIR.

**NEW HOLLYWOOD.** "New Hollywood" is a term used to describe the era in studio filmmaking from roughly the mid-1960s to the early 1980s when new trends merged, partly due to the aftermath of the collapse of the classic studio system and partly due to the emergence of a new generation of directors, many of whom had been educated in film schools and most of whom were highly conscious of their relationship with their predecessors in film. The New Hollywood was also greatly enabled by social changes in the United States in the 1960s and 1970s, which led to the collapse of the **Production Code** and opened new possibilities for Hollywood filmmaking. The movement is also sometimes referred to as the "American New Wave," in reference to the French New Wave, which exercised a considerable influence on the New Hollywood, especially in its early years, when films such as **Bonnie and Clyde** (1967) clearly showed such influence in their departure from the classic Hollywood style.

The New Hollywood films were marked by a number of stylistic innovations, largely having to do with intrusive editing as opposed to the "invisible" editing of classic Hollywood films. However, the New Hollywood films also departed from classical Hollywood films in their content, which was more youth oriented, more sexually frank, and generally more realistic in its treatment of a variety of issues and themes than that of classic Hollywood films.

It became particularly clear that a new era had arrived by the mid-1970s, when a variety of new young directors had emerged to become dominant forces in Hollywood. **Woody Allen, Robert Altman, Hal Ashby, Dennis Hopper, Stanley Kubrick, Mike Nichols,** and **Roman Polanski** are among the directors often associated with the movement, though its central figures were probably **Peter Bogdanovich, Francis Ford Coppola, Brian De Palma, Martin Scorsese, George Lucas,** and **Steven Spielberg**. However, the stupendous box-office success of the films of the latter two directors is also often cited as a key factor in the end of the New Hollywood era, as studios began to put more emphasis on commercial blockbusters than on interesting and innovative filmmaking. Michael Cimino's *Heaven's Gate* (1980), which oddly (and disastrously, in a commercial sense) combined the budgetary excess of a blockbuster with the artistic aspirations of the best New Hollywood films, is often cited as the death knell of the New Hollywood era. Coppola's extravagant *One from the Heart* (1982) then not only finished off the New Hollywood but virtually killed off the **musical** as well.

The success of New Hollywood filmmakers helped to make the 1970s one of the richest decades in American film history. Twenty films from the 1970s are on the **American Film Institute**'s 2007 list of the 100 greatest films of all time—more than any other decade.

**NEW LINE CINEMA.** Founded in 1967 to produce and distribute **independent films**, New Line Cinema grew to become an important Hollywood studio, especially as the co-producer and U.S. distributor of the *Lord of the Rings* **trilogy** (2001–2003). However, New Line has operated as a subsidiary of Time Warner since 1996 and has now been merged with their **Warner Bros.** Studios. At its peak, New Line was involved with an average of 10–12 films per year; it continues to produce films under its own brand but now releases or distributes less than half that number yearly. The company originally gained success with the re-release and distribution of the 1936 antimarijuana film *Reefer Madness*, which warned against marijuana use with such over-the-top hysteria that it became a camp hit on college campuses across the United States. The company also released many of the campy films of director **John Waters** early in its history, as well as providing the U.S. distribution for a number of important foreign films.

Nevertheless, New Line soon fell upon hard times until the studio was resurrected with the success of the *Nightmare on Elm Street* sequence of

**horror** films (featuring dreamstalker Freddy Krueger), beginning in 1984 and extending through the 2010 remake of the original film, with six sequels and two television series in between, in addition to the 2003 spin-off *Freddy vs. Jason* (2003). Thus, the studio is still referred to in some circles as "the House that Freddy Built."

New Line has been involved in the production and/or distribution of a number of interesting and innovative films, including *Glengarry Glen Ross* (1992), *Seven* (1995), *Boogie Nights* (1997), and *Dark City* (1998). However, the company has come to specialize in franchises of related films and in remakes of earlier films. In addition to the *Nightmare on Elm Street* and *Lord of the Rings* films, the company took over the *Texas Chainsaw Massacre* horror franchise in 1990 and the *Friday the 13th* horror franchise in 1993; it has also been involved with such sequences as the *Austin Powers* films (1997–2002), the *Blade* films (1998–2004), and the *Final Destination* films (2000–2009).

**NEWMAN, ALFRED (1901–1970).** Alfred Newman was one of the leading composers of **music** for film during the **Golden Age** of Hollywood. He received a total of more than 40 **Academy Award** nominations for his music, including nominations in 20 consecutive years from 1938 through 1957. Altogether, he composed music that was used in more than 200 films, though many of them were without screen credits.

Newman served as the music director for **Twentieth Century Fox** from 1940 to 1960, composing music for many of their films during that time. It was also during this period that he developed the "Newman System," a method for synchronizing a musical score with a film that is still in use today. He worked as a freelance composer after leaving Fox in 1960. His nine **Oscar** wins include awards for the scores of *Alexander's Ragtime Band* (1938), *Tin Pan Alley* (1940), *The Song of Bernadette* (1943), *With a Song in My Heart* (1952), *Love Is a Many-Splendored Thing* (1955), *The King and I* (1956), and *Camelot* (1967).

Newman was the father of film composer **Thomas Newman** and the uncle of film and popular music composer **Randy Newman**.

**NEWMAN, PAUL (1925–2008).** In a film career that lasted more than 50 years, Paul Newman was one of the great figures of the American cinema, as well as one of the great humanitarians of his era. After studying acting at Yale University and in New York, Newman made several appearances on the stage and on television before making his film debut with an important supporting role in *The Silver Chalice* (1954). He then broke through into starring roles with his performance as Rocky Graziano in the 1956 boxing **biopic** *Somebody Up There Likes Me* (1956). After several more roles in both film and television, he solidified his position as a top Hollywood star by starring in no less than four different films in 1958. These films included *The Long, Hot Summer*; *The Left Handed Gun*; *Rally 'round the Flag, Boys*; and *Cat on a Hot Tin Roof*, the latter of which won him the first of his eight **Academy Award** nominations for Best Actor in a Leading Role.

Newman continued to appear frequently in film through the 1960s, starring in such key films as *Exodus* (1960), *The Hustler* (1961, *Hud* (1963), and *Cool Hand Luke* (1967), receiving Best Actor **Oscar** nominations for the latter three of these. In 1969, he paired with **Robert Redford** in one of his best-known films, **Butch Cassidy and the Sundance Kid**. The two would be successfully paired again in *The Sting* (1973), another hit.

Newman continued to star in highly commercial projects, such as *The Towering Inferno* (1974), but also began to appear in quirkier projects, such as his two films with **Robert Altman** in the 1970s: *Buffalo Bill and the Indians, or Sitting Bull's History Lesson* (1976) and *Quintet* (1979). He also starred in *Slap Shot* (1977), an ice hockey film that has become a **cult** classic. He then began the 1980s by winning Oscar nominations for Best Actor in two consecutive years, for *Absence of Malice* (1981) and *The Verdict* (1982).

Then moving into his late fifties, Newman began to specialize in playing older characters who have been largely defeated by life but maintain just enough energy to keep going. In 1986, he received a special Oscar for his lifetime of achievement in film, but he still had much to achieve. One of the most interesting of his later performances was his reprisal of the role of pool hustler Fast Eddie Felson in *The Color of Money* (1986), a sequel to *The Hustler*. This role won him his only Oscar for Best Actor in a Leading Role. *The Hudsucker Proxy* (1994), *Nobody's Fool* (1995), and *Twilight* (1998) were among Newman's most interesting films of the 1990s, as he continued to play starring roles into his seventies.

In 2002, Newman received a Best Supporting Actor Oscar nomination for his performance in *The Road to Perdition*. His last film performance was as the voice of Doc Hudson in the **animated film** *Cars* (2006), from **Pixar**. He also directed and produced several films during his career, including *Rachel, Rachel* (1968), which received an Oscar nomination for Best Picture.

In his later years, Newman became well known as a racing car enthusiast, winning several national championships as a driver in Sports Car Club of American road races, competing successfully into his seventies. He was also a prominent liberal political activist, philanthropist, and humanitarian, particularly as the founder of a line of food products from which all after-tax profits were donated to charities. At the time of his death, proceeds from the Paul Newman brand of food products and generated nearly $300 million in such donations. In 1994, he won the Jean Hersholt Humanitarian Award from the **Academy of Motion Picture Arts and Sciences**.

**NEWMAN, RANDY (1943– ).** Randy Newman had already had a successful career as a composer and performer of popular songs (and had composed here and there for television and film) when he turned, in the 1980s, to a focus on composing for film. That new emphasis got to a strong start when Newman wrote the **music** for **Milos Forman**'s *Ragtime* (1981), receiving **Academy Award** nominations for both Best Score and Best Song for his work on that film. Newman received a second Best Score **Oscar** nomination for his work on *The Natural* (1984), whose central theme is one of his best-known works.

When Newman again received both Best Score and Best Song Oscar nominations for *Toy Story* (1995), the first **Pixar** film, it brought his total number of Oscar nominations to eight, firmly establishing him as a leading Hollywood composer. It also started a fruitful partnership between Newman and Pixar that would see him write the music for *A Bug's Life* (1998); *Toy Story 2* (1999); *Monsters, Inc.* (2001); and *Cars* (2006). Newman has received a total of seven Oscar nominations for the music he wrote for these five Pixar films, finally winning his first Oscar for Best Song for "If I Didn't Have You" from *Monsters, Inc.*

Newman received two Best Song Oscar nominations for music from **Disney**'s *The Princess and the Frog* (2009), bringing his total number of nominations to 19. Other films for which Newman wrote Oscar-nominated music include *Parenthood* (1989), *Avalon* (1990), *The Paper* (1994), *James and the Giant Peach* (1996), *Pleasantville* (1998), *Babe: Pig in the City* (1998), and *Meet the Parents* (2000). Among other films for which he wrote music was *¡Three Amigos!* (1986), for which he also co-wrote the screenplay.

Newman is the nephew of esteemed film composer **Alfred Newman** and the cousin of film composer **Thomas Newman**.

**NEWMAN, THOMAS (1955– ).** Thomas Newman had established himself as a solid composer of film **music** in films such as **Robert Altman**'s *The Player* (1992) when he finally made his breakthrough with two **Academy Award** nominations for Best Score in a single year, for *The Shawshank Redemption* (1994) and *Little Women* (1994). He also received two **Oscar** nominations (for Best Song and Best Score) in 2009, both for *WALL-E* (2008). In between, he received six other nominations, though to date he has yet to win an Oscar.

Newman's other Oscar nominations were for the scores of *Unstrung Heroes* (1995), *American Beauty* (1999), *Road to Perdition* (2002), *Finding Nemo* (2003), *Lemony Snicket's A Series of Unfortunate Events* (2004), and *The Good German* (2006). Other notable films scored by Newman include *The People vs.*

*Larry Flynt* (1996), *Mad City* (1997), *The Green Mile* (1999), *Erin Brockovich* (2000), *Cinderella Man* (2005), and *Revolutionary Road* (2008).

Newman is the nephew of esteemed film composer **Alfred Newman** and the cousin of film and popular music composer **Randy Newman**.

**NICHOLS, MIKE (1931– ).** Born Michael Peschkowsky in Berlin, Mike Nichols came to the United States as a child when his Jewish family fled the Nazis in 1939. He began his show business career in improvisational **comedy**, soon forming a comedy team with Elaine May, a young comic who would later become a successful screenwriter. After some early experience directing stage plays, Nichols got off to an impressive start in film, directing *Who's Afraid of Virginia Woolf?* (1966) and *The Graduate* (1967), receiving **Academy Award** nominations for Best Director for both films and winning the award for the second.

*Catch-22* (1970), *Carnal Knowledge* (1971), and *The Day of the Dolphin* (1973) were also notable films, though Nichols would not return to his initial level of success until *Silkwood* (1983), which won him another **Oscar** nomination for Best Director, as did *Working Girl* (1988). His films *The Birdcage* (1996) and *Primary Colors* (1998) were both scripted by May. Other recent films directed by Nichols include *Wolf* (1994), *Closer* (2004), and *Charlie Wilson's War* (2007).

Nichols has also produced a number of his own films and received a Best Picture Oscar nomination as the co-producer of *The Remains of the Day* (1993), which he did not direct.

**NICHOLSON, JACK (1937– ).** Jack Nicholson is one of the most recognized, respected, and awarded actors of his generation. After a slow start that included appearances in a number of television programs and an apprenticeship in the low-budget shop of **Roger Corman**, he began to attract attention with his role in *Easy Rider* (1969), for which he received an **Academy Award** nomination for Best Actor in a Supporting Role. *Five Easy Pieces* (1970) was his first major starring role; it also won him the first of his eight **Oscar** nominations for Best Actor in a Leading Role.

Nicholson received such nominations in three consecutive years in the mid-1970s, for *The Last Detail* (1973), **Chinatown** (1974), and *One Flew over the Cuckoo's Nest* (1975), winning his first Oscar for the latter. *Chinatown* was a particularly important film that anticipated Nicholson's appearances in several more **neo-noir** films in the coming years, including a sequel, *The Two Jakes* (1990); the 1981 remake of *The Postman Always Rings Twice*; and *Blood and Wine* (1996). The late 1970s saw Nicholson star in two unusual **Westerns**, *The Missouri Breaks* (1976) and *Goin' South* (1978). One of his most memorable performances was in the **horror** film *The Shining* (1980), while *Terms of Endearment* (1983) won him an Oscar for Best Supporting Actor.

Nicholson received additional Best Leading Actor Oscar nominations for *Prizzi's Honor* (1985) and *Ironweed* (1987), while gaining considerable attention for his over-the-top performance as the Joker in **Tim Burton**'s *Batman* (1989), foreshadowing his later comic performance in dual roles in Burton's *Mars Attacks!* (1996). In between, Nicholson starred in several other films, including the **biopic** *Hoffa* (1992) and the horror film *Wolf* (1994). He also gained another Best Supporting Actor Oscar nomination for *A Few Good Men* (1992).

Nicholson has appeared less frequently in film in recent years but continues to play prominent roles in key films. He won another Best Actor Oscar for his starring role in the **romantic comedy** *As Good As It Gets* (1997) and scored another Best Actor nomination for *About Schmidt* (2002). Other recent films include *Anger Management* (2003), *Something's Gotta Give* (2003), and *The Bucket List* (2007).

Nicholson has also occasionally served as a writer, producer, and director, including the direction of his own films *Goin' South* and *The Two Jakes*.

**NORTH, ALEX (1910–1991).** The American modernist composer Alex North worked extensively in film, producing some of the most innovative and influential film scores in Hollywood history. North was nominated for a total of 14 **Academy Awards** for Best Score (and one for Best Song, for "Unchained Melody" from the 1955 film *Unchained*), but never won a competitive award. He was, however, given a special lifetime achievement **Oscar** in 1986.

Among North's leading contributions to innovation in film **music** were the jazz-based score for *A Streetcar Named Desire* (1951) and the modernist score for *Viva Zapata!* (1952), both for director **Elia Kazan**, with whom North had been associated since they worked together on the leftist documentary *People of the Cumberland* in 1937; that same year, North wrote the score for another leftist **documentary** (in support of the antifascist Republicans of the Spanish Civil War), *Heart of Spain*.

It was not until 1951 (with *Streetcar*, **Otto Preminger**'s *The 13th Letter*, and the film adaptation of Arthur Miller's *Death of a Salesman*) that North moved into Hollywood film, but he would ultimately become far better known for his film music than for his classical compositions or his music for the stage. Among his Oscar-nominated scores are those for *The Rose Tattoo* (1955), *The Rainmaker* (1956), *Spartacus* (1960), *Cleopatra* (1963), *Who's Afraid of Virginia Woolf?* (1956), and *Dragonslayer* (1981).

North wrote the original score for **Stanley Kubrick**'s *2001: A Space Odyssey* (1968), but the score was famously rejected by Kubrick, who had earlier worked successfully with North on *Spartacus*.

**NUGENT, FRANK S. (1908–1965).** Frank S. Nugent was a journalist and film reviewer, as well as a screenwriter and a script doctor of screenplays written by others. He is especially well known for the 11 screenplays he wrote for director **John Ford**, including the classic **Western** *The Searchers* (1956). Other Westerns written by Nugent for Ford's direction include *Fort Apache* (1948), *3 Godfathers* (1948), *She Wore a Yellow Ribbon* (1949), and *Wagon Master* (1950). Other films he wrote for Ford include *The Quiet Man* (1952), *Mister Roberts* (1955, completed by **Mervyn LeRoy** due to Ford's battles with alcohol), and *Donovan's Reef* (1963).

Nugent also wrote films in a variety of genres for other directors, but none approached the success he had with Ford. Nugent's only **Academy Award** nomination came for the screenplay of *The Quiet Man*. He served as the president of the **Writers' Guild of America** from 1957 to 1958.

**NYKVIST, SVEN (1922–1906).** The Swedish cinematographer Sven Nykvist is known especially for his work with Swedish director Ingmar Bergman, though he also had a productive career in Hollywood film as well. Moreover, he won American **Academy Awards** for Best Cinematography for two of his Swedish films with Bergman, *Cries and Whispers* (1972) and *Fanny and Alexander* (1982). He also received a third **Oscar** nomination for Best Cinematography for one of his American films, *The Unbearable Lightness of Being* (1988).

The effectiveness of Nykvist's simple, naturalistic style of cinematography has made him one of the most respected cinematographers of all time. Moreover, his collaboration with Bergman is credited with having exercised a strong influence on the evolution of the director's style, beginning with their early work together in the 1950s. In addition to the Oscar-winning films, Nykvist's work on Bergman's *Persona* (1966), especially in its use of close-ups, is considered particularly important in terms of its influence on other cinematographers.

Nykvist also worked with other leading European directors, as well as with some of Hollywood's best-known directors. American-produced films on which he served as the principal cinematographer include Richard Fleischer's *The Last Run* (1971), Louis Malle's *Pretty Baby* (1978), Alan J. Pakula's *Starting Over* (1979), Bob Rafelson's *The Postman Always Rings Twice* (1981), **Norman Jewison**'s *Agnes of God* (1985), and Nora Ephron's *Sleepless in Seattle* (1993). His most extensive collaboration with American directors was with **Woody Allen**, a great admirer of Bergman who employed Nykvist as his cinematographer on a series of films, including *Another Woman* (1988), *Crimes and Misdemeanors* (1989), and *Celebrity* (1998).

Nykvist was also an occasional director and screenwriter; the Swedish film *Oxen* (1991), which he both wrote and directed, was nominated for an Oscar for Best Foreign Language Film.

# O

**ODETS, CLIFFORD (1906–1963).** One of the most distinguished American playwrights of his generation, Clifford Odets was a particularly important figure in the left-wing theater of the 1930s. His first play, *Waiting for Lefty* (1935), is considered a classic of 1930s proletarian literature. Odets moved into screenwriting with *The General Died at Dawn* (1936). In 1939, his play *The Golden Boy* was adapted to film, though he did not write the screenplay. Odets did, however, write the screenplays for *Deadline at Dawn* (1946), based on a novel by Cornel Woolrich, and *Wild in the Country* (1961), based on a novel by J. R. Salamanca.

Odets co-wrote the screenplays for *Humoresque* (1946) and *Sweet Smell of Success* (1957). Among films adapted by other writers from Odets's plays are *Clash by Night* (1952), *The Country Girl* (1954), and *The Big Knife* (1955).

Called before the **House Un-American Activities Committee** (HUAC) in 1952, Odets provided cooperative testimony and thus avoided the **blacklist**. Though all of those he named to the committee as possible leftist sympathizers in the Hollywood film industry had been named previously, Odets later expressed strong remorse over his testimony.

**OLIVIER, LAURENCE (1907–1989).** A distinguished stage actor known especially for his performances in the plays of William Shakespeare, Sir Laurence Olivier (knighted in 1947) also had an extensive career in both British and American film. After appearing in numerous British films of the 1930s, he topped off the decade with his performance in the American-produced *Wuthering Heights* (1939), for which he gained the first of his nine **Academy Award** nominations for Best Actor, tying him with **Spencer Tracy** for the most all-time nominations in that category. Olivier followed with another **Oscar**-nominated performance in **Alfred Hitchcock**'s *Rebecca* (1940) and gained considerable critical acclaim for his performance in *Pride and Prejudice* the same year, establishing him as a Hollywood star.

Olivier followed with several other highly regarded performances in the 1940s, culminating in his star turn in *Hamlet* (1948), which won him his only Oscar for Best Leading Actor. He also starred in three other high-profile Shakespeare adaptations, *Henry V* (1944), *Richard III* (1955), and *Othello*

(1965), all of which won him Oscar nominations for Best Actor. He also won Best Actor nominations for *The Entertainer* (1960), *Sleuth* (1972), and *The Boys from Brazil* (1978). He gained his only Oscar nomination in the Best Supporting Actor category for *Marathon Man* (1976). Among the best known of the numerous other films in which he appeared are *Spartacus* (1960), *Nicholas and Alexandra* (1971), *A Bridge Too Far* (1977), and *The Bounty* (1984).

*ON THE WATERFRONT.* One of the key films of the 1950s and probably the most important film of director **Elia Kazan**'s career, *On the Waterfront* (1954) was nominated for 12 **Academy Awards** and won eight, including the five major categories of Best Picture, Best Director, Best Actor, Best Actress, and Best Screenplay. The film is set on a New Jersey waterfront, where most of the longshoremen who keep the docks running live and work under miserable conditions, made worse by the fact that the local longshoremen's union, headed by gangster Johnny Friendly (Lee J. Cobb), is so corrupt that the longshoremen have no real union representation. Friendly and his minions rule the entire waterfront, exploiting both the workers and the shipping companies for their own profit.

*On the Waterfront* is probably best remembered for the performance of its star, **Marlon Brando**, and for the way its plot, which involves an investigation of the union by the state crime commission, seems to echo the investigations of supposed communist activity in Hollywood by the **House Un-American Activities Committee** (HUAC). In particular, the film's sympathetic treatment of this investigation and of the decision of protagonist Terry Malloy (Brando), to testify against the union leaders before the commission has been widely interpreted as an attempt on the part of Kazan and screenwriter **Budd Schulberg** to justify their own cooperative testimony before HUAC.

*On the Waterfront* shows genuine concern for the exploitation of the dock workers; however, its presentation of a corrupt union as the principal culprit in this exploitation leaves largely unexamined the role of the shipping companies, even though the profits of these companies from this exploitation are acknowledged in the film to be far greater than those realized by the corrupt officials of the union. Meanwhile, the film's positive figures, such as Malloy, are political innocents who have no understanding of the role played by the capitalist system in the exploitation of workers. Their naive perspective helps to reduce the film to a simple opposition between good and evil.

**ORION PICTURES.** Orion Pictures Corporation, founded in 1978, went on to become one of the most successful **independent film** studios, producing a number of respected and award-winning films, before a series of financial failures led to the bankruptcy of the studio in 1992, even though it had dominated two consecutive **Academy Award** celebrations with *Dances with Wolves* (1990) and *Silence of the Lambs* (1991). The company continued to operate under bankruptcy protection until 1996, when it emerged, soon to be sold to **Metro-Goldwyn-Mayer** (MGM), which continues to use the Orion brand name.

Formed by a group of former executives at **United Artists** who had grown unhappy with their former employer, Orion was from the beginning run by experienced Hollywood insiders who had, in their last years at United Artists, overseen the production of three consecutive Best Picture **Oscar** winners. The company nevertheless got off to a slow start, and most of its first films were unsuccessful. However, during its heyday in the 1980s, Orion served as the distributor for the films of director **Woody Allen** and for such prestige products as *Amadeus* (1984), which gained 11 Academy Award nominations and won eight Oscars, including Best Picture. Films such as the Best Picture winner *Platoon* (1986) also enhanced the reputation of the studio for being involved with high-quality films. The decade ended, however, with a series of expensive box-office failures, and Orion never recovered.

**OSCAR.** The designation "Oscar" is often used as a synonym for the **Academy Award**, though Oscar is also used to designate the statuette that is given to Academy Award recipients. The statuette itself was designed under the supervision of **Metro-Goldwyn-Mayer** (MGM) art director Cedric Gibbons, and the design has changed little since the first statuette was cast in 1928. This design features the streamlined nude figure of a knight, 34 cm (13.5 in) in height, holding a sword and standing on a reel of film. It is made of britannium (a tin alloy) and plated with gold, weighing in at 3.85 kg (8.5 lbs).

In order to preserve resources for the war effort, temporary plaster Oscars were given out during World War II; recipients then traded them in for regular gold-plated Oscars after the war was over. Recipients of the award must agree to a legal restriction that forbids them to sell the statuette on the open market.

**O'SULLIVAN, MAUREEN (1911–1998).** The Irish-born Maureen O'Sullivan was the first Irish actor to rise to stardom in Hollywood. Recruited by **Twentieth Century Fox** to come to America, she made several minor appearances for that and other studios, then moved to **Metro-Goldwyn-Mayer** (MGM), where she eventually drew major attention for her performance as Lady Jane Parker in *Tarzan the Ape Man* (1932). Some of that attention was for her near-nude costuming in several scenes of this film, but she soon moved into a series of prestige films, many adapted from classic literary works, though mostly in supporting roles.

O'Sullivan also appeared as Jane Parker in several *Tarzan* sequels, including *Tarzan and His Mate* (1934), *Tarzan Escapes* (1936), *Tarzan Finds a Son!* (1939), *Tarzan's Secret Treasure* (1941), and *Tarzan's New York Adventure* (1942). However, she also appeared in supporting roles in such films as *The Thin Man* (1934), *David Copperfield* (1935), *Anna Karenina* (1937), and *Pride and Prejudice* (1940). Her career included a number of genres, including such light fare as *A Day at the Races* (1937) and *Bonzo Goes to College* (1953).

O'Sullivan retired from show business for several years following her last *Tarzan* film, but returned with an important role in the **film noir** classic *The Big Clock* (1948). She continued to act well into the 1990s, though most of her appearances after 1948 were on television. Among her later film performances was an appearance in **Woody Allen**'s *Hannah and Her Sisters* (1986), which starred her daughter, Mia Farrow.

# P

**PACINO, AL (1940– ).** One of the great American film actors of his generation, Al Pacino was still relatively unknown after years as a struggling young actor when he burst onto the scene as Michael Corleone in *The Godfather* (1972). Reprising that role in the *Godfather* sequels in 1974 and 1990, Pacino made Corleone one of the most recognized characters in the history of American cinema. He received **Academy Award** nominations for Best Supporting Actor for *The Godfather* and for Best Actor in a Leading Role for *The Godfather: Part II*, in between winning another **Oscar** nomination for Best Leading Actor for *Serpico* (1973).

Altogether, Pacino has received eight Oscar nominations for either Best Supporting Actor or Best Leading Actor; for 1992, he was nominated in both categories, for *Glengarry Glen Ross* and *Scent of a Woman*, respectively. He won his only Oscar for the latter film. Pacino's bravura performance in *Dog Day Afternoon* (1976) won him his fourth consecutive Oscar nomination, by which time he was widely recognized as one of Hollywood's leading talents.

Subsequent performances in films such as . . . *And Justice for All* (1979), *Scarface* (1983), *Sea of Love* (1989), *Dick Tracy* (1990), *Frankie and Johnny* (1991), *Carlito's Way* (1993), *Heat* (1995), *City Hall* (1996), *Donnie Brasco* (1997), and *The Insider* further established both his reputation and his versatility, though he remained something of a specialist in crime and **gangster films**. He has continued to appear regularly in films into his seventies, though his films of the 21st century have been less well received than his earlier efforts. In both *Heat* and *Righteous Kill* (2008), Pacino appeared onscreen with fellow acting legend **Robert De Niro**.

Pacino won both an Emmy and a **Golden Globe** for Best Actor for his performance in the HBO television miniseries *Angels in America* (2004). He has also directed three films: *Looking for Richard* (1996), *Chinese Coffee* (2000), and *Wilde Salome* (2010).

**PARAMOUNT ANTITRUST CASE.** *United States v. Paramount Pictures, Inc.*, also known as the Hollywood Antitrust Case, the Paramount Antitrust Case, or simply the Paramount Case, was a landmark 1948 decision in which the U.S. Supreme Court ruled that the operation of an extensive chain of theaters by studios such as **Paramount Pictures** was a violation of federal antitrust laws. The decision had far-reaching consequences not only for Paramount but also for the other **major studios**, which similarly owned their own chains of theaters, in which they could exert control over which films were exhibited. As a result, the **Golden Age** of the Hollywood studio system was brought to an end, and the major studios would never again exercise the same kind of dominance over the film industry that they had once enjoyed.

Concerns over antitrust violations within the film industry began during the **silent film** era, when major studios first began to build their own chains of theaters. In 1938, the federal government finally brought suit against all the major studios for unfair trade practices due to the control they exercised over the booking of films in their own theaters. In 1940, the case was temporarily settled with a consent decree that required the major studios to institute significant reforms. By 1943, the suit was reinstated due to unsatisfactory compliance with this decree on the part of the studios. The case went to trial in 1945 and reached the Supreme Court in 1948. Though the case was referred to legally as *United States v. Paramount Pictures, Inc.*, all of the major studios were in fact named in the suit, and the implications of the ruling, which went strongly against the studios, applied to all of them.

As a result of the ruling, the studios were forced to divest themselves of their holdings in theaters (or vice versa, as in the case of **Metro-Goldwyn-Mayer** (MGM), which was owned by Loew's Theatres). Coupled with the subsequent investigations of supposed communist activity in Hollywood by the **House Un-American Activities Committee** (HUAC) and the rise of television as a rival, this ruling led to dramatic changes in the film industry, which was in a state of crisis over the coming years.

*United States v. Paramount* was also a landmark case that has had far-reaching implications beyond the movie business and is the basis of much antitrust law concerning the vertical integration of various businesses.

**PARAMOUNT PICTURES.** Paramount Pictures is one of Hollywood's **major studios**, joining **Twentieth Century Fox** and **Warner Bros.** as the only major studios of the **Golden Age** of Hollywood from the 1930s and 1940s to remain a major in the 21st century. Though it is currently a subsidiary of the media conglomerate Viacom, the company now known as Paramount has been continuously in operation since its inception in 1916, which makes it America's oldest existing studio. Actually, Paramount had its origins in **Adolph Zukor**'s founding of the Famous Players Film Company in 1912; Paramount Pictures Corporation was then founded by theater-owner W. W. Hodkinson in 1914 to provide national distribution for films produced by others, including Zukor's company and Jesse L. Lasky's Lasky Feature Show Company. By 1916, Zukor had engineered a merger of his company, Lasky's, and Paramount to form the entity that soon became known as Paramount Pictures.

Hodkinson's Paramount had been the first film distributor to operate nationwide. The availability of this national network, combined with Zukor's business skills and the talent of figures such as actors **Mary Pickford** and **Douglas Fairbanks** and Lasky's chief director, **Cecil B. DeMille**, helped the new Paramount Pictures to quickly become the biggest Hollywood studio. Paramount managed to maintain its position as a major studio through the transition to the talkies, though the Depression of the 1930s hit the studio harder than some others, allowing **Metro-Goldwyn-Mayer** (MGM) to supplant Paramount as the biggest of the major studios in that decade.

Nevertheless, Paramount continued to churn out dozens of films per year, drawing upon the appeal of major stars such as **Claudette Colbert, Gary Cooper, Bing Crosby, Marlene Dietrich, Dorothy Lamour, Carole Lombard**, the **Marx Brothers**, and **Mae West**. Paramount's ongoing power was also closely tied to its relationship with the extensive national chain of theaters originally built by Zukor in the 1920s. However, in 1948, the U.S. Supreme Court ruled, in *United States v. Paramount Pictures, Inc.* (better known as the **Paramount Antitrust Case**) that the relationship between Paramount and its chain of theaters was a violation of federal antitrust laws.

Paramount was forced to divest itself of its theater holdings, with United Paramount Theaters spun off as a separate entity. Other major studios were forced to do likewise, and the studios never again exercised the power they had had during the Golden Age. Paramount went into decline, releasing most of its contract players and producing far fewer films. DeMille remained at the studio, however, and one of their biggest hits of the 1950s was his **biblical epic** *The Ten Commandments* (1956). The studio failed to keep up with changing times, however, and it was on the verge of collapse when it was sold in 1966 to Charles Bluhdorn's Gulf and Western Industries. Bluhdorn installed a young **Robert Evans** as head of the studio, which subsequently produced a series of hits, including *The Godfather* (1972), which restored some of the studio's former luster.

Film franchises such as the *Star Trek* and *Indiana Jones* sequences brought Paramount success over the coming years. In 1993, Paramount was acquired by Viacom, making it a part of one of the world's largest media corporations. The studio remains a major player in both film and television production and distribution. Paramount Home Entertainment is also a major player in the home video market.

**PARSONS, LOUELLA (1881–1972).** Louella Parsons was a highly influential Hollywood gossip columnist whose reports on the activities of various figures in the film industry, via her newspaper column and radio show, could have a substantial impact on the careers of those individuals. As a result, she was a figure both respected and feared in Hollywood circles.

After a brief try at writing film scripts, Parsons began writing what was apparently the first gossip column in the United States in 1914, for the *Chicago Record Herald*. In 1918, William Randolph Hearst bought the paper, and Parsons's column was cancelled; by 1922, however, she was working for Hearst, writing a similar column for the *New York American*. A bout with tuberculosis in 1925 caused Parsons to move to Arizona, then to Los Angeles, where she resumed her career writing a column for the *Los Angeles Examiner*. This column was soon syndicated in hundreds of papers around the world, and Parsons's career as an influential Hollywood figure was launched.

In 1928, Parsons added a regular radio show to her repertoire, further increasing both her audience nationwide and her clout in Hollywood. Often scooping her competitors with the juiciest stories about the private lives of well-known actors and other figures in the film industry, Parsons, with the support of Hearst, soon gained a power rivaled among columnists only by her one-time friend **Hedda Hopper**, with whom she eventually developed a bitter rivalry.

Parsons became a highly recognizable figure to film audiences, making cameo appearances in several films. She maintained her powerful position through the 1930s and 1940s, but her influence diminished through the 1950s, partly due to the coming of television. By the time she retired in 1965, she was no longer the powerful figure she had once been.

**PATHÉ.** Pathé, or Pathé Frères, was the name of several film-related enterprises headed by the Pathé brothers of France, beginning in 1896. Pioneering in the development of technologies for the recording and projection of films, the company soon became the world's largest producer of such equipment. They also moved into the production of films, including the establishment of a unit for such production in the United States in 1914. This unit, located in Fort Lee, New Jersey, produced many short **silent films**, including the well-known *Perils of Pauline* series and newsreels produced under the name Pathé News.

In 1923, Pathé sold off its U.S. operations, which were subsequently renamed Pathé Exchange. This unit was then acquired by **RKO Pictures** in a complicated series of negotiations that stretched from 1928 to 1931. RKO continued to use the Pathé name, primarily for the production of newsreels, until 1947, when the Pathé unit of RKO was sold to **Warner Bros.** Warners continued to use the Pathé label for newsreel production until 1956, when it discontinued the production of newsreels and sold off the Pathé name and library to Studio Films, Inc., which changed its own name to Pathé Pictures soon after, but was never an important factor in the film business.

**PECK, GREGORY (1916–2003).** Gregory Peck was one of the leading film actors of his generation. He appeared in dozens of films in a career that spanned more than half a century, beginning with *Days of Glory* and *The Keys of the Kingdom* (both 1944, the latter winning him an **Academy Award** nomination for Best Actor) to the television remake of *Moby Dick* (1998), the original 1956 film version of which had starred Peck as Captain Ahab. Also a noted humanitarian and liberal political activist, Peck won the Jean Hersholt Humanitarian Award in 1968 and was awarded the Presidential Medal of Freedom on 1969. He was voted the 12th greatest male screen legend of all time in a 1999 poll conducted by the **American Film Institute**.

Peck followed his auspicious 1944 debut with a series of key roles in such important films as *Spellbound* (1945), *The Yearling* (1946), *Duel in the Sun* (1946), *Gentleman's Agreement* (1947), and *The Paradine Case* (1947), quickly establishing himself as one of **Twentieth Century Fox**'s (and Hollywood's) top stars. Both *The Yearling* and *Gentleman's Agreement* won him **Oscar** nominations for Best Actor, as did *Twelve O'Clock High* (1949).

However, Peck did not win an Oscar until his performance as Atticus Finch in *To Kill a Mockingbird* (1962), widely regarded as his greatest role. In between, he had starred in some of the most important films of the 1950s, including *Roman Holiday* (1953), *The Man in the Gray Flannel Suit* (1956), *Moby Dick*, and *On the Beach* (1959). He remained a top star through the 1960s; in 1962 alone, he starred in *Cape Fear* (1962) and *How the West Was Won* (1962), in addition to *To Kill a Mockingbird*. Other key films featuring Peck in the 1960s included *Mirage* (1965), *Arabesque* (1966), and *Marooned* (1969).

Peck began to appear less frequently in the 1970s, but still starred in such films as *I Walk the Line* (1970), *The Omen* (1976), *MacArthur* (1977), and *The Boys from Brazil* (1978), the latter alongside fellow icon **Laurence Olivier**. He was still playing starring roles in theatrical films as late as *The Old Gringo* (1989) and *Other People's Money* (1991). He played a supporting role in **Martin Scorsese**'s 1991 remake of *Cape Fear*.

**PECKINPAH, SAM (1925–1984).** Sam Peckinpah was one of the most distinctive directors of his generation, known especially for his depiction of graphic violence and for his revisionist work in the **Western** genre, often employing Mexican settings. After extensive early work as a television writer, especially of Westerns, Peckinpah broke into film direction with the Western *Ride the High Country* (1962). He next both directed and co-wrote the Western *Major Dundee* (1965), then achieved major success as the director and co-writer of *The Wild Bunch* (1969), which gained him his only **Academy Award** nomination, for Best Screenplay.

*Straw Dogs* (1971) and *The Getaway* (1972) saw Peckinpah move into crime thrillers, but he soon moved back into the realm of unusual Westerns with *Pat Garrett and Billy the Kid* (1973) and *Bring Me the Head of Alfredo Garcia* (1974). He followed with a **spy film**, *The Killer Elite* (1975), and a **war film**, *Cross of Iron* (1977), while *Convoy* (1978) was a trucker film with the sensibilities of a Western. Health problems exacerbated by drugs and alcohol limited his output from that point, though he did return to direct an additional spy film, *The Osterman Weekend*, in 1983.

**PENN, ARTHUR (1922– ).** Director Arthur Penn amassed an impressive and critically acclaimed body of work in the 1960s and 1970s, often showing the influence of his theatrical background and of international cinema, especially the French New Wave. After an extensive apprenticeship as a television director in the 1950s, Penn broke into film with *The Left Handed Gun* (1958) and *The Miracle Worker* (1962), the latter of which gained him an **Academy Award** nomination as Best Director. He first achieved truly major success, however, with ***Bonnie and Clyde*** (1967), one of the key films of the 1960s. That film received 10 **Oscar** nominations, including Best Picture and Best Director, though it won only in the categories of Cinematography and Best Supporting Actress.

Penn followed with a series of unusual and innovative films in a variety of genres, including *Alice's Restaurant* (1969), a **satirical comedy** drama about the counterculture of the 1960s that won Penn another Best Director Oscar nomination; the revisionist **Western** *Little Big Man* (1970); the **neo-noir** film *Night Moves* (1975); and *The Missouri Breaks* (1976), another unusual Western. *Four Friends* (1981) was a serious look back at the 1960s counterculture that received positive critical attention but little commercial success. The thrillers *Target* (1985) and *Dead of Winter* (1987) were less successful, and the farcical *Penn & Teller Get Killed* (1989) received little notice.

**PENN, SEAN (1960– ).** One of the most intense and talented actors of his generation, Sean Penn has also demonstrated unusual versatility as an actor. After breaking in as a teen actor on television, Penn moved into film with an important supporting role in *Taps* (1981). He then delivered a memorable performance as the stoner Jeff Spicoli in *Fast Times at Ridgemont High* (1982), moving into a serious starring role in the crime drama *Bad Boys*

(1983). Other major roles followed, including those in *Racing with the Moon* (1984), *Shanghai Surprise* (1986), *Colors* (1988), *Casualties of War* (1989), and *We're No Angels* (1989).

Often sharing the screen with well-known actors such as **Robert De Niro**, **Al Pacino**, and **Robert Duvall**, Penn developed a reputation as an actor's actor. In 1995, his performance in *Dead Man Walking* won Penn his first **Academy Award** nomination for Best Actor in a Leading Role, a nomination he would also receive for *Sweet and Lowdown* (1999), *I Am Sam* (2001), *Mystic River* (2003), and *Milk* (2008), winning the award for the latter two films. His performance in *21 Grams* (2003) was also notable.

Penn, who is noted for his political activism and for his battles with paparazzi, is also a writer, producer, and director. He served in all three capacities for such films as *The Crossing Guard* (1995) and *Into the Wild* (2007).

**PERKINS, ANTHONY (1932–1992).** Anthony Perkins was a gifted actor who appeared widely in both film and television in the 1950s, including a role in *Friendly Persuasion* (1957) that gained him an **Academy Award** nomination for Best Supporting Actor. It was, however, his iconic role as Norman Bates in **Alfred Hitchcock**'s *Psycho* (1960) that established him as an important presence in American film. Unfortunately, that role made such an indelible impression that it haunted Perkins through the remainder of his career, making it difficult for him to get roles other than ones that were similar to the one he had played in *Psycho*. Indeed, the majority of his film appearances through the remainder of the 1960s were in French films, including his starring role in *Le procès* (*The Trial*, 1962), **Orson Welles**'s adaptation of the Franz Kafka novel.

An important supporting role in **Mike Nichols**'s *Catch-22* (1970) was part of a minor comeback in Hollywood film. He appeared in several high-profile films in the 1970s, though only in supporting roles. These appearances included those in *The Life and Times of Judge Roy Bean* (1972), *Murder on the Orient Express* (1974), *Mahogany* (1975), and *The Black Hole* (1979).

In the 1980s, Perkins finally gave in to the legacy of his role in *Psycho*, reprising his role as Norman Bates in *Psycho II* (1983) and *Psycho III* (1986), the latter of which he also directed. In between, his role in *Crimes of Passion* (1984) was similar, though exaggerated almost to the point of being a parody of his *Psycho* character. He also used some of the same persona n his dual role as Dr. Jekyll and Mr. Hyde in *Edge of Sanity* (1989). By this time battling AIDS, he made several more appearances on television from 1990 to 1992 — including one more turn as Bates in the 1990 made-for-TV film *Psycho IV: The Beginning* — before ultimately succumbing to the disease.

**PICKFORD, MARY (1892–1979).** Known as "America's Sweetheart," the Canadian-born Mary Pickford (birth name Gladys Smith) became one of the first superstars of American film, ultimately appearing in more than 200 **silent films** and a total of over 50 feature-length films, most of which were silent. She was named the 24th greatest female screen legend of all time in a 1999 poll conducted by the **American Film Institute**, one of only two silent-film actresses on the list. (**Lillian Gish** was 17th.) Pickford transitioned to the talkies with *Coquette* (1929), for which she won the **Academy Award** for Best Actress in a Leading Role. In general, however, she did not fare well in the sound era, and by 1933 she had retired from acting.

Pickford began her film career in 1909, appearing in more than 50 silent shorts in that year alone, quickly becoming the favorite actress of the **Biograph** film studio and its chief director, **D. W. Griffith**. Though she was also attracted to stage acting, she gave up the stage for film in 1913, when she signed a new contract with **Adolph Zukor** as part of the founding of his Famous Players group of stars, which later became **Paramount** studios. By 1916, a new contract with Zukor gave Pickford considerable creative control over her film projects.

In 1919, Pickford sought still more autonomy when she joined fellow superstars Griffith, **Charles Chaplin**, and **Douglas Fairbanks** to form **United Artists**, a new studio dedicated to giving more creative control to these artists. She married Fairbanks the following year, forming Hollywood's most glamorous couple. In the following years, Pickford had notable success as the producer and star of such films as *Pollyanna* (1920), *Little Lord Fauntleroy* (1921), *Sparrows* (1926), and *My Best Girl* (1927), the latter two of which, her last two silents, are particularly highly regarded by critics.

After her retirement from acting, Pickford served as a producer for several more films, finally retiring from work in film altogether in 1949. In 1976 she received a special Academy Award for her career achievements in film.

**PIXAR.** Pixar Animation Studios is the industry leader in the production of state-of-the-art **animated films** (produced via **computer-generated imagery**) for children and families. The company began as the computer graphics group of **George Lucas**'s **Lucasfilm** studio, but was then sold off to Steve Jobs in 1986. Under Jobs's leadership, the company evolved from what at first was primarily a computer hardware company into an important film production company, producing a number of innovative short computer-animated films before making a major breakthrough with *Toy Story* (1995), the first film to be entirely generated using computer animation. That film and its sequel, *Toy Story 2* (1999), feature anthropomorphic toys as their central characters and thus offer rich possibilities for the comarketing of toys and other related merchandise, something that has come to be a key feature of the company's business, which has also included particularly strong DVD sales.

The *Toy Story* films make considerable use of imagery from **science fiction**, which has also become a trademark of Pixar films, echoing the company's own use of state-of-the-art technologies in producing their films. For example, one of the central characters in the *Toy Story* sequence is "Buzz Lightyear," a toy spaceman marketed in conjunction with a children's science fiction television program. Similarly, the Pixar film *Monsters, Inc.* (2001) makes use of the common science fictional conceit of parallel worlds, while building centrally, though ironically, upon the tradition of the **monster movie**.

The consistent commercial success of Pixar's films, buoyed by the fact that they have released an average of less than one film per year, is unprecedented in Hollywood history. Their greatest commercial success came with the undersea adventure *Finding Nemo* (2003), grossed over $867 million in international box-office receipts, making it the highest grossing animated film of all time, though it now ranks second behind **DreamWorks**'s *Shrek 2* (2004). In addition, every feature film released by Pixar has been a major success, and the release of each Pixar film is treated as a major event in children's popular culture, partly due to their successful efforts at branding, furthered by the extensive marketing that is enabled by the resources of **Disney**, of which Pixar has been, since 2006, a wholly owned subsidiary. The company's films before that time had all been distributed by Disney.

Pixar's success also owes a great deal to the quality of their films, which not only employ envelope-pushing animation but also clever storytelling (and effective use of recognizable elements derived from other works of popular culture). While Disney's films have sometimes been criticized as being simplistic and as talking down to children, Pixar's films tend to be complex and intelligent. Pixar often explores surprising territory for **children's films**, as in *WALL-E* (2008), a postapocalyptic science fiction film that includes important space opera elements and features a title character that is a robot. Meanwhile, their next film, *Up* (2009), includes a number of elements of the sf adventure genre and also features a protagonist who is an old man disappointed by life. Such elements have helped Pixar to dominate the **Academy Award** for Best Animated Feature, given since 2001. Of the nine awards given thus far, Pixar has won five, including the last three, for *Ratatouille* (2007), *WALL-E*, and *Up*.

*Up* was also the first Pixar film to be released in digital 3D, now the company's preferred format. In the fall of 2009, *Toy Story* and *Toy Story 2* saw brief theatrical re-releases in 3D, preparing audiences for the 2010 release of *Toy Story* in the format. *See also* LASSETER, JOHN.

**POITIER, SIDNEY (1927– ).** The first major African American star in Hollywood history, Sidney Poitier opened the way for numerous other black actors who followed him. After a successful beginning as a stage actor, Poitier broke into film with a major role in the antiracist **film noir** classic *No Way Out* (1950), in which he played a medical doctor, pointing the way toward the numerous future roles in which he would go against traditional Hollywood stereotyping of black characters.

Roles in films such as *Cry, the Beloved Country* (1952), *Blackboard Jungle* (1955), *Edge of the City* (1957), and *The Defiant Ones* (1958) quickly followed, establishing Poitier as a major presence in American film. He received an **Academy Award** nomination for Best Actor in a Leading Role for the latter film, becoming the first African American actor to be nominated for a competitive **Oscar**. Then, after another important performance in *A Raisin in the Sun* (1961), Poitier became the first black actor to win a competitive Oscar when he won the Best Actor Award for *Lilies of the Field* (1963).

Poitier has received no further competitive Oscar nominations, though he reached the pinnacle of his stardom when he starred in three high-profile pictures in 1967 alone: *To Sir, With Love*; *In the Heat of the Night*; and *Guess Who's Coming to Dinner?* He continued to play major roles through the 1970s, also moving into directing with the **Western** *Buck and the Preacher* (1972), in which he also starred. Key to Poitier's work of the 1970s was a trilogy of **comedies** that he directed as well as starred in (opposite Bill Cosby): *Uptown Saturday Night* (1974), *Let's Do It Again* (1975), and *A Piece of the Action* (1977). After the latter film, he took more than a decade off from acting, in the meantime directing the **comedies** *Stir Crazy* (1980) and *Hanky Panky* (1982) and the dramatic **musical** *Fast Forward* (1985).

Then in his sixties, Poitier returned to acting in 1988 with starring roles in the thrillers *Shoot to Kill* and *Little Nikita*. He also directed Cosby in the comedy *Ghost Dad* (1990). Poitier has continued to act occasionally, though most of his appearances since 1990 have been on television. In 2002 he was given a special Academy Award for his career achievements in film. In 1999, he was named the 22nd greatest male film legend of all time in a poll conducted by the **American Film Institute**.

**POLANSKI, ROMAN (1933– ).** Though known as much for his personal problems as for his artistic achievements in film, Roman Polanski is undeniably one of the most gifted directors of his generation. Born in France but of Polish descent, Polanski began his directing career in Poland; his first feature-length film, *Knife in the Water* (1962), is still an acknowledged classic of European cinema. *Repulsion* (1965), an English-language film made in Great Britain, further cemented Polanski's burgeoning reputation, gaining the attention of Hollywood. In 1968, he moved to the United States, where he wrote and directed *Rosemary's Baby* (1968), which raised the American **horror** film to the level of true cinematic art and marked Polanski as a rising star in Hollywood. It also gained him an **Academy Award** nomination for Best Screenplay.

In 1969, Polanski's pregnant wife, actress Sharon Tate, was murdered by the Charles Manson gang in a case that attracted tremendous public attention. Troubled by the event, Polanski returned to Europe and did not release another film until *The Tragedy of Macbeth* (1971), an adaptation of Shakespeare's play. He then followed with *What?* (1972), a European farce with art-house sensibilities that drew little attention at the time, but has since become something of a **cult** hit. He then returned triumphantly to Hollywood with *Chinatown* (1974), one of the key films in the **neo-noir** resurgence of the 1970s and indeed a key film of that decade as a whole. Polanski received his first **Oscar** nomination for Best Director for that film.

Polanski returned to European film with *The Tenant* (1976) and was then driven into European exile after a judge reneged on a plea deal after his conviction for the statutory rape of a 13-year-old girl in 1977. Polanski's first film made in exile was *Tess* (1979), a commercial and critical success that gained him his second Oscar nomination for Best Director. His subsequent work, mostly in France, was made in English but generally drew relatively little attention in the United States, though *Frantic* (1988) is a superb thriller that features American megastar **Harrison Ford** in the lead role.

Films such as *Death and the Maiden* (1994) and *The Ninth Gate* (1999) also featured big-name American stars but had limited success with American audiences. However, *The Pianist* (2002), a film about the Holocaust in Poland that was produced and directed by Polanski, won major acclaim, including the Palme d'Or at the Cannes Film Festival and seven Oscar nominations. Polanski, as producer, was nominated in the Best Picture category; he won the award, his only Oscar, as Best Director. That film reflected Polanski's own experience as a nominally Jewish child during World War II, hiding out from the Nazis while both his parents were interned in concentration camps.

Polanski followed in 2005 with *Oliver Twist* (2005), an adaptation of the Charles Dickens novel. He was still at work on the atmospheric political thriller *The Ghost Writer* when he was arrested (at the request of the American authorities) while receiving a lifetime achievement award in Switzerland. He remained under house arrest while fighting extradition to the United States, while the film nevertheless premiered at the Berlin Film Festival in February 2010, winning Polanski the Silver Bear for Best Director. Switzerland eventually denied the extradition request, and Polanski was released. The film has seen only limited release in the United States.

Polanski has also made numerous appearances as an actor, often in his own films.

**POLEDOURIS, BASIL (1945–1906).** Basil Poledouris was a prolific composer of **music** for both film and television. Although his music is known more for its popularity than its virtuosity (he was never nominated for an **Academy Award**), much of his music holds up well over time. His score for *Conan the Barbarian* (1982), for which he received a Saturn Award nomination from the Academy of Science Fiction, Fantasy, and Horror Films (but did not win the award), is particularly well respected and is sometimes mentioned as being among the most effective film scores ever written.

Poledouris became something of a specialist in writing music for **fantasy** and **science fiction** films. Among the most prominent films for which he wrote the scores are *The Blue Lagoon* (1980), *Red Dawn* (1984), *Conan the Destroyer* (1986), *Iron Eagle* (1986), *Robocop* (1987), *The Hunt for Red October* (1990), *Free Willy* (1993), and *Starship Troopers* (1997).

**POLLACK, SYDNEY (1934–2008).** After an extensive apprenticeship as a television director in the early 1960s, Sydney Pollack moved into feature film in 1965 and scored his first major success with *They Shoot Horses, Don't They?* (1969), which gained him the first of his three **Academy Award** nominations for Best Director. He then went on to direct some of the highest-profile films of the 1970s and 1980s.

Films such as *The Way We Were* (1973) and *Three Days of the Condor* (1975) remain among the best-remembered works of 1970s cinema. *Absence of Malice* (1981) was an important film as well, helping to solidify Pollack's reputation as a director of thrillers. However, his most successful film was a **romantic comedy**, *Tootsie* (1982), which gained him a Best Picture **Oscar** nomination as co-producer, as well as his second nomination for Best Director. Pollack then scored wins in both of those categories for *Out of Africa* (1985).

Pollack also won Best Picture nominations as the co-producer of *Michael Clayton* (2007) and *The Reader* (2008), but most of the later films he directed—including *Havana* (1990), *The Firm* (1993), *Sabrina* (1995), *Random Hearts* (1999), and *The Interpreter* (2005)—were only moderate successes. In addition to his work as a director and producer, Pollack made numerous appearances as an actor on both film and television.

**POSTMODERNISM.** Though much debated as a cultural and historical phenomenon (partly because it is still evolving), postmodernism has generally been recognized as an important (and perhaps even dominant) mode of cultural production in the Western world since about the 1970s. Used as a derogatory term by critics concerned with the poverty of American mass culture in the 1950s, the term "postmodernism" first came to the forefront of critical discussions of contemporary culture in the late 1960s, when critics such as Ihab Hassan celebrated postmodernism as a radical new form of cultural production, congruent with the oppositional political movements of that decade. At about the same time, French poststructuralist theorists such as Jean-François Lyotard began to embrace postmodernism as well, and postmodernism and poststructuralism have been closely associated ever since. In general, however, the most insightful readings of the politics of postmodernism have been performed by Marxist critics such as Fredric Jameson, who have been highly suspicious of the subversive and antiauthoritarian energies often attributed to postmodernism, seeing it instead as a cultural phenomenon that, at best, has limited critical potential and, at worst, works in the interests of the global capitalist hegemony.

From this point of view, postmodernism represents the reduction of culture to commerce as capitalist commodification penetrates into every aspect of life. As such, postmodernism as a concept is particularly relevant to the understanding of popular culture (such as film), in which a profit motive exerts an overt influence on cultural production. Indeed, while many observers have seen television as the quintessential form of postmodernist culture, much has been said about postmodernism in film as well.

Typical characteristics of a film that might be described as postmodernism include the following: an intense self-awareness within the film of its status as a cultural artifact, with a resulting foregrounding of technique (such as intrusive camera movements or angles); a conscious (and often nostalgic) recycling of elements and motifs from earlier films, either through direct allusion or stylistic pastiche; fragmented narrative structures that reflect a loss of a sense of history as a continuous narrative process; a questioning of the boundary between fiction and reality; and an expectation of weakened emotional response from audiences, resulting either in ironic detachment (with no attempt at emotional connection) or in the use of increasingly powerful images in an attempt to connect emotionally with audiences.

These basic characteristics can play out differently in different films, reflecting the complex roots of postmodernism in both avant-garde art and popular culture. Thus, some postmodernist filmmakers pursue serious experiments with form and content, tending to make their work unpopular and obscure, though some serious postmodernist filmmakers (such as David Lynch) have gained widespread attention, if not major box-office success. Others, on the other hand, tend to be more playful, as in the fond recycling of elements from previous popular film genres in the films of **Quentin Tarantino** or the reveling in visual images (often at the expense of narrative coherence) in the films of **Tim Burton**.

Other well-known American filmmakers often considered to be postmodernists include **Woody Allen**, **Robert Altman**, **Joel and Ethan Coen**, **Brian De Palma**, and **Gus Van Sant**, though the roots of postmodernism in film can be traced back at least as far as *Citizen Kane* (1941).

**POVERTY ROW.** Though the emerging American film industry of the early 20th century came very quickly to be dominated by large and powerful **major studios**, many smaller studios came and went, producing mostly low-budget (and generally low-quality) films. These studios came collectively to be known as the "Poverty Row" studios both because of their low budgets and because of the small amount of revenue typically generated by their films. These films, however, did fill a niche market, especially in the era before television, when film played a more crucial role in the day-to-day entertainment of the American populace. By the end of the 1950s, with television growing more and more powerful as a cultural force and the major studios in disarray, the term Poverty Row had generally fallen out of use though new studios such as **American International** continued to specialize in low-cost, quickly made films. **Republic Pictures**, founded in 1935 through the merger of six preexisting studios, was the most important of the Poverty Row studios, occasionally even venturing into relatively big-budget features.

**PREMINGER, OTTO (1905–1986).** Born in Austro-Hungary, Otto Preminger began his career as a film and theater director in Vienna, coming to the United States in 1935 at the behest of **Twentieth Century Fox**, which had been scouting for talent in Europe. Preminger got off to a slow start in Hollywood, directing several minor films in an early career dogged by battles with Fox production head **Darryl F. Zanuck**. However, Preminger scored a major success with the highly regarded **film noir** *Laura* (1944), which won him the first of his two **Academy Award** nominations for Best Director.

Films such as *Fallen Angel* (1945), *Daisy Kenyon* (1947), *Whirlpool* (1949), *Where the Sidewalk Ends* (1950), and *Angel Face* (1952) further established Preminger's credentials as a leading director of film noir. Even *River of No Return* (1954), a **Western** featuring **Marilyn Monroe**, had noir sensibilities and featured film noir icon **Robert Mitchum** in the lead opposite Monroe. Gritty dramas such as *The Man with the Golden Arm* (1955) and *Anatomy of a Murder* (1959) were also informed by Preminger's noir background; the latter won a Best Picture **Oscar** nomination for Preminger as producer. In between, however, he directed the historical drama *Saint Joan* (1957); he also directed two **musicals** in the 1950s that broke new ground by featuring African American casts: *Carmen Jones* (1954) and *Porgy and Bess* (1959).

Many of these films pushed the boundaries of the **Production Code** (and eventually contributed to its demise), and Preminger's *The Moon Is Blue* (1953) was even released without code approval (because it used the forbidden word "virgin"), becoming the first studio film to be thus released since the full implementation of the code in 1934. Then, as the director of *Exodus* (1960), Preminger played a key role in breaking the Hollywood **blacklist** by insisting that blacklisted screenwriter **Dalton Trumbo** be given open onscreen credit for writing the film. *Advise & Consent* (1962) was a political thriller that again challenged the strictures of the Production Code by featuring a homosexual subplot. Preminger, however, had seen his greatest days of success. He received his second Best Director Oscar nomination for *The Cardinal* (1963), but subsequent films such as *In Harm's Way* (1965), *Bunny Lake Is Missing* (1965), and *Hurry Sundown* (1967) were not received well by critics.

Preminger also served as a producer on most of the films he directed. He made a number of appearances as an actor as well, mostly in films directed by others.

**PRESLEY, ELVIS (1935–1977).** Known to fans of his **music** as "The King," Elvis Presley was one of the central figures of 20th-century American popular culture. Though certainly more important for his contributions to the evolution of Rock and Roll music than for his work in film, he nevertheless had an extensive career in film as Hollywood sought to convert his vast fame and popularity into box-office gold.

Presley moved into film as the star of *Love Me Tender* (1956), then quickly followed with *Loving You* (1957), *Jailhouse Rock* (1957), and *King Creole* (1958). All were formulaic **musical comedies**, designed to foreground Presley's musical performances; they were also commercially successful. Presley's show-business career was then put on hold while he served in the U.S. military from 1958 to 1960. He then returned with another successful musical comedy that used his military service as a tie-in, *G. I. Blues* (1960).

Presley attempted more serious roles in *Flaming Star* (1960) and *Wild in the Country* (1961), but with limited success; fans clearly preferred the formula of the earlier films, to which he returned in *Blue Hawaii* (1961). Most of his subsequent films stuck to the formula as well, and the more than two dozen films he ultimately made in the 1960s were almost universally panned by critics. Still, films such as *Kid Galahad* (1962), *Viva Las Vegas* (1964), *Roustabout* (1964), *Girl Happy* (1965), *Spinout* (1966), and *Speedway* (1968) often had a considerable amount of action and remain watchable for more than their camp value.

In addition to his own career as an actor, Presley's highly recognizable music has been used on the soundtracks of literally hundreds of films.

**PREVIN, ANDRÉ (1929– ).** The German-born André Previn immigrated with his family to the United States in 1938; he has since gone on to become one of the most prominent American composers and conductors of his generation. Previn has served terms as the **music** director of the Houston, Pittsburgh, and Los Angeles Philharmonic Orchestras, as well as conducting for many classical recordings (often with the London Symphony Orchestra) and composing many classical pieces of his own. Previn's film scores, composed over the period 1949–1975, are highly regarded and have won him a total of 11 **Academy Awards** for Best Score, in addition to two nominations for Best Song.

Previn has won the **Oscar** for Best Score four times, for *Gigi* (1958), *Porgy and Bess* (1959), *Irma la Douce* (1963), and *My Fair Lady* (1964). He has composed the music for films in a variety of genres, ranging from the modern-day **Western** *Bad Day at Black Rock* (1954), to the **romantic comedy** *Designing Woman* (1957), to the drama *Elmer Gantry* (1960), to the dystopian **science fiction** film *Rollerball* (1975). Previn also conducted the orchestras that recorded many of his scores.

**PRICE, VINCENT (1911–1993).** Though he was never particularly respected for his acting talents, Vincent Price's distinctive performances, especially in **horror** movies, made him an iconic figure of American cinema. Indeed, Price appeared in the horror genre as early as 1939, when he had a supporting role in the **Boris Karloff** vehicle *Tower of London*. However, most of his performances of the 1940s and 1950s were in more mainstream fare, including such notable films as the **film noir** classic *Laura* (1944). *The Song of Bernadette* (1943), and *The Ten Commandments* (1956).

However, it is unquestionably for his performances in the horror genre that Price will be best remembered. After most of his performances of the late 1950s had been on television, he turned to horror in the **science fiction**/horror hybrid *The Fly* (1958), then moved into full-scale horror with *House on Haunted Hill* (1959). Several other horror films quickly followed, but it was with **Roger Corman**'s *House of Usher* (1960), based on a short story by Edgar Allan Poe, that Price began his most memorable sequence of starring roles in horror films. Corman's film adaptations of the writings of Poe for **American International Pictures** ultimately became an important franchise, all but one of which starred Price. Price's Poe films included *The Pit and the Pendulum* (1961), *Tales of Terror* (1962), *The Raven* (1963), *The Haunted Palace* (1963), *The Masque of the Red Death* (1964), and *The Tomb of Ligeia* (1964).

Among other things, Price's films have been named as a major creative inspiration by director **Tim Burton,** and one of Price's last performances was in Burton's *Edward Scissorhands* (1993).

**PRODUCTION CODE.** The Motion Picture Production Code was a series of restrictions on the content of Hollywood film adopted by the film industry as a form of self-**censorship,** designed both to counter the public perception of film as a morally suspect form and to prevent the imposition of censorship from outside the industry. Adopted in 1930, the code remained in effect until 1968, by which time it was clear that the code was out of step with the changing mores of American society. The code was drafted by former U.S. Postmaster Will B. Hays, who resigned his cabinet post in 1922 to become the head of the Motion Picture Producers and Distributors of America (MPPDA), charged with creating a better public image of the film industry.

The code (often referred to as the Hays Code), established three general principles. First, no film should be produced that would tend to lower the moral standards of its audience. Second, films should present "correct standards of life." Finally, no film should ridicule the law (natural or human) or show sympathy with the violators of the law. It then spelled out a number of specific restrictions, most of which were oriented toward limiting the representation of sexuality, violence, or criminality on the screen. Though it was not fully enforced until 1934, the code had a major impact on Hollywood film from that time until the 1960s, when it began to appear more and more anachronistic. The Code was abandoned in 1968 after a series of incidents — including controversies over approval of the 1964 Holocaust film *The Pawnbroker* and the defiant release by **Metro-Goldwyn-Mayer** (MGM) of the film *Blowup* (1966) without code approval — made it clear that the code was no longer viable. It was replaced by a film rating system instituted by the **Motion Picture Association of America** (MPAA), to which the MPPDA had changed its name in 1945.

**PULP FICTION.** *Pulp Fiction* (dir. **Quentin Tarantino,** 1994) was one of the key films of the 1990s. Not only did it make a star of director Quentin Tarantino, but it also revived the career of actor **John Travolta** and made a central contribution to the **independent film** boom of the 1990s. Indeed, the self-consciously cool *Pulp Fiction* was so commercially successful that it virtually demolished the boundary between independent film and mainstream Hollywood film. Meanwhile, Tarantino's film has exercised a powerful influence on subsequent films, especially with its fragmented narrative structure and its use of elements of the pop cultural past.

The very title of *Pulp Fiction* evokes the 1950s, when the pulp fiction publishing phenomenon was at its peak, while numerous aspects of the film reference the **film noir** tradition of the 1940s and 1950s. There is, however, little genuine nostalgia for the 1950s in *Pulp Fiction*, which is very much a hip film of the 1990s, drawing upon elements of popular film and **music** from a variety of decades to construct a postmodern cultural stew. Even the film's title music is a composite, beginning with the California surfer music of "Misirlou" by Dick Dale and the Del-Tones (1962), then abruptly switching styles and even decades (the transition marked by a sound effect like the turning of a radio dial) to the cool urban 1970s funk of "Jungle Boogie" by Kool and the Gang.

The rest of the soundtrack is similarly diverse; it was also crucial to the film's commercial success, and the soundtrack itself remained on *Billboard*'s Top 200 albums chart for more than 100 weeks, selling more than three million copies. *Pulp Fiction* was nominated for a total of seven **Academy Awards**, including Best Picture, Best Director, and Best Actor (Travolta). However, it won the award only for Best Original Screenplay, by Tarantino and Roger Avary. *See also* POSTMODERNISM.

# R

**RAFT, GEORGE (1901–1980).** After several minor appearances, George Raft made his breakthrough in film with a convincing supporting performance as a gangster in *Scarface* (1932). He would subsequently become one of the actors most closely associated with the **gangster film** genre, culminating in his appearance in the classic gangster film **comedy** *Some Like It Hot* (1959), though his career was by that time greatly in decline, partly due to his turning down roles in such key films as *High Sierra* and *The Maltese Falcon* (both 1941).

Among Raft's other best-known films in the crime and gangster vein were *The Glass Key* (1935), *Each Dawn I Die* (1939), and *They Drive by Night* (1940). However, he also appeared in a number of other kinds of films, as when he played the lead role in the drama *Manpower* (1941) and the French Foreign Legion adventure *Outpost in Morocco* (1949). Raft was also a talented dancer who appeared in **musicals** such as *Bolero* (1934).

***RAGING BULL.*** Named the greatest **sports movie** of all time in a 2008 poll conducted by the **American Film Institute**, *Raging Bull* (dir. **Martin Scorsese**, 1980) is one of the key films of the boxing film subgenre and one of the most important of director Scorsese's films. A **biopic** that narrates the life of boxer Jake LaMotta (played by **Robert De Niro**), *Raging Bull* takes us from the beginnings of LaMotta's career as a boxer through his retirement to Florida after that career, vividly depicting its protagonist both as a boxer and as a deeply flawed human being. The film vaguely continues the tradition, established in earlier boxing films, of treating boxing as a metaphor for American individualist alienation and competition, though it fails to explore the economic dimension of this metaphor (and thus to treat boxing specifically as a metaphor for capitalism).

The film does suggest that LaMotta's propensity for violence is very much a product of his social environment, while noting the ways in which corruption in the boxing business often limited LaMotta's opportunities in the sport. Otherwise, it generally focuses on LaMotta's individual story (both personal and professional) and avoids any real engagement with social issues. Though it is thus weak as a "message" picture, *Raging Bull* is justifiably admired for its technical achievements, including its moody black-and-white photography and the brilliant acting of De Niro in the lead role. Particularly important in this regard are the film's highly realistic fight scenes, which are regarded as some of the most effectively staged sports sequences ever put on film.

*Raging Bull* was nominated for eight **Academy Awards,** including Best Picture and Best Director, though it won only for Best Editing and Best Actor (De Niro).

**RAIMI, SAM (1959– ).** Beginning from his roots in low-budget **horror** films, Sam Raimi has gone on to become one of Hollywood's most successful directors, producers, and writers. After several minor efforts, his career was launched when he wrote, directed, and produced the **horror** film *The Evil Dead* (1981), an **independent film** that has gone on to become a major **cult** classic. Among his subsequent efforts were two sequels to this original film, *Evil Dead II* (1987) and *Army of Darkness* (1992), which he both wrote and directed. At the other end of the film industry spectrum, Raimi also directed all three of the big-budget, slickly produced *Spider-Man* films (2002, 2004, 2007), which together represent one of the most commercially successful franchises in film history, as well as some of the most respected **superhero films** in history.

Raimi has also directed a variety of other films, ranging from the dark, relatively low-budget superhero film *Darkman* (1990), to the **Western** *The Quick and the Dead* (1995), to the stylish **neo-noir** film *A Simple Plan* (1998), to the baseball film *For Love of the Game* (1999). He has also returned to the horror genre with *The Gift* (2000) and *Drag Me to Hell* (2009), the latter of which contains some of the self-parodic energy of the *Evil Dead* films.

Raimi has also made several small appearances as an actor. His credits as a producer include several of his own films as well as several films directed by others. However, as a producer he is probably best known as the executive producer of the syndicated television series *Hercules: The Legendary Journeys* (1995–1999) and *Xena: Warrior Princess* (1995–2001). As a writer, he has not only scripted several of his own films, but also co-wrote *The Hudsucker Proxy* (1994), with directors **Joel and Ethan Coen.** Raimi and the Coens also co-wrote *Crimewave* (1985), directed by Raimi. In fact, Raimi has worked with the Coens (with whom he once shared an apartment) on several projects and in several capacities.

**RAMIS, HAROLD (1944– ).** Harold Ramis is a successful actor, writer, producer, and director, best known for his involvement with a number of now-classic **comedies** in the 1990s. For example, Ramis directed *Caddyshack*

(1980), *Vacation* (1983), and *Groundhog Day* (1993), the latter of which he also co-wrote and co-produced. He co-wrote and costarred in *Ghost Busters* (1984) and *Ghost Busters II* (1989), while his writing credits also include *Caddyshack* and *Caddyshack II* (1988), as well as *Animal House* (1978), *Meatballs* (1979), *Stripes* (1981), and *Back to School* (1986).

Ramis, a Chicago native, started out as a member of that city's "Second City" improvisational comedy troupe, working there with such future stars as John Belushi and **Bill Murray**, the latter of whom would later work with Ramis on many of his film projects. His work there and in subsequent television projects eventually led him into film, beginning with co-writing the script for *Animal House*, starring Belushi. The success of that film launched Ramis into a career that made him a central figure in American film comedy over the next decade.

Ramis's most prominent appearances as an actor were in the *Ghost Busters* films, though he has appeared in more than a dozen films altogether. His most recent directorial credits include the cloning comedy *Multiplicity* (1996) and the comic **film noir** *The Ice Harvest* (2005). In addition, he both directed and co-wrote the comic **gangster films** *Analyze This* (1999) and *Analyze That* (2002), the supernatural comedy *Bedazzled* (2000), and the prehistoric comedy *Year One* (2009).

**RAT PACK.** "Rat Pack" was the popular designation given to a group of performers known not only for their work together in film and other venues but also for their personal friendship (and high-rolling lifestyles) outside of such performances. The group was first centered, in the early 1950s, on legendary actor **Humphrey Bogart**, but became more famous as a group entity after Bogart's 1957 death, when **Frank Sinatra** became the most prominent member of a group that also included Sammy Davis Jr., Peter Lawford, Dean Martin, and comedian Joey Bishop.

Various members of the Rat Pack often appeared together in live performances in venues such as Las Vegas. They were also seen together on television and in a number of films, most notably the 1960 heist film *Ocean's Eleven*, which featured all of the above-named performers. Lawford was the brother-in-law of U.S. President John F. Kennedy, and the group publically supported Kennedy's 1960s presidential campaign, though Kennedy later distanced himself from the group due to Sinatra's reported ties to organized crime. An angry Sinatra subsequently effectively ostracized Lawford from the group, but the other members of the group remained associated with one another through the rest of their lives.

Several female performers were also associated with the Rat Pack, largely through their personal relationships with its central participants. Many of these women were important film stars in their own rights, including actresses **Lauren Bacall**, **Ava Gardner**, **Judy Garland**, **Shirley MacLaine**, and **Marilyn Monroe**. *See also* BRAT PACK.

**RAY, NICHOLAS (1911–1979).** Nicholas Ray weathered concerns about his possible leftist political leanings and his potentially controversial lifestyle to remain a successful Hollywood director through the 1950s. In the 1960s, as his Hollywood career waned, Ray gained additional critical attention when members of the French New Wave (especially Jean-Luc Godard) identified Ray as a key influence on their own work and as a distinctive American film auteur. Though he was never nominated for an **Academy Award** for his directorial efforts, Ray has also been identified as an important influence on such directors as the German Wim Wenders and the Americans **Martin Scorsese**, **Jim Jarmusch**, and **Dennis Hopper**.

Ray's distinctive use of lighting to produce atmospheric effects, combined with his natural sympathy for social outsiders, made him a master of the **film noir**. He began his directorial career in 1949 with the release of two stylish noir films, *Knock on Any Door* and *They Live by Night*, though the latter of these had actually been filmed two years earlier. Ray made several other film noirs as well, including *In a Lonely Place* (1950) and *On Dangerous Ground* (1952). He also directed the unusual **Western** *Johnny Guitar* (1954) somewhat in the noir mode.

Ray's best-known film is *Rebel without a Cause* (1955), still one of Hollywood's classic expressions of the alienation of America's youth—and the best-known film of its young star **James Dean**. Ray's *The True Story of Jesse James* (1957) continued to explore the angst of young outsiders and was in fact also intended as a vehicle for Dean, but starred Robert Wagner due to Dean's untimely death. In *Bitter Victory* (1957), Ray tried his hand at the **war film**, and he even turned to the **biblical epic** with *King of Kings* (1961), but his troubles with drugs and alcohol and his rumored bisexuality were quickly making this chronicler of outsider angst an outsider in Hollywood.

The historical drama *55 Days at Peking* (1963), set in China during the 1900 Boxer Rebellion, was Ray's last major film. His collapse on the set during the shooting of this film was indicative of the growing health problems that ended his career for more than a decade, though he did direct a couple of minor films in the 1970s. Dying of cancer, he then collaborated with Wenders in the direction of *Lightning over Water* (1980), a fictionalized account of Ray's own last days that features a director named "Nicholas Ray" who is dying of cancer while struggling to make his last film in collaboration with Wenders.

**RAZZIE AWARDS.** The Golden Raspberry Awards, better known as the "Razzies," are a series of awards given annually to recognize the year's worst achievements in film. Founded by writer and publicist John J. B. Wilson in 1981, the Razzies are generally given out at a ceremony held the day before the annual **Academy Awards** ceremony. They function as humorous opposites of the **Oscars**; given generally with good humor, the Razzies have become a popular annual event with extensive national media coverage.

The Razzies particularly began to receive increased attention after Bill Cosby became the first recipient of the "honor" to show up at the ceremony to accept the award—for Worst Actor and Worst Screenplay, for what was also named the Worst Picture, *Leonard Part 6*. In 1996, **Paul Verhoeven** accepted the award for Worst Director for Worst Picture winner *Showgirls*, while **Halle Berry** showed up to collect the worst actress award for *Catwoman* in 2005, three years after she had won the Oscar for Best Actress for *Monster's Ball* (2001). In 2010, Sandra Bullock accepted the Razzie for Worst Actress for *All about Steve* (2009), one night before she won the Oscar for Best Actress for *The Blind Side* (2009).

Several Razzie Award winners for Worst Picture have been commercial hits, including the box-office smash *Transformers: Revenge of the Fallen* (2009).

**REAGAN, RONALD (1911–2004).** An actor of limited talent, Ronald Reagan appeared primarily in **B-movies**, some of which have become minor **cult** classics because of the combination of their laughable badness—as in the case of *Bedtime for Bonzo* (1951)—and Reagan's later fame as governor of California (1967–1975) and president of the United States (1981–1989). However, Reagan did make memorable appearances in some notable films, including major supporting roles in *Knute Rockne All American* (1940) and *Kings Row* (1942). Indeed, his last film appearance was in one of his best films, the 1964 remake of *The Killers*, in which he played a brutish gangster.

Reagan's greatest visibility in show business came as a corporate television pitch man for various products in the 1950s and early 1960s and as the president of the **Screen Actors Guild** (SAG) from 1947 to 1952, during the peak of the investigations into supposed communist activity in Hollywood conducted by the **House Un-American Activities Committee** (HUAC). Though these investigations have come to be almost universally regarded as a sensationalist witch hunt, they were enthusiastically supported by Reagan, which helped to enable the career-crippling **blacklist** of a number of prominent Hollywood figures.

Married to actress **Jane Wyman** from 1940 until their divorce was finalized in 1949, Reagan entered politics in the 1960s, serving as the governor of

California from 1967 to 1975 and president of the United States from 1981 to 1989.

**REDFORD, ROBERT (1936– ).** Charles Robert Redford Jr. appeared widely on television in the first half of the 1960s, then moved into film, ultimately becoming one of the most popular film actors of his generation. His first important screen role was as the star of *Barefoot in the Park* (1967), opposite **Jane Fonda**. He then achieved major stardom in *Butch Cassidy and the Sundance Kid* (1969, alongside **Paul Newman**). Several subsequent starring roles in films such as *The Candidate* (1972) and *The Way We Were* (1973) solidified Redford's star status. Then, reuniting with Newman in *The Sting* (1974), Redford began to receive more critical acclaim for his acting, including an **Academy Award** nomination for Best Actor.

In the mid-1970s, Redford remained one of Hollywood's top box-office draws, while films such as *The Great Gatsby* (1974), *The Great Waldo Pepper* (1975), *Three Days of the Condor* (1975), and *All the President's Men* (1976) further established him as a serious and versatile actor. The political concerns of the latter film reflected Redford's own liberal and political activism, which gained greater visibility during this period. Starring roles in *A Bridge Too Far* (1977) and *The Electric Horseman* (1979) followed, after which Redford moved into directing with *Ordinary People* (1980), winning the **Oscar** for Best Director for this inaugural effort.

Redford continued to appear regularly as an actor through the 1980s, with films such as *The Natural* (1984) and *Out of Africa* (1985) being particularly prominent. Soon, however, films such as *The Milagro Beanfield War* (1988) and *A River Runs through It* (1992) were beginning to make him more important as a director than as an actor. He was also becoming a successful producer, serving as both director and co-producer of *Quiz Show* (1994), which was nominated for a Best Picture Oscar and for which he received his second Oscar nomination for Best Director.

Redford's most recent appearances as an actor have included starring roles in *The Horse Whisperer* (1998), *The Last Castle* (2001), and *Lions for Lambs* (2007), which he also directed. He also directed *The Conspirator* (2010), a post–Civil War film centering on investigations into the assassination of Abraham Lincoln. Some of the most important films for which he has served as producer or executive producer include *A Civil Action* (1998) and *The Motorcycle Diaries* (2004).

In recent decades, Redford's name has been associated particularly closely with the Sundance **Film Festival**, of which he served as the founding chair and through which he has helped to promote the development of **independent film** since 1978.

**REITMAN, IVAN (1946– )**. Born in Slovakia, Ivan Reitman grew up in Canada (where he moved with his family in 1950) and ultimately became a key figure in Hollywood as a producer and as the well-known director of a number of key **comedies**, most notably *Ghost Busters* (1984) and *Ghost Busters II* (1989). Indeed, after a few forgettable early efforts, Reitman directed a string of successful comedies from 1979 to 1990, beginning with *Meatballs* (1979) and *Stripes* (1981), which starred **Bill Murray**, one of the stars of the *Ghost Busters* films. Reitman also directed **Arnold Schwarzenegger** in two comedies that played off of the star's action-hero image, *Twins* (1988) and *Kindergarten Cop* (1990).

Reitman has been less active as a director since 1990, though films such as the political comedy *Dave* (1993) and the **science fiction** comedy *Evolution* (2001) had some success. Since 1990, however, Reitman (who got his first important film credit as the producer of *Animal House* in 1978) has actually worked more widely as a producer than as a director. He was, for example, the executive producer of *Beethoven* (1992) and *Beethoven's 2nd* (1993), as well as the producer of *Space Jam* (1996) and *Private Parts* (1997). Reitman was nominated for a Best Picture **Academy Award** as the co-producer of *Up in the Air* (2009).

**REMICK, LEE (1935–1991)**. After several appearances on television, Lee Remick broke into film as a teenage baton-twirler in **Elia Kazan**'s *A Face in the Crowd* (1957). She followed with another supporting role in *The Long, Hot Summer* (1958), then moved into lead roles in such notable films as *Anatomy of a Murder* (1959), *Wild River* (1960), and *Days of Wine and Roses* (1962), receiving an **Academy Award** nomination for Best Actress for the latter.

The promise of Remick's early career was never quite fulfilled. Subsequent roles in films such as *Baby the Rain Must Fall* (1965) and *Sometimes a Great Notion* (1970) kept her on the Hollywood radar, but most of her performances after 1970 were on television, mostly in miniseries or made-for-TV films. One of her more prominent later roles in film was as the female lead (opposite **Gregory Peck**) in the **horror** film *The Omen* (1976).

Remick also performed frequently on the stage, winning a Tony Award nomination in 1966 for her performance in *Wait until Dark*.

**REPUBLIC PICTURES**. Republic Pictures was an **independent film** studio that actively operated from 1935 to 1959, producing numerous films, with a specialization in low-budget **B-movies**, especially **Westerns**. However, they did produce some films that were notable for their artistic aspirations, such as **Orson Welles**'s film adaptation of *Macbeth* (1948), as well as some higher-grade Westerns, including a number of the films of **John Ford**, as well as **Nicholas Ray**'s *Johnny Guitar* (1954).

Republic was founded when Herbert J. Yates amalgamated six different small low-budget studios that were all using the facilities of Yates's Consolidated Film Industries for technical processing of their films. Yates himself became head of the new studio. Indeed, very much a film factory, Republic eventually began to produce films at several different budget levels, which essentially functioned as "brands," ranging from their very low-budget "Jubilee" films that typically cost around $50,000 to make to fairly high-budget "Premiere" films that could cost a million dollars or more and that typically attracted well-known directors from other studios.

Republic was one of the first studios to realize that television might be more than a competitor, establishing a new unit, Hollywood Television Service, in 1951 to market its catalogue for broadcast on television. Some of the serials made by Republic in the 1930s were rebroadcast on television in the 1950s, but Republic did not itself move extensively into production of new programming for television. With even the **major studios** struggling in the 1950s, Republic did not survive the decade, and essentially ceased production of new films by 1959. However, Republic Pictures continued to exist as a corporate entity, and the sales of its older films to the merging (and content-hungry) cable television business were so successful in the 1980s that National Telefilm Associates (which had bought the Republic library in 1961) bought the corporate name and logo and began using it for new productions for both film and television.

In the 1990s, Republic became a subsidiary of Viacom-**Paramount**, but corporate reshuffling of Viacom and its holdings led to a split between Republic's television properties (now owned by CBS Television) and its film properties (now owned by Paramount).

**REYNOLDS, DEBBIE (1932– ).** Singer, dancer, and actress Debbie Reynolds was a key figure in the attempt by **Metro-Goldwyn-Mayer** (MGM) to revive the movie **musical** in the 1950s. After several minor roles, Reynolds gained major attention as young Kathy Selden in *Singin' in the Rain* (1952), opposite **Gene Kelly** and Donald O'Connor. That led to a string of starring roles in other musicals, including *The Affairs of Dobie Gillis* (1953), *The Tender Trap* (1955, with **Frank Sinatra**), *Tammy and the Bachelor* (1957), and *The Mating Game* (1959), though Reynolds's close association with the musical, a declining genre, limited her stardom.

Reynolds's starring role in *The Unsinkable Molly Brown* (1964) led to an **Academy Award** nomination for Best Actress, something that is relatively rare for the star of a musical. Starring roles in such films as *The Singing Nun*

(1966) and *Divorce American Style* (1967) followed. Reynolds then starred in her own self-titled television sitcom from 1969 to 1970, famously canceled by the NBC network after Reynolds protested the airing of cigarette commercials during the show.

Most of Reynolds's roles since 1970 have been on television, though she has made occasional film appearances and has lent her voice to several **animated films**. Married to Eddie Fisher from 1955 to 1959, Reynolds is the mother of actress Carrie Fisher.

**RITT, MARTIN (1914–1990).** Though he directed only just over two dozen films and never won an **Academy Award**, Martin Ritt was arguably one of the most important directors in Hollywood during a career that spanned more than 30 years directing feature films. Ritt began his career in the 1930s as a playwright for the Federal Theater Project, a government-sponsored group noted for the typically leftist political leanings of its participants. He then moved on to the even more left-leaning Group Theater in New York where he refined the sense of political responsibility and sympathy for life's unfortunates that he would maintain throughout his directorial career, the beginning of which was delayed because he was placed on the **blacklist** due to suspicions concerning his political sympathies. He finally broke into film in 1957 with the **film noir** *Edge of the City* and a film adaptation of William Faulkner's novel *The Hamlet*. The latter film, entitled *The Long, Hot Summer*, helped to make a star of actor **Paul Newman**, who later also starred in *Hud* (1963), a film for which Ritt received his only **Oscar** nomination for Best Director. In between, Ritt directed several other films, including another Faulkner adaptation, *The Sound and the Fury* (1959).

In 1964, Ritt directed *The Outrage*, essentially an American remake of the classic Japanese film *Rashomon* (1950), again starring Newman. In 1965, he directed the classic Cold War **spy film** *The Spy Who Came In from the Cold*, demonstrating further versatility, as he did with *The Brotherhood* (1968), a Vietnam-themed **gangster film**. *The Molly Maguires* (1970) combined the labor film with issues concerning ethnicity (in this case of Irish immigrant miners), while *The Great White Hope* (1970) and *Sounder* (1972) both focused on racism.

In the second half of the 1970s, Ritt directed *The Front* (1976), an important film that drew upon Ritt's own experiences with being blacklisted from both film and television, and a horse-racing film, *Casey's Shadow* (1978). In 1979, he directed his best-known film, *Norma Rae* (1979), a commercial and critical hit that dealt with labor activism and gender, as his career continued to stand out from the usual Hollywood fare for its serious engagement with important social and political issues.

Of the four films directed by Ritt in the 1980s, the **romantic comedy** *Murphy's Romance* (1985) was the most successful, though *Nuts* (1987) was an effective return to the serious treatment of topical issues that marked his entire career. His last film, *Stanley & Iris* (1990), similarly continued the engagement with class issues that had been a concern of Ritt's work since the 1930s.

**RKO PICTURES.** One of the "Big Five" majors of Hollywood's **Golden Age**, RKO Pictures produced and distributed some of the most memorable films of the 1930s and 1940s. RKO (which stands for Radio-Keith-Orpheum) was formed at the end of the 1920s through a series of complicated corporate maneuvers spearheaded by the Radio Corporation of America (RCA) and its parent company, General Electric (GE), in an attempt to take advantage of the merging interest in sound film by producing films using the Photophone Process developed by GE and controlled by RCA. The new company included the Keith-Albee-Orpheum chain of theaters (thus accounted for the other letters in the new company's name), and its formation was complete in 1930, when RKO acquired Pathé, formerly the U.S. arm of the French film studio Pathé Frères.

From the beginning, then, RKO was a large, vertically integrated company with powerful corporate backing. Spearheaded by the success of such efforts as the **musical** *Rio Rita* (1929), RKO quickly expanded its output, especially after **David O. Selznick** took the helm as production chief in 1931. Under Selznick, the company produced such notable films as the **screwball comedy** *A Bill of Divorcement* (1932), in which Katharine Hepburn made her film debut, and the landmark *King Kong* (1933). Unfortunately, RKO's ambitious expansion plans were unsuited to the economic climate of the Depression, and the company, with Selznick having already departed, soon faltered. It filed for bankruptcy in 1933, remaining in receivership until 1940.

Despite its financial condition, the studio remained in operation and produced a number of important films in the 1930s, most notably in the realms of screwball comedy and of musicals featuring actor/dancer **Fred Astaire**, whom Selznick had signed to a contract during his tenure. RKO, with its extensive theater holdings, also became an important distributor of films made by smaller studios. For example, from 1936 to 1954, they distributed all of the shorts and features made by **Disney**, at that time a small independent studio. RKO remained on the cutting edge of film technology as well, while also producing a number of high-profile films such as *Gunga Din* and *The Hunchback of Notre Dame* (both 1939) that helped to pull the company out of receivership.

The studio's turn toward greater artistic quality culminated in their 1941 release of **Orson Welles**'s *Citizen Kane* (1941). Now widely regarded as the greatest film ever made, *Citizen Kane* was not a financial success for the studio, which distributed the film only in a limited release due to pressure from William Randolph Hearst and the Hearst newspaper chain. Welles's *The Magnificent Ambersons* (1942) was another artistic success and financial failure. The company fared better in the remainder of the 1940s, with prestige successes such as **Alfred Hitchcock**'s *Notorious* (1946), *The Best Years of Our Lives* (1946), and several films by director **John Ford** in the late 1940s. However, RKO came in the course of the 1940s to rely more and more on low-cost, quickly made **B-movies**, including a number of **horror** films produced by Val Lewton and **film noirs** by such directors as **Edward Dmytryk** and **Nicholas Ray**, often featuring a young **Robert Mitchum**.

Industrialist Howard Hughes acquired a controlling interest in RKO in 1948, the year the **Paramount Antitrust Case** would lead to a chaotic shake-up of the film industry. Years of decline followed, as Hughes's capricious and intrusive management style was disastrous in the environment of crisis in which the industry soon found itself. Hughes sold off the studio to General Tire and Rubber in 1955; it ceased active production in 1957 and essentially went out of business in 1959. However, the RKO catalog remained an important holding for General Tire, which resumed film production in 1981 with a new subsidiary, RKO Pictures, Inc. That company, though under new ownership, continues to operate as RKO Pictures LLC, now a small **independent film** studio.

**ROACH, HAL (1892–1992).** The director and producer Hal Roach had one of the longest and most prolific careers in Hollywood history. He began work in film as an extra in 1912, becoming fascinated by the business. He then used the money from an inheritance to found his own production company in 1915 and went into business directing and producing his own films, beginning with *Willie Runs the Park* (1915), starring his friend **Harold Lloyd**. Roach and Lloyd made dozens of **silent film** shorts over the next several years, before transitioning into features in the early 1920s.

Roach's success as a producer of **comedies** during these early years was rivaled only by that of **Mack Sennett**. Releasing his films through **Pathé** and then **Metro-Goldwyn-Mayer** (MGM), Roach converted his studio to sound early on, in 1928. In the 1930s, he gradually shifted from short films to features, beginning with *Pardon Us* (1931), featuring his most successful comedy team, **Stan Laurel and Oliver Hardy**. The Laurel and Hardy comedies would remain an important Roach product through most of the 1930s, though they were phased out by 1940. Also of particular importance in the 1930s were the "Our Gang" (or "Little Rascals") shorts, which had begun as silents in 1922 and continued to be produced by Roach until 1938, when he sold the rights to the series to MGM.

In the late 1930s, Roach began to concentrate on producing bigger-budget films, such as *Topper* (1937) and *Of Mice and Men* (1939), a rare foray into serious drama. Drafted into the military, Roach oversaw the production of training films during World War II. After the war, Roach, always interested in the latest technological advances, became the first producer to begin making all of his films in color. As the 1950s proceeded, he was also among the first filmmakers to begin marketing his film library for broadcast on television. Perhaps more importantly, he also shifted many of his studio's resources to the production of programming for television quite early on, beginning in 1948.

Roach retired from active production in 1955, selling his interest in Hal Roach Studios to his son Hal Jr. However, he occasionally served as a consultant on various film projects during his retirement. In his career, Roach won two **Academy Awards** for Best Short Subject and was nominated for a third. In 1984, he received an honorary **Oscar** for his career contributions to film. Altogether, Roach directed approximately 150 films and produced well over 1,000.

**ROBBINS, TIM (1958– ).** Though never a top-level Hollywood star, Tim Robbins has had a long and productive acting career that has seen him appear in some of the most notable films of his generation. He has also directed several films, including the political **satire** *Bob Roberts* (1992), the capital-punishment commentary *Dead Man Walking* (1995), and *Cradle Will Rock* (1999), about the leftist theater scene in New York in the late 1930s. He received an **Academy Award** nomination for Best Director for the second of these films. Robbins also wrote these three films, which clearly reflect his liberal political beliefs, about which he has been quite vocal.

After a number of appearances on television, Robbins broke into film with supporting roles in such films as *Toy Soldiers* (1984) and *The Sure Thing* (1985). He then moved into bigger films with *Top Gun* (1986) and had a much bigger role in *Howard the Duck* (1986), though that film was a notorious failure. Robbins then made his breakthrough as young pitcher "Nuke" LaLoosh in the 1988 baseball film *Bull Durham*. That performance launched Robbins into leading roles in such films as *Miss Firecracker* (1989), *Cadillac Man* (1990), and *Jacob's Ladder* (1990).

In 1992, Robbins made his directorial debut with *Bob Roberts*, in which he also starred as the title character, a right-wing folk singer and senatorial candidate. He also attracted his first major critical acclaim as an actor for his performance in **Robert Altman**'s Hollywood satire *The Player*, winning the Best Actor award at the Cannes **Film Festival**. He followed with smaller roles in two other Altman films, *Short Cuts* (1993) and *Prêt-à-Porter* (1994), as well as lead roles in **Joel and Ethan Coen**'s *The Hudsucker Proxy* (1994) and in the much admired prison film *The Shawshank Redemption* (1994).

Robbins was less active as an actor over the next several years, though he did have important roles in such films as *Mission to Mars* (2000) and *Human Nature* (2001). He then received his only **Oscar** nomination as an actor for his performance in *Mystic River* (2003), which won him the award for Best Supporting Actor. He has played mostly supporting roles since that time—including a high-profile appearance in **Steven Spielberg**'s *War of the Worlds* (2003), though he did win critical approval for his lead role in *The Secret Life of Words* (2005). *See also* SPORTS MOVIES.

**ROBERTS, JULIA (1967– ).** Propelled to major stardom for her **Oscar**-nominated roles in *Steel Magnolias* (1989) and *Pretty Woman* (1990), Julia Roberts became one of Hollywood's most popular (and highly paid) female leads of the next 20 years. While Roberts's films of the 1990s, from thrillers such as *Sleeping with the Enemy* (1991) and *The Pelican Brief* (1993) to **romantic comedies** such as *Something to Talk About* (1995), *My Best Friend's Wedding* (1997), and *Runaway Bride* (1999) met with mixed responses from critics, she remained popular with audiences. She then won her greatest critical acceptance (and the **Academy Award** for Best Actress in a Leading Role) for *Erin Brockovich* (2000).

Roberts's follow-up, *The Mexican* (2001), was not a great success, but she continued her status as a top star in such films as *Mona Lisa Smile* (2003), *Closer* (2004), *Charlie Wilson's War* (2007), and *Eat Pray Love* (2010). However, most of her more recent performances have been in supporting roles, as in *Ocean's Eleven* (2001), *Full Frontal* (2002), and *Ocean's Twelve* (2004), all with *Erin Brockovich* director **Steven Soderbergh**.

As of 2010, the cumulative gross receipts of Roberts's films made her the top-grossing female star in Hollywood history.

**ROBESON, PAUL (1898–1976).** Widely regarded as one of the most gifted performers of his generation, Paul Robeson's talents extended beyond singing and acting to include achievements as an athlete, lawyer, and political activist. Unfortunately, his vocal support of leftist political causes combined with racial prejudice to impose serious limits on his career, especially in film.

Despite the few opportunities that were available to black actors at the time, Robeson managed to break into acting with a lead role in the 1925 silent drama *Body and Soul* (1925). He then went on to land starring roles in such films of the 1930s as *The Emperor Jones* (1933), *Song of Freedom* (1936), and *King Solomon's Mines* (1937), as well as playing a prominent role in the high-profile **musical** *Show Boat* (1936).

Robeson's most important role of the 1940s was on Broadway, where he starred as the title character in Shakespeare's *Othello* from 1943 to 1945. After World War II, Robeson became increasingly outspoken in his criticism of American racism. Coming at a time when Hollywood was increasingly under fire for what many saw as the dangerously leftist political beliefs of many individuals in the film business, Robeson's activism at this time brought a complete end to his film career and limited his other opportunities in show business as well.

For the last three decades of his life, Robeson remained a vocal supporter of socialist, antiracist, and anticolonial positions. During his period he was kept under continual surveillance by the U.S. government and suffered considerable persecution, including the revocation of his passport from 1950 to 1958 and widespread attempts to erase his name from accounts of American cultural history. As a result, Robeson was for a time better known abroad (he spent much of his career living and working in Great Britain) than in the United States. However, Robeson's name has recently been restored in many historical accounts, which acknowledge him as a pioneer not only in show business but as an early professional football player and a 1923 graduate of Columbia Law School.

**ROBINSON, EDWARD G. (1893–1973).** Edward G. Robinson appeared in **silent films** as early as 1916, but his major fame came with the advent of the talkies, especially after his starring role in the pioneering **gangster film** *Little Caesar* (1931). Robinson would be associated with that genre throughout the rest of his long career, though he performed in a number of genres and even occasionally went against his tough-guy image to play sensitive types, as in **Fritz Lang**'s **films noir** *The Woman in the Window* (1944) and *Scarlet Street* (1945).

The Hungarian-born Robinson came to the United States with his family at the age of 10. After an early career on the stage, he moved into film. Then, after the success of *Little Caesar* he played a number of gangster or tough-guy roles in films such as *Five Star Final* (1931), *Smart Money* (1931, with fellow gangster-film icon **James Cagney**), *Tiger Shark* (1932), *Kid Galahad* (1937), and *A Slight Case of Murder* (1938). To counter **Production Code** concerns that his films glorified crime, Robinson sometimes played a crime fighter, as in *Bullets or Ballots* (1936), where he played an undercover police detective who seeks to infiltrate the mob.

In the 1940s, Robinson became one of the central actors of the film noir, in which his most notable role was probably as insurance investigator Barton Keyes in **Billy Wilder**'s classic *Double Indemnity* (1944), a role that combined his earlier tough-guy image with his emerging sensitive image.

Other key film noirs in which Robinson starred include **Orson Welles**'s *The Stranger* (1946), *The Red House* (1947), and *Key Largo* (1948), in which he returned to his gangster persona.

Though he was never literally blacklisted and though he supplied cooperative testimony before the **House Un-American Activities Committee**, Robinson's career was damaged in the early 1950s because of suspicions of his leftist political leanings. As a result, he played fewer and less prominent roles in the first half of that decade, though films such as *Vice Squad* (1953) and *A Bullet for Joey* (1955) again featured Robinson as a crime-fighting police official, the latter showing him in action against a communist agent. In 1956, he played a prominent role in **Cecil B. DeMille**'s **biblical epic** *The Ten Commandments*, though the appearance seemed to do little to boost his career.

In the following years, Robinson played few important roles, though his roles in *A Hole in the Head* (1959), *Seven Thieves* (1960), *The Outrage* (1964), and *The Cincinnati Kid* (1965) were notable. His last film appearance was a memorable one as he once again played a sensitive character in the **science fiction** thriller *Soylent Green* (1973). That same year he was given an honorary **Academy Award** for his career achievements, though he was never nominated for a competitive **Oscar**.

**RODRIGUEZ, ROBERT (1968– ).** Texan Robert Rodriguez rose to prominence in Hollywood in the 1990s as the director of a sequence of stylish, self-consciously cool, ultra-violent films. *El Mariachi* (1992), shot in Spanish for around $7,000, launched Rodriguez's career, achieving enough success that Rodriguez was able to make a follow-up with a much higher budget (and in English) as *Desperado* (1995). From there, Rodriguez moved on to direct one of the four segments of *Four Rooms* (1995), one of the other directors of which was **Quentin Tarantino**, with whom Rodriguez would subsequently collaborate on several projects and whose films share numerous characteristics with those of Rodriguez.

Tarantino played a key role as an actor in Rodriguez's spectacularly violent, tongue-in-cheek vampire thriller *From Dusk till Dawn* (1996), set in Mexico. *The Faculty* (1998), meanwhile, was another **horror** film with an alien invasion theme. With *Once upon a Time in Mexico* (2003), Rodriguez then completed the "El Mariachi" trilogy.

Rodriguez's career took an important turn with the graphic-novel adaptation *Sin City* (2005), a commercial and critical success that featured a number of stylistic and technical innovations, especially involving the use of digital imagery. That film also led Rodriguez to resign from the Directors' Guild of America (DGA) when the organization refused to allow Frank Miller, author of the original graphic novels, to receive an onscreen credit as co-director of the film. This move was a sign of Rodriguez's independence from the Hollywood scene; he has also written and produced most of his films, which have generally been made by his own production company, Troublemaker Studios, which he operates out of his Austin, Texas, home.

Tarantino "guest" directed one sequence within *Sin City*, then again teamed with Rodriguez in 2007 to codirect the "Grindhouse" double-feature, with Tarantino directing one feature (*Death Proof*) and Rodriguez directing the other (the over-the-top zombie film *Planet Terror*). This film was typical of Rodriguez's fascination with excessive, even campy, violence, though he has also pursued a sort of parallel career as a director of **children's films**, made partly for the benefit of Rodriguez's own five children. These films include such features as *The Adventures of Shark Boy and Lava Girl* (2005) and *Shorts* (2009), but more importantly include the trilogy of *Spy Kids* films that appeared yearly from 2001 to 2003, with a fourth installment scheduled for release in 2011.

**ROGERS, GINGER (1911–1995).** Ginger Rogers enjoyed a long and productive career as a Hollywood actress, appearing in more than 70 films and receiving an **Academy Award** for Best Actress for her performance in *Kitty Foyle: The Natural History of a Woman* (1940). However, Rogers—who was named the 14th greatest female film legend of all time in a 1999 poll conducted by the **American Film Institute**—is best known for her series of appearances in **musicals** opposite **Fred Astaire**, generally as his love interest and dance partner.

After a number of appearances in smaller films, Rogers achieved prominence as a musical star on Broadway in *Girl Crazy* in 1932, then with her performances in *42nd Street* and *Gold Diggers of 1933* (both 1933). That same year, she appeared in her first film with Astaire, *Flying Down to Rio*. Over the next several years, Astaire and Rogers costarred in such films as *The Gay Divorcee* (1934), *Roberta* (1935), *Top Hat* (1935), *Follow the Fleet* (1936), *Swing Time* (1936), *Shall We Dance* (1937), *Carefree* (1938), and *The Story of Vernon and Irene Castle* (1939). The last of these films lost money for struggling **RKO Pictures**, but as a whole these films transformed the Hollywood musical, shifting the focus from large-scale production numbers to smaller numbers involving the dance performances of the two stars.

*Kitty Foyle* represented a new direction for Rogers that led to her appearances in a wider variety of roles, including **Billy Wilder**'s *The Major and the Minor* (1942), *Tender Comrade* (1943), *Lady in the Dark* (1944), and *Heartbeat* (1946). Rogers then reunited with Astaire for still another musical in *The Barkleys of Broadway* (1949).

The film was a success, but Rogers, one of the highest-paid performers in Hollywood in the 1940s, would never recover her earlier level of stardom. Good roles became harder to find as she entered her forties, though films such as the drama *Storm Warning* (1950), the **screwball comedy** *Monkey Business* (1952), the **romantic comedy** *We're Not Married!* (1952), and the drama *Black Widow* (1954) continued to provide highlights through the first half of the decade. Rogers continued to perform until 1987, but most of her appearances after 1957 were on television.

**ROMANTIC COMEDY.** Romantic comedy is probably the single most important subgenre of American film **comedy**. In romantic comedies, a potential couple (usually a man and a woman) undergoes a variety of humorous travails (often via a sequence of misunderstandings or accidental mishaps) on the road toward the establishment of a successful romantic connection. The genre has been prominent in film since the **silent film** days, when films such as **Charles Chaplin**'s *City Lights* (1931) helped to establish the parameters of the form.

Indeed, a 2007 poll conducted by the **American Film Institute** named *City Lights* the greatest romantic comedy of all time. With the coming of sound, film narratives became more complex, and the obstacles to romance in romantic comedy became more complicated. Among other things, this development gave rise to a new form of romantic comedy, the so-called **screwball comedy**, in which the difficulties encountered by the couple include the fact that they are seemingly mismatched (often in terms of social class) to begin with, but in which the comedy involved in their courtship is particularly farcical, often involving elements of **slapstick**.

From films such as *It Happened One Night* (1934) and *Twentieth Century* (1934) to films such as *Ball of Fire* (1941), *The Lady Eve* (1941), and *Arsenic and Old Lace* (1944), the screwball comedy—spearheaded by such renowned directors as **Frank Capra** and **Howard Hawks**—was the most interesting form of romantic comedy in American film. Meanwhile, **Katharine Hepburn** and **Spencer Tracy**—in films such as *Woman of the Year* (1942), *Adam's Rib* (1949), and *Desk Set* (1957)—virtually created their own subgenre of romantic comedy, with two strong protagonists struggling to establish a balance of power in their relationship.

In the 1950s, films such as *Roman Holiday* (1953), *How to Marry a Millionaire* (1953), *Sabrina* (1954), *The Seven Year Itch* (1955), and *Love in the Afternoon* (1957) still often contained elements of screwball comedy, but tended to rely less on farcical comedy and to focus more on sexual attraction. Such comedies, with **Billy Wilder** as the most important director, were often a bit edgier and more cynical than their predecessors. Meanwhile, by the end of the decade, Wilder's *Some Like It Hot* (1959), perhaps the greatest romantic comedy of the decade (and voted by the **American Film Institute** in 1999 as the funniest film of all time), was really more of an antiromantic comedy that turned to self-parody, playing with the conventions of the genre.

Wilder's *The Apartment* (1960) added an unusually large dose of social commentary (on the sexism and corruption of corporate culture) to the romantic comedy, but as a whole the genre became less important in the 1960s, as American film strove for greater engagement with the real social and political world. Later, when films such as **Hal Ashby**'s *Harold and Maude* (1971, featuring a particularly unusual couple) and **Woody Allen**'s *Annie Hall* (1977, in which the couple does not wind up together in the end) helped the genre to begin a comeback in the 1970s, they often did so by putting offbeat twists on the conventions of the genre. Thus, *Tootsie* (1982), a highlight of the early 1980s, relies centrally on a cross-dressing theme in its exploration of gender relations.

By the late 1980s and early 1990s, romantic comedy was in the midst of a full-scale resurgence as an American film genre. Films such as *The Princess Bride* (1987), *Moonstruck* (1989), *When Harry Met Sally . . .* (1989), and *Pretty Woman* (1990) showed how versatile the genre could be, while films such as *Sleepless in Seattle* (1993) and *You've Got Mail* (1998) demonstrated the ongoing viability of all-out sentimentality in romantic comedy. In addition, films such as *There's Something about Mary* (1998) and *50 First Dates* (2004), showed that contemporary romantic comedy could still be successfully combined with broad farce—as it often had been in the screwball days.

**ROMERO, GEORGE A. (1940– ).** After years of work making short films and television commercials, George Romero became a **horror** film legend with the release of *Night of the Living Dead* (1968), an ultra-low-budget black-and-white film that would come to be regarded as one of the landmark classics of its genre. That film, along with several other low-budget efforts that followed it, including most notably *The Crazies* (1973) and the unusual vampire film *Martin* (1977), solidified Romero's reputation for being able to use low-budget horror films to make serious social commentary.

In 1978, Romero directed *Dawn of the Dead*, the first of several sequels in the *Dead* series, which has itself exercised an immense influence on subsequent zombie films. Working with a substantially higher budget than the first film, Romero here produced another important classic of the vampire genre, and one that was a substantial commercial success. A subsequent sequel, *Day of the Dead* (1985), was less successful in theaters but has done well in home video sales, joining the first two films as **cult** classics of the horror genre. Another sequel, *Land of the Dead* (2005), had the biggest budget and produced the most overt social commentary of the entire sequence in its foregrounding of issues of class-based inequality. *Diary of the Dead* then returned to Romero's low-budget roots with a film that was released primarily on DVD, though it did see a limited theatrical release. *Survival of the Dead* (2010), the latest film in the sequence, was also a relatively low-budget effort.

In addition to the *Dead* series, Romero has directed a number of other horror-related films, including *Knightriders* (1981), *Creepshow* (1982), *Monkey Shines* (1988), *Two Evil Eyes* (1990), *The Dark Half* (1993), and *Bruiser* (2000). Romero has written most of his own films and has occasionally served as a producer, including serving as an executive producer for the 2010 remake of *The Crazies*.

**ROONEY, MICKEY (1920– ).** Beginning as a child star in the late 1920s, Mickey Rooney has gone on to have one of the longest and most productive careers of any actor in the history of American film. Born Joe Yule, young Rooney began his career playing "Mickey McGuire" in dozens of short films from 1927 to 1934, at one point legally changing his name to that of the character so that the series could have the right to use the name without paying royalties to the comic strip on which it was originally based. Then, as Mickey Rooney, he moved into a series of features as a teenage star in the late 1930s, including the early "Andy Hardy" films and the first of a string of successful **musicals** alongside **Judy Garland**. During this period, he also played a serious dramatic role in *Boy's Town* (1938).

In 1939, Rooney received a special Juvenile **Academy Award** for his career achievements as a young actor; the next year he received a regular **Oscar** nomination for Best Actor in a Leading Role for *Babes in Arms* (1939), one of his films with Garland, directed by **Busby Berkeley**. Rooney received another such Oscar nomination for *The Human Comedy* (1943), remaining one of Hollywood's most bankable stars through the early 1940s. However, his career was interrupted in 1944 by nearly two years of military service, during which time he served primarily as an on-air radio personality for the American Forces Network.

After the war, Rooney returned to the Andy Hardy character with *Love Laughs at Andy Hardy* (1946), but he never quite recovered the momentum of his earlier career. Nevertheless, he performed in a variety of roles in both film and television through the 1950s, including occasional appearances in notable films such as *The Bridges at Toko-Ri* (1954) and *The Bold and the Brave* (1956), for which he received a Best Supporting Actor Oscar nomination. He even starred in another Andy Hardy film as late as 1958, with *Andy Hardy Comes Home*. By the 1960s and 1970s, he transitioned primarily to supporting roles in film, including a role in *The Black Stallion* (1979) that won him another Oscar nomination for Best Supporting Actor. He also became more prominent as a performer on both television and the stage, continuing to work in those venues through the 1990s.

In 1983, Rooney received a special Academy Award for his lifetime of achievement in film. In the first decade of the 21st century, he played a number of small roles in film and also worked as a television pitch man.

**ROSHER, CHARLES (1885–1974).** The London-born Charles Rosher was one of the top cinematographers of the **silent film** era but continued to work widely in Hollywood film until the mid-1950s. After beginning his career as a newsreel cameraman in Great Britain, Rosher came to the United States in 1909 and quickly became one of the most sought-after cinematographers in the emerging American film industry. In 1929, Rosher won the first **Academy Award** for Best Cinematography for his work, along with Karl Struss on **F. W. Murnau**'s *Sunrise* (1927); he would go on to receive a total of six **Oscar** nominations for cinematography, winning the award a second time for *The Yearling* (1946).

The first full-time professional cameraman working in Hollywood, Rosher was instrumental in defining the profession, in which he was active as one of the founders of the American Society of Cinematographers. He worked in a variety of genres for a number of studios, winning additional Oscar nominations for *The Affairs of Cellini* (1934), *Kismet* (1944), *Annie Get Your Gun* (1950), and *Show Boat* (1951). The latter two were part of an attempt by **Metro-Goldwyn-Mayer** (MGM) to revive the **musical** in the 1950s. Rosher, who worked exclusively for MGM in the 1950s, shot many of the films involved in that effort, also including *Pagan Love Song* (1950), *The Story of Three Loves* (1953), *Kiss Me Kate* (1953), and *Jupiter's Darling* (1955).

Other notable films shot by Rosher include *Sparrows* (1926), *Rockabye* (1932), *Moulin Rouge* (1934), *Little Lord Fauntleroy* (1936), and *Ziegfeld Follies* (1945).

**ROSS, HERBERT (1927–2001).** Though his overall output was relatively small, Herbert Ross directed some of the most memorable films of the 1970s and 1980s. Ross, whose directorial career stretched from *Goodbye, Mr. Chips* (1969) to *Boys on the Side* (1995), was also a successful Broadway choreographer who worked on several dance-related films, including *The Turning Point* (1977), for which he received an **Academy Award** nomination for Best Director; he also received a Best Picture nomination as the co-producer of that film.

Some of Ross's early films included *The Owl and the Pussycat* (1970) and *Funny Lady* (1975), both starring **Barbra Streisand**. In 1975, he also directed *The Sunshine Boys*, an adaptation of a play by Neil Simon. He would go on to direct several adaptations of Simon's plays, including *The Goodbye Girl* (1977), *California Suite* (1978), and *Max Dugan Returns* (1983).

Though not a commercial hit, one of Ross's most interesting films was the 1981 **musical** *Pennies from Heaven* (1981), based on a BBC miniseries by Dennis Potter. Films such as *Footloose* (1984) and *Steel Magnolias* (1989), on the other hand, were hits and have become iconic works of American popular culture. Ross also drew considerable attention for *True Colors* (1991), a fictionalized account of Bill Clinton's election to the U. S. presidency.

**ROSSEN, ROBERT (1908–1966).** After early work writing and directing for the stage, Robert Rossen started his film career as a screenwriter in the 1930s, then moved into directing in the 1940s, helming a number of important films. His early writing credits include *Marked Woman* (1937), *Racket Busters* (1938), and *The Roaring Twenties* (1939). He then scripted such films as *The Sea Wolf* (1941), *Edge of Darkness* (1943), and *The Strange Love of Martha Ivers* (1946) before moving into directing in 1947.

The year 1947 saw the release of the successful crime drama *Johnny O'Clock* (1947), which Rossen both wrote and directed; that year, he also directed the noir boxing film *Body and Soul* (1947), still considered a classic of its type. In 1949, he had another major success as the writer and director of *All the King's Men*, receiving **Academy Award** nominations in both capacities.

A member of the Communist Party from 1937 to 1947, Rossen was unable to work in Hollywood from 1949 to 1954, though his cooperative testimony before the **House Un-American Activities Committee** in 1953 (after an uncooperative appearance in 1951) eventually led to his removal from the **blacklist**. In 1954, he returned as the writer and director of *Mambo*, then followed by writing and directing *Alexander the Great* (1956) and directing *Islands in the Sun* (1957). He then scored one of his greatest successes with *The Hustler* (1961), receiving **Oscar** nominations for Best Director, Best Screenplay, and (as producer) for Best Picture. However, he directed only one more film, *Lilith* (1964), which he also wrote. *See also* FILM NOIR; SPORTS MOVIES.

**RÓZSA, MIKLÓS (1907–1995).** The Hungarian-born Miklós Rózsa was one of the most popular and successful composers of film **music** in a career that stretched from the British film *Knight without Armour* (1937) into the 1980s. In between, he scripted some of the most memorable scores in film history, receiving a grand total of 17 **Academy Award** nominations in various music categories. He won the Best Music **Oscar** for *Spellbound* (1945), *A Double Life* (1947), *Julius Caesar* (1953), and *Ben-Hur* (1959).

Among the Oscar nominations for Best Score received by Rózsa are those for the **historical epics** *Quo Vadis* (1951) and *El Cid* (1961). In addition to *Ben-Hur*, he also composed the scores for the **biblical epics** *King of Kings* (1961) and *Sodom and Gomorrah* (1962). Rózsa was a particularly important composer of **film noir** scores, receiving Oscar nominations for his scores for **Double Indemnity** (1944) and *The Lost Weekend* (1945), as well as composing the scores for *The Strange Love of Martha Ivers* (1946), *The Killers* (1946), *The Naked City* (1948), and *Criss Cross* (1949). A stroke in 1982 ended his career as a film composer, shortly after he had composed the music for *Dead Men Don't Wear Plaid*, a loving spoof of the film noirs for which he had earlier written so much effective music.

**RUSSELL, JANE (1891–1986).** Known more for her voluptuous looks than for her talents as an actress, Jane Russell was a popular pinup girl with American servicemen during World War II and a top Hollywood sex symbol in the years following the war. Signed to a seven-year contract by **Howard Hughes** in 1940, Jane Russell got off to a slow start, with her first film *The Outlaw* (directed by Hughes himself) not being released until 1943 (and not receiving a wide release until 1946) due to difficulties with **censorship**, primarily over the displays of Russell's ample cleavage in the film.

These difficulties, however, helped to promote Russell's image as a sex symbol, though her career still proceeded slowly, with only two more films *Young Widow* (1946) and *The Paleface* (1948) in the 1940. Her film career reached its zenith in the early 1950s, with starring roles in such films as *His Kind of Woman* (1951), *The Las Vegas Story* (1952), *Son of Paleface* (1952), *Montana Belle* (1952), and *Gentlemen Prefer Blondes* (1953). In *The French Line* (1954), produced by Hughes's **RKO Pictures**, Russell appeared in a skimpy costume that raised eyebrows at the time.

In the mid-1950s, Russell starred in *Gentlemen Marry Brunettes* (1955) and *Fuzzy Pink Nightgown* (1957), produced by an **independent film** company set up by Russell and her husband, former Los Angeles Rams quarterback Bob Waterfield. She did not appear in another film until 1966, when she starred in the **Westerns** *Johnny Reno* and *Waco*. The films did not, however, signal a comeback, and Russell subsequently made only a couple of minor appearances in film. She also enjoyed a minor career as a singer and stage performer.

# S

**SALT, WALDO (1914–1987).** Waldo Salt was a successful Hollywood screenwriter whose career was brought to a halt by his placement on the **blacklist** at the beginning of the 1950s. Salt's first credit as a screenwriter came for *The Shopworn Angel* (1938). He also wrote the screenplays for *The Wild Man of Borneo* (1941), *Tonight We Raid Calais* (1943), and *Rachel and the Stranger* (1948), while also making uncredited contributions to several other screenplays, including that for *The Philadelphia Story* (1940). His last screenwriting credit before his blacklisting was for the medieval adventure *The Flame and the Arrow* (1950).

Post-blacklist, Salt had several television writing credits beginning in 1955 (sometimes using the pseudonym "Mel Davenport"), but did not write another screenplay until *Taras Bulba* (1962). He then had only a few minor other credits until the beginning of his comeback period in 1969. In fact, he enjoyed the best years of his career in its last decade, from 1969 to 1978. During that period he received **Academy Awards** for Best Screenplay for *Midnight Cowboy* (1969) and *Coming Home* (1978), in between receiving another nomination, for *Serpico* (1973). He also wrote *The Gang That Couldn't Shoot Straight* (1971) and *The Day of the Locust* (1975) during this period.

The Waldo Salt Screenwriting Award has been given annually at the Sundance **Film Festival** since 1992 for best screenwriting in a film screened at that year's festival.

**SARANDON, SUSAN (1946– ).** Susan Sarandon has crafted a long and successful career that has made her one of Hollywood's most respected actors. After several minor appearances in film and television, Sarandon stepped into starring roles in film with *The Front Page* (1974) and followed as the female lead in *The Rocky Horror Picture Show* (1975), one of the top **cult** hits of all time. Several other key roles followed, including one in the controversial *Pretty Baby* (1978). Sarandon's **Oscar** nomination for *Atlantic City* (1980) moved her into an even more prominent position; however, her subsequent role in the controversial vampire film *The Hunger* (1983) somewhat slowed her rise to major stardom, though that film has also gained minor cult status.

Key roles in *The Witches of Eastwick* (1987) and *Bull Durham* (1988) helped Sarandon to regain the momentum that would propel her into major stardom in the first half of the 1990s, during which she scored four **Academy Award** nominations for Best Actress in five years though in her late forties, usually a difficult time for Hollywood actresses. Altogether, she received Oscar nominations for Best Actress in a Leading Role for her performances in *Atlantic City*, *Thelma & Louise* (1991), *Lorenzo's Oil* (1992), and *The Client* (1994). She won the award for her performance in *Dead Man Walking* (1995).

Since 1995, Sarandon has maintained a prominent presence in American film, continuing to play lead roles in such films as *Speed Racer* (2008) and *Solitary Man* (2009), while transitioning gracefully into supporting roles in such films as *In the Valley of Elah* (2007), *The Lovely Bones* (2009), and *Wall Street: Money Never Sleeps* (2010). She has also done voiceover work in such films as *James and the Giant Peach* (1996) and *Cats & Dogs* (2001), while making several guest appearances on television.

Sarandon has appeared in several films directed by her long-time partner **Tim Robbins**, including *Bob Roberts* (1992), *Dead Man Walking*, and *Cradle Will Rock* (1999). Like Robbins, she is well known for her liberal social and political activism.

**SATIRE.** While Hollywood films are noted for their tendency to avoid controversy, numerous American films have strong satirical components. Many films are almost purely satirical, making satire an important subgenre of film **comedy**. However, despite its use of humor, satire often makes serious and important points about weighty social and political issues.

Some film satires belong to the literary tradition of the comedy of manners and are intended to satirize the behavior and mores of particular social groups. The rich have been a favorite target of such film satires, especially since the 1930s, when films such as *My Man Godfrey* (1936) lampooned the rich, providing entertainment to audiences struggling with the grim economic realities of the Great Depression. Such satires were also particularly prominent in the "greed" decade of the 1980s, including such examples as *Trading Places* (1983), *Down and Out in Beverly Hills* (1986), and *Less Than Zero* (1987). More recent examples of such satire include *The Nanny Diaries* (2007).

Such comedies have also frequently dealt with the shallowness and grasping materialism of suburban and upper-middle-class life, as in *The Graduate* (1967) or *American Beauty* (1999), though the latter is ultimately more grim than comedic. Similarly, numerous films specifically satirize capitalism and its numbing effect on ethics and morality, such as *Wall Street* (1987) and

*American Psycho* (2000). Among these films are satires of specific industries or businesses, such as the advertising industry in *Will Success Spoil Rock Hunter?* (1957), the tobacco industry in *Thank You for Smoking* (2005), or the fashion industry in *The Devil Wears Prada* (2006). Particularly prominent among such satires are those of various aspects of show business, including the Hollywood film industry. Key Hollywood satires include such films as **Sunset Blvd.** (1950), *The Bad and the Beautiful* (1952), *The Player* (1992), and *Mulholland Drive* (2001). Television has also come under particular scrutiny in films such as *A Face in the Crowd* (1957) and *Network* (1976), while media culture in general is satirized in such films as *Being There* (1979) and *Natural Born Killers* (1994).

Political satire has also long been a prominent aspect of American film. The electoral process itself is satirized in such films as *Meet John Doe* (1941), *State of the Union* (1948), *The Best Man* (1964), *The Candidate* (1972), *Bob Roberts* (1992), *Bulworth* (1998), and *Silver City* (2004). Closely related are films about the machinations of those in political power (often in an attempt to get re-elected); such films range from *The Great McGinty* (1940) to *Wag the Dog* (1997) and can also be considered to include such films as *The Great Dictator* (1940), **Charles Chaplin**'s lampoon of Adolf Hitler.

Finally, an important element of American film satire is the legacy of anti-war films that dates back to such commentaries on World War I as the **silent film** *The Big Parade* (1925) and the early sound film *All Quiet on the Western Front* (1930). As early as the 1950s, films such as *The Naked and the Dead* (1958) began to cast a more critical eye on the once-glorified World War II, while antiwar satires became particularly popular during the Vietnam War era, when such films as *Catch-22* (1970) and *MASH* (1970) were perceived as critiques of the American involvement in Vietnam, though they were set in World War II and the Korean War, respectively. Meanwhile, one of the greatest (and funniest) antiwar satires of all time was *Doctor Strangelove or: How I Learned to Stop Worrying and Love the Bomb* (1964), which lampooned the Cold War arms race. *See also* SHOW BUSINESS FILMS.

**SAYLES, JOHN (1950– ).** The screenwriter and director John Sayles has come to be regarded as the epitome of the **independent film** artist. Though sometimes writing screenplays for other directors to help finance his own projects, he is best known for his own series of inexpensive self-financed films in which he has grappled with a number of important social and political issues.

Like so many others in the film industry, Sayles began his career working for **Roger Corman**, writing screenplays for such films as *Piranha* (1978) and *Battle beyond the Stars* (1980). He used money made from the first of these to help finance his first directorial effort *Return of the Secaucus Seven* (1979), which he also wrote, just as he has written the screenplays for all of his films, including the Spanish-language film *Men with Guns* (1997). In the 1980s, Sayles continued to use the proceeds from writing films for others—such as *Alligator* (1980), *The Howling* (1981), *Clan of the Cave Bear* (1986)—along with his stipend from a MacArthur Foundation "genius grant" to make his own films, gaining an increasing reputation as a director with such films as *Lianna* (1983), *The Brother from Another Planet* (1984), *Matewan* (1987), and *Eight Men Out* (1988).

Sayles's success allowed the budgets of his films to gradually increase, and *Eight Men Out* was by far his most commercial effort to date, though he continued to refuse to compromise his politics or his desire for independence. In 1989, Sayles created the television series *Shannon's Deal*, which he also produced, though it ran (on the NBC network) for only 16 episodes in 1990 and 1991. He then returned to film with *City of Hope* (1991), *Passion Fish* (1992), *The Secret of Roan Innish* (1994), and *Lone Star* (1996), his most commercially successful film.

Sayles received **Academy Award** nominations for Best Screenplay for both *Passion Fish* and *Lone Star*, which he followed with the intense, but decidedly noncommercial *Men with Guns*. He continued his independent path with such politically charged films as *Limbo* (1999), *Sunshine State* (2002), *Casa de los babys* (2003), *Silver City* (2004), *Honeydripper* (2007), and *Amigo* (2010). He has written less widely for others in recent years, though he wrote the screenplay for the big-budget **fantasy** film *The Spiderwick Chronicles* (2008).

Sayles, one of whose unproduced screenplays reportedly inspired **Steven Spielberg**'s *E.T.: The Extra-Terrestrial*, was commissioned by Spielberg to write the screenplay for *Jurassic Park IV*, though production of that film has been repeatedly delayed. Sayles has also frequently appeared as an actor, both in his films and in films directed by others. A published author of both novels and short stories, he has also directed several **music** videos for Bruce Springsteen.

**SCHARY, DORE (1905–1980).** Studio executive Dore Schary oversaw the unsuccessful attempts of **Metro-Goldwyn-Mayer** (MGM) to regain its former glory in the 1950s, but the tide of the times was against the studio. Schary also had a successful career as a writer in the 1930s and early 1940s, before turning primarily to producing, and then becoming production chief at **RKO Pictures** in 1947, then becoming MGM's production chief in 1948.

Schary received an **Academy Award** nomination for co-writing the screenplay for *Boy's Town* (1938) and for co-writing the original story for

*Edison: The Man* (1940). He won the **Oscar** for co-writing the original story for *Boy's Town*. In the 1950s, he received three nominations as a producer of **documentaries**. In the latter part of his career, he wrote and produced such films as *Lonelyhearts* (1958) and *Act One* (1963).

Schary was also a playwright who both wrote and produced the 1960 film adaptation of his successful Broadway play *Sunrise at Campobello*. It is, however, as the production chief and later president of MGM from 1948 to 1956 that Schary is best remembered, despite his lack of success in restoring the studio's flagging fortunes. Actually, 1948, the year of both the **Paramount Antitrust Case** and the initial **House Un-American Activities Committee** (HUAC) hearings into supposed subversive activity in the film industry, was the worst possible time to take over a studio. In addition, Schary's initial work was made more difficult by high expectations (he was expected to be a "new **Thalberg**") and by ongoing battles with MGM head **Louis B. Mayer**, who favored light, wholesome fare, as opposed to the politically liberal Schary, who preferred serious, realistic, socially engaged films.

In 1951, Schary won the battle with Mayer when the latter was deposed by MGM's corporate rulers, and Schary was made president of the studio. MGM had some notable successes in the early 1950s but never regained its former glory, and Schary resigned from the studio in 1956. He was notable during his tenure at the studio for being one of the few studio executives in Hollywood who was openly critical of HUAC's Hollywood investigations, which he regarded as an illegal and unjustified witch hunt. He was also politically active as national chairman of B'nai B'rith's Anti-Defamation League.

**SCHENCK, JOSEPH M. (1878–1961).** The Russian-born Joseph M. Schenck was a pioneering film executive who played a major role in the early evolution of the American film industry. Schenck came to the United States with his family and entered the entertainment business, first as an amusement park concessions operator, then as a park owner. He soon entered the film business, and (along with his brother Nicholas) became partners with **Marcus Loew** in 1912, helping to build Loew's chain of theaters.

After parting ways with Loew, Schenck moved to Hollywood and began producing films. In 1916, he met and married **silent-film** star Norma Talmadge. Schenck eventually becoming the studio head at **United Artists** in 1924, working to help the fledgling studio build its own chain of theaters. In 1933, Schenck joined with **Darryl F. Zanuck** to form Twentieth Century Pictures, which merged with Fox Film Corporation in 1935 to form **Twentieth Century Fox**, with Schenck as chairman.

In 1936, Schenck became embroiled in investigations of illegal payoffs made by the Hollywood studios to keep peace with labor unions that reportedly had mob ties. These investigations eventually led to his conviction on charges of income tax evasion in 1941 and his imprisonment in 1946, though he was pardoned by President Harry S. Truman four months into his prison term. He immediately returned to Fox as production head, in which capacity he promoted the early career of **Marilyn Monroe**.

In 1953, Schenck was given an honorary **Oscar** by the **Academy of Motion Picture Arts and Sciences**, which he had helped to found in 1927. Also in 1953, he partnered with Michael Todd to help market Todd's highly successful Todd-AO widescreen process.

*SCHINDLER'S LIST.* One of the most talked-about films of the early 1990s, *Schindler's List* (dir. **Steven Spielberg**, 1993) still stands as one of the most effective cinematic explorations of the experiences of European Jews in the midst of the Nazi Holocaust in the years before and during World War II. Named the eighth greatest film of all time in a 2007 poll conducted by the **American Film Institute** (AFI), *Schindler's List*, based on the 1982 Australian novel *Schindler's Ark*, by Thomas Keneally, relates the story of Oskar Schindler (played by Liam Neeson), a German industrialist who helped numerous Jews escape from the Nazis.

The winner of the **Academy Award** for Best Picture, as well as six other **Oscars**, *Schindler's List* begins in 1939 when Schindler has just arrived in Krakow, Poland, hoping to profit from the emerging world war. At first, he helps Jews by employing them in his factory, thus saving them from being sent to concentration camps, but he does so only because they provide cheap labor and increase his profits. Eventually, however, Schindler finds that he cannot stand by and allow the continuing extermination of the Polish Jews without doing what he can to help as many as possible of them to escape extermination, even when he must go to considerable risk and expense to do so. *Schindler's List* is thus the story of one ordinary man who does the right thing, by extension serving as a rebuttal to those who would claim that there was nothing ordinary Germans could do to oppose the Holocaust.

*Schindler's List* uses highly effective black-and-white photography, and one of its seven Oscars (it was also nominated for five others) went to **Janusz Kaminski** for Best Cinematography. It also famously uses color to identify a little girl who is seen at several points wearing a red coat, then seen in the red coat late in the film in the midst of a pile of bodies. However, the film has been praised mostly for the effective treatment of its subject matter, though some have criticized it for focusing on the successful salvation of the relatively few Jews on Schindler's list, rather than on the extermination of the many more who were not.

**SCHRADER, PAUL (1946– ).** Though never nominated for an **Academy Award**, Paul Schrader has long been one of Hollywood's most respected screenwriters, as well as being a successful director. His earliest screenplays, including those for *The Yakuza* (1974), **Brian De Palma**'s *Obsession* (1976), and (especially) **Martin Scorsese**'s *Taxi Driver* (1976), gained considerable attention for Schrader and identified him as one of the key writers of the **New Hollywood** of the time. Among other things, Schrader was typical of the New Hollywood in that he had academic training in film studies, worked as a film critic, and showed a strong awareness of European and Japanese cinemas.

Schrader established himself further with a series of films that he both wrote and directed, including *Blue Collar* (1978), *Hardcore* (1979), and *American Gigolo* (1980). In the process, he became known for the consistent social consciousness that informs his films, as in the demonstration of a concern for the working class in *Blue Collar* or the interrogation of American morality in *American Gigolo*. Since 1980, Schrader has actually worked more as a director than as a writer, though he has contributed to the scripts for additional notable films directed by Scorsese, including ***Raging Bull*** (1980), *The Last Temptation of Christ* (1988), and *Bringing Out the Dead* (1999). Notable scripts written by Schrader for other directors include *The Mosquito Coast* (1986) and *City Hall* (1996).

Schrader both wrote and directed the 1982 **horror** remake *Cat People* (1982), as well as the **biopic** *Mishima: A Life in Four Chapters* (1985), the rock **music** drama *Light of Day* (1987), the crime drama *Light Sleeper* (1992), the Elmore Leonard adaptation *Touch* (1997), and the dramas *Affliction* (1997), *Forever Mine* (1999), and *The Walker* (2007). Films directed, but not written, by Schrader include the biopics *Patty Hearst* (1988) and *Auto Focus* (2002, about actor Bob Crane), as well as *The Comfort of Strangers* (1990) and *Adam Resurrected* (2008). Such films also include the made-for-TV film *Witch Hunt* (1994), about the notorious congressional investigations into supposed communist activity in Hollywood in the 1940s and 1950s, and the controversial *Dominion: Prequel to the Exorcist* (2005).

**SCHULBERG, BUDD (1914–2009).** Seymour Wilson "Budd" Schulberg was an important Hollywood screenwriter, as well as a successful novelist. The son of early **Paramount** executive B. P. Schulberg, Schulberg had a direct inroad into the film industry. However, early in his career, he was better known as the writer of such novels as *What Makes Sammy Run?* (1941), *The Harder They Fall* (1947), and *The Disenchanted* (1950) than as a screenwriter. *The Harder They Fall* was adapted to film (with a screenplay by Philip Yordan) in 1956, by which time Schulberg had achieved major success as a screenwriter for writing **Elia Kazan**'s *On the Waterfront* (1954), which won him the **Academy Award** for Best Writing for the story and screenplay.

Schulberg worked with Kazan again when he scripted another important film, *A Face in the Crowd* (1957). His name was also closely linked with that of Kazan because, like the director, he provided friendly testimony before the **House Un-American Activities Committee** hearings into supposed communist infiltration of the film industry in 1951. Ironically, while this testimony allowed Schulberg to escape the **blacklist**, it also made a number of enemies in the film industry, where he subsequently seldom worked. Other than his two films with Kazan, his only other important work in film after 1951 was as the writer and co-producer of **Nicholas Ray**'s *Wind across the Everglades* (1958).

Schulberg also wrote a number of scripts for television and was a successful sportswriter who was inducted into the Boxing Hall of Fame in 2002 for his writing about that sport.

**SCHWARZENEGGER, ARNOLD (1947– ).** The Austrian-born Arnold Schwarzenegger first came to prominence as a competitive bodybuilder, winning the Mr. Universe title at age 22, after a move to the United States the year earlier in order to further his competitive career. He ultimately won seven prestigious Mr. Olympia titles; his success as a superstar bodybuilder also helped him to get into films, when (as "Arnold Strong") he played the role of Hercules in the 1970 film *Hercules in New York*, though his German accent was still so strong that his speaking part was dubbed by another actor. In 1973, he had a small part as a gangster's strongman in Robert Altman's *The Long Goodbye*, in which his character was a deaf-mute, thus solving the problem of his strong accent. He had his first speaking role (and his first credit under his real name) in *Stay Hungry* (1976).

Schwarzenegger gained additional attention with his central presence in the 1977 bodybuilding documentary *Pumping Iron*. In 1982, he had the starring role in the sword-and-sorcery epic *Conan the Barbarian*. The film was a major step forward in his career. However, lest the role of the laconic, muscle-bound barbarian seem to be the part of a lifetime for a bodybuilder who was still struggling with English, Schwarzenegger found an even better fit for his skill set in **James Cameron**'s *The Terminator* (1984), in which he played the virtually unstoppable killer cyborg of the title. That role, which he would reprise in *Terminator 2: Judgment Day* (1991) and *Terminator 3: Rise of the Machines* (2003), made him a major Hollywood star—so much so that the scenario of the two latter films was modified to make him a hero, rather than a villain.

In the meantime, he became Hollywood's most bankable action star, appearing in such action-oriented **science fiction** films as the futuristic **satire**

*The Running Man* (1986) and the violent alien invasion drama *Predator* (1987). In such films, Schwarzenegger managed to overcome his limited acting skills and lack of facility with English through his commanding physical presence and a surprising onscreen charisma that reflected his sharp intelligence and senses of irony. With films such as *Commando* (1985), *Raw Deal* (1986), and *Red Heat* (1988), he became a top action star outside of science fiction as well.

In 1990, Schwarzenegger starred in **Paul Verhoeven**'s *Total Recall* (1990), though here he played a somewhat more vulnerable protagonist than his usual virtual superhumans. His career punctuated by occasional changes of pace such as the **comedies** *Twins* (1988) and *Kindergarten Cop* (1990), Schwarzenegger continued to be an important action star into the 1990s (and into his fifties), though both the action comedy *The Last Action Hero* (1993) and the **spy film** *True Lies* (1994, again directed by Cameron) can be taken as spoofs of precisely the sorts of films that had made Schwarzenegger a superstar in the 1980s, suggesting that his career might have passed its peak. That perception was surely reinforced by his turn as Mr. Freeze in the disastrous 1997 **superhero** flick *Batman & Robin*. **Action films** such as the supernatural thriller *End of Days* (1999) and the cloning drama *The 6th Day* (2000) failed to return Schwarzenegger to his former glory, and his third *Terminator* film was generally judged to be far inferior to the first two.

By the time of the release of the spoofy adventure *Around the World in Eighty Days* (2004), in which he had a minor cameo role, Schwarzenegger seemed a farcical parody of his former self as an actor, but he had by this time emerged elsewhere as someone to be taken seriously indeed when he was elected governor of California in the recall election of late 2003. A moderate Republican in a typically Democratic state, he was easily re-elected in 2006. He returned to film with a small role in *The Expendables* (2010).

**SCIENCE FICTION.** Science fiction film got off to a slow start in the history of American cinema. Prior to the 1950s, the major entries in the genre from the United States included **comedies** from **Twentieth Century Fox**, such as *Just Imagine* (1930) and *It's Great to Be Alive* (1933); **monster movies**, such as *Frankenstein* (1931) and *King Kong* (1933); serials such as the Flash Gordon and Buck Rogers sequences of the 1930s; and the mad scientist film *Dr. Cyclops* (1940). All of that changed in 1950, however, as the race between *Destination Moon* and *Rocketship X-M* to be the first major sf film released in the new decade was a sign of big things to come. The rest of the 1950s saw a major boom in the production of science fiction films in the United States, making sf film one of the key cultural phenomena of the decade.

The year 1951 was a particularly rich one, as the boom went into full swing. In this year, *The Thing from Another World* became the first of the many alien invasion films of the 1950s, while Arch Oboler's *Five* was the first Cold War film to depict the after-effects of a nuclear apocalypse, while also commenting on such important themes as racism. *When Worlds Collide* treated the catastrophic destruction of the Earth in a collision with another planet as a chance for a new start, in a disaster motif that also clearly reflected the nuclear fears of the time. *The Day the Earth Stood Still* was probably the most important sf film of the year, providing a warning against the Cold War arms race that demonstrated the potential of sf film to address complex contemporary issues in a thoughtful manner.

As the decade proceeded, a rich array of sf films began to appear, dominated by the alien invasion narrative, the postapocalyptic film, and the monster movie, all reflecting in key ways the anxious, and often paranoid, tenor of the times. Yet some of these films were quite complex and nuanced, as when the *Creature from the Black Lagoon* trilogy (1954–1956) addresses concerns about unethical scientific research that can be related to concerns over the arms race, but also involves themes related to gender and domestic relations in the 1950s. *Invasion of the Body Snatchers* (1956), often seen as a paradigmatic expression of anticommunist hysteria, could also be read as an expression of anxieties over other threats, including anticommunism itself. In that same year, *Forbidden Planet* provided an especially sophisticated warning against the threat of nuclear weapons—and against the dangers posed by unrestrained technological development as a whole, laced with a liberal dose of Freudian psychology. That film also broke new ground in the development of visual effects, while attempting to give sf film a new cultural legitimacy by basing its narrative on William Shakespeare's *The Tempest*. Meanwhile, *The Incredible Shrinking Man* (1957) addressed a number of the domestic anxieties of the 1950s, including the embattled state of American masculinity.

By the end of the 1950s, however, American science fiction film had come more and more to be regarded in Hollywood as especially suitable fare for the teenage audiences that were becoming an increasingly important segment of the filmgoing demographic. This vein included interesting and valuable films such as *The Blob* (1958), but most of the films produced in the late 1950s for teen audiences were low-budget affairs, often laughably bad as films. New studios such as **American International Pictures** began to dominate the genre, specializing in ultra-low-budget teen movies. As a result, the science fiction films of the 1950s as a whole are still often associated in the public mind with cheap effects, bad acting, and ludicrous scripts—as in the case of *Plan 9 from Outer Space* (1959), often identified as the worst film ever made. Relatively high-budget color films for fairly broad audiences, such as George

Pal's *The Time Machine* (1960), based on a novel by H. G. Wells, and Irwin Allen's *The Lost World* (1960), based on a novel by Sir Arthur Conan Doyle, did occasionally still appear, but became more and more rare as the new decade of the 1960s proceeded.

**Disney**'s *The Absent-Minded Professor* (1961), a lighthearted mad scientist film for children and families, suggested potential new directions for sf film, while films such as Byron Haskin's *Robinson Crusoe on Mars* (1964) provided occasional highlights, but all in all the 1960s were a slow decade in American sf film until 1968, when *Planet of the Apes* was a major box-office hit that also provided thoughtful commentary on issues from the Cold War arms race to racism. Meanwhile, **Stanley Kubrick**'s *2001: A Space Odyssey*, a British–American co-production, broke new aesthetic ground, using a classical **music** soundtrack and special visual effects of unprecedented sophistication to help produce a film that was self-consciously intended to be a genuine work of art rather than mere entertainment. The success of such films spurred a minor renaissance in American sf film in the coming years. However, with the Vietnam War and the Watergate scandal hovering over American society like twin dark clouds, the sf films of the early 1970s were almost universally dark in tone, dominated by such works of dystopian film as *A Clockwork Orange*, another joint U.S./U.K. production directed by Kubrick, and *THX 1138*, the first film from future *Star Wars* creator **George Lucas**, both released in 1971. Other key works of this era included Richard Fleischer's *Soylent Green* (1973) and Michael Anderson' *Logan's Run* (1976). On the other hand, **Woody Allen**'s farcical *Sleeper* provided a parodic rejoinder to the dystopian films of the early 1970s, though even it had certain dark undertones.

This darkness was lifted with the release of *Star Wars* in 1977, providing rollicking feel-good entertainment with vaguely mythical undertones, while looking nostalgically back on the serials of the 1930s. The good vs. evil moral certainties of this film were clearly a major attraction for audiences, though it also helped that the film broke new ground in the use of high-tech **special effects**, pointing toward a bold new future in sf filmmaking. Meanwhile, **Steven Spielberg**'s *Close Encounters of the Third Kind*, also released in 1977, was one of the most sophisticated (both technically and thematically) alien invasion films ever made, suggesting that the minor renaissance of the early 1970s was quickly becoming a major new boom. This suggestion was quickly verified with the release of *Alien* and *Star Trek: The Motion Picture* in 1979, followed by the first *Star Wars* sequel, *The Empire Strikes Back* in 1980, then by *Blade Runner* and *E.T.: The Extra-Terrestrial* in 1982. Topped off with *The Return of the Jedi* in 1983 and **James Cameron**'s *The Terminator* in 1984, the period from 1977 to 1984 was probably the richest in sf film history. Indeed, though this boom slowed a bit after 1984, the release of *Aliens* in 1986, *Robocop* in 1987, and *The Abyss* in 1989 provided important high points through the rest of the 1980s. The *Back to the Future* trilogy (1985–1990) provided popular lighthearted sf fare during this period.

The 1990s got off to a good start as well, with films such as *Total Recall* (1990) and *Terminator 2: Judgment Day* (1991) providing thoughtfulness as well as rousing entertainment—and propelling **Arnold Schwarzenegger** to superstardom. Meanwhile, the *Alien* franchise continued to provide highlights with *Alien³* (1992) and *Alien: Resurrection* (1997). The **computer-generated imagery** that helped produce the dinosaurs of Spielberg's *Jurassic Park* (1993) provided another milestone in the history of visual **special effects**, while films such as *Twelve Monkeys* (1995) and *Dark City* (1998) demonstrated that there was still room for the quirky and the unusual in a field increasingly dominated by big-budget blockbusters. **Tim Burton**'s *Mars Attacks!* (1996) and the first *Men in Black* film (1997) were successful sf **comedies**, the latter itself becoming a blockbuster hit. Meanwhile, *Independence Day* (1996), an alien-invasion narrative with the structure of a **disaster** film, was just behind *Jurassic Park* as the top-grossing sf films of the decade—and two of the highest grossing films of all time. And the decade ended on a high note, with the huge commercial success of *Star Wars: Episode I—The Phantom Menace* and the commercial and critical success of *The Matrix* (1999), a U.S.–Australian co-production now widely regarded as the first truly successful cyberpunk film. The underappreciated **animated** film *The Iron Giant* (1999) was another end-of-the-decade highlight.

Highlights of the new millennium in American sf film have included two more *Star Wars* sequels, two sequels to *The Matrix*, and two more *Terminator* films. Meanwhile, the *Star Trek* film franchise, which seemed on the verge of extinction with the failure of *Star Trek: Nemesis* (2002) gained renewed life with the success of the prequel/reboot of 2009, suggesting that the franchise effect remained strong in sf film. And 2009 ended with the release of Cameron's *Avatar*, which would go on to become the highest grossing film of all time.

Nonfranchise highlights of the first decade of the new millennium included Spielberg's *Artificial Intelligence: A. I.* (2001) and *Minority Report* (2002). Truly original sf films such as *Donnie Darko* (2001) and *Serenity* (2005) gained a **cult** following, while big-budget effects-driven extravaganzas such as *I, Robot* (2004), *Transformers* (2007), and *Transformers: Revenge of the Fallen* (2009) raked in huge takes at the box office. Science fiction **children's films** became more and more prominent during the decade, culminating in **Pixar**'s release of *WALL-E* in 2008, followed by an unprecedented spate of children's sf films in 2009. Another important phenomenon of this decade was a flurry of remakes of earlier classics, including *Planet of the Apes* (2001), *Solaris* (2002), *War of the Worlds* (2005), and *The Day the Earth Stood Still* (2008). However, though spiced up with state-of-the-art **special effects**, these remakes were generally less impressive and interesting than the originals. *See also* CARPENTER, JOHN; CORMAN, ROGER; GILLIAM, TERRY; WISE, ROBERT.

**SCORSESE, MARTIN (1942– ).** One of the key participants in the **New Hollywood** movement of the 1970s, director Martin Scorsese has gone on to become one of the most respected figures in American film. In addition to directing some of the most important American films of his generation, the film-school graduate Scorsese has also showed an intense awareness of film history and has actively worked to promote awareness of some of the important films of the past, especially in **film noir**. After five unsuccessful nominations for the **Academy Award** for Best Director (and two for Best Screenplay), Scorsese finally won a Best Director **Oscar** for *The Departed* (2006).

Scorsese drew attention for his early student films, especially *I Call First* (1967), which would be reissued as *Who's That Knocking at My Door?* and is still watched today. He then moved into more mainstream film with *Boxcar Bertha* (1972) and (more importantly) the neo-noir film *Mean Streets* (1973), which showed characteristics of many of his later films, including the fact that it featured actor **Robert De Niro** in a key role. *Alice Doesn't Live Here Anymore* (1974) was also a successful film directed by Scorsese, but his first truly major film came in 1976, when he directed De Niro in *Taxi Driver*, one of the iconic films of the 1970s.

Scorsese followed with *New York, New York* (1977), a big-budget **musical** tribute to his home city that was a box-office failure. *The Last Waltz* (1978) was a **documentary** about the last concert of The Band. Scorsese then directed the boxing **biopic** *Raging Bull* (1980), perhaps his most respected film. His other notable directorial efforts of the 1980s included *The King of Comedy* (1982), the uncharacteristic dark **comedy** *After Hours* (1985), *The Color of Money* (1986), and the highly controversial *The Last Temptation of Christ* (1988). Scorsese then began the 1990s with another classic, the **gangster film** *Goodfellas* (1990).

Most of Scorsese's films of the 1990s were relatively minor, ranging from the 1991 remake of *Cape Fear*, to the period piece (and literary adaptation) *The Age of Innocence* (1993), to the gangster film *Casino* (1995), to *Kundun* (1997, a biopic about the Dalai Lama). His more recent films have shown considerable variety. Many have been high-profile, relatively big-budget efforts, including the period piece *Gangs of New York* (2002), the **Howard**

**Hughes** biopic *The Aviator* (2004), the crime drama *Departed*, and the dark thriller *Shutter Island* (2010).

**SCOTT, GEORGE C. (1927–1999).** An acclaimed Shakespearean and Broadway stage actor, George C. Scott also went on to be one of the most admired film actors of the second half of the 20th century. His first important roles in film were as a supporting player in *Anatomy of a Murder* (1959) and in **Robert Rossen**'s *The Hustler* (1961), both of which won him **Academy Awards** for Best Supporting Actor. Scott followed in the role of General Buck Turgidsen in **Stanley Kubrick**'s *Dr. Strangelove or: How I Learned to Stop Worrying and Love the Bomb* (1964), one of his most memorable roles. However, Scott continued to perform primarily on Broadway and television through the 1960s.

Scott received his greatest acclaim for his film work in the title role in the combined **war film** and **biopic** *Patton* (1970), winning the **Oscar** for Best Actor in a Leading Role. However, he famously declined the award, feeling that the entire award process pitted actors against one another in an inappropriate way. Nevertheless, he was again nominated for the Oscar for his lead role in *The Hospital* (1971). Now a top name in Hollywood, Scott followed with starring roles in such films as *The New Centurions* (1972), *Oklahoma Crude* (1973), *The Day of the Dolphin* (1973), *Islands in the Stream* (1977), and even the comic **musical** *Movie Movie* (1978). He started strong in the 1980s with the supernatural **horror** film *The Changeling* (1980) and the intense drama *Taps* (1981).

However, Scott's film career had lost some of its momentum by this time, partly because he continued to devote much of his energy to the stage. Most of his appearances after *Taps* were on television, though he continued to appear both on the stage and in film until his final film performance in a supporting role in *Gloria* (1999).

**SCOTT, RIDLEY (1937– ).** The British director and producer Ridley Scott first made his mark with the classic **science fiction** films *Alien* (1979) and *Blade Runner* (1982), and would later become the successful director of a number of highly commercial **special effects**-driven **action films**. Together, these films have made him the most commercially successful British director in Hollywood history.

Scott began his career in British television, then gained the attention of Hollywood with his direction of the period **war film** *The Duellists* (1977). Still little known in the United States, he was then tapped to direct *Alien* and *Blade Runner*, launching his career as a successful Hollywood director. Scott moved into **fantasy** with *Legend* and into crime drama with *Someone* *to Watch over Me* (1987), but did not have his next major success until *Thelma & Louise* (1991), about two women on the run from the law and from patriarchal society as a whole. This important film won him his first **Academy Award** nomination for Best Director. However, his other films of the 1990s—including *1492: Conquest of Paradise* (1992), *White Squall* (1996), and *G. I. Jane* (1997)—were less successful.

Scott achieved another major hit—and received another **Oscar** nomination—for *Gladiator* (2000), then followed with another high-profile hit in *Hannibal* (2001) and another Oscar nomination for *Black Hawk Down* (2001). His more recent films have received considerable attention from the public, but less admiration from critics. Still, *American Gangster* (2007), *Body of Lies* (2008), and *Robin Hood* (2010) were box-office hits, and Scott remains a much sought-after director with numerous films in development, including a proposed two-part prequel to *Alien*.

Scott has also served as a producer for most of the films he has directed, as well as producing or executive producing several films directed by others. He has also executive produced the television series *Numb3rs* (2005–2010) and *The Good Wife* (2009–2010). He is the older brother of **Tony Scott**, also a successful director.

**SCOTT, TONY (1944– ).** The British director Tony Scott has helmed a number of successful Hollywood films, known primarily for his fast-paced action sequences. Scott first gained attention as the director of the controversial **horror** film *The Hunger* (1983), then moved into American film with two major hits, *Top Gun* (1986) and *Beverly Hills Cop II* (1987). His record since that time has been uneven (and critics have often been unkind to his work), but he continues to direct big-budget A-list projects.

In the 1990s, Scott directed such big-budget **action films** as *Days of Thunder* (1990), *Crimson Tide* (1995), and *Enemy of the State* (1998). However, his most critically successful film of the decade was the **Quentin Tarantino**-scripted *True Romance* (1993), a gritty, violent, lower-budget effort.

Scott's success in the 21st century has been spotty. *Spy Game* (2001) was not a hit, and *Domino* was a major failure at the box office and with critics. On the other hand, *Man on Fire* (2004), *Déjà Vu* (2006), and *The Taking of Pelham 1 2 3* (2009), all featuring **Denzel Washington**, were modest successes at the box office and received some critical praise, though mostly for their technical style (especially the **special effects** and **action** sequences), rather than their substance.

Scott has also directed several successful made-for-television movies, including *RKO 281* (1999), about the making of *Citizen Kane*. He has also produced or executive produced a number of films, as well as serving as an executive producer for the television series *Numb3rs* (2005–2010) and *The Good Wife* (2009–2010), along with his older brother, **Ridley Scott**.

**SCREEN ACTORS GUILD.** The Screen Actors Guild (commonly referred to as SAG) is the principal labor organization that represents actors who perform in film and television, with more than 200,000 members. SAG was founded in 1933 in an effort to oppose the exploitation of actors in a growing film industry, providing them with collective representation that could counter the growing corporate clout of the Hollywood studios. By 1937, aided by the passage of the National Labor Relations Act, which gave more power to labor unions, SAG had gained the exclusive right to represent actors in collective bargaining with the studios.

Though SAG was one of the labor unions investigated for communist infiltration by the **House Un-American Activities Committee** (HUAC) when its Hollywood hearings began in 1947, the union at the time was headed by arch-conservative **Ronald Reagan**, who served as a confidential informant for HUAC. Soon after the initial hearings, SAG forced its officers to take an anticommunist pledge. Meanwhile, the union divorced itself from actors blacklisted as a result of the HUAC hearings and provided no support for them. The union would later express regret for this stance, but it did enable them to solidify their power as the sole actors' union in the film industry and to extend their work into the burgeoning television industry in the 1950s.

SAG remains the exclusive representatives of film actors, though it shares the representation of television and new media performers with its sister union, the American Federation of Television and Radio Artists (AFTRA). Among its other activities, SAG has given annual Screen Actors Guild Awards since 1995 to recognize the best performances by individuals and ensembles in film and television.

**SCREEN WRITERS GUILD.** *See* WRITERS GUILD OF AMERICA.

**SCREWBALL COMEDY.** Screwball **comedy** is a form of **romantic comedy** in which a couple, seemingly ill matched due to differences in temperament, social class, or other circumstances, negotiates a series of comical obstacles on their way to establishing a romantic relationship. The form arose in the 1930s, partly in response to the new complexities in plot and characterization that were made possible by the coming of sound, and the screwball comedy quite often makes use of rapid and witty exchanges of dialogue between the two protagonists. The screwball comedy also frequently contains social commentary that can be seen as a response to the Depression; its theme of a class-based mismatch between the two protagonists typically involves a depiction of the richer party (usually the woman) as spoiled and out of touch with the daily realities faced by ordinary people. Finally, the screwball comedy also tends to hint at (though only hint at) sexuality more clearly than most romantic comedies of the same period; it can thus also be seen partly as a strategy for getting around the restrictions placed on sexual content in Hollywood film by the Motion Picture **Production Code** of 1930.

From films such as *It Happened One Night* (1934) and *Twentieth Century* (1934) to films such as *Ball of Fire* (1941), *The Lady Eve* (1941), and *Arsenic and Old Lace* (1944), the screwball comedy—spearheaded by such renowned directors as **Frank Capra** and **Howard Hawks**—was the most interesting form of romantic comedy in American film. Other key films during this period included *My Man Godfrey* (1936), *Bringing Up Baby* (1938), and *The Philadelphia Story* (1940). After World War II, the heyday of screwball comedy was over, though films such as *Monkey Business* (1952) and *Some Like It Hot* (1959) continued many of the characteristics of screwball comedy. The latter is notable for the way its cross-dressing motifs enact the themes of disguise and misrecognition that often occur in screwball comedy.

With the coming of the 1960s and the possibility of representing sexuality more frankly on the screen, screwball comedy fell out of favor in Hollywood, though films that could be considered screwball comedies continued to appear. Thus, elements of screwball comedy can be found in such films as *When Harry Met Sally . . .* (1989) and *You've Got Mail* (1998). Screwball comedy has been a particularly important influence on the films of **Joel and Ethan Coen**, most of whose films continue some elements of screwball comedy; many of their films—such as *The Hudsucker Proxy* (1994), *O Brother, Where Art Thou?* (2000), *Intolerable Cruelty* (2003), and *Burn after Reading* (2008)—can be considered specifically as contemporary revisions of the genre.

**SEARCHERS, THE.** *The Searchers* (dir. **John Ford**, 1956) is widely regarded as one of the greatest **Westerns** of all time and has, along with *Stagecoach* (1939), become one of the signature films of John Ford, probably the single director who is most closely associated with the genre. Indeed, *The Searchers* was named the greatest Western of all time in a 2008 poll conducted by the **American Film Institute** (AFI), while the 2007 AFI list ranked it the 12th greatest film of all time.

To some extent, the film, which revolves around the kidnapping of a young white girl by a Native American raiding party that massacres her family, draws upon the tendency of earlier Westerns to depict Native Americans as bloodthirsty savages. On the other hand, *The Searchers* is far more nuanced in its treatment of Native Americans than most films that came before it and is in general one of the most complex and intelligent Westerns ever made.

*The Searchers* features Western icon **John Wayne** as Civil War veteran Ethan Edwards, who sets out with his adoptive nephew, Martin Pawley (Jeffrey Hunter), in an attempt to rescue the kidnapped girl, Debbie Edwards (**Natalie Wood**). After years of searching, they finally find Debbie, now a young adult who is fully assimilated into the culture of the Comanche Indians, a wife of Cicatriz, or "Scar" (Henry Brandon), chief of the band that abducted her. At first, Edwards is tempted to kill Debbie, feeling that she is suffering a fate worse than death. Ultimately, however, Debbie is rescued and welcomed back into the fold, while the film is bitterly critical of the virulent racism of Edwards toward Native Americans, suggesting that this racism has led to genocide.

*The Searchers* thus foreshadows the more sympathetic treatment of Native Americans that would come to characterize Westerns in the coming years, including Ford's own *Cheyenne Autumn* (1964), and culminating in the **Oscar**-winning *Dances with Wolves* (1990). In addition to its thematic importance, *The Searchers* is regarded as one of the finest examples of Ford's mastery of the art of filming Western landscapes.

**SEBERG, JEAN (1938–1979).** Though her career was relatively brief (and though much of her career was spent in France), Jean Seberg is still one of the most remembered actresses in Hollywood film history. A young Seberg broke into film by playing the title role in **Otto Preminger**'s *Saint Joan* (1957) and followed with a key role in Preminger's *Bonjour tristesse* (1958). She also had an important role in *The Mouse That Roared* (1959), made in Great Britain. However, when reviews of her performances in all three of these films were negative, she moved to France and continued her career there, becoming a key performer in French New Wave films.

Seberg's best known role was as the female lead in Jean-Luc Godard's classic *À bout de souffle* (*Breathless*, 1960). She also had a lead role in **Robert Rossen**'s *Lilith* (1964).

**SELZNICK, DAVID O. (1902–1965).** David O. Selznick was one of the best-known and most successful film producers in Hollywood history, though he also became known as the epitome of the meddling producer who interfered with the work of his directors. Though involved in the production of numerous important films, he is perhaps best known as the force behind the production of *Gone with the Wind* (1939). After early work as an editor and then producer at **Metro-Goldwyn-Mayer** (MGM) and **Paramount**, he became the head of production at **RKO Pictures** in 1931, with the reputation for being something of a boy wonder. His tenure at RKO was brief but successful in terms of the quality of the pictures he produced. However, the economic climate of the Depression put RKO in financial difficulty, and by 1933 Selznick had returned to MGM to establish his own production unit to supplement the unit headed by **Irving G. Thalberg**, whose productivity was suffering due to health reasons. Selznick again produced several successful films in this new capacity, but in 1935 left to realize his dream of forming his own **independent film** production company.

Selznick International Pictures, distributing its films through **United Artists**, was one of the great successes in the American film industry of the second half of the 1930s, producing such films as *The Prisoner of Zenda* (1937) and *The Adventures of Tom Sawyer* (1938) and culminating in the hugely successful release of the *Gone with the Wind*, which won eight **Academy Awards**, including Best Picture. Selznick was then instrumental in bringing British director **Alfred Hitchcock** to the United States, beginning with the production of *Rebecca* in 1940, which became the second consecutive Selznick-produced film to win the Best Picture **Oscar**. In 1940, he also received the Irving G. Thalberg Award for career achievement.

After *Rebecca*, Selznick cut back on the production of films, often developing projects (such as several of Hitchcock's subsequent films) and then selling them to others to do the actual production. Selznick did produce Hitchcock's *Spellbound* (1945) and *The Paradine Case* (1947), as well as the controversial **Western** *Duel in the Sun* (1946), starring actress **Jennifer Jones**, whom he would eventually marry in 1949. Though uncredited, Selznick was also a co-producer of the much respected **film noir** *The Third Man* (1949). He was involved in the production of relatively few films in the 1950s, eventually retiring after *A Farewell to Arms* (1957) due to worsening health.

**SENNETT, MACK (1880–1960).** The Canadian-born Mack Sennett (birth name Mikall Sinnott) was one of the most important innovators in the early history of **silent film**, especially in the development of **slapstick comedy** as an important mode in silent film. Sennett ultimately produced more than 1,000 films (mostly silent), while acting in and directing more than 300 each, though most of his acting and directing credits were early in his career, before 1915.

After early work as a performer and director for **Biograph**, Sennett founded **Keystone Studios** in 1912. That company was at the forefront of developments in the film industry over the next several years. They built the first fully enclosed film studio in the world and there they made films that gave many important performers their starts in the business, including **Bing Crosby**, **W. C. Fields**, Mabel Normand, **Gloria Swanson**, and (most importantly) **Charles Chaplin**.

Making his mark with early short **comedies** featuring frenetic chase scenes and other scenes of anarchic mayhem (such as a series of films featuring the "Keystone Cops"), Sennett quickly became a success. However, he soon moved primarily into producing, leaving the acting to the numerous talented performers whom he discovered and leaving the directing to Chaplin and others.

In 1915, Sennett joined with **D. W. Griffith** and Thomas Ince to form **Triangle Pictures** Corporation, of which Keystone continued to operate as an autonomous unit. In 1917, however, Sennett left to form his own **independent film** production company, which produced some feature-length films, but continued to specialize in comedy shorts into the 1920s, while the bigger studios focused more and more on features. In the latter part of the 1920s, he began to distribute his films through **Pathé**, then switched to **Educational Pictures**. He transitioned into sound film in the 1930s but continued to concentrate on shorts.

Sennett enjoyed some memorable successes in the 1930s, including a series of shorts featuring Crosby and several feature films starring Fields, made in conjunction with and distributed through **Paramount**. By 1933, however, Depression-era conditions had caused Sennett's studio to fail, forcing Sennett himself to file for bankruptcy. Sennett's attempted comeback included the direction and production of several comedy shorts in 1934 and 1935—such as *The Timid Young Man* (1935), starring **Buster Keaton**—but he never regained his earlier momentum and retired from active filmmaking at that point.

**SEXPLOITATION FILM.** The sexploitation film is a category of exploitation film that relies primarily on nudity and sexual material to attract audiences. Usually independently produced with very low budgets and questionable production values, sexploitation films emerged in the United States around the beginning of the 1960s after several court rulings had made the exhibition of such films legal and as the **Production Code** began to lose its grip on the film industry.

Originally playing mostly in **grindhouse** and drive-in theaters, many early sexploitation films (known as "nudie cuties") justified their heavy use of nudity by being set in nudist camps and were thus extensions of the nudist camp films of the 1950s. Other films, sometimes known as "roughies," included heavy doses of sex-related violence, usually against women. Among the first of these films to appear was *Lorna* (1964), directed by Russ Meyer, who would go on to become the most widely known director of sexploitation films. Meyer had also pioneered in the nudie cuties with *The Immoral Mr. Teas* (1959), while the success of his films ultimately allowed him to move into higher-budget sexploitation films such as *Faster, Pussycat! Kill! Kill!* (1965) and *Vixen!* (1968), which have become **cult** classics.

Sexploitation films gained a larger audience and even moved into some mainstream theaters by the end of the 1960s, enabling Meyer to make *Beyond the Valley of the Dolls* (1970) for **Twentieth Century Fox**. Scripted by noted film critic **Roger Ebert**, who had become an admirer of the **satirical** aspects of Meyer's films, as well as their tendency toward a sort of low-brow surrealism, this film nevertheless gained an X rating (equivalent to the later NC-17) and remained in the sexpoitation mode. Ebert also scripted Meyer's later sexploitation films *Up!* (1976) and *Beneath the Valley of the Ultra-Vixens* (1979). By this time, however, Meyer's career as a director had run its course, as had the sexploitation film itself, replaced on one end of the spectrum by the exploration of more sexual material in mainstream films and on the other end of the spectrum by pornographic films, which explored more explicit and hard-core sexual material than the sexploitation films ever had.

**SHEARER, NORMA (1902–1983).** The Canadian-born Norma Shearer rose to major stardom in **silent film** in the 1920s and continued to be a well-known actress until her retirement in 1942. Though she originally played wholesome roles, her career took an important turn with her starring role in *The Divorcée* (1930), after which she was often cast as a sophisticated (and sexually liberated) woman of the world. Shearer won the 1930 **Academy Award** for Best Actress for that film, in a year in which she was also nominated in that category for *Their Own Desire* (1929). She followed with another such nomination for *A Free Soul* (1931).

Married to **Irving G. Thalberg** from 1927 until his death in 1936, Shearer was a major force in the film industry during those years and for several years afterward. Ultimately, she became best known for her starring roles in several "prestige" films later in the 1930s, including *The Barretts of Wimpole Street* (1934), **George Cukor**'s *Romeo and Juliet* (1936), and *Marie Antoinette* (1938), again receiving **Oscar** nominations for Best Actress for those three films, and *The Women* (1939). In 1939, she starred alongside **Joan Crawford** and Rosaline Russell in Cukor's *The Women*. Subsequently, she starred in **Mervyn LeRoy**'s anti-Nazi film *The Escape* (1940) and reunited with Cukor for *Her Cardboard Lover* (1942).

Shearer sank into relative obscurity after her retirement from film, but her reputation has enjoyed a resurgence in recent years, when she has come to be seen as a feminist pioneer whose roles provided strong models for young women.

**SHORE, HOWARD (1946– ).** The Canadian Howard Shore is a prominent composer of **music** for films, known primarily for his work with Canadian director David Cronenberg and for composing the scores for the *Lord of the*

*Rings* **trilogy.** Shore won **Academy Awards** for Best Score for both the first and the third entries in that trilogy: *The Fellowship of the Ring* (2001) and *The Return of the King* (2003). He also won an **Oscar** for Best Song from co-writing the song "Into the West," which appeared in the latter film.

Shore also received a **Golden Globe** award for Best Score for *The Return of the King* and followed it with another for *The Aviator* (2004), making him the first composer to win that award in consecutive years. Among the dozens of other films for which Shore has composed the music are *Big* (1988), *The Silence of the Lambs* (1991), *Philadelphia* (1993), *Ed Wood* (1994), *Dogma* (1999), *High Fidelity* (2000), *The Departed* (2006), and *The Twilight Saga: Eclipse* (2010).

Shore has also worked widely as a composer of concert music, touring conductor, and on television, where his most prominent role was as musical director of *Saturday Night Live* from 1975 to 1980, during which he appeared in a number of sketches, most often as the leader of the group "Howard Shore and His All-Nurse Band."

**SHOW BUSINESS FILMS.** Since the very beginnings of American film, one of its favorite subjects has been the film business itself and, by extension, show business as a whole. An early example was Buster Keaton's *Sherlock, Jr.* (1924), in which Keaton's character steps from the world of reality into the world of film, but only in his dreams. The genre of films about the film industry was already well established in the 1920s, when such **silent films** as James Cruze's *Hollywood* (1923) and **King Vidor**'s *Show People* (1928) offered audiences a view of the world behind the camera, increasing the sense of realism with numerous cameos by well-known personages from the film industry. These films, along with the early sound film *Movie Crazy* (1932), starring silent-screen legend **Harold Lloyd**, also poke good-natured fun at both the film industry and the public's fascination with it.

Many early sound films were either **musicals** or rather direct adaptations of stage plays, and a number of the show business films of the 1930s were explicitly about the staging of plays or musicals, ranging from the elaborately staged *Gold Diggers of 1933* (1933) to the more modest *Babes in Arms* (1939), featuring a young **Mickey Rooney** and **Judy Garland** as two young performers struggling to stage their own show. Meanwhile, *A Star Is Born* (1937) was an effective **satire** of the exploitation of a talented young and upcoming performer by the Hollywood star-making machine.

This satire was so effective that the film was remade in both 1954 and 1976, with a third remake rumored to be in the works for a 2012 release. Meanwhile, a certain amount of satire (usually gentle) has been typical of show business films since the 1930s. Thus, **Preston Sturges**'s *Sullivan's*

*Travels* (1942) pokes some fun at Hollywood's tendency toward light, escapist entertainment during the dark days of the Depression but ultimately concludes that such entertainment is valuable in helping audiences through hard times. *All about Eve* (1950) is more serious in its indictment of the ambition and backbiting that are often necessary for success in show business, but focuses on the stage rather than film.

Also in 1950, **Nicholas Ray**'s *In a Lonely Place* was a genuinely dark postwar film about Hollywood, but it contains very little real criticism of the film industry. The unhappy outcome of this film, in fact, derives almost exclusively from the personal demons of protagonist Dixon Steele (**Humphrey Bogart**), a bitter and violent screenwriter. That same year, one of the greatest show business films, **Billy Wilder**'s *Sunset Blvd.*, acknowledged the tragedies that can occur when once-famous celebrities lose their fame due to changing circumstances such as the shift from silent to sound film. Ultimately, though, *Sunset Blvd.* again concludes that filmmakers create wonderful worlds of the imagination, whatever the collateral damage.

***Singin' in the Rain*** (1952) also explores the fallout of the transition to sound in the film industry, but in a lighter mode. One of the great musicals of all time, this film calls attention to the element of illusion that informs film as a medium; its central plot line concerns an attempt to deceive audiences by secretly substituting the voice of another actress for that of a popular silent screen star who is attempting to make the transition to talkies but has an awful voice. That same year saw a more serious satire in **Vincente Minnelli**'s much respected *The Bad and the Beautiful* (1952). Here, an actress, director, and screenwriter, who have all formerly worked for fallen film mogul Jonathan Shields (**Kirk Douglas**), have turned their backs on him because his ruthless drive to succeed has caused him to betray them all, one by one. Yet, in the course of the film, which narrates these perceived betrayals in flashback, all of the characters come to realize that their association with Shields has been beneficial to their lives and their careers. He thus emerges as a sort of capitalist hero, making tough decisions that his employees might resent at the time but that ultimately work to the advantage of all. **Robert Aldrich**'s *The Big Knife* (1955), based on a play by **Clifford Odets**, is a particular dark commentary on the toll that show business can take on those who work in it, focusing on a prominent film actor who is ultimately driven to suicide by personal and professional pressures.

By the late 1950s, Hollywood was beginning to focus its satire on television, as films such as *Will Success Spoil Rock Hunter?* (1957) and **Elia Kazan**'s *A Face in the Crowd* (1957) made the new medium look either ridiculous or sinister. Numerous films about television have followed, with a special focus on television news. Sidney Lumet's *Network* (1976), for example, is bitterly critical of the tendency of television to turn news into entertainment. Later developments in the American media have made *Network* seem prescient. Thus, in **Gus Van Sant**'s *To Die For* (1995), television news has been thoroughly converted into show business, and television journalists are big-time media stars. Meanwhile, television coverage turns a minor hostage situation into a media spectacle in Costa-Gavras's *Mad City* (1997), leading to tragedy.

A particularly scathing indictment of the media culture of the 1990s can be found in **Oliver Stone**'s *Natural Born Killers* (1994), which includes television news in a sweeping critique of contemporary American culture and in particular that culture's fascination with violence. Meanwhile, if such films suggested the corruption of the American media by the 1990s, another film of the same year, **Robert Redford**'s *Quiz Show*, reminded audiences that television was already corrupt even in the simpler days of the 1950s. On the other hand, **George Clooney**'s *Good Night, and Good Luck* (2005) would present pioneering 1950s television newsman Edward R. Murrow in a positive light.

The most important film about filmmaking of the 1960s was not an American film, though Federico Fellini's Italian classic *8 1/2* (1963) has influenced numerous subsequent American films, including **Woody Allen**'s *Stardust Memories* (1981), which is essentially a reinscription of *8 1/2* but with Allen's biography substituted for Fellini's as a central source of material. In the meantime, **Robert Altman** produced one of the most important show business films with *Nashville* (1975), though that film has implications that go well beyond the country **music** industry that is its central focus. In addition, Altman followed with a satirical treatment of the entire ethos of fame and spectacle that informs American show business with *Buffalo Bill and the Indians* (1976).

Indeed, many of Altman's films are self-conscious revisions of specific film genres. From the 1970s on, in fact, whether it be attributed to **postmodernism** or simply to the growing prominence of directors and others trained in film schools, American film came to be informed more and more by examinations of its own legacies, so that many films from that time forward have been implicitly about filmmaking and the film industry, even if they were not explicitly so. Meanwhile, with *The Player* (1992), Altman produced one of the most effective overt satires of the film industry, helping, along with **Joel and Ethan Coen**'s *Barton Fink* from the previous year, to trigger a new cycle of films about Hollywood.

Subsequent films about the film industry have included **biopics** about particularly colorful or important figures within the film industry, such as *Chaplin* (1992) and *Ed Wood* (1994), while satires of Hollywood and its role in American society have included such films as *Swimming with Sharks*

(1994), *Wag the Dog* (1997), and Allen's *Hollywood Ending* (2002). Also in this category is **David Mamet**'s *State and Main* (2000), which satirically explores the comic impact of the arrival of a Hollywood film crew on a typical American small town. **John Waters**'s *Cecil B. Demented* (2000), takes it for granted that mainstream Hollywood films are little more than insipid, commercialized pablum designed for mindless consumption by infantile audiences. Starting from this premise, Waters then turns his satirical focus not on the products of Hollywood studios but on the outlaw underground cinema of which he himself is one of the better known practitioners.

The films of David Lynch, which are always to an extent about the process of filmmaking, have also included explicit treatments of the Hollywood film industry in *Mulholland Drive* (2001) and *Inland Empire* (2006). Meanwhile, the work of **Quentin Tarantino** is essentially compilations of motifs seen before in film, while he follows Altman in often basing his films on specific genres, though Tarantino tends to celebrate the genres he draws upon, which have often received relatively little critical acclaim, such as Hong Kong martial arts films, spaghetti **Westerns**, and ultraviolent "grindhouse" movies. And several recent films have been explicitly about even more lowly regarded movies, as in the treatment of the pornographic film industry in *Boogie Nights* (1997), *Wonderland* (2003), and *Southland Tales* (2006).

Popular music, especially rock music, has been the topic of numerous films as well. The films of **Elvis Presley**, for example, were typically little more than showcases for his music. Among the more prominent films about real-life rock stars are *The Buddy Holly Story* (1977; *La Bamba* (1987), about Richie Valens; and **Oliver Stone**'s *The Doors* (1991). Cameron Crowe's *Almost Famous* (2000) explores the world and culture of rock music through a thinly fictionalized account of its director's days as a teenage rock music journalist. In addition, **documentaries** about rock music, often based on specific concerts or festivals, have often produced interesting results, as in the cases of *Monterey Pop* (1968), *Gimme Shelter* (1970), *Woodstock* (1970), and **Martin Scorsese**'s *The Last Waltz* (1978).

Meanwhile, *The Rutles—All You Need Is Cash* (1978) is a satirical mockumentary about a fictional rock group based rather transparently on the Beatles. In a similar vein is the **cult** classic rock mockumentary *This Is Spinal Tap* (1984), which follows a fictional rock group through their various travails. Meanwhile, fictional rock stars have also been the subject of numerous films. Straight fictional accounts of the rock music scene range from the 1976 remake of *A Star Is Born*, to *That Thing You Do!* (1996), to *Rock Star* (2001). Also, of note is the fictional *Across the Universe* (2007) that relates the culture of the 1960s largely through the music of the Beatles, which provides its soundtrack.

**SHYAMALAN, M. NIGHT (1970– ).** Born in Pondicherry, India, the son of two Indian medical doctors, M. Night Shyamalan grew up in Penn Valley, Pennsylvania, a suburb of Philadelphia. He had written and directed two small, **independent films** when he finally made his way into the Hollywood spotlight in 1999 as the co-writer of *Stuart Little* and as the writer and director of the supernatural thriller *The Sixth Sense*, a huge hit that became one of the most talked-about films of the year. That film established his reputation as a maker of supernaturally themed films with twist endings, a reputation much of his subsequent work has reinforced. Shyamalan followed as the writer, director, and producer of *Unbreakable* (2000), a highly unusual **superhero** narrative that contains a number of **science fiction** elements. In 2002, he moved fully into science fiction territory as the writer, director, and producer of *Signs*, an alien-invasion narrative with strong religious resonances. *The Village* (2004) and *Lady in the Water* (2006), two lackluster supernatural thrillers followed, but Shyamalan again drew considerable attention (though lukewarm reviews) with *The Happening* (2008), an unusual environmentalist tale in which the Earth itself appears to issue a warning to the human race that they had better start taking better care of their environment lest the environment be forced to defend itself against them. He followed with an action-oriented fantasy, *The Last Airbender* (2010); a live-action film (the first installment of a planned trilogy) based on the anime-influenced American animated television series *Avatar: The Last Airbender*.

**SIEGEL, DON (1912–1991).** The Cambridge-educated Donald Siegel began his work in film in the montage department at **Warner Bros.**, then moved into directing in 1945, mostly in low-budget genre films, including **film noir**, **Westerns**, and **science fiction**. Though known more as a craftsman than an artist, Siegel quickly developed a reputation for getting the most out of meager resources, and many of his early films are still well remembered. Meanwhile, though he continued to concentrate on relatively inexpensive genre films, he did eventually move into bigger-budget projects, especially in the 1970s.

Siegel's early films include such **film noirs** and crime dramas as *The Verdict* (1946), *The Big Steal* (1949), *Riot in Cell Block 11* (1954), and *Baby Face Nelson* (1957). He also directed such Westerns as *The Duel at Silver Creek* (1952) and *Flaming Star* (1960). However, easily the most important of his early films was the science fiction drama *Invasion of the Body Snatchers* (1956), widely regarded as one of the films that best captured the spirit of anxiety that pervaded American society in the 1950s.

In the 1960s, Siegel directed such notable crime dramas as *The Killers* (1964) and *Madigan* (1968). He then directed **Clint Eastwood** in *Coogan's Bluff* (1968), beginning an association with the actor that would be the richest collaboration of his career. Siegel subsequently directed Eastwood in the Western *Two Mules for Sister Sara* (1970) and the violent crime drama *Dirty Harry* (1971), two films that are classics of their kind. He also directed Eastwood in *The Beguiled* (1971) and *Escape from Alcatraz* (1979), meanwhile directing such notable films as *Charley Varrick* (1973) and *The Shootist* (1976). Siegel finished his career with a turn toward **comedy** in *Rough Cut* (1980) and *Jinxed!* (1982).

**SILENT FILM.** While attempts to develop technologies for the recording of synchronized soundtracks date back to the mid-1890s, technical problems with this approach dictated that, for the first four decades of its existence, American cinema was a primarily "silent" medium, in that films were generally distributed as visual images only, without integrated soundtracks. However, even these "silent" films were typically accompanied, in actual exhibition, by **music** that was performed live. Meanwhile, any dialogue or narrative exposition that was felt to be necessary to accompany silent films was supplied through the use of brief passages of onscreen text known as "intertitles." In general, however, silent film depended upon lighting and special photographic techniques to supply atmosphere and upon the gestures of its actors to convey emotion and personality.

Silent films were shot almost exclusively in black and white, though there were experiments with various techniques (including hand-painting) for adding localized color, while tinting for atmospheric effect was sometimes supplied by dipping the film in dyes. The vast majority of silent films were quickly made (often in a week or less) and were quite short in duration (perhaps only two to three minutes, though slightly longer films became common as time went on). Thus, Edwin S. Porter's *The Great Train Robbery* (1903), often considered the first American narrative film, was only 11 minutes long. Meanwhile, it is generally recognized that silent film moved forward dramatically as an art form with the early work of director **D. W. Griffith**, who became the principal director for the **Biograph Company**, subsequently directing nearly 500 short films for them before leaving the company in 1913 because of his commitment to making longer films, which they opposed.

Soon afterward, Griffith directed, for his own self-named company, *The Birth of a Nation* (1915), a three-hour-plus epic that was controversial for its racist content but that became easily the biggest box-office hit of the silent film era, demonstrating once and for all that audiences could and would sit through feature-length films. Griffith himself followed with the even more ambitious *Intolerance* a year later, but this elaborate and expensive work was a box-office failure that essentially ended Griffith's reign as the most successful director in the film business. Feature-length films, however, continued to grow in popularity and gradually became the dominant form in American film.

While Griffith worked in a number of genres, he specialized in serious dramas; however, some of the most successful filmmakers of the silent era were devoted to **comedy**, often using broad forms of **slapstick** humor that could achieve their effects without the benefit of integrated sound. One of the most important pioneers in this sense was director **Mack Sennett**, who acted in and directed more than 300 silent film comedies. Ultimately, however, it was as a producer (of more than 1,100 films) and as an entrepreneur that Sennett is best remembered. For one thing, he gave starts to such illustrious figures as **Charles Chaplin** (probably the biggest individual star of the silent film era), Mabel Normand, **Gloria Swanson**, and **W. C. Fields**. For another, he helped to shape the film industry, founding his own **Keystone Studios** in 1912, building for it the first totally enclosed film stage and studio. In 1915, he joined the newly founded **Triangle Film Corporation** (along with Griffith and Thomas Ince), making Keystone a unit of that larger entity. In 1917, all three of these principles left Triangle, and Sennett founded the Mack Sennett Comedies Corporation. His short films remained popular through the 1920s, though the tide of history was against them and shorts were essentially rendered passé by the coming of sound, though Sennett did issue the first short talkie in 1928.

The experiences of pioneering filmmakers such as Sennett and Griffith as entrepreneurs indicate the extent to which the silent film era was a period of rapid evolution and innovation not only in the technology and aesthetics of filmmaking but also in the business of film, as efficient means needed to be found for financing, production, distribution, and exhibition of films. Indeed, film had begun very much as a business, with **Thomas Edison**, who viewed the new medium primarily as a profit-making enterprise, being the key driving force behind its early development. By the time Sennett and Griffith founded their own companies in the 1910s, artists were already feeling restricted by the emphasis placed on profits by their corporate bosses and were seeking means of gaining greater creative control over their work.

Perhaps the most important artist-driven company of the silent era was **United Artists**, founded by Griffith, Chaplin, **Douglas Fairbanks**, and **Mary Pickford**, though even this formidable alliance of artists was ultimately unable to compete successfully against the larger corporate interests that eventually emerged as Hollywood's **major studios**. Part of this result had to do with the increasing growth of feature-length films, which made films much more expensive to produce and which made it very advantageous to have well-organized systems in place for the distribution of films, including through extensive studio-owned theater chains, which remained a dominant factor in the film business until the end of the 1940s.

The growth of features greatly limited the opportunities for experimentation that had been offered by the relatively quick and inexpensive short films of earlier times. Thus, the film business of the 1920s came to be dominated by such major features as Griffith's *Way Down East* (1920), *Ben-Hur* (1925), and **King Vidor**'s *The Big Parade* (1925) and *The Crowd* (1928). Meanwhile, the growing global importance of American cinema was signaled by the fact that numerous important European directors were lured to Hollywood to work, producing such masterworks as **F. W. Murnau**'s *Sunrise* (1927). Meanwhile, top stars of the silent shorts transitioned into features with such films as *Sparrows* (1926), and *My Best Girl* (1927), both starring Mary Pickford.

Even Chaplin, a master of the short form, moved into features with *The Kid* in 1921, ultimately producing two classic silent features, *The Gold Rush* (1925) and **City Lights** (1931). The latter was a sort of last-ditch effort to preserve the silent film form, which had by this time essentially been supplanted by the new sound films, generally acknowledged to have begun with *The Jazz Singer* (1927). Indeed, sound film became such a force after the success of that film that several silent films already in production—including the classic *All Quiet on the Western Front* (1930)—were scrapped and remade as sound films.

**SIMMONS, JEAN (1929–2010).** Born in London, Jean Simmons got her start as a teenage actress in Great Britain, appearing in a number of roles, including those of the young Estella in *Great Expectations* (1946) and of Ophelia in **Laurence Oliver**'s *Hamlet* (1948). The latter role won her an **Academy Award** nomination for Best Actress in a Supporting Role and gained the attention of Hollywood. In 1950, **Howard Hughes** bought Simmons's contract from British producer Otto Rank and Simmons soon came to Hollywood to work for Hughes's **RKO Pictures**. There, she made several films, including a performance in **Otto Preminger**'s **film noir** *Angel Face* (1952) that remains one of her best-known roles.

Freed from her contract with RKO via a lawsuit, Simmons appeared in a number of important films in the coming years, including *The Robe* (1953), *Guys and Dolls* (1955), *The Big Country* (1958), *Elmer Gantry* (1960), and *Spartacus* (1960). Her appearances in film diminished in the 1950s, though she did receive an **Oscar** nomination for Best Actress in a Leading Role for her performance in *The Happy Ending* (1969).

From that point forward, Simmons appeared primarily on television and the stage, though she did occasionally appear in film, including a late role in the British film *Shadows in the Sun* (2009).

**SIMON, NEIL (1927– ).** Neil Simon was one of Broadway's most successful playwrights from the early 1960s to the 1990s. He also wrote widely for television in the 1960s and eventually became particularly well known for the film adaptations of his plays, including films that he himself scripted. Simon's play *Come Blow Your Horn* was adapted to film with a script by Norman Lear in 1963. Simon himself scripted the film adaptations of his plays *Barefoot in the Park* (1967) and *The Odd Couple* (1968), establishing himself as an important presence in Hollywood.

Simon received an **Academy Award** nomination for Best Adapted Screenplay for *The Odd Couple* and would receive a similar nomination for his adaptations of his plays *The Sunshine Boys* (1975) and *California Suite* (1978). In a reversal of his usual procedure, he received an **Oscar** nomination for Best Original Screenplay for *The Goodbye Girl* (1977), then later adapted that film to Broadway.

Other original screenplays written by Simon include those for *The Out of Towners* (1970), *The Heartbreak Kid* (1972), *Murder by Death* (1976), *The Cheap Detective* (1978), *Seems Like Old Times* (1980), *Max Dugan Returns* (1983), and *The Odd Couple II* (1998). Other Simon plays that he himself adapted to the screen include *Plaza Suite* (1971), *The Prisoner of Second Avenue* (1975), *I Ought to Be in Pictures* (1982), *Brighton Beach Memoirs* (1986), and *Lost in Yonkers* (1993).

**SINGIN' IN THE RAIN.** Named the fifth greatest film of all time in a 2007 poll conducted by the **American Film Institute** (AFI), *Singin' in the Rain* (dir. **Gene Kelly** and **Stanley Donen**, 1952) is one of Hollywood's best-loved **musicals**, featuring some of its most memorable musical scenes, as in the film's title number, in which star and co-director Gene Kelly literally sings and dances in the rain. Featuring a number of elaborate production numbers, *Singin' in the Rain* is in many ways reminiscent of the **Busby Berkeley** musicals of the 1930s. However, *Singin' in the Rain* is very much a film about the making of a film, demonstrating a new self-consciousness in the American film industry that would never have been found in a film of the 1930s.

The film deals specifically with the coming of the talkies, perhaps the single most significant event in the history of the American cinema. It centers on the transition of **silent film** stars Don Lockwood (Kelly) and Lina Lamont (Jean Hagen) into sound, a transition that is complicated by the fact that Lamont has a horrible, grating voice that forces the studio to make sure that she never actually speaks in public, lest her glamorous (and highly profitable) image be destroyed. Meanwhile, when Lockwood and Lamont make their first talkie, Lamont's speaking and singing voice has to be dubbed over by that of aspiring young actress Kathy Selden (**Debbie Reynolds**).

After numerous complications, Selden is revealed as the voice behind Lamont, and her own career is launched. Meanwhile, she and Lockwood seem poised to live together happily ever after in a quintessential Hollywood happy ending that reinforces the film's classic song-and-dance numbers. On the other hand, the theme of Hollywood trickery runs throughout the film, from the studio's various fake publicity campaigns, to Lockwood's manufactured aristocratic background, to the dubbing, to Lockwood's courtship of Selden in an empty studio where he uses various bits of Hollywood illusion to create a romantic mood. Though treated as **comedy**, the film's acknowledgment that Hollywood tends to deceive its audiences in a variety of ways provides a surprisingly serious undercurrent that reflects the fundamental tensions that informed the American film industry in the early 1950s. *See also* SHOW BUSINESS FILMS.

**SINGLETON, JOHN (1968– ).** John Singleton is one of the most important African American filmmakers of his generation. After studying film at the University of Southern California, he honed his craft making **music** videos, then burst onto the Hollywood scene as the writer and director of *Boyz n the Hood* (1991), a gripping inner-city drama that won him **Academy Award** nominations for Best Director and Best Screenplay. He has since become known for his depiction of inner-city life (especially in Los Angeles) in films such as *Poetic Justice* (1993), *Higher Learning* (1995), and *Baby Boy* (2001), which he wrote directed and produced.

Singleton moved in a slightly different direction with *Rosewood* (1997), a historical drama about a racist massacre in Florida in 1932, which he only directed. In 2000, he moved in a more commercial direction as the writer, director, and producer of the **blaxploitation** classic *Shaft* (2000). He went back to directing only with *2 Fast 2 Furious* (2003) and *Four Brothers* (2005), which again showed greater versatility. He has not made a feature film since that time, but has been named as the director of the upcoming **superhero** movie *Luke Cage*, scheduled for release in 2011.

**SIODMAK, ROBERT (1900–1973).** The German-born Robert Siodmak was one of the key Hollywood directors of the 1940s. After a successful early career in German film, he fled from the Nazis, first to Paris and then to the United States, where he resumed his career as a filmmaker. His first American film was the **B-movie comedy** *West Point Widow* (1941). He continued to direct low-budget films over the next several years, including the **horror** film *Son of Dracula* (1943). With *Phantom Lady* (1944), he moved into **film noir**, a genre on which he would place an indelible stamp, following with such films as *Christmas Holiday* (1944) and the noir classic *The Killers* (1946), which earned him his only **Academy Award** nomination for Best Direction.

*The Dark Mirror* (1946), *Cry of the City* (1948), *Criss Cross* (1949), and *The File on Thelma Jordan* (1950) were also important film noirs directed by Siodmak. His final noir film in Hollywood, *Deported* (1950), was unsuccessful, as was his turn to adventure with *The Crimson Pirate* (1952). Siodmak then returned to Germany and worked in Europe through most of the remainder of his career, achieving success with such films as *Die Ratten* (1955, *The Rats*) and *Nachts, wenn der Teufel kam* (1957, *The Devil Strikes at Night*). He returned to Hollywood to direct one last film there, the **biopic** *Custer of the West* (1967).

**SIRK, DOUGLAS (1900–1987).** Douglas Sirk began his film career in his native Germany, then fled the Nazis, arriving in the United States to direct his first American film, the anti-Nazi thriller *Hitler's Madman* (1943). He directed several more films in the 1940s, then made his most important contributions in the 1950s, directing a series of films that achieved commercial success but were generally dismissed by critics as unimportant melodramas with more style than substance. However, his work would ultimately be reassessed by critics (especially in France and Great Britain) as some of the finest films of the decade. Marxist critics, for example, focused on the irony that underlies his films, while Sirk's focus on female characters in domestic settings also brought him renewed attention from feminist critics in the 1970s and beyond.

Among Sirk's more successful films of the 1950s were *Magnificent Obsession* (1954), *All That Heaven Allows* (1955), *Written on the Wind* (1956), *There's Always Tomorrow* (1956), and *Imitation of Life* (1959). Then, at the height of his popularity, Sirk returned to Europe and retired from filmmaking, though he did return to direct several short German films in the 1970s.

**SLAPSTICK.** Slapstick is a broad form of physical **comedy** in which characters humorously experience exaggerated (and often absurd) violence. It was a dominant form of American silent comedy, as its physical nature was well suited to that largely nonverbal form. The form evolved from centuries-old stage traditions such as the *Commedia dell'arte* and was refined into a cinematic art by **silent film** comedians such as **Charles Chaplin**, **Buster Keaton**, and the Keystone Kops. However, it has continued to be a major form of humor in American film until the present day.

In the era of sound film, performers such as the Three Stooges have relied primarily on slapstick to achieve comic effects in their films. Other comic forms, such as **anarchic comedy** and **screwball comedy** also often include slapstick as part of their comic arsenals, though slapstick has, over the years, fallen somewhat into disrepute as an unsophisticated way to get cheap laughs.

Thus, in recent feature films it has been seen primarily in intentionally low-brow farcical films. However, from the 1940s onward, the most important uses of slapstick have been in **animated films**, especially in short cartoons such as the *Tom and Jerry* series, from **Metro-Goldwyn-Mayer** (MGM). Cartoon characters (who can emerge unscathed from any amount of mayhem) are perfect objects for the violence of slapstick comedy.

**SMITH, WILL (1968– ).** After an early career as a rapper (the "Fresh Prince" of "DJ Jazzy Jeff and the Fresh Prince"), Will Smith had a successful stint as a television actor on the sitcom *The Fresh Prince of Bel-Air* (1990–1996), then moved into film, ultimately becoming one of the top box-office draws of his generation. After a couple of minor film appearances, Smith drew considerable critical approval for his performance in *Six Degrees of Separation* (1993), then moved into more commercial projects with *Bad Boys* (1995). By the time of his performance as a wise-cracking fighter pilot in the **science fiction** blockbuster *Independence Day* (1996), he had become a top Hollywood star.

Smith followed with another major hit with the science fiction **comedy** *Men in Black* (1997), then moved into the realm of **action films** with *Enemy of the State* (1998) and the tongue-in-cheek **Western** *Wild, Wild West* (1999). The latter was an infamous failure both commercially and critically. *The Legend of Bagger Vance* (2000) was also unsuccessful, but Smith achieved his greatest critical recognition yet in the title role in the **biopic** *Ali* (2001), which won him an **Academy Award** nomination for Best Actor.

Smith next starred in two successful sequels, *Men in Black II* (2002) and *Bad Boys II* (2003), then again achieved box-office success in science fiction with the action- and effects-driven *I, Robot* (2004). *Hitch* (2005) was a moderately successful comedy, while the drama *The Pursuit of Happyness* (2006) won Smith another **Oscar** nomination for Best Actor. The postapocalyptic science fiction film *I Am Legend* (2007) and the unusual **superhero movie** *Hancock* (2008) were big commercial hits that solidified Smith's status as a box-office draw, while *Seven Pounds* (2008) was a return to smaller and more thoughtful drama.

**SNOW WHITE AND THE SEVEN DWARFS.** The first feature-length **animated film** in history, *Snow White and the Seven Dwarfs* (dir. David Hand, 1937) was a huge success that made **Walt Disney** a leading figure in **children's film** (especially animated film for children), even though his company remained relatively small through his lifetime. *Snow White* flew in the face of the conventional belief that animated films could not hold an audience for more than a few minutes. Meanwhile, it established many of the basic conventions of its genre, which would be dominated by the **Disney** Company for decades to come.

Based on a fairy tale but considerably simplifying and sanitizing its source material, *Snow White* makes heavy use of **music**, magic, animal characters, and **slapstick** violence, while purging its story of any hint of sexuality. It also features a relatively passive female protagonist who is a princess deprived of her proper place, then restored to that place through the intervention of an active male hero. Similar characteristics would remain central to most of Disney's films of the next three decades and would then return to prominence with the Disney renaissance that began at the end of the 1980s and extended through the 1990s.

*Snow White* received an **Academy Award** nomination for Best Music, while Disney himself was given an honorary **Oscar** to signify the importance of the film as a cinematic innovation. In a 2008 poll conducted by the **American Film Institute** (AFI), it was named the greatest animated film of all time.

**SODERBERGH, STEVEN (1963– ).** Steven Soderbergh is an American director and producer who first gained widespread attention with the **independent film** *Sex, Lies, and Videotape* (1989), which he wrote and directed. He also directed such big-budget mainstream films as *Out of Sight* (1998), *Traffic* (2000), *Erin Brockovich* (2000), and *Ocean's Eleven* (2001) and its two sequels. However, despite such successes, he has maintained an interest in independent, noncommercial projects, directing such films as *Kafka* (1991), *Schizopolis* (1993), *Underneath* (1995), *Full Frontal* (2002), *Bubble* (2005), the two-part *Che* (2008, a **biopic** about revolutionary Ernesto "Che" Guevara), and *The Informant!* (2009). Other films directed by Soderbergh, such as *King of the Hill* (1993) and *The Limey* (1999), seemed aimed at larger audiences but did not succeed commercially.

Throughout his career, Soderbergh has shown a special interest in **neo-noir** filmmaking and in innovative filmmaking technologies, such as the use of digital video, rather than film. This interest in technology has sometimes meshed with an interest in **science fiction**. In 2002, he wrote and directed the remake of the classic Soviet film *Solaris*. He also executive produced the experimental green-screen film *Able Edwards* (2004), a sort of science fiction remake of ***Citizen Kane***, and the innovative *A Scanner Darkly* (2006), based on a novel by Philip K. Dick.

Soderbergh has also produced most of the films he has directed, as well as producing or executive producing a number of films directed by others. The latter include *Suture* (1993), *Pleasantville* (1998); *Far from Heaven* (2002); *Keane* (2004); *Syriana* (2005); *Good Night, and Good Luck* (2005), *Michael Clayton* (2007); and *Solitary Man* (2009).

Soderbergh received **Academy Award** nominations for Best Director for *Sex, Lies, and Videotape* and *Erin Brockovich*, then won that award for *Traffic*.

*SOME LIKE IT HOT.* Named the funniest movie of all time in a 2000 poll conducted by the **American Film Institute** (AFI), *Some Like It Hot* (dir. **Billy Wilder**, 1959) is a sort of combination of the **film noir** (of which director Billy Wilder was a leading practitioner) and the **screwball comedy**. The result is not only highly entertaining but also poses important questions about the nature of gender as a performance, rather than a biological imperative.

The plot of *Some Like It Hot* is simple: two struggling musicians, Jerry and Joe (played by **Jack Lemmon** and **Tony Curtis**, respectively), witness a gangland slaying in Chicago, then flee the mob by posing as women and joining an all-woman band that is headed for Florida. On the train to Florida, they meet and become smitten by the band's sultry vocalist, "Sugar Kane" (played by **Marilyn Monroe**). Meanwhile, the gangsters from Chicago coincidentally arrive at the same Florida hotel where the band is staying (and playing). To complicate matters further, millionaire Osgood Fielding III (Joe E. Brown) falls in love with Jerry's female alter ego, "Daphne."

Predictably, given that the film is a **comedy**, Joe and Jerry escape the gangsters, while love blooms, with Joe and Sugar together at the end of the film. The film's most interesting twist, however, occurs when Fielding decides to go ahead with his plans to marry "Daphne," despite the fact that he discovers Jerry's true identity. Perhaps because of its potentially controversial subject matter, *Some Like It Hot* did not receive an **Academy Award** nomination, though it did receive a total of six **Oscar** nominations in such major categories as Best Director, Best Screenplay (Wilder and I. A. L. Diamond) and Best Actor in a Leading Role (Lemmon). However, it won the Oscar only for Orry-Kelly's costume design.

**SONY PICTURES ENTERTAINMENT.** Sony Pictures Entertainment is a division of the Japanese technology and media conglomerate Sony, involved in the production and distribution of films and television programming. Sony Pictures came into being when Sony acquired **Columbia Pictures** in 1989. While maintaining the Columbia brand and logo, Sony has since expanded its holdings in the entertainment industry to become one of Hollywood's **major studios**, producing "**independent films**" under the Sony Pictures Classics label and merging Columbia Pictures with TriStar Pictures in 1998 to form the Columbia TriStar Motion Picture Group. Sony also continues to produce television programming under Columbia's "Screen Gems" label, as well as specialty and low-budget films under the Screen Gems label, as well as the Destination Films and Triumph Film labels.

**SPACEK, SISSY (1949– ).** Sissy Spacek is one of the most respected American film actresses of her generation. After several minor roles, mostly on television, she gained attention with her lead role in **Terrence Malick**'s *Badlands* (1973), then received an **Academy Award** nomination for Best Actress in a Leading Role for her performance in **Brian De Palma**'s *Carrie* (1976). She followed with a solid performance in **Robert Altman**'s *3 Women* (1977), then won the **Oscar** for Best Actress for her performance as Loretta Lynn in the **biopic** *Coal Miner's Daughter* (1980).

Spacek's career was at its peak in the 1980s, though she withdrew from acting in the last few years of the decade to raise her children on a farm. By this time, however, she had received Oscar nominations for her performances in the dramas *Missing* (1982), *The River* (1984), and *Crimes of the Heart* (1986). She returned to acting in the 1990s, when she made important appearances in such films as *JFK* (1991), *Affliction* (1997), and *The Straight Story* (1999), while making several appearances on television as well.

Transitioning gracefully into more mature roles, Spacek continued to make important film appearances through her fifties. She received her sixth Oscar nomination for Best Actress for *In the Bedroom* (2001) and has also appeared in such films as *Nine Lives* (2005), *North Country* (2005), *Lake City* (2008), and *Four Christmases* (2008).

*SPARTACUS.* *Spartacus* (dir. **Stanley Kubrick**, 1953) is an important film, both because of its own merit as a work of cinematic art and because of the key role it played in breaking the Hollywood **blacklist** by openly employing blacklist writer **Dalton Trumbo**, a member of the **Hollywood Ten**, to write the screenplay. Meanwhile, the use of Trumbo was appropriate both because the film is explicitly about resistance to tyranny and because it was based on a 1951 novel by leftist writer Howard Fast, written mostly while Fast was in prison for his political beliefs.

Both the film and the novel of *Spartacus* are based on a real historical event, a famous rebellion, ending in 71 BC, in which the gladiator Spartacus led a rebel army composed of slaves and other gladiators in a two-year war against the power of Rome. While ultimately unsuccessful, this rebellion would long stand as a source of inspiration for the left, as when the communist rebels who nearly took control of the German government under the leadership of Rosa Luxemburg and Karl Liebknecht in 1919 referred to themselves as "Spartacists." Moreover, like the novel, the film clearly suggests parallels between Roman slavery and American slavery, while also indicating parallels between the Roman exploitation of slave labor and the exploitation of proletarians in modern capitalist America.

Nevertheless, *Spartacus* is not really a radical film. For one thing, it was an extremely expensive film that had to seek a mass audience in order to recover its production costs. In its attempt to attract and please such an audience, it mutes its political message, while making a number of concessions to the conventions of Hollywood cinema. Spartacus (played by **Kirk Douglas**, who was also the film's executive producer) espouses a personal ideology that sounds suspiciously similar to Jeffersonian democracy, while the film pays an excessive amount of attention to Hollywood motifs such as Spartacus's romance with the former slave Varinia (**Jean Simmons**). In addition, the film, a genuine epic with a consistent tone of grandeur, sometimes seems to get carried away with its own status as gorgeous spectacle. But the very splendor of the film makes it unique among left-leaning works of the American cinema, which have seldom had access to the budgets required to produce such a grand epic.

*Spartacus* is a long, epic film that gives audiences a view of numerous aspects of Roman society. It is probably best remembered, however, for its ending, in which Marcus Licinius Crassus (**Laurence Olivier**), the first consul of Rome and commander-in-chief of the Roman armies, defeats the rebel army and searches among the dead and the prisoners, hoping to identify Spartacus. In the process, he offers a reprieve from crucifixion for all of the prisoners if they will identify Spartacus. Spartacus comes forward and cries, "I am Spartacus!" But then another voice cries out the same, and eventually all of the prisoners proclaim themselves to be Spartacus, serving the double function of defeating Crassus's desires and making the point that, in a very real sense, they all *are* Spartacus, the symbol of their collective effort. Frustrated, Crassus orders them all crucified, saving a few for gladiatorial contests; soon the Appian Way is lined with the bodies of 6,000 crucified rebels hanging on crosses, Spartacus among them.

*Spartacus* was nominated for six **Academy Awards** though it was not nominated for Best Film, Best Screenplay, or Best Director; it won in four of the nominated categories, including Best Color Cinematography. The film was re-released in a significantly abridged form in 1967 but restored to its original length in 1991. Indeed, one scene cut from the original, in which Crassus makes homoerotic suggestions to Antoninus, then his slave, was added in the 1991 restoration.

**SPECIAL EFFECTS.** While film is primarily a photographic medium, a variety of techniques (generally grouped under the rubric of "special effects" to make items or actions appear on the screen that were not actually present during the filming. This is especially the case in certain genres, such as **action films** (which typically depict scenes too dangerous and violent to be enacted in reality) and **science fiction** and **fantasy** films (which typically include the depiction of technologies, settings, and creatures that do not exist in the real world).

The French magician and pioneering filmmaker Georges Méliès is usually credited with having created the first cinematic special effects, and his short film *Voyage dans la lune* (*A Trip to the Moon*), an adaptation of an 1867 novel by Jules Verne, is often considered the first science fiction film. In order to provide facilities for the production of the impressive special effects in his films, Méliès also constructed what is generally considered to be the first motion picture studio. His films employed a variety of techniques, such as double exposure and overexposure of negatives; running films backward; and fast, slow, and stop motion. He also achieved the first color effects in film, having color effects hand-painted, frame-by-frame, onto some of his films.

The special photographic techniques used by Méliès have been used, in one way or another, by filmmakers ever since that time. However, through much of cinema history, special visual effects have been achieved simply by creating and then filming physical models of the devices, settings, and creatures appearing in a film. Some of these physical techniques are as simple as employing painted backgrounds to create the illusion that the action being filmed is taking place in futuristic cities or distant planets. Techniques of back projection (projecting a moving image onto a screen behind the actors during filming) have similarly been used to create moving backgrounds. Makeup and costuming constitute an important part of this category of special effects, and any number of aliens and other science fiction or **horror** film creatures have been produced simply by placing human actors in elaborate makeup and costumes.

A particularly important breakthrough in physical special effects came in 1925, with the release of *The Lost World*, in which adventurers discover an enclave inhabited by a variety of exotic and prehistoric creatures that were produced by filming moveable physical models in stop-motion animation. These models were built by Willis O'Brien, who would employ similar techniques to even better effect in producing the landmark creatures of ***King Kong*** (1933). O'Brien used the same technologies in *Son of Kong* (1933) and *Mighty Joe Young* (1949), helping to establish further the viability of stop-motion animation as a technique. The technique of stop-motion animation then reached its pinnacle in the work of O'Brien's protégé, Ray Harryhausen, who became the dominant figure in the world of special effects for American science fiction and fantasy throughout the boom in sf cinema of the 1950s.

Harryhausen's elaborate models were used to create special effects, via the stop-motion technique that came to be known as Dynamation, for such films as *The Beast from 20,000 Fathoms* (1953), *It Came from Beneath the Sea* (1955), *20 Million Miles to Earth* (1957), and *First Men in the Moon*

(1964). Harryhausen's techniques had the advantage that they were relatively inexpensive. However, model-building for science fiction film reached a new level of sophistication (and costliness) with the release in 1968 of **Stanley Kubrick**'s *2001: A Space Odyssey*, which employs a variety of highly complex (and convincing) futuristic spacecraft and other futuristic hardware, including the representation of the interior and exterior of the spacecraft *Discovery* in unprecedented detail. Special photographic effects director Douglas Trumbull and other crew members achieved these effects partly through the simple expedient of building large, complex models, which they were able to do because of the availability of an unusually large budget for the film. However, a number of innovative strategies were also used to film these models, including the use of front-projection (aka retroflective matting), a technique that allowed for the creation of much more detailed and believable backgrounds than could have been achieved by painted backdrops or back-projection. This technique had never before been used so extensively but has been widely used ever since. It involves placing a separate scenery projector at right angles to the camera. A special mirror splits the light coming out of the projector, with about half of it reflected forward onto a backdrop, which then reflects the image back to the camera, where it is combined in-camera with the actual scene being filmed.

Special effects technology took a major step forward with the release of **George Lucas**'s *Star Wars* (1977), a film whose runaway success was largely due to the effectiveness of its special effects. *Star Wars* employed a number of complex models filmed using computer-controlled cameras. But it became best known for its pioneering use of blue-screen technologies, in which action was filmed in front of a blank blue screen, the background images to be filled in later. The blue screens of *Star Wars* would soon be replaced by the use of a **green screen**, but the basic technique remained the same and has since become a staple of sf film, largely supplanting the front-projection techniques of *2001: A Space Odyssey*.

*Star Wars* also made unprecedented use of **computer-generated imagery** (CGI), which had been pioneered in the films *Westworld* (1973) and *Future World* (1976). From that point forward, CGI became more and more dominant as a technique for the generation of special effects for film, with Lucas's own **Lucasfilm** and its special-effects arm **Industrial Light and Magic** (ILM) leading the way, producing effects not just for Lucas's *Star Wars* films but for hundreds of other films as well. As computer technology itself improved, the sophistication with which computer-generated special effects could be produced improved as well. This phenomenon led to the thematization of CGI itself in such films as the *Matrix*. It also spurred the spread of effects-dominated films from science fiction into action films such as the *Mission: Impossible* sequence, as well as to the production of such films as the *Lord of the Rings* **trilogy** at the beginning of the 21st century. **Superhero films** such as the *Spider-Man* sequence and the resurrected Batman sequence—*Batman Begins* (2005) and *The Dark Knight* (2008)—also received a substantial boost from the use of CGI in the new century.

In fact, CGI technologies had improved in the 1990s to the point that, in 1995, the new studio **Pixar** (a spin-off of Lucasfilm) produced an entire film (*Toy Story*) by computer animation. Pixar has gone on to become the industry leader in the production of computer-animated family films, while computer animation itself has largely supplanted traditional hand animation as a technique for producing such films.

By 2001, with the release of the big-budget joint U.S.–Japanese production *Final Fantasy: The Spirits Within*, sf filmmakers were fast approaching the ability to produce entire photorealistic films by computer animation, though the human characters in this film still look a bit more like video-game characters than real actors. For example, 2004 saw the release of such films as the Japanese *Casshern*, the French *Immortel (ad Vitam)*, and the American *Able Edwards* and *Sky Captain and the World of Tomorrow* (the latter actually a joint British–Italian–American production), all of which were shot entirely in front of green screens, using live actors, with all backgrounds added later by computer. *Immortel* even made extensive use of computer-generated human characters to supplement the characters portrayed by human actors, while *Sky Captain* used one computer-generated character (based on recorded images of legendary actor **Laurence Olivier**) as well. With the release of *WALL-E*, computer generation of science fictional backgrounds and hardware reached a new level of sophistication (though the film made no attempt at photorealistic depiction of human characters), suggesting a bright future for computer animation of sf films, a future that was already becoming a reality with the release of such films as **James Cameron**'s *Avatar*, one of the most complex, sophisticated (and expensive) films ever made.

**SPIELBERG, STEVEN (1946– ).** Steven Spielberg has been one of the most successful directors in American film since the release of the breakthrough blockbuster hit *Jaws* in 1975. Though his work spans many different genres, Steven Spielberg is arguably most important as a director of **science fiction** films, a film genre he entered with the alien-invasion classic *Close Encounters of the Third Kind* (1977), which he also wrote. This film, along with *Star Wars*, ushered in one of the most productive periods in the history of sf film, a period that also included *E.T.: The Extra-Terrestrial* (1982), which was both directed and produced by Spielberg. A huge hit, this film, following on Spielberg's success as the director of the first Indiana Jones film,

*Raiders of the Lost Ark* (1981), solidified his reputation as box-office gold. Though he produced or executive produced several more films with sf themes in the coming years, it was not until 1993, with the much-hyped release of *Jurassic Park*, that Spielberg returned to the helm as director of a science fiction film, though this one was a **monster movie**, a genre whose relation with science fiction is sometimes considered tenuous. Spielberg returned to all-out science fiction, both scripting and directing the Pinocchio-inspired robot story *Artificial Intelligence: AI* in 2001, completing a project originally conceived by **Stanley Kubrick**, who died before he was able to begin the film. Spielberg followed as the director of *Minority Report* (2002), a stylish futuristic thriller that was another major box-office hit. Spielberg's remake of *War of the Worlds* in 2005 was greeted with lukewarm response by critics, but was another commercial success. In 2008, Spielberg released his fourth Indiana Jones film, *Indiana Jones and the Kingdom of the Crystal Skull*, this time taking the archaeological adventurer into the realm of the alien-invasion narrative. Spielberg has also executive produced such high-profile sf film sequences as the *Back to the Future* films and the *Men in Black* films, directed by others.

Though he has also had some notable failures—such as *1941* (1979) and *Hook* (1991), Spielberg has also had considerable success outside the realm of science fiction, directing such important films as *The Color Purple* (1985), *Schindler's List* (1993), and *Saving Private Ryan* (1998), winning the **Academy Award** for Best Director for the latter two of these. He also received Best Director nominations for *Close Encounters of the Third Kind*, *Raiders of the Lost Ark*, and *E.T.*, while receiving Best Picture nominations as the producer of *E.T.*, *The Color Purple*, and *Munich* (2005), all of which he directed, and *Letters from Iwo Jima* (2006), directed by **Clint Eastwood**. Spielberg won the Best Picture **Oscar** as the producer of *Saving Private Ryan*.

Spielberg has been an important figure in the entertainment industry well beyond his work as a director, writer, and producer of individual films. His production company, **Amblin Entertainment**, has been involved not only in the production of Spielberg's own films, but in the production of numerous films directed by others. They have made especially important contributions in the area of family and **children's films**. Spielberg was also one of the founders of the **DreamWorks** studio in 1994 and has remained active in that enterprise ever since.

In addition to his work in film, Spielberg has been particularly important as an executive producer behind a number of television series. He joined with **Warner Bros.** to produce innovative updated cartoon series in the spirit of Warner's *LooneyToons* series, including *Tiny Toon Adventures* (1990–1995) and *Animaniacs* (1993–1998), as well as the *Animaniacs* spin-off *Pinky and* *the Brain* (1995–1998). Spielberg has also been the driving force behind such important television miniseries as *Band of Brothers* (2001) and *The Pacific* (2010).

**SPORTS MOVIES.** Competitive sports have provided subject matter for a number of important American films, both fictional and reality-based. Any number of popular American sports have provided such material, as in the football films *The Longest Yard* (1974), *Heaven Can Wait* (1978), and *Friday Night Lights* (2004), the basketball films *Hoosiers* (1986) and *He Got Game* (1998), and even the ice hockey films *Slap Shot* (1977) and *Miracle* (2004). Even golf has produced a number of notable films, including the classic **comedy** *Caddyshack* (1980) and *Tin Cup* (1996). There have also been successful sports **documentaries**, such as the much-acclaimed basketball film *Hoop Dreams* (1994).

Competitive sports have built-in plots and built-in heroes, so they are in many ways ideally suited as the material for films. Indeed, they feature such clear-cut oppositions that they have often been the basis for **children's films**, as in the cases of *The Bad News Bears* (baseball, 1976, remade in 2005), *The Mighty Ducks* (ice hockey, 1992), *Space Jam* (basketball, 1996), and *Like Mike* (basketball, 2002). In addition, sports are often seen to represent phenomena larger than themselves, and they can function that way in films as well. Particularly notable in this regard are films based on boxing and baseball, which function particularly often as parables of larger experiences in American life.

Boxing films have often had particularly strong political implications, presenting the competition within the sport as representative of the competitive ethos in American society as a whole, while presenting the often tragic lives of boxers within the business of boxing as representative of the exploitation of workers within capitalist society. An early examples of such films is *The Golden Boy* (1939), based on a play by leftist playwright **Clifford Odets**. Here, an aspiring concert violinist is driven to take up prizefighting to make his way amid the cutthroat world of American capitalism. The tragic ending of the play is converted into a happy ending in the film, but the film version nevertheless manages to make many of Odets's points about the difficulty of getting ahead in capitalist society without becoming ruthless or dishonest.

*The Golden Boy* is the forerunner of a number of important politically charged boxing films, especially those made in the mode of **film noir**, including *Body and Soul* (1947), *Champion* (1949), and *The Set-Up* (1949). In this context, one might also mention **Robert Rossen**'s *The Hustler* (1961), about the difficult life of a pool hustler, which has very much the texture of a boxing film.

*Rocky* (1976) went very much against the tragic grain of the boxing film tradition with an uplifting story about the triumph of an underdog (even though the title character, played by **Sylvester Stallone**, actually loses his most important fight). *Rocky* was a huge success that became an emblematic work of American popular culture, triggering a series of sequels: *Rocky II* (1979), *Rocky III* (1982), *Rocky IV* (1985), *Rocky V* (1990), and *Rocky Balboa* (2006), though in general each sequel was more lowly regarded than the one before. Meanwhile, **Clint Eastwood**'s *Million Dollar Baby* (2004) was a successful return to the tragic mode, with the twist that the boxer involved is a woman.

Other effective boxing films have been **biopics** based on the lives and careers of real boxers, such as *Somebody Up There Likes Me* (1956), about Rocky Graziano; **Martin Scorsese**'s highly regarded *Raging Bull* (1980), about Jake LaMotta; *The Hurricane* (1999), about Rubin "Hurricane" Carter; **Michael Mann**'s *Ali* (2001), about Muhammad Ali; and *Cinderella Man* (2005), about Jim Braddock.

Baseball films have also often been based on the lives of real-world players, such as *The Pride of the Yankees* (1942, about Lou Gehrig), *The Jackie Robinson Story* (1950), *The Pride of St. Louis* (1952, about "Dizzy" Dean), *The Babe* (1992, about Babe Ruth), and *Cobb* (1994, about Ty Cobb). In addition, **John Sayles**'s *Eight Men Out* (1988) also involves real players; it is a dramatized account of the infamous 1919 "Black Sox" scandal that treats its baseball players as exploited workers, thus linking it to the tradition of boxing films.

Among the many notable fictional films based on baseball are *Bang the Drum Slowly* (1973), **Barry Levinson**'s *The Natural* (1984), and the Kevin Costner vehicle *Field of Dreams* (1989). One of the most admired fictional baseball films is *Bull Durham* (1988), set not in the major leagues but in the minors, where players struggle to make it to the majors. Much praised for its realistic depiction of the lives of minor league ballplayers, this film was written and directed by Ron Shelton, himself a former minor leaguer. Baseball has been the basis for a particularly wide variety of films, as in the **musical** *Damn Yankees* (1958) or in *Major League* (1989), a particularly successful baseball **comedy** that spawned two sequels.

Some successful sports movies have focused on sports outside the American mainstream, usually by making them part of a larger story, as when the bicycling film *Breaking Away* (1979) becomes a more general coming-of-age story or when the women's roller derby film *Whip It* (2009) becomes a parable of feminist independence. Also notable in this sense is Eastwood's *Invictus* (2009), which presents the story of South Africa's victory in the 1995 Rugby World Cup as part of that country's post-apartheid interracial healing process under the leadership of Nelson Mandela (played by **Morgan Freeman**).

**SPY FILMS.** Films about espionage and secret agents have been around about as long as films themselves and were particularly popular in British **silent films** of the World War I era. British director **Alfred Hitchcock** became a master of the form in the 1930s, before coming to the United States, bringing with him his mastery of the form. While there were earlier American examples of the form—such as the **Great Garbo** vehicle *Mata Hari* or the **Marlene Dietrich** film *Dishonored* (both 1931)—the form first became truly prominent during World War II with the arrival of Hitchcock and with the rise of anti-Nazi spy films such as *Confessions of a Nazi Spy* (1939) and *The Fallen Sparrow* (1943). **Fritz Lang**, who had earlier pioneered the spy film in Germany, contributed the anti-Nazi spy films *Hangmen Also Die!* (1943) and *Cloak and Dagger* (1946).

After World War II, the spy film gradually evolved from an anti-Nazi to an anticommunist format, leading to a sort of golden age for the form by the 1960s, when such films became immensely popular in the United States. Among the most important of the Cold War–era spy films are *The Manchurian Candidate* (1962), *The Quiller Memorandum* (1966), *The Parallax View* (1974), and *Three Days of the Condor* (1975).

Sequences of spy novels became particularly rich sources of material for films during this period, as filmmakers drew upon the realistic depictions of the world of espionage by writers such as Len Deighton—whose work inspired the Harry Palmer series of spy films, beginning with *The Ipcress File* (1965)—and John Le Carré—whose work inspired several films, including *The Spy Who Came in from the Cold* (1965, made in Great Britain by American director **Martin Ritt**).

By far the most important of the novel sequences that inspired spy films, of course, was the series of novels by Ian Fleming about British secret agent James Bond. Beginning with *Dr. No* (1962), the Bond films quickly became the centerpiece of the spy film genre, with Scottish actor **Sean Connery** in the title role. Though these films were originally British-produced, they eventually became joint U.S.–UK productions, beginning with *For Your Eyes Only* (1981), with Roger Moore now in the title role, though Connery would return for one more Bond film in the aptly titled *Never Say Never Again* (1983). The sequence has continued through several lead actors and more than 20 "official" James Bond films, the latest being *Quantum of Solace* (2008), with English actor Daniel Craig as Bond.

The Bond films, which moved away from gritty realistic and into increasingly fantastic territory, often involving strong elements of **science**

**fiction**, exercised an immense influence on the evolution of the spy film genre. Among other things, they spawned numerous direct imitations and responses, as when actor Dean Martin's Matt Helm character—in films such as *The Silencers* (1966) and *The Ambushers* (1967)—was openly marketed as a sort of American Bond. The over-the-top nature of the Bond films also inspired parody, as in the case of *Casino Royale* (1967), which was loosely based on the Fleming novel of that title but was an overt parody of the more mainstream Bond sequence. Meanwhile, other films, such as *Our Man Flint* (1966) and its sequel *In Like Flint* (1967) parodied the spy film genre as a whole, with special relevance to the Bond sequence.

By the mid-1970s, Watergate-era domestic paranoia had somewhat supplanted Cold War paranoia, and the classic spy film turned more to domestic thrillers. The true spy film then made something of a comeback in the 1990s, as the end of the Cold War introduced new complications and anxieties into the global political scene. Novelists once again provided fertile material, as Jack Clancy's CIA agent Jack Ryan became the central figure in such early-1990s films as *The Hunt for Red October* (1990), *Patriot Games* (1992), and *Clear and Present Danger* (1994). **James Cameron**'s *True Lies* (1994), meanwhile, was a stylish example of the spy film genre that also poked good-natured fun at itself and at the genre.

Though women spies had been featured in film at least as early as *Mata Hari* and *Dishonored* and in Cold War films such as *Modesty Blaise* (1967), the genre has long been dominated by male protagonists. Women spies came to new prominence in the 1990s, however, especially with the popularity of Luc Besson's French film *Nikita* (1990), which spawned an American remake (*Point of No Return*, 1993) and a Canadian television series (*La femme Nikita*, 1997–2001).

This film, along with **Brian De Palma**'s *Mission: Impossible* (1996), which spawned sequels in 2000 and 2006, marked a turn toward more spectacular **special effects**-driven **action** sequences in the spy film genre. Meanwhile, the resurgence of the genre also produced a resurgence in parody, as the sequence of Austin Powers films—including *Austin Powers: International Man of Mystery* (1997), *Austin Powers: The Spy Who Shagged Me* (1999), and *Austin Powers in Goldmember* (2002). These popular films most specifically spoofed the 1960s-era Bond films but were also nostalgic send-ups of the 1960s as a whole.

Particularly successful among recent spy films have been the sequence of Jason Bourne films, based on the novels of Robert Ludlum. With **Matt Damon** in the title role, these films thus far have included *The Bourne Identity* (2002), *The Bourne Supremacy* (2004), and *The Bourne Ultimatum* (2007).

**STALLONE, SYLVESTER (1946– ).** Sylvester Stallone was one of Hollywood's top box-office draws from the mid-1970s until the beginning of the 1990s, largely on the basis of his iconic roles as Rocky Balboa and John Rambo in the film franchises starring those characters. After several minor roles, his breakthrough came with *Rocky* (1976), in which he received **Academy Award** nominations for both Best Leading Actor and Best Screenplay Written Directly for the Screen. That film, in fact, received a total of 10 **Oscar** nominations and won three Oscars, including that for Best Picture. It was ranked the 57th greatest film of all time in a 2007 poll conducted by the **American Film Institute** (AFI).

*Rocky II* (1979) and *Rocky III* (1982) failed to achieve the critical respect of the original *Rocky* but were commercially successful films both written by and starring Stallone, who moved into the director's chair for those films as well. Then, in 1982, Stallone scored his first success outside of the *Rocky* franchise when he starred in and co-wrote the ultra-violent *First Blood*, the first Rambo **action film**. *Rambo: First Blood Part II* (1985) and *Rambo III* (1988) were also commercial successes, but *Rocky IV* (1985) and *Rocky V* (1990) seemed to suggest that the *Rocky* franchise was in decline.

These franchises helped to make the muscular Stallone a 1980s action star exceeded only by **Arnold Schwarzenegger** in his box-office appeal. On the other hand, Stallone's success outside his two central franchises was limited, and some of his films—such as *Rhinestone* (1984), *Oscar* (1991), and *Judge Dredd* (1995)—were infamously bad. Still, he had minor successes with such films as *Lockup* (1989), *Tango & Cash* (1989), *Cliffhanger* (1993), and *Demolition Man* (1993).

Stallone received critical praise for his performance in *Cop Land* (1997), but by 2000 his reputation had waned to the point that he was given a special **Razzie Award** as the worst actor of the 20th century. He has not fared well in the 21st century either, beginning with poorly received performances in *Get Carter* (2000) and *Driven* (2001). Stallone would return, with only limited success, to his two best-known roles with *Rocky Balboa* (2006) and *Rambo* (2008), both of which he also wrote and directed. He also wrote, directed, and starred in *The Expendables* (2010), featuring an all-star cast of action stars, including cameos by Stallone's old rivals, Schwarzenegger and **Bruce Willis**.

*STAR WARS AND SEQUELS.* The original *Star Wars* (dir. **George Lucas**, 1977) (now conventionally referred to as *Star Wars: Episode IV—A New Hope*) caused a sensation upon its release in 1977, helping to initiate an explosion of production in **science fiction** film over the next several years. Moreover, the innovative **special effects** of *Star Wars* were on the cutting edge of a revolution in the **computer-generated imagery** (CGI) that continues to this day and that has had a dramatic impact on the visual texture of sf film. However, despite its technical innovations, *Star Wars* is at heart a nostalgic film that looks back to the sf serials of the 1930s, featuring a simple narrative of good vs. evil in which good triumphs against all odds.

*Star Wars* introduced some of the best-known characters and settings in the history of sf film. Meanwhile, the two immediate sequels, *Stars Wars: Episode V—The Empire Strikes Back* (1980) and *Star Wars: Episode VI—The Return of the Jedi* (1983) helped to contribute to the formation of a compelling and gradually expanding mythology that made the fictional context of the films seem believable, despite the sometimes farfetched or muddled nature of its narrative.

The *Star Wars* sequence (1977–2008) was in hiatus from 1983 to 1999, when the release of *Star Wars: Episode I—The Phantom Menace* became one of the most anticipated events in global film of the late 20th century. This film also initiated a second "prequel" trilogy of *Star Wars* films that also went on to include *Star Wars: Episode II—Attack of the Clones* (2002) and *Star Wars: Episode III—Revenge of the Sith* (2005). In keeping with the focus of the first three *Star Wars* films on building a detailed mythological framework, the prequel trilogy does a great deal to fill in the backgrounds of the characters and political oppositions of the first trilogy.

A seventh *Star Wars* film, the computer-animated *Star Wars: The Clone Wars*, was only a modest success in 2008, but together the seven *Star Wars* films have taken in nearly $2 billion at the box office (over $3.5 billion adjusted to 2005 dollars), making *Star Wars* the most lucrative film franchise of all time. *Star Wars* is also the center of a multimedia empire, having inspired one of the most successful licensing and merchandising campaigns in film history. In addition to toys and other merchandise, the *Star Wars* "expanded universe" now includes an extensive sequence of video games, comic books, novels, fan fiction, animated television series, and made-for-TV films.

A 2008 poll conducted by the **American Film Institute** named the original *Star Wars* the second greatest science fiction film of all time.

**STEIGER, ROD (1925–2002).** Rod Steiger had a long and productive acting career that stretched from early television performances at the beginning of the 1950s to his appearance in four different films in 2001 and one more in 2002. His breakthrough in film came with his performance in *On the Waterfront* (1954), for which he received an **Academy Award** nomination for Best Supporting Actor. Steiger turned down the title role in the award-winning film *Marty* (1955), which he had played in a television version in 1953. Indeed, most of his roles in the remainder of the 1950s were on television, though he did have important parts in such films as *The Big Knife* (1955), *Oklahoma!* (1955), and *The Harder They Fall* (1956).

In the 1960s, Steiger for the first time moved primarily into film acting, especially after his performance in *The Pawnbroker* (1964) earned him an **Oscar** nomination for Best Actor in a Leading Role. He followed with an important role in *Doctor Zhivago* (1965), then won the Best Actor Oscar for his performance in *In the Heat of the Night* (1967). From that point up to the time of his death he remained one of Hollywood's busiest film actors, while still making occasional television appearances as well.

Steiger appeared in a wide variety of films in the latter decades of his career, in both starring and supporting roles, showing a particularly effective ability to portray real historical figures in a convincing manner. Some of the highlights include his star turns in *The Illustrated Man* (1969), *Waterloo* (1970, in which he played Napoleon Bonaparte), *Mussolini: Ultimo atto* (1974, in which he played Benito Mussolini), and *W. C. Fields and Me* (1976, in which he played **W. C. Fields**). Some of his most prominent supporting roles were in *Lucky Luciano* (1973), *Lion of the Desert* (1981, in which he again played Mussolini), *Mars Attacks!* (1996), and *The Hurricane* (1999).

**STEINER, MAX (1888–1971).** The Vienna-born Max Steiner was a child prodigy who already had numerous achievements as a composer to his credit when he arrived in the United States in 1914. After composing accompanying **music** for the **silent film** *The Bondman* (1916), he worked outside of film (largely on Broadway) until 1929. From that point he would go on to become one of Hollywood's most prolific and respected composers of film music, though the majority of his work involved uncredited contributions to film scores prior to 1934, when his scores for *The Gay Divorcee* and *The Lost Patrol* both earned **Academy Award** nominations for Best Score. From that point, Steiner received at least one Best Score **Oscar** nomination virtually every year until his final nomination, for *Battle Cry* (1955). Along the way, he earned a total of 24 Best Score nominations, although he won the award only three times, for *The Informer* (1935); *Now, Voyager* (1942); and *Since You Went Away* (1944).

Steiner specialized in lush scores with a classical feel; he was also particularly successful with dramatic scores for **film noir**. His other credits include the scores for some of the best-known films in Hollywood history, including those for **King Kong** (1933) and **The Searchers** (1956) as well as the Oscar-nominated scores for **Gone with the Wind** (1939) and *Casablanca* (1942). Some of the other notable films for which Steiner composed the scores include *Little Women* (1933), *The Life of Emile Zola* (1937), *Sergeant York* (1941), *Mildred Pierce* (1945), *The Big Sleep* (1946), *The Treasure of the Sierra Madre* (1948), *Key Largo* (1948), *The Flame and the Arrow* (1950), *The Caine Mutiny* (1954), and *Spencer's Mountain* (1963)

**STEVENS, GEORGE (1904–1975).** George Stevens was one of the most successful directors in Hollywood, especially in the 1950s, when he directed some of the decade's most memorable films. Stevens started his film career as a cameraman on numerous films, including many of those made by **Stan Laurel and Oliver Hardy**. He also directed a number of shorts before moving into features with *The Cohens and Kellys in Trouble* (1933). He subsequently directed several minor films, then made his breakthrough with *Alice Adams* (1935), starring **Katharine Hepburn**.

Stevens followed as the director of a number of important films with some of Hollywood's top stars, including the **musical** *Swing Time* (1936), starring **Fred Astaire** and **Ginger Rogers**; the adventure film *Gunga Din* (1939), starring **Cary Grant**; and *Woman of the Year* (1942), with Hepburn and **Spencer Tracy**. He also received his first **Academy Award** nomination for Best Director for *The More the Merrier* (1943). Meanwhile, during World War II, Stevens served in the U.S. military, heading a film unit that shot some of the most memorable footage of the war, including coverage of the D-Day invasion, the Allied capture of Paris, and the liberation of the Dachau concentration camp.

It was, however, in the 1950s when Stevens truly reached his professional peak, beginning with *A Place in the Sun* (1951), for which he won the Best Director **Oscar**, as well as a Best Picture nomination as the producer of that film. He was again nominated for Best Director and as the producer of the Best Picture for *Shane* (1953), *Giant* (1956), and *The Diary of Anne Frank* (1959), winning the Best Director Oscar for *Giant*. From there, however, he went into semiretirement. His only subsequent directorial credits were for *The Greatest Story Ever Told* (1965) and *The Only Game in Town* (1970).

Stevens received the **Irving G. Thalberg** Award for career achievement in 1954.

**STEWART, DONALD OGDEN (1894–1980).** Donald Ogden Stewart was one of Hollywood's leading screenwriters of the 1930s and 1940s, then had his career derailed in the 1950s when he was placed on the **blacklist**. He began his film career by writing an adaptation of the play *Brown of Harvard* for a 1926 **silent film**, but his career picked up momentum with the coming of sound. He was nominated for an **Academy Award** for Best Writing, Original Story for *Laughter* (1930), then wrote the screenplays for such films of the 1930s as *Red Dust* (1932), *The Barretts of Wimpole Street* (1934), and *Marie Antoinette* (1938), while making contributions to the scripts for several more films, including *The Prisoner of Zenda* (1937) and *The Women* (1939).

Stewart won the **Oscar** for Best Screenplay for *The Philadelphia Story* (1940). He then wrote the screenplays for numerous other films in the 1940s, including *A Woman's Face* (1941), *Keeper of the Flame* (1942), and *Life with Father* (1947). Suspected of communist sympathies (largely for his anti-Nazi activism in the years leading to World War II), Stewart was blacklisted at the beginning of the 1950s. In response, he moved to Great Britain in 1950 and lived there for the rest of his life.

While Stewart contributed to several screenplays in the 1950s without credit—and wrote the script for *Escapade* (1955) under the name Gilbert Holland—he would never write another script with credit under his own name.

**STEWART, JAMES (1908–1997).** James Stewart was one of Hollywood's biggest stars in a career that stretched for more than half a century and included a number of the greatest films in American history along the way. In a poll conducted by the **American Film Institute** (AFI) in 1999, he was named the third greatest male screen legend of all time. Excelling in roles in which he played ordinary, down-to-earth characters forced to deal with extraordinary difficulties, Stewart was a key **Metro-Goldwyn-Mayer** (MGM) star during that studio's greatest years. He also broke new ground after World War II, when he returned from military service in the air force (in which he rose to the rank of colonel while flying active combat missions) to become one of the first major stars to work as an independent, without a studio contract.

After his first onscreen credit, in *The Murder Man* (1935), Stewart built a solid, if unremarkable, portfolio of supporting roles, plus a few starring roles in relatively minor films. He broke through into major stardom in 1939, starring in five films that year, including roles opposite **Marlene Dietrich** in the comic **Western** *Destry Rides Again*, opposite **Claudette Colbert** in the crime comedy *It's a Wonderful World*, opposite **Joan Crawford** in the **musical** *The Ice Follies of 1939*, and opposite **Carole Lombard** in the **romantic comedy** *Made for Each Other*. It was, however, his title role in **Frank Capra**'s *Mr. Smith Goes to Washington* in that year that propelled Stewart to major stardom, winning him the first of his five **Academy Award** nominations for Best Actor in a Leading Role.

Several important roles in 1940 and 1941 followed, including a starring role, alongside **Cary Grant** and **Katharine Hepburn**, in *The Philadelphia Story* (1940). Stewart won the Best Leading Actor **Oscar** for that film. His military service then kept him out of the movies from 1941 to 1946, when he returned in Capra's *It's a Wonderful Life*, a film that was not a big success at the time but that has gone on to become one of the most beloved films in American film history. It also won him another Oscar nomination for Best Actor. After several less remarkable films, Stewart then starred in **Alfred Hitchcock**'s *Rope* (1948), beginning an association with the director that would ultimately see him also play the lead roles in Hitchcock's classic films

*Rear Window* (1954) and ***Vertigo*** (1958), as well as *The Man Who Knew Too Much* (1956).

Stewart was one of Hollywood's most sought-after actors through the 1950s, proving that an independent actor could, in fact, succeed in the film business and leading the way for more and more actors to work without studio contracts. Among his numerous films of the 1950s were *Harvey* (1950) and *Anatomy of a Murder* (1959), for which he received his final two Oscar nominations for Best Actor. Along the way, he starred in numerous other films, including *The Glenn Miller Story* (1954), *Strategic Air Command* (1955), and *The Spirit of St. Louis* (1957).

Stewart also starred in a number of important Westerns, beginning with *Winchester '73* (1950), which began an important association with director **Anthony Mann**. It was also his first film as a freelance actor working for a percentage of the film's profits rather than a studio salary. Other highly successful Westerns made with Mann during the 1950s included *Bend of the River* (1952), *The Naked Spur* (1953), *The Far Country* (1954), and *The Man from Laramie* (1955). Stewart also starred in the Westerns *Broken Arrow* (1950) and *Night Passage* (1957), while continuing to serve in the air force reserves through the decade, rising to the rank of brigadier general.

In the early 1960s, Stewart continued to specialize in Westerns, starring in a sequence of such films directed by **John Ford**, including *Two Rode Together* (1961), *The Man Who Shot Liberty Valance* (1962), and *Cheyenne Autumn* (1964), while also appearing in *How the West Was Won* (1962), co-directed by Ford. After the mid-1960s, he began to scale back his appearances in film, though he did star in such Westerns as *Shenandoah* (1965), *Bandolero!* (1968), and *The Cheyenne Social Club* (1970), while playing a minor supporting role to **John Wayne** in *The Shootist* (1976). Stewart, essentially in retirement, partly due to his failing hearing, subsequently made only a few minor appearances in film, though he did appear several times on television, including an appearance as late as 1992.

In 1985, Stewart was given an honorary Academy Award on the occasion of the 50th anniversary of his first credited screen appearance.

**STONE, OLIVER (1946– ).** The often controversial Oliver Stone has been one of the most visible directors in Hollywood since bursting into prominence with two remarkable (and highly political) films in 1986: *Salvador* (dealing with U.S. interventions in Central America) and *Platoon* (dealing with the U.S. war effort in Vietnam, where Stone himself had served in combat in 1967–1968). These films established Stone's reputation for being able to produce compelling dramas that treat sensitive political topics, a reputation that would be solidified with several more politically charged films in the coming years.

Stone started his career primarily as a screenwriter. Indeed, he won an **Academy Award** for Best Screenplay for *Midnight Express* (1978) nearly a decade before he became known as a director. He also wrote or co-wrote the screenplays for *Conan the Barbarian* (1982), *Scarface* (1983), and *Year of the Dragon* (1985) early in his career. Stone received **Oscar** nominations for Best Screenplay for both *Salvador* and *Platoon*, winning the Best Director Oscar for the latter, a film that also won for Best Picture.

Stone followed his initial directorial success as the writer and director of *Wall Street* (1987) and *Talk Radio* (1988), the former of which would become one of the iconic films of the 1980s with its exploration of the capitalist greed that was perhaps the most important distinguishing characteristic of the decade. Stone followed with another Vietnam-themed picture in *Born on the Fourth of July* (1989), for which he received Oscar nominations for Best Screenplay and (as producer) Best Picture, while winning his second Oscar for Best Director. He followed with the same three nominations for *JFK* (1991), one of the most controversial films of the 1990s.

*The Doors* (1991), a film about the 1960s rock group, was also an exploration of American culture in that decade, though it and Stone's third Vietnam film, *Heaven & Earth* (1993) were somewhat less successful than Stone's earlier films. *Natural Born Killers* (1994), meanwhile, was a stylistic tour de force, though many felt that its attempt to critique the fascination with violence in American culture actually fed that fascination. *Nixon* (1995), Stone's **biopic** about the controversial U.S. president, also met with a mixed reception, though many found it a highly effective (and balanced) exploration of the life and career of its subject.

The **neo-noir** film *U-Turn* (1997) was a departure for Stone in that he did not write the script for the film, which for once seemed designed mostly as an entertainment. Stone returned to writing his own films with *Any Given Sunday* (1999), an exploration of contemporary American culture through the lens of professional football. Since that time, he has continued to explore controversial topics, though with limited success.

His **documentaries** about Fidel Castro (*Comandante*, 2003) and South American politics (*South of the Border*, 2009) drew relatively little attention. *Alexander* (2004) was Stone's move into the big-budget epic, but was panned by critics and avoided by audiences. *World Trade Center* (2006) was an effective drama about the 9/11 bombings in New York, but provided little in the way of actual commentary or illumination about that event. *W.* (2008) was an unusual (and, for many, surprisingly sympathetic) effort at a **biopic** about a sitting president (George W. Bush), but again received lackluster responses from critics and audiences. *Wall Street: Money Never Sleeps* (2010) was a sequel to the original *Wall Street*, made in response to the recent near-collapse of the U.S. financial system.

**STOPPARD, TOM (1937– ).** The Czech-born Tom Stoppard is one of the leading British playwrights of his era, one of the leading practitioners of **postmodernism** in the theater. He has also become a successful screenwriter, scripting several of the most notable films of the 1980s and 1990s.

Stoppard wrote a number of scripts for television and film in the 1960s and 1970s, including those for **Joseph Losey**'s *The Romantic Englishwoman* (1975) and **Otto Preminger**'s *The Human Factor* (1979). It was, however, as the co-writer of **Terry Gilliam**'s *Brazil* (1985) that Stoppard had his first major success in film, receiving an **Academy Award** nomination for Best Screenplay. He followed as the writer of **Steven Spielberg**'s *Empire of the Sun* (1987) and of such novel adaptations as *The Russia House* (1990) and *Billy Bathgate* (1991). He won an **Oscar** for Best Screenplay as the co-writer of *Shakespeare in Love* (1998), which won a total of seven Oscars, including that for Best Picture.

Stoppard adapted his play *Rosencrantz & Guildenstern Are Dead* to the screen in 1990, also serving as the director of that film.

**STORARO, VITTORIO (1940– ).** Vittorio Storaro is one of Italy's leading cinematographers, known particularly for his work with director Bernardo Bertolucci. Storaro has also worked extensively in Hollywood film, beginning with **Francis Ford Coppola**'s *Apocalypse Now* (1979), for which he won an **Academy Award** for Best Cinematography. He followed with another **Oscar** for **Warren Beatty**'s *Reds* (1981) and would win another for Bertolucci's internationally co-produced *The Last Emperor* (1987). Storaro was also nominated for an Oscar for Best Cinematography for Beatty's *Dick Tracy* (1990).

Storaro also served as the chief cinematographer for the Beatty-directed *Bulworth* (1998), as well as on the ill-fated *Ishtar* (1987), in which Beatty starred. Storaro also worked again with Coppola on *Tucker: The Man and His Dream* (1988) and on Coppola's segment of the anthology film *New York Stories* (1989). Since *Bulworth*, Storaro has worked primarily in international films, though he did shoot the U.S.-produced *Picking Up the Pieces* (2000) and *Exorcist: The Beginning* (2004).

**STREEP, MERYL (1949– ).** One of the most esteemed actresses of her generation, Meryl Streep has shown unusual staying power, successfully starring in major films from *Kramer vs. Kramer* (1979) through *It's Complicated*

(2009). One of Streep's earliest performances was in *The Deer Hunter* (1978), for which she also received a Best Supporting Actress Oscar nomination. After *Kramer vs. Kramer* she moved primarily into leading roles, including Oscar-nominated turns in *The French Lieutenant's Woman* (1981), *Silkwood* (1983), *Out of Africa* (1985), *Ironweed* (1987), *Evil Angels* (1988), *Postcards from the Edge* (1990), *The Bridges of Madison County* (1995), *One True Thing* (1998), and *Music of the Heart* (1999).

Other films in which Streep has appeared range from the **Woody Allen**-directed comedy *Manhattan* (1979), to the **children's film** *Lemony Snicket's A Series of Unfortunate Events* (2004), to the **musical** *Mama Mia!* (2008), demonstrating a versatility for which she has been widely praised. Along the way, she has played a wide variety of roles and has received a total of 16 **Academy Award** nominations for Best Actress, three for supporting roles and 13 for leading roles. She has won one Best Supporting Actress Oscar (for *Kramer vs. Kramer*) and one Best Leading Actress Oscar, for *Sophie's Choice* (2002). She has received three nominations for Best Actress in a Leading Role in her late fifties, for her performances in *The Devil Wears Prada* (2006), *Doubt* (2008), and *Julie & Julia* (2009).

**STREISAND, BARBRA (1942– ).** Though she first became known as a singer (and is still one of the most successful female recording artists of all time), Barbra Streisand also became a top box-office draw in several key Hollywood films and eventually became an important woman director. Streisand broke into film in a big way, winning the **Academy Award** for Best Actress in a Leading Role for her very first film performance, as Fanny Brice in the **biopic** *Funny Girl* (1968), adapted from the Broadway hit in which she had also starred. She followed with starring roles in *Hello, Dolly!* (1969), *On a Clear Day You Can See Forever* (1970), *The Owl and the Pussycat* (1970), and *What's Up, Doc?* (1972), showing a particular penchant for playing offbeat characters in comic roles. Then, in *The Way We Were* (1973), she proved she could handle a serious dramatic role, winning another **Oscar** nomination for Best Actress.

Streisand had important starring roles in *Funny Lady* (1975), *A Star Is Born* (1976), and *All Night Long* (1981), one of her few box-office failures. She also starred in *Yentl* (1983), which she produced and directed. She subsequently cut back on her work as an actor; her only other film performance of the 1980s was in **Martin Ritt**'s *Nuts* (1987), which she also produced. She then had her greatest success as a director and producer with *The Prince of Tides* (1991), in which she also starred. That film was nominated for an Academy Award for Best Picture, though Streisand's only nomination was as its producer.

Streisand also directed, produced, and starred in *The Mirror Has Two Faces* (1996). She then took a hiatus from film acting (and directing) and did not appear in another film until the **comedy** *Meet the Fockers* (2004), her first appearance since 1987 in a film she did not direct.

Streisand has received numerous recording industry honors, including nine Grammy Awards. She has received two Oscar nominations for Best Original Song, for **music** from *A Star Is Born* and *All Night Long*, winning the award for the former.

**STURGES, PRESTON (1898–1959).** Preston Sturges was one of the first successful Hollywood directors who also wrote the screenplays for all of his own films. Indeed, Sturges had been a successful screenwriter throughout the 1930s when he first made the leap (accompanied by considerable studio publicity from **Paramount**) into directing with *The Great McGinty* (1940), for which he won the **Academy Award** for Best Original Screenplay. The success of that film started a sequence in which Sturges became one of the most successful directors of the early 1940s, continuing with *Christmas in July* (1940) and then with his two most memorable films: *Sullivan's Travels* and *The Lady Eve* (1941).

Sturges took the **screwball comedy** in sophisticated new directions, partly thanks to his own mastery of intricate dialogue. In 1942, he wrote and directed another success, *The Palm Beach Story*. He then received **Oscar** nominations for Best Screenplay for two films that he also directed that were released in 1944: *The Miracle of Morgan's Creek* and *Hail the Conquering Hero*. However, *The Great Moment*, also released in 1944, was not a success; that failure topped off a series of battles between Sturges and Paramount that led to his departure from the studio.

With backing from **Howard Hughes**, Sturges became an independent producer and was for a time the only Hollywood director to also both produce and write his own films. However, his first release under the new agreement, *The Sin of Harold Diddlebock* (1947), featuring **silent film** icon **Harold Lloyd**, was not a success. Sturges wrote and directed *Unfaithfully Yours* (1948) and *The Beautiful Blonde from Bashful Bend* (1949) for **Twentieth Century Fox**. He then began another film with Hughes, *Vendetta* (1950), but the partnership fell apart in the midst of the making of that film. Sturges directed one French film in the mid-1950s, but his Hollywood career was at that point over.

*SUNSET BLVD.* One of the true classics of American cinema, *Sunset Blvd.* (dir. **Billy Wilder**, 1950) is one of the great Hollywood films about the film industry itself and about **show business** in general. A 2007 poll conducted by the **American Film Institute** (AFI) named *Sunset Blvd.* the 16th greatest film of all time.

Clearly reflecting the anxiety that pervaded Hollywood (and America) at the beginning of the 1950s, *Sunset Blvd.* suggests, among other things, that the movies must respond to social and historical change in order to remain relevant. The film features one-time silent-film superstar Norma Desmond, played by **Gloria Swanson**, whose over-the-top performance is a highlight of the film. Unable to adapt to the coming of the talkies, Norma has lived for 20 years in the seclusion of her posh, but now somewhat rundown, mansion on Sunset Boulevard. However, Desmond still dreams of a comeback, believing that her fans still love her.

Unfortunately, Desmond has completely lost touch with the outside world, and her attempts to return to Hollywood through an alliance with struggling screenwriter Joe Gillis (**William Holden**) lead to disaster for both of them. Indeed, in a famous narrative move, the entire film is narrated by Gillis in flashback—after his body has been found floating in Desmond's pool at the beginning of the film. This beginning sets the overall dark tone of the film, which has much in common with **film noir**, a form of which director and co-writer Wilder was one of the great masters. Yet the film also has its darkly comic moments, creating a mixed atmosphere that is appropriate to its am-bivalent treatment of the film industry as both sinister and wondrous.

At the most obvious level, *Sunset Blvd.* warned that Hollywood needed to keep up with the rapidly changing American society that surrounded it at the beginning of the 1950s. In this sense, the film anticipated the attempts of Hollywood to make more socially relevant films in the 1950s, even while the Cold War climate of anticommunist hysteria made it necessary to eschew any genuine systemic critique of American society. At a less obvious level, one can also see the reclusive Desmond as an allegorical suggestion of America's former isolationism, now made obsolete by America's participation in World War II and subsequent involvement in the global politics of the Cold War.

**SUPERHERO FILM.** Films based on the exploits of superheroes (usually from comic books) have become some of Hollywood's most successful prod-ucts of the early 21st century. Actually, superhero films have been around for some time, as in the 15-part serial that ran in 1943 based on the superhero character the Phantom, who had begun to appear in a King Features syndi-cated comic strip in 1936, thus predating the debut of Superman by two years. Superman himself appeared in animated serials made for theaters as early as 1942 and was featured in a self-titled live-action serial in 1948, starring Kirk Alyn as the Man of Steel. Alyn returned for a second serial, *Atom Man vs. Superman*, in 1950, though he would be replaced by George Reeves in the

1951 feature *Superman and the Mole Men*—a theatrical release of the pilot episode of the upcoming television series, *Adventures of Superman.*

*Superman and the Mole Men* can thus claim to be the first feature film based on material from the comics, even if it was a spillover from a TV series. That series itself was a major success in the 1950s, especially with younger viewers, though superhero films made few additional inroads into theaters between that film and *Superman: The Movie*, in 1978. Indeed, one of the few examples of a superhero film in the intervening years was *Batman* (1966), also an offshoot of a television series, in this case the ultra-campy 1960s *Batman* series that featured Adam West as Batman.

Advances in **special effects** technology and the success of such films as **Star Wars** (1977) paved the way for *Superman: The Movie*, the first important superhero film. That film was a big hit, paving the way for a string of sequels. However, the Superman franchise was still regarded in Hollywood as a one-of-a-kind special case, so that Superman films remained the only major example of superhero film until the release of **Tim Burton**'s *Batman* (1989), which revived the form after the Superman film franchise had declined into campy self-parody. Burton's sequel, *Batman Returns* (1992), was also a success, but that franchise itself declined into self-parody with two subsequent films, directed by Joel Schumacher.

Superhero films gained a new importance in Hollywood when the major properties of Marvel Comics, after preliminary success with *Blade* (1998), began to be adapted to film with Bryan Singer's big-budget *X-Men* (2000), a huge box-office hit that was also an impressive demonstration of state-of-the-art technology for adaptation of superhero comics to film. That film triggered a string of sequels and opened the way for other successful Marvel superhero adaptations, including the *Spider-Man* films that appeared in 2002, 2004, and 2007, becoming one of the most commercially successful film franchises of all time.

In the meantime, the two leading superheroes from DC Comics continued to have an impact in Hollywood. The venerable Superman franchise received a moderately successful reboot with the release of Singer's *Superman Returns* (2006). Even more successful was the revival of the Batman franchise with Christopher Nolan's *Batman Begins* (2005) and *The Dark Knight Returns* (2008), the latter of which became just the fourth film to reach the billion-dollar mark in global box-office receipts.

Marvel's Iron Man character also became the basis for successful film adaptations in 2008 and 2010. Meanwhile, the acquisition of Marvel by **Disney** at the end of 2009 signaled a recognition of the ongoing potential of Marvel's heroes as the bases for films, though many of their leading characters had already been licensed to others, including **Sony**, which has the rights to the Spider-Man franchise. *See also* ANIMATED FILM; FANTASY.

**SWANSON, GLORIA (1899–1983).** Gloria Swanson was a top star of **silent film**, known especially for her work with director **Cecil B. DeMille**. She later enjoyed only limited success in sound film, but is now remembered best for her role as Norma Desmond in **Billy Wilder**'s *Sunset Blvd.* (1950), a film about an aging former silent-film star hoping to make a comeback in the talkies (and in which DeMille plays an important role).

After some early roles in **slapstick comedies**, Swanson moved to **Paramount** and began her work with DeMille, in which she became a top star. Such films as *Don't Change Your Husband* (1919), *Male and Female* (1920), and *Why Change Your Wife?* (1920) were hugely successful, making Swanson famous, though as much for her elaborate costuming (both in the films and in her public appearances outside of film) as for her acting. Swanson also worked with a number of other directors through the remainder of the 1920s, becoming a powerful figure in the industry with an unusual amount of creative control over her projects. **Raoul Walsh**'s *Sadie Thompson* (1928), in which Swanson played the title character, was a highlight of the final years of silent film.

Swanson enjoyed a brief career in the talkies from 1929 to 1934, but her limited success there caused her to withdraw from acting in favor of other pursuits. She briefly returned to film to star in *Father Takes a Wife* (1941), then did not appear again until *Sunset Blvd.* By this time, she was hosting her own television variety show, making her a pioneer in that venue; she later made a number of guest appearances on television as an actress.

# T

**TARANTINO, QUENTIN (1963– ).** Though his films have been criticized for their excessive violence (and for relying more on style than substance), Quentin Tarantino has been one of the most prominent directors in Hollywood since the release of his first major film, *Reservoir Dogs* (1992), which he also wrote. Tarantino was then propelled to major directorial stardom with the release of ***Pulp Fiction*** (1994), one of the highlights of American film in the 1990s and a key work in the rise of **independent film** in that decade.

Tarantino received an **Academy Award** nomination for Best Director for *Pulp Fiction*, winning the **Oscar** for Best Original Screenplay (along with co-writer Roger Avary) for that film. The film itself won the Palme d'Or at the Cannes **Film Festival**, as well as seven Oscar nominations, including that for Best Picture. *Pulp Fiction* firmly established Tarantino's reputation for featuring graphic violence, snappy dialogue, popular **music**, and homages to previous films in his work. Indeed, Tarantino (who once famously worked as a video store clerk) is known as a movie buff's filmmaker, and all of his films are as much about filmmaking and film history as they are about their ostensible subject matter.

Tarantino followed *Pulp Fiction* with the stylish *Jackie Brown* (1997), which draws upon various crime film traditions, including **blaxploitation**, though this film attracted less attention than his earlier ones. He then followed with the highly controversial *Kill Bill: Vol. 1* (2003) and *Kill Bill: Vol. 2* (2004), which were widely criticized not only for their excessive violence but for breaking what was really one film into two in an attempt to generate more income. Nevertheless, these films, which draw upon the Hong Kong martial arts film, as well as the spaghetti **Western** and the 1970s revenge film, did attract some praise and have become **cult** favorites.

Tarantino next teamed with **Robert Rodriguez** to direct the "Grindhouse" double-feature (2007), an overt homage to the **grindhouse** films of the 1970s. Tarantino's half of this effort was *Death Proof*, which draws upon a variety of grindhouse genres, including the slasher film, as well as car films such as *Vanishing Point* (1971). That effort was Tarantino's least successful, both commercially and critically, but he bounced back with his next film, receiving Oscar nominations for both Best Director and Best Original Screenplay for *Inglourious Basterds* (2009), a film that was itself nominated for a total of eight Oscars, including that for Best Picture, though it won only in the Best Supporting Actor category (Christoph Waltz). This **war film** set in World War II plays fast and loose with history, ultimately becoming a tale of what might have happened (including the assassination of Hitler), rather than what actually happened.

In addition to writing or co-writing all of his own films—and **Tony Scott's** *True Romance* (1993)—Tarantino has appeared as an actor in small roles in several of his own films as well as in films directed by others, most notably in his friend Rodriguez's *From Dusk till Dawn* (1996). In addition to producing *Death Proof*, he has also been an executive producer for several films directed by others, including *From Dusk till Dawn*, *Hostel* (2005), and *Hell Ride* (2008).

**TAYLOR, ELIZABETH (1932– ).** Elizabeth Taylor began as a child actress in the early 1940s, then rose to become one of the top Hollywood stars over the next 20 years. A 1999 poll conducted by the **American Film Institute** (AFI) named her the seventh greatest female legend in film history.

Born in England to American parents, Taylor returned to the United States with her family shortly before World War II. She began acting in film at the age of nine, in *There's One Born Every Minute* (1942). She received particularly positive reviews for her supporting performance in *Lassie Come Home* (1943). More roles followed, and she was then catapulted to stardom for her starring role in *National Velvet* (1944).

After more successful adolescent roles, Taylor (though still a teenager) transitioned into adult leads by the end of the 1940s. In the 1950s, she starred in such notable films as *A Place in the Sun* (1950), *Ivanhoe* (1951), and *Giant* (1956), becoming a top box-office draw renowned for both her beauty and her acting talent, while her personal life became the object of much public fascination as well. She then reached the zenith of her acting career with a string of **Oscar**-nominated lead performances in *Raintree County* (1957), *Cat on a Hot Tin Roof* (1958), and *Suddenly, Last Summer* (1959), finally winning the **Academy Award** for Best Actress in a Leading Role for *Butterfield 8* (1960).

Taylor's starring role in the big-budget **historical epic** *Cleopatra* (1963) was her most notorious appearance, partly because the film itself was an infamous failure and partly because of her infamous on-set romance with costar **Richard Burton**. *The Sandpiper* (1965), opposite then-husband Burton was more successful, and Taylor then won another Best Actress Oscar for her performance in *Who's Afraid of Virginia Woolf?* (1967), again opposite Burton, as the two played a battling married couple whose troubles in some ways mirrored the tempestuous relationship of the real-world actors.

Burton and Taylor again played warring lovers in *The Taming of the Shrew* (1967). Indeed, Taylor starred in four films in 1967 alone, including *The Comedians* and *Dr. Faustus*, both with Burton, and *Reflections in a Golden Eye*, opposite **Marlon Brando**. She remained busy as a film actress through the 1970s, but never again quite reached the level of her earlier success. After her performance in *The Mirror Crack'd* (1980), Taylor's subsequent performances have been mostly on television.

Taylor has become a prominent activist, especially in support of AIDS-related charities. In 1993 she was given the Jean Hersholt Humanitarian Award for that aspect of her career.

**TEMPLE, SHIRLEY (1928– ).** Shirley Temple performed in her first film at the age of three, then became a star for her performance in *Bright Eyes* (1934), launching a career that made her the most successful child actor in film history. Temple appeared in numerous films in the 1930s, many of which were major box-office hits. She received a special juvenile **Academy Award** in 1935 for her appearances in several films the year before.

Films such as *Curly Top* (1935), *Dimples* (1936), *Wee Willie Winkie* (1937), *Heidi* (1937), *Rebecca of Sunnybrook Farm* (1938), and *The Little Princess* (1939) made Temple a major star; she was Hollywood's top box-office draw from 1935 to 1938, and Temple-themed licensed merchandise became highly popular. However, *The Blue Bird* (1940), a fantasy clearly influenced by *The Wizard of Oz* (1939), was not a notable success. Temple, now entering adolescence, performed less frequently through the 1940s in order to pursue her schooling.

Her star status fading, Temple retired from acting in 1950 upon her marriage to Charles Alden Black, though she did return briefly to show business in 1958, hosting a television anthology series of fairy-tale adaptations.

**THALBERG, IRVING G. (1899–1936).** Irving G. Thalberg was a pioneering film producer whose knack for overseeing the development of hit films earned him the reputation of being a "boy wonder" in Hollywood. Indeed, by the age of 21, he became the executive in charge of production for the California operations of **Universal Studios**, where he quickly showed an ability to impose his vision on older, well-established directors. In 1924, he left Universal to join **Louis B. Mayer** at the latter's self-named studio, which later became part of **Metro-Goldwyn-Mayer** (MGM), which Thalberg, as production chief, helped to mold into Hollywood's leading studio.

Thalberg oversaw the production of dozens of films, putting his stamp on all of them, though he refused to allow his name to be listed in onscreen credits. Unfortunately, heart problems caused by complications from a childhood bout with rheumatic fever plagued Thalberg throughout his adult life, limiting his productivity. He died of pneumonia at the age of 37, with several films still in production. His contributions to the evolution of the film industry have been recognized in the establishment of the Irving G. Thalberg Memorial Award, given periodically by the **Academy of Motion Picture Arts and Sciences** for career contributions in the production of films.

**TIERNEY, GENE (1920–1991).** Though her film career at first sputtered, Gene Tierney became one of **Twentieth Century Fox**'s top stars in the 1940s, appearing at the beginning of the decade in such films as **John Ford**'s *Tobacco Road* (1941) and Josef von Sternberg's *The Shanghai Gesture* (1941). She moved into star status in *Heaven Can Wait* (1943). In 1944 she starred in **Otto Preminger**'s **film noir** classic *Laura* (1944), still her best-remembered role, following with a performance in *Leave Her to Heaven* (1945) that won her her only **Academy Award** nomination for Best Actress in a Leading Role.

Tierney received additional critical praise for her performances in *The Razor's Edge* (1946) and (especially) *The Ghost and Mrs. Muir* (1947), then reunited with Preminger for another classic film noir, *Whirlpool* (1949). She starred in two more successful film noirs in 1950: Preminger's *Where the Sidewalk Ends* and Jules Dassin's *Night and the City* (1950). She appeared in a number of additional films in the early 1950s, but by the middle of the decade mental health problems had driven her out of acting and into shock treatment.

Tierney returned to acting with a major role in Preminger's *Advise & Consent* (1962). She also had supporting roles in *Toys in the Attic* (1963) and *The Pleasure Seekers* (1964), but would never regain her star status.

**TIOMKIN, DIMITRI (1894–1979).** The Russian-born Dimitri Tiomkin came to the United States in 1925 and to Hollywood in 1930, subsequently becoming one of the film industry's leading composers. He was nominated for a total of 22 **Academy Awards** for Best Song or Best Score for films released from 1939 to 1969. He won a total of four **Oscars**, including those for both Best Song and Best Score for *High Noon* (1952), becoming the first composer to win those double awards for the same film.

Tiomkin's first score was for *Resurrection* (1931), though he rose to prominence as a composer later in the decade when he began writing the **music** for a series of films directed by **Frank Capra**, including *Lost Horizon* (1937) and *Mr. Smith Goes to Washington* (1939), for which he received his first Oscar nomination for Best Score. Tiomkin also scored Capra's *Meet John Doe* (1941) and received Oscar nominations for Best Score for such films of the 1940s as *The Corsican Brothers* (1941), *The Moon and Sixpence* (1942), *The Bridge of San Luis Rey* (1944), and *Champion* (1949).

Heavily influenced by European classical music traditions, Tiomkin was a leading force behind the tendency for **Golden Age** Hollywood films to have a classical tone. He was at his peak in the 1950s, winning Best Song and Best Score Oscar nominations for both *The High and the Mighty* (1954) and *Friendly Persuasion* (1956), as well as *High Noon*. He scored three films for **Alfred Hitchcock** during the decade, including *Strangers on a Train* (1951), *I Confess* (1952), and *Dial M for Murder* (1954), as well as the earlier *Shadow of a Doubt* (1943).

Tiomkin received three more double Oscar nominations in the 1960s, for *The Alamo* (1960), *Town without Pity* (1961), and *55 Days at Peking* (1963). He was particularly successful with the scores for **Westerns**, providing the music for such films as *The Big Sky* (1952), *Gunfight at the O.K. Corral* (1957), *Rio Bravo* (1959), and *The Young Land* (1959), in addition to *High Noon* and *The Alamo*. He also wrote a considerable amount of music for television, including the theme songs for the Western series *Gunsmoke* and *Rawhide*.

**TO KILL A MOCKINGBIRD.** Based on the classic novel by Harper Lee, *To Kill a Mockingbird* (dir. Robert Mulligan, 1962) is one of the best-known films in Hollywood history. Rated the 25th greatest film of all time in a 2007 poll conducted by the **American Film Institute** (AFI), it was named the greatest courtroom drama of all time in a 2008 AFI poll. It is also the signature film of its well-known star, **Gregory Peck**.

In the film, Peck plays virtuous Southern lawyer Atticus Finch, whom the AFI named the greatest film hero of all time in a 2003 poll. Though the film covers a number of events, its central dramatic focus concerns Finch's courageous defense of a young black man charged with raping a white woman, which forms the centerpiece of the film's (and novel's) critique of racism and bigotry. This critique is made all the more effective because much of the film is presented from the point of view of Finch's children, whose innocence provides a counterpoint to the evils of the world around them, which they gradually come to discover. Another key element of the film involves the children's fascination with neighbor "Boo" Radley (**Robert Duvall**, in his first film role), rumored to be a dangerous monster but ultimately found to be harmless.

*To Kill a Mockingbird* received a total of eight **Academy Award** nominations, including those for Best Picture and Best Director. It won the **Oscar** in three categories, including Peck's award for Best Actor in a Leading Role and the award to Horton Foote for Best Adapted Screenplay.

**TOLAND, GREGG (1904–1948).** Gregg Toland is one of the most legendary cinematographers in American film history, best known for his work on *Citizen Kane* (1941), for which he designed special lenses that enabled the use of deep-focus photography that deviated greatly from the shallow depth of field then prevalent in Hollywood films. Actually, by the time of *Citizen Kane*, Toland had already worked extensively in film, beginning as a cameraman for the **silent film** *The Bat* (1926) and receiving his first solo credit for cinematography in 1931 for *Palmy Days*. He had shot such important films as *Wuthering Heights* (1939) and *The Grapes of Wrath* (1940) and had, especially in *The Long Voyage Home* (1940), already begun to experiment with lenses and special lighting schemes to facilitate deep focus photography.

Toland showed a knack for innovation as early as the beginnings of sound film, when he developed a mechanism to quiet camera noise so that the camera would not disrupt the sound being recorded. He was especially effective at using shadows to produce interesting atmospheric effects, pointing the way for the important use of such techniques in **film noir**. In addition to *Citizen Kane*, he shot such important films of the 1940s as *The Little Foxes* (1941), *Ball of Fire* (1941), and *The Best Years of Our Lives* (1946), though his career was cut short when he died of a heart attack at the age of 44.

Toland received **Academy Award** nominations for Best Cinematography for *Les misérables* (1935), *Dead End* (1937), *Intermezzo: A Love Story* (1939), *The Long Voyage Home*, and *Citizen Kane*, winning the award for *Wuthering Heights*.

**TOURNEUR, JACQUES (1904–1977).** The son of a French film director who worked briefly in Hollywood in the 1920s, Jacques Tourneur started his own Hollywood career in 1934 and continued to work there for more than 30 years. Most of Tourneur's films were low-budget affairs, but several became classics of their kind, especially the **horror** films he made for producer Val Lewton, including *Cat People* (1942) and *I Walked with a Zombie* (1943). Those films propelled Tourneur into A-list efforts (though he never attained true big-budget status), and subsequent films such as the **film noir** classics *Out of the Past* (1947) and *Berlin Express* (1948) are among the highlights of that genre.

The **Western** *Stars in My Crown* and the adventure *The Flame and the Arrow* (both released in 1950) demonstrated Tourneur's ability to work successfully in a variety of genres. He directed several Westerns during the 1950s, then returned to horror with *Night of the Demon* (1959). In the 1960s, Tourneur returned to lower-budget horror films with *The Comedy of Terrors* (1963) and *City in the Sea* (1965), both starring **Vincent Price**. He also directed a number of television episodes in the 1960s, including one episode each of the well-known series *Bonanza* (in 1960) and *The Twilight Zone* (1964).

**TOWNE, ROBERT (1934– ).** Robert Towne has written some of the most successful screenplays in Hollywood in a career that has stretched from **Roger Corman**'s low-budget *Last Woman on Earth* (1960) to the upcoming remake of **Alfred Hitchcock**'s 1935 film *The 39 Steps*, scheduled for release in 2011. In between, he not only wrote numerous successful screenplays but also became one of Hollywood's most sought-after script doctors, working to improve screenplays written by others.

Towne achieved his first major success as a screenwriter with *The Last Detail* (1973), for which he received the first of his four Academy Award nominations for Best Screenplay. The next year he scored his only **Oscar** win in that category for *Chinatown*, still his most highly regarded film. Another nomination followed for *Shampoo* (1975). That was his last credited screenplay of the 1970s, and his screen credits for writing in the 1980s included only the minor films *Personal Best* (1982) and *Tequila Sunrise* (1988), both of which he also directed. However, Towne also co-wrote *Greystoke: The Legend of Tarzan, Lord of the Apes* (1984), for which he was credited as P. H. Vazak (the name of his dog), because he was dissatisfied with the script. Ironically, he received his fourth Oscar nomination for Best Screenplay for that film.

Towne made something of a comeback in the 1990s, scoring commercial successes with such films as *Days of Thunder* (1990), *The Firm* (1993), and the first two *Mission: Impossible* films (1996 and 2000). He also wrote and directed *Without Limits* (1998) and *Ask the Dust* (2006), which is (like *Chinatown*) a period piece set in Los Angeles.

Films to which Towne has contributed as an uncredited script doctor include several projects involving **Warren Beatty**, such as *Bonnie and Clyde* (1967), *The Parallax View* (1974), and *Heaven Can Wait* (1978).

***TOY STORY.*** *Toy Story* (dir. **John Lasseter**, 1995) is a historically important film, both because it was the first feature-length **animated film** to be produced entirely by **computer-generated imagery** (CGI) and because it was the first feature released by **Pixar**, then a small, struggling company but soon to become a dominant force in **children's film**. *Toy Story* was a genuine landmark in animated film, historically comparable, in many ways, to ***Snow White and the Seven Dwarfs*** in the way it introduced an entirely new form to feature film. In recognition of this fact, director Lasseter was given a Special Achievement **Academy Award** for the film. A 2008 poll conducted by the **American Film Institute** (AFI) named *Toy Story* the sixth greatest animated film of all time, the highest ranking of any non-**Disney** film (though it was distributed by Disney for Pixar, and Pixar itself would later be acquired by Disney).

*Toy Story* is an extremely warm, charming, and sentimental film that easily overcomes any concerns that an entirely computer-generated film might somehow seem cold and mechanical—or that *Toy Story* itself might turn out to be a mere technological curiosity. Some of the film's warmth comes from the lovability of the characters, enhanced by the voice performances of well-known actors **Tom Hanks** and Tim Allen in the roles of the film's central toy-characters, Woody (a talking cowboy doll) and Buzz Lightyear (a spaceman action figure), respectively. Some of the warmth comes from **Randy Newman**'s **Oscar**-nominated score, including the song "You've Got a Friend in Me," which also won an Oscar nomination for Best Song. In addition, a key secret to the success of *Toy Story* is in its storytelling (it also won an Oscar nomination for its screenplay, written by, among others, Joss Whedon, who would soon become better known for his creation of television's *Buffy the Vampire Slayer*).

Ultimately, though, *Toy Story* is most remarkable for the quality of its computer animation, which was so effective that it quickly revolutionized animation, making computer animation the standard and hand animation a curiosity. On the other hand, the animation of *Toy Story* is relatively simple, with its toy characters being far easier to portray effectively than living animals or humans. The narrative (focusing on older toys who fear being made obsolete by newer, shinier models) is simple as well, yet it resonates with multiple meanings that help to make the film attractive to adults, as well as children.

Among other things, the obsolescence of toys can be taken as a marker of the fleeting nature of childhood itself. Toys become obsolete not just because they are replaced by newer, more technologically sophisticated toys but also because children grow older, enter new phases, change interests, and start to be amused by different things. This message applies to the world of film as well. After all, the narrative in *Toy Story* of the transition in toy technology from the charming but rather simple Woody to the fancy, high-tech Buzz can also be taken as an allegory of the history of children's animated film—and particularly of the transition from Disney to Pixar. The message seems to be the reassuring one (aimed perhaps at both the film's audiences and Disney executives) that, just as there is still room for lovable old Woody in *Toy Story*, so too will there still be a place in children's film for the kinds of films that Disney has traditionally made.

*Toy Story* can be taken as a critique of consumer culture in its emphasis on the fact that toys should be regarded as more than mere commodities. Ironically, its toy characters were perfect as the basis for an extensive comarketing campaign in which virtually every toy in the film was produced and marketed to children who had been made eager to possess the toys by watching the film.

Pixar released successful sequels to *Toy Story* in 1999 and 2010.

**TRACY, SPENCER (1900–1967).** Spencer Tracy was one of Hollywood's most distinguished actors in a film career that stretched from the early days of sound film to the 1967 hit *Guess Who's Coming to Dinner?* He was named the ninth greatest male screen legend of all time in a 1999 poll conducted by the **American Film Institute** (AFI).

Tracy's first feature film was **John Ford**'s *Up the River* (1930), in which he starred, with **Humphrey Bogart** as a key supporting player. After starring in a variety of films in the early 1930s, he received the first of his nine **Academy Award** nominations for Best Actor in a Leading Role for *San Francisco* (1936). He then followed by winning that award two years in a row, for *Captains Courageous* (1937) and *Boys Town* (1938).

Tracy received no **Oscar** nominations in the 1940s, though he did star in such notable films as *Woman of the Year* (1942), *Keeper of the Flame* (1942), *Without Love* (1945), *The Sea of Grass* (1947), *State of the Union* (1948), and *Adam's Rib* (1949). All of these films costarred **Katharine Hepburn**, with whom Tracy formed one of the most successful onscreen couples in Hollywood history. Beginning during the making of the first of these films, they also became an off-screen couple and that relationship, though sometimes troubled, would continue until Tracy's death, though they never married because Tracy was already married and, as a Catholic, could not get a divorce from his first wife.

Tracy scored a number of notable successes in the 1950s, including *Father of the Bride* (1950), *Bad Day at Black Rock* (1955), and *The Old Man and the Sea* (1958), for which he received additional Oscar nominations for Best Actor. *Desk Set* (1957), another **romantic comedy** with Hepburn, was also a highlight of the decade.

Tracy continued to be an effective leading man into his sixties, winning further Oscar nominations for *Inherit the Wind* (1960), *Judgment at Nuremberg* (1961), and the posthumously released *Guess Who's Coming to Dinner*, the latter again pairing him with Hepburn in what would be his last screen role. That brought his total of Oscar nominations for Best Actor to nine, tying him with **Laurence Olivier** for the most in Hollywood history.

**TRAVOLTA, JOHN (1954– ).** After a number of minor television roles, John Travolta burst into the public consciousness as high-schooler Vinnie Barbarino in the series *Welcome Back, Kotter*, which ran from 1975 to 1979.

His success in that role also catapulted him into the movies. Important roles in **Brian De Palma**'s *Carrie* (1976) and the made-for-TV film *The Boy in the Plastic Bubble* (1977) were followed by two films that made him a top Hollywood star: *Saturday Night Fever* (1977) and *Grease* (1978). Travolta received an **Academy Award** nomination for Best Actor in a Leading Role for the first of these, though his performances in these films were perhaps more notable for his dance moves than for his acting.

De Palma's *Blow Out* (1981) gave Travolta a chance at a more serious dramatic role, while *Staying Alive* (1983) allowed him to reprise his role as Tony Manero from *Saturday Night Live*. However, this film was less successful than the original, and Travolta's other films of the 1980s fared poorly as well, with *Urban Cowboy* (1980) being a particularly notable failure. *Perfect* (1985) did not do much better, and by the end of the decade he was reduced to starring in such light **comedies** as *Look Who's Talking* (1989) and *Look Who's Talking, Too* (1990).

Though the latter two films had some commercial success, it appeared in the early 1990s that Travolta's days as a top Hollywood star were over. He then delivered his most highly regarded performance as hit-man Vincent Vega in **Quentin Tarantino**'s *Pulp Fiction* (1994), earning him his second **Oscar** nomination for Best Actor, 17 years after the first.

Now again an elite star, Travolta subsequently starred in a number of high-profile projects in the following years. *Get Shorty* (1995), *Face/Off* (1997), *A Civil Action* (1998), and *Primary Colors* (1998) did well enough for Travolta to continue being cast in leading roles in A-list projects. *Battlefield Earth* (2000), however, was another major failure, both commercially and critically, which was a particular disappointment to Travolta because it was based on the writings of L. Ron Hubbard, the founder of the Church of Scientology, of which Travolta had been a member since 1975.

Since that time, Travolta has continued to appear regularly in film as both a hero and a villain. Some recent highlights include *Ladder 49* (2004), *Be Cool* (2005, reprising his role from *Get Shorty*), *Wild Hogs* (2007), and *Old Dogs* (2009). Demonstrating versatility, Travolta has also cross-dressed to star as Edna Turnblad in the 2007 remake of the **musical** *Hairspray* and provided the voice of the title character in the **children's film** *Bolt* (2008).

**TRIANGLE FILM CORPORATION.** During its brief heyday (1915–1919), the Triangle Film Corporation was one of the most important producers of **silent films**. Founded in 1915 by brothers Harry and Roy Aitken, the studio initially featured the combined talents of silent film superstars **D. W. Griffith**, Thomas Ince, and **Mack Sennett** (thus the "triangle" in the name). The company released more than three dozen short films in 1916, in addition to Griffith's epic *Intolerance* (1916), the most important film produced by the new company. Triangle released even more films in 1917, but the quality of the films soon began to suffer as the company struggled to keep up its high-quantity output. By 1917, Griffith, Ince, and Sennett had all left the studio for other endeavors, and the studio went into decline.

Triangle released dozens of films again in 1918, but by 1919 their output had dwindled to less than two dozen, and they released only one more film after 1919. By this time, their production facilities had been bought by **Samuel Goldwyn** for the use of his own Goldwyn Pictures Corporation.

**TRUMBO, DALTON (1905–1976).** Screenwriter Dalton Trumbo was one of the most prominent members of the **Hollywood Ten**, who were at the very center of the Hollywood blacklist of the 1950s. By 1947, Trumbo had already written the screenplays for more than two dozen films—including *Kitty Foyle, The Story of a Woman* (1940), for which he received an **Academy Award** nomination for Best Screenplay. His uncooperative testimony before the **House Un-American Activities Committee** (HUAC) in October 1947 officially removed him from the film business for over a decade. However, after serving a prison term for contempt of Congress, Trumbo moved to Mexico and there continued to write screenplays, many of which were produced in Hollywood using fronts or pseudonyms for the writing credits.

Even before his prison term, Trumbo co-wrote the screenplay for the **film noir** classic *Gun Crazy* (1950), through the front Millard Kaufman, and the groundbreaking **science fiction** film *Rocketship X-M*, without screen credit. Trumbo has the distinction of having written two **Oscar**-winning screenplays while on the **blacklist**, for *Roman Holiday* (1953, originally credited to a front, McLellan Hunter) and *The Brave One* (1956, originally credited to Trumbo's pseudonym, Robert Rich). He also has the distinction of being the writer who first broke the blacklist, receiving onscreen credit for writing two major films released in 1960, *Spartacus* and *Exodus*.

Trumbo never quite regained the momentum of his earlier career and subsequently wrote few important films, though *The Sandpiper* (1965) and *Papillon* (1973) were notable exceptions. He also both wrote and directed the film adaptation of his own 1939 antiwar novel, *Johnny Got His Gun* (1971).

**TURNER, LANA (1921–1995).** Famously discovered at a Hollywood drugstore, Lana Turner began her acting career at the age of 16 in *They Won't Forget* (1937). She subsequently played a number of supporting ingénue roles, in films such as *Love Finds Andy Hardy* (1938), but moved into more mature roles in the early 1940s, in such films as *Johnny Eager* (1941) and *Ziegfeld*

*Girl* (1941). She achieved major success as a sultry femme fatale in the **film noir** classic *The Postman Always Rings Twice* (1946).

Now regarded as one of Hollywood's sexiest leading ladies, Turner was known for her platinum blonde hair and her form-fitting attire, which early on earned her the nickname of "the Sweater Girl." She remained a top star through the 1950s, appearing in such films as *The Bad and the Beautiful* (1952), *Betrayed* (1954), and *Peyton Place* (1957), receiving her only **Academy Award** nomination for Best Actress for the latter film.

*Imitation of Life* (1959) was a major commercial success. By this time Turner was as famous for her tempestuous personal life as for her acting, including a string of seven husbands and a high-profile case involving the killing of her mob-related lover Johnny Stompanato, apparently by Turner's teenage daughter. Turner's popularity quickly waned in the 1960s. She appeared in only a handful of films in the decade, by the end of which she was reduced to starring in **B-movies** such as *The Big Cube* (1969). Turner subsequently appeared mostly on television, receiving positive critical attention for her recurring role in the prime-time soap opera *Falcon Crest* in 1982 and 1983.

**TWENTIETH CENTURY FOX.** Formed in 1935 via the merger of Fox Film Corporation and Twentieth Century Pictures, the Twentieth Century Fox Film Corporation has been one of the **major studios** in the film industry ever since. Since 1985, the studio (now often referred to simply as "Fox") has been a subsidiary of Rupert Murdoch's media conglomerate News Corporation.

At the time of the initial merger, Twentieth Century Pictures was a relatively small enterprise, while the larger Fox was beginning to flounder beneath the weight of the Depression economy. With **Darryl F. Zanuck** as production chief, the new Twentieth Century-Fox (the hyphen was dropped in 1985) began to groom a stable of new young stars, including **Henry Fonda** and **Gene Tierney**. They also had notable successes with some of their existing stars, especially a young **Shirley Temple**, who reached the height of her popularity in the years following the merger.

Immediately after World War II, Twentieth Century Fox had released such serious-minded films as *The Razor's Edge* (1946) and *Gentlemen's Agreement* (1947), but the company soon began to suffer, along with the rest of the film industry, as a result of the rise of television. In addition, the company was hard hit by the 1948 **Paramount Antitrust Case**, which forced them to divest themselves of the extensive chain of theaters that had been the principal asset brought by Fox into the original merger.

In 1953, with the industry as a whole seeking to produce spectacular films that could give audiences an experience they could not get from television,

Fox released the big-budget **biblical epic** *The Robe*, using a refinement of the French-developed CinemaScope process, to which Fox had acquired the exclusive rights. The film was a huge success, and Fox announced plans to begin releasing all of their films in CinemaScope. Other studios, allowed access to the process by Fox, soon began using it as well, ensuring enough product to make it worthwhile for theaters to convert their equipment to the process.

CinemaScope increased business for Fox in the mid-1950s, but the company had again fallen on hard times by the beginning of the 1960s, a situation that was then exacerbated in the early 1960s by the demise of **Marilyn Monroe**, the studio's top star, and by the critical and commercial failure of the hugely expensive **historical epic** *Cleopatra* (1963). Zanuck was installed as the chairman of the studio and immediately instituted emergency measures that kept the company afloat long enough to produce such hits as *The Sound of Music* (1965) and the **science fiction** films *Fantastic Voyage* (1966) and *Planet of the Apes* (1968), restoring the studio to solvency.

Science fiction has, in fact, been particularly important to Twentieth Century Fox. One of the most important films produced by the company in the 1950s had been the alien invasion narrative *The Day the Earth Stood Still* (1951), a courageous film that counseled international cooperation and criticized the arms race during the height of Cold War hysteria. Fox again struggled in the early 1970s, but sf film again brought success to the studio with the 1977 release of **Star Wars** (co-produced with **Lucasfilm**), at that time easily the biggest hit in the company's long and illustrious history. Fox followed with what would become another science fiction classic with the release of *Alien* in 1979, establishing the studio as a leading player in the science fiction film boom of 1977 to 1984, during which time they also distributed the second and third *Star Wars* films.

The success of *Star Wars* made Fox an attractive acquisition for News Corporation in 1985, while the studio itself welcomed the takeover due to problems caused by the flight of major investor Marc Rich from income tax evasion charges. Science fiction continued to be a key part of the company's success over the coming years with the release of such films as *Aliens* (1986) and *The Abyss* (1989), both directed by **James Cameron**. In the 1990s, Fox scored another huge blockbuster hit with *Independence Day* (1996), while the decade ended with the Fox-distributed *Star Wars: Episode 1—The Phantom Menace* (1999), one of the biggest hits in film history and the beginning of a second trilogy of *Star Wars* films. Fox followed with other sf films, including Cameron's *Avatar* (2009), which became the biggest box-office hit in film history.

Fox has also had notable successes in television production, including the founding of its own broadcast network in 1986.

# U

**ULMER, EDGAR G. (1904–1972).** The Austrian-born director Edgar G. Ulmer is widely regarded as one of the greatest practitioners of low-budget filmmaking. He first came to Hollywood as an assistant to famed director **F. W. Murnau** in 1926, working on set design for the film *Sunrise* (1927). He subsequently had a long career in Hollywood as a director of low-budget **B-movies**, during which he became known as a master of getting the maximum mileage out of limited resources. His 1934 **horror** film *The Black Cat*, for example, is one of the classics of that genre, while his 1945 **film noir** *Detour* has achieved near legendary status. He also directed several other film noirs, including *The Strange Woman* (1946) and *Ruthless* (1948).

Ulmer was a master of low-budget **science fiction** as well. His 1951 alien-invasion film *The Man from Planet X*, while a bit technically crude, has some interesting noirish visuals and is a thoughtful meditation on the kind of paranoid xenophobia that was fueling the Cold War arms race. Ulmer also directed *The Amazing Transparent Man* (1960), a less interesting mad scientist film. That same year, he directed *Beyond the Time Barrier*, an enjoyable little postapocalyptic film involving time travel. In 1961, Ulmer directed the sf adventure film *L'Atlantide*, a French-Italian co-production made in Italy.

**UNITED ARTISTS.** Though it has had a troubled financial history, United Artists was still the most extensive and successful attempt on the part of cinematic artists to gain artists greater creative control over their work. The studio was founded in 1919 as a joint effort of superstars **Charles Chaplin, D. W. Griffith, Douglas Fairbanks**, and **Mary Pickford**. The original agreement called for each of the four principals to produce five films per year. However, feature-length films were just becoming the dominant form in the industry and were also becoming more complex and expensive, which quickly made it impossible for the four founders to meet the terms of the agreement.

This reality soon brought financial difficulty to the company. By 1924, Griffith had departed for other pursuits, and the company hired seasoned film executive **Joseph Schenck** to run the studio and try to get it on a firmer financial footing. Schenck brought new talent and resources to the company, but United Artists was particularly hard hit by the end of the **silent film** era, which virtually ended the careers of Fairbanks and Pickford and sent Chaplin into semiretirement, producing only one sound film in the 1930s and that one—*Modern Times* (1936)—with only limited dialogue.

By the end of the 1940s, United Artists was virtually out of business, but the company was somewhat resuscitated in the 1950s under the new management of lawyers Arthur Krim and Robert Benjamin and new production manager Arnold Picker. Directors such as **John Huston**, **Otto Preminger**, **Stanley Kramer**, and **Billy Wilder** worked with the studio during the decade, as United Artists profited from the breakdown of the old studio system—which had been greatly facilitated by the 1948 **Paramount Antitrust Case**, which came about as the eventual result of a 1942 lawsuit filed against the studios by Society of Independent Motion Picture Producers, many of whose principals (including Pickford and Chaplin) had formerly been associated with United Artists.

In 1962, United Artists became the major distributor for *Dr. No*, launching the James Bond **spy film** franchise, which was hugely profitable for the company. Most of the company's successes by this time were in fact as distributors of films produced by other companies, including *The Graduate* (1967) and *In the Heat of the Night* (1967), films the success of which helped to make the company a lucrative property, leading Krim and Benjamin to sell the controlling interest in United Artists company to the American insurance conglomerate Transamerica, though they stayed on to continue to run the company.

United Artists continued to both produce and distribute successful films, with franchises such as the Bond films and the Pink Panther films providing an important part of their business. Relations with the parent company were not always good, however. In 1978, Krim and Benjamin left after the latest dispute with Transamerica to help found a new studio, **Orion Pictures**. By 1980, the box-office disaster *Heaven's Gate* (1980) caused further trouble between United Artists and Transamerica, which decided to sell the studio to **Metro-Goldwyn-Mayer** (MGM).

United Artists has remained affiliated with MGM since 1981, through several changes in ownership/management and considerable financial turmoil. As of this writing, the combined company is virtually moribund and is seeking still another new owner.

**UNITED STATES V. PARAMOUNT PICTURES, INC.** *See* PARAMOUNT ANTITRUST CASE.

**UNIVERSAL STUDIOS.** Founded in 1912 as the Universal Film Manufacturing Company under the leadership of **Carl Laemmle**, Universal Studios is one of the world's oldest film studios. With directors such as **Erich von Stroheim** working with the studio, Universal produced a number of prestigious **silent films** in its early years, including von Stroheim's *Blind Husbands* (1919) and *Foolish Wives* (1922). The company was incorporated as Universal Pictures Company, Inc., in 1925, by which time it had already been on the forefront of numerous innovations, such as giving onscreen credit to performers in films, thus facilitating their marketing as "brand" names.

Universal lacked the resources (especially extensive company-owned theater chains) to compete directly with the **major studios**, and the company was further troubled by the departure of production chief **Irving G. Thalberg** in 1925. Laemmle made his son, Carl Jr., the head of Universal Pictures in 1928 as a 21st birthday present. The younger Laemmle proved to be a fairly effective studio chief, convincing his father to modernize the studio and its operations and overseeing the production of films such as the classic **war film** *All Quiet on the Western Front* (1930).

Having had success with **horror** movies starring Lon Chaney in the 1920s, Universal produced a series of distinctive and now-classic **monster movies** in the early 1930s, including *Dracula* (1931), *Frankenstein* (1931), *The Mummy* (1932), *The Black Cat* (1934), and *The Bride of Frankenstein* (1935). However, Carl Jr.'s move into more expensive productions in the mid-1930s ultimately spelled the end for himself and his father at Universal. By 1936, production problems with the lavish **musical** *Show Boat* led to the ouster of both Laemmles from Universal by its creditor Standard Capital Corporation, even though that picture would ultimately prove to be a great critical and commercial success.

Much of Universal's output in the 1940s involved sequels to the classic monster movies of the 1930s, making the company a pioneer in the development of the phenomenon of film franchises. During this period and through the 1950s, the company also developed such franchises as the low-budget "Francis the Talking Mule" and "Ma and Pa Kettle" sequences, as well as a series of films starring comedians **Lou Abbott and Bud Costello**, several of which were spoofs of **science fiction** or of the company's own monster movies, including *Abbott and Costello Meet Frankenstein* (1948), *Abbott and Costello Meet the Invisible Man* (1951), and *Abbott and Costello Go to Mars* (1953).

The company, now operating as Universal-International, was also a central force in the science fiction film boom of the 1950s, producing such classic films as *It Came from Outer Space* (1953), the *Creature from the Black Lagoon* trilogy (1954–1956), and *The Incredible Shrinking Man* (1957). By the late 1950s, however, the financially troubled company was concentrating on increasingly low-budget efforts such as *The Thing that Couldn't Die* (1958) and *The Leech Woman* (1960); in 1963 they served as the U.S. distributor for Toho Studios' 1962 film *Kingu Kongu tai Gojira* (***King Kong** vs. Godzilla*). Indeed, their activity in science fiction film in the 1960s was mostly limited to the U.S. distribution of Toho products and other international productions, such as *Fahrenheit 451* (1966). By the 1970s, under the ownership of the entertainment conglomerate MCA since 1962, Universal was primarily a television production company.

Universal continued to be involved in the production or distribution of a number of important films, including **Seven Spielberg**'s blockbuster hit *Jaws* (1975), the success of which helped to keep the company solvent in troubled times. Universal also produced a number of science fiction and **disaster** films in the 1970s, including *Airport* (1970) and its three sequels of the decade, as well as *Earthquake* (1974). Interestingly, though, the company largely sat out the major ***Star Wars**-*fueled sf film boom of 1977–1984, concentrating its efforts in science fiction during this period on television productions such as *Battlestar Galactica* (1978–1979) and *Buck Rogers in the 25th Century* (1979–1981), the former being so similar to *Star Wars* that it triggered a lawsuit from **Twentieth Century Fox**, the producers of *Star Wars*. Universal did co-produce (with Spielberg's **Amblin Entertainment**) *E.T.: The Extra-Terrestrial* (1982) during this period, also later working with Amblin to co-produce the immensely successful *Back to the Future* trilogy (1985–1990).

In 1997, Universal began distributing films by the new **DreamWorks** studio, but Paramount's takeover of DreamWorks in 2005 ended that arrangement. By this time, Universal had become part of the media conglomerate NBC Universal, a subsidiary of the General Electric Corporation whose holdings include a number of cable television networks. The company still owns the rights to most of its considerable film library.

# V

**VALENTINO, RUDOLPH (1895–1926).** The Italian-born Rudolph Valentino (birth name Rodolfo Guglielmi) soared to unprecedented heights of fame as a male sex symbol in his relatively brief career as a **silent film** star. Valentino came to the United States in 1913. Though he had appeared in over three dozen films (including a number of shorts beginning as early as 1914), his starring roles in such early features as *The Four Horsemen of the Apocalypse* and *The Sheik* (1921) made him a screen idol, known for his dashing and exotic sex appeal.

Subsequent features, including *Blood and Sand* (1922) and *The Son of the Sheik* (1926), further increased his star status with women, though Valentino was becoming increasingly unpopular with American male audiences, who found his image effeminate and a threat to American manhood. In many ways, Valentino's early death only served to increase his legendary status. Since his death, he has been the subject of a number of films, including the recent critical success *Good Night Valentino* (2003).

**VAN PEEBLES, MELVIN (1932– ).** The actor, director, producer, and screenwriter Melvin Van Peebles was one of the leading pioneers in African American film. He began making short films in the United States in the 1950s, then made his first feature, *The Story of a Three-Day Pass* (198), while working in France. That film drew the attention of Hollywood and enabled him to make his first American feature, *The Watermelon Man* (1970), for **Columbia Pictures**. It was, however, with the independently made *Sweet Sweetback's Baadasssss Song* (1971), which he wrote, directed, produced, scored, and starred in, that Van Peebles made his most important contribution to film, helping to trigger a surge in the production of African American films in the 1970s and in particular helping to inspire the **blaxploitation** cycle of that decade.

Since that time Van Peebles has been involved in a number of projects as an actor, director, writer, and musician. One of the most notable of these was *Panther* (1995), an account of the history of the Black Panther Party directed by his son, Mario Van Peebles, scripted by Melvin based on his own novel.

Mario also directed *Baadasssss* (2003), a documentary about the making of *Sweet Sweetback's Baadasssss Song.*

**VAN SANT, GUS (1952– ).** Gus Van Sant has directed some of Hollywood's most interesting films since he first gained positive critical attention for his low-budget **independent film** *Mala Noche* (1985), about a doomed gay love affair. This film allowed Van Sant, who had been making television commercials, to move permanently into filmmaking, though his initial efforts to pitch ideas to **Universal Studios** proved fruitless. Van Sant then made a major breakthrough with the critically acclaimed *Drugstore Cowboy* (1989), about a group of drug addicts who support their habits by robbing drug stores.

Van Sant, one of Hollywood's first openly gay directors, has often treated gay and other marginalized cultures in his work, though in a matter-of-fact way that eschews judgment or political statements. The success of *Drugstore Cowboy* allowed Van Sant to make the highly experimental *My Own Private Idaho* (1991), a modern retelling of the story of Shakespeare's Henry IV and Henry V plays focusing on gay street hustlers, based on a script Van Sant had been working on for years.

*My Own Private Idaho* again drew praise from critics, though it was not a big commercial success. Van Sant then turned in a more commercial direction with *Even Cowgirls Get the Blues* (1993), an adaptation of a novel by countercultural novelist Tom Robbins. The film was a commercial and critical failure, but Van Sant returned to success with *To Die For* (1995), a **satire** of the American media culture of celebrity made for **Columbia Pictures**, his first film for a **major studio** and the first film directed, but not written, by Van Sant.

Van Sant returned to independent film with *Good Will Hunting* (1997), written by Ben Affleck and **Matt Damon**. The film was a runaway hit that received nine **Academy Award** nominations, including Best Picture and Best Director. That success allowed Van Sant to make another pet project in 1998, a shot-by-shot exact remake of **Alfred Hitchcock**'s *Psycho* (but in color and with a contemporary cast) that was mostly judged a failure, though it was certainly an interesting experiment in **postmodernism.**

Van Sant returned to mainstream success with *Finding Forrester* (2000), then scored another critical triumph with *Elephant* (2003), which won the Palme d'Or at the Cannes **Film Festival**, even though it met with a divided response in the United States. Since that time, Van Sant has focused mostly on experimental projects, though he again gained major attention (and another **Oscar** nomination for Best Director, as well as seven other nominations) for *Milk* (2008), a **biopic** about slain gay San Francisco politician Harvey Milk.

**VERHOEVEN, PAUL (1938– ).** The Dutch director Paul Verhoeven had early success in the Netherlands, but was almost entirely unknown in the United States when he was tabbed to direct *Robocop* (1987), a **science fiction satire** for which Verhoeven's over-the-top style was well suited. Verhoeven followed that film with the **Arnold Schwarzenegger** vehicle *Total Recall* (1990), another sf film with strong satirical components. Verhoeven then scored a mainstream success with the **neo-noir** thriller *Basic Instinct* (1992), followed by controversy and critical derision for *Showgirls* (1995). The director has never shied away from controversy, however, and in 1997 he directed the film adaptation of *Starship Troopers*, Robert A. Heinlein's most controversial novel. The film was controversial as well: It seemed to want to critique the violence and militarism of Heinlein's novel via Verhoeven's trademark satire, but was taken by many as a violent, militaristic film in its own right. Verhoeven followed with *Hollow Man* (2000), a sort of combination of an invisible man narrative with a Jekyll-and-Hyde mad scientist narrative. That film features superb **special effects** but is otherwise unremarkable.

Verhoeven returned to Europe to make *Black Book* (2006), set during World War II. In 1999, his earlier European work was recognized when his film *Turkish Delight* (1973) was named the best Dutch film of the 20th century at the Netherlands Film Festival.

**VERTIGO.** A recognized classic of the American cinema, *Vertigo* (dir. **Alfred Hitchcock**, 1958) is one of the most respected films of its esteemed director and is certainly his most stylistically complex. *Vertigo* was ranked the ninth greatest film of all time in a 2007 poll conducted by the **American Film Institute** (AFI).

*Vertigo* can also be seen as an early example of **postmodernism** in film, with its questioning of the boundary between fiction and reality and its portrayal of human identity as more performance than essence. In the film, police detective Scottie Ferguson (**James Stewart**) has been forced into retirement by a fear of heights that gives him vertigo and makes it difficult for him to do his job properly. When an old college chum hires Ferguson to follow his wife, Madeleine (Kim Novak), to make sure she does no harm to herself, Ferguson develops an obsession with the woman, only to have her (apparently) die from a suicidal fall that he is unable to prevent due to his condition.

Later, Ferguson meets (and essentially stalks) a shopgirl who resembles Madeleine, then sets about trying to transform her into a new Madeleine, only to discover that she and Madeleine really are the same person and that "Madeleine's" earlier suicide "death" had been part of an elaborate ruse designed to cover up the murder of the "real" Madeleine. Unfortunately, Ferguson's reaction to this discovery quickly leads to the woman once again falling to her death, this time for real, as a stunned Ferguson looks on.

Numerous elements of *Vertigo* are unlikely, even preposterous, as Hitchcock seems to revel in his ability to engage audiences no matter how farfetched the events or how unlikeable his protagonist. Meanwhile, two climactic kisses between Ferguson and "Madeleine" are staged with elaborately overdone camerawork, suggesting the constructed and artificial nature of their passion and of romance in general, informing the film with a postmodernist emotional skepticism.

This skepticism may have been a bit ahead of its time and out of step with the 1950s, which might account for the fact that *Vertigo* received little recognition from the **Academy Awards**, winning no **Oscars** and receiving only two nominations, for Best Sound and Best Art Direction.

**VIDOR, KING (1894–1982).** King Vidor was one of the most important directors in Hollywood in a career that stretched from 1913 to 1959, though he actually returned in 1980 to direct a short **documentary**. Vidor began as a director of short **silent films**, ultimately moving into features and directing two silent film classics, *The Big Parade* (1925) and *The Crowd* (1928), the latter of which (an exploration of the new mass society brought about by the recent rise of consumer capitalism in the United States) is widely considered to be his masterpiece.

Vidor received an **Academy Award** nomination for Best Director for *The Crowd*, which itself was nominated for Best Picture. He quickly followed with an additional nomination for his first sound film, *Hallelujah!* (1929), a groundbreaking **musical** with an African American cast. He also received an **Oscar** nomination for *The Champ* (1931), an early boxing film. Other highlights of the 1930s included *Our Daily Bread* (1934), a sort of sequel to *The Crowd*, and *The Citadel* (1938), for which he received another Oscar nomination for Best Director.

Other important films directed by Vidor include *Stella Dallas* (1937), *Duel in the Sun* (1946), *The Fountainhead* (1949), and *War and Peace* (1956), for which he received his final Oscar nomination as Best Director. He also directed (without onscreen credit) the Kansas scenes of *The Wizard of Oz* (1939).

All in all, Vidor, who also scripted most of the most important films he directed, received five Oscar nominations for Best Director, but won none. He was, however, given a special Oscar in 1979 in recognition of his lifetime achievements in film.

**VON STERNBERG, JOSEF (1894–1969).** The Vienna-born Josef von Sternberg was one of the first Hollywood directors to develop a reputation as a self-conscious maker of art rather than simply as a producer of entertainments. Many of his early works, such as the **silent films** *Underworld* (1927) and *The Dragnet* (1928, now lost) and the early sound film *Thunderbolt* (1929), were crime and **gangster films**, but showed an uncommon emphasis on style and innovative cinematography.

Though often thought of as one of the many European directors who were recruited by Hollywood in the 1920s in an attempt to bring greater creative artistry to American film, von Sternberg actually grew up largely in New York City and New Jersey and began his career in film in the United States. He did, however, move to Germany after the failure of *Thunderbolt* and began making films there, including *The Blue Angel* (1930), which was filmed in dual German- and English-language versions. That film starred von Sternberg's young protégée **Marlene Dietrich**, with whom he soon returned to Hollywood to make a series of films, including *Morocco* (1931) and *Shanghai Express* (1932), both of which won **Academy Award** nominations for Best Director for von Sternberg. His other films with Dietrich included *Dishonored* (1931), *Blonde Venus* (1932), *The Scarlet Empress* (1934), and *The Devil Is a Woman* (1935).

With Dietrich's stardom having passed its peak, von Sternberg's career declined in the latter 1930s as well, though he did later make important contributions to the genre of **film noir**, including *The Shanghai Gesture* (1941) and *Macao* (1952). His last film was the **John Wayne** vehicle *Jet Pilot* (1957).

**VON STROHEIM, ERICH (1885–1957).** The Austrian-born Erich von Stroheim is one of the most legendary figures of the early years of American cinema. Having come to the United States, he began working in film there in 1914. His first credited **silent film** as a director was *Blind Husbands* (1919), which he quickly followed with *The Devil's Passkey* (1920) and *Foolish Wives* (1922), all made for the Universal Film Manufacturing Company, a forerunner of **Universal Studios**.

By this time, von Stroheim had developed a reputation for devotion to artistic quality, often at the expense of practicality, and his early battles with Universal production chief **Irving G. Thalberg** are the stuff of Hollywood legend. Stroheim's next film, *Greed* (1924), is even more legendary. This attempt to make a detailed film adaptation of Frank Norris's novel *McTeague* (1899) resulted in numerous delays and cost overruns and in a first cut of over nine hours in length. Von Sternberg's resistance to cutting the film then led to his removal by Thalberg, with whom von Sternberg had moved to **Metro-Goldwyn-Mayer** (MGM); a dramatically shortened version of the film was then edited by others and released, though it was unsuccessful. The longer version is now lost.

This commercial fiasco was followed by *The Merry Widow* (1925), von Stroheim's biggest commercial success. *Queen Kelly* (1929), starring **Gloria Swanson**, was another controversial film plagued by von Stroheim's battles with Swanson and producer Joseph Kennedy, leading to von Stroheim's removal in midproduction, though he did receive sole onscreen credit as the director. The difficulties surrounding the production of this film made von Stroheim a virtual outcast in Hollywood, and he was credited as the director of only one more (minor) film, *Hello, Sister!* (1933)—on which he again had to get an assist from other directors, including **Raoul Walsh**, in order to complete.

Von Stroheim also worked extensively as an actor, a career that in fact extended well beyond his years as a director. This career included an important role as the aristocratic German aviator von Rauffenstein in Jean Renoir's *Grand Illusion* (1937) and several roles as German villains in American World War II films. His best-known role, however, is probably as former silent-film director Max von Mayerling in **Billy Wilder**'s *Sunset Blvd.* (1950), opposite Swanson.

# W

**WALLIS, HAL B. (1898–1986).** Hal B. Wallis was one of the most successful film producers in Hollywood history. After beginning work in the publicity department at **Warner Bros.** in 1923, Wallis moved into production and eventually served as a producer and executive producer for more than 300 films. His first work as a producer was for the pioneering **gangster film** *Little Caesar* (1931). In the 1930s, Wallis typically worked behind the scenes without onscreen credit, but by the 1940s was generally credited onscreen.

In the 1940s, Wallis served as the producer or executive producer of a number of classic films for Warner Bros., including *High Sierra* (1941), *Sergeant York* (1941), *The Maltese Falcon* (1941), and ***Casablanca*** (1942). The latter received the **Academy Award** for Best Picture, an award that typically goes to the producer. When **Jack Warner** insisted on accepting that award himself in the name of Warner Bros., Wallis responded by leaving Warners and going into **independent film** production.

Wallis subsequently produced such films as *The Strange Love of Martha Ivers* (1946), *The Rose Tattoo* (1955), *Becket* (1964), and *Anne of the Thousand Days* (1969), the latter three of which all received **Oscar** nominations for Best Picture, the only nominations for which Wallis was personally named. Most of his films after 1944 were made by his own company, Hall Wallis Productions, though he occasionally produced films through other studios, especially **Paramount Pictures**.

A total of 16 films produced by Wallis at Warners were nominated for Best Picture, although only *Casablanca* won the award. However, Wallis did received the **Irving G. Thalberg** Memorial Award for his work as a producer in both 1939 and 1944 and still stands as one of only two individuals to have won that award multiple times. (**Darryl F. Zanuck** won the award three times.)

**WALSH, RAOUL (1887–1980).** Raoul Walsh had a long and successful career as a Hollywood director, stretching from numerous short **silent films**, to classic silent features such as *The Thief of Bagdad* (1924) and *Sadie Thompson* (1928, in which Walsh himself costarred), to a number of important sound films in genres such as the **Western** and **film noir**.

397

Walsh was on the cutting edge when he directed the widescreen Western *The Big Trail* (1930), starring **John Wayne** in his first credited screen role. After directing mostly **B-movies** for **Paramount** during the rest of the 1930s, Walsh moved to **Warner Bros.** and into bigger projects such as the **gangster film** *The Roaring Twenties* (1939), the noirish **Humphrey Bogart** vehicle *High Sierra* (1940), and the Western *They Died with Their Boots On* (1941), starring **Errol Flynn**.

Later in the 1940s, Walsh directed such Westerns as *Cheyenne* (1947) and *Silver River* (1948), as well as the film noir classic *White Heat* (1949). By this time, however, Walsh was again being relegated to lower-budget projects. His contract with Warners expired in 1953. He made a number of additional films as a freelance director, including the Civil War drama *Band of Angels* (1957, with **Clark Gable**) and the World War II drama *The Naked and the Dead* (1958), based on the novel by Norman Mailer. Most of his latter films were minor ones, however, and he retired from directing in 1964.

Known more as a competent maker of commercial films than as an artist, Walsh never received an **Academy Award** nomination. He also wrote and produced a number of films.

**WANGER, WALTER (1894–1968).** Walter Wanger was one of Hollywood's most prominent producers in a career that stretched from his uncredited work on the **Marx Brothers** film *Cocoanuts* (1929) to the **historical epic** *Cleopatra* (1963), a box-office disaster that nevertheless won Wanger his only **Academy Award** nomination for Best Picture. In between, he produced some of Hollywood's most important films, specializing in socially conscience dramas such as *Gabriel over the White House* (1933), *You Only Live Once* (1937), *Blockade* (1938), *Scarlet Street* (1945), *Smash-Up: The Story of a Woman* (1947), *Riot in Cell Block 11* (1954), and *I Want to Live!* (1958), the latter two of which were prison films influenced by Wanger's own incarceration after he was convicted of the 1951 shooting of the agent (and suspected lover) of his wife, actress **Joan Bennett**.

Though most of his early work was done for **Paramount Pictures**, Wanger branched out, forming his own company, Walter Wanger Productions, beginning with the 1934 film *The President Vanishes*. The company was subsequently involved in the production of a number of important films, including *The Trail of the Lonesome Pine* (1936), *Stagecoach* (1939), *The Long Voyage Home* (1940), and *Invasion of the Body Snatchers* (1956).

Wanger was nominated for the **Irving G. Thalberg** Memorial Award in 1939 and was given an honorary Academy Award in 1946 for his service as the president of the **Academy of Motion Picture Arts and Sciences** from 1939 to 1945. He was granted another special Academy Award in 1949 for the production of *Joan of Arc* (1948), but refused to accept the award to protest the fact that this film did not receive an **Oscar** nomination for Best Picture.

**WAR FILM.** War inherently involves the kind of conflict and human drama on which movies thrive, so it is not surprising that movies about war have long been a central genre of American film. The war film is also a rather flexible genre that overlaps with many others, including the **biopic**, the **historical epic**, **science fiction**, or even **comedy**. On the other hand, films about actual combat can be difficult and expensive to make, so it is not surprisingly that such films were fairly unusual in the early years of American film. In the **silent film** era, **D. W. Griffith**'s groundbreaking *The Birth of a Nation* (1915), often considered the founding work of American feature-length film, deals with the end and aftermath of the Civil War. If the era of feature-length silent film thus began with a war movie, it also effectively ended with one, as **Lewis Milestone**'s *All Quiet on the Western Front* (1930), originally conceived as a silent film, ultimately became one of the first major sound films. It was also one of the first antiwar films, depicting combat during World War I as grim and brutal, rather than grand and heroic. In between, notable war films included **Charles Chaplin**'s war comedy *Shoulder Arms* (1918) and the groundbreaking *The Big Parade* (1925), which focused on the horrors of World War I.

War movies were not a major force in Hollywood in the 1930s, though the classic *Gone with the Wind* (1939) deals with events surrounding the Civil War. *Sergeant York* (1941) was an important World War I film, released just two months before the bombing of Pearl Harbor drew the United States into World War II. The war movie first became a truly major genre during World War II, when any number of films were made in support of the American war effort, including such classics as *Casablanca* (1942) and *For Whom the Bell Tolls* (1943). Several films—including *The North Star* (1943), *Mission to Moscow* (1943), *Song of Russia* (1943), and *Counter-Attack* (1945)—were explicitly pro-Soviet, made in support of the U.S.–Soviet alliance during the war. More common were films that focused on pro-American propaganda, generally combined with anti-Nazi or anti-Japanese propaganda, including such films as *Guadalcanal Diary* (1943), *Destination Tokyo* (1943), *Thirty Seconds over Tokyo* (1944), *Objective, Burma!* (1945), and *The Story of G. I. Joe* (1945).

World War II remained the focus of the war film genre long after the end of that war, though subsequent films were more nuanced and less equivocally pro-war. Some, such as **William Wyler**'s *The Best Years of Our Lives* (1946), focused on the postwar experiences of soldiers returning from the war, while others, such as Mark Robson's *Home of the Brave* (1949), employed the war film as social commentary—in this case to critique racism both within the military and in American society as a whole. Robson's film thus anticipated such later works as *Glory* (1989), which focuses on the experiences of black soldiers fighting for the Union in the Civil War.

Films such as **Billy Wilder**'s *Stalag 17* (1953) focused on specialized aspects of World War II—in this case on the experiences of American airmen held in the German prisoner-of-war camp. Some films even began to make antiwar statements, such as **Raoul Walsh**'s *The Naked and the Dead* (1958), though that film significantly toned down the critique of the American war machine that is contained in the Normal Mailer novel on which it was based. Meanwhile, **Stanley Kubrick**'s *Paths of Glory* (1957) returned to World War I in treating war with skepticism. Still, other postwar films continued to treat war in general and World War II in particular as settings for the presentation of exciting adventures, as in the **John Wayne** vehicle *The Sands of Iwo Jima* (1949) or *D Day the Sixth of June* (1956). Such films also tended toward an established formula in which a small band of buddies (usually of diverse ethnic and cultural backgrounds) struggles together to survive the rigors of war. The romantic *From Here to Eternity* (1953) was a particularly memorable film about the Japanese bombing attack on Pearl Harbor, while *The Bridge on the River Kwai* (1957), a joint British–American production about British and American war prisoners forced into labor by their Japanese captors, is still a much-admired classic.

American war movies moved toward more realistic depiction of battle scenes in such films as *The Longest Day* (1962), an epic film depicting the D-Day invasion of Normandy from both Allied and German perspectives. On the other hand, the film, featuring an impressive ensemble cast of well-known stars, is hardly balanced, presenting the Allies largely as heroic and the Germans largely as bumbling incompetents. Other notable World War II films of the 1960s included *The Guns of Navarone* (1961), *The Great Escape* (1963), *The Dirty Dozen* (1967), and *Where Eagles Dare* (1968). *Patton* (1970) was an important biopic with particular emphasis on the role of its title figure, General George S. Patton, in World War II, while *Tora! Tora! Tora!* effectively detailed the Japanese bombing of Pearl Harbor, largely focusing on the Japanese themselves.

By the end of the 1960s, of course, the American experience in Vietnam was leading to a popular reconsideration of attitudes toward war in general, which would soon be reflected in American film. Actually, the first major film directly based on the war in Vietnam was the John Wayne vehicle *The Green Berets* (1968), a propaganda piece designed to support the American war effort. The first films to criticize the American involvement in Vietnam typically did so indirectly, as in **Robert Altman**'s *MASH* (1970), which is ostensibly about the absurdity of certain aspects of the Korean War.

Particularly prominent in this category were a number of **Westerns** that rather transparently deployed the genocidal destruction of Native Americans and their culture as an allegorical replacement for the havoc being wrought at the time by American forces in Vietnam. Such anti–Vietnam War Westerns included *The Professionals* (1966); *The Wild Bunch* (1969), *Little Big Man* (1970), *Soldier Blue* (1970), *Two Mules for Sister Sara* (1970), and *Ulzana's Raid* (1972). Collectively, these films suggested that the Vietnam War was enabled by a tendency in the American national psyche toward violence and hatred of the Other that has been present throughout the history of the United States.

Eventually, major Vietnam War films (most of which can be characterized as antiwar films) began to appear, beginning with **Francis Ford Coppola**'s *Apocalypse Now* (1979). **Oliver Stone**'s *Platoon* (1986) and Kubrick's *Full Metal Jacket* (1987) were also particularly prominent films that dealt critically with the American experience of combat in Vietnam, while films such as **Hal Ashby**'s *Coming Home* (1978) and Stone's *Born on the Fourth of July* (1989) focused on the postwar experiences of Vietnam War veterans. Michael Cimino's *The Deer Hunter* (1978) is a sweeping saga that attempts to follow the lives of its major characters before, during, and after the war. Finally, *Heaven and Earth* (1993) completed Stone's Vietnam trilogy, adding a new dimension with its focus on the war-related experiences of a Vietnamese woman.

Of course, movies based on World War II continued to appear as well, as in **Samuel Fuller**'s *The Big Red One* (1980). **Steven Spielberg**'s *Schindler's List* (1993) was a highly acclaimed account of the efforts of a German industrialist to save a group of Jews from Nazi persecution during World War II, heralding a return of that conflict to a prominent place in American film, a return that was spurred by the fact that the 50th anniversary of the end of World War II in 1995 seemed to trigger a wave of nostalgia for the relative moral verities of that conflict. Spielberg's *Saving Private Ryan* (1998) was a particularly graphic account of the D-Day invasion of the beaches of Normandy, though it in many ways looked back to the classic World War II films in its focus on heroism and masculine bonding. In the same year, Terrence Malick's *The Thin Red Line* was a grimly realistic but less traditional account of combat, focusing on the battle of Guadalcanal in the Pacific.

Other notable recent films about the conflict in the Pacific include **Clint Eastwood**'s 2006 dual accounts of the Battle of Iwo Jima, *Flags of Our Fathers* (from the American perspective) and *Letters from Iwo Jima* (from the Japanese). **Quentin Tarantino**'s *Inglourious Basterds* (2009), centered on an Allied plot to assassinate Adolf Hitler, with stylistic touches borrowed from the Italian spaghetti Western. In the meantime, films about more recent American military involvements in the Middle East and elsewhere had begun to appear. For example, **Michael Moore**'s **satirical** *Canadian Bacon* (1995) suggested the way in which events such as the first Gulf War of 1991 extended the mentality of the Cold War, with the United States desperately looking for enemies against which to define itself; this film in many ways anticipated Moore's much-acclaimed **documentary** about the 2003 invasion of Iraq, *Fahrenheit 9/11* (2004). Rod Lurie's *Deterrence* (1999) similarly builds upon the Gulf War of 1991, while Jonathan Demme's *The Manchurian Candidate* (2004)—a remake of John Frankenheimer's 1962 Cold War classic—was an even more direct attempt to move from the Cold War to the Gulf War as cinematic material.

Edward Zwick's *Courage under Fire* (1996) was the first major Hollywood film based on the 1991 Gulf War, while **Sam Mendes**'s *Jarhead* (2005) has the distinction of being the first major film about the first Gulf War that was made after the beginning of the second. It also suggests parallels between the U.S. involvements in the Middle East and the earlier experience in Vietnam, as does David O. Russell's *Three Kings* (1999), a hip, stylish effort that nevertheless provides some of the most telling and trenchant commentary on the American involvement in Iraq. Meanwhile, **Ridley Scott**'s *Black Hawk Down* (2001) deals with the first major American military experience after the first Gulf War, the near-disastrous intervention in Somalia in the fall of 1993. Films related to the 2003 Iraq War include *In the Valley of Elah* (2006) and *Home of the Brave* (2006). Finally, in recent years, wars related to the American "war on terror" have begun to appear, but the very nature of this phenomenon means that such films—such as Scott's *Body of Lies* (2008)—tend to collapse the distinction between the war film and the **spy film**.

**WARNER BROS.** Warner Bros. Entertainment (though "Bros." is an abbreviation for "Brothers," the name is now officially given as "Bros." in company documents) is one of the major producers of films and other entertainments in the United States. Founded by the titular four brothers, immigrants from Poland, the company grew slowly at first but eventually attained **major studio** status. It retains that status to this day, though it is now a subsidiary of the Time Warner media conglomerate.

The Warners opened their first movie theater in 1903 and gradually expanded their participation in the film business until they opened their own movie studio in Hollywood in 1918. Here, Sam and **Jack Warner** produced films, while Harry and Albert Warner headed the firm's business operations back in New York. At first a relatively small, struggling enterprise, the company (incorporated in 1923 as Warner Brothers Pictures, Inc.) had a major breakthrough with the release of *The Jazz Singer* (1927), using a synchronized soundtrack supplied by their own Vitaphone process. This film propelled the industry into the sound era and Warners into major-studio status, moving into a new, larger studio in Burbank, California, and expanding their holdings in movie theaters.

With **Darryl F. Zanuck** as production head, the company scored numerous successes in the early 1930s, though they struggled financially due to the economic climate of the Depression. The company produced a wide variety of films, including elaborately staged **musicals** such as *Gold Diggers of 1933* (1933) and *42nd Street* (1933). They also released the first all-color musical—*On with the Show*—in 1929 and generally led the way in the evolution of color film, as they had with sound. However, the company became particularly associated in the early 1930s with gritty, realistic black-and-white films that directly engaged the difficulties of the Depression era, including a successful string of **gangster films**, including *Little Caesar* (1931), *The Public Enemy* (1931), and *I Am a Fugitive from a Chain Gang* (1932).

**Hal B. Wallis** succeeded Zanuck as production chief in 1933, while the imposition of the **Motion Picture Code** in 1934 curbed Warner Brothers' gangster films and other "problem" pictures to some extent. By the end of the decade, with stars such as **Bette Davis** and **Humphrey Bogart** leading the way, Warner Brothers was turning a profit. They also began to produce more prestigious films, such as the **biopics** *The Story of Louis Pasteur* (1935) and *The Life of Emile Zola* (1937), both starring Paul Muni. The latter film won the studio its first **Academy Award** for Best Picture.

Arguably, however, the studio's most important contribution to American popular culture in the 1930s came with the introduction of the "Looney Toons" cartoon shorts, designed to be shown in theaters prior to feature films. Hugely popular, these cartoons, featuring such characters as Bugs Bunny and Daffy Duck, became a mainstay of American popular culture for decades and are still popular today, even though they were ostensibly replaced in the 1990s by reboots such as the *Tiny Toon Adventures* and *Animaniacs* television series co-produced by Warner Bros. and **Amblin Entertainment**, with **Steven Spielberg** as executive producer.

Warner Bros. scored huge successes in the early 1940s with such films as *Casablanca* and *Yankee Doodle Dandy* (1942). With Bogart at his peak and a stable of female stars (including Davis, **Joan Crawford**, and **Olivia de Havilland**) scoring numerous successes, the war years were particularly good ones for Warner Bros. Soon afterward, however, they began to struggle, along with all of the other Hollywood studios. Warners, however, had particular problems in the late 1940s and through the 1950s due to battles between the company (and especially studio head Jack Warner) and a number of their leading performers.

In the course of the 1950s, Warner Bros. significantly expanded into television and the recording industry, though feature films remained their flagship product. In 1967, Jack Warner sold controlling interest in the company to Seven Arts Productions. The new studio, renamed Warner Bros.-Seven Arts, was then acquired in 1969 by Kinney National Company, a conglomerate whose holdings included parking lots, funeral homes, and National Allied Publications, publishers of DC Comics. That company soon spun off its non-entertainment assets and refocused its holdings with Warner Bros. at the core, renaming itself Warner Communications.

Through the 1970s and 1980s, Warner Bros. scored numerous successes, depending largely upon the drawing power of big-name stars, though it also generated substantial profits from taking its leading DC Comics characters onto the screen with such films as *Superman* (1978) and *Batman* (1989). Meanwhile, Warner Communications merged with publisher Time, Inc., in 1989 to form the Time Warner conglomerate of which it is still today. (That company was actually acquired by Internet company AOL in 2000, but the subsequent collapse of Internet stocks led AOL to be pushed into the background of the resultant merged entity, and eventually spun off into a separate company.)

With the tremendous success of franchises such as the Harry Potter film series and of films such as the Batman vehicle *The Dark Knight* (2008), Warner Bros. has turned huge profits in recent years. In 2009, Warners became the first studio to gross more than $2 billion in the United States in a single year. In addition to Warner Bros. Pictures, Time Warner now releases films through a variety of subsidiaries, including New Line Cinema, Castle Rock Entertainment, and HBO Films, the latter in association with the company's successful HBO subscription cable television channels. In terms of both total revenue and total market capitalization, Time Warner is the world's second largest media conglomerate, behind the Walt **Disney** Company.

**WARNER, JACK (1892–1978).** Jack Warner joined siblings Harry, Sam, and Albert to found the **Warner Bros.** film studio, which has remained one of America's **major studios** since the end of the 1920s. The company opened its first Hollywood studio in 1918, with Jack and Sam in charge of production and Harry and Albert in charge of business operations back in New York. After Sam died in 1927, Jack remained in charge of the company's Hollywood operations, though top producers such as **Darryl F. Zanuck** and **Hal B. Wallis** were in charge of actual production into the mid-1940s.

Jack Warner's tyrannical management style led to many conflicts with performers and other employees over the years, as well as with Albert and (especially) Harry back in New York. After Jack secretly acquired control of the company in 1956 via a carefully crafted scheme, he was permanently estranged from his brothers. Jack continued to manage the company alone into the mid-1960s, scoring a number of successes in film and expanding the company's operations in television and the recording industry. By this time, however, Warner was increasingly regarded as something of a relic of Hollywood's **Golden Age** and he eventually left the company entirely in 1969 (when the studio was taken over by Kinney National Company), after years of erosion in his power there.

Warner pursued a career as an independent producer from 1969 to 1972, but scored no major successes and was soon forced to retire altogether due to his failing health.

**WASHINGTON, DENZEL (1954– ).** Denzel Washington is one of the most successful American film actors of his generation and one of the leading African American actors in film history. After several early minor appearances, Washington attracted major attention as Dr. Phillip Chandler on the television medical drama *St. Elsewhere* from 1982 to 1988. During the run of that show, Washington received an **Academy Award** for Best Actor in a Supporting Role for his performance in *Cry Freedom* (1987). He then went on to receive a second such nomination for the much-admired Civil War drama *Glory* (1989).

Now much sought after in Hollywood, Washington followed with a series of important roles, including starring roles in two films by **Spike Lee**, *Mo' Better Blues* (1990) and the epic **biopic** *Malcolm X* (1992), for which Washington received an **Oscar** nomination for Best Actor in a Leading Role. A variety of starring roles followed, including a reunion with Lee for *He Got Game* (1998). Washington then received another Best Actor Oscar nomination for his performance in *Hurricane* (1999) and followed with an Oscar win for his leading role in *Training Day* (2001), becoming just the second African American actor (after **Sidney Poitier**) to win that award.

Indeed, though a number of Washington's films have foregrounded race issues, he has largely transcended race, playing numerous lead roles in which race is not a key issue. His films have ranged from the supernatural thriller *Fallen* (1998) to the postapocalyptic drama *The Book of Eli* (2010), from the family-oriented football drama *Remember the Titans* (2000) to the time-travel thriller *Déjà vu* (2006). The latter was one of several collaborations with director **Tony Scott**. Washington has appeared in a number of action-oriented crime dramas (usually on the side of the police), though he starred in *American Gangster* (2007) as drug kingpin Frank Lucas. *See also* ACTION FILM.

**WATERS, JOHN (1946– ).** John Waters is one of America's best-known makers of **independent films**. Many of his early films, famed for their outrageously bad taste, have become **cult** classics, including *Pink Flamingos* (1972), *Female Trouble* (1974), *Desperate Living* (1977), and *Polyester* (1981). Among other things, these films became known for their offbeat casts of regulars (including actress Mink Stole and drag queen Divine), who became known as the "Dreamlanders."

Many of the Dreamlanders (joined by newcomer Ricki Lake and singers Sonny Bono and Deborah Harry) were also featured in *Hairspray* (1988), though this film represented a movement toward the mainstream and is still Waters's best-known work. *Cry-Baby* (1990), featuring a young **Johnny Depp**, former kidnapped heiress Patricia Hearst, and former porn star Traci Lords (among others), was somewhat in the same spirit, while the Kathleen Turner vehicle *Serial Mom* (1994) was Waters's most mainstream film yet, though it was still a decidedly offbeat comedy.

*Pecker* (1998) was a movement back away from the mainstream, while *Cecil B. DeMented* (2000) spoofed the marginal filmmaking world of which Waters himself had long been an important part. His latest directorial effort was *A Dirty Shame* (2004), a comic exploration of the underground subculture of sex addiction in Waters's native Baltimore, where his films are typically set.

**WAXMAN, FRANZ (1906–1967).** Born in the German province of Silesia (now a part of Poland), Franz Waxman was one of Hollywood's most successful composers of film **music** in a career that stretched from *The Bride of Frankenstein* (1935) to *Lost Command* (1966). He began his career in German film in 1930s, then moved to Paris and finally the United States to escape the Nazis. He quickly became a sought-after composer in Hollywood and received his first **Academy Award** nomination for Best Score for *The Young in Heart* (1938). He went on to receive a total of 12 **Oscar** nominations for his film scores, winning twice, for **Sunset Blvd.** (1950) and *A Place in the Sun* (1951).

Other films for which Waxman's scores received Oscar nominations include **Alfred Hitchcock**'s *Rebecca* (1940) and *Suspicion* (1941), as well as *Objective, Burma!* (1945), *The Silver Chalice* (1954), *The Nun's Story* (1959), and *Taras Bulba* (1962). Important scores that did not receive Oscar nominations include those for *The Philadelphia Story* (1940), *Woman of the Year* (1942), and *Mister Roberts* (1955), as well as two more films with Hitchcock, *The Paradine Case* (1947) and *Rear Window* (1954).

Waxman also composed extensively for television. Outside of the film and television world, Waxman is particularly well known for his *Carmen*

*Fantasie*, an extremely difficult piece for violin and orchestra. However, that piece first appeared as part of a film score, in *Humoresque* (1946), another film for which Waxman's score was Oscar-nominated. In 1947, he founded the annual Los Angeles International Music Festival, of which he served as the head for the next two decades.

**WAYNE, JOHN (1907–1979).** Born Marion Morrison, John Wayne was one of the most popular film stars of all time, even though his outspoken conservative and sometimes racist politics (which included a rabid anticommunism in the 1950s and a strong support for the U.S. war effort in Vietnam in the 1960s and 1970s), drew the ire of many. Wayne was named the 13th greatest male screen legend of all time in a 1999 poll conducted by the **American Film Institute** (AFI).

After early work as a prop man, Wayne played a number of bits parts in movies, especially for **John Ford**, a director with whom he would have a long and successful partnership. He got his first big break when he was cast as the lead in **Raoul Walsh**'s *The Big Trail* (1930), a lavish spectacle that was the first major **Western** of the sound era. That film was a box-office failure, but the role launched a career that would see Wayne star in more than 100 films, becoming probably the leading star of both Westerns and **war films**.

Known for his distinctive voice and swaggering walk, Wayne was a charismatic star, though he attracted relatively little critical acclaim, partly because he specialized in genre films. He did receive three **Academy Award** nominations for Best Actor in a Leading Role, including those for *Sands of Iwo Jima* (1949) and *The Alamo* (1960, which he also directed), but he won only for *True Grit* (1969). Wayne was a major box-office draw whose name (which eventually became virtually synonymous with a particular conservative brand of Americanism) made any film in which he appeared an identifiable and easily marketable brand.

Wayne appeared in dozens of Westerns and other films in the 1930s, but it was not until his starring role as the Ringo Kid in Ford's *Stagecoach* (1939) that he became the biggest star of the genre, which itself gained more respect after that film. Wayne would continue to make Westerns up until his last film, *The Shootist* (1976), starring in some of the greatest Westerns of all time, including Ford-directed classics such as *Fort Apache* (1948), *She Wore a Yellow Ribbon* (1949), *Rio Grande* (1950), *The Searchers* (1956), and *The Man Who Shot Liberty Valance* (1962). He also starred in a number of Westerns directed by **Howard Hawks**, including *Red River* (1948), *Rio Bravo* (1959), *El Dorado* (1966), and *Rio Lobo* (1970).

Wayne did not serve in World War II, as **Republic Pictures** sought and obtained a draft deferment for its biggest star. He did, however, become a star of films made to support the U.S. war effort, remaining a leading star of war films throughout the rest of his career. Highlights of his career in this genre included **William Wellman**'s *The High and the Mighty* (1954), Ford's *The Wings of Eagles* (1957), the epic World War II film *The Longest Day* (1962), **Otto Preminger**'s *In Harm's Way* (1965), and the only major pro-Vietnam War film made during the U.S. military involvement there, *The Green Berets* (1968), which he also directed.

Wayne's status as an American icon was recognized when he was awarded a special Congressional Gold Medal in 1979, just weeks before his death. In 1980, Wayne was posthumously awarded the Presidential Medal of Freedom by President Jimmy Carter.

**WEISMULLER, JOHNNY (1904–1984).** The Hungarian-born Johnny Weismuller rose to fame as a swimmer in the 1920s, when he won five Olympic gold medals and dozens of national championships in the United States. That fame carried him into a successful acting career in which he played Edgar Rice Burroughs's Tarzan in a series of films for **Metro-Goldwyn-Mayer** (MGM), beginning with *Tarzan the Ape Man* (1932). After six Tarzan films with MGM, Weismuller made six more lower-budget Tarzan films with **RKO Pictures**, ending with *Tarzan and the Mermaids* (1948).

Now too old to continue the Tarzan role, Weismuller made another series of 13 jungle pictures as Jungle Jim, beginning with *Jungle Jim* (1948) and ending with *Jungle Man-Eaters* (1954). He also played Jungle Jim in a 1955–1956 television series, then played a fictionalized version of himself (as a Jungle Jim–like character) in three more jungle films in 1954 and 1955, because the television series by that time had acquired the rights to the "Jungle Jim" name. Weismuller then retired from acting, though he made a brief cameo appearance in *Won Ton Ton: The Dog Who Saved Hollywood* (1976).

**WELLES, ORSON (1915–1985).** The actor and director Orson Welles is widely recognized as one of the few true geniuses of American cinema. After an early career acting and directing for the stage earned him the reputation of a prodigy, Welles gained national attention with the notorious live broadcast in 1938 of an adaptation of H. G. Wells's *War of the Worlds*, which many viewers took as a news report of an actual Martian invasion. Welles was then brought to Hollywood by **RKO Pictures**, which was seeking to gain artistic respectability by hiring the young phenom, who was given unprecedented creative freedom.

Welles used this freedom to direct, co-write, and star in *Citizen Kane* (1941), widely believed to be the greatest film ever made. Welles won the only competitive **Academy Award** nominations of his career for the film, including those for Best Director and Best Actor; he won the **Oscar** for Best Screenplay, along with **Herman J. Mankiewicz**. Unfortunately, it was also a controversial film and a box-office failure, partly due to the efforts of William Randolph Hearst (on whose life the story of Kane was partly based) to suppress the showing of the film. Welles followed as the writer and director of *The Magnificent Ambersons* (1942), another classic, but his further battles with the studio during the making of this film eventually led RKO to change the ending of the film without Welles's approval and in violation of his contract.

Welles also appeared in the hastily made *Journey into Fear* (1943) for RKO, but was unable to complete his wartime documentary about the Brazilian carnival, *It's All True*. By this time, his relations with RKO were shattered and few studios wanted to hire him as a director, given his growing reputation for being difficult to work with. However, he did find work as an actor in such films as *Jane Eyre* (1943), for **Twentieth Century Fox**.

Welles returned to directing with the classic **film noirs** *The Stranger* (1946) and *The Lady from Shanghai* (1947), also starring in both, but his battles with **Columbia Pictures** head **Harry Cohn** during the making of the latter virtually ended his Hollywood career as a director. Welles did direct a low-budget film adaptation of Shakespeare's *Macbeth* in 1948, but by this time he had left the United States for exile in Europe given the political climate of anticommunist hysteria that was sweeping America and having a major impact on the American film industry.

While in Europe, Welles starred in the British film noir classic *The Third Man* (1949), but produced relatively little as a director, though *Mr. Arkadin* (1955) has gained considerable critical attention over the years. He then returned to Hollywood to direct another classic, *Touch of Evil* (1958), which many feel to be second only to *Citizen Kane* among his films in importance. But the film was not a box-office success and did little to repair his relations with the Hollywood film industry.

Subsequently, Welles directed such literary adaptations as *The Trial* (1962), based on the novel by Franz Kafka, and *Chimes at Midnight* (1965), based on a combination of several Shakespeare plays featuring the character of Falstaff, whom Welles played in the film. He subsequently worked on a number of **independent films** (many left unfinished) and made several appearances in both film and television (including his notorious series of TV commercials in the 1970s for Paul Masson wine). He also used his distinctive booming voice in a number of voiceover roles, but his career as a frontline Hollywood director and lead actor was over by the beginning of the 1960s. He did, however, receive a Golden Globe nomination for Best Motion Picture Actor in a Supporting Role for his performance in *Butterfly* (1982).

In 1971, Welles was given a special Academy Award for his lifetime of achievement in film, accepting the award in a prerecorded speech that is still considered one of the historical highlights of the Academy Award ceremonies. For his work as an actor, he was named the 16th greatest screen legend of all time in a 1999 poll conducted by the **American Film Institute** (AFI).

**WELLMAN, WILLIAM (1896–1975).** William Wellman was one of the leading directors in the **Golden Age** of Hollywood. His career began in the **silent film** era, when he had a brief acting career, then directed such features as *Wings* (1927), the winner of the first **Academy Award** for Best Picture. Wellman himself received three **Oscar** nominations for Best Director—for *A Star Is Born* (1937), *Battleground* (1949), and *The High and the Mighty* (1954)—though he never won that award. His only Oscar win was for Best Screenplay as the co-writer of *A Star Is Born*.

Wellman was a fast worker noted for turning out his films on time, but not without considerable turmoil on the set, partly because of his own flamboyant personality and partly because of his dislike of male actors, whom he regarded as effeminate and narcissistic. It is perhaps for this reason that he had some of his greatest successes with films starring **John Wayne**, an actor at least as macho as Wellman. In any case, Wellman directed some of the most memorable films in Hollywood history, in a variety of genres. His films included the early **gangster film** *The Public Enemy* (1931) and the adventure film *Beau Geste* (1939), **war films** such as *Story of G. I. Joe* (1945), and **Westerns** such as *The Ox-Bow Incident* (1943).

Wellman retired after directing two films released in 1958: *Darby's Rangers* and *Lafayette Escadrille*.

**WEST, MAE (1893–1980).** Though she was a top star for less than a decade and appeared in a total of only a dozen films, Mae West has become an almost mythical figure, one of the most recognizable personages in 20th-century American popular culture. She was named the 16th greatest female screen legend of all time in a 1999 poll conducted by the **American Film Institute** (AFI).

A star in vaudeville before she moved into film, West was known as much for the spicy double entendres that filled her dialogue as for her voluptuous figure. She debuted in film with a supporting role in *Night after Night* (1932), then burst into stardom in 1933 as the female lead in *She Done Him Wrong* and *I'm No Angel*, both opposite **Cary Grant**.

Several more films in the 1930s failed to fulfill the promise offered by these early roles, though *Go West Young Man* (1937) was something of a highlight. West then made her best-known film, opposite **W. C. Fields**, in

*My Little Chickadee* (1940). That film represented her last major success, however. She starred in *The Heat's On* (1943), then retired from the screen until she returned to appear in *Myra Breckinridge* (1970), a campy sex **comedy** somewhat in the spirit of her own earlier films. She also appeared in *Sextette* (1978), but she maintained a public presence throughout her life due to her **musical** recordings and her appearances on the stage and occasionally on television.

A sex symbol whose appeal included a projected strength and independence and a breaker of taboos both on the screen and off, West would eventually become something of a feminist icon, despite her raunchy image.

**WESTERN.** Perhaps the most distinctively American of all film genres because of the way in which it directly reflects the history of the United States, the Western is essentially as old as American film itself. Indeed, Edwin S. Porter's *The Great Train Robbery* (1903), generally acknowledged to be the first fictional narrative film, was a Western. Westerns remained popular throughout the **silent film** period, as cowboy stars such as **Tom Mix** (who made more than 300 silent Westerns) rose to the very pinnacle of Hollywood megastardom. The Western remained popular after the transition to sound as well, with singing cowboys such as **Gene Autry** dominating the genre through the 1930s, though the Western during this period developed something of a reputation as a lowbrow genre, falling out of favor with the **major studios.**

The Western began to achieve more critical respect with the rise of **John Ford** as the first great Western film director of the sound era. Many film historians locate Ford's *Stagecoach* (1939) as the first great Western film (it was Ford's first Western of the sound era, though he had made numerous silent Westerns), and that film certainly established many of the conventions that would dominate the genre in years to come. Most importantly, Ford made striking use of Western landscapes in this film, while featuring a complex protagonist who was something of an antihero (played by **John Wayne**, who would go on to become the Western's greatest star). Unfortunately, *Stagecoach* also featured Native Americans who were depicted largely as undifferentiated and murderous savages, a tendency that would mark (and mar) the Western for years to come. Ford's Westerns, in particular, demonstrated the ability of the genre to take on almost mythic dimensions in making a crucial contribution to the development of the national cultural identity of the United States.

The Western is a complex and versatile genre whose influence extends into numerous other genres as well. To an extent, though, the history of the genre can be separated into two major phases, depending on the dominant treatment of the central motif of the struggle for control of the opportunities provided by the wealth and the vastness of the American West. In the first phase, which extends from *Stagecoach* into the 1960s, with Ford as the most important director, the struggle is primarily about the taming of the West, as individualist cowboy heroes battle the wild terrain and wild Indians of the West to try to carve out a place for themselves in the new land. In the second phase, which extends from the 1960s to the present, the dominant trope involves the waning of the West, as these individualist cowboys, having helped to tame the West, now face the threat posed by the growing corporatization and routinization of this once wild region.

*Drums along the Mohawk* (1939), Ford's first color film, was a frontier drama set in New York during the Revolutionary War. Though set in the East, it should still be considered a Western and extends many of the conventions established by *Stagecoach*, including battles against savage Indians. Ford's military service slowed the progress of his career (and of the Western) during World War II, but he returned with the romantic Western *My Darling Clementine* (1946). Over the next decade and a half, Ford directed some of the most important Westerns of all time, including *Fort Apache* (1948), *Rio Grande* (1950), *The Searchers* (1956), and *The Man Who Shot Liberty Valance* (1962), all of which extended, but often complicated, the conventions of the Western that Ford's own earlier films had helped to establish. By the time of *Cheyenne Autumn* (1964), Ford had completely shifted his earlier portrayal of the conflict between white settlers and Native Americans, now showing the latter in a highly sympathetic light.

In addition to Ford's films of this first phase of the Western, other highlights included **Howard Hawks's** *Red River* (1948), **Fred Zinnemann's** *High Noon* (1952), **George Stevens's** *Shane* (1953), **Robert Aldrich's** *Apache* (1954), and **Nicholas Ray's** *Johnny Guitar* (1954), which used the form to explore a number of serious issues of concern to American society in the postwar years, while also beginning to treat Native Americans in more nuanced ways. The **B-movie** Western during this period still tended to concentrate on battles between virtuous whites and savage Indians, but the appearance of *The Magnificent Seven* in 1960 announced the beginning of the end of the first phase of the Western. Wayne, however, continued to make Westerns in the older, more heroic vein to the end of his career, with such well-known films as *The Sons of Katie Elder* (1965), *El Dorado* (1966), *True Grit* (1969), *Rio Lobo* (1970, the last film directed by Hawks), and *The Shootist* (1976).

Highlights of the 1960s included the rise of the so-called spaghetti Western, an Italian-made version of the Western, most of the examples of which were Italian–American co-productions and featured American stars, the most important of whom was **Clint Eastwood**, who was featured in such films as *A Fistful of Dollars* (1964), *For a Few Dollars More* (1965), and *The Good, the Bad, and the Ugly* (1966). These films re-energized the Western, endowing it with self-parodic humor and a new moral complexity, embodied in Eastwood's laconic, enigmatic characters. Eastwood then brought this character back home to the United States in such films as *Hang 'Em High* (1968), *Two Mules for Sister Sara* (1970), *High Plains Drifter* (1973), and *The Outlaw Josie Wales* (1976), virtually establishing a subgenre of his own.

The other important development in the Western during the 1960s was the rise of the "anti-Western," which often challenged the established conventions of the genre, while at the same time shifting the emphasis from the taming of the West to the waning of the West. Some key films in this category included *The Professionals* (1966), ***Butch Cassidy and the Sundance Kid*** (1969), Abraham Polonsky's *Tell Them Willie Boy Is Here* (1969), **Sam Peckinpah**'s *The Wild Bunch* (1969), and **Robert Altman**'s *McCabe and Mrs. Miller* (1971). Many of these films used the Western form to comment indirectly on the American involvement in Vietnam, as did *Little Big Man* (1970), *Soldier Blue* (1970), and *Ulzana's Raid* (1972).

The appearance of Mel Brooks's genre parody *Blazing Saddles* (1974) in many ways marked the beginning of a decline in the popularity of the Western, though important examples continued to appear, mostly again in the anti-Western and waning-of-the-West veins. Especially impressive were Michael Cimino's much-maligned *Heaven's Gate* (1980) and Eastwood's widely acclaimed *Unforgiven* (1992). Other notable recent films that have indicated the versatility and continuing relevance of the Western include **Kevin Costner**'s *Dances with Wolves* (1990, a pro–Native American film that became the highest grossing Western of all time), Kurt Russell's *Tombstone* (1993), **Jim Jarmusch**'s enigmatic *Dead Man* (1995), and *3:10 to Yuma* (2007, a remake of the 1957 film of the same title). The Western has also demonstrated its vitality through the appearance of a number of films set in the contemporary era (rather than the typical 19th-century setting of the classic Western), but still conforming to many of the conventions of the genre. Important films in this category include **Quentin Tarantino**'s *Kill Bill 2* (2004) and **Joel and Ethan Coen**'s *No Country for Old Men* (2007).

**WEXLER, HASKELL (1922– ).** Haskell Wexler is one of the most respected American cinematographers of his generation. He has been nominated for the **Academy Award** for Best Cinematography five times, winning twice, for *Who's Afraid of Virginia Woolf?* (1966) and *Bound for Glory* (1976). He has also had a substantial career as a director of films such as *Medium Cool* (1969) and *Latino* (1985), as well as politically charged **documentaries** such as *Underground* (1976), *Bus Rider's Union* (1999), and *From Wharf Rats to Lords of the Docks* (2007).

It is, however, as a cinematographer that Wexler will be best remembered. After work as a cameraman for low-budget documentary films and television, he moved into A-list films as the cinematographer for **Elia Kazan**'s *America, America* (1963). His work on that film gained considerable attention, and he was soon working steadily, leading up to his **Oscar** for *Who's Afraid of Virginia Woolf?*, for which he won the last Oscar to be given specifically for black-and-white cinematography. Other films for which his camerawork gained Oscar nominations include *One Flew over the Cuckoo's Nest* (1975), **John Sayles**'s *Matewan* (1987), and *Blaze* (1989).

Other key films shot by Wexler include *In the Heat of the Night* (1967), *The Thomas Crown Affair* (1968), *Coming Home* (1978), *Colors* (1988), *Other People's Money* (1991), and three more films with Sayles: *The Secret of Roan Innish* (1994), *Limbo* (1999), and *Silver City* (2004).

In 1993, Wexler was given a lifetime achievement award from the American Society of Cinematographers. In 2007, he received a similar award from the Independent Documentary Association.

**WHALE, JAMES (1889–1957).** After some success as a theater director in his native England, James Whale moved into film and soon scored a major success with *Frankenstein* (1931), one of the definitive classics of the **horror** film genre. Whale followed with such important horror films as *The Old Dark House* (1932), *The Invisible Man* (1933), and *Bride of Frankenstein* (1935). However, he soon grew wary of being pigeon-holed as a director of horror films and attempted to branch out more into other genres, including the **musical**, in which he had notable success with *Show Boat* (1936).

*The Man in the Iron Mask* (1939) was another notable film directed by Whale, but he would never again achieve the success he had had with horror films in the first half of the 1930s. He directed only two more feature films in the 1940s.

Whale was one of the few openly (if discreetly) gay directors working in Hollywood during his career. Christopher Bram's 1995 novel *Father of Frankenstein* is based on the final years of Whale's life. It brought the director newfound prominence, especially after it was adapted to film as *Gods and Monsters* in 1998.

**WIDMARK, RICHARD (1914–2008).** Richard Widmark was an iconic actor of the **film noir**, usually playing crazed and sadistic villains, though he later branched out into more positive roles. He began his career as the vicious killer Tommy Udo in the film noir *Kiss of Death* (1947), earning his only **Academy Award** nomination, for Best Actor in a Supporting Role, for his performance in that film. He then followed with appearances in a series of important film noirs, including *The Street with No Name* (1948), *Road House* (1948), *Night and the City* (1950), *Panic in the Streets* (1950), *No Way Out* (1950), and *Pickup on South Street* (1953).

As Widmark began to move beyond film noir, he appeared in a variety of genres, especially **Westerns** and **war films**. And, though he remained primarily a supporting actor in these films, he became a well-known figure for his performances in such films as *Broken Lance* (1954), *Saint Joan* (1957), *The Alamo* (1960), *Judgment at Nuremberg* (1961), and *How the West Was Won* (1962). By the time of *The Bedford Incident* (1965) and *Madigan* (1968), he was often appearing in lead roles.

Widmark followed *Madigan* to star as the title character in a television series of the same title (1972–1973). Afterward, he returned primarily to supporting roles in film, including *Murder on the Orient Express* (1974), but by this time the quality of the films in which he appeared was beginning to decline. Late highlights include his appearances in *Twilight's Last Gleaming* (1977), *Coma* (1978), *Against All Odds* (1984), and *True Colors* (1991), his last theatrical film. The majority of his appearances from 1980 onward were in made-for-TV movies.

**WILDE, CORNEL (1915–1989).** The Hungarian-born Cornel Wilde moved to the United States and went on to have a successful career as a dashing leading man in Hollywood films. A former champion fencer, he got his first break in acting in 1940 when he was hired as a fencing instructor for **Laurence Olivier**'s Broadway production of *Romeo and Juliet*, subsequently also winning the role of Tybalt in that play. That performance greatly aided his movement into film, including an early supporting role in *High Sierra* (1941), starring **Humphrey Bogart**. More supporting roles followed; he then had the lead role as Frédéric Chopin in the **biopic** *A Song to Remember* (1945), which earned him his only **Academy Award** nomination, for Best Actor in a Leading Role.

Wilde starred in a variety of films in the remainder of the 1940s, including the historical drama *Forever Amber* (1947) and the **film noirs** *Leave Her to Heaven* (1945), *Road House* (1948), and *Shockproof* (1949). Often cast in "exotic" roles because of his dark good looks, Wilde starred as Aladdin in *A Thousand and One Nights* (1945) and as the Persian poet of the title in *Omar Khayyam* (1957). His lead role in **Cecil B. DeMille**'s *The Greatest Show on Earth* (1952) was another highlight of Wilde's career in the 1950s. He returned to film noir to star in *The Big Combo* (1955), which he produced through his own production company.

Wilde both produced and directed a number of subsequent films in which he starred, including *Storm Fear* (1955), *The Devil's Hairpin* (1957), *Maracaibo* (1958), *Sword of Lancelot* (1963), *The Naked Prey* (1966), *Beach Red* (1967), and *Sharks' Treasure* (1975). By the 1970s, however, his acting career was in decline, and he returned mostly to supporting roles. He appeared in only one film in the 1980s but made several appearances on television in that decade.

**WILDER, BILLY (1906–2002).** The Austrian-born Billy Wilder was one of greatest directors in Hollywood history, as well as one of its most successful screenwriters. Wilder worked in a number of genres, but was a particular master of the **film noir** and the **romantic comedy**. The Jewish Wilder began his career as a screenwriter in Germany in 1929, then moved to France to escape the Nazis. He directed one film there before moving on to the United States. Wilder arrived in Hollywood in 1933 and resumed his career as a screenwriter, contributing to a number of scripts during the 1930s while honing his skills with English.

Wilder achieved his first major success as a Hollywood screenwriter with *Ninotchka* (1939), for which he shared the **Academy Award** nomination for Best Screenplay with **Charles Brackett**, with whom he would collaborate on 13 screenplays between 1938 and 1950. Wilder and Brackett also shared the Best Screenplay **Oscar** nomination for *Ball of Fire* (1941). In 1942, Wilder turned to directing with *The Major and the Minor* (1942), which he also co-wrote with Brackett.

Wilder's first major success as a director came with the film noir classic *Double Indemnity* (1944), with he co-wrote with Raymond Chandler and for which he received Oscar nominations for both Best Screenplay and Best Director. Wilder followed the next year by winning the Oscars for both Best Director and Best Screenplay for *The Lost Weekend*, which he co-wrote with Brackett. Wilder and Brackett shared another Best Screenplay nomination for *A Foreign Affair* (1948), which Wilder directed. They then shared an Oscar win for Best Writing, Story, and Screenplay, for *Sunset Blvd.* (1950), for which Wilder also received a Best Director nomination.

Wilder would win only one more Best Director Oscar, for *The Apartment* (1960), for which he also won Oscars for Best Screenplay and, as the producer, Best Picture. In between, he directed and co-wrote some of the most memorable films of the 1950s, including *The Big Carnival* (1951), *Stalag 17* (1953), *Sabrina* (1954), *The Seven Year Itch* (1955), *The Spirit of St. Louis* (1957), and *Some Like It Hot* (1959), the latter of which again won him dual Oscar nominations for Best Screenplay and Best Director.

After *The Apartment*, Wilder directed only four more films in the 1960s, of which *Irma la Douce* (1963) was probably the most important, though he also received another Oscar nomination for Best Screenplay for *The Fortune Cookie* (1966). He wrote and directed a total of four films in the 1970s, including *The Private Life of Sherlock Holmes* (1970) and *The Front Page* (1974). He then ended his career with *Buddy Buddy* (1981), starring Jack Lemmon, with whom he had worked on a number of films.

Wilder received the prestigious **Irving G. Thalberg** Memorial Award in 1988 for his career achievements in film. Altogether, he received a total of 12 Oscar nominations for Best Screenplay (winning three) and eight for Best Director (winning two).

**WILLIAMS, JOHN (1932– ).** The American composer John Williams is one of the most honored composers of film **music** in Hollywood history, having received a total of 45 **Academy Award** nominations, winning five Best Score **Oscars**. Williams has written some of the most recognizable scores in film history, including those for most of the films of director **Steven Spielberg** and the first three films in the Harry Potter film series. Williams's best-known music, however, may have been that for two films in the late 1970s, *Star Wars* (1977) and *Superman* (1978).

Though sometimes criticized for the excessively romantic bombast of his film scores, Williams has remained one of the most sought-after composers in Hollywood since those films. He has been especially important in **science fiction**, and his music has become so thoroughly associated with the genre that even science fiction films not scored by Williams have often had scores that were intentionally crafted to sound as if Williams had written them. In addition to all five *Star Wars* sequels, other science fiction films scored by Williams include all Spielberg's sf films, including *Close Encounters of the Third Kind* (1977), *E.T.: The Extra-Terrestrial* (1982), *Jurassic Park* (1993), *The Lost World: Jurassic Park* (1997), *A.I.: Artificial Intelligence* (2001), *Minority Report* (2002), and *War of the Worlds* (2005).

Williams's Oscar wins for Best Score were for *Fiddler on the Roof* (1971), Spielberg's *Jaws* (1975), the original *Star Wars*, *E.T.*, and Spielberg's *Schindler's List* (1993). Other notable films for which he has written the scores include *The Killers* (1964), *The Long Goodbye* (1973), *Raiders of the Lost Ark* (1981), *Born on the Fourth of July* (1989), *Home Alone* (1990), *JFK* (1991), *Nixon* (1995), and *Saving Private Ryan* (1998).

Williams began composing scores for films in the late 1950s and continues as of this writing, having been tapped to write the score for the upcoming sf film *Interstellar*, slated for release in 2012 with Spielberg as director.

**WILLIS, BRUCE (1955– ).** After his breakthrough role in the television series *Moonlighting* (1985–1989), Bruce Willis has gone on to become a top box-office star in film. Though his biggest commercial success has come in **action** thrillers such as the four *Die Hard* films in which he has starred as John McClain, Willis has also starred in some of the most interesting and unusual films of his generation.

After limited success in such films as *Blind Date* (1987) and *Sunset* (1988), the blockbuster *Die Hard* (1988) proved that Willis could be a major success on the big screen. Though several of his subsequent films were less than successful, *Die Hard 2* (1990) was another major hit. Willis then had a major role in **Quentin Tarantino**'s *Pulp Fiction* (1994) that did a great deal to prove his versatility as an actor.

Willis followed in 1995 as the star of the third *Die Hard* film, as well as of **Terry Gilliam**'s highly unusual **science fiction** drama, *Twelve Monkeys* (1995). Willis followed with another lead role in a highly unusual sf film, Luc Besson's *The Fifth Element* (1997). Willis subsequently starred in two films with supernatural and superhuman themes directed by **M. Night Shyamalan**, *The Sixth Sense* (1999) and *Unbreakable* (2000).

Willis had a key role in **Robert Rodriguez**'s innovative *Sin City* (2005), then reunited with Rodriguez, playing a supporting role in *Planet Terror* (2007). Other films in which he has appeared include such varied efforts as *In Country* (1989), *Billy Bathgate* (1991), *Last Man Standing* (1996), *Armageddon* (1998), *The Story of Us* (1999), *The Whole Nine Yards* (2000), *Alpha Dog* (2006), and *Cop Out* (2010).

In 1998, Bruce Willis became the first prominent actor to act in a performance for capture and use in a videogame, in *Apocalypse* for the Sony PlayStation system. *See also* ACTION FILM.

**WISE, ROBERT (1914–2005).** Robert Wise had a long and varied career as a successful Hollywood film director. He began his career as a film editor on such illustrious works as **Orson Welles**'s *Citizen Kane* (1941) and *The Magnificent Ambersons* (1942), the former of which won him an **Academy Award** nomination for Best Editing. Wise also started as a director, though somewhat inauspiciously, on the latter film, when **RKO Pictures** asked him to direct a new, more upbeat ending for the film while Welles was away in South America on another project. Wise directed the sequence, which was the ending ultimately released in theaters, though many subsequent critics have felt this ending undermined the entire film.

Wise continued his career with two early **horror** films for producer **Val Lewton** that are still worth watching today: *The Curse of the Cat People* (1944) and *The Body Snatcher* (1945). He also directed several competent

**Westerns** and was the director of at least one film, *The Set-Up* (1949), that is now considered a **film noir** classic and one of the best boxing dramas ever made. In 1951, he moved into **science fiction**, directing *The Day the Earth Stood Still* (1951), which still stands as one of the most important classics of the genre.

Wise directed another classic boxing film with *Somebody Up There Likes Me* (1956), a **biopic** about Rocky Graziano. He received an Academy Award nomination for Best Director for *I Want to Live!* (1958). He then directed another important film noir, *Odds against Tomorrow* (1959), one of numerous films that he also produced. The latter included some truly classic films, such as the **musicals** *West Side Story* (1961) and *The Sound of Music* (1965), both of which won him **Oscars** as Best Director and, as producer, for Best Picture.

Wise received his fourth and final Best Director nomination for *The Sand Pebbles* (1966). He returned to science fiction for two of the most important films in that genre of the 1970s, *The Andromeda Strain* (1971) and *Star Trek: The Motion Picture* (1979). In 1967, Wise received the prestigious **Irving G. Thalberg** Memorial Award for his career achievements in film.

**THE WIZARD OF OZ.** *The Wizard of Oz* (dir. **Victor Fleming**, 1939) is one of the best-known and best-loved films in American cinematic history, widely considered to be the greatest **children's films** of all time. Based on a classic turn-of-the-century children's novel by L. Frank Baum but adapted to reflect the realities of the Depression decade in which it was produced, *The Wizard of Oz* was ranked as the 10th greatest film of all time in a 2007 poll conducted by the **American Film Institute** (AFI).

A lavish live-action **musical** *The Wizard of Oz* is perhaps most notable for its contrast between the drab, sepia-toned Depression-era Kansas in which it begins (the scenes in which were directed by **King Vidor**) and the brilliantly colored magical land of Oz (the scenes in which were directed by Fleming, who replaced initial director **George Cukor**). In the film, protagonist Dorothy Gale (**Judy Garland**) is carried (house and all) to Oz by a tornado that hits her family farm. There, her house lands on and kills the Wicked Witch of the East, triggering a chain of events that have become among the most famous in film history.

Of course, the film (differing from the novel, in which Oz is real) stipulates that Dorothy's adventure in Oz is a mere dream she experiences while unconscious from a head injury. In the end, after receiving help from a number of colorful sidekicks on her quest to find the titular wizard and to elude the attacks of the Wicked Witch of the West, Dorothy learns that all she needs is to be able to believe that she has the power to return home just by clicking the heels of her ruby slippers together, and magically she can do it. The film thus potentially delivers a message about feminine confidence and capability, even if the more fundamental point would seem merely to be an endorsement of good old American individualism and the power of positive thinking—a mode of thought that, in 1939, was becoming more and more difficult as the Depression lingered on year after year while the world drifted toward war.

*The Wizard of Oz* was only a moderate commercial success upon its initial release; it did, however, receive six **Academy Award** nominations, including one for Best Picture, though it won only two, for Best Original Score and Best Song, the now iconic "Over the Rainbow." The film itself did not gain the iconic status it now enjoys until the annual television showings that began in 1959 and that constituted an important part of the cultural framework of a whole generation of American children. It has since become one of the American films most alluded to by other films and works of popular culture.

**WOOD, NATALIE (1938–1981).** Born Natasha Zacharenko, Natalie Wood began her career as a four-year-old child actor and went on to become a top Hollywood star before her early death. After a couple of small, uncredited appearances in film, Wood began to draw attention for her work in such important films as *Miracle on 34th Street* and *The Ghost and Mrs. Muir* (both 1947). She worked regularly in film from that point forward, then received an **Academy Award** nomination for Best Actress in a Supporting Role for her breakthrough performance in *Rebel without a Cause* (1955).

Wood followed that performance with an important role in the classic **Western** *The Searchers* (1956). She appeared in several more films in the following years, including a starring role as the title character in *Marjorie Morningstar* (1958), opposite **Gene Kelly**. It was not, however, until 1961 that she took a significant step toward greater stardom with her lead roles in *Splendor in the Grass* and *West Side Story*, the former of which won her an **Academy Award** nomination for Best Actress in a Leading Role.

Wood received another such nomination for her performance in *Love with the Proper Stranger* (1963). Other key films in which she appeared in the 1960s included *Gypsy* (1962), *Sex and the Single Girl* (1964), *The Great Race* (1965), and *Bob & Carol & Ted & Alice* (1969). She appeared less regularly in film in the 1970s, when most of her roles were on television, though she starred in the **science fiction disaster** film *Meteor* (1979). Her last film was another sf thriller, *Brainstorm* (1983).

**WRITERS GUILD OF AMERICA (WGA).** The Writers Guild of America is a labor union that represents the collective interests of television and film writers, as well as some radio news employees. It consists of two separate affiliated organizations, the Writers Guild of America East (WGAE) and the Writers Guild of America West (WGAW). The two wings exist because they have separate histories; the WGAE began when the Authors' League of America split into two branches, one for print writers and one (the Dramatists Guild) for radio and stage dramatists, while the WGAW began as a revival of the old Screen Writers Guild in the same year.

The two branches first became affiliated in 1933, and the current name and configuration was adopted in 1954, by which time film and television writing had become the primary emphasis of both groups. The WGA did little to resist the **blacklist** of screenwriters during the anticommunist scare of the 1950s, even though many of those blacklisted had been among the original founders of the Screen Writers Guild. In more recent years, the WGA has represented its members more actively, including a highly publicized strike in 2007–2008 over income from DVD sales of films and television programs.

In addition to providing collective bargaining and other benefits (such as pensions and health insurance) to its members, the WGA is actively involved in establishing rules to determine onscreen writing credits for film and television writers. The two wings of the WGA also jointly administer the annual Writers Guild of America Awards, given for outstanding achievement in writing for film and television. In film, the awards are given for Best Original Screenplay, Best Adapted Screenplay, and Best Documentary Feature Screenplay. A number of television awards are given, based on genre, including awards for best writing for a dramatic series, comedy series, episodic drama, episodic comedy, daytime serial, and animation, among others.

**WYLER, WILLIAM (1902–1981).** In addition to working as a producer and screenwriter, William Wyler was one of the leading directors of the **Golden Age** of Hollywood. Born to a Jewish family in the French region of Alsace, Wyler came to the United States in 1921 and soon began to work in the film industry. Somewhat irresponsible in his youth, Wyler got off to a slow start, but by 1925 had become a director of **silent films** for **Universal Studios**, whose chief, **Carl Laemmle**, was a cousin of his mother. Specializing in **Westerns**, he had success and soon transitioned into sound film with such features as *The Love Trap* (1929) and *Hell's Heroes* (1930).

Later in the 1930s, Wyler left Universal to work with **Samuel Goldwyn**, directing some of the most important films of the latter half of the decade, including *Dodsworth* (1936) and *Wuthering Heights* (1939), both of which won him **Academy Award** nominations for Best Director. He continued as a top director for three more decades, famed for his craftsmanship and attention to detail, which often demanded numerous takes from his actors.

Altogether, Wyler received 12 **Oscar** nominations for Best Director, including Oscar wins for *Mrs. Miniver* (1942), *The Best Years of Our Lives* (1946), and *Ben-Hur* (1959). He twice received double nominations for Best Director and, as producer, Best Film, for *Roman Holiday* (1953) and *Friendly Persuasion* (1956). Other important films directed by Wyler include *Dead End* (1937), *The Little Foxes* (1941), *The Desperate Hours* (1955), *The Big Country* (1958), *The Children's Hour* (1961), and *Funny Girl* (1968).

Wyler was given the **Irving G. Thalberg** Memorial Award for his career achievements at the 1966 Academy Award ceremonies, the same year he received his final nomination for Best Director, for *The Collector* (1965).

**WYMAN, JANE (1917–2007).** Though the majority of her career (roughly from 1955 onward) was spent almost exclusively on television, Jane Wyman also had an extensive career as a film actress, especially in the 1940s and early 1950s. She began her career as a teenager with small roles from 1932 to 1937, when she had her first starring role, in *Public Wedding* (1937). Still, she appeared in relatively minor films (in both starring and supporting roles) over the next several years, until she gained major attention for her performance in **Billy Wilder**'s *The Lost Weekend* (1945). She followed that film with a starring role in *The Yearling* (1946), for which she received her first **Academy Award** for Best Actress in a Leading Role.

Wyman won the Best Actress **Oscar** for her performance in *Johnny Belinda* (1948) and later received additional nominations for *The Blue Veil* (1951) and *Magnificent Obsession* (1954). After *All That Heaven Allows* (1955), however, Wyman performed mostly on television, playing only occasional roles in film, including *Pollyanna* (1960) and *How to Commit Marriage* (1969). Her most important late role was in the prime-time soap opera *Falcon Crest*, in which she starred from 1981 to 1990 as villainous matriarch Angela Channing, drawing considerable critical praise.

Wyman was married to fellow actor **Ronald Reagan** from 1940 to 1949, when they divorced. He later became the first U.S. president to have been divorced.

**YOUNG, LORETTA (1913–2000).** Born Gretchen Young, Loretta Young had one of the longest and most prolific careers in the history of Hollywood actors. Mostly uncredited with small roles in her earliest films (beginning at the age of four), Young transitioned into larger roles and started using the name "Loretta" in her teen years, as in the Lon Chaney vehicle *Laugh, Clown, Laugh* (1928). She moved seamlessly into sound film, appearing in numerous features in the 1930s, when she proved herself a serviceable star in dozens of mostly minor films. She gradually began to appear in bigger films in the 1940s, as when she starred opposite **Orson Welles** in *The Stranger* (1946).

The next year, Young's performance in *The Farmer's Daughter* (1947) won her the **Academy Award** for Best Actress in a Leading Role. She won another Best Actress **Oscar** nomination for *Come to the Stable* (1949). She thus entered the 1950s at the peak of her stardom but made only a few more films—including the interesting **film noir** *Cause for Alarm!* (1951)—before shifting to television as the host and star of her own series, *The Loretta Young Show* (1953–1961). All of her subsequent appearances were on television.

# Z

**ZANUCK, DARRYL F. (1902–1979).** Darryl F. Zanuck was one of the most important studio executives in Hollywood history. His career began as a screenwriter and producer in the **silent film** era and extended through nearly five decades until his retirement as the head of **Twentieth Century Fox** in 1971. Along the way, he was involved in many of the most important films of those five decades, including *42nd Street* (1933), *Young Mr. Lincoln* (1939), *The Grapes of Wrath* (1940), *Gentleman's Agreement* (1947), *All about Eve* (1950), *The Man in the Gray Flannel Suit* (1956), *The Longest Day* (1962), and *Tora! Tora! Tora!* (1970).

After early work mostly as a writer, Zanuck first became an executive at **Warner Bros.** in 1929, rising quickly to become their production head by 1931. In 1933, he left Warners (after numerous battles with Harry Warner) to join the fledgling Twentieth Century Films, which merged with Fox Film Corporation in 1935 to form **Twentieth Century Fox**, with Zanuck as production chief.

After numerous successes, Fox found itself in difficulty by the mid-1950s, partly due to the rise of television and partly due to the loss of its extensive chain of theaters due to the **Paramount Antitrust Case** of 1948. Zanuck resigned as production chief in that year and moved to Europe, where he worked as an independent producer. Zanuck returned to head Fox in 1962, making his son, Richard D. Zanuck, head of production. Zanuck remained as the head of the studio until 1971, when he was forced out after a power struggle against a group that included his son.

Zanuck has the distinction of having won the **Irving G. Thalberg** Memorial Award for contributions to the production of motion pictures four times, in 1938, 1939, 1945, and 1951. Zanuck still occasionally wrote scripts even during his tenure as an executive. He was nominated for an **Academy Award** for Best Screenplay for *"G" Men* (1935).

**ZEMECKIS, ROBERT (1951– ).** The writer, producer, and director Robert Zemeckis has been involved in some of Hollywood's most successful and innovative films. Fresh out of film school, Zemeckis became a protégé of

**Steven Spielberg.** His first two films—*I Wanna Hold Your Hand* (1978) and *Used Cars* (1980)—both starred Kurt Russell and were produced by Spielberg. They drew some critical praise but had little commercial success. Even *1941* (1979), a Spielberg-directed film that Zemeckis co-wrote with frequent partner Bob Gale, was a commercial failure. *Romancing the Stone* (1984), produced by its star, **Michael Douglas,** was only slightly more successful. But Zemeckis then struck commercial gold with *Back to the Future* (1985), a film executive-produced by Spielberg that won a Best Screenplay **Oscar** nomination for Zemeckis and Gale.

That film spawned successful sequels in 1989 and 1990. In between, Zemeckis directed *Who Framed Roger Rabbit* (1988), a commercial hit remarkable for its sophisticated integration of animation and live action that demonstrated an interest in envelope-pushing technologies that would mark the rest of Zemeckis's career. The 1990s were less productive for Zemeckis as a filmmaker, partly because of his extensive involvement as executive producer of the HBO television series *Tales from the Crypt* (1989–1996). He did, however, direct what many view as his most important film in the decade in *Forrest Gump* (1994), for which he won the **Academy Award** for Best Director, while the film won for Best Picture.

*Cast Away* (2000), featuring *Forrest Gump* star **Tom Hanks,** was another commercial success, but Zemeckis's most notable films of the 2000s were probably *The Polar Express* (2004) and *Beowulf* (2007), partly because of their innovative use of performance capture animation technology, continuing Zemeckis's long interest in digital filmmaking. Digital technologies were also used extensively in *A Christmas Carol* (2009), though this megabudget film was not a big success at the box office

**ZIMMER, HANS (1957– ).** The German composer Hans Zimmer began writing film **music** in Great Britain in the 1980s and has been one of Hollywood's top composers of film scores since his breakthrough score for *Rain Man* (1988), which won him his first **Academy Award** nomination for Best Score. In 1989 he wrote the scores for *Black Rain* (1989), *Twister* (1989), and *Driving Miss Daisy* (1989) and has been a prolific composer of film scores ever since.

Zimmer composed the scores for many of the most interesting and successful films of the 1990s, including the **Oscar**-winning score for **Disney's** *The Lion King* (1994). Other Oscar-nominated scores composed by Zimmer in the 1990s included those for *The Preacher's Wife* (1996), *As Good As It Gets* (1997), *The Prince of Egypt* (1998), and *The Thin Red Line* 1998). He also composed the scores for *Thelma & Louise* (1991), *True Romance* (1993), *Something to Talk About* (1995), and *The Rock* (1996) in the decade.

In the 2000s, Zimmer has received Oscar nominations for Best Score for *Gladiator* (2000) and *Sherlock Holmes* (2009). He also composed the scores for *Batman Begins* (2005), *The Dark Knight* (2008), and *Inception* (2010), all with British director Christopher Nolan, and for several animated films, including *Shark Tale* (2004), *Madagascar* (2005), *The Simpsons Movie* (2007), *Kung Fu Panda* (2008), and *Madagascar: Escape 2 Africa* (2008).

**ZINNEMAN, FRED (1907–1997).** Known for his ability to solicit fine performances from his actors, the Austrian-born Fred Zinneman was one of Hollywood's most successful and versatile directors from the mid-1940s to the mid-1960s. Zinneman directed a number of short films in the 1930s, then moved into features in the early 1940s. His first major film was *The Seventh Cross* (1944), a hit that starred **Spencer Tracy**. Zinneman received an **Academy Award** nomination for Best Director for *The Search* (1948). He was at the height of his creative powers in the 1950s, when he won a Best Director **Oscar** for *From Here to Eternity* (1953) and received another such nomination for *High Noon* (1952), which would ultimately become his most respected film.

Other prominent films directed by Zinneman in the 1950s included *Oklahoma!* (1955) and *The Nun's Story* (1959), for which he received another Best Director Oscar nomination. He received another such nomination for *The Sundowners* (1960), for which he received a Best Picture nomination as the producer. He won for both Best Director and Best Picture for *A Man for All Seasons* (1966) and received another Best Director nomination late in his career for *Julia* (1977). His last film was *Five Days One Summer* (1982).

**ZSIGMOND, VILMOS (1930– ).** The Hungarian-born Vilmos Zsigmond became a naturalized citizen of the United States in 1962 and subsequently became one of Hollywood's leading cinematographers. He worked extensively as a cinematographer for both film and television in the 1960s, then moved into more important projects in the 1970s, including **Robert Altman**'s *McCabe & Mrs. Miller* (1971) and *The Long Goodbye* (1973). He won the **Academy Award** for Best Cinematography for **Steven Spielberg**'s *Close Encounters of the Third Kind* (1977).

Zsigmond has subsequently received **Oscar** nominations for Best Cinematography for *The Deer Hunter* (1978), *The River* (1984), and **Brian De Palma**'s *The Black Dahlia* (2006). He has also shot a number of other important films along the way, including Spielberg's *The Sugarland Express* (1974) and De Palma's *Obsession* (1976) and *Blow Out* (1981), as well as *Deliverance* (1972) and *Heaven's Gate* (1980).

**ZUKOR, ADOLPH (1873–1976).** The Hungarian-born Adolph Zukor came to the United States in 1889 and was already a successful businessman when he entered the film business in 1903, subsequently becoming one of its important pioneers. In 1912 he founded the film distribution company Famous Players in Famous Plays, which evolved into Famous Players Film Company by the next year, when it also began producing its own films. This company eventually evolved into **Paramount Pictures**, of which Zukor served as president until 1936, when he cut back on his activity and became chairman of the board, a position he held until his retirement in 1959.

A major figure behind the turn from an emphasis on short films to an emphasis on features, Zukor was credited as a producer on nearly 100 films between 1912 and 1938 and listed as the "presenter" of hundreds of others. His organization of Paramount as an integrated production, distribution, and exhibition company provided a key model for the film industry until the 1948 **Paramount Antitrust Case** broke up the kind of vertical integration that he had pioneered.

Zukor received an honorary **Academy Award** in 1949, with an inscription noting that he had been called the "father of feature film in America."

# Bibliography

## CONTENTS

## INTRODUCTION

The American film industry has long been accompanied by a wide range of printed publications, from industry trade magazines such as *Variety* (founded in 1905) and the *Hollywood Reporter* (1930), to reviews of films in newspapers, to fan magazines, to books aimed at fans, to detailed and sophisticated academic studies. This bibliography is a guide to resources in the latter two areas, with the brief addition at the end of a number of key websites that provide information about film online, which is rapidly becoming the most widely accessed source of information about film.

Serious studies of film in the United States are at least as old as the Payne Fund Studies, which began in 1929 and were aimed primarily at determining the effect of movie viewing on American children. These studies ultimately produced such book-length summaries as Henry James Forman's *Our Movie Made Children* (1934) and Edgar Dale's *How to Appreciate Motion Pictures: A Manual of Motion-Picture Criticism Prepared for High-School Students* (1938). In retrospect, they seem biased, based on an assumption that any impact of movie viewing on children would probably be negative, but they set the tone for many subsequent discussions of film, which have tended to assume a similar negative view.

European theorists such as Hugo Munsterberg, Rudolf Arnheim, Sergei Eisenstein, and Siegfried Kracauer led the way in terms of serious attention to the theoretical aspects of film, while many of the first serious critical studies of specific American films and film phenomena were produced by European critics and theorists as well—as when French critics Nino Frank and Jean-Pierre Chartier identified the phenomenon they called "film noir" in 1946, or when French critics associated with the journal *Cahiers du cinéma*, led by André Bazin, often wrote glowingly of the work of film directors (including American directors) whom they regarded as "auteurs" with distinct individual visions.

The American academic critic Andrew Sarris began to expand on this work in "auteur theory" from a specifically American point of view in the early 1960s, eventually developing his work into the publication of *The American Cinema: Directors and Directions 1929–1968*, first published in 1968. By this time, the study of film in American universities, which actually had its roots well before World War II, was rapidly expanding, producing not only a new generation of highly self-conscious filmmakers but also a new generation of sophisticated critics—and new markets for their criticism.

After Sarris's landmark book, auteur theory remained the dominant approach in American film studies for several years, until it began to be challenged by more theoretically informed approaches in the 1970s, influenced both by French structuralism and poststructuralism and by a desire, growing out of the political movements of the 1960s, to develop more politically relevant forms of film criticism. Thus, important works such as Robert Sklar's *Movie-Made America* (first published in 1975) emphasized the contributions of external social forces in determining the nature of film production. Eventually, works such as Thomas Schatz's *The Genius of the System* (1988) have demonstrated the important role played by forces (in this case, studio policies during the Golden Age) other than the director in the production of a film, posing further challenges to the director-oriented assumptions of auteur theory.

Thus, since the 1960s, the academic study of film has been marked by a growing variety in approaches, making academic film criticism a burgeoning enterprise, while books on film for more general audiences (with biographies of film stars leading the way) have remained a major category of American publishing as well. Film guides by popular reviewers such as Roger Ebert or Leonard Maltin have aimed at giving general viewers information about which films the public might want to watch, while more advanced guides such as James Monaco's classic *How to Read a Film*, first published in 1977, have tried to give audiences a more advanced appreciation of film and to provide them with more sophisticated techniques for the viewing and interpretation of films.

Studies on the history of film, either in general or in terms of specific genres and categories of film, gradually became more and more common as well. Gerald Mast's *A Short History of the Movies* (which deals with both American and international cinema), first published in 1971, has been popular as a textbook in college course on film history and is, as of this writing, now in its 11th edition. Historical accounts became especially popular as the 20th century drew to a close and film critics and scholars began to think in terms of summarizing the century. Decade-by-decade historical accounts of American cinema, such as the "History of the American Cinema" series begun by the University of California Press in the 1990s and the more recent "Screen Decades" sequence published by Rutgers University Press, have provided particularly valuable assessments of American film from the end of the 19th century to the early years of the 21st century. The British

Film Institute has also published a particularly valuable "Film Classics" series (which covers international cinema, including a significant number of American films), each volume of which provides a detailed discussion of one specific film.

Given the large amount of published material concerning American film, this bibliography cannot claim to be complete. It is hoped, however, that it includes most of the most important studies of various aspects of American films, as well as providing examples of most of the different types of studies of American film. Because of space limitations, this bibliography has been limited to book-length studies, though there is a vast amount of material published in individual articles in magazines and journals that is relevant and valuable as well. (Many of the most valuable of these, however, have been collected in book-length works.)

## GENERAL STUDIES

Biskind, Peter. *Easy Riders, Raging Bulls: How the Sex-Drugs-and-Rock 'n' Roll Generation Saved Hollywood*. New York: Simon and Schuster, 1999.

———. *Gods and Monsters: Thirty Years of Writing on Film and Culture*. London: Bloomsbury, 2005.

———. *Seeing Is Believing: How Hollywood Taught Us to Stop Worrying and Love the Fifties*. New York: Pantheon, 1983.

Bogdanovich, Peter. *Peter Bogdanovich's Movie of the Week*. New York: Ballantine, 1999.

Everson, William K. *American Silent Film*. New York: Da Capo Press, 1998.

Kobel, Peter. *Silent Movies: The Birth of Film and the Triumph of Movie Culture*. New York: Little, Brown, 2007.

Mast, Gerald, and Bruce F. Kawin. *A Short History of the Movies*. 11th ed. Boston: Longman, 2010.

Monaco, James. *How to Read a Film: Movies, Media, and More*. 30th anniv. ed. New York: Oxford University Press, 2009.

Ray, Richard B. *A Certain Tendency of Hollywood Cinema, 1930–1980*. Princeton, N.J.: Princeton University Press, 1985.

Ross, Steven. *Working-Class Hollywood: Silent Film and the Shaping of Class in America*. Princeton, N.J.: Princeton University Press, 1998.

Sarris, Andrew. *The American Cinema: Directors and Directions, 1929–1968*. New York: Da Capo Press, 1996.

Schatz, Thomas. *The Genius of the System: Hollywood Filmmaking in the Studio Era*. New York: Henry Holt, 1988.

Sklar, Robert. *Movie-Made America: A Cultural History of American Movies*. Rev. ed. New York: Vintage-Random House, 1994.

## SPECIFIC HISTORICAL PERIODS

Balio, Tino. *Grand Design: Hollywood as a Modern Business Enterprise, 1930–1939*. Berkeley: University of California Press, 1995.

Bergman, Andrew. *We're in the Money: Depression America and Its Films*. New York: New York University Press, 1971.

Bordwell, David, Janet Staiger, and Kristin Thompson. *The Classical Hollywood Cinema: Film Style and Mode of Production to 1960*. New York: Columbia University Press, 1985.

Bowser, Eileen. *The Transformation of Cinema, 1907–1915*. Berkeley: University of California Press, 1994.

Cook, David A. *Lost Illusions: American Cinema in the Shadow of Watergate and Vietnam, 1970–1979*. Berkeley: University of California Press, 2000.

Corrigan, Timothy, ed. *American Cinema 2000–2009: Themes and Variations*. New Brunswick, N.J.: Rutgers University Press, forthcoming.

Crafton, Donald. *The Talkies: American Cinema's Transition to Sound, 1926–1931*. Berkeley: University of California Press, 1999.

Dixon, Wheeler Winston, ed. *American Cinema of the 1940s: Themes and Variations*. New Brunswick, N.J.: Rutgers University Press, 2005.

Fischer, Lucy, ed. *American Cinema of the 1920s: Themes and Variations*. New Brunswick, N.J.: Rutgers University Press, 2009.

Friedman, Lester, ed. *American Cinema of the 1970s: Themes and Variations*. New Brunswick, N.J.: Rutgers University Press, 2007.

Gaudreault, André, ed. *American Cinema 1890–1909: Themes and Variations*. New Brunswick, N.J.: Rutgers University Press, 2009.

Grant, Barry K., ed. *American Cinema of the 1960s: Themes and Variations*. New Brunswick, N.J.: Rutgers University Press, 2008.

Hark, Ina Rae, ed. *American Cinema of the 1930s: Themes and Variations*. New Brunswick, N.J.: Rutgers University Press, 2007.

Holmlund, Chris, ed. *American Cinema of the 1990s: Themes and Variations*. New Brunswick, N.J.: Rutgers University Press, 2008.

Jacobs, Lea. *The Decline of Sentiment: American Film in the 1920s*. Berkeley: University of California Press, 2008.

James, David E. *Allegories of Cinema: American Film in the Sixties*. Princeton, N.J.: Princeton University Press, 1989.

Keil, Charlie, and Ben Singer, eds. *American Cinema of the 1910s: Themes and Variations*. New Brunswick, N.J.: Rutgers University Press, 2009.

Lev, Peter. *The Fifties: Transforming the Screen, 1950–1959*. Berkeley: University of California Press, 2003.

Monaco, Paul. *The Sixties, 1960–1969*. Berkeley: University of California Press, 2001.

Musser, Charles. *The Emergence of Cinema: The American Screen to 1907*. Berkeley: University of California Press, 1994.

Prince, Stephen, ed. *American Cinema of the 1980s: Themes and Variations.* New Brunswick, N.J.: Rutgers University Press, 2007.

———. *A New Pot of Gold: Hollywood under the Electronic Rainbow, 1980–1989.* Berkeley: University of California Press, 2000.

Ray, Robert B. *The ABCs of Classic Hollywood.* New York: Oxford University Press, 2008.

Schatz, Thomas. *Boom and Bust: The American Cinema in the 1940s.* New York: Scribner's, 1997.

## GENRES AND MODES

### Blaxploitation Films

Howard, Josiah. *Blaxploitation Film: The Essential Reference Guide.* Guildford, UK: FAB Press, 2008.

James, Darius. *That's Blaxploitation!: Roots of the Baadasssss 'Tude (Rated X by an All-Whyte Jury).* New York: St. Martin's Griffin, 1995.

Koven, Mikel J. *Blaxploitation Films.* Harpenden, U.K.: Kamera Books, 2010.

Lawrence, Novotny. *Blaxploitation Films of the 1970s: Blackness and Genre.* London: Routledge, 2007.

Sims, Yvonne D. *Women of Blaxploitation: How the Black Action Film Heroine Changed American Popular Culture.* Jefferson, N.C.: McFarland, 2006.

### Children's Film

Booker, M. Keith. *Disney, Pixar, and the Hidden Messages in Children's Film.* Westport, Conn.: Praeger, 2009.

Brode, Douglas. *From Walt to Woodstock: How Disney Created the Counterculture.* Austin: University of Texas Press, 2004.

———. *Multiculturalism and the Mouse: Race and Sex in Disney Entertainment.* Austin: University of Texas Press, 2006.

Byrne, Eleanor, and Martin McQuillan. *Deconstructing Disney.* London: Pluto Press, 1999.

Davis, Amy M. *Good Girls and Wicked Witches: Women in Disney's Feature Animation.* Bloomington: Indiana University Press, 2007.

Jackson, Kathy Merlock. *Images of Children in American Film.* Lanham, Md.: Scarecrow Press, 1995.

Sammond, Nicholas. *Babes in Tomorrowland: Walt Disney and the Making of the American Child, 1930–1960.* Durham, N.C.: Duke University Press, 2005.

Wojcik-Andrews, Ian. *Children's Films: History, Ideology, Pedagogy, Theory.* New York: Garland, 2000.

Zipes, Jack. *Breaking the Magic Spell: Radical Theories of Folk and Fairy Tales.* Rev., exp. ed. Lexington: University Press of Kentucky, 2002.

## Comedies

Beach, Christopher. *Class, Language, and American Film Comedy.* Cambridge: Cambridge University Press, 2008.

Byrge, Duane. *The Screwball Comedy Films: A History and Filmography, 1934–1942.* Jefferson, N.C.: McFarland, 2004.

Cavell, Stanley. *Pursuits of Happiness: The Hollywood Comedy of Remarriage.* Cambridge, Mass.: Harvard University Press, 1984.

Clayton, Alex. *The Body in Hollywood Slapstick.* Jefferson, N.C.: McFarland, 2007.

Dale, Alan. *Comedy Is a Man in Trouble: Slapstick in American Movies.* Minneapolis: University of Minnesota Press, 2002.

Everson, William K. *Hollywood Bedlam: Classic Screwball Comedies.* Secaucus, N.J.: Carol Publishing, 1994.

Gehring, Wes D. *Romantic vs. Screwball Comedy: Charting the Difference.* Lanham, Md.: Scarecrow Press, 2002.

———. *Screwball Comedy: A Genre of Madcap Romance.* Westport, Conn.: Greenwood, 1986.

Glitre, Kathrina. *Hollywood Romantic Comedy: States of the Union, 1934–1965.* Manchester: Manchester University Press, 2006.

Hallenbeck, Bruce G. *Comedy-Horror Films: A Chronological History, 1914–2008.* Jefferson, N.C.: McFarland, 2009.

Harvey, James. *Romantic Comedy in Hollywood: From Lubitsch to Sturges.* New York: Da Capo Press, 1998.

Horton, Andrew S., ed. *Comedy/Film/Theory.* Berkeley: University of California Press, 1991.

Jeffers, Tamar. *Romantic Comedy: Boy Meets Girl Meets Genre.* London: Wallflower, 2007.

Karnick, Kristine Brunovska, and Henry Jenkins, eds. *Classical Hollywood Comedy.* London: Routledge, 1994.

Kendall, Elizabeth. *The Runaway Bride: Hollywood Romantic Comedy of the 1930s.* New York: Alfred A. Knopf, 1990.

Krutnik, Frank, ed. *Hollywood Comedians: The Film Reader.* London: Routledge, 2003.

Mast, Gerald. *The Comic Mind: Comedy and the Movies.* Chicago: University of Chicago Press, 1979.

Matthews, Nicole. *Comic Politics: Gender in Hollywood Comedy after the New Right.* Manchester: Manchester University Press, 2001.

McCabe, Bob. *The Rough Guide to Comedy Movies.* London: Rough Guides, 2005.

Merton, Paul. *Silent Comedy.* New York: Random House, 2007.

Mitchell, Glenn. *A–Z of Silent Film Comedy: An Illustrated Companion.* London: Batsford, 2003.

Mortimer, Claire. *Romantic Comedy.* London: Routledge, 2010.

Neale, Steve, and Frank Krutnik. *Popular Film and Television*. London: Routledge, 1990.

Rickman, Gregg. *The Film Comedy Reader*. New York: Limelight, 2004.

Rubinfeld, Mark D. *Bound to Bond: Gender, Genre, and the Hollywood Romantic Comedy*. Westport, Conn.: Praeger, 2001.

Sikov, Ed. *Screwball: Hollywood's Madcap Romantic Comedies*. New York: Random House, 1991.

Waldau, Paul. *Film Comedy*. London: Wallflower, 2002.

Weales, Gerald. *Canned Goods as Caviar: American Film Comedies of the 1930s*. Chicago: University of Chicago Press, 1985.

## Cult Films

French, Carl, and Philip French. *Cult Movies*. Billboard Books, 2000.

Hoberman, J., and Jonathan Rosenbaum. *Midnight Movies*. New York: Da Capo Press, 1991.

Jancovich, Mark. *Defining Cult Movies: The Cultural Politics of Oppositional Taste*. Manchester: Manchester University Press, 2003.

Mathijs, Ernest, and Xavier Mendik, eds. *The Cult Film Reader*. New York: Open University Press, 2008.

Peary, Danny. *Cult Movies: The Classics, the Sleepers, the Weird, and the Wonderful*. New York: Gramercy Books, 1998.

Simpson, Paul. *The Rough Guide to Cult Movies*. London: Rough Guides, 2001.

## Documentaries

Alexander, William. *Film on the Left: American Documentary Film from 1931 to 1942*. Princeton, N.J.: Princeton University Press, 1981.

Aufderheide, Patricia. *Documentary Film: A Very Short Introduction*. New York: Oxford University Press, 2007.

Barnouw, Eric. *Documentary: A History of the Non-Fiction Film*. 2nd ed. New York: Oxford University Press, 1993.

Chanan, Michael. *The Politics of Documentary*. London: Palgrave Macmillan, 2008.

Ellis, Jack C., and Betsy A. McLane. *A New History of Documentary Film*. New York: Continuum, 2005.

Grant, Barry Keith, and Jeannette Sloniowski, eds. *Documenting the Documentary: Close Readings in Documentary Film and Video*. Detroit, Mich.: Wayne State University Press, 1998.

Kahana, Jonathan. *Intelligence Work: The Politics of American Documentary*. New York: Columbia University Press, 2008.

McEnteer, James. *Shooting the Truth: The Rise of American Political Documentaries*. Westport, Conn.: Praeger, 2005.

Nichols, Bill. *Introduction to Documentary*. Bloomington: Indiana University Press, 2001.


## Fantasy Films

Booker, M. Keith. *Red, White, and Spooked: The Supernatural in American Culture*. Westport, Conn.: Praeger, 2008.

Fowkes, Catherine A. *The Fantasy Film: Wizards, Wishes, and Wonders*. Malden, Mass.: Wiley-Blackwell, 2010.

Singer, Michael. *Bring Me That Horizon: The Making of* Pirates of the Caribbean. New York: Disney Editions, 2007.

Smith, Jim, and J. Clive Matthews. The Lord of the Rings*: The Films, the Books, the Radio Series*. London: Virgin Books, 2004.

Young, R. G. *The Encyclopedia of Fantastic Film: Ali Baba to Zombies*. New York: Applause Books, 2000.


## Film Noir and Neo-Noir

Ballinger, Alex, and Danny Graydon. *The Rough Guide to Film Noir*. London: Rough Guides, 2007.

Borde, Raymond, and Etienne Chaumeton. *A Panorama of American Film Noir, 1941–1953*. 1955. Trans. Paul Hammond. San Francisco: City Lights Books, 2002.

Broe, Dennis. *Film Noir, American Workers, and Postwar Hollywood*. Gainesville: University Press of Florida, 2009.

Bould, Mark. *Film Noir from* Berlin *to* Sin City. London: Wallflower, 2005.

Bould, Mark, Kathrina Giltre, and Greg Tuck, eds. *Neo-Noir*. London: Wallflower, 2009.

Conard, Mark T. *The Philosophy of Neo-Noir*. Lexington: University Press of Kentucky, 2007.

Dickos, Andrew. *Street with No Name: A History of the Classic American Film Noir*. Lexington: University Press of Kentucky, 2002.

Dixon, Winston Wheeler. *Film Noir and the Cinema of Paranoia*. New Brunswick, N.J.: Rutgers University Press, 2009.

Doane, Mary Ann. *Femmes Fatales*. London: Routledge, 1991.

Grant, Barry Keith, ed. *Film Noir Reader III*. Austin: University of Texas Press, 2003.

Hillier, Jim, and Alastair Phillips. *100 Film Noirs*. London: British Film Institute, 2009.

Hirsch, Foster. *Detours and Lost Highways: A Map of Neo-Noir*. New York: Limelight, 1999.

Kaplan, E. Anne, ed. *Women in Film Noir*. London: British Film Institute, 2008.

Keaney, Michael F. *Film Noir Guide: 745 Films of the Classic Era, 1940–1959.* Jefferson, N.C.: McFarland, 2003.

Krutnik, Christopher. *In a Lonely Street: Film Noir, Genre, Masculinity.* London: Routledge, 1991.

Martin, Richard. *Mean Streets and Raging Bulls.* Lanham. Md.: Scarecrow Press, 1999.

Mayer, Geoff, and Brian McConnell. *Encyclopedia of Film Noir.* Westport, Conn.: Greenwood Press, 2007.

Muller, Eddie. *Dark City: The Lost World of Film Noir.* New York: St. Martin's, 1998.

Naremore, James. *More Than Night: Film Noir in Its Contexts.* Berkeley: University of California Press, 1998.

Palmer, R. Barton. *Hollywood's Dark Cinema: The American Film Noir.* New York: Twayne, 1994.

———, ed. *Perspectives on Film Noir.* New York: G. K. Hall, 1996.

Porfirio, Robert, Alain Silver, and James Ursini, eds. *Film Noir Reader 3: Interviews with Filmmakers of the Classic Noir Period.* New York: Limelight, 2004.

Robson, Eddie. *Film Noir.* London: Virgin Books, 2005.

Schwartz, Ronald. *Neo-Noir: The New Film Noir Style from* Psycho *to* Collateral. Lanham, Md.: Scarecrow Press, 2005.

Silver, Alain, and James Ursini, eds. *Film Noir Reader.* New York: Limelight, 1996.

———. *Film Noir Reader 2.* New York: Limelight, 2004.

———. *Film Noir Reader 4: The Crucial Films and Themes.* New York: Limelight, 2004.

Silver, Alain, and Elizabeth Ward, eds. *Film Noir: An Encyclopedic Reference to the American Style.* 3rd ed. Woodstock, N.Y.: Overlook Press, 1992.

Spicer, Andrew. *Film Noir.* New York: Longman, 2002.

———. *Historical Dictionary of Film Noir.* Lanham, Md.: Scarecrow Press, 2010.

## Gangster Films

Grieveson, Lee, Esther Sonnet, and Peter Stanfield. *Mob Culture: Hidden Histories of the American Gangster Film.* New Brunswick, N.J.: Rutgers University Press, 2005.

Hardy, Phil, ed. *The Overlook Film Encyclopedia: The Gangster Film.* Woodstock, N.Y.: Overlook Press, 1998.

Leitch, Thomas M. *Crime Films.* Cambridge: Cambridge University Press, 2002.

Mason, Fran. *American Gangster Cinema: From* Little Caesar *to* Pulp Fiction. New York: Palgrave Macmillan, 2002.

McCarty, John. *Bullets over Hollywood: The American Gangster Picture from the Silents to* The Sopranos. New York: Da Capo Press, 2005.

Munby, Jonathan. *Public Enemies, Public Heroes: Screening the Gangster from Little Caesar to* Touch of Evil. Chicago: University of Chicago Press, 1999.

Parrish, James Robert. *The Great Gangster Pictures*. Lanham, Md.: Scarecrow Press, 1976.

———. *The Great Gangster Pictures II*. Lanham, Md.: Scarecrow Press, 1987.

Shadoian, Jack. *Dreams and Dead Ends: The American Gangster/Crime Film*. 2nd ed. New York: Oxford University Press, 2003.

Silver, Alain, ed. *The Gangster Film Reader*. New York: Limelight, 2007.

Smith, Jim. *Gangster Films*. London: Virgin, 2004.

Stephens, Michael L. *Gangster Films: A Comprehensive, Illustrated Reference to People, Films, and Terms*. Jefferson, N.C.: McFarland, 2008.

## Horror Films

Carroll, Noel. *The Philosophy of Horror: Or, Paradoxes of the Heart*. London: Routledge, 1990.

Clover, Carol J. *Men, Women, and Chain Saws: Gender in the Modern Horror Film*. Princeton, N.J.: Princeton University Press, 1993.

Dika, Vera. *Games of Terror:* Halloween, Friday the Thirteenth, *and the Films of the Stalker Cycle*. London: Associated University Presses, 1990.

Grant, Barry Keith, ed. *The Dread of Difference: Gender and the Horror Film*. Austin: University of Texas Press, 1996.

Grant, Barry Keith, and Christopher Sharratt, eds. *Planks of Reason: Essays on the Horror Film*. Rev. ed. Lanham, Md.: Scarecrow Press, 2004.

Humphries, Reynold. *The American Horror Film*. Edinburgh: Edinburgh University Press, 2003.

Hutchings, Peter. *Historical Dictionary of Horror Cinema*. Lanham, Md.: Scarecrow Press, 2008.

———. *The Horror Film*. New York: Pearson Longman, 2004.

Jancovich, Mark, ed. *Horror: The Film Reader*. London: Routledge, 2001.

Jones, Darryl. *Horror: A Thematic History in Fiction and Film*. London: Arnold, 2002.

Kinnard, Roy. *Horror in Silent Films: A Filmography, 1896–1929*. Jefferson, N.C.: McFarland, 1999.

Paul, William. *Laughing Screaming: Modern Hollywood Horror and Comedy*. New York: Columbia University Press, 1995.

Phillips, Kendall R. *Projected Fears: Horror Films and American Culture*. Westport, Conn.: Praeger, 2008.

Silver, Alain, and James Ursini, eds. *Horror Film Reader*. New York: Limelight, 2004.

Skal, David J. *Hollywood Gothic: The Tangled Web of Dracula from Stage to Screen*. London: Deutsch, 1990.

——. *The Monster Show: A Cultural History of Horror*. Rev. ed. London: Faber and Faber, 2001.

Spadoni, Robert. *Uncanny Bodies: The Coming of Sound Film and the Origins of the Horror Genre*. Berkeley: University of California Press, 2007.

Twitchell, James P. *Dreadful Pleasures: An Anatomy of Modern Horror*. Oxford: Oxford University Press, 1985.

Worland, Rick. *The Horror Film: An Introduction*. Malden, Mass.: Wiley-Blackwell, 2006.

## Independent Films

Biskind, Peter. *Down and Dirty Pictures: Miramax, Sundance, and the Rise of Independent Film*. New York: Simon and Schuster, 2004.

Hillier, Jim, ed. *American Independent Cinema: A Sight and Sound Reader*. London: British Film Institute, 2008.

Holmlund, Chris, and Justin Wyatt, eds. *Contemporary American Independent Film: From the Margins to the Mainstream*. London: Routledge, 2004.

King, Geoff. *American Independent Cinema*. Bloomington: Indiana University Press, 2005.

Levy, Emanuel. *Cinema of Outsiders: The Rise of American Independent Film*. New York: New York University Press, 2001.

Merritt, Greg. *Celluloid Mavericks: A History of American Independent Film Making*. New York: Da Capo Press, 1999.

Tzioumakis, Yannis. *American Independent Cinema: An Introduction*. New Brunswick, N.J.: Rutgers University Press, 2006.

Winter, Jessica. *The Rough Guide to American Independent Film*. London: Rough Guides, 2006.

## Musicals

Altman, Rick. *The American Film Musical*. Bloomington: Indiana University Press, 1988.

——, ed. *Genre, the Musical: A Reader*. London: Routledge, Kegan, and Paul, 1982.

Barrios, Richard. *A Song in the Dark: The Birth of the Musical Film*. 2nd ed. New York: Oxford University Press, 2009.

Cohan, Steve. *Hollywood Musicals, the Film Reader*. London: Routledge, 2002.

Dunne, Michael. *American Film Musical Themes and Forms*. Jefferson, N.C.: McFarland, 2004.

Feuer, Jane. *The Hollywood Musical*. 2nd ed. Bloomington: Indiana University Press, 1993.

Muir, John Kenneth. *Singing a New Tune: The Rebirth of the Modern Film Musical from* Evita *to* De-Lovely *and Beyond*. New York: Applause Books, 2005.

Parkinson, David. *The Rough Guide to Film Musicals*. London: Rough Guides, 2007.

Tyler, Don. *The Great Movie Musicals: A Viewer's Guide to 168 Films That Really Sing*. Jefferson, N.C.: McFarland, 2010.


## Postmodernism in Film

Booker, M. Keith. *Postmodern Hollywood: What's New in Film and Why It Makes Us Feel So Strange*. Westport, Conn.: Praeger, 2007.

Brooker, Peter, and Will Brooker, eds. *Postmodern After-Images: A Reader in Film, Television, and Video*. London: Arnold, 1997.

Degli-Esposti, Cristina, ed. *Postmodernism in the Cinema*. New York: Bergahn Books, 1998.

Denzin, Norman K. *Images of Postmodern Society: Social Theory and Contemporary Cinema*. London: Sage, 1995.

Jameson, Fredric. *Postmodernism; or, The Cultural Logic of Late Capitalism*. Durham, N.C.: Duke University Press, 1991.


## Science Fiction Films

Baxter, John. *Science Fiction in the Cinema*. New York: Paperback Library, 1970.

Booker, M. Keith. *Alternate Americas: Science Fiction Film and American Culture*. Westport, Conn.: Praeger, 2006.

———. *Historical Dictionary of Science Fiction Cinema*. Lanham, Md.: Scarecrow Press, 2010.

———. *Monsters, Mushroom Clouds, and the Cold War: American Science Fiction and the Roots of Postmodernism, 1946–1964*. Westport, Conn.: Greenwood Press, 2001.

Brosnan, John. *Future Tense: The Cinema of Science Fiction*. New York: St. Martin's Press, 1978.

Clarens, Carlos. *An Illustrated History of Horror and Science-Fiction Films: The Classic Era, 1895–1967*. 1967. New York: Da Capo Press, 1997.

Kaveney, Roz. *From* Alien *to* The Matrix: *Reading Science Fiction Film*. London: I. B. Tauris, 2005.

King, Geoff, and Tanya Krzywinska. *Science Fiction Cinema: From Outerspace to Cyberspace*. London: Wallflower, 2000.

Kuhn, Annette, ed. *Alien Zone: Cultural Theory and Contemporary Science Fiction Cinema*. London: Verso, 1990.

———, ed. *Alien Zone II: The Spaces of Science Fiction Cinema*. London: Verso, 1999.

Redmond, Sean, ed. *Liquid Metal: The Science Fiction Film Reader*. London: Wallflower, 2004.

Rickman, Gregg, ed. *The Science Fiction Film Reader*. New York: Limelight, 2004.

Sardar, Ziauddin, and Sean Cubitt, eds. *Aliens R Us: The Other in Science Fiction Cinema*. London: Pluto, 2002.

Scalzi, John. *The Rough Guide to Sci-Fi Movies*. London: Rough Guides, 2005.

Sobchack, Vivian. *Screening Space: The American Science Fiction Film*. 2nd ed. New Brunswick, NJ: Rutgers University Press, 1997.

Telotte, J. P. *A Distant Technology: Science Fiction Film and the Machine Age*. Middletown, Conn.: Wesleyan University Press, 1999.

———. *Replications: A Robotic History of the Science Fiction Film*. Urbana: University of Illinois Press, 1995.

———. *Science Fiction Film*. Cambridge: Cambridge University Press, 2001.

## Sports Films

Didinger, Ray, and Gene Macnow. *The Ultimate Book of Sports Movies: Featuring the 100 Greatest Sports Films of All Time*. Philadelphia, Penn.: Running Press, 2009.

Edelman, Rob. *The Great Baseball Films: From* Right Off the Bat *to* A League of Their Own. Secaucus, N.J.: Citadel Press, 1994.

Erickson, Hal. *The Baseball Filmography, 1915 through 2001*. 2nd ed. Jefferson, N.C.: McFarland, 2010.

Most, Marshall G., and Robert Rudd. *Star, Stripes, and Diamonds: American Culture and the Baseball Film*. Jefferson, N.C.: McFarland, 2006.

Romano, Frederick V. *The Boxing Filmography: American Features, 1920–2003*. Jefferson, N.C.: McFarland, 2004.

Schoenecke, Michael K., Deborah A. Carmichael, and Ron Briley, eds. *All-Stars and Movie Stars: Sports in Film and History*. Lexington: University Press of Kentucky, 2008.

Streible, Dan. *Fight Pictures: A History of Boxing and Early Cinema*. Berkeley: University of California Press, 2008.

Williams, Randy. *Sports Cinema: 100 Movies. The Best of Hollywood's Heroes, Losers, Myths, and Misfits of the Silver Screen*. New York: Limelight, 2006.

Wood, Stephen C., and J. David Pinkus, eds. *Reel Baseball: Essays and Interviews on the National Pastime, Hollywood, and American Culture*. Jefferson, N.C.: McFarland, 2003.

## Spy Films

Black, Jeremy. *The Politics of James Bond: From Fleming's Novels to the Big Screen*. Westport, Conn.: Praeger, 2001.

Britton, Wesley A. *Beyond Bond: Spies in Fiction and Film*. Westport, Conn.: Praeger, 2005.

——. *Onscreen and Undercover: The Ultimate Book of Movie Espionage.* Westport, Conn.: Praeger, 2006.

Chapman, James. *Licence to Thrill: A Cultural History of the James Bond Films.* London: I. B. Tauris, 2008.

Comentale, Edward P., Stephen Watt, and Skip Willman, eds. *Ian Fleming and James Bond: The Cultural Politics of 007.* Bloomington: Indiana University Press, 2005.

Di Leo, Michael. *The Spy Who Thrilled Us: A Guide to the Best of Cinematic James Bond.* New York: Limelight, 2004.

Lisanti, Tom, and Louis Paul. *Film Fatales: Women in Espionage Films and Television, 1962–1973.* Jefferson, N.C.: McFarland, 2002.

Miller, Toby. *Spyscreen: Espionage on Film and TV from the 1930s to the 1960s.* Oxford: Oxford University Press, 2003.

Rubenstein, Leonard. *The Great Spy Films.* Secaucus, N.J.: Citadel Press, 1981.

Wark, Wesley K. *Spy Fiction, Spy Films and Real Intelligence.* London: Routledge, 1991.

White, Rosie. *Violent Femmes: Women as Spies in Popular Culture.* London: Routledge, 2007.

## Superhero Films

Booker, M. Keith. *May Contain Graphic Material: Comic Books, Graphic Novels, and Film.* Westport, Conn.: Praeger, 2007.

Burke, Liam. *Superhero Movies.* Harpenden, U.K.: Pocket Essentials, 2008.

Gordon, Ian, Mark Jancovich, and Matthew P. McAllister, eds. *Film and Comic Books.* Jackson: University Press of Mississippi, 2007.

Hughes, David. *Comic Book Movies.* London: Virgin Books, 2003.

Kaveney, Roz. *Superheroes!: Capes and Crusaders in Comics and Films.* London: I. B. Tauris, 2008.

Muir, John Kenneth. *The Encyclopedia of Superheroes on Film and Television.* Jefferson, N.C.: McFarland, 2008.

Rossen, Jake. *Superman vs. Hollywood: How Fiendish Producers, Devious Directors, and Warring Writers Grounded an American Icon.* Chicago: Chicago Review Press, 2008.

## War Films

Adair, Gilbert. *Hollywood's Vietnam: From* The Green Berets *to* Apocalypse Now. New York: Proteus, 1985.

Basinger, Jeanine. *The World War II Combat Film: Anatomy of a Genre.* Middletown, Conn.: Wesleyan University Press, 2003.

Chambers, John Whiteclay, II, and David Culbert. *World War II, Film, and History.* New York: Oxford University Press, 1996.

Corrigan, Timothy. *A Cinema without Walls: Movies and Culture after Vietnam.* New Brunswick, N.J.: Rutgers University Press, 1991.

Davenport, Robert. *The Encyclopedia of War Movies: The Authoritative Guide to Movies about Wars of the Twentieth Century.* New York: Facts on File, 2004.

Dick, Bernard F. *The Star-Spangled Screen: The American World War II Film.* Lexington: University Press of Kentucky, 2006.

Dittmar, Linda, and Gene Michaud. *From Hanoi to Hollywood: The Vietnam War in American Film.* New Brunswick, N.J.: Rutgers University Press, 1990.

Doherty, Thomas. *Projections of War: Hollywood, American Culture, and World War II.* New York: Columbia University Press, 1999.

Eberwein, Robert. *The Hollywood War Film.* Oxford: Wiley-Blackwell, 2009.

Koppes, Clayton R., and Gregory D. Black. *Hollywood Goes to War: How Politics, Profit, and Propaganda Shaped World War II Movies.* Berkeley: University of California Press, 1990.

Rollins, Peter C., and John E. O'Connor, eds. *Why We Fought: America's Wars in Film and History.* Lexington: University Press of Kentucky, 2008.

Schneider, Steven Jay, ed. *101 War Movies You Must See before You Die.* Hauppage, N.Y.: Barron's Educational, 2009.

Slocum, J. David, ed. *Hollywood and War: A Film Reader.* London: Routledge, 2006.

## Westerns

Buscombe, Edward. *100 Westerns.* London: Palgrave Macmillan, 2008.

Carter, David. *The Western.* Harpenden, Hertfordshire: Oldcastle Books, 2008.

Hughes, Howard. Stagecoach *to* Tombstone: *The Filmgoers' Guide to Great Westerns.* London: I. B. Tauris, 2008.

Kitses, Jim. *Horizons West: Directing the Western from John Ford to Clint Eastwood.* London: Palgrave Macmillan, 2008.

Kitses, Jim, and Gregg Rickman, eds. *The Western Reader.* New York: Limelight, 2004.

Lusted, David. *The Western.* London: Longman, 2003.

McGee, Patrick. *From* Shane *to* Kill Bill: *Rethinking the Western.* Oxford: Wiley-Blackwell, 2006.

Simmon, Scott. *The Invention of the Western Film: A Cultural History of the Genre's First Half Century.* Cambridge: Cambridge University Press, 2003.

Simpson, Paul. *The Rough Guide to the Western.* London: Rough Guides, 2006.

Slotkin, Richard. *Gunfighter Nation: The Myth of the Frontier in Twentieth-Century America.* 1992. Norman: University of Oklahoma Press, 1998.

Tompkins, Jane. *West of Everything: The Inner Life of Westerns.* New York: Oxford University Press, 1993.

Varner, Paul. *Historical Dictionary of Westerns in Cinema.* Lanham, Md.: Scarecrow Press, 2008.

Wright, Will. *Sixguns and Society: A Structural Study of the Western.* Berkeley: University of California Press, 1977.


## THEMATIC STUDIES

### The Blacklist

Bernstein, Walter. *Inside Out: A Memoir of the Blacklist.* New York: Knopf, 1996.
Buhle, Paul, and Dave Wagner. *Blacklisted: The Film Lover's Guide to the Hollywood Blacklist.* London: Palgrave Macmillan, 2003.
———. *The Hollywood Blacklistees in Film and Television, 1950–2002.* London: Palgrave Macmillan, 2004.
Caute, David. *The Great Fear: The Anti-Communist Purge under Truman and Eisenhower.* New York: Simon and Schuster, 1978.
Ceplair, Larry. *The Marxist and the Movies: A Biography of Paul Jarrico.* Lexington: University Press of Kentucky, 2007.
Ceplair, Larry, and Steven Englund. *The Inquisition in Hollywood.* Rev. ed. Berkeley: University of California Press, 1983.
Dick, Bernard F. *Radical Innocence: A Critical Study of the Hollywood Ten.* Lexington: University of Kentucky Press, 1989.
Dmytryk, Edward. *Odd Man Out: A Memoir of the Hollywood Ten.* Carbondale: Southern Illinois University Press, 1996.
Freedland, Michael. *Hollywood on Trial: McCarthyism's War against the Movies.* London: Robson Books, 2007.
Hellman, Lillian. *Scoundrel Time.* Boston: Little, Brown, 1976.
Horne, Gerald. *The Final Victim of the Blacklist: John Howard Lawson, Dean of the Hollywood Ten.* Berkeley: University of California Press, 2006.
Krutnik, Frank. *"Un-American" Hollywood: Politics and Film in the Blacklist Era.* New Brunswick, N.J.: Rutgers University Press, 2007.
Navasky, Victor S. *Naming Names.* New York: Viking, 1980.


### Feminism and Gender

Carson, Diane, Linda Dittmar, and Janice R. Welsch, eds. *Multiple Voices in Feminist Film Criticism.* Minneapolis: University of Minnesota Press, 1994.
De Lauretis, Teresa. *Technologies of Gender: Essays on Theory, Film, and Fiction.* Bloomington: Indiana University Press, 1987.
Erens, Patricia, ed. *Issues in Feminist Film Criticism.* Bloomington: Indiana University Press, 1991.
Kaplan, E. Ann. *Feminism and Film.* New York: Oxford University Press, 2000.
Mulvey, Laura. *Visual and Other Pleasures.* Bloomington: Indiana University Press, 1989.

Silverman, Kaja. *The Acoustic Mirror: The Female Voice in Psychoanalysis and Cinema.* Bloomington: Indiana University Press, 1988.


## Politics and Film

Booker, M. Keith. *Film and the American Left: A Research Guide.* Westport, Conn.: Greenwood Press, 1999.

———. *From Box Office to Ballot Box: The American Political Film.* Westport, Conn.: Praeger, 2007.

Christensen, Terry. *Reel Politics: American Political Movies from* Birth of a Nation *to* Platoon. London: Basil Blackwell, 1987.

Crowdus, Gary, ed. *The Political Companion to American Film.* Chicago: Lakeview Press, 1994.

Davies, Philip, and Brian Neve, eds. *Cinema, Politics and Society in America.* New York: St. Martin's, 1981.

Franklin, Daniel P. *Politics and Film: The Political Culture of Film in the United States.* Lanham, Md.: Rowman and Littlefield, 2006.

Gianos, Philip L. *Politics and Politicians in American Film.* Westport, Conn.: Praeger, 1999.

Giglio, Ernest. *Here's Looking at You: Hollywood, Film, and Politics.* New York: Peter Lang, 2004.

Giovacchini, Saverio. *Hollywood Modernism: Film and Politics in the Age of the New Deal.* Philadelphia, Penn.: Temple University Press, 2001.

Lawson, John Howard. *Film in the Battle of Ideas.* New York: Masses and Mainstream, 1953.

Monteath, Peter. *The Spanish Civil War in Literature, Film, and Art.* Westport, Conn.: Greenwood, 1994.

Neve, Brian. *Film and Politics in America: A Social Tradition.* London: Routledge, 1992.

Roffman, Peter, and Jim Purdy. *The Hollywood Social Problem Film: Madness, Despair and Politics from the Depression to the Fifties.* Bloomington: Indiana University Press, 1981.

Rosenbaum, Jonathan. *Movies as Politics.* Berkeley: University of California Press, 1997.

Ryan, Michael, and Douglas Kellner. *Camera Politica: The Politics and Ideology of Contemporary Hollywood Film.* Bloomington: Indiana University Press, 1988.

Zaniello, Tom. *Working Stiffs, Union Maids, Reds, and Riffraff: An Organized Guide to Films about Labor.* Ithaca, N.Y.: ILR Press, 1996.


## Studios and Hollywood History

Dick, Bernard F. *Columbia Pictures: Portrait of a Studio.* Lexington: University Press of Kentucky, 1991.

Eames, John Douglas. *The MGM Story: The Complete of Sixty-Five Roaring Years.* New York: Crown, 1975.

Eames, John Douglas, and Robert Abele. *The Paramount Story: The Complete History of the Studio and Its Films.* New York: Simon and Schuster, 2004.

Fernett, Gene. *Hollywood's Poverty Row, 1930–1950,* Satellite Beach, Fla.: Coral Reef, 1973.

Finler, Joel W. *The Hollywood Story.* New York: Crown, 1988

Gabler, Neal. *An Empire of Their Own: How the Jews Invented Hollywood.* New York: Anchor, 1989.

Gomery, Douglas. *The Hollywood Studio System: A History.* London: British Film Institute, 2008.

Hirschhorn, Clive. *The Columbia Story.* London: Hamlyn, 1999.

——. *The Universal Story.* New York: Crown, 1983.

——. *The Warner Bros. Story.* New York: Crown, 1979.

Jewell, Richard B. *The RKO Story.* New York: Crown, 1982.

Kimmel, Daniel M. *The Dream Team. The Rise and Fall of DreamWorks: Lessons from the New Hollywood.* Chicago: Ivan R. Dee, 2006.

LaPorte, Nicole. *The Men Who Would Be King: An Almost Epic Tale of Moguls, Movies, and a Company Called DreamWorks.* Boston: Houghton Mifflin Harcourt, 2010.

Mordden, Ethan. *The Hollywood Studios.* New York: Knopf, 1988.

Paik, Karen. *To Infinity and Beyond!: The Story of Pixar Animation Studios.* San Francisco: Chronicle Books, 2007.

Price, David A. *The Pixar Touch: The Making of a Company.* New York: Vintage, 2009.

Schickel, Richard, and George Perry. *You Must Remember This: The Warner Bros. Story.* Philadelphia: Running Press, 2008.

Solomon, Aubrey. *Twentieth Century-Fox: A Corporate and Financial History.* Lanham, Md.: Scarecrow Press, 1988.

Vaz, Mark Cotta. *Industrial Light & Magic: Into the Digital Realm.* New York: Del Rey, 1996.

Vieira, Mark A. *Hollywood Dreams Made Real: Irving Thalberg and the Rise of M-G-M.* New York: Harry N. Abrams, 2008.

Wasko, Janet. *Understanding Disney: The Manufacture of Fantasy.* London: Polity, 2001.

## INDIVIDUAL FILMS

Barr, Charles. *Vertigo.* London: British Film Institute, 2008.

Braudy, Leo. *On the Waterfront.* London: British Film Institute, 2008.

French, Karl. *Apocalypse Now.* London: Bloomsbury, 1998.

Friedman, Lester D. *Arthur Penn's* Bonnie and Clyde. Cambridge: Cambridge University Press, 1999.

Hayes, Kevin J., ed. *Martin Scorsese's* Raging Bull. Cambridge: Cambridge University Press, 2005.

Krämer, Peter. *2001: A Space Odyssey*. London: British Film Institute, 2010.

Polan, Dana B. *Pulp Fiction*. London: British Film Institute, 2008.

Rushdie, Salman. *The Wizard of Oz*. London: British Film Institute, 2008.

Schickel, Richard. *Double Indemnity*. London: British Film Institute, 2008.

Staggs, Sam. *Close-Up on Sunset Boulevard: Billy Wilder, Norma Desmond, and the Dark Hollywood Dream*. New York: St. Martin's Griffin, 2003.

## PERSONNEL

### Actors

Basinger, Jeanine. *Silent Stars*. Middletown, Conn.: Wesleyan University Press, 2000.

Costello, Ben. *Jack and Walter: The Films of Lemmon and Matthau*. Chandler, Ariz.: Five Star Publications, 2009.

Sklar, Robert. *City Boys: Cagney, Bogart, Garfield*. Princeton, N.J.: Princeton University Press, 1992.

#### Bud Abbott and Lou Costello

Cox, Stephen, and John Lofflin. *The Abbott & Costello Story: Sixty Years of "Who's on First."* 2nd ed. Nashville, Tenn.: Cumberland House, 1997.

Miller, Jeffrey S. *Horror Spoofs of Abbott and Costello: A Critical Assessment of the Comedy Team's Monster Films*. Jefferson, N.C.: McFarland, 2004.

Nollen, Scott Allen. *Abbott and Costello on the Home Front: A Critical Study of the Wartime Films*. Jefferson, N.C.: McFarland, 2004.

#### Jean Arthur

Oller, John. *Jean Arthur: The Actress Nobody Knew*. New York: Limelight, 2004.

#### Fred Astaire

Epstein, Joseph. *Fred Astaire*. New Haven, Conn.: Yale University Press, 2009.

Levinson, Peter. *Puttin' on the Ritz: Fred Astaire and the Fine Art of Panache, A Biography*. New York: St. Martin's, 2009.

## Gene Autry

George-Warren, Holly. *Public Cowboy No. 1: The Life and Times of Gene Autry.* New York: Oxford University Press, 2009.

## Lauren Bacall

Greenberger, Howard. *Bogey's Baby.* New York: St. Martin's, 1978.
Quirk, Lawrence J. *Lauren Bacall: Her Films and Career.* Secaucus, N.J.: Citadel Press, 1986

## Theda Bara

Genini, Ronald. *Theda Bara: A Biography of the Silent Screen Vamp, with a Filmography.* Jefferson, N.C.: McFarland, 2001.

## Warren Beatty

Biskind, Peter. *Star: How Warren Beatty Seduced America.* New York: Simon and Schuster, 2010.
Finstad, Suzanne. *Warren Beatty: A Private Man.* New York: Harmony, 2005.

## Joan Bennett

Kellow, Brian. *The Bennetts: An Acting Family.* Lexington: University Press of Kentucky, 2004.

## Ingrid Bergman

Leamer, Lawrence. *As Time Goes By: The Life of Ingrid Bergman.* New York: Harper and Row, 1986.
Spoto, Donald. *Notorious: The Life of Ingrid Bergman.* Cambridge, Mass.: Da Capo Press, 2001.

## Halle Berry

Naden, Corinne J., and Rose Blue. *Halle Berry.* Philadelphia, Penn.: Chelsea House, 2002.

## Humphrey Bogart

McCarty, Clifford. *The Complete Films of Humphrey Bogart.* New York: Carol Publishing, 1990.
Sperber, A. M., and Eric Lax. *Bogart.* New York: William Morrow, 1997.

*Marlon Brando*

Kanfer, Stefan. *Somebody: The Reckless Life and Remarkable Career of Marlon Brando*. New York: Vintage-Random House, 2009.
Schickel, Richard. *Brando: A Life in Our Times*. New York: Atheneum, 1991.

*Yul Brynner*

Capua, Michelangelo. *Yul Brynner: A Biography*. Jefferson, N.C.: McFarland, 2006.

*Richard Burton*

Bragg, Melvyn. *Richard Burton: A Life*. New York: Warner Books, 1990.

*James Cagney*

Dickens, Homer. *The Films of James Cagney*. Secaucus, N.J.: Citadel Press, 1972.
McCabe, John. *Cagney*. New York: Da Capo Press, 1999.

*Montgomery Clift*

Lawrence, Amy. *The Passion of Montgomery Clift*. Berkeley: University of California Press, 2010.

*Claudette Colbert*

Dick, Bernard F. *Claudette Colbert: She Walked in Beauty*. Jackson: University Press of Mississippi, 2008.

*Sean Connery*

Pfeiffer, Lee, and Philip Lisa. *The Films of Sean Connery*. New York: Citadel Press, 2001.
Silver, Alain, and Paul Duncan. *Connery*. Los Angeles: Taschen, 2009.

*Gary Cooper*

Thomson, David. *Gary Cooper*. London: Faber and Faber, 2010.

*Joan Crawford*

Cowie, Peter. *Joan Crawford: The Enduring Star*. New York: Rizzoli, 2009.

*Bing Crosby*

Prigozy, Ruth, and Walter Raubicheck, eds. *Going My Way: Bing Crosby and American Culture*. Rochester, N.Y.: Rochester University Press, 2007.

*Bette Davis*

Schickel, Richard, and George Perry. *Bette Davis: Larger Than Life*. Philadelphia, Penn.: Running Press, 2009.

*James Dean*

Dalton, David. *James Dean: The Mutant King*. Chicago: Chicago Review Press, 2001.

*Olivia De Havilland*

Becker, Heinz. *The Films of Olivia De Havilland*. New York: Citadel Press, 1986.

*Dorothy Dandridge*

Bogle, Donald. *Dorothy Dandridge: A Biography*. New York: Boulevard Books, 1997.

*Bette Davis*

Quirk, Lawrence J. *Fasten Your Seat Belts: The Passionate Life of Bette Davis*. New York: W. Morrow, 1990.
Ringgold, Gene. *The Films of Bette Davis*. Secaucus, N.J.: Citadel Press, 1966.
Schickel, Richard, and George Perry. *Bette Davis: Larger Than Life*. Philadelphia, Penn.: Running Press, 2009.
Sikov, Ed. *Dark Victory: The Life of Bette Davis*. New York: Henry Holt, 2007.

*Doris Day*

Kaufman, David. *Doris Day: The Untold Story of the Girl Next Door*. New York: Virgin Books USA, 2008.

*Robert De Niro*

Brode, Douglas. *The Films of Robert De Niro*. New York: Citadel Press, 2001.

## Johnny Depp

Blitz, Michael, and Louise Krasniewicz. *Johnny Depp: A Biography*. Westport, Conn.: Greenwood Press, 2007.

## Marlene Dietrich

Riva, Maria. *Marlene Dietrich*. New York: Ballantine, 1994.
Spoto, Donald. *Blue Angel: The Life of Marlene Dietrich*. New York: Doubleday, 1992.

## Kirk Douglas

Douglas, Kirk. *The Ragman's Son: An Autobiography*. New York: Simon and Schuster, 1988.
Munn, Michael. *Kirk Douglas*. New York: St. Martin's, 1985.
Thomas, Tony. *The Films of Kirk Douglas*. Secaucus, N.J.: Citadel Press, 1972.

## Faye Dunaway

Hunter, Allan. *Faye Dunaway*. New York: St. Martin's, 1986.

## Clint Eastwood

Eliot, Marc. *American Rebel: The Life of Clint Eastwood*. New York: Harmony Books, 2009.
Engel, Leonard, ed. *Clint Eastwood, Actor and Director: New Perspectives*. Salt Lake City: University of Utah Press, 2007.

## Douglas Fairbanks

Vance, Tony, and Tony Maietta. *Douglas Fairbanks*. Berkeley: University of California Press, 2008.

## W. C. Fields

Curtis, James. *W. C. Fields: A Biography*. New York: Knopf, 2003.
Louvish, Simon. *Man on the Flying Trapeze: The Life and Times of W. C. Fields*. New York: W. W. Norton, 1997.

## Errol Flynn

Flynn, Errol. *My Wicked, Wicked Ways: The Autobiography of Errol Flynn*. New York: Putnam, 1960.

Hurst, Lincoln Douglas. *Errol Flynn: The True Adventures of a Real-Life Rogue.* Lanham, Md.: Scarecrow Press, 2010.


## Henry Fonda

Collier, Peter. *The Fondas: A Hollywood Dynasty.* New York: Putnam, 1991.
Goldstein, Norm. *Henry Fonda.* New York: Holt, Rinehart, and Winston, 1982.
Thomas, Tony. *The Films of Henry Fonda.* New York: Citadel Press, 1990.


## Jane Fonda

Anderson, Christopher P. *Citizen Jane: The Turbulent Life of Jane Fonda.* New York: Henry Holt, 1990.
Hershberger, Mary. *Jane Fonda's War: A Political Biography of an Antiwar Icon.* New York: New Press, 2006.


## Clark Gable

Essoe, Gabe. *The Films of Clark Gable.* Secaucus, N.J.: Citadel Press, 1970.
Harris, Warren G. *Clark Gable: A Biography.* New York: Harmony Books, 2002.
———. *Gable and Lombard.* New York: Simon and Schuster, 1974.


## Greta Garbo

Paris, Barry. *Garbo.* Minneapolis: University of Minnesota Press, 2002.
Vieira, Mark A. *Greta Garbo: A Cinematic Legacy.* New York: Harry N. Abrams, 2005.


## Ava Gardner

Server, Lee. *Ava Gardner: "Love Is Nothing."* New York: St. Martin's Griffin, 2007.


## John Garfield

Gelman, Howard. *The Films of John Garfield.* Secaucus, N.J.: Citadel Press, 1975.
Nott, Robert. *He Ran All the Way: The Life of John Garfield.* New York: Limelight, 2003.
Swindell, Larry. *Body and Soul: The Story of John Garfield.* New York: Morrow, 1975.

*Judy Garland*

Clarke, Gerald. *Get Happy: The Life of Judy Garland.* New York: Random House, 2000.
Frank, Gerold. *Judy.* New York: Da Capo Press, 1999.


*Lillian Gish*

Affron, Charles. *Lillian Gish: Her Legend, Her Life.* Scribner, 2001.
Oderman, Stuart. *Lillian Gish: A Life on Stage and Screen.* Jefferson, N.C.: McFarland, 2000.


*Paulette Goddard*

Morella, Joe, and Edward Z. Epstein. *Paulette: The Adventurous Life of Paulette Goddard.* New York: St. Martin's, 1985.


*Gloria Grahame*

Curcio, Vincent. *Suicide Blonde: The Life of Gloria Grahame.* New York: Morrow, 1989.


*Gene Hackman*

Hunter, Allan. *Gene Hackman.* New York: St. Martin's, 1987.


*Tom Hanks*

Gardner, David. *The Tom Hanks Enigma: The Biography of the World's Most Intriguing Movie Star.* London: John Blake, 2007.


*Jean Harlow*

Stenn, David. *Bombshell: The Life and Death of Jean Harlow.* New York: Doubleday, 1993.


*Rita Hayworth*

Kobal, John. *Rita Hayworth: The Time, the Place, and the Woman.* New York: Berkley Books, 1982.
McLean, Adrienne L. *Being Rita Hayworth: Labor, Identity, and Hollywood Stardom.* New Brunswick, N.J.: Rutgers University Press, 2004.

*Audrey Hepburn*

Spoto, Donald. *Enchantment: The Life of Audrey Hepburn*. New York: Harmony Books, 2006.
Woodward, Ian. *Audrey Hepburn*. New York: St. Martin's, 1984.


*Katharine Hepburn*

Britton, Andrew, and Robin Wood. *Katharine Hepburn: Star as Feminist*. New York: Columbia University Press, 2004.
Dickens, Homer, and Lawrence J. Quirk. *The Films of Katharine Hepburn*. New York: Carol Publishing, 1990.
Kanin, Garson. *Tracy and Hepburn*. New York: Viking Press, 1971.
Verlhac, Pierre-Henri. *Katharine Hepburn: A Life in Pictures*. San Francisco: Chronicle Books, 2009.


*Charlton Heston*

Rovin, Jeff. *The Films of Charlton Heston*. Secaucus, N. J.: Citadel Press, 1977.


*William Holden*

Capua, Michelangelo. *William Holden: A Biography*. Jefferson, N.C.: McFarland, 2009.
Quirk, Lawrence J. *The Complete Films of William Holden*. New York: Citadel, 1986.


*Bob Hope*

McCaffrey, Donald W. *The Road to Comedy: The Films of Bob Hope*. Westport, Conn.: Praeger, 2004.


*Rock Hudson*

Bret, David. *Rock Hudson*. London: Robson, 2004.


*Samuel L. Jackson*

Hudson, Jeff. *Samuel L. Jackson: The Unauthorised Biography*. London: Virgin, 2004.


*Jennifer Jones*

Epstein, Edward Z. *Portrait of Jennifer: A Biography of Jennifer Jones*. New York: Simon and Schuster, 1995.

*Boris Karloff*

Bojarski, Richard, and Kenneth Beale. *The Films of Boris Karloff.* Secaucus, N.J.: Citadel Press, 1974.
Lindsay, Cynthia. *Dear Boris: The Life of William Henry Pratt a.k.a. Boris Karloff.* New York: Knopf, 1975.


*Buster Keaton*

Carroll, Noël. *Comedy Incarnate: Buster Keaton, Physical Humor, and Bodily Coping.* Malden, Mass.: Wiley-Blackwell, 2009.
Smith, Imogen Sara. *Buster Keaton: The Persistence of Comedy.* Chicago: Gambit, 2008.


*Gene Kelly*

Yudkoff, Alan. *Gene Kelly: A Life of Dance and Dreams.* New York: Back Stage Books, 1999.


*Grace Kelly*

Spoto, Donald. *High Society: The Life of Grace Kelly.* New York: Harmony Books, 2009.


*Veronica Lake*

Lenburg, Jeff. *Peekaboo: The Story of Veronica Lake.* New York: St. Martin's, 1983.


*Burt Lancaster*

Buford, Kate. *Burt Lancaster: An American Life.* New York: Knopf, 2000.
Fishgall, Gary. *Against Type: The Biography of Burt Lancaster.* New York: Scribner, 1995.
Hunter, Allan. *Burt Lancaster: The Man and His Movies.* New York: St. Martin's, 1984.


*Vivien Leigh*

Edwards, Anne. *Vivien Leigh: A Biography.* New York: Simon and Schuster, 1977.
Walker, Alexander. *Vivien: The Life of Vivien Leigh.* New York: Grove Press, 1994.

### Carole Lombard

Ott, Frederick, W. *The Films of Carole Lombard*. Secaucus, N.J.: Citadel Press, 1972.

Swindell, Larry. *Screwball: The Life of Carole Lombard*. New York: Morrow, 1975.

### Béla Lugosi

Lenning, Arthur. *The Immortal Count: The Life and Films of Béla Lugosi*. Lexington: University Press of Kentucky, 2003.

### The Marx Brothers

Gardner, Martin. *The Marx Brothers as Social Critics: Satire and Comic Nihilism in Their Films*. Jefferson, N.C.: McFarland, 2009.

Louvish, Simon. *Monkey Business: The Lives and Legends of the Marx Brothers*. New York: St. Martin's Griffin, 2001.

### Steve McQueen

Porter, Darwin. *Steve McQueen, King of Cool: Tales of a Lurid Life*. New York: Blood Moon Productions, 2009.

Terrill, Marshall. *Steve McQueen: Portrait of an American Rebel*. London: Plexus, 2008.

### Burgess Meredith

Meredith, Burgess. *So Far, So Good: A Memoir*. Boston: Little, Brown, 1994.

### Robert Mitchum

Server, Lee. *Robert Mitchum: Baby, I Don't Care*. London: Faber and Faber, 2002.

### Tom Mix

Jensen, Richard D. *The Amazing Tom Mix: The Most Famous Cowboy of the Movies*. New York: iUniverse, 2005.

### Marilyn Monroe

Mailer, Norman. *Marilyn: A Biography*. New York: Grosset and Dunlap, 1993.

Morgan, Michelle. *Marilyn Monroe: Private and Undisclosed*. New York: Carroll and Graf, 2007.

Spoto, Donald. *Marilyn Monroe: The Biography*. New York: HarperCollins, 1993.

Summers, Anthony. *Goddess: The Secret Lives of Marilyn Monroe*. New York: Macmillan, 1985.

### Paul Newman

Levy, Shawn. *Paul Newman: A Life*. New York: Harmony Books, 2009.

Newman, Paul, and A. E. Hotchner. *In Pursuit of the Common Good: Twenty-Five Years of Improving the World, One Bottle of Salad Dressing at a Time*. Updated ed. New York: Broadway Books, 2008.

Quirk, Lawrence J. *Paul Newman: A Life*. Updated ed. Lanham, Md.: Taylor Trade, 2009.

### Jack Nicholson

McDougal, Dennis. *Five Easy Decades: How Jack Nicholson Became the Biggest Movie Star in Modern Times*. Hoboken, N.J.: Wiley, 2008.

McGilligan, Patrick. *Jack's Life: A Biography of Jack Nicholson*. New York: W. W. Norton, 1996.

Parker, John. *Jack: The Biography of Jack Nicholson*. London: John Blake, 1997.

### Laurence Olivier

Coleman, Terry. *Olivier*. New York: Henry Holt, 2005.

Spoto, Donald. *Laurence Olivier: A Biography*. New York: HarperCollins, 1992.

### Maureen O'Sullivan

Fury, David. *Maureen O'Sullivan: "No Average Jane."* Minneapolis, Minn.: Artist's Press, 2006.

### Al Pacino

Feeney, F. X., and Paul Duncan. *Pacino*. Los Angeles: Taschen, 2009.

### Gregory Peck

Fishgall, Gary. *Gregory Peck: A Biography*. New York: Scribner, 2002.

Haney, Lynn. *Gregory Peck: A Charmed Life*. New York: Da Capo Press, 2005.

*Anthony Perkins*

Bergan, Ronald. *Haunted Life: A Biography of Anthony Perkins.* Boston: Little, Brown, 1995.

*Mary Pickford*

Brownlow, Kevin. *Mary Pickford Rediscovered.* New York: Harry N. Abrams, 1999.
Whitfield, Eileen. *Mary Pickford: The Woman Who Made Hollywood.* Lexington: University Press of Kentucky, 2007.

*Sidney Poitier*

Goudsouzian, Aram. *Sidney Poitier: Man, Actor, Icon.* Chapel Hill: University of North Carolina Press, 2003.
Poitier, Sidney. *The Measure of a Man: A Spiritual Autobiography.* San Francisco: HarperSanFrancisco, 2007.

*Elvis Presley*

Tracy, Kathleen. *Elvis Presley: A Biography.* Westport, Conn.: Greenwood, 2006.
Zmijewski, Steve, and Boris Zmijewski. *Elvis: The Films and Career of Elvis Presley.* Secaucus, N.J.: Citadel Press, 1976.

*George Raft*

Yablonsky, Lewis. *George Raft.* New York: iUniverse, 2000.

*Paul Robeson*

Duberman, Martin B. *Paul Robeson.* New York: Knopf, 1988.
Nollen, Scott Allen. *Paul Robeson: Film Pioneer.* Jefferson, N.C.: McFarland, 2010.
Robeson, Paul. *Here I Stand.* Boston: Beacon Press, 1971.
Stewart, Jeffrey C. *Paul Robeson: Artist and Citizen.* New Brunswick, N. J.: Rutgers University Press, 1998.

*Edward G. Robinson*

Beck, Robert. *The Edward G. Robinson Encyclopedia.* Jefferson, N.C.: McFarland, 2008.

Gansberg, Alan L. *Little Caesar: A Biography of Edward G. Robinson.* Lanham, Md.: Scarecrow Press, 2004.

### Arnold Schwarzenegger

Krasniewicz, Louis, and Michael Blitz. *Arnold Schwarzenegger: A Biography.* Westport, Conn.: Greenwood, 2006.

### George C. Scott

Sheward, David. *Rage and Glory: The Volatile Life and Career of George C. Scott.* New York: Applause Books, 2008.

### James Stewart

Eliot, Marc. *Jimmy Stewart: A Biography.* New York: Harmony Books, 2006.
Fishgall, Gary. *Pieces of Time: The Life of James Stewart.* New York: Scribner's, 1996.
Pickard, Roy. *Jimmy Stewart: A Life in Film.* New York: St. Martin's, 1993.

### Gloria Swanson

Quirk, Lawrence J. *The Films of Gloria Swanson.* New York: Citadel Press, 1988.

### Elizabeth Taylor

Spoto, Donald. *A Passion for Life: The Biography of Elizabeth Taylor.* New York: HarperCollins, 1995.
Taraborrelli, J. Randy. *Elizabeth.* New York: Warner Books, 2006.
Walker, Alexander. *Elizabeth: The Life of Elizabeth Taylor.* New York: Grove Press, 2001.

### Gene Tierney

Vogel, Michelle. *Gene Tierney: A Biography.* Jefferson, N.C.: McFarland, 2005.

### Spencer Tracy

Fisher, James. *Spencer Tracy: A Bio-Bibliography.* Westport, Conn.: Greenwood, 1994.

Kanin, Garson. *Tracy and Hepburn.* New York: Viking Press, 1971.
Swindell, Larry. *Spencer Tracy: A Biography.* New York: World, 1969.


*Lana Turner*

Valentino, Lou. *The Films of Lana Turner.* New York: Citadel Press, 1979.


*John Wayne*

Munn, Michael. *John Wayne: The Man behind the Myth.* New York: NAL, 1995.
Roberts, Randy, and James S. Olson. *John Wayne: American.* New York: Free Press, 1995.


*Mae West*

Louvish, Simon. *Mae West: It Ain't No Sin.* New York: St. Martin's Griffin, 2007.
Watts, Jill. *Mae West: An Icon in Black and White.* New York: Oxford University Press, 2003.


## Directors

Waxman, Sharon. *Rebels on the Backlot: Six Maverick Directors and How They Conquered the Hollywood Studio System.* New York: HarperCollins, 2005.


*Robert Aldrich*

Silver, Alain, and James Ursini. *What Ever Happened to Robert Aldrich?: His Life and His Films.* New York: Limelight, 1995.


*Woody Allen*

Conard, Mark T., and Aeon J. Skoble, eds. *Woody Allen and Philosophy: You Mean My Whole Fallacy Is Wrong?* Open Court, 2004.
Hirsch, Foster. *Love, Sex, Death, and the Meaning of Life: The Films of Woody Allen.* 2nd ed. Cambridge, Mass.: Da Capo Press, 2001.


*Robert Altman*

Kagan, Norman. *American Skeptic: Robert Altman's Genre—Commentary Films.* Ann Arbor, Mich.: Pierian Press, 1982.
O'Brien, Daniel. *Robert Altman, Hollywood Survivor.* New York: Continuum, 1995.

Self, Robert T. *Robert Altman's Subliminal Reality*. Minneapolis: University of Minnesota Press, 2002.

## Jack Arnold

Reemes, Dana M. *Directed by Jack Arnold*. Jefferson, N.C.: McFarland, 1988.

## Hal Ashby

Beach, Christopher. *The Films of Hal Ashby*. Detroit, Mich.: Wayne State University Press, 2009.

## Busby Berkeley

Rubin, Martin. *Showstoppers: Busby Berkeley and the Tradition of Spectacle*. New York: Columbia University Press, 1993.

## Kathryn Bigelow

Jermyn, Deborah, and Sean Redmond, eds. *The Cinema of Kathryn Bigelow: Hollywood Transgressor*. London: Wallflower, 2003.

## Peter Bogdanovich

Yule, Andrew. *Picture Shows: The Life and Films of Peter Bogdanovich*. New York: Limelight, 2004.

## Tim Burton

Burton, Tim. *Burton on Burton*. 2nd, rev. ed. Ed. Mark Salisbury. London: Faber and Faber.

McMahan, Alison. *The Films of Tim Burton: Animating Live Action in Contemporary Hollywood*. New York: Continuum, 2005.

Page, Edwin. *Gothic Fantasy: The Films of Tim Burton*. London: Marion Boyars, 2007.

Woods, Paul A. *Tim Burton: A Child's Garden of Nightmares*. London: Plexus, 2007.

## James Cameron

Keegan, Rebecca Winters. *The Futurist: The Films of James Cameron*. New York: Crown, 2009.

### Frank Capra

Carney, Raymond. *American Vision: The Films of Frank Capra.* Cambridge: Cambridge University Press, 1986.

Gehring, Wes D. *Populism and the Capra Legacy.* Westport, Conn.: Greenwood Press, 1995.

Maland, Charles J. *Frank Capra.* Boston: Twayne, 1980.

### John Carpenter

Cumbow, Robert C. *Order in the Universe: The Films of John Carpenter.* Metuchen, N.J.: Scarecrow Press, 1990.

### John Cassavetes

Fine, Marshall. *Accidental Genius: How John Cassavetes Invented American Independent Film.* New York: Miramax Books, 2005.

### Charles Chaplin

Flom, Eric L. *Chaplin in the Sound Era: An Analysis of the Seven Talkies.* Jefferson, N.C.: McFarland, 1997.

Maland, Charles J. *Chaplin and American Culture.* Princeton, N.J.: Princeton University Press, 1991.

Schickel, Richard. *The Essential Chaplin: Perspectives on the Life and Art of the Great Comedian.* Chicago: Ivan R. Dee, 2006.

Vance, Jeffrey. *Chaplin: Genius of the Cinema.* New York: Harry N. Abrams, 2003.

### Joel and Ethan Coen

Levine, Josh. *The Coen Brothers: The Story of Two American Filmmakers.* Toronto: ECW Press, 2000.

### Francis Ford Coppola

Bergan, Ronald. *Francis Ford Coppola Close-Up: The Making of His Films.* New York: Thunder's Mouth Press, 1998.

Schumacher, Michael. *Francis Ford Coppola: A Filmmaker's Life.* New York: Crown, 1999.

### Roger Corman

McGee, Mark Thomas. *Roger Corman, the Best of the Cheap Acts.* Jefferson, N.C.: McFarland, 1988.

Morris, Gary. *Roger Corman*. Boston: Twayne, 1985.

Naha, Ed. *The Films of Roger Corman: Brilliance on a Budget*. New York: Arco, 1982.

## George Cukor

Bernardoni, James. *George Cukor: A Critical Study and Filmography*. Jefferson, N.C.: McFarland, 1985.

McGilligan, Patrick. *George Cukor, a Double Life: A Biography of the Gentleman Director*. New York: St. Martin's, 1991.

## Michael Curtiz

Kinnard, Roy, and R. J. Vitone. *The American Films of Michael Curtiz*. Metuchen, N.J.: Scarecrow Press, 1986.

Robertson, James C. *The Casablanca Man: The Cinema of Michael Curtiz*. New York: Routledge, 1993.

## Cecil B. DeMille

Eyman, Scott. *Empire of Dreams: The Epic Life of Cecil B. DeMille*. New York: Simon and Schuster, 2010.

Ringgold, Gene. *The Films of Cecil B. DeMille*. New York: Citadel Press, 1969.

## Brian De Palma

Dworkin, Susan. *Double De Palma: A Film Study with Brian De Palma*. New York: Newmarket Press, 1984.

Peretz, Eyal. *Becoming Visionary: Brian De Palma's Cinematic Education of the Senses*. Stanford, Calif.: Stanford University Press, 2007.

## Blake Edwards

Wasson, Sam. *A Splurch in the Kisser: The Movies of Blake Edwards*. Middletown, Conn., Wesleyan University Press, 2009.

## Robert Flaherty

Barsam, Richard Meran. *The Vision of Robert Flaherty: The Artist as Myth and Filmmaker*. Bloomington: Indiana University Press, 1988.

Rotha, Paul. *Robert J. Flaherty: A Biography*. Philadelphia: University of Pennsylvania Press, 1983.

## Victor Fleming

Sragow, Victor. *Victor Fleming: An American Movie Master*. New York: Pantheon, 2008.

## John Ford

Bogdanovich, Peter. *John Ford*. Rev., enlarged ed. Berkeley: University of California Press, 1978.
Eyman, Scott. *Print the Legend: The Life and Times of John Ford*. Baltimore, Md.: Johns Hopkins University Press, 2001.

## John Frankenheimer

Armstrong, Stephen B. *Pictures about Extremes: The Films of John Frankenheimer*. Jefferson, N.C.: McFarland, 2008.
Pratley, Gerald. *The Films of John Frankenheimer: Forty Years in Film*. Bethlehem, Penn.: Lehigh University Press, 1998.

## Samuel Fuller

Dombrowski, Lisa. *The Films of Samuel Fuller: If You Die, I'll Kill You*. Middletown, Conn.: Wesleyan University Press, 2008.

## Terry Gilliam

Marks, Peter. *Terry Gilliam*. Manchester: Manchester University Press, 2009.

## D. W. Griffith

Henderson, Robert M. *D. W. Griffith: His Life and Work*. New York: Oxford University Press, 1972.
Schickel, Richard. *D. W. Griffith: An American Life*. New York: Limelight, 2004.
Simmon, Scott. *The Films of D. W. Griffith*. Cambridge: Cambridge University Press, 1993.

## Howard Hawks

Hillier, Jim, and Peter Wollen. *Howard Hawks: American Artist*. London: British Film Institute, 1997.
Wood, Robin. *Howard Hawks*. Detroit, Mich.: Wayne State University Press, 2006.

## Alfred Hitchcock

Allen, Richard, and S. Ishii Gonzalès, eds. *Alfred Hitchcock: Centenary Essays.* London: British Film Institute, 1999.

Brill, Lesley. *The Hitchcock Romance: Love and Irony in Hitchcock's Films.* Princeton, N.J.: Princeton University Press, 1988.

Corber, Robert J. *In the Name of National Security: Hitchcock, Homophobia, and the Political Construction of Gender in Postwar America.* Durham, N.C.: Duke University Press, 1993.

Freedman, Jonathan, and Richard Millington, eds. *Hitchcock's America.* New York: Oxford University Press, 1999.

Spoto, Donald. *The Art of Alfred Hitchcock: Fifty Years of His Motion Pictures.* 2nd ed. New York: Anchor-Doubleday, 1992.

Sterritt, David. *The Films of Alfred Hitchcock.* Cambridge: Cambridge University Press, 1993.

Wood, Robin. *Hitchcock's Films Revisited.* New York: Columbia University Press, 1989.

## Dennis Hopper

Rodriguez, Elena. *Dennis Hopper: A Madness to His Method.* New York: St. Martin's, 1988.

## John Huston

Brill, Lesley. *John Huston's Filmmaking.* Cambridge: Cambridge University Press, 1997.

Kaminsky, Stuart M. *John Huston.* Boston: Houghton Mifflin, 1978.

## Jim Jarmusch

Suarez, Juan A. *Jim Jarmusch.* Urbana: University of Illinois Press, 2007.

## Elia Kazan

Pauly, Thomas H. *An American Odyssey: Elia Kazan and American Culture.* Philadelphia, Penn.: Temple University Press, 1983.

Schickel, Richard. *Elia Kazan: A Biography.* New York: Harper Perennial, 2006.

## Stanley Kramer

Spoto, Donald. *Stanley Kramer, Filmmaker.* New York: Putnam, 1978.

## Stanley Kubrick

Kagan, Norman. *The Cinema of Stanley Kubrick*. New York: Grove, 1972.
Nelson, Thomas Allen. *Kubrick, Inside a Film Artist's Maze*. Bloomington: Indiana University Press, 1982.
Rhodes, Gary D., ed. *Stanley Kubrick: Essays on His Films and Legacy*. Jefferson, N.C.: McFarland, 2008.

## Fritz Lang

Gunning, Tom. *The Films of Fritz Lang: Allegories of Vision and Modernity*. London: British Film Institute, 2008.

## Spike Lee

Massood, Paula, ed. *The Spike Lee Reader*. Philadelphia, Penn.: Temple University Press, 2008.

## Joseph Losey

Gardner, Colin. *Joseph Losey*. Manchester: Manchester University Press, 2004.
Palmer, James, and Michael Riley. *The Films of Joseph Losey*. Cambridge: Cambridge University Press, 1993.

## Ernst Lubitsch

Eyman, Scott. *Ernst Lubitsch: Laughter in Paradise*. Baltimore, Md.: Johns Hopkins University Press, 2000.
Paul, William. *Ernst Lubitsch's American Comedy*. New York: Columbia University Press, 1987.

## George Lucas

Hearn, Marcus. *The Cinema of George Lucas*. New York: Harry N. Abrams, 2005.
Pollock, Dale. *Skywalking: The Life and Films of George Lucas*. New York: Harmony Books, 1983.

## Terrence Malick

Michaels, Lloyd. *Terrence Malick*. Urbana: University of Illinois Press, 2008.
Morrison, James, and Thomas Schur. *The Films of Terrence Malick*. Westport, Conn.: Praeger, 2003.

Patterson, Hannah, ed. *The Cinema of Terrence Malick: Poetic Visions of America*. 2nd ed. London: Wallflower Press, 2007.

### Joseph L. Mankiewicz

Geist, Kenneth L. *Pictures Will Talk: The Life and Films of Joseph L. Mankiewicz*. New York: Da Capo Press, 1983.

### Anthony Mann

Basinger, Jeanine. *Anthony Mann*. Middletown, Conn.: Wesleyan University Press, 2007.
Darby, William. *Anthony Mann: The Life and Films*. Jefferson, N.C.: McFarland, 2009.

### Lewis Milestone

Millichap, Joseph R. *Lewis Milestone*. Boston: Twayne, 1981.

### Vincente Minnelli

Griffin, Mark. *A Hundred or More Hidden Things: The Life and Films of Vincente Minnelli*. New York: Da Capo Press, 2010.
Levy, Emanuel. *Vincente Minnelli: Hollywood's Dark Dreamer*. New York: St. Martin's, 2009.

### Michael Moore

Bernstein, Matthew. *Michael Moore: Filmmaker, Newsmaker, Cultural Icon*. Ann Arbor: University of Michigan Press, 2010.
Rapoport, Roger. *Citizen Moore: An American Maverick*. London: Methuen, 2007.

### F. W. Murnau

Eisner, Lotte H. *Murnau*. Berkeley: University of California Press, 1973.

### Sam Peckinpah

Seydor, Paul. *Sam Peckinpah: The Western Films, a Reconsideration*. Urbana: University of Illinois Press, 1999.
Weddle, David. *If They Move . . . Kill 'Em!: The Life and Times of Sam Peckinpah*. New York: Grove Press, 2001.

## Roman Polanski

Ain-Krupa, Julia. *Roman Polanski: A Life in Exile*. Santa Barbara, Calif.: Praeger, 2009.

Feeney, F. X., and Paul Duncan. *Roman Polanski*. Los Angeles: Taschen, 2006.

Mazierska, Eva. *Roman Polanski: The Cinema of a Cultural Traveller*. London: I. B. Tauris, 2007.

Morrison, James. *Roman Polanski*. Urbana: University of Illinois Press, 2007.

Orr, John, and Elzbieta Ostrowska, eds. *The Cinema of Roman Polanski: Dark Spaces in the World*. London: Wallflower Press, 2006.

## Sydney Pollack

Meyer, Janet L. *Sydney Pollack: A Critical Filmography*. Jefferson, N.C.: McFarland, 2008.

## Otto Preminger

Fujiwara, Chris. *The World and Its Double: The Life and Work of Otto Preminger*. London: Faber and Faber, 2008.

Hirsch, Foster. *Otto Preminger: The Man Who Would Be King*. New York: Knopf, 2007.

## Vincent Price

Meikle, Denis. *Vincent Price: The Art of Fear*. London: Reynolds and Hearn, 2003.

Williams, Lucy Chase. *The Complete Films of Vincent Price*. Secaucus, N.J.: Citadel Press, 2000.

## Nicholas Ray

Andrew, Geoff. *The Films of Nicholas Ray: The Poet of Nightfall*. London: Charles Letts, 1991.

Eisenschitz, Bernard. *Nicholas Ray: An American Journey*. Trans. Tom Milne. London: Faber and Faber, 1993.

## Robert Redford

Quirk, Lawrence J., and William Schoell. *The Sundance Kid: An Unauthorized Biography of Robert Redford*. Lanham, Md.: Taylor Trade, 2006.

## Martin Ritt

Jackson, Carlton. *Picking Up the Tab: The Life and Movies of Martin Ritt*. Bowling Green, Ohio: Bowling Green State University Popular Press, 1994.
Whitaker, Sheila. *The Films of Martin Ritt*. London: British Film Institute, 1972.

## Robert Rodriguez

Rodriguez, Robert. *Rebel without a Crew: Or, How a 23-Year-Old Filmmaker with $7,000 Became a Hollywood Player*. New York: Dutton, 1995.

## George Romero

Fallows, Tom, and Curtis Owen. *George A. Romero*. Harpenden, U.K.: Pocket Essentials, 2009.
Paffenroth, Kim. *Gospel of the Living Dead: George Romero's Visions of Hell on Earth*. Waco, Tex.: Baylor University Press, 2006.

## Mickey Rooney

Marill, Alvin H. *Mickey Rooney: His Films, Television Appearances, Radio Work, Stage Shows, and Recordings*. Jefferson, N.C.: McFarland, 2004.
Ray, Robert G. *The Avant-Garde Finds Andy Hardy*. Cambridge, Mass.: Harvard University Press, 1995.

## Robert Rossen

Casty, Alan. *The Films of Robert Rossen*. New York: Museum of Modern Art, 1969.

## John Sayles

Bould, Mark. *The Cinema of John Sayles: Lone Star*. London: Wallflower, 2009.

## Paul Schrader

Kouvaros, George. *Paul Schrader*. Urbana: University of Illinois Press, 2008.

## Martin Scorsese

Friedman, Lawrence S. *The Cinema of Martin Scorsese*. New York: Continuum, 1998.

Kelly, Mary Pat. *Martin Scorsese: A Journey.* New York: Thunder's Mouth Press, 1996.

*Ridley Scott*

Raw, Lawrence. *The Ridley Scott Encyclopedia.* Lanham, Md.: Scarecrow Press, 2009.
Schwartz, Richard A. *The Films of Ridley Scott.* Westport, Conn.: Praeger, 2001.

*Robert Siodmak*

Alpi, Deborah Lazaroff. *Robert Siodmak: A Biography, with Critical Analyses of His Films Noirs and a Filmography of All His Works.* Jefferson, N.C.: McFarland, 1998.

*Douglas Sirk*

Klinger, Barbara. *Melodrama and Meaning: History, Culture, and the Films of Douglas Sirk.* Bloomington: Indiana University Press, 1994.

*Steven Soderbergh*

Wood, Jason. *Steven Soderbergh.* Harpenden, U.K.: Pocket Essentials, 2002.

*Steven Spielberg*

Gordon, Andrew M. *Empire of Dreams: The Science Fiction and Fantasy Films of Steven Spielberg.* Lanham, Md.: Rowman and Littlefield, 2007.
Jackson, Kathi. *Steven Spielberg: A Biography.* Westport, Conn.: Greenwood, 2007.

*George Stevens*

Moss, Marilyn Ann. *Giant: George Stevens, a Life on Film.* Madison: University of Wisconsin Press, 2004.

*Oliver Stone*

Kagan, Norman. *The Cinema of Oliver Stone.* New York: Continuum, 1995.
Kunz, Don, ed. *The Films of Oliver Stone.* Lanham, Md.: Scarecrow Press, 1997.
Toplin, Robert Brent, ed. *Oliver Stone's USA: Film, History, and Controversy.* Lexington: University Press of Kentucky, 2003.

## Quentin Tarantino

Clarkson, Wensley. *Quentin Tarantino: The Man, the Myths and His Movies.* London: John Blake, 2007.

Smith, Jim. *Tarantino.* London: Virgin Books, 2005.

Woods, Paul A. *King Pulp: The Wild World of Quentin Tarantino.* London: Plexus, 1998.

## Melvin Van Peebles

Van Peebles, Melvin. *Sweet Sweetback's Baadasssss Song: A Guerrilla Filmmaking Manifesto.* New York: Thunder's Mouth Press, 2004.

## Gus Van Sant

LoBrutto, Vincent. *Gus Van Sant: His Own Private Cinema.* Santa Barbara, Calif.: Praeger, 2010.

## Paul Verhoeven

Van Scheers, Rob. *Paul Verhoeven.* London: Faber, 1997.

## King Vidor

Durgnat, Raymond, and Scott Simmon. *King Vidor, American.* Berkeley: University of California Press, 1988.

## Josef von Sternberg

Baxter, John. *Von Sternberg.* Lexington: University Press of Kentucky, 2010.

## Erich von Stroheim

Koszarski, Richard. *Von: The Life and Films of Erich von Stroheim.* Rev. and exp. ed. New York: Limelight, 2004.

## Orson Welles

Bazin, André. *Orson Welles: A Critical View.* Trans. Jonathan Rosenbaum. New York: Harper and Row, 1978.

Beja, Morris, ed. *Perspectives on Orson Welles.* New York: G. K. Hall, 1995.

Callow, Simon. *Orson Welles.* London: Jonathan Cape, 1995.

Higham, Charles. *The Films of Orson Welles*. Berkeley: University of California Press, 1970.

——. *Orson Welles: The Rise and Fall of an American Genius*. New York: St. Martin's, 1985.

*William Wellman*

Thompson, Frank T. *William A. Wellman*. Metuchen, N.J.: Scarecrow Press, 1983.

*Billy Wilder*

Phillips, Gene D. *The Life and Controversial Films of Billy Wilder*. Lexington: University Press of Kentucky, 2009.

Sikov, Ed. *On Sunset Boulevard: The Life and Times of Billy Wilder*. New York: Hyperion, 1998.

Zolotow, Maurice. *Billy Wilder in Hollywood*. New York: Limelight, 2004.

*Robert Wise*

Keenan, Richard C. *The Films of Robert Wise*. Lanham, Md.: Scarecrow Press, 2007.

*Robert Zemeckis*

Kagan, Norman. *The Cinema of Robert Zemeckis*. Lanham, Md.: Taylor Trade, 2003.

## Other Personnel

Barbas, Samantha. *The First Lady of Hollywood: A Biography of Louella Parsons*. Berkeley: University of California Press, 2005.

Berg, A. Scott. *Goldwyn: A Biography*. New York: Knopf, 1989.

Bernstein, Matthew. *Walter Wanger: Hollywood Independent*. Minneapolis: University of Minnesota Press, 2000.

Bigsby, C. W. E., ed. *The Cambridge Companion to David Mamet*. Cambridge: Cambridge University Press, 2004.

Custen, George Frederick. *Twentieth Century's Fox: Darryl F. Zanuck and the Culture of Hollywood*. New York: Basic Books, 1997.

Dick, Bernard F. *Hal Wallis: Producer to the Stars*. Lexington: University Press of Kentucky, 2004.

——. *The Merchant Prince of Poverty Row: Harry Cohn of Columbia Pictures*. Lexington: University Press of Kentucky, 2009.

Eliot, Marc. *Walt Disney: Hollywood's Dark Prince.* New York: Carol Communications, 1993.

Evans, Robert. *The Kid Stays in the Picture.* New York: Hyperion, 1994.

Gabler, Neal. *Walt Disney: The Triumph of the American Imagination.* New York: Vintage, 2007.

Goldman, William. *Adventures in the Screen Trade.* New York: Warner Books, 1983.

Hanson, Peter. *Dalton Trumbo, Hollywood Rebel: A Critical Survey and Filmography.* Jefferson, N.C.: McFarland, 2001.

Henderson, Sanya Shoilevska. *Alex North, Film Composer: A Biography, with Musical Analyses of* A Streetcar Named Desire, Spartacus, The Misfits, Under the Volcano, *and* Prizzi's Honor. Jefferson, N.C.: McFarland, 2009.

Herr, Christopher J. *Clifford Odets and American Political Theatre.* Westport, Conn.: Praeger, 2003.

Kelly, Katharine E., ed. *The Cambridge Companion to Tom Stoppard.* Cambridge: Cambridge University Press, 2001.

MacAdams, William. *Ben Hecht: The Man behind the Legend.* New York: Scribner, 1990.

Martin, Jeffrey Brown. *Ben Hecht, Hollywood Screenwriter.* Ann Arbor, Mich.: University of Michigan Research Press, 1985.

Schary, Dore. *Heyday: An Autobiography.* Boston: Little, Brown, 1979.

Schickel, Richard. *The Disney Version: The Life, Times, and Art of Walt Disney.* 1968. 3rd ed. Chicago: Ivan R. Dee, 2007.

Schulberg, Budd. *Moving Pictures: Memoirs of a Hollywood Prince.* Chicago: Ivan R. Dee, 2003.

Vieira, Mark A. *Irving Thalberg: Boy Wonder to Producer Prince.* Berkeley: University of California Press, 2009.

Watts, Steven. *The Magic Kingdom: Walt Disney and the American Way of Life.* Columbia: University of Missouri Press, 2001.

## REFERENCE WORKS

Berry, S. Torriano, and Venise T. Berry. *Historical Dictionary of African American Cinema.* Lanham, Md.: Scarecrow Press, 2007.

Gritten, David. *Halliwell's Film Guide 2008.* London: HarperCollins UK, 2008.

Katz, Ephraim. *The Film Encyclopedia: The Complete Guide to Film and the Film Industry.* 6th ed. New York: Collins Reference, 2008.

Maltin, Leonard. *Leonard Maltin's Classic Movie Guide: From the Silent Era through 1965.* 2nd ed. New York: Plume, 2010.

———. *Leonard Maltin's Movie Guide.* New York: Plume, 2010.

Slide, Anthony. *The New Historical Dictionary of the American Film Industry.* Lanham, Md.: Scarecrow Press, 1998.

*Videohound's Golden Movie Retriever.* Detroit, Mich.: Gale Cengage, 2010.

## INTERNET RESOURCES

Academy of Motion Picture Arts and Sciences. http://www/oscars.org [accessed 6 July 2010].

American Film Institute. http://www.amc.com [accessed 6 July 2010].

Berardinelli, James. http://www.reelviews.net [accessed 6 July 2010].

*Box Office Mojo.* http://www.boxofficemojo.com [accessed 6 July 2010].

Cinema.com. http://www.cinema.com [accessed 6 July 2010].

Dirks, Tim. *Filmsite.* http://www.filmsite.org [accessed 6 July 2010].

Early Cinema. http://www.EarlyCinema.com [accessed 6 July 2010].

Ebert, Roger. *rogerebert.com.* http://www.suntimes.com/ [accessed 6 July 2010].

*The Internet Movie Database.* http://www.imdb.com [accessed 6 July 2010].

Movie Review Query Engine. http://www.mrqe.com [accessed 6 July 2010].

Rotten Tomatoes Movie Reviews. http://www.rottentomatoes.com [accessed 6 July 2010].

# About the Author

**M. Keith Booker** is the James E. and Ellen Wadley Roper Professor of English at the University of Arkansas, where he is also the director of the Program in Comparative Literature and Cultural Studies. Before devoting himself to literary and cultural studies, Professor Booker spent 14 years on the scientific research staff of the Oak Ridge National Laboratory. He is the author or editor of dozens of books on literature, popular culture, and literary and cultural theory. His books on film include *Film and the American Left: A Research Guide* (1999); *Monsters, Mushroom Clouds, and the Cold War: American Science Fiction and the Roots of Postmodernism, 1946–1964* (2001); *Alternate Americas: Science Fiction Film and American Culture* (2006); *From Box Office to Ballot Box: The American Political Film* (2007); *Postmodern Hollywood: What's New in Film and Why It Makes Us Feel So Strange* (2007); *May Contain Graphic Material: Comic Books, Graphic Novels* (2007); *Disney, Pixar, and the Hidden Messages in Children's Films* (2009); and *Historical Dictionary of Science Fiction Cinema* (2010). Other books include *Joyce, Bakhtin, and the Literary Tradition: Toward a Comparative Cultural Poetics* (1995); *A Practical Introduction to Literary Theory and Criticism* (1996); *Colonial Power, Colonial Texts: India in the Modern British Novel* (1997); *The African Novel in English: An Introduction* (1998); *The Post-Utopian Imagination: American Culture in the Long 1950s* (2002); *TV: Innovative Television Series from* The Twilight Zone *to* The X-Files (2003), *Science Fiction Television* (2004); *Drawn to Television: Prime-Time Animated Series from* The Flintstones *to* Family Guy (2006); *Red, White, and Spooked: The Supernatural in American Culture* (2008); and *The Science Fiction Handbook* (with Anne-Marie Thomas, 2009).

Breinigsville, PA USA
07 March 2011
257073BV00003B/2/P